MONGOLIA
CHAHAR
KIRIN
Kirin
SUIYUAN
Suiyuan
Changchiakow (Kalgan)
Peiping (Peking)
Tientsin
Dairen (Jap.)
Seoul
Taiyüan
HOPEI (CHIHLI)
Weihaiwei (Br.)
SHANSI
Tsinan
Tsingtao
YELLOW R.
Yenan
SHANTUNG
Loyang
Kaifeng
KIANGSU
Sian
SHENSI
HONAN
ANHWEI
Nanking
Shanghai
HUPEI
YANGTZE R.
Hankow
Chungking
CHEKIANG
Nanchang
Changsha
KIANGSI
KWEICHOW
HUNAN
Foochow
Kweiyang
FUKIEN
Amoy
KWANGSI
TAIWAN
KWANGTUNG
Canton
Nanning
Hong Kong (Br.)
Macao
Kwangchow (Fr.)
HAINAN

HOOVER INSTITUTION PUBLICATIONS

China's Nation-Building Effort, 1927-1937

China's Nation-Building Effort, 1927-1937

The Financial and Economic Record

Arthur N. Young

Former Financial Adviser to China

1971
Hoover Institution Press
Stanford University

The Hoover Institution on War, Revolution and Peace, founded at Stanford University in 1919 by the late President Herbert Hoover, is a center for advanced study and research on public and international affairs in the twentieth century. The views expressed in its publications are entirely those of the authors and do not necessarily reflect the views of the Hoover Institution.

Hoover Institution Publications 104
Standard Book Number 8179-1041-7
Library of Congress Card Number 70-123350
Printed in the United States of America

Preface

Seldom if ever in a brief span of years has any country seen changes as swift and dramatic as those affecting China during the second quarter of this century. The warlords of the chaotic twenties gave way to the Nationalists, who strove from 1927 to 1937 to build the country into a nation. In mid-1937, Japan's drive for hegemony in East Asia, after her seizure of Manchuria and encroachment in North China, led to war and the occupation of China's most productive areas. The events of the war led, in turn, to the Communist takeover on the mainland in 1949. Thus China changed from a pro-Western and fairly open society, based mostly on free enterprise, to a socialistic and totalitarian state.

Impressed by the Communist takeover, writers and students of Chinese affairs often tend to lump together the years between the fall of the empire in 1911 and 1949 as an interregnum of uninterrupted confusion. This approach is essentially Marxist in assuming the historical inevitability of a Communist revolution. It is not warranted by the facts. Focusing on the transformation that the Communists wrought after 1949, it ignores the major transformation which the Nationalists brought about after they had set up their capital at Nanking in 1927. It also ignores China's promising outlook in mid-1937, tragically interrupted by Japan, when on many fronts there had been great progress, with signs of further progress rather than collapse.

The Nationalists' nation-building effort from the twenties to mid-1937 largely overcame the disintegration that followed the fall of the imperial regime in 1911. The Nationalists put an end to major regional militarism; created a government able to speak internationally for China; and put the country on the road to becoming a strong, unified, and developing nation. Key factors in the accomplishment were Sun Yat-sen's ideology of nationalism, which took advantage of the many-sided urge for reform and modernization; the government's political and military skill; and the strengthening of the finances. A weakness, however, was the inadequate attention to reforms in the traditional economic and social system—partly because of the urgency of consolidating central authority, partly because of the orientation of the leaders, and partly because of difficulties with Japan.

For the decade from 1927 to 1937, attention has centered primarily on political events, notably on the Nationalists' confrontation with the Communists and on China's relations with Japan and the other powers. Financial and economic developments during these years were of first importance but have been neglected or, when discussed, have often been incorrectly presented. Although this book deals primarily with financial and economic affairs, internal political and social matters as well as international relations are necessarily interwoven in the story.

As the record set forth in the following pages will show, the accomplishments of Nationalist China were impressive under the extremely difficult conditions prevailing in the prewar decade 1927 to 1937. Mention of the Nationalists all too often conjures up only the charge that the regime was nothing more than one of "corruption and inefficiency." This charge, which dates especially from the middle forties, did not derive from the words of uninformed critics alone. It was spread by Communist propaganda, and was echoed by leftists and others who accepted it uncritically and without regard for what had happened before the forties. Justice demands that the record be viewed objectively.

There was indeed corruption and inefficiency. Less developed countries generally suffer from traditional systems of exploitation that are not easily changed, and China was no exception. Widespread corruption can be eradicated only by effective public administration, backed by public opinion. And a good bureaucracy must be adequately and regularly paid. Achievement of these things in a largely traditional society is far from easy and calls for prolonged effort. This type of orderly change, however, is an alternative to the brutal and indiscriminate liquidation of the economically successful and of moderate liberal elements that has characterized Communist takeovers. Such takeovers have been only the prelude to other forms of exploitation by a minority.

The corruption and inefficiency I observed in China during the prewar decade were certainly no worse than what I found in other less developed countries where I have worked. In many respects, indeed, the situation in China was better, and notable progress was being made—witness the fiscal reforms recounted in this volume. Many leaders and officials at every level were trying, often with much success, to improve public administration and eliminate abuses.

The deterioration during and after the war was the primary cause of the repeated accusations of corruption and inefficiency. The disruption and suffering of over eight years of bitter warfare explain much. For more than half of this time, China confronted alone and with little outside aid an enemy far stronger than herself. When China did gain allies after Pearl Harbor, aid was little and late. Early in the war the government lost its chief economic base and a large part of its experienced personnel, and was forced into medieval West China. Also, in addition to the bitter struggle with Japan for survival, the government had to contend with the Communists' drive for power. The structure was too fragile to withstand such a strain. The country suffered incalculable losses and was racked by galloping inflation, which creates corruption and inefficiency in any country.

Concerning the war years, I have written elsewhere that "... China's resistance was almost a miracle ..." and that "The marvel is, not that there were failures and sordid happenings, but that the National Government lasted through the war at all."* Yet I felt obliged to conclude that "... however reasonable the explanation, failures took place ..." and that "... the corruption went beyond what could be deemed excusable as due to inflation and confusion."† In the postwar years, enormous difficulties continued to confront the Nationalists, and the record from 1945 until the withdrawal to Taiwan cannot be called good. The government has since, however, done much to redeem itself by effecting notable economic progress and reforms on Taiwan.

After the Nationalists' takeover in 1927-1928, the obstacles to progress were great. Social and institutional problems hampered efforts for consolidation and development. The militarists of provinces and regions were not prepared to disband their troops and cede authority to central control. Their disruptive action was responsible for civil wars that were particularly serious until 1931. The Communists remained in strength in Central China until 1934, when they were driven to the distant northwest. There they remained a continuing though greatly diminished

*Arthur N. Young, *China and the Helping Hand, 1937-1945* (Cambridge, 1963), pp. vii-ix.
†*Ibid.*, p. 422.

threat. The Kuomintang party was divided, the Canton faction in particular repeatedly making trouble until removed from regional power in 1936. These pressing problems entailed a costly drain on finances, and diverted resources and attention from development and reform.

China and Japan were on a collision course after 1927-1928. The nationalism that took over in China could not be denied. In Japan, despite the efforts of moderate leaders, a key part of the drive for Japanese hegemony in East Asia was for domination of China. This trend was inexorable. It probably became inevitable once Japan failed to discipline the militarists who assassinated Marshal Chang Tso-lin in Manchuria in 1928. It grew much stronger after the Japanese seizure of Manchuria in 1931-1932, while the Western powers and Russia stood by. That seizure took from China one of her richest areas, curtailed her revenues, and added to costs of defence. But Japan's pressure on China also brought support to the government as it strove to strengthen the country against the aggressor.

China's transformation during the prewar decade was most notable in the growth of central authority and in the improvements in fiscal and monetary affairs. The contrast to the chaos of the warlord period that preceded is striking. By 1937 the government was in substantial control of the chief parts of the country, with the exception of Japanese-occupied Manchuria and parts of North China where Japan was encroaching. Important elements in promoting progress were the large increase of revenues, to far beyond what Peking had ever enjoyed, and the highly successful monetary reform of 1935. The strengthening of the government and its positive policy toward economic development, along with recovery of the economy beginning in 1935, greatly improved the prospects for economic progress. The forward movement was especially strong in 1936-1937. As shown in this book, the financial improvement and economic growth were excellent in face of all the difficulties, and they contrasted strongly with the retrogression that most of the world experienced during the depression of the thirties.

China's progress was achieved mainly by self-help. The only direct prewar credits by foreign governments were the two American credits of 1931-1933 totaling US $26 million (utilized). Further support, having a total equivalent of the order of US $100 million, came from remitted British Boxer Indemnity funds and credits partly guaranteed by European governments.

The American silver purchases, which buttressed the currency reform already adopted by China, were not credits but exchanges of China's silver for dollars. Private foreign investment began to play an important part in promoting progress only in the latter part of the decade.

Foreign financial and technical advice and aid in administration were vital—mostly well-received and at times eagerly sought. This advice and aid were provided not by foreign governments but by relatively few experts, who were engaged by China directly or, in some branches of economic reconstruction, were recommended by the League of Nations. I well recall the satisfaction, at times even enthusiasm, with which I and my foreign associates worked with our Chinese colleagues, especially in the latter part of the prewar decade. This episode shows the key importance for financial and economic development of having a government with leaders resourceful under difficulties, striving by self-help to improve public order and administration, and ready to accept advice—even though receiving little foreign financial aid.

China's financial and economic progress in the prewar decade was a pioneer effort in the field of economic development. It antedated the widespread interest since World War II in the promotion of the progress of less developed countries, and the provision of large-scale foreign grants and credits. China's effort merits the careful attention of countries seeking development and of those providing aid.

This book is at once a history and a memoir. In addition to my recollections, I have used, with the consent of the Chinese government, the papers that I gathered and preserved intact while serving as Financial Adviser to China from 1929 to 1947. Because of the loss of many official records during and after the war, my data on some subjects are more complete than those available elsewhere. I have also used the records of the Department of State; the Morgenthau *Diaries* and the presidential papers in the Roosevelt Library at Hyde Park, New York; and the great volume of official and private materials published about the period. In addition, I have talked with many participants in the events with which this book deals.

My participation related more to financial matters than to economic development. Nevertheless, for completeness, I have included a discussion of the economy and its progress. This discussion, in Part IV, is based on data I obtained at the time, supplemented by data drawn from other sources. Parts of my treatment of development do not have the depth of the treatment of fiscal and monetary matters with which I was concerned at first-hand and for which I have primary and often unique data. I believe, however, that my account of development substantially indicates what happened, although I recognize that further detailed study, especially of sources in Chinese, could present a more complete picture.

The outbreak of Sino-Japanese hostilities in July 1937 checked the publication of official Chinese materials covering the latter part of the period treated. And the fighting that followed diverted attention from events that occurred before the war. Thus, much pertinent information is unavailable or has not been adequately analyzed. Consequently, appraisals of the events have often been defective. In this account, with the aid of materials not previously available, I have tried to describe objectively the course of financial and economic events and have included an appraisal. Whether I have been fair will be for the reader to judge.

In this book, Part I summarizes the setting in which the Nationalists took over in 1927-1928 and describes their first measures to consolidate their position and prepare for rehabilitation and progress. Part II describes the quest for fiscal stability, and Part III treats monetary affairs. Part IV deals with the development and modernization of the economy, and with the roles played by the Chinese and by foreign financial and technical advisers. Part V contains an overall view of the period.

Pasadena, California ARTHUR N. YOUNG
February, 1971

Acknowledgments

For reading the manuscript and offering comments that enabled me to improve the presentation, I am indebted to Kia-ngau Chang, formerly head of the Bank of China and Minister of Railways and now of the Hoover Institution on War, Revolution and Peace; to Franklin L. Ho, formerly of Nankai University and later of Columbia University; and to Yuan-li Wu of the Hoover Institution. For reading parts of the manuscript and offering helpful comments, I am indebted to William L. Bond, formerly in charge of operations in China of the China National Aviation Corporation; to J. Lossing Buck, formerly of the University of Nanking; to F. Chang, former head of the Chinese Customs Administration; to John K. Chang of Lafayette College; to John B. Condliffe of the Stanford Research Institute; to Owen L. Dawson, former Agricultural Attache of the American Embassy in China; to Jo F. Freeman, formerly accountant of the Central Bank of China; to Stanley K. Hornbeck, formerly Chief of the Division of Far Eastern Affairs of the Department of State; to Byrd L. Jones of the University of Massachusetts; to William M. Leary, Jr., of the University of Victoria, British Columbia; to L. K. Little, formerly of the Chinese Customs Service and later Inspector General of Customs; to Oliver C. Lockhart, formerly Financial Adviser to China and Associate Director General of the Salt Revenue Administration; to Ramon H. Myers of Harvard University; to Joseph Spencer of the University of California at Los Angeles; to K. C. Yeh of the Rand Corporation; to John Parke Young, formerly Chief of the Division of International Finance of the Department of State; and to Mrs. John Parke Young, formerly of the Department of State. Throughout, my wife, Nellie May Young, has provided invaluable suggestions, criticisms, and encouragement.

For additional help in a number of ways, I am indebted to John K. Fairbank of Harvard University; to Roy L. Hofheinz, Jr., of Harvard University; to Marius B. Jansen of Princeton University; to David Maynard, formerly of the American Foreign Service; to P. K. Mok of Occidental College; to Mrs. P. K.

Mok, Librarian of Orientalia at the University of California at Los Angeles; and to E. O. Reischauer of Harvard University.

For aid in access to materials I am indebted to the authorities of the Archives of the United States; to Elizabeth B. Drewry, Director, and Joseph W. Marshall of the Franklin D. Roosevelt Library; to the East Asian Research Center of Harvard University; and to John T. Ma, Curator-Librarian, East Asian Collection, Hoover Institution. I am grateful to the Hoover Institution for a grant to cover some of the costs of preparation of this volume. My thanks go also to Mrs. Lucille Lozoya for typing the manuscript, to Mrs. Joyce King for help with tables, and to Miss Ruth Hersch for editorial suggestions. Finally, I wish to thank Harvard University Press for permission to quote from *After Imperialism: The Search for a New Order in the Far East, 1921-1931*, by Akira Iriye (1965); and Chi-ming Hou, *Foreign Investment and Economic Development in China, 1840-1937* (1965).

For this work as it stands and for any errors and omissions, those who have helped me are of course in no way responsible.

A.N.Y.

Contents

Appendixes

List of Tables

List of Charts

Cartoons

Part One

The Setting and the Nationalist Takeover

1: Introduction

Developments in China from the fall of the empire in 1911 to the Nationalist takeover in 1927-1928 have been fully described elsewhere. Therefore, in this chapter, I shall only summarize the situation during this period with regard to foreign rights and interests; the state of government, the finances, and the economy; the growth of Chinese nationalism; China's relations with the powers; and relations among the powers with respect to China.

The setting of this period was well stated by R. H. Tawney who visited China early in the prewar decade. Under the empire the political system was "... crumbling from within at the moment when it was assailed by growing pressure from without ... the old regime could neither resist change nor initiate it, so that everything in the end gave way together. As a consequence, economic, political and intellectual movements, which elsewhere made their way by gradual stages and small increments of growth, are, in the China of today, in simultaneous ferment ... —all these, and much else, have been crowded into the space of little more than a generation."[1]

A century of conflict and imperialism had left a legacy of special foreign rights and interests in and adjoining China.[2] Hong Kong was British, and certain nearby areas were leased to Britain. Macao was Portuguese. Formosa (Taiwan) was a Japanese colony. The Liaotung (or Kwantung) Peninsula was leased to Japan. Control of this area along with special railway rights gave Japan a strong economic hold and a sphere of influence in southern Manchuria. Russia had special railway rights and a sphere of influence in northern Manchuria. The ports of Weihaiwei and Kwangchouwan were leased to Britain and France, respectively.

There were foreign-ruled concessions and settlements in the treaty ports, the chief of which were the International Settlement and French Concession at Shanghai and the concessions at Tientsin, Hankow, and Canton.

The Sino-foreign Customs and Salt revenue services were

British-dominated but internationally staffed. Tariffs were held to a low level by old treaties. Foreign vessels could engage in coastwise and river trade.

Under the system of extraterritoriality (extrality) foreigners were subject only to courts of their own nationality. They were not subject to Chinese jurisdiction. Because of the peculiar laws and customs of the "barbarians," China originally wanted the system. Later, however, extrality came to be lumped with the other special rights and privileges of foreigners as an objectionable provision of the unequal treaties.

The chief powers had the right to station troops in Peking and to maintain communications to the sea. Foreign troops also could be stationed elsewhere, notably at Shanghai. Foreign warships had the use of coastal waterways and rivers.

The regime of special foreign rights was naturally most obnoxious to China. In particular, the presence of foreign troops on Chinese soil was a humiliation. It was the clash accompanying maneuvers of Japanese troops outside Peiping on July 7, 1937, that was to usher in the war.

The agreements for special foreign rights were mostly ended by the latter part of World War II after China became an ally. Thereafter, about the only thing remaining that could properly be called imperialism was the position of Hong Kong, with its adjoining leased territory, and Macao.

The republican period from 1911 to 1928 saw political confusion with repeated civil wars. From 1920 to 1928, Peking's writ hardly ran beyond the city's walls and the adjoining area that the warlord heading the government happened to control. Rival generals, most of whose names are no longer important, fought to rule at Peking. Regionalism was strong, and lesser warlords sought to retain or enlarge their control of provinces and regions. As there was no central government able to speak for China as a whole, it came to be said that China was not a nation but a geographical expression. "Chaos and China have become almost synonymous terms," said Sir John Jordan, long-time British Minister to China. H. G. W. Woodhead confirmed this view: "Administrative chaos has never previously attained the proportions which we witness today, and it must be obvious that to obtain national statistics on any subject is now a matter of absolute impossibility."[3]

Resources of the governments at Peking were meager indeed. Budgets were based on nothing more than a pious hope as to what the revenue and expenditure would be if the government of the day controlled the country. After 1919-1920, no formal budgets were prepared. A draft budget for 1925 showed an outlay of C $310 million,* but a published report by Wellington V. K. Koo, covering his three and a half months as Finance Minister in 1926, showed actual receipts and payments averaging only about C $1 million monthly, of which about half was from loans.[4] Salaries and payments due from most government organs fell into arrears, except for those that had a cash flow such as the telegraphs and railways. Remittances to diplomatic officers and students abroad likewise largely ceased. There was no central bank, and customs funds together with such salt revenue funds as came into the government's hands were deposited in foreign banks.

The Peking regimes were caught in a vicious circle. Lacking funds, they could not gain authority. And lacking authority, they could not develop a system of nationwide revenues. Except for the foreign-run customs and salt revenue services, medieval fiscal practices prevailed.

The customs revenue came from duties fixed under treaties (dating from 1842) that limited rates to 5 per cent. In 1858, the rates were converted to specific duties based on prices then prevailing. Since these duties remained unchanged during long periods when prices rose, the actual yield became much less than 5 per cent. Meanwhile, customs revenue was pledged to secure loans contracted to pay a heavy indemnity to Japan after the war of 1894-1895, the Boxer Indemnity of 1901, and a loan of 1913 that was largely unproductive. These debts totaled over US $600 million. From 1921 to 1927, payments for foreign debt took over three-fourths of the net customs revenue, and payments on internal loans took nearly all the rest. During this period, customs funds released to the government or used to support specific governmental outlays amounted to less than 2 per cent of the net customs revenue.[5]

The salt revenue, next in importance to customs, was mostly lost to Peking in the twenties because of local seizures. By 1927-1928, the disposable salt revenue did not cover foreign loan service, equivalent to about US$5 million yearly. Receipts from the lesser taxes on wine and tobacco, stamp dues, and the Peking

*In this book, I use the symbol C$ to represent Chinese dollars or *yuan*, and US$ for American dollars. The value of the Chinese dollar in 1925 to 1928 averaged a little less than US$0.50 (Appendix 10).

octroi (collected at the city's gates on movement of goods) were but a few million yearly.

The Peking regimes lived largely on foreign and local loans until about 1920. But the revenues could not even provide for the government's basic needs, let alone debt payments. So, as the finances deteriorated, well over half of the debt fell into arrears. Governments with such poor credit could no longer find lenders. When the Nationalists took over at Peking in 1928, only the customs-secured foreign debt and about US $6 million of the foreign railway debt of about US $150 million (equivalents) were being duly paid. Railway receipts, like other revenues, were largely retained by the local authorities. Practically all the internal debt was in default.

In the rural areas, where about four-fifths of the people lived, there was bitter suffering and loss from the incessant civil wars of the twenties. Men were impressed for service and labor, vast amounts of property were looted or destroyed, local production and markets were disrupted, and rail transport as well as water transport was interrupted. Banditry was rife. These events were to a large extent responsible for the agrarian crisis inherited by the Nationalists which was so widely noted in the thirties. Economic and social conditions were also aggravated by persisting evils. Landlords often exploited the farmers. In both rural and urban areas, people often suffered from abuses by moneylenders and corrupt officials.

Roads and airways hardly existed. Foreign trade was the lowest per capita of any important country. Measured in gold, trade showed little growth during the twenties. It did, however, expand considerably in Manchuria because of the increased export of soy beans and their products. Meanwhile, industrial production progressed despite the confusion. Various light industries were established during World War I when China was cut-off from many foreign sources of supply. These industries continued to develop, largely in the treaty ports where they were in the hands of both Chinese and foreigners.

The currency standard and money in circulation varied from place to place, although the silver dollar was gaining as a standard. There were different units of silver, and copper coins were unrelated to silver or to one another. In several regions, depreciated paper money was in circulation. China was a paradise for moneychangers who took their toll at every turn.

Paralleling the chaotic state of affairs during these years, however, was a growing urge throughout the country to find for China a place in the world corresponding to the talents, numbers, and past achievements of her people. The principles of national sovereignty and self-determination, which Woodrow Wilson enunciated during World War I, had a strong impact on China. But the Paris Peace Conference of 1919 failed to apply them to China. It confirmed Japan's seizure in 1914-1915 of the former German rights in Shantung Province, China's "Holy Land" where Confucius and Mencius had lived and taught. On May 4, 1919, Peking students demonstrated in protest. This demonstration gave rise to the May Fourth Movement, a political, social, and cultural movement of great import in Chinese history. The movement called for equality for China among the nations, reform of outworn traditional attitudes, and modernization using western technology.[6]

The changed and potentially threatening situation in the Far East after World War I led the United States to have the Washington Conference of 1921-1922 deal with Pacific and Far Eastern affairs as well as limitation of armaments. The Washington agreements sought to create better relations, especially in Pacific affairs, among the United States, Britain, France, and Japan. The treaties aimed at ensuring China's integrity; at strengthening her finances by agreeing to hold a conference to arrange for limited increase of tariff rates; and at creating a framework of cooperation in which China could gradually progress politically and economically. A special commission was to study extraterritoriality. The powers agreed not to take advantage of unsettlement to seek further special privileges. During the Conference, Japan agreed to restore to China the rights at Tsingtao and in the Shantung Peninsula that she had obtained from Germany under the Versailles Treaty of 1919. A further check on national rivalries in China was the Consortium agreement of 1920 by which leading financial groups in Britain, France, Japan, and the United States, with the support of their governments, agreed to cooperate in future loan business in China.

Rising Chinese nationalism was far from satisfied because of the failure of China to gain full sovereignty at the Conference. The treaty powers felt that disturbed conditions and lack of real central authority in China precluded any radical change in the status of foreign rights. The Conference left full sovereignty a problem for the future. Foreign governments, although frustrated by the impotence of the Peking regimes, nevertheless continued to deal with the government of the moment, even though it was powerless to speak for China as a whole. They also dealt, as they deemed appropriate, with regional and local rulers.

For these governments there was no real alternative because of their policy of not interfering in the internal affairs of other states. But Russia, which had not been invited to Washington, had no such inhibitions. About 1920, Russia began moving actively to expand her influence in China. She sent Communist agents to China where they soon established contact with Sun Yat-sen, who from the middle nineties was promoting his movement for revolution, reform, and modernization. Viewing Sun's movement as likely to succeed, they hoped it would become an instrument for Communism. Sun was no believer in Communism. Because the help he needed was not available from the West, he accepted advice and funds from Russia. Chinese Communists were allowed to join as individuals the Kuomintang Party which Sun led.

Russia also sent diplomatic agents to China. In 1924, to the embarrassment of the other powers, she proposed that the Chinese and Russian envoys have the rank of ambassador—China and the other powers exchanged ministers only. In 1924 Russia also agreed with Peking to cancel all Tsarist treaties. This action meant granting tariff autonomy, remitting the Russian portion of the Boxer Indemnity, and ending extrality. But Russia was careful to retain her hold on the Chinese Eastern Railway in Northern Manchuria.[7]

Unhappily, France delayed approval of the Washington treaties until mid-1925, because of the controversy over paying the French share of the Boxer Indemnity in gold or paper francs. By the time the Tariff Conference met at Peking in the fall of 1925, new factors had emerged. Nationalism was much stronger. Besides the burgeoning Nationalist movement in the south, the regime at Peking was calling for much more definite progress in restoring China's sovereignty than was contemplated at Washington. Besides Russia's actions already described, Germany had agreed in 1921 to tariff autonomy for China, subject to most-favored-nation treatment, and to give up extrality.

In view of the changed situation, the Peking Tariff Conference went far beyond what had been intended at Washington three years earlier. It agreed that the powers should grant tariff autonomy by treaty. Tentatively it accepted new tariff rates that

China could enforce from January 1, 1929. But the conference ended without formal agreements because of the civil war that overthrew the Peking regime in the spring of 1926.

Although not recognized until later, the end of this conference also ended the last serious effort of the Western powers and Japan to work together for a better order in the Far East. Thereafter the powers tended to deal separately with China. Analyzing what happened in this period, Akira Iriye has said:

> The three years following the Washington Conference saw many changes in the Far Eastern scene, not of the powers' making but due largely to the Soviet initiative. . . .
>
> The Soviet initiative came before other powers had time to put into effect the new ideas of international relations which they had formulated as an alternative to imperialist power politics. They had failed to make good their promises to assist China to emerge as a sovereign nation, nor had they given a substantial content to the "spirit of the Washington Conference." The Soviet successes in north and south China were a challenge to the Washington powers precisely because they were successful; Soviet policy had achieved what they had visualized but not implemented—a new order of Sino-foreign relations. The Sino-Soviet *rapprochement* could mean the emergence of a parallel system of international relations in the Far East, challenging the structure of the Washington treaties. Although the powers had hoped to have enunciated universal principles and prescribed new rules for the conduct of all countries, the Soviet initiative and the Chinese response seemed to reduce them to the status of partial doctrines and particularistic rules.
>
> Such a trend is clear now, but to the policy makers of the 1920's the basic nature of the Soviet initiative was only dimly discernible. The result was that the Washington powers failed to work out a systematic joint strategy to cope with the challenge.[8]

The Nationalists' rise to power, which started in the early twenties, may be summarized in the light of these trends. Their movement centered in South China where it was sparked by Sun Yat-sen's preaching of the three principles of nationalism, democracy, and the people's livelihood. The first Kuomintang congress in January 1924 called for a bold program:

> All unequal treaties are to be abolished: foreigners' leased territories, consular jurisdiction, foreigners' management of customs duties, all political power exercised by foreigners in China at the cost of Chinese sovereignty. New treaties are to be concluded based on recognition of China as an equal and sovereign nation.[9]

Reflecting aspirations of the Chinese people, the Nationalist movement seemed more and more the wave of the future. The Nationalists, with their capital at Canton, came to control much of South China. Their experience and leadership were preparing them for responsibility on a greater scale. They were building financial resources under the energetic management of Tse-vung (T. V.) Soong. Their published reports for 1926 and early 1927 showed an organized government, with receipts at the yearly rate of about 100 million Canton dollars, the value of which then equaled about 75 to 80 per cent of the ordinary silver dollar.[10] That income far exceeded the few millions available yearly to Peking.

By the spring of 1927, the Nationalists succeeded in the first phase of the Northern Expedition launched in July 1926. They marched to the Yangtze and took over most of the southern half of China. The Expedition was more than a drive against the Peking regime. It became a phase of the continuing struggle of the moderate and rightist elements against the leftist factions for control of the revolution. Chiang Kai-shek, with the chief power in the armed forces, led the moderates and rightists. The leftists included regular Kuomintang members, but the Communists were the most aggressive element. The Communist strength lay in propaganda and infiltration. Political agents trained largely by them moved ahead of the troops, stirring revolt and infiltrating opposing forces.

The leftist group captured Hankow, where it set up a radical regime in what they claimed to be the Nationalist capital. Meanwhile, Chiang sought and gained control of the Shanghai-Nanking region—China's economic heart, which he saw was needed as the base for future power. The capture of Nanking in March 1927 was marked by anti-foreign outrages and murder, generally regarded as provoked by Communist elements. Hu Shih considered that the extremists' aim at Nanking was to provoke large-scale foreign intervention, and thus start an "imperialist" war which the Communists considered a precondition for capturing the revolution.[11] At this stage, there was what American Minister John V. A. MacMurray described as "a hurly-burly of aspirants to the functions of government."[12]

Chiang moved decisively and outmaneuvered his opponents. "There is an alertness and mobility in the man," said a contemporary commentator, "to which neither civilians nor militarists are accustomed ... to strike quickly at the very heart of the problem."[13] He was able to purge the Communist elements from the lower Yangtze area with the aid of Kwangsi troops.[14] On April 18, 1927, he and his associates set up the Nationalist capital at Nanking.

In Shanghai, the Nationalists promptly gained public confidence, including that of the bankers. They were able to issue, as of May 1, a loan of C $30 million for "extraordinary military expenses." This and subsequent loans made it possible to finance the continuing revolution.

Meanwhile, the Kuomintang leftists and the Communists were quarreling in Hankow. In July they split when the Communists, directed by Stalin, tried to seize control. The move failed; the Russian advisers departed; and Hankow acknowledged Nanking as the capital. In April 1928, the Peking regime raided the office of the Soviet military attache at Peking. Seized documents disclosed financial and military aid from Russia to Chiang's opponents as well as plots to control the Kuomintang. The documents also called for provoking anti-foreign incidents without leading to Japanese intervention.[15]

The leftist collapse at Hankow was followed by a period of consolidation. Chiang withdrew from leadership in August, but before the end of the year he returned to power. In the spring of 1928, the Northern Expedition was resumed. The northern warlords suffered reverses and their armies disintegrated; their leader, Marshal Chang Tso-lin, withdrew to Manchuria. In June, the Nationalists entered the gates of Peking. The city's name, which means "Northern Capital," was changed to Peiping, meaning "Northern Peace."

The Nationalist revolution at last had triumphed. By catching the people's ear with the slogans of Sun Yat-sen's program, the Nationalists had won "the mandate of Heaven."

2: First Measures, 1928

China was unified in name only when in mid-1928, following the collapse of the ineffective Peking regime, the National Government assumed nationwide responsibility. The new government faced a forbidding array of problems—international, internal, political, military, and economic. The Western powers and Japan were sympathetic to ending the outmoded treaty restrictions on China's tariff autonomy, but new agreements had to be made. Furthermore, the government had to consolidate its internal authority, and military and political consolidation was closely related to financial and economic action.

The government was, in effect, a coalition of diverse elements. Regional leaders and warlords gave lip service, but their loyalty was uncertain or improbable. Only the lower Yangtze region was solidly under government control. Elsewhere the degree of control varied; in many areas it was only nominal. The Kwangsi leaders, from South China, held the Peiping-Tientsin area. In the northeastern provinces (Manchuria), Marshal Chang Hsueh-liang had thrown in his lot with Nanking and raised the new national flag in the latter part of 1928; however, he expected to retain most of the revenues and, as far as Manchuria was concerned, to conduct most of the relations with Japan and Russia. In the Canton region in the south, control was uncertain. In the northwest, Marshals Feng Yu-hsiang and Yen Hsi-shan had moved arsenal machinery inland and threatened revolt. In the west and southwest, the local warlords were practically independent. And the Communists, after the purge of 1927 and the departure of the Russian advisers, had retreated to the mountainous area of Kiangsi Province, southwest of Shanghai, where they continued to plot the takeover of China.

Military operations continued after mid-1928 with little interruption, the first aim being to eliminate or absorb elements of the old Peking armies. The government was obliged to maintain large armies that were a burden on the people and a drain on the treasury. Chiang clearly saw the necessity for a strong government if China's national aspirations were to be realized. Other leaders opposed him, seeking either to keep full regional control or to displace him as leader. Not until the spring of 1929 did the government succeed in gaining full control of the important Hankow region of central China, up-river from Nanking. Despite setbacks, the basic task of consolidation and unification was pushed actively during the prewar decade, and notable progress had been made by 1937. The task, however, was not complete when Japan's attack began a new era for China.

Financial and economic consolidation was bound up with political and military control. Effective central government depended on the receipt of adequate revenue from the entire country and on control of the railways and other nationwide communications. In 1928, although accepting the government's nominal rule, Chiang's rivals retained most of the national revenues, except customs, collected in their areas.

The new rulers had yet to prove themselves. They suffered from the lack of experienced administrators. They had to contend with the age-old idea that official "squeeze," if moderate, was entirely ethical, and with the all too common practice of official rapacity. Charges of greed and corruption on the part of members of the regime were frequent. The new government itself was divided in outlook between the traditional and the modern, and at all levels these two elements were striving for ascendency. The task of consolidating the Nationalist victory, unifying the huge land mass of China, and reforming its largely medieval structure and attitudes was tremendous. Accomplishment was bound to be spotty and imperfect.

Organizing a government

Although the National Government set up its capital at Nanking in April 1927, no formal scheme of organization was adopted until after the takeover at Peking in mid-1928. In August, the Fourth Plenary Session of the Kuomintang Party adopted a basic plan. This plan gave rise to the Organic Law promulgated October 4, 1928, in the following terms (translated):

> The Kuomintang of China, in order to establish the Republic of China on the Basis of the Three Principles of the People and the Constitution of Five Powers, which form the underlying principle of the revolution, having conquered all opposition by military force and having now brought the Revolution from the military stage to the educative stage, deem it necessary to construct a framework for the Constitution of Five Powers with a view to developing the ability of

> the people to exercise political power, so that constitutional government may soon come into existence and political power be restored to the people; and, further, in view of the responsibilities hitherto entrusted to the Party for the guidance and supervision of the Government, do hereby ordain and promulgate the following Organic Law of the National Government.

This law provided for a president and a State Council of 12 to 16 members. Under the Council, five Yuans were created: the Executive Yuan, the Legislative Yuan, the Judicial Yuan, the Control Yuan, and the Examination Yuan. The Yuan heads were members of the State Council. The Executive Yuan was by far the most important, and comprised 15 ministries and commissions. The law also provided for 28 provincial governments, each with a chairman named by the National Government. In practice, many chairmen were named in recognition of the *de facto* authority they already had.

The Organic Law made it clear that a period of tutelage was necessary before popular government could be established. The tutelage was to be under the guidance of the Kuomintang. Thus, the theory of government was borrowed extensively from Russia. An organization chart issued at the time of promulgation showed the Kuomintang at the top, above the Government. This chart described the Kuomintang as the "Body of registered electors in provinces, special districts, and overseas constituencies, who have been examined with respect to their loyalty and who have taken the oath of allegiance to the National Government."

To create a legal system, the National Government promulgated "The Civil Code of the Republic of China" on May 23, 1929. This code was formulated after extensive study by a group of experts named by the Legislative Yuan in the fall of 1928. The motivation for the development of this code was recognition of the need for a modern judicial system as a precondition of the abolition of extrality. It was by dint of judicial reforms that Japan had been able to end extrality in 1899. China's treaties with several countries provided for abolition of extrality when Chinese laws and administration warranted such action.[1]

Formulating an economic and financial program

The government immediately recognized the urgency of economic and financial rehabilitation. To plan a suitable program, the National Economic Conference met at Shanghai from June 20 through 30, 1928. The National Financial Conference met at Nanking during the first ten days of July. The Economic Conference was composed primarily of private businessmen and financial experts. The Financial Conference was composed of national and provincial officials who were to be charged with carrying out the financial program. Both conferences were advisory. Their work resulted in preparation of a comprehensive program relating to revenue, expenditure, debt, banking, and currency.

The objective of the Economic Conference was stated as follows by Finance Minister T. V. Soong:

> Now that the war is over, we shall have to raise enormous funds to rehabilitate the country, to restore peace and order, to disband the surplus troops, to restore the dilapidated railways, to care for famine-stricken areas which have served as the battlefield. In this work of rehabilitation, the people must have a voice. The Ministry of Finance has not waited until high-flown plans are formulated for the participation of the people in government. We have called together responsible non-political persons, representatives of the tax-payers, to criticize us, to help us, and to guide us. This is, so far as I know, the first conference of its nature to be held in China. Its success will be a step forward in democratic institutions in China.[2]

In August, a plenary session of the Central Executive Committee of the Kuomintang substantially adopted the program recommended by the two conferences. That program was an important guide for the National Government although circumstances —notably continuing regionalism, revolts of warlords, and Japanese aggression—interfered with its full implementation.

Both conferences had concluded that control of expenditure was of major importance. Soong was in favor of a strict budget, which China had not had under the warlords, and urged that a strong Budget Committee be set up to exercise control. Data presented to the conferences showed that the military establishment, as it existed in the summer of 1928, would cost at least C $360 million a year. Total revenue after making debt payments was estimated at not more than C $300 million. A recommendation was made to reduce military expenditures to C $192 million by reducing the armies. The conferences suggested that a special loan be raised for costs of disbandment and that disbanded troops be used temporarily on public works.

Demarcation of national and provincial revenues was essential since local authorities were retaining most of the revenues that came into their hands. In addressing the Financial Conference, with provincial officials present, Soong said:

> Without coming to a definite understanding with the military authorities to let taxation alone, without arranging with the provincial authorities to give a free hand to the Ministry of Finance in the control of national revenue, and finally without knowing what our actual income is, all talk of unifying China is idle.[3]

The conclusions of the Conference were that national revenues should include the customs; taxes on salt, tobacco and wine, and mining; stamp dues; and revenue from government enterprises and property. *Likin,* the burdensome tax collected by the provinces on the inland movement of goods, should be abolished as soon as practicable, but meanwhile should become a national revenue. Since the provinces were receiving large revenue from *likin* they should be given the land tax, long a national revenue. They should also retain miscellaneous business taxes and licenses of a local character. Provincial and local authorities should not detain national revenues. The systems of taxes and tax administration were to be improved, and new taxes on incomes, inheritance, and consumption were to be introduced.

As to debt, the new government as a successor to Peking should recognize old obligations in principle, and should devise means to liquidate the debt that had fallen into arrears. The new leaders, now facing national responsibility, realized the need to modify the policy of the first Kuomintang Congress in January 1924, which had declared that China should not repay those foreign loans that were "contracted by an irresponsible government, such as the Peking government, to maintain the power of the war lords."[4]

The conferences called for creation of a Central Bank that alone should have the right of note issue. The coinage should be unified on the basis of the silver dollar, and the *tael* should be abolished as a monetary unit. Ultimately China should adopt the gold standard.

The financial situation in the early months of the new government, and the program to deal with it, appear clearly from Soong's memorandum of January 11, 1929, to the Third Plenary Session of the Military Conference at Nanking. The government had full financial control only in four provinces: Kiangsu, Chekiang, Anhwei, and Kiangsi. The first two alone yielded a surplus, as all the receipts of the other two went for military costs. These four were the only provinces to supply full reports of receipts and payments—the other provinces sent either partial data or none at all. Soong's program was to centralize and reorganize the finances and establish full control of national revenues and expenditures throughout the country; to have power to appoint and remove staff; and to limit military outlay.[5] In the period ahead, as the account that follows will show, progress in controlling military expenditure was far from satisfactory. But in the rest of the program progress was noteworthy.

Feeling the need of expert foreign advice, the government engaged Professor E. W. Kemmerer of Princeton University to bring the Commission of Financial Experts to China for a year's service. There were indications that for some members of the new government a further motive for engaging this group was the hope that it would help in obtaining a loan in the United States—because previous Kemmerer missions in Latin America had done so. But Soong had no illusions on this point. In his first annual report for 1928-1929 (page 7), he recognized the prior need for settling debts in arrears and for "sound public financing in the future on a basis honorable to China and satisfactory to prospective bondholders."

At this stage, creation of viable finances and rehabilitation of the economy after the revolution took priority over economic development. Yet Sun Yat-sen's long-range program of development was not forgotten, and several primary steps were taken. These steps included the completion of agreements to begin air services and the creation of the National Reconstruction Commission, the National Highway Planning Commission, the Ministry of Agriculture and Mining, the Ministry of Health, and the Ministry of Railways. Not until 1931, however, did the government begin to give attention to more comprehensive plans for development (Chapters 13 and 14).

Recovering tariff autonomy

China had reason to feel outraged by the working of the tariff restrictions of the unequal treaties. These restrictions deprived the government of much needed revenue and prevented it from adopting protective duties should it so desire. Not even China's need for more revenue to meet heavy payments on the loans floated in Europe in 1895-1898, to pay the war indemnity to Japan, could move the powers to revise the specific duties dating from 1858 that yielded much less than an effective 5 per cent. The difficulty of getting so many powers to agree, combined with the greed of traders anxious to keep the *status quo*, prevented action. Rates were finally revised after the powers imposed the heavy Boxer Indemnity of 1901. The next revision was made in 1918 as a result of China's joining the Allies in World War I. But that revision proved inadequate since the yield at the time of the Washington Conference of 1921-1922 was estimated at only about 3 per cent.

That Conference agreed to immediate revision to an effective 5 per cent. Recognizing that this increase would not be enough, the Conference agreed further that a tariff conference would meet in China to set the rates of a general surtax of 2-1/2 per cent, with 5 per cent on luxuries. But this modest reform was delayed for over three years, when France delayed ratification. When the Peking Tariff Conference finally met in the fall of 1925 to give effect to the surtaxes, the plan was outdated. China then asked for full tariff autonomy.

In November 1925 the representatives of the powers and China unanimously agreed to recognize by treaty a new tariff, specifying rates that would tentatively take effect on January 1, 1929. China was to abolish *likin* simultaneously. The Conference continued in session and gave attention to arrangements for immediate application of the surtaxes granted under the Washington treaty as well as to problems concerning abolition of *likin* and defaulted debts. In the spring of 1926, however, a coup overthrew the Peking government. And in the summer the Nationalists began the Northern Expedition, which soon captured Hankow and overran much of China south of the Yangtze River. Since there was no authority able to speak for China as a whole, the Peking conference petered out.[6]

In the fall of 1926, the Nationalists began to levy the 2-1/2 and 5 per cent surtaxes at Canton. They also levied special taxes on kerosene, gasoline, tobacco, and wine. Similar levies soon spread throughout the country, creating a hodgepodge of rates and practices, with the proceeds retained locally. By the spring of 1928 the surtaxes were yielding at the yearly rate of about C $32 million in Nationalist areas and about C $6 million in areas controlled by Peking. The special taxes brought in about as much more. The new levies were administered not by the Customs but by special bureaus, sometimes working closely with the Customs.[7] Peking, however, wanted the Customs to collect the surtaxes. The Inspector General, Sir Francis Aglen, objected and was dismissed. But for the time being the special bureaus continued to collect the surtaxes.[8]

The powers protested the surtaxes since treaties permitting the new duties had not been concluded. But their efforts failed. On December 18, 1926, Britain proposed that the powers agree to the immediate unconditional grant to China of the right to impose these duties. Britain regarded this as "a sympathetic adjustment ... to the equitable claims of the Chinese." The United States, though sympathetic to the proposal, could not act by executive authority but only through a new treaty, duly ratified.[9]

So the matter dragged on, until the Nationalists took over at Peking in June 1928. Since negotiations with the powers collectively for tariff autonomy had failed, China turned to individual negotiations, first with the United States. On July 25, the Soong-MacMurray treaty was signed, granting to China full tariff autonomy. At that time, as the Economic Adviser of the Department of State, I participated in framing the language of the treaty—not dreaming that before long I would be representing the interests of China in further international negotiations on the subject. One problem in July 1928 was to find a way to maintain equal American rights without using the phrase "most-favored-nation" to which China objected. We had devised in the State Department the phrase, used in this and other treaties made with China, that treatment would be "in no way discriminatory."

The chief European powers followed suit in treaty negotiations before the end of 1928. In general, the agreements were like the one with the United States, but Britain obtained a promise that for at least a year the duties on British goods should be those set forth in the 1926 draft schedule. China hoped to introduce the new tariff January 1, 1929, but negotiations with Japan had not been concluded. Finally, in January, Japan agreed conditionally and the tariff became effective from February 1. The negotiations with Japan were difficult. Japan sought an agreement on the settlement of debts. The agreement of January 1929, negotiated by Soong, provided that China should hold a conference to discuss the debts and meanwhile should set aside C $5 million yearly to be applied later to debt payments. China undertook also to abolish *likin* within two years, and stated that the rates of the new tariff would mostly be those drafted at the Peking Conference in 1926.[10] But this agreement did not convey Japan's agreement to tariff autonomy, which required further negotiations.

The new tariff of 1929 superseded the 2-1/2 and 5 per cent surtaxes from February 1, 1929. It also eliminated the need for the special taxes on imported goods collected by the special bureaus all over the country. It was not easy to abolish these bureaus, but to the credit of the government it was done. The government also asserted its right to receive the entire proceeds of customs revenue. This solid accomplishment was a major step toward fiscal centralization. But temporary local enjoyment of part of the customs revenue had whetted local appetites, causing trouble in several instances, as described in Chapter 3.

Receipts from the higher tariff rates gave a major boost to the finances of the new government. In 1924 through 1928, customs revenue averaged C $121 million yearly. It rose to C $244 million in 1929, C $290 million in 1930, and C $385 million in 1931.*

Salt revenue

China's salt tax came into worldwide prominence in 1913 when President Woodrow Wilson withdrew support from an American banking group planning to participate in the Reorganization Loan that was secured on that tax.[11] He objected to loan conditions that would "include not only the pledging of particular taxes, some of them antiquated and burdensome, to secure the loan but also the administration of those taxes by foreign agents."[12] China and the foreign groups, however, went ahead, and the Salt administration was duly organized under British auspices.

By the 1913 agreement, China undertook "to take immediate steps for the reorganization with the assistance of foreigners of the system of collection of the salt revenues" (Article V). The Chief Inspectorate of Salt Revenue was set up in charge of a Chinese Chief Inspector, Chang Hu, and a British Associate Chief Inspector, Sir Richard Dane, who was also Adviser to the Central Salt Administration. In each salt-producing district there was a branch office with one Chinese and one foreign District Inspector, jointly responsible for collecting and handling the revenue. The agreement provided for depositing collections in foreign banks, paying collection costs, and turning over the surplus to the government.[13]

*Part of the increase reflected the depreciation of silver. But prices in China rose much less than silver fell, so a substantial real gain of revenue resulted. The worldwide depression did not cause great damage to China immediately because she was on the silver standard and the slump in silver prices and in the exchange value of China's currency avoided a deflation for the time being.

Under the 1913 agreement, the Inspectorate became a semi-independent career service for both Chinese and foreign officers. Dane was an experienced officer of the Indian civil service, who had been in charge of the Indian salt tax. With the collaboration of his Chinese colleagues, he carried through a notable reorganization of the Salt administration during his five years of tenure. Salt revenue grew to be second only to customs in yield. One clause of the agreement provided for customs security for the 1913 loan when the yield of the customs should become sufficient. From 1917, the Customs provided the funds for the loan service, but until 1930, the Salt administration made the payments to the banks.

Two other foreign loan issues of the Peking government were charged upon and paid from salt revenue: the Anglo-French loan of 1908 and the Crisp Loan of 1912. The Hukuang Railway Loan of 1911 also had salt security in the amount of about C $1.4 million yearly.

After 1920, the provincial authorities detained more and more of the salt revenue. By 1927, although the Salt administration collected yearly about C $60 million, the service of these loans of 1908-1912 was only partly met because the central government received only about C $3 million. In the first half of 1928, the funds provided for debt service were only a small fraction of the amount needed. In 16 of the 22 districts, Inspectorate functions had been disturbed. In some districts they were taken over by local officials and Inspectorate offices were closed or their functions suspended.

Thus the affairs of the Salt administration were at a low ebb when the National Government took over at Peking in mid-1928. Finance Minister Soong saw clearly the value of keeping the organization as an effective revenue-collecting agency for the central government. He also saw the importance of restoring loan payments. On September 25, 1928, he issued a statement that the new government "is anxious to maintain the national credit even before complete unification of finance has been achieved, and before the entire Salt revenue has become centralized under the Ministry of Finance." He announced that each salt district would forthwith be assigned monthly loan quotas sufficient to provide an annual total of C $10 million. That sum sufficed to cover what was due for one year's service—payment of arrears was left for later attention.

There was nationalistic opposition to the position of the Salt administration as a somewhat autonomous revenue agency in which foreigners took the leading part in management. On November 16, 1928, Soong announced changes in the former arrangements, to make the administration "an effective part of the National Government under the exclusive control of the Ministry of Finance." The Ministry rather than that administration would assume "full responsibility for . . . loan service." The system of deposits in foreign banks, with collection costs and debt service paid and the surplus remitted to the government, had broken down and was now ended. The representatives of Britain, France, and Japan issued a statement critical of the "unilateral action." The Associate Chief Inspector, Frederick Hussey-Freke, presented a brief in support of the previous status, but accepted confirmation in his post by the new government. He explained in a statement that the new arrangements were the best that could be made under the circumstances.[14]

The terms of the Reorganization Loan agreement of 1913 had certainly been infringed, but the infringement was only nominal and the bondholders suffered no real damage. Payments on this loan were amply covered with customs revenue after 1917, and the other loan agreements called for no special procedure as to salt revenue. Had the changes of 1928 not been made, the government would have found it hard to keep radical elements in line and to gain support for such policies as recognition of the old Peking debts, restoration of payments on the salt-secured foreign loans, and maintenance of Sino-foreign collaboration in handling salt and customs revenues.

Other revenues

The need for money to continue the Northern Expedition led the Nationalists to begin revenue reforms in 1927, after establishing their capital at Nanking and before the takeover in North China. These reforms led to development of the consolidated tax system. This system was based on the principle that taxes on taxable commodities should be paid once and for all at the source at which the commodities are produced.

Prior to 1928, the factories of foreign tobacco-manufacturing companies in the international settlements had paid no tax to China in view of the old treaty provisions. Chinese companies located in the settlements were also free from taxation. Since the central government and the provincial and local authorities had imposed a great variety of taxes on rolled tobacco, the settlements became centers of huge smuggling operations.

In January 1928, Soong made a major breakthrough by arranging for the producing companies to pay specified taxes. This change was made with the understanding that these taxes would be the only ones the companies would pay on rolled tobacco, and that the government would reimburse them if they had to pay additional taxes in specified areas. At first these areas included Kiangsu, Chekiang, Anhwei, Kiangsi, and Fukien Provinces; in the spring of 1929 they were extended to include Hupeh, Hunan, Honan, Hopei, Kwangtung, and Kwangsi. However, since the government did not have full control of the regimes in all these provinces, some of the collections were retained locally.

It was not easy to make these arrangements. Because of the tax-exempt position of the foreign companies, their governments intervened during the negotiations. Finally, to circumvent the treaty difficulties and at the same time to recognize the foreign rights under the treaties while they existed, the government agreed to exempt from taxation at the factory one case of foreign-made cigarettes and one box of foreign-made cigars each month. For the companies, the *quid pro quo* was freedom from the burdensome and often arbitrary exactions and bribery that previously impeded their operations.

Similarly, the government arranged that the oil companies pay a special tax on kerosene, but be immune from other exactions. That tax became security for a loan of C$40 million, which was used to help to finance the Northern Expedition in 1928. The tax became an import duty when the new tariff took effect on February 1, 1929, and the security of the loan was transferred accordingly.

In connection with these arrangements, the government used its increased authority throughout the country to end provincial and local levies on the items concerned. Sometimes it had to let the provincial authorities temporarily retain part or all of the revenue collected on the new basis. In 1928 it did not have enough control to extend the arrangements to the Northeastern Provinces (Manchuria), Shansi, and the provinces of the northwest and southwest.

Besides adoption of these broad new measures, the new government moved to improve existing taxes. The historic wine and tobacco tax was being collected in various forms and at different rates (these did not apply to rolled tobacco). Although a national revenue, it was mostly operated by the provinces and little reached the central government. Because of the unsettled conditions and differing practices in the provinces, the government could not undertake drastic changes at once. Moreover, reform was especially difficult for wine, because production, distribution, and consumption were not concentrated. In January 1929, the government appointed a commission of experienced administrators to devise improvements. In August, it prescribed a uniform tax rate of 20 per cent and a procedure for registering persons engaged in those trades and for using a standard report form. It also began moves to do away with tax farming, and the Finance Ministry was able to recognize some of the collecting bureaus. The result was that, whereas before 1928 the central government got practically nothing from this revenue, in the first fiscal year ending June 30, 1929, the yield was C $3.5 million. Thereafter it grew severalfold.

The stamp tax presented special problems because a system of tax farming had developed. Under this system, local groups contracted with the tax collector to take a fixed amount of stamps for a particular kind of business or a region. Because the contracted payments enabled tax collectors to turn over regular revenue to higher authorities, the tax farmers did not insist on actual attachment of the stamps, and commonly retained them.

In November 1927, the Nationalists, before taking over at Peiping, issued provisional regulations for the stamp tax. Documents and cosmetics were added to the list of taxable items. The policy of the Finance Ministry was to enforce use of uniform stamps to be sold at post offices, even though the revenue did not necessarily come to the central government; to move to end the tax farming system, although this was to take some time; and to make agreements to apply the tax to Chinese in the foreign settlements.

The old *likin* tax on goods in transit had long been a source of difficulties. This tax was collected at about 700 barriers throughout the country on the main trade routes by land and water. It was originally imposed in the 1850's to raise revenues for the government to put down the Taiping Rebellion. Literally *likin* meant a tax of one-tenth of 1 per cent. But the amount became subject to arbitrary arrangement, giving rise to much corruption. Rates up to 10 per cent became frequent and even more was sometimes charged. The system was a grave obstruction to trade and costly to operate. It burdened the people with higher prices for goods that were mainly necessities. But the revenue was large. The provinces, however, were taking most of it even though it was a national revenue. The National Government committed itself to abolish *likin,* but it could do little until it gained wider control. One step was to give the land tax to the provinces in exchange for their claims on *likin.* In the fall of 1930, the government declared that *likin* would be abolished at the beginning of 1931 (Chapter 3).

The results of the reforms in the revenue system were gratifying. In the fiscal year ending June 30, 1929, the first after the takeover at Peiping, the revenue available to the government after the payments on debts and the Boxer Indemnity was C $274 million. That was quite a change from the few millions at the disposal of the Peking regimes in their later years. And producers and the people began to benefit from improvement of the financial system and its administration, especially from the action taken to get rid of irregular and arbitrary exactions.[15]

Loans and restoration of credit

The National Government, after taking over at Shanghai in the spring of 1927, had to borrow heavily to maintain its existence and to finance its drive to take over North China. To borrow, it had to convince the Shanghai bankers and the public that it was worthy of credit. And, having borrowed, it had to carry out strictly the terms of the loans. It could accomplish these things because it collected the 2-1/2 per cent surtax and developed new taxes on tobacco and kerosene and gasoline. These revenues were pledged to secure loans and were paid over to a commission composed of representatives of banking interests and public bodies, operating under a government mandate. This commission, the 2-1/2 per cent Surtax Treasury Bonds Sinking Fund Commission, strengthened public confidence in the issues and rendered important service until supplanted in 1932 by the National Loans Sinking Fund Administrative Commission. A considerable market for the new bonds promptly developed.

Prior to July 1, 1928, when the National Government began

its first fiscal year as a national regime, it issued at Shanghai the following loans in the nominal amount of C $136 million:

Date of issue	Amount, millions	Interest rate, %	Security
May 1, 1927	C$30	8.4	Shanghai customs 2-1/2% surtax
October 1, 1927	40	9.6	ditto
April 1, 1928	16	9.6	Rolled tobacco tax
May 1, 1928	6	8	Stamp tax
June 1, 1928	4	8	ditto
June 30, 1928 (half of loan issued in December)	40	8	Kerosene and gasoline tax
Total	C$136		

These loans were indispensable. First, they enabled the government to maintain a position of strength in Central and South China in 1927 vis-a-vis the dissidents within the Kuomintang. Second, they were used to finance the Northern Expedition, which the Nationalists resumed from Nanking in April 1928.

In mid-1928, nearly all of China's foreign debt, except customs-secured debt, was in default. The new government realized that settlement of defaulted debts was vital if China's damaged credit at home and abroad was to be restored. The government felt the need of foreign loans and investment to aid in rehabilitation and development. There was then no prospect of loans by friendly governments, and private lenders would be deterred so long as old debts were not being paid. The Economic and Financial Conferences of mid-1928 urged steps to settle the debts, and the government recognized in principle, as a successor, the foreign and domestic debts of the Peking regimes. As already mentioned, resumption of payments on the salt-secured foreign loans in September 1928 showed a serious intention to deal with the debts.

The breakdown of the Peking Conference of 1925-1926 thwarted the plans of the powers to agree with China on a program to apply to debt payment part of the revenue from higher tariffs. The powers thereafter were not effectively cooperating in the matter. Japan alone continued pressing for some commitment by China, which led to the undertaking to set aside C $5 million yearly in the first instance for debt settlement. Japan wanted a settlement of the Nishihara loans of 1917-1918 and other debts (Chapter 5). These loans were a sore topic in China because of the circumstances of issue, and an agreement about them was not then politically feasible. The upshot was agreement with Japan in January 1929, as mentioned above, to hold a conference to discuss debts.

The Central Bank of China

Recognizing the need for a modern financial system, the new government created the Central Bank of China with a charter sanctioned on October 6, 1928.[16] In 1913, the Peking government had created the Bank of China, intending it to become a central bank. But during the successive weak regimes it was forced into unsound practices in North China, although its Shanghai office managed to establish enough autonomy to maintain parity of its notes there.

The governor of the Central Bank was Finance Minister Soong. He had been head of the Kuomintang's central bank at Canton and had managed it with a large degree of success. The new bank had nine directors, appointed by the government, of whom three represented respectively private banking, commerce, and industry. The capital was C $20 million, provided by the government. The bank was given the right to issue notes, to mint and circulate coins, to deal in foreign exchange, and to handle the issuance and service of public loans. Following the tradition of the Bank of England, it had separate banking and issue departments. Notes were to have a reserve of 60 per cent in silver or gold coin or bullion and 40 per cent in government bonds or commercial paper.

The Central Bank began operations on November 1, 1928, with its head office in Shanghai. It promptly established branches at Nanking and other leading cities. Its most immediate function was to act as the government's fiscal agent. But it had the potential to become a major factor for monetary reform. From the start it was conservatively managed and began to gain public confidence.

Meanwhile the predecessor central bank at Canton continued as an entirely separate local institution. Its operations were in terms of the "small money" silver currency of that area, where the "dollar" represented by five 20-cent depreciated coins was worth around 70 to 75 per cent of the ordinary silver dollar.

Monetary reform

Although monetary reform had been discussed from time to time since about 1900, little had been done about it. The basic problems were the adoption of a definitive monetary standard and the creation of a uniform and convenient monetary circulation.

The National Financial Conference of July 1928 recommended the silver dollar as the basic unit. The dollar would replace the silver *taels,* money of account whose fine silver content varied from place to place. Subsidiary coins would be issued convertible into silver dollars. The Conference also recommended that the government work toward ultimate adoption of the gold standard. Seignorage profits on subsidiary coin would be set aside as a reserve to that end.

Fundamental measures of monetary reform had to wait. The fiscal problem of making ends meet was more urgent, and occupied the government's chief attention in the early period. Meanwhile, two currency operations incidental to the Northern Expedition called for liquidation. The leftist regime at Hankow, which briefly claimed to be the National Government, had issued paper money through a since defunct central bank and also through the Bank of China and the Bank of Communications. Although this money had become almost valueless, the Nanking authorities felt a moral and practical obligation to do something about it. The solution was to redeem the notes at face value in special bonds totaling C $45 million. These bonds bore interest of only 2-1/2 per cent, and were redeemable by drawings from the sixth to the 25th year.

A second note issue needing attention was that put out by the Nationalists to finance in part the march from Nanking to the north. This issue consisted of 8.7 million in notes of "small money" dollars. Since 12 of the 10-cent notes equaled a "big" dollar, the issue was equivalent to C $7.25 million. The government announced that this issue would be redeemed in full at par as from December 7, 1928. This redounded to the new government's credit. But since the notes were redeemable on demand at any office of the Central Bank, Bank of China, or Bank of Communications, they were not promptly withdrawn. Thus a new complication of "small money" notes was added to an already over-complicated currency.

Communications

China's railways were in a sad state when the Nationalists took power in 1928. Creation of a railway network had made some progress in the first two decades of this century, but came to an almost complete halt with the breakdown of the central government in the twenties. In 1928, much of the line was not in effective operation. Local warlords had seized railways and their revenues, and most of the debt was in default. The number of locomotives and passenger cars in China south of the Great Wall seriously decreased from 1925 to 1929. The warlord Marshal Chang Tso-lin had taken some equipment to Manchuria, but the cooperative attitude of his son and successor, Marshal Chang Hsueh-liang, suggested that much of it might be returned. Both lines and equipment had deteriorated to the point where a great amount was barely usable.

Sun Yat-sen's grand plan for China's development called for 100,000 miles of railways. His son, Sun Fo, became Minister of Railways in 1928 and promptly announced plans for the rehabilitation and gradual expansion of the railway network. But little beyond rehabilitation could be done until greater progress had been made with unification of the country and development of more solid governmental finances.

Apart from a few progressive cities, most roads were mere tracks traversable only by carts. In 1928, dirt roads passable for motor traffic totaled perhaps 18,000 miles, with about half as much more partly built or being built. There were not even roads from Shanghai to nearby Nanking and Hangchow. In all of China there were perhaps 20,000 motor vehicles, mostly motor cars in the chief cities. So distinctive was their use that in 1928 Kweichow Province issued a dollar coin bearing the image of a motor car.

There were no functioning air lines in 1928. In the years after World War I China had bought a number of planes for commercial service. Air mail postage stamps were issued as early as 1920, and there had been some sporadic service. But the military had long since taken over the planes. Early in 1929, Minister Sun Fo set up the China National Aviation Corporation, which was later to play such a large and honorable part in the development of civil aviation in China.

In transportation the beginnings were small, but at least the rehabilitation of communications was started, and there was promise for the future.

International relations

The new government and popular opinion in China welcomed as important steps forward the recovery of tariff autonomy, the greater integration of the Customs and Salt revenue services into the Finance Ministry, and the arrangements for foreign companies to pay certain taxes. But unresolved problems of economic importance concerned extrality and the status of international settlements and concessions, especially Shanghai. China's push to end extrality stalled promptly when the powers insisted on the need first to improve drastically Chinese administration of justice. As to Shanghai, the powers felt that the stability there benefited China as well as foreign interests. Certain foreigners, especially some of the British, felt that Shanghai might be made a sort of international enclave from which foreign enterprise could work for the development and modernization of China. A study of the Shanghai situation by Justice Richard Feetham of South Africa, commissioned by the Shanghai Municipal Council, argued that rendition of the settlement to China was a matter of decades, not years. But such an attitude failed to take into account the burgeoning nationalism of China. The ideas of the Feetham report were strongly rejected by Chinese official and popular opinion.[17] China's predominant stake in Shanghai Settlement affairs was recognized by increasing Chinese participation in its rule. But it took the war to bring about rendition to China of the several foreign settlements and concessions.

The procedure of bilateral negotiations for tariff autonomy, begun on American initiative, was an indication that the program of the Washington treaty powers with regard to cooperative dealings with China was breaking down. In 1928-1929, and until Japan invaded Manchuria in 1931, the relations of these powers as to Chinese affairs remained generally harmonious. But the powers dealt with China independently.

The United States sought closer ties with China and recognized the new government by signing the tariff treaty of 1928, following Secretary of State Frank B. Kellogg's conclusion that the government was "demonstrating a capacity to establish itself in China as the accepted government."[18] In the summer of

1928, Sun Fo was welcomed when he came to the United States to solicit American official and business support. It was he who arranged for the Commission of Financial Experts headed by Kemmerer. Britain and the chief European powers were also taking a favorable view of the new government's prospects, evidenced later in 1928 by signing treaties granting tariff autonomy. Britain in particular was paying special attention to Chinese matters because of the heavy British investments in enterprises and loans as well as interest in the Customs and Salt administrations.

Japan was in a special position. Her attitude concerning Manchuria was crucial for future world history. After defeating Russia in 1904-1905, Japan succeeded to the Russian sphere of influence in South Manchuria. That included railway rights and a lease of Liaotung Peninsula, which contained the port of Dairen and the naval base of Port Arthur. Thus an impetus was provided for full control of the area.

Aided by newly available Japanese materials, Akira Iriye tells what was going on behind the scenes in mid-1928:

> Given the picture of Sino-American *rapprochement,* Japan had to decide on a new course of action. It could either retract its strong stand in China and seek friendly relations with the Nationalists, bring about renewed understanding with the United States and other powers in order to solve the China question within the framework of international cooperation, or pursue the policy of consolidating its interests in Manchuria regardless of the attitudes of Nanking and Washington. In the summer and early fall of 1928 all these policies were tried simultaneously.[19]

Japanese military elements had already shown that they could not be controlled by the civilian authorities or even by the War Ministry at Tokyo. In May 1928, Japanese and Chinese troops clashed at Tsinan in Shantung Province, the basic cause being the arbitrary action of the Japanese commander who was apparently seeking prestige for his army. In June, Japanese junior officers assassinated Marshal Chang Tso-lin in Manchuria by blowing up his train near Mukden; despite the Emperor's backing, the civilian government proved unable to punish them. In the summer of 1928, the General Staff at Tokyo advocated a unilateral policy for Manchuria, and spoke of the possibility of military action to set up a puppet regime. Japan was also negotiating locally on Manchurian affairs. Thus the seeds were already present for the creation of Manchukuo in the fall of 1931, and for an inevitable clash with China which was to involve the United States.[20]

The leaders of Japan's civil government, however, sought improved relations with China. In the fall of 1928, Premier Tanaka sent friendly personal messages to Chiang, and told his envoy that Japan wanted to aid the Nationalists, now that they seemed "to be entering a constructive phase of their revolution." The Sino-Japanese agreement on tariffs and debts was made in January 1929. In March, the Tsinan incident was settled. Japan recognized the National Government on June 3, 1929. Meanwhile, in the summer of 1928, Japan sought better relations concerning China matters with the United States, Britain, and the other treaty powers. But Japan's attitude concerning Manchuria, as well as such unilateral action as in the Tsinan affair, stood as an obstacle.[21]

China's relations with Russia continued to be strained after Chiang's purge of the Communists in the lower Yangtze Valley and other action against them, and expulsion of the Russian advisers. He denounced, however, the Peking government's raid on the office of the Soviet military attache in 1928. But some time was to elapse before Sino-Russian relations became normalized.

Summary

In its early months, the new government accomplished a great transformation. Formally organized at Nanking, it had gained both internal and international recognition as the government of China. An authority was finally emerging that seemed likely to be able to speak for China as a whole. Furthermore, the Nationalists were giving effect to the fundamental aspiration of China's people to see their country restored to a position of equality and stature in the world.

A beginning had been made with major reforms, based on a far-reaching program of financial and economic reorganization. The new government was gaining vitally needed income and becoming solvent, thanks to its tariff autonomy, its rehabilitation of the salt and other revenues, and its ability to borrow at Shanghai. The state of the finances under T. V. Soong's able management contrasted strongly with the meager resources that had rendered the Peking regimes impotent. Despite leftist opposition, the new government had recognized Peking's debts in principle and had taken the first steps to deal with debts in arrears. The leaders were anxious for foreign loans, but realized that they would not be forthcoming without debt settlements. The Central Bank of China had been created. Expert foreign advisers had been engaged in an effort to effect monetary and fiscal reforms. A beginning had been made in restoring and improving the railways and other communications.

Yet grave problems remained. The confusion of the twenties could not be changed into order overnight. Unification was only nominal, regionalism strong, and Chiang's leadership and conception of a strong central government was still challenged. The heavy military burden that was necessary impeded financial reforms and economic progress. Traditional attitudes and old institutions resisted change: the acceptance of moderate official "squeeze"; the *likin* charges on movement of goods; the opium habit and the accompanying racket; the exploitation practiced by many landlords and moneylenders; the tendency of those gaining wealth to invest in land and moneylending rather than in enterprises; the tendency of enterprises to distribute earnings rather than reinvest a suitable proportion; the multiplication of unneeded staff in both government and business; and a currency that consisted of money of endless variety, differing from place to place. The inertia of hundreds of millions of illiterate and poor though industrious people, living in millions of farms and many thousand villages, was a stubborn obstacle to modernization. Progress could only be gradual and intermittent.

Internationally, the new government in its early months had made a good start toward improving relations with the Western powers and in some areas with Japan. But serious problems with Japan and Russia still remained and were later to lead to conflict.

Part Two

Fiscal Affairs

3: The Quest for Fiscal Stability: Building Revenues

Conduct of the national finances was not easy under the conditions of 1927-1937. The government was in constant need of money, but was firmly resolved not to rely upon paper money financing. Thus it had to raise money in hard silver up to the currency reform of November 1935, and from then until the Japanese attack on July 7, 1937, in a convertible currency firmly held at par.

To make ends meet, the government first had to develop dependable revenues. Although revenues grew rapidly they were outpaced by rising expenditures, and resulting deficits had to be financed by heavy borrowing from banks and the public. The effort to keep the country solvent became a struggle.

The expenditures, revenues, and deficits of the National Government during the period are summarized in Table 1.* Details are shown in Appendix 1.

Completing tariff autonomy

Japan alone of the chief powers withheld agreement to tariff autonomy when accepting the new tariff effective February 1, 1929. The new duties were substantially those agreed upon at the Peking Tariff Conference in 1926. The rates were moderate, from 7-1/2 up to 27-1/2 per cent on some luxuries. Rates on textiles and other main imports from Japan were in the lower part of the scale. But Japan, before agreeing to tariff autonomy, sought a *quid pro quo.*

Negotiations began early in 1930 and were concluded in May. China agreed not to increase for three years the rates on certain cotton goods, sea products, and wheat flour, and for one year the rates on a number of other items. Japan undertook to maintain for three years her existing duties on certain Chinese exports. China declared that she had ordered abolition of *likin* as from October 10, 1930, and stated her intention to end other

*Figures in tables throughout this volume may not add to totals because of rounding. A billion is here used to mean a thousand million.

similar charges as soon as possible. China also confirmed the annual allocation of C $5 million from customs revenue for debt consolidation, and agreed to hold a conference on or before October 1, 1930, to discuss settlement of debts in arrears. Having satisfied Japan by these agreements, China at last attained full tariff autonomy, thereby ending one of the servitudes of the unequal treaties and gaining recognition of an important sovereign right.

Table 1

Expenditures, revenues, and deficits of the National Government from 1929 to 1937[a]

Year ending June 30	Expenditure excluding balances at end of the period, millions	Revenue, unborrowed, excluding balances at beginning of the period,[b] millions	Deficit covered by borrowing	
			Amount, millions	Percentage of expenditure
1929	C$434	C$334	C$100	23.0
1930	585	484	101	17.3
1931	775	558	217	28.0
1932	749	619	130	17.4
1933	699	614	86	12.3
1934	836	689	147	17.6
1935	941	745	196	20.8
1936	1073	817	256	23.8
1937	1167	870	297	25.4

[a]Source: Finance Ministry, for 1929 to 1935 from published reports, and for 1935 to 1937 from unpublished data stated to be final.

[b]For fiscal years before 1934 to 1935, costs of revenue collection were shown as deductions from revenue. Thereafter they were shown as expenditures, as explained in the Ministry's Report for 1934-1935, p. 16n. These costs are treated here as expenditures.

After attainment of tariff autonomy, the Customs continued to account separately for the 5 per cent duties and the additional revenue received from the new and higher rates. This was because certain internal loans were secured on the surplus revenue from the 5 per cent duties, after payments on the foreign debts that enjoyed priority. There were disadvantages in the separate accounting besides the extra clerical work in the preparation of documents and accounts. Later, when silver slumped, the yield of the 5 per cent duties fell short of covering foreign debt payments, although these obligations continued to be paid because they enjoyed full security of customs revenue. But, as a result of maintaining separate accounts, dissident elements that temporarily seized the Customs were encouraged to claim receipts over and above the proceeds of the 5 per cent duty.

Abolition of the separate accounting became possible after the reorganization of the internal loans in February 1932. At that time, the internal loans secured on the surplus of the 5 per cent duties were given general customs security, subject only to the prior charges for foreign debts. The separate accounting was ended as of March 1, 1932, and the last vestige of the old tariff servitude disappeared.

Status of the Customs

China had a clear legal obligation under the agreement for the 1898 loan that the Customs administration "shall remain as at present constituted during the currency of this loan," which was until 1943 (Article 6). Also China informed Britain in 1898 that she intended that a British subject act as Inspector General of Customs so long as British trade with China exceeded that of any other country.[1] By 1929, China's trade with the United Kingdom was much less than with Japan or the United States; but trade of the British Empire, aided in particular by the trade of Hong Kong, still predominated. The distribution of trade by countries is shown in Appendix 23.

Understandably, foreign participation in revenue collection was not pleasing to nationalistic sentiments. The First Kuomintang Congress in 1924 called for ending "foreigners' management of customs dues," as noted in Chapter 1. But when the Nationalists, with the moderate elements in control, held the responsibility for ruling China, they recognized both the legal obligation and the advantage of maintaining and supporting the venerable Inspectorate General of Customs. In 1933 T. V. Soong commented:

> At the time that the National Government was removed to Nanking, many grievances were harbored against the Customs Service by the Government and people. It was said that the Customs had become an *imperium in imperio;* that it was an adjunct of Legation Street; that the word of the Inspector-General had become law in

> national finances; that the Inspector-General had played the role of king-maker to every Finance Minister at Peking; that the Customs funds were deposited almost *in toto* with foreign banking institutions, and had served merely to build up their credit to the neglect of Chinese banks; and that the higher ranks of the Service were exclusively occupied by foreigners and were not open to Chinese.[2]

An additional criticism then current, which Soong did not mention, was the alleged high costs of collection. Prior to tariff autonomy, the costs were about 10 per cent of the relatively small revenue collected. In 1929-1930, the costs remained about the same, but the proportion fell to 6 to 7 per cent as revenue rose. Since the higher tariff rates invited smuggling, the Customs had to develop a costly preventive service, with vessels and guards, and costs again took about 10 per cent of revenue. The Customs treated its people well, and in return gave good value to China.

Soong went on to say that the grievances were "not indigenous" to the Service. As Minister he made the Customs administration an integral part of his Ministry. In his first published annual report, for the fiscal year ending June 30, 1929, he said (page 3) that "Until the summer of 1928 the Customs Administration ... was a thoroughly denationalized administration." But under the new policy, "while the administrative integrity of the Customs with its civil service traditions would be maintained, the Customs should concern itself solely with the collection of revenue in implicit obedience to the orders of the government and divest itself of all political and extraneous functions and associations." He also put an end to the discrimination that prevented Chinese from holding high rank in the service. "For 50 years," he said, "no Chinese reached the rank of Commissioner of Customs." Promotion was to be based solely on merit. Selected Chinese in the service would be given training abroad, and capable Chinese would be recruited; foreigners would be recruited only if needed for technical reasons and only with the approval of the Ministry. The Customs gave effect to this policy of naming more Chinese to higher posts, and by 1937 about one-third of the commissioners at the various ports were Chinese. These changes, Soong believed, were beneficial to the Customs Service by making it "a purely National non-partisan institution." The ability and energy of Minister Soong and his aide, F. Chang, the Chief of the Customs Bureau, went far to promote the efficient operation of the Customs in the changed situation.

In accordance with Minister Soong's policy of developing financial administration of a modern type, starting in 1932 important changes were made in the procedure for the handling of customs monies and the payment of foreign debts. These changes relieved the Customs of extraneous fiscal functions, which it had been performing because China formerly lacked more appropriate means of handling them. The quality of the personnel in the Finance Ministry responsible for fiscal functions had greatly improved after the Nationalist takeover. In addition, the newly created Central Bank was functioning well. Key officials in effecting the improved procedures were Loy Chang, chief of the Loan Department of the Ministry and Temou Hsi, head of the Banking Department of the Central Bank. They worked closely with advisers Young and Lynch, members of the Kemmerer Commission who were engaged for continuing service in 1929.

The changes in procedure were worked out in cooperation with the Customs and gained the agreement of the bankers concerned. For years the foreign banks had been the depositories of the customs revenue and had administered the service of foreign debts.[3] But from March 1, 1932, the revenue was concentrated in the Central Bank, which transferred to foreign banks in Chinese currency the sums needed for foreign debt payments in accordance with the loan agreements. A few months later, the system was further modified, and the Central Bank made the payments in foreign currency against payments that the Customs made to it in silver. The Central Bank bought the foreign currency from the foreign banks that acted as agents for the loans. A substitute procedure was then devised whereby the Central Bank made direct payments to the agents for the debts out of foreign currencies that it received under operation of the customs gold unit system, as described on pages 46 to 48.

During these years, there was no serious movement or agitation to overthrow the Customs system, whose operation was based on agreements and traditions dating back many years. Responsible elements in the government and among the public realized that precipitate action would impair China's credit both at home and abroad. Although official and public opinion in general wanted to see a wholly Chinese service, the prevailing attitude was that the changes should come by evolution. Clearly there was no lack of Chinese who, with training, could effectively operate the system. But the crux was whether this could be done on a civil service basis, with a customs service able to resist pressures for patronage and special privileges.

Struggle for Customs integrity

Full receipt of customs revenue by the central government was vitally important. The customs was security for most of the debt, foreign and domestic. Domestic bonds were important both as reserves of the banking system and as assets of numerous individuals and enterprises. The government, hard-pressed by the costs of consolidating its political and military position, badly needed the revenue that remained after payment of debt charges. Maintenance of the integrity of the Customs service, with its tradition of fairly administering the revenues, was essential.

Yet, several times seizure of customs revenue and interference with customs integrity threatened or caused grave damage to China. Rebellious military and political leaders wanted the revenue both for themselves and to deprive the government of means of thwarting them. And in 1932, Japan seized the Customs in Manchuria when taking over that region. In each case, those making the seizures recognized an obligation to contribute in some fashion to the cost of debt service. In practice, this recognition did not go beyond words.

Sun Yat-sen's Kuomintang regime at Canton set a dangerous precedent in 1923 by presenting to the diplomatic body "the claim of the Southwestern provinces for their share of the customs surplus." In its note, Canton said it wanted the money for "constructive purposes," and referred to "the so-called government at Peking" as one of the factions that had "accidental possession of the offices and archives" there. The diplomatic body warned that the powers would forcibly resist interference with the Customs. There was a naval demonstration by vessels of Britain, France, Japan, Portugal, and the United States. American action was influenced by a feeling that failure to join in the demonstration would encourage Canton to act. Canton abandoned the effort at seizure.[4]

When in 1926 plans for formal agreement by the powers to the 2-1/2 per cent customs surtax and a 5 per cent surtax on luxuries failed, Canton began levying the surtaxes. Early in 1927, the Peking Government ordered their general enforcement. But the proceeds were not remitted to Peking.[5] And as of May 1, 1927, the National Government, which had not then taken over at Peking, issued a loan secured on the proceeds of these taxes at Shanghai. So there were precedents of a sort for later regional attempts at taking part of the customs revenue. Nevertheless in 1928-1929 Nanking was able to consolidate under its control the collection of the old 5 per cent duties and the new surtaxes. This was an important accomplishment.

In the spring of 1930, a rebellion was started by warlords and politicians jealous of the growing success of the Nanking government led by Chiang Kai-shek. The leaders were the northern warlords Yen Hsi-shan and Feng Yü-hsiang, the Kwangsi warlord Li Tsung-jen, and the leftist politician Wang Ching-wei, who in 1940 was to become the chief collaborator with the Japanese. About May 1, General Yen let it be known that his group planned to seize the Tientsin Customs and take all the revenue except for the proceeds of the old 5 per cent duties, which would be remitted to Shanghai. On June 16, Yen's agents removed the commissioner and installed in his place B. Lenox Simpson, a British writer with the pseudonym Putnam Weale. Simpson ran a loose administration, to curry favor with certain business elements.

Nanking at once ordered that the Tientsin customhouse be temporarily closed and that duty on goods bound for Tientsin be collected at other ports. Finance Minister Soong denounced the seizure, saying that it "strikes at the very root of China's national credit." To avoid interrupting the service of internal bonds issued in 1928 on the security of the 2-1/2 per cent customs surtax at Tientsin, the government remitted to Tientsin in August the funds needed for a current payment. In September, the government forces, aided by the intervention of Marshal Chang Hsueh-liang of Manchuria, decisively defeated the rebellious generals. Simpson abandoned his post, and the legitimate customs officers took over. Two weeks later, Simpson was assassinated at Tientsin, under circumstances that never became clear.

The next interference came in the spring of 1931, when dissident leaders tried to set up a rival National Government at Canton. The leaders included Sun Fo, Li Tsung-jen, and Wang Ching-wei, who had formerly been in the leftist groups associated with the Communists. In June, the Canton group moved to seize the Customs in South China. The revolt was serious, especially since Chiang was busy fighting the Communists in Kiangsi Province. Because the government was not in a position to put down the revolt immediately, the Customs issue was temporarily compromised. Canton paid its *pro rata* share of collection costs and remitted to Shanghai the proceeds of the old 5 per cent duties. The compromise, making the best of a bad situation, was unfavorable to Nanking because the 5 per cent duties fell short of covering the proportionate quota for foreign debts, leaving nothing for internal loans—most of which had previously been issued with the concurrence of the rebelling leaders. But it had the merit of preserving the integrity of the Customs service.

The Canton revolt dragged on until after Japan's move to take over Manchuria beginning September 18, 1931. Then an expedition from Canton against Nanking was under way. It was a sad commentary on the psychology of revolt that the great flood of the summer of 1931 in central China led the leaders at Canton to conclude, as I put it in a letter of the time to a friend, that the flood "afforded the opportunity of a life time to undertake a military expedition against the Government." But Japan's action shocked the leaders of the revolt into seeing the urgent need for national unity. A peace conference at Shanghai several weeks later patched up the internal difficulties, and the South China Customs offices were restored to government control.

In the latter part of 1933, certain Fukien leaders revolted and seized the Customs. But the government quickly put down this revolt.

By far the most serious seizure followed the Japanese creation of the puppet state of Manchukuo in 1931-1932. The customhouses of Manchuria provided about 15 per cent of total customs revenue in 1927-1931. The fact that Japan had joined in the naval demonstration of 1923 against the attempted seizure of the Customs at Canton did not deter certain Japanese sources from intimating that separatist movements in China offered a precedent for Customs seizure.[6] The seizures in Manchuria took place in the spring of 1932, and included a takeover in the leased territory of Dairen, despite a Sino-Japanese agreement of 1907 providing for a customhouse there under the Inspectorate General of Customs. The Japanese in Manchukuo offered to contribute a quota of revenue for foreign debt service but nothing for internal loans. No contributions were actually made, and the Japanese even retained about two-thirds of the customs funds on hand at the time of seizure.

The Japanese civil government intimated a wish to reach a

settlement, such as letting China have the customs revenue of Dairen, which was a substantial part of the total seized. The British also tried to mediate in the summer of 1932 and again in 1935-1936. But no way was found to make an agreement that would avoid implied recognition of Japan's seizure of Manchuria.

Gold basis for import duties

The slump in the value of silver had long been a problem for China. From 1873 to 1895 the value of silver had halved, doubling the cost in local currency of acquiring gold currencies. The difficulty became acute after China contracted the large sterling loans of 1895-1898 to pay the indemnity to Japan. And the need to pay the Boxer indemnity after 1900 made matters much worse. In 1896, Viceroy Li Hung-chang put forward a plan prepared by Sir Robert Hart, Inspector General of Customs, for payment of duties on a gold basis. But this plan was rejected. Again in 1900-1901, Hart argued for such a plan. He proposed giving the *Haikwan tael,* in which duties were paid, a gold value equal to that prevailing when the fixed tariff was set in 1858. But Hart's wise proposal was shouted down by representatives of the powers because it would have added greatly to burdens on trade. After unseemly higgling about favorable rates on their exports to China, and with small regard to China's interests, in 1902 the powers at last agreed to a revised schedule calling for higher duties in terms of silver.[7]

In 1928-1929, China had to pay the equivalent of about US $35 million yearly on debts due in gold.* But revenues were in silver. From 1921 to 1928 the price of silver did not vary widely, and the average value of China's silver dollar was about US $0.50. After wide fluctuations that value was roughly the same as in 1895. In 1928, it was fairly steady around US $0.45. But in 1929 decline set in that was to take the silver dollar to a low of about US $0.20 in 1931. The rates are shown in Appendix 10.

*The government had issued internal loans in C$ secured on the cancelled German and Austro-Hungarian portions of the Boxer Indemnity and on the remitted Russian portion. Although the C$ equivalent of these portions depended on the rate of exchange, the loan payments were not made in foreign currency. Hence payments in respect of these three portions are excluded from this figure, which includes other customs and salt revenue charges equal to about US$30 million and US$5 million, respectively. At this time little was being paid on railway debts.

In 1929 the slump in silver threatened to wipe out much of the gain from tariff autonomy. Most tariff rates were set in specific sums in *Haikwan taels* per unit of goods imported. The *Haikwan tael* equaled 581.83 grains of fine silver, and it eventually was abolished in 1933, being converted to C $1.558. At the exchange rates of May 1929, the yearly cost of debt payments in foreign currency had risen to about C $83.5 million, compared with about C $78 million in 1928.

Clearly the remedy was to collect revenue on a gold basis. In the 1920's, I had observed in France the success of collecting certain revenues on a gold basis, to counteract the slumping franc. This gave me the idea, in the spring of 1929, of proposing a similar measure for China. The Kemmerer Commission formally recommended it in May, repeating the recommendation in October.

On January 15, 1930, the government announced that from February 1* import duties would be collected in terms of a customs gold unit (CGU) equal to U $0.40, or 19.7265 pence sterling, or 0.8025 yen. Specific duty rates were converted from the former rates in *Haikwan taels* to the new unit for the period February 1, to March 15, on the basis of average exchange rates of the last quarter of 1929, namely, Hk. Tls. 1 = CGU 1.50. As of March 15, the conversion would be at Hk. Tls. 1 = CGU 1.75, being the approximate rate in January 1929, the month prior to adoption of the new tariff. Dollars, *taels,* and other local currencies would be accepted for duty payment at rates to be officially announced. These rates, which from March 1, 1930, were announced daily, approximated the actual market rates of exchange for the various currencies. When a revision of the tariff was promulgated on January 1, 1931, rates were stated in CGU.

A statement by Minister Soong on January 15, 1930, pointed out that the change was needed to safeguard the finances, and to add to China's ability to pay its foreign obligations, in the face of the slump in silver. The change, he said, would restore duty payments to the same proportion of dutiable value as that of a year earlier when tariff autonomy was agreed. He pointed out that the increase in duty would be mostly but 2 or 3 per cent of the value of imported goods after March 15, and less in the

*The application of the gold unit tariff from February 1, 1930, was consistent with the Sino-British agreement that the rates of the tariff of February 1, 1929, would remain the maximum rates applied to British goods for at least a year.

meantime. The public accepted the change with little objection, and the transition took place smoothly. Some customs officers, however, grumbled about making the change. But this discontent was unofficial, and the Customs loyally gave effect to the measure, while claiming the credit for Sir Robert Hart.

As of May 1, 1931, the Central Bank issued CGU bank notes to facilitate duty payments. There was discussion of using these notes as a step toward the gold standard. But this was not done because a much broader policy was involved. The notes were secured by a reserve of 100 per cent, comprising at least 60 per cent in gold or deposits payable in gold, with the balance in acceptances or other obligations payable in gold. The notes did not prove very popular because it was more convenient to pay duty from a CGU bank account or by purchase of a cashier's order for the exact amount of duty. Circulation was less than CGU1 million during most of the prewar years.

After a few months, the Central Bank fixed its rates to make it advantageous for payers of duty to buy CGU at the bank for duty payments, rather than to pay the silver equivalent directly. Many importers established CGU accounts at the Bank. Others bought CGU cashier's checks. This procedure was first set up only at Shanghai, but soon extended to other ports—the Bank of China acting for the Central Bank where the latter did not have branches. In 1930, only 12 per cent of total import duty was received directly in CGU. But the figure rose to 63 per cent in 1931, 75 per cent in 1932, and 88 per cent in 1933.

Beginning in the spring of 1931, the government had an overage of CGU, which by 1933 was several million CGU monthly, to sell in the market for silver currency. Formerly the government had to buy exchange with silver currency for debt service from the banks named in the loan agreements. The banks knew when payments had to be made, and the government felt that they often rigged exchange rates in their favor. Now such a situation could be avoided since the government could pay directly from its balances abroad. The right to do this was clear under some agreements, but under others the banks handling debt service questioned the right. The issue was compromised by the government paying an extra 1/8 per cent commission to settle the latter cases.

Collection of duties on a gold basis was a reform of first importance. Eighteen months later *Finance and Commerce* of Shanghai stated, on July 22, 1931, that "it would probably be no exaggeration to say . . . that . . . the collection of the revenue in the form of gold units saved the country from financial disaster." The measure protected the government to a large extent from the slump in silver, which carried the Chinese dollar down from about US $0.45 in January 1929 to about US $0.20 in February 1931. The reform removed from the finances a major speculative risk. It ensured maintenance of foreign debt payments; otherwise the financial difficulties of the thirties might have forced default as in so many other countries.

Moreover, the higher revenue from duties automatically resulting from the slump in silver was invaluable to the government while it was consolidating its authority. Putting down the revolts of warlords and the Communists in these years was costly. Increased revenue was vital to the government's survival, and the additional millions that the reform produced were of utmost importance in a difficult time.

The Central Bank also derived important benefits. Until early 1930 it had no balances or correspondents abroad. The CGU system showed the need for these arrangements. With the guidance of Fenimore B. Lynch, the Bank's adviser and an experienced international banker, the Bank established direct relations with banks in New York and London. It thus became an important factor in the foreign exchange market, acquiring needed experience in exchange transactions, handling foreign business matters for the government, and gaining prestige at home and abroad along with substantial profits on exchange operations. The Bank was able to build up reserves in New York and London. By the time of the currency reform of November 1935, the Bank was well able to handle maintenance of stability of rates of exchange. Thus the CGU system was a major step toward currency reform.

When the American dollar was devalued in 1934, the equivalent value of the CGU was adjusted from US $0.40 to US $0.6775.

Tariff policy

China did not hesitate to use actively her freedom of action in tariff matters. The 1929 tariff, the first under tariff autonomy, was only the first of many changes. Most of these changes were increases, although the government to its credit took occasion to eliminate many old and burdensome charges on movement of goods and to rely mainly on import duties. The first tariff change was the collection of import duties on a gold basis from February 1, 1930 (see the preceding Section). This raised rates slightly in terms of the gold value of imports. But in terms of silver values the increase resulting from the CGU system became greater as silver slumped until about the end of 1932.

At the beginning of 1931 rates were raised, some to as much as 60 per cent. Compared with the 1929 tariff, 43 per cent of the rates were unchanged; nearly 10 per cent were decreased; and 21 per cent showed increases *ad valorem* of 2-1/2 per cent, 9 per cent by 5 or 7-1/2 per cent, and 17 per cent by 10 per cent or more. Important increases were enacted for matches, chinaware, sugar, cement, glass, soap, cosmetics, artificial silk, and woollen goods.

The new tariff of January 1, 1931, was primarily a revenue measure, but it also had elements of protection. It reduced duties on some industrial materials, and raised other rates to protect certain industries. One purpose of the higher general level of duties was to compensate for removal of a variety of troublesome old-time obstacles to trade. The government abolished coast trade duties, transit dues, and "native customs" levied on movement of imported goods to destinations away from the immediate area (beyond 50 *li* or roughly 16 2/3 miles) of treaty ports. That reform did away with revenue badly needed by the government, but the hope was that improved domestic trade would amply justify the change. For revenue reasons, however, the government retained under the name of "interport duties" relatively low duties, mostly about 2 to 3 per cent, on native goods moved from one treaty port to another for consumption in China.

The export tariff was revised effective June 1, 1931. The old rates were based on valuations of 1858. The new rates were based on value and were partly 5 per cent and partly 7-1/2 per cent, with many items free of export duty. At the same time, the remaining native customs duties were completely ended.

A surtax of 10 per cent on customs duties was imposed from December 1, 1931, with the rate to drop to 5 per cent after the following July. This was to meet extraordinary costs of the great Yangtze flood of the summer of 1931. This surtax was used as security for the American Flood Relief Loan of about US $9 million for the purchase of wheat. The surtax did not apply to rates bound under the agreement of 1930 with Japan until after expiration of the three-year term in May 1933.

Further considerable increases in the import tariff took place during 1932-1933. In July 1932, the question was whether to retain the customs surtax at 10 per cent after July 31; to raise rates on a variety of items; or to do both. The advisers and others in the government favored only keeping the surtax at 10 per cent, but the government decided to keep the 10 per cent surtax and also to raise various rates. The revision, effective August 3, 1932, applied largely to luxuries and raised most rates on the items affected by more than half. This increase followed the Japanese seizure of the Customs in Manchuria, and was largely a move to replace the lost revenue.

In May 1933, the three-year limit on duties on leading Japanese goods expired, and a new import tariff effective May 22 greatly increased duties on many items, notably cotton goods, sea products, and paper. The increase was urged as a revenue measure, but the desire for tariff protection, notably by the cotton textile interests, had a part in affecting policy. Advisers Lockhart and Young, along with some members of the Tariff Commission, feared a loss of revenue or at best little or no increase. They urged moderation and reduction of some rates, but with little success. One important result of higher duties was the severe loss of revenue from sugar. There was active smuggling especially from Formosa. Also the Canton authorities set up a sugar monopoly, which apparently was not so much concerned with promoting local production as with importing sugar free of duty to be mixed with the local product. It was hard for the government to deal with the abuse because of regionalism and its weak position in South China in this period.

The higher duties of May 1933 especially affected imports from Japan, although the rates were not discriminatory. Japan protested strongly, and accompanied her protest with aggressive pressure in the north. Although not openly recognizing the pressure, the government put in effect a new tariff from July 1934. This revision reduced rates on important items of interest to Japan, notably cotton goods, sea products, and paper. But rates were raised on kerosene and gasoline, wool and woollen goods, chemicals, machinery and other items. The revision was generally considered to be unfavorable to Western trade interests.

The level of rates is roughly indicated by the relation of revenue to imports, since prohibitive rates were not important. Before 1929 the proportion was about 4 per cent. It rose to 10 per cent in 1930, about 15 per cent in 1931 and 1932, 20 per cent in 1933, and over 25 per cent in 1934-1937. The higher proportions, however, partly reflected the smaller demand for imports because of the acute depression in China.

China thus moved in a few years from an extremely low tariff to a high level of duties. The rates, while not always maximizing revenue, were still productive. Yield rose from C $134 million in 1928 to a peak of C $388 million in 1931. It stayed well over C $300 million in the following years despite disturbed economic and political conditions. The yield by classes of revenue is shown in Table 2.

Politics of high tariffs

The high duties that followed China's hard won tariff autonomy not only brought in much needed revenue and encouraged some local producers, but gave rise to grave problems. They seriously complicated China's drive for national unity and independence. The internal issues mainly concerned Canton and the deep-seated regionalism of South China. The external issues mainly concerned relations with Japan.

Smuggling quickly became a major problem. Under the pre-1929 low tariff it had not been important. But now it became acute, first in South China. Hong Kong was practically a free trade area. Other havens for smugglers were Macao and Kwangchowan, ports controlled, respectively, by Portugal and France. The Japanese colony of Formosa was also a convenient base for smuggling, and "puff-puff" boats plied from there to many points in South China.

The government began negotiations with Hong Kong in 1929 to combat smuggling. Negotiations proved difficult, and by the time a draft agreement was ready, a large vested interest in smuggling had emerged in South China. Canton strongly opposed concluding the proposed agreement with Hong Kong. Nanking's authority in the south was weak, and matters went from bad to worse. Official organs in the south, especially the Navy and Salt revenue authorities, openly engaged in smuggling. Major items smuggled included sugar, textiles, oil products, and motor vehicles. Officially protected smuggling was ended only in mid-1936, when the National Government finally established control in the south. Meanwhile, huge sums of revenue were lost, and legitimate trade suffered.

To combat smuggling, the Customs developed a Preventive Service. Numerous substations were set up along the coast, a

Table 2

Customs revenue from 1927 to 1937[a]

Year	Import duty, millions	Export duty, millions	Coast trade duty, millions	Inter-port duty, millions	Transit dues, millions	Native customs, millions	Tonnage dues, millions	Revenue surtax, millions	Flood relief surtax, millions	Total, millions
1927	C$54	C$40	C$4	--	C$5	C$6	C$4	--	--	C$113
1928	72	42	4	--	5	6	5	--	--	134
1929	167	57	6	--	4	7	5	--	--	245
1930	212	55	6	--	3	10	5	--	--	292
1931	315	48	--	C$16	--	3	5	--	C$2	388
1932	236	27	--	21	--	--	4	C$5	19	312
1933	266	23	--	18	--	--	4	14	14	340
1934	260	25	--	17	--	--	4	14	14	335
1935	250	21	--	13	--	--	4	14	14	316
1936	255	24	--	14	--	--	4	14	14	325
1937	261	29	--	20	--	--	3	15	15	343

[a] Source: Inspectorate General of Customs.

radio net was created, and a fleet of armed vessels was acquired. Hundreds of junks and motor boats were seized. The cost of combatting smuggling was heavy.

By far the most serious smuggling and evasion took place in North China after the Japanese, in the latter part of 1935, created the East Hopei Autonomous Government, north of the Peiping-Tientsin area. The East Hopei region promptly became a paradise for smugglers, since the Japanese military forcibly interfered with the preventive work of the Customs. The *North China Daily News* of May 5, 1936, thus quoted a man returned from Peitaiho:

> I saw no smuggling. I only saw 38 vessels of all sorts and sizes lying out in the bay and discharging cargo into dozens of sampans, and the beach as busy as the Bund here in Tientsin in the height of the shipping season. You can't call that smuggling any more. That's Free Trade.

A smuggler offered to bring in "anything you want, anything except, perhaps, an elephant." Besides evasion of import duties, the region was an exit point for silver exported contrary to Chinese regulations.

Japan's action in East Hopei was costly to the Chinese Government. Loss of revenue ran into millions monthly. Smuggled goods began to flood the northern half of China. Legitimate imports could not compete with duty-free goods. The Japanese action, directed by the military leaders in Manchuria and North China, had a double motive. It was intended to bring pressure for a Japanese-controlled autonomous region in North China. And it was a protest against the tariff rates affecting Japanese goods. Japanese officials indicated that they would stop the racket if China reduced duties on Japanese imports.[8]

China and the friendly powers protested to Japan. But to little avail. China tried to combat the smuggling by organizing a bureau to prevent smuggling by rail, and by setting up land barriers to block exits to southern markets. These measures had some effect in reducing smuggling, and caused losses to smugglers. But conditions remained unsatisfactory. There was little change until Japan seized the North China ports in the summer of 1937.[9]

The discontent of Japanese business interests with China's high tariff policy merged with the aggressive ideas of the militarists who wanted China to become a Japanese satellite. The idea grew that not only Manchuria but all of China should become an economic preserve for Japan—a source of raw materials and low tariff if not a preferential market for exports. Thus China's exercise of tariff autonomy came to be a factor in the march of events that led to the extension of Japanese aggression from Manchuria into North China, and to the all-out fighting that began with the incident at the Marco Polo bridge on the Double Seventh of 1937.

Salt as a revenue source

Salt taxation is said to date back at least to the Chou dynasty in the 12th century B.C. Over the years, revenue was raised by a system that amounted to tax farming, with monopolies granted to merchants in particular areas. The arrangements gave large gains to the merchants, revenue to the state, and squeeze to the bureaucracy.[10]

Since salt meets an essential physical need, and there is no practicable substitute, its taxation was an obvious recourse under conditions existing in China. China's salt consumption has been estimated at about 20 pounds yearly per capita, the figure being large because salt was the primary food preservative. The needs of rich and poor for salt are alike, hence the tax amounted to a poll tax. In the 1930's, on the average, the total of taxes on salt equaled about three-fourths of the retail price, which was then about twice as high as in the United States.

Although the salt tax was burdensome, the new National Government's fiscal needs had to take precedence. The government needed all the money it could gather, and replacement of the salt tax by other revenues could not be seriously considered. Experience since creation of the Salt Inspectorate in 1913 showed that salt could be a productive revenue source. The Inspectorate's organization covered the entire country, and had brought the revenue under central control. Consequently, the government promptly turned to restoring the Inspectorate. In Chapter 2, I described the Inspectorate's setup and development as well as the action of the government in 1928 relating to collection of salt revenue. This action marked the start of a continuing drive to rehabilitate the service nationwide, integrate it into the Finance Ministry, and restore to schedule the salt-secured loans that had fallen into arrears.

The system as the Nationalists inherited it was extremely complex. There were 800 to 900 offices and suboffices spread over China's vast area. The Inspectorate's authority varied from province to province. Rates of tax were far from uniform in the different districts, with numerous surtaxes and fees. The tax burden varied even within a given district because of local efforts to tax salt. This lack of uniformity promoted smuggling from low tax to high tax areas.

The complexities and abuses of the system were thus described by F. A. Cleveland, Associate Chief Inspector, in 1934:

> The existing system ... is nondescript. It is an inheritance from past bargaining between corrupt officials and groups of organized exploiters of the salt trade—a remaining complexity of interlocking and conflicting monopolies granted by officials to merchants in exchange for ready cash. The trade is thereby left incumbered by a maze of grants to licensees in the nature of special privileges—subsequently enlarged on by practices not of record which have gained sanctity as customs. No one has as yet been able to fathom all the constituent intricacies of the salt merchandising organization.... And the most baffling features ... remain because beneficiaries of this system—many of whom now have no direct relation to the salt business as such—have gained an economic, social or political status or influence which has protected the system.
>
> No branch of revenue administration could be made more simple, or more inexpensive to operate, than this one—assuming uniformity of imposts in different areas. There is only one commodity to be brought under control; and this control could be first made effective at the source of supply.[11]

The efforts to reform the salt revenue, described on pages 57 to 59, paid off in a notable growth of yield. In 10 districts where conditions were relatively favorable for enforcement of the new policies, revenue grew from an average of C $34 million in 1914-1928, and C $38 million in 1929, to C $111 million in 1933. In the remaining districts, excluding Manchuria which the Japanese seized in 1931-1932, the growth was from an average of C $37 million in 1914-1928 and C $23 million in 1929 to C $48 million in 1933.[12]

The yield of salt revenue from 1913 to 1937 is shown in Table 3. The figures have to be taken with reservations. At all times certain offices were not under Inspectorate control, and they were subject to various degrees of local interference. These offices generally rendered supporting accounts, but in some cases revenue items were affected by collusion with the salt trade. Also in some cases the proceeds of various local surtaxes were not reported. The government always had to tolerate some local retentions. During the 1920's, these amounts became so great that little net revenue remained for the central government. Thereafter, the situation improved greatly. About 30 per cent of gross revenue was retained in 1930-1932, dropping to 24 per cent in fiscal 1933 and 13 per cent in 1934, after which date the item does not appear in the accounts.[13]

The government extensively substituted subsidies for retentions, thus benefiting as collections improved. In 1934, the government issued a loan of C $12 million for railway construction in Kiangsi Province, secured on a local salt surtax that later was converted to a subsidy. In 1935 the government took over a measure of fiscal control in Szechwan Province and collected the salt revenue, from it granting a subsidy to the province. Secured on that subsidy, the government issued a loan of C $70 million for rehabilitation, refunding provincial debts, and suppression of bandits and Communists.

Salt was very important as a revenue source. Although the customs yielded much more total revenue, it was heavily charged with debt payments. The revenue freely at the government's disposal in the 1930's from customs and salt was of the same order of size.

In 1931-1932, the Japanese seizure of Manchuria caused a loss of about 15 per cent of salt revenue collections. Hence, the growth of the revenue shown in Table 3 is even more impressive

Table 3
Revenue collected by the Salt administration from 1913 to 1937[a]

Calendar year	Revenue, millions	Year	Revenue, millions	Year	Revenue, millions
1913	C$19	1921	C$95	1929	C$85
1914	68	1922	98	1930	130
1915	81	1923	91	1931	155
1916	81	1924	88	1932	145[b]
1917	82	1925	92	1933	159
1918	88	1926	86	1934	176
1919	88	1927	60	1935	184
1920	90	1928	54	1936	218
				1937	213

[a]Source: Annual reports of the Finance Ministry, and for 1936 and 1937, from the Inspectorate's *Advance Annual Report for 1937*, April 1938.

[b]Including C$3 million from Manchuria. Collections there were about C$25 million yearly in the immediately preceding period.

than the figures indicate. Loan quotas from Manchuria were not sent after March 1932. China protested the seizure in communications to Japan, the Lytton Commission of the League of Nations, and the friendly foreign governments. But, as in the case of the Customs, the Japanese militarists would not send quotas unconditionally. No way was found to obtain loan quotas without implying recognition of Manchukuo.

The system of quotas for foreign debt payments from each district worked well. Nearly all districts duly remitted the quotas, although intermittent revolts caused some interruptions. The chief problem regions, apart from Manchuria, were the Canton area and Szechwan. Eventually, however, quotas were forthcoming from these areas. The restoration of the Inspectorate and the success of the quota system made possible resumption of payments on the salt-secured foreign loans.

Reform of the salt revenue

The first and basic problem facing the new government in improving the salt revenue was to gain control of the producing districts. In mid-1928 it controlled the salt revenue only in the lower Yangtze region. From that low point there was rapid progress, as Minister Soong thus described it in his first annual report covering fiscal 1928-1929 (page 4):

> .. the Government in consolidating its authority enabled the Ministry to spread its area of control throughout the Yangtze Valley, into Hopei, Shantung and the Southwest. Where its authority extends the Ministry strives to secure uniformity of the rate of taxation and methods of collection, to consolidate the various surtaxes under the sole control of the Salt Inspectorate, to abolish the old system of farming out taxes, to institute better control of the preventive service, and to extend the depot system so that revenue can be collected at the source. . . .
>
> .. it has been abundantly shown in the brief period that the revenue is capable of rapid improvement, given a modicum of peace and sound administration.

The government continued its struggle to extend its area of control. By the fall of 1929, Soong's report said that 60 per cent of collections went to the central government. The outbreak of major civil war caused a setback, as did further intermittent disturbances. But the government persisted. By 1937, most of the revenue was under its control, although it still had to turn over some of the revenue collected to provincial authorities or to subsidize them in other ways.

As control extended, the Inspectorate was able to collect surtaxes formerly collected by provinces. It worked toward greater uniformity in rates, finding it easier to raise the lower rates than to reduce the higher. There was also some consolidation of rates, but a large part of the system of surtaxes continued. Continuing urgent need for money made it politically hard to reduce rates even though reduction could have added to revenue by lessening evasion.

The Inspectorate, supported by the Ministry, waged a fight against the abuses deeply embedded in the system. Tax farmers often had paid a sum for the right to collect the tax, which amounted to giving a monopoly to special interests. These monopolies became in some places a sort of intangible property that could be transferred, leased, or even inherited. Depots and works to control salt at the source were inadequate. Many ingenious ways were devised to defraud the revenue. Salt merchants squeezed salt by means of nonstandard weights and wastage allowances. An early measure to control this abuse was by the use of the new *picul* of 50 kilograms or 110.23 pounds. Those transporting salt by boat, carts, or on animals often sold as they went. Salt was frequently of poor quality. One practice of those pilfering salt was to adulterate it by adding sand to maintain the weight. Where salt was monopolized, the lack of competition removed an incentive to provide good quality. Smuggling took place on a large scale, with merchants, officials, and guards often in collusion. Organized banditry and piracy preyed upon the salt trade.

The Legislative Yuan in March 1931 adopted a law calling for uniform and lower rates, the end of monopolies and freedom of trade, improvement of salt depots and works, taxation at the source, and quality inspection. The Inspectorate was already working along those lines, and continued to do so. But full enforcement of these desirable provisions depended on extension of the government's control, and on provision of funds by the hard-pressed treasury for the needed construction.

Because of abuses, much potential revenue was lost. In 1931 the gross revenue from salt was C $155 million. But Cleveland estimated in a report of December 12, 1931, to Soong that revenue loss was probably C $70 million, of which C $40 million was from smuggling and C $30 million from squeeze. He estimated that tax farmers took a further C $30 million from the public in profits. He urged paying adequate wages and salaries to personnel on a civil service basis; adopting uniform rates; reforming the system of having Salt Commissioners parallel with the Inspectorate; strengthening custody of salt; and improving the revenue guards and preventive service.

Until 1932 there had been a dual system, with the government maintaining a separate Salt Bureau with a national organization to oversee nominally the Sino-foreign Inspectorate. There were Salt Commissioners in the districts, along with the Inspectorate, and their activities all too often related to abuses and smuggling. In 1932, Minister Soong merged the two organizations at the top, and locally wherever it was politically feasible, naming the Chinese district salt officials concurrently as Commissioners. Like many other reforms, this change could only be accomplished gradually. The budget for Salt Commissioners fell from C $4 million in 1932-1933 to about half a million in 1935-1936. This reform was not extended to South China (Kwangtung) until 1936, and had not been extended to Shansi and Yunnan Provinces when hostilities began in mid-1937. In Kwangtung the revenue from salt grew by 40 per cent in the year following abolition of the Commissioner's office.[14]

The Inspectorate embarked upon a comprehensive program of constructing depots and other works at places of salt production to bring about better control. Formerly salt was heaped up in various places with little supervision. Smuggling was a serious problem since it was highly organized in collusion with officials and guards. Also there were bandits who seized salt. To combat smuggling, the Inspectorate purged undesirable elements wherever it could do so. Minister Soong took great personal interest in developing revenue guards. A training school was organized, and the guards were equipped as a para-military force. They were well-enough trained and equipped to give a good account of themselves when used in the fighting at Shanghai early in 1932 when the Japanese attacked. By 1934, this force comprised 27,000 special police and 18,000 men in the special regiments. Soong's political enemies even called the guards his army.

The abuses that grew up over long years could not be easily eradicated. Yet progress was made in curtailing them progressively. It is clear that the Salt administration made a notable record of achievement from its rehabilitation that began in 1928 to the outbreak of hostilities in mid-1937.

Working of the Sino-foreign Salt administration

When the Nationalists rehabilitated the salt revenue in 1928, as described in Chapter 2, the changes affecting the Inspectorate were deemed necessary for internal political reasons and to remove the implication of a foreign-directed receivership for China's finances. Although the changes infringed the 1913 loan agreement, the foreign protests were not insistent. Apart from the fact that the protests could not be made effective, loan payments did not depend on salt revenue because the loan had been well-secured on customs revenue since 1917. The agreements for certain loans prior to 1913 provided for salt security, but did not specify any arrangements for collecting the revenue. The Finance Ministry's assumption of responsibility for salt revenue rehabilitation was accompanied by a large growth of salt revenue and restoration of payments on the pre-1913 foreign loans. Within about five years, the prices of the 1913 bonds and the earlier salt-secured bonds of 1908 and 1912 more than doubled on the London market (Table 10).

From 1913 to 1931, the Associate Chief Inspector was always British, as had been the Chief Inspector of Customs from the beginning in the middle of the 19th century. But in February 1931, Minister Soong named as Associate Chief Inspector an American, Frederick A. Cleveland, who had had an extensive career in public administration and accounting. Although there was no understanding by China that the post should always be filled by a British subject, some British publicists tried to represent that the action was a breach of faith. An unfounded rumor was even telegraphed to London that Cleveland favored a moratorium on loan payments, causing a slump in the price of Chinese bonds.[15] Apart from Cleveland being much better qualified for the post than the man he replaced, the government felt it desirable to engage an American because a Britisher already held the Customs post and because relations between China and the United States were becoming closer.

Cleveland justified his appointment by bringing about improvement of procedures of administration and accounting. He retired in 1935 and was succeeded by Oliver C. Lockhart, who continued concurrently in his previous work as Financial Adviser with special reference to taxation. Lockhart continued with measures to strengthen the administration of the salt revenues.

Clearly the Sino-foreign system reduced corruption, helped

toward more mature attention to difficult problems, and resulted in more effective administration than a wholly Chinese organization could have provided under existing conditions. The participation of the foreign associates helped to protect the revenue. Trained and experienced Chinese officers could match the technical competence of the foreign staff, and they had greater rapport with the people and deeper knowledge of Chinese conditions. The foreign staff, however, could better resist pressure from civil and military authorities and the salt trade for action contrary to the public interest. The cooperative efforts of the Chinese and foreign personnel resulted in a large growth of revenue, improvement of the quality of salt, and notable progress in doing away with deep-rooted malpractices.

The changes in the salt revenue system dictated by rising nationalism altered the Inspectorate's semi-independent status. The Finance Ministry supported the principle of civil service, yet made various political appointments. Chinese and foreign officers continued to have nominal joint authority and responsibility. But the arrangements were ended whereby the foreign co-chief and district officers took the leadership in management. The position of foreign and Chinese officers was in practice reversed. In view of the changed conditions, some experienced officers left the service.

Cooperation between Chinese and foreign officers was still enjoined, and financial transactions, release of salt, and personnel action required joint signatures. But the wave of nationalism was weakening the position of the foreign personnel. Chinese officers often acted alone on such administrative matters as dealing with producers and merchants. Because Finance Ministry approval was needed on important matters, the approval was sometimes obtained by direct communication between the Chinese chief officer and the Ministry without participation of his foreign colleague. The smooth working of the joint arrangement largely depended on the personalities of the Chinese and foreign officers at the different levels. It was easy for friction to develop, with the Chinese officer feeling that his colleague was interfering, and the foreigner feeling that he was being ignored. Lockhart, as Associate Director General, appreciated that changes that recognized the rising nationalism were inevitable. But he felt that in China's best interests the evolution should take place openly rather than by undermining the agreements and the position of foreign staff.

Matters came to a head when an Organic Law for the Salt administration was adopted by the Legislative Yuan in July 1936. It became effective on April 1, 1937. It reflected nationalistic trends, and parts of it cast doubt on the prerogatives of the foreign associate head and the foreign members of the staff. Instead of "Inspectorate," the organization became the Directorate General of Salt Administration, and its Chinese title suggested a reduction in status. Lockhart pointed out to Finance Minister Kung parts of the law that he felt changed the established arrangements or were at best ambiguous. Article 9 was translated to read that the Associate Director General was to assist the Director General. There was a corresponding provision regarding district officers in Article 17.

The time was peculiarly inappropriate for a change. Because of Japan's increasingly aggressive action, China badly needed the support of the Western Powers. This support was affected by confidence in China's policies toward foreign interests. Also China was actively negotiating settlements of debts in arrears, including arrangements to pledge salt security (Chapter 5). It was important to China's credit that confidence be retained in that security. Lockhart pointed this out to Minister Kung, indicating his understanding that the government did not wish to change materially the former arrangements for Sino-foreign cooperation, and stating the hope that the Minister would clarify the matter in regulations and instructions. The representatives of the bondholders also asked for an interpretation. In a letter of May 25, 1937, which I drafted with Lockhart's concurrence, the Minister assured the representatives that "in our interpretation and implementation of this law the foreign associate officials continue to have joint responsibility as to essential functions and thus no material change in the established practice is being introduced." The Directorate General issued circular instructions on these lines.

Nevertheless, the position of the foreign officers was in fact impaired. In July 1936, the Ministry of Audit urged cutting their pay and reducing their number—there were then 36.[16] The Chinese officers tended to feel that the new law gave them the upper hand, despite the Ministry's interpretation. The growing nationalism during these years is understandable. Developing countries wish to get rid of foreign direction or constraint in the management of their affairs as rapidly as conditions permit, regardless of any loss of efficiency. And in China during these years the Chinese staff was gaining experience and growing in effectiveness. Also the reforms and suppression of established malpractices naturally made enemies, and in some quarters the stricter ideas of foreign officers were resented.

The prewar trend to nationalization of salt affairs was stimulated after outbreak of the Sino-Japanese hostilities in mid-1937, and gained momentum during and after 1938. The Sino-foreign salt administration gradually disintegrated during the war and was not revived.[17]

Excise tax reforms

The development of the system of excises, other than taxes on salt, after the takeover of the National Government in mid-1928, was largely an extension of the measures adopted in 1927-1928 after the capital was set up at Nanking. These measures, described in Chapter 2, included the arrangements made with the foreign manufacturers of tobacco and with importers of oil products to pay specified taxes. These taxes were paid with the understanding that the government would refund the amount of further taxes if collected in areas under central control. This agreement was a notable breakthrough in China's struggle to change the old international arrangements limiting her power of taxation.

The successful working of these new tax measures, as well as other early measures to improve the operation of the old wine and tobacco tax and stamp tax, depended on extension of the central authority. As the government strove to make its weight felt throughout the country, taxation was always a major issue. The aim was to apply the principles of division of revenue sources between the government and the provinces, as determined in 1928 at the conferences described in Chapter 2. The government sought control of the taxes, even though it might have to pay a price. The provinces had their revenue problems, and throughout the period under review the government had to negotiate arrangements providing for various degrees of local retention of parts of specific revenues and subsidies. In the thirties, roughly 15 per cent of the consolidated taxes and over half of the wine and tobacco tax went to the provinces.

Extension of fiscal control throughout the country involved many difficulties and setbacks. An important event was extension of central control to Szechwan, where the Internal Revenue Administration took over on August 1, 1935. That control was part of an overall settlement between the government and the province that was to prove vitally important when the fighting forced removal of the capital to Chungking in 1938.

The task of tax reform was extremely formidable under the conditions of 1928. The new government, said Finance Minister Soong, inherited "a motley collection of taxes, surtaxes and miscellaneous imposts which were levied without any pretence at system by innumerable bureaus all over the country."[18] In 1928, over 130 national and local tax offices were located in Shanghai alone. His program was to simplify the system and consolidate the administration; tax the production at the source; consolidate taxes on the same commodity; and improve administration and accountability for revenues and eliminate leakage.[19]

Soong's ideas were reinforced by the recommendations in 1929 of the Kemmerer Commission. Its *Report on Revenue Policy,* prepared by Lockhart, urged China to concentrate on improving existing revenue sources rather than to experiment with untried sources. There was little tradition of administrative efficiency and control in tax matters apart from the Customs and Salt services, and there were no recognized techniques and standards of performance in tax matters. The report said (page 1):

> Furthermore, there is little or no comprehension on the part of taxpayers that taxes are a contribution to the expense of maintaining essential public services, and all too little evidence of the recognition of this truth in practical ways by public servants themselves. This is an historical situation, the statement of which implies neither praise nor blame.
>
> The realization that taxes are in fact a contribution to collective purposes, not a mere "one-sided" compulsory exaction of wealth by the government (or, it may be, by officials, largely for their private and personal benefit), must be gradually built up through the devotion of public funds to useful public purposes.

The report went on to say that the process of building up a proper view of taxation—a common problem in less developed countries—would be furthered by improving tax administration and by devoting revenues to public purposes such as education, public health and order, and economic improvement, rather than to civil war or salaries for a multiplicity of officials. China, said the report, should tax a limited number of commodities of wide consumption; avoid multiple taxes on the same item; and get rid of burdensome taxes on trade such as *likin* and native customs and coast trade duties. Besides the report on revenue policy, the Commission recommended taxes on matches and cement, and presented a plan for revising the stamp tax.

The government was generally in accord with these recommendations, and was already moving in the directions indicated, although planned reforms often had to wait because of disturbed conditions. The system of excises was extended. The nucleus was the tax on rolled tobacco which became a major revenue source. The flour tax was devised in mid-1928 to replace *likin* charges on flour. Next were added the tax on flue-cured tobacco (1930); cotton yarn, matches, cement, foreign-style wine, liquor, and beer (1931); mineral products (1933); and alcohol (1935).

A first step in reorganization was to create the Consolidated Tax Administration to administer the new excises. Soong recruited modern-type men for the revenue service. Payment of taxes was evidenced by affixing revenue stamps when practicable, or by issuing receipts and permits to accompany shipments. Arrangements were made with the authorities of the Shanghai International Settlement for inspection, and in September 1933 about 600 inspectors were in 190 Settlement factories. These arrangements placed on a more equal footing tax-payers in the Settlement and throughout the country. Regional offices of the Administration were created. The two offices in charge of the old wine and tobacco tax and the stamp tax were merged into one Administration. In 1932 it and the Consolidated Tax Administration were combined into the Internal Revenue Administration. This Administration together with the Customs and Salt Revenue Administrations provided a logical organization, to which was added in 1936 a separate office to take charge of the newly adopted income tax.

Lockhart as Financial Adviser with special reference to taxation participated in devising the specific tax measures and developing their working, and he contributed significantly to their success. He continued his advisory work on taxation concurrently after being named co-chief of the Salt Revenue Administration in 1935. His collaboration in tax matters was aided by the presence of an able and dedicated head of the Internal Revenue Administration, Tse Tsok-kai. That office won the respect of the community as one of the best-working branches of the government.

Of particular importance was the abolition of *likin,* the burdensome *octroi* or transit tax. The two-year period for abolition ended in December 1930, according to the understanding given to Japan as a condition of agreeing to the tariff effective early in 1929. Abolition of *likin* and similar levies was ordered, in a mandate of January 1930, to take effect on October 10, 1930. Because of civil war, the date was postponed until January 1, 1931.

The measure involved major problems. *Likin* besides burdening trade was "the fountain-head of political corruption" because of the extortion and squeeze to which it gave rise.[20] The 1928 plan for allocation of revenues gave the land tax to the provinces and provided that *likin* would be a national revenue. But the provinces did little to improve and develop the land tax, and they still collected *likin* to a considerable extent. They received much of the estimated C $80 to C $100 million yearly yield from *likin.*

The government made a serious effort to abolish *likin,* and the degree of success exceeded the general expectation. The abolition proceeded gradually as the government's control was extended during the thirties. Minister Johnson reported in January 1934 that "abolition has been almost complete" in the territory which the government controlled.[21] To meet the loss of revenue from *likin,* the government introduced in early 1931 excise taxes on cotton yarn, matches, and cement. Besides subsidizing the provinces with about C $20 million yearly, it authorized a provincial business tax, planned and administered under central supervision.

At the time of ordering abolition of *likin,* the government also ended transit and coast trade dues. Native customs duties, comprising duties on junk-borne trade, were ended in two stages on January 1 and June 1, 1931. The dues and duties thus ended yielded about C $20 million yearly.

The ending of these charges on movement of goods was a most constructive move, designed to promote trade and relieve the people of heavy burdens. These burdens much exceeded the revenue going to government, because there were heavy costs of collection by a host of officials and also irregular exactions.

A sizable irregular source of revenue that persisted was from opium. This revenue did not figure in the official accounts of the National Government, although some military units received it. But it was received by various provincial and local authorities, and in some provinces was for a time an important revenue source. In Szechwan Province and elsewhere some rulers forced farmers to grow opium poppies, and placed heavy taxes on opium shops. Fragmentary data and estimates indicate that annual revenue at the various levels may have been of the order of C $100 million yearly.[22] Opium was grown extensively in the southwest and west. There was clandestine traffic on vessels plying the Yangtze and other rivers and coastal waterways, often involving military personnel. Civil officers found it difficult and dangerous to interfere. Opium shops were licensed in various places. In 1936-1937, the government was making some headway in reducing and suppressing the growth, traffic, and use of opium. Unhappily, Japanese were heavily involved in North China, and the Japanese Concession at Tientsin was described in February 1937 as "the headquarters . . . for a vast opium and narcotic industry that has spread its tentacles throughout the Far East and has direct connections with the narcotic rings in Europe and the Americas." In June 1937, at the Opium Advisory Commission of the League of Nations, the Japanese representative deplored the situation and undertook to report it to his government.[23]

Direct taxes

The government's tax system relied almost wholly on indirect taxes: tariffs, salt taxes, and commodity taxes, all of which bore disproportionately on the masses of the people. To remedy this situation, income taxes were an obvious measure if practicable. An income tax adopted in 1914 became effective in 1921. But its yield in that year was C $10,311.69,[24] and it became a dead letter. In 1929, the Kemmerer Commission recommended against adopting either a general or partial income tax, and later Lockhart recommended against it on several occasions. The objections were found both in the lack of accounting practice, and in difficulties of administration. The Commission favored such a tax, perhaps begun partially or tentatively, when conditions made possible its successful introduction.

In 1935, the government proposed an income tax with moderate and progressive rates, and it became law in mid-1936.[25] The tax was on (a) "profit-seeking business enterprises," with rates from 3 to 10 per cent; (b) "emoluments and salaries of public functionaries, people practicing free professions, and those engaged in other profitable vocations," with rates from 0.05 to 20 per cent; and (c) "interest accrued from government bonds, corporation debentures, and stocks and banking deposits," taxed at 5 per cent (translated). The profits tax was complicated since it was based on return on capital. The method combined collection at source and declared returns. The tax was made effective from October 1, 1936, on income from public functionaries and from government bonds, with full effectiveness from January 1, 1937. The measure was considered experimental, and many in the government realized the difficulties of enforcement.

Experienced observers quickly recognized that the law as adopted could not be operated successfully as a general law applicable throughout the country. Lockhart and I, had we been consulted on this project, would have considered the experiment premature. Since 1928, China had made notable progress in improving public administration, and was creditably operating the Internal Revenue Administration on an all-Chinese basis. Yet an income tax is complicated at best. Success was bound to depend on more than the presence of competent administrators —even had they been available in sufficient numbers, which they were not. There was a need for the general practice of accounting with adequate standards as well as for the general acceptance of the obligation to pay the tax, together with confidence that it would be fairly and comprehensively enforced. The public in China, especially after the misgovernment and exploitation of the 1920's, was steeped in the idea of concealment of wealth and profits from the government.

The law had defects, such as failure to tax income from rural and urban real estate. It applied to wages as low as C $30 per month, on which the tax was C $0.05, and to income on capital of C $2000. To assess and collect such taxes effectively should have been seen as out of the question. Many of the officers charged with operating the law sincerely tried to make it work well, but their task was impossible. In practice, the tax applied mostly to the captive income from salaries of public functionaries and from bonds and bank deposits. The hostilities supervened soon after the tax took effect, thus compounding the difficulties. The yield in the first fiscal year ending June 30, 1937, was C $7 million, and during the war was roughly 3 to 4 per cent of total nonborrowed revenue.

The age-old land tax was long a major revenue of the imperial governments. But it was based on assessments and valuations that had not been changed for generations. Sir Robert Hart of the Customs unsuccessfully urged reform in 1904, saying that the tax "has hitherto been levied in a way that takes most from the people and hands least to the Government, while both exactions and malpractices flourish under it." Hart and others believed that, with proper reform, the land tax could readily produce several times its current yield.[26] In 1912, the new republican government confirmed the land tax as a national revenue, and its yield in 1913 was C$82 million. But provinces were permitted to collect additional levies up to 30 per cent, or more in special cases. A result was that numerous surtaxes were added. In some places, the tax was collected 60 or more years in advance.[27]

In 1928, the land tax was given to the provinces and the salt tax and various excises to the central government, according to the principles then agreed concerning division of revenue. The *hsiens* as well as the provinces obtained a large part of their revenue from land.

The land tax as it existed in the prewar decade was a heavy and inequitable burden on the rural population. Much land was not on the tax rolls—surveys indicated nearly a fourth in the Yangtze Delta and half in an area of Szechwan.[28] A study of the tax as of 1934 in Chekiang Province by a League of Nations group headed by Sir Arthur Salter and including Franklin Ho and other competent Chinese economists concluded that the tax bore much more heavily on poorer than richer districts. They found a multiplicity of exactions, legal and extra-legal. Calculations based on the area of taxable land, tax rates, and yield showed wholesale evasion. There were no proper or accurate tax rolls. Collectors received only nominal pay, and the system thus made for evasion and extortion.[29]

It was not so much the old basic tax but the surcharges that aggravated the burdens. The surcharges were repeatedly raised during the civil wars of the twenties and thirties. No less than 673 different surtaxes on land tax, including 147 in Kiangsu and 73 in Chekiang, were reported in a study of the Rural Reconstruction Commission. In 1933, the amount of these surcharges ranged from 81 to 173 per cent of the land tax proper.[30] Although the Land Law of 1930 provided that taxes on improved farm land should not exceed 1 per cent of value, with higher rates allowed on unimproved land, rates remained much higher.[31]

Various proposals were made for land tax reform. In 1929, the

Kemmerer Commission noted the need for an effective land tax as part of the revenue system. The Commission urged proceeding as promptly as possible with surveys and land registration, as the first step toward a proper land tax. The League of Nations group also urged this later, with simplification, equalization, and reduction of burdens as the first step. Economists in private Chinese institutions also studied the problem and proposed reforms.

Nationwide reform of the land tax would have been a major undertaking. The government took a number of steps toward that end. The land law of 1930 provided for a limit on land taxes, as mentioned above, and contained provisions designed to reform conditions of tenure (Chapter 14). The Second National Financial Conference in 1934 called for the abolition of exorbitant taxes, including those on land, and for land survey and registration. Following the Conference, the Finance Ministry reported that about 5000 items of taxes had been abolished, including surtaxes on land that produced C $49 million of revenue. Pilot projects of land registration and tax reform were begun with good results in several *hsiens,* and expansion of the measures so devised was begun or under consideration in several provinces.[32] In May 1937, the government adopted a program for general land survey and registration. Although beginnings were made, the progress with land reform in the country as a whole was far from satisfactory. The hostilities supervened before there could be substantial change in the basic situation.

In addition to the serious social and political effects of failure to reform the land tax, the fiscal consequences were momentous. A properly adjusted tax on rural and urban land could have provided large revenue. Agriculture in the thirties produced from 60 to 70 per cent of China's gross national product.[33] But total revenue from land was less than 10 per cent of total national and local tax revenue in 1936. The government's giving up the land tax to the provinces in 1928, coupled with the failure to draw adequate revenue at any level from the largest sector of the economy, seriously impaired its ability to cover growing expenditures from noninflationary revenues. That failure was important in the prewar decade, but proved much more grave during the war after 1937. The more modernized commercial and industrial regions, which provided most of the national revenue, were lost to Japan in the early months of fighting. The land tax in kind was indeed developed during the second half of the war, to become the chief single revenue source. Meanwhile, the main fiscal resource had to be paper money inflation.

China's lack of progress in dealing with the land tax contrasts strongly with what took place earlier in Japan, after the Meiji restoration. There a nationwide survey was followed by a change from taxation in kind to a money tax based on assessed values. The land tax was set at 3 per cent of land value, which in turn was fixed at 8.5 times the average annual value of crop yield. The aim was to provide a dependable source of revenue that would be easy to collect and hard to evade. The tax became Japan's largest source of revenue for many years. The reform was effectively carried out but required nine years.[34] In China it would have taken much longer.

Provincial and local revenues

No comprehensive data of actual provincial revenues are available, but budgetary estimates are available for most provinces. Approximate totals by years were C $362 million for 1931, C $360 million for 1932, C $358 million for 1933, C $384 million for 1934, C $453 million for 1935, and C $534 million for 1936. These figures include data from the special municipalities of Nanking, Shanghai, Peiping, Tientsin and Tsingtao. The *hsien* (county) revenues are available only for 1936-1937, and the estimated total was C $190 million.[35] The total estimated for the provinces, special municipalities, and *hsiens* was about C $724 million as of 1936.

The land tax was the most important source of provincial revenue, and with the tax on transfer of title deeds represented perhaps 35 to 40 per cent of the total. After abolition of *likin* the business tax was substituted, but it yielded less than one-fifth of the total, and failed to produce the amount of revenue obtained from *likin*. The rest of the revenue was derived from public properties and enterprises, administrative charges, and a variety of lesser taxes. Various provinces borrowed, largely for reconstruction, and for 1935-1936 incomplete data show estimated receipts of C $19 million from loans.[36] Subsidies to provincial and local governments from Nanking according to Finance Ministry data were respectively C $55, C $99, and C $86 million in the last three prewar fiscal years (Appendix 1). Those figures averaged more than 10 per cent of total estimated revenue of provincial and local bodies in 1936.

The government pressed provinces and *hsiens* to improve their revenue systems. Provinces were required under the budget law of 1932 to submit their budgets to the government for approval. Most did so after the earlier years of the decade, although action on them was slow. Important provinces not submitting budgets during most of the decade, until the central authority was extended to them, were Kwangtung, Kwangsi, and Szechwan. After the collapse of the dissident movement in 1936, the government examined the fiscal situation in Kwangtung and took steps to put things in order. The government found that of a total revenue of 54 million Canton dollars, one-fourth came from the gambling tax and 18 per cent from opium. The *hsiens* were required to submit their budgets to the provincial governments for approval, and the provincial governments in turn were required to transmit the *hsien* budgets to Nanking. As of 1935, budgets of more than half of the 1941 *hsiens* were reported to the central authorities. That provided opportunity to check whether the *hsiens* complied with the aforementioned decision to abolish oppressive and illegal taxes.[37]

Revenue growth and distribution: the overall tax burden

The Nationalists developed sizable fiscal resources even before the overthrow of the Peking regime in mid-1928. A report covering the year ended May 31, 1928, showed the following receipts (millions of C $): salt, 21; "customs and land tax," including the 2-1/2 per cent customs surtax and kerosene tax, 15; wine and tobacco tax, 9; provincial remittances, 10; other, 35; loans, 61; total, 151.[38]

After the government became established on a nationwide basis, its total receipts excluding loans grew from C $334 million in fiscal 1929 to C $870 million in fiscal 1937 (Table 1). The overall growth was even more striking than the figures show because of the loss of about C $50 million yearly of customs and salt revenue in Manchuria after 1931. The figures in Table 1 somewhat overstate the real growth to 1931, because of the considerable price rise; but for 1931 to 1935 when prices were falling, the growth in real terms was greater than the figures show (Table 15). The prospect in 1937 was for further growth. Revenue administration was improving, and China was emerging from deflation and depression, which was aggravated by the

American silver-buying program. Unhappily, Japan's attack in mid-1937 reversed the promising prospect, and largely destroyed the main revenue sources.

The revenue yield is shown in detail in Appendix 1, and its distribution in Table 4. The customs was by far the largest source. The yield grew rapidly after tariff autonomy, and was over half the total. Then the proportion shrank, partly because other revenues grew faster, partly because of depressed foreign trade in the mid-thirties, and partly because of Japanese-sponsored smuggling in North China.

Table 4

Distribution of revenues from 1929 to 1937[a]

Year ending June 30	Customs	Salt	Other Taxes	Miscellaneous
1929	53.5%	9.0%	11.0%	26.5%
1930	57.0	25.2	11.0	6.8
1931	56.1	26.9	12.2	4.8
1932	59.8	23.2	16.5	0.6
1933	53.1	25.8	15.9	5.2
1934	51.3	25.7	19.	4.1
1935	47.3	22.4	17.3	12.9
1936	33.3	22.6	20.4	23.7
1937	43.4	22.7	22.2	11.7

[a] Source: Finance Ministry, for 1929 to 1935 from published reports, and for 1935 to 1937 from unpublished data stated to be final.

Salt revenue after it was reorganized provided about one-fourth of the total. The share of other internal taxes grew from 11 to 22 per cent in the period, largely because of the development of the rolled tobacco tax and the introduction of the tax on cotton yarn. Miscellaneous revenues included considerable sums from the railways in 1935-1936, and fairly large unspecified items in some years. Part of the miscellaneous revenues represented book transactions (Appendix 1, note d).

Since debt payments heavily burdened the customs, the free revenue available to the government at the close of the period came in roughly equal parts from customs, salt, and the other internal taxes.

As of 1936-1937, the total yearly revenue in China proper comprised C $870 million for the central government, plus approximately C $534 million for the provinces and C $190 million for the *hsiens*. The total was about C $1,594 million. Assuming for purposes of calculation a population of 500 million, the tax burden averaged a little over C $3 per capita. To that however should be added something for the irregular exactions of various militarists and a host of officials. And something should be subtracted because the provincial figure represented estimates, which apparently somewhat exceeded actual revenues.

In absolute terms, the average burden would not seem heavy. But it bore unduly upon those least able to support it, in particular, the poor farmer. This was especially true in the 1930's, when many farmers were pressed to or below the level of subsistence after many years of civil wars with looting and conscription of soldiers and laborers, aggravated by the sharp drop of agricultural prices accompanying the depression. The tax system as a whole was highly regressive—many well-to-do paid no direct taxes and were burdened only slightly by excise and customs duties.

4: The Quest for Fiscal Stability: Expenditures, Deficits, and Borrowing

Although revenues much more than doubled in the prewar decade, deficits covered by borrowing were about one-fifth of total expenditures (excluding changes in balances). By far the chief cause of deficits was heavy military outlay, which forced the borrowing. As borrowing grew, the debt payments became heavier, especially because loans had to be repaid within a brief period.

Objects of expenditure

Outlay caused by internal disturbances and trouble with Japan dominated the finances through the prewar decade. Military costs plus debt payments were 84 per cent of all payments in 1928-1929, and in 1929-1937 never fell much below two-thirds. Details of expenditure for the fiscal years ended June 30, 1929-1937, are shown in Appendix 1.

By the summer of 1929, said Finance Minister Soong in his first published report for 1928-1929, the government was near to balancing current income and outgo without borrowing. A Disbandment Conference early in 1929 set the yearly military budget at C$192 million plus costs of disbandment. But that figure quickly became unrealistic. Soon the Kwangsi leaders revolted, and later in 1929 there were other revolts, the most serious being that led by Marshall Feng Yu-hsiang in the northwest. Drawing a lesson from these events and from the progress of the economy in intervals of internal peace, Soong concluded that with peace and order the government would be able to devote sizable funds to constructive purposes and restoring the national credit. In solving the problem of internal peace, he concluded, "lies indeed the future of democratic government, economic reconstruction, foreign relations and financial progress, and therefore it constitutes the one challenge to the statesmanship of the Government and the Party together with the support of the entire nation."[1]

Unhappily for China, the revolts continued sporadically until 1936. The last serious threat in these years was by the Communists in Kiangsi Province south of the Yangtze. But after several campaigns they were driven to the far northwest. Their retreat was the famous "long march." This retreat was mostly through territory outside the control of the government, where the inefficient armies of local warlords were unable to contain and destroy the determined Communist remnants. By 1935 there was substantial internal peace in the most important economic areas, although the South China dissidents were not definitely dislodged until mid-1936. Paralleling the internal improvement, the growing threat from Japan gave rise to heavy costs for military development.

Minister Soong, until leaving office late in 1933, tried repeatedly to bring expenditures under better control. His report for 1929-1930 recognized that they "do not present any approach to proper proportion in their intrinsic importance," but that the constant state of disturbance "rendered any choice or discretion in allotting funds entirely out of the question" (page 7). He clearly recognized that the constant state of emergency caused by both internal and external pressures left the government where it could "provide for nothing beyond the minimum of bare existence." He longed for conditions that would permit "the creation of a stable currency, the development of domestic industries, the revival of the tea and silk trades, the opening up of new lines of communication, the promotion of mass education and public health" (page 10). Finally, Soong pointed out the need for lessening the burdens of military costs and debt repayment.

In pressing to control military costs Soong more than once offered his resignation. His attitude is shown in his statement of June 11, 1932:

> But shall the government embark on a course of fresh borrowing and repeat the tragedy of the past? . . . Is it not possible to continue a process of rigid economy and seek reforms from within? Are banditry and communism purely military phenomena, and could we hope for quick success by an old-fashioned and costly military drive? Have not banditry and communism thriven on political, military and economic maladjustments, and will they not respond better to a systematic, if unspectacular, combination of politico-military-economic treatment? . . . Can we not by dint of patience, hard work and continual personal sacrifices bring ourselves to weather this crisis so that we may emerge from the world depression with a bal-

> anced budget and a peaceful countryside? The answers to these questions rest not with any Minister of Finance.[2]

On July 8, Soong returned to duty from partial retirement after assurances limiting the payments sought by the military.

His successor in the fall of 1933, H. H. Kung, also tried to hold down military costs. But the situation was out of civilian hands.

For the period 1928 through 1937, military costs plus subsidies and revenue transfers to local authorities were about one-half of total outlay. Debt payments consumed 31 per cent, and government overhead including costs of revenue collections, 13 per cent.

Outlay for education, culture, and reconstruction, the term commonly used to signify economic development, was shown separately only in the accounts for fiscal years 1934 through 1937, as follows (millions):

	1934	1935	1936	1937
Education and culture	C$13	C$32	C$37	C$42
Reconstruction (development)	7	26	88	54
Capital for government banks and other government enterprises		74	33	29
Total	C$20	C$133	C$158	C$125

The accounts for 1928-1929 show C $20 million allocated for initial capital of the Central Bank. There should be added also part of the Boxer Indemnity payments used for the purposes stated above, roughly amounting to C $100 million for the fiscal years 1928 through 1937 (Chapter 5). This amount chiefly comprised payments to the United States and Britain, remitted for China's use. For the four years tabulated above, such remitted payments would add about C $60 million to the totals shown. In these four years, total outlay for education, culture, and economic development was about one-eighth of total expenditures in the general budget.

Some large expenditures for development were not included

in the general budget. Chief of these were for railways, whose finances were autonomous, and lesser amounts were for telecommunications. These agencies had a cash flow that enabled them to use considerable funds for development. Over 2000 miles of railway were built during the prewar decade, and existing lines, plant, and equipment were notably improved (Chapter 14). Expenditures for these railway purposes in that period were of the order of C $100 million. Provincial governments also took active part in promoting development as described below.

A program deserving special emphasis was the handling of relief and rehabilitation after the great Yangtze River flood of the summer of 1931. This flood was one of the greatest natural calamities on record, affecting many millions of people. The government acted vigorously to meet the emergency, aided by an American credit of US $9.2 million for wheat and flour. Total expenditures were C $70 million, of which donations mostly from Chinese provided about one-tenth. The success of the program, showing the ability of the government to act efficiently, added materially to confidence in the government throughout the country. The operation is described further in Chapter 16.

In addition to the American credit of 1931 for flood relief, the American Cotton and Wheat Loan of 1933, of which US $17.1 million was utilized, was spent entirely for productive purposes. These included highways and other development work, rehabilitation of areas recovered from the Communists, public health, and education. The net proceeds of this credit so spent were about C $38 million (Chapter 16).

The burden of debt payments was heavy throughout. At times it was close to 40 per cent of the total expenditure, and in 1936-1937 about one-fourth. That burden was largely the result of borrowing heavily in the local market at a discount, for repayment over a brief period. Foreign debt payments equivalent to about US $30 million yearly from the budget, plus about US $10 million from the railways and communications, were not a serious problem in the balance of payments. But provision of funds to cover service of internal and foreign debts was continually a major budgetary problem, second only to military outlay.

Provincial and local expenditures

The total expenditures of provinces and the special municipalities of Nanking, Shanghai, Peiping, Tientsin, and Tsingtao are estimated as follows (calendar years in millions of C $): 362 for 1931; 360 for 1932; 358 for 1933; 384 for 1934; 453 for 1935; and 534 for 1936.

Partial data for 1935-1936 indicate 16 per cent spending for public safety; 16 per cent for construction, industry, communications, and public health; 14 per cent for education; and the rest for general administration, judicial administration, and debt service. For *hsiens,* the estimated yearly total is C $190 million.[3] Particulars of the objects of their expenditures are not available.

The situation in the twenties was quite different from that in the thirties. A compilation of provincial budgets for various dates in the twenties showed total estimated outlay of C $275 million, of which 68 per cent was for the military. Only 3 per cent was for the categories of education, agriculture, and communications.[4] As to outlay for armed forces the data do not permit of specific quantitative comparisons. But the greatly reduced allocations in the thirties for "public safety," as compared with military outlay, reflect the efforts of the National Government to centralize military power in its hands and get rid of warlords, the cost of whose surviving armies was either incorporated into the national budget or met to a reduced extent from provincial revenues augmented by subsidies from Nanking. The budgets of the thirties also show a great change as to outlay for constructive purposes. The data cited above suggest that the increase of provincial outlay for education, development, and public health was of the order of tenfold compared with the twenties.

Some provinces spent considerable sums for development, especially for roads, railways, telephones, dykes, and irrigation. Shansi and Chekiang Provinces each financed several hundred miles of railway largely by provincial resources, and most provinces carried out extensive programs of road building (Chapters 14 and 15). Kwangsi, wrote a correspondent of the *North China Daily News* (May 18, 1936), was becoming a "model province." Peace and order were being maintained despite a cut in military forces. There was "a considerable degree of self-government." The province had "established a sound budget system," education was being promoted, and 7 per cent of the administrative budget was allotted for public health.

But provincial development was not always without its drawbacks. In 1934 a group of Chinese and foreign experts led by Sir

Arthur Salter investigated conditions in Chekiang Province. Under Governor Chang Ching-kiang that province had been specially active in developing roads, railways, and utilities. The experts reported that the provincial Bureau of Reconstruction spent C $20 million in the calendar years 1932 and 1933, including C $5.8 million for roads and C $4.5 million for railways. The ordinary and extraordinary provincial expenditures of C $31 million for 1932-1933 included C $8 million for service of loans that were mainly for reconstruction.[5] The experts found that while considerable development had been accomplished, there were serious disadvantages at least in the short run. Taxes and especially surtaxes on land had sharply increased, becoming "in the poorer districts an almost intolerable burden on agricultural life." So far there had been little discernible gain for the rural people, who made little use of the roads and railways. Some utilities had been constructed at unduly high cost and were under-utilized.[6]

Budgets, accounts, and fiscal control

When the Nationalists took over the government there was no real national system of budgets, accounting, and fiscal control. Budgets existed only on paper. The last of these was for 1919-1920, and it was to this that the later Peking regimes hoped sometime to revert.[7] Then and later the budget did not include all the receipts and payments of organs of the central government. Certain administrative receipts, such as those of the judiciary and the Ministry of Education, were omitted from the budget. A much more important exclusion resulted from the fact that the Ministries of Railways and Communications, with relatively large financial operations, operated independently of the Finance Ministry. Some military authorities collected and disposed of irregular revenues, including receipts from opium. There were also the provincial and local budgets, whose total in 1936-1937 was of the order of 70 per cent of the national budget (page 79).

T. V. Soong in his report for 1928-1929 urged the need for "a budget to replace the present haphazard, hand-to-mouth, wasteful methods, by virtue of which the Ministry must depend upon expedients rather than operate on policies. . . . Without a budget of some sort, however imperfect it may be, . . . all thorough-going financial plans are rendered impossible, and publicity, which is the mainspring of public confidence and provides the moral sanction for taxation, is difficult to furnish." The main difficulty was "the inability of the Government to foresee and curb military expenditures" (pages 9-10).

Before the start of the fiscal year in mid-1929, Soong took the first steps toward budgetary reform. He circulated to all branches of government forms for submitting estimates of receipts and expenditures. These were to be sent to the Finance Ministry for scrutiny and comment; then to the Finance Committee of the Central Political Council; and after approval to the Ministry and Bureau of Audit for enforcement. Practically all the collecting and disbursing organs sent in their estimates, except in areas outside government control.

Meanwhile the Kemmerer Commission was at work on the problem. Frederick A. Cleveland was the senior adviser and William Watson assisted, both staying on for a time after the end of the Commission's work. The Commission's report of 1929 proposed adoption by law of a detailed procedure for a system of budgeting, accounts, and fiscal control. Soong approved the principles involved, but wanted the plan so far as his Ministry was concerned put into effect by administrative action. The Ministry's Department of Accounts adopted a new comprehensive accounting system as of January 1, 1931, and instituted a plan for 10-day reports. But progress with the new procedures had to be gradual because of problems of personnel and the difficulty of changing old procedures. In 1931, the Directorate General of Budgets, Accounts, and Statistics was created as an independent office. It did not, however, directly prepare basic records of financial transactions, but used the data of the Finance Ministry.

Preparation of complete and accurate reports of receipts and expenditures was difficult, especially in the earlier years when various areas were disturbed by fighting. The statements of expenditures in the published reports of the Finance Ministry, according to a report of the Department of Accounts, showed generally payments by the Ministry rather than actual outgo of the disbursing organs. The civil organs often did not for the most part report at all their actual outgo and, where they did, reports were often incomplete and late.[8] Auditing of receipts and payments, outside the chief revenue collecting organs, was far from adequate in the civilian branches of government, let alone the military.

A major weakness in Nationalist finance was lack of fiscal

control of the military. The large amounts asked by the military were paid over in lump sums. They were then disbursed to lower echelons in lump sums. A commander got a lump sum for so many troops, who were not paid individually. This procedure encouraged a commonly employed practice by commanders to pocket the pay of nonexistent, absent, or dead troops. Thus, the higher authorities could not know just how many troops were available at a given time and place. Certainly the practice made for corruption and inefficiency in he army. That, in turn, reflected on the army's prestige as an internal force, and in some areas gave color to the charge that government forces were not too different from those of the warlords. Failure to reform drastically the old army system was a major weakness throughout the prewar decade, and thereafter during the war.

The budgeted and actual expenditures are shown in Table 5. Expenditures exceeded the budget in five of the nine fiscal years. Until 1935, budgets were promulgated too late to be of full use. Thereafter they were promulgated in time. But that did not bring effective budgetary control, because the Executive did not feel limited by the budget and authorized additional outlay in situations considered an emergency.

When announcing the currency reform of November 1935 the government declared its intention to balance the budget within 18 months. After that period balance had not been attained. The situation was much improved by recovery from the depression, but spending pressures were such that fiscal stabilization was still in doubt.

Table 5

Budgeted and actual expenditures from 1929 to 1937[a]

Year ending June 30	Budget, millions	Expenditures,[b] millions	Year ending June 30	Budget, millions	Expenditures,[b] millions
1929	C$492	C$434	1934	C$828	C$836
1930	619	585	1935	918	941
1931	712	775	1936	957	1073
1932	893	749	1937	991	1167
1933	788	699			

[a] Source: Budget data through fiscal 1935 from Chang Wei-ya, *The Money and Finance of China* (in Chinese) (Taipei, 1951), p. 87, and thereafter from Finance Ministry. Data of expenditures from Finance Ministry (Appendix 1).

[b] Excluding balances at end of the period.

Statistics of receipts and expenditures: evaluation of differing data

In presenting and analyzing the fiscal data I use those prepared contemporaneously by the Finance Ministry. These data I consider the authoritative and best available statement, reasonably consistent *inter se,* and comparable with the Ministry's official data for the war period. The Ministry published in English and Chinese its annual reports for the fiscal years ended June 30 from 1929 through 1935. No reports for fiscal 1936 and 1937 were published, but the Ministry's statements of receipts and expenditures for those two periods were contemporaneously furnished to me as final. These are included in Appendix 1.

Unfortunately differing sets of data exist which have misled several writers. One of these sets was prepared by the Directorate General of Budgets, Accounts, and Statistics. Another set was published in 1943 by the Finance Ministry. Still another unpublished set was prepared for presentation to Laughlin Currie, who visited China in 1941 as an emissary of President Roosevelt.

Some writers have seen nefarious motives in the failure to publish the 1936 and 1937 reports. Y. C. Wang has stated that "fear of divulging" a large increase in note issue "was undoubtedly the main reason behind Kung's decision to suspend" them. Actually the figures of note issue were regularly and accurately published in the Central Bank's *Bulletin* and elsewhere. D. S. Paauw saw "no genuine explanation" of failure to issue the reports.[9]

The real explanation is simple. I was charged with preparing the draft of the reports for fiscal years 1929 through 1935, although Ministers Soong and Kung made changes so that the reports would be their own. I left China just after the close of the fiscal year ended June 30, 1936, partly on leave and partly to negotiate debt settlements in the United States and was absent until February 1937. I then began work on the 1936 report but soon afterward Kung left to attend the coronation in London. There was never to my knowledge any suggestion of omitting the reports. Rather, besides recognition of responsibility to give a public accounting, they were viewed as an opportunity to publicize the progress made in several fields, despite difficulties. While Kung was away, outbreak of the Sino-Japanese fighting on July 7, 1937, forced concentration on matters more urgent than completing the 1936 report and preparing one for the 1937 fiscal year that had just ended.

The Directorate General of Budgets, Accounts, and Statistics published on February 27, 1936, through *Kuo Min News Agency* its own set of figures for fiscal 1934. This set differed little from the Ministry's figures in the annual report published a year earlier, and did not attract much attention. I recommended—unsuccessfully—to Minister Kung in a letter of March 20, 1936, that there be only a single standard publication. When the Directorate's figures for fiscal 1935 were published on February 4, 1937, through *Central News*, some items differed widely from those in the Ministry's annual report published six months earlier. Existence of the two official reports with unexplained differences brought unfavorable comment at the time. In 1940, the Directorate published in the *Statistical Abstract* (Chung-hua min-kuo t'ung chi t'i yao, Chungking, 1940, page 144) its figures for the last four prewar fiscal years through 1937.

The Directorate did not compile its own data but rather presented the Ministry data in a different form. Table 6 contains a comparison of the four-year figures of the Ministry and Directorate for the fiscal years 1934 through 1937, for such items as nonborrowed receipts, the two major items of expenditure for the military and debt, and the balancing totals of receipts and expenditure. The year by year figures show considerable differences, especially for 1934-1935. The four-year totals do not, however, greatly differ. The relatively small differences in the totals seem capable of explanation by differences in accounting methods and by inclusions and exclusions from preceding and following periods.

To compound the difficulty, the Finance Ministry issued in 1943 entirely different sets of figures for the prewar period, in the *Public Finance Yearbook, Supplement* (Ts'ai-cheng nien-chien, hsu-pien, Chungking, 1943, pages 107-111).[10] For fiscal 1937, total receipts and expenditures are shown as C $1973 million and C $1894 million, respectively, excluding beginning and ending balances. Those figures compare with C $1206 million and C $1167 million, respectively, in the contemporaneous Ministry figures (Appendix 1). Customs receipts are inexplicably shown as C $636 million, whereas the Inspectorate General's contemporaneous figure was C$379 million. In the 1943 presentation, the figures for the other revenues and for military and other expenditures are of the same general magnitude as in the Ministry and Directorate data. But there is a major difference in that the 1943 presentation shows for fiscal 1937 receipts of C $679 million from borrowing and C $835 million for debt service. The Ministry's contemporaneous figures (Appendix 1) show C $336 million received from borrowing, compared with the Directorate's C $330 million. As to debt service, the contemporaneous Ministry and Directorate figures are C $305 million and C $249 million, respectively. Had there been a major net increase in borrowing in 1936-1937, as Paauw deduced from the 1943 figures, presumably it would have shown up in larger listings of outlay for military or other specific items and not only under the head of debt service.

When the 1943 document appeared, I was in the United States and did not learn of it until long afterward. The 1943 figures of borrowing and debt service, to the extent that they are correct, seem to include gross figures of turnover instead of net figures, and also to include in some form the unissued balance of the 1936 consolidation loan. The total of expenditures of C $1894 million (excluding balances) for the last prewar year, however determined, is clearly misleading. In the first war year, 1937-1938, expenditures greatly increased over the last prewar year and also general prices were higher. Yet the Ministry figure of C $2091 million for that year, which was given me contemporaneously as final, is only slightly greater than the aforementioned C $1894 million. Apparently it was realized later in the Ministry that the 1943 figures were not comparable with the Ministry's definitive figures for the prewar and war periods. Whatever the method used in 1943, it was abandoned in presenting the wartime fiscal statistics in the *Public Finance Yearbook, 1948* (Section III, pages 98-101), which were on a basis comparable with the Ministry's prewar data.[11]

Figures for 1932-1937 were prepared for Roosevelt's representative Laughlin Currie in 1941, and I received them later upon my return to Chungking from Washington. Those figures are of the same general magnitude as the Ministry figures in Appendix 1 except for one item. In the data given Currie, gross receipts and payments of government enterprises are included instead of net figures. The total of payments in these data for 1936-1937 for example is C $1583 million, including gross enterprise payments of C $362 million. That total is C $416 million greater than the contemporaneous Ministry figure of C $1167, which includes net enterprise payments. I do not know the reason for departing from the earlier Ministry figures, and I have

Table 6

Comparison of six items of fiscal statements prepared by the Finance Ministry and Directorate General of Budgets, Accounts, and Statistics, fiscal years ended June 30, 1934 to 1937[a]

	Amounts (millions) in indicated year					
	1934	1935	1936	1937		Total
Nonborrowed receipts:						
Ministry	C$689	C$745	C$817	C$870		C$3121
Directorate	718	776	669	812		2975
Receipts from "bank loans and overdrafts":						
Ministry	91	36	128	113	368	
Less payments on same		30	5	7	42	
						326
Receipts from "loans":	79	43	373	114	566	
Directorate						
Less payments on "loans" and "others"	18	157	46	6	227	339

(Continued)

Table 6 (Continued)

Comparison of six items of fiscal statements prepared by the Finance Ministry and Directorate General of Budgets, Accounts, and Statistics, fiscal years ended June 30, 1934 to 1937[a]

	Amounts (millions) in indicated year				
	1934	1935	1936	1937	Total
Military expenditures:					
Ministry	373	388	390	521	1672
Directorate	362	368	366	451	1547
Debt service expenditures[b]:					
Ministry	245	237	294	305	1081
Directorate	226	361	223	249	1059
Total receipts and expenditures:					
Ministry	896	1031	1182	1251	4360
Directorate	898	1212	1107	1195	4412

[a] Sources: For Ministry data, Appendix 1; Directorate General of Budgets, Accounts, and Statistics, *Statistical Abstract of the Republic of China*, 1940 (Chung-hua Min-kuo t'ung chi t'i yao, Chungking, 1940), p. 144.

[b] Including Boxer Indemnity and the fund of C$5 million set aside yearly for readjustment of debts. The Ministry figure for 1935 takes account of the deduction of C$32 million for "refund of principal and interest" on obligations held by the Treasury.

seen no other compilations incorporating these gross data. Although the departure was unfortunate, I see no ulterior purpose.

In summary, the authentic figures of receipts and payment for fiscal years 1928 through 1935 are those published in the Finance Ministry's annual reports, and the ones for fiscal 1936 and 1937 are those the Ministry contemporaneously prepared on a similar basis (Table 1 and Appendix 1). Publication of the figures for fiscal 1936 and 1937 was planned but did not occur only because of successive absences of Adviser Young and Minister Kung, followed by the outbreak of the Sino-Japanese fighting. There was no ulterior motive, as has been charged, for lack of publication. The reports of the Directorate-General of Budgets, Accounts, and Statistics used Ministry data and not those independently gathered. Those reports contain figures differing year by year from Ministry reports, but the four-year totals are similar (Table 6). In 1943, the Ministry published figures for 1934 through 1937 prepared on a basis different from that used contemporaneously, apparently using some gross rather than net figures, especially for debt transactions. That basis was abandoned in the *Public Finance Yearbook 1948,* which contains the authoritative figures of wartime receipts and payments on a basis comparable with prewar data.

The confusion of data has been more unfortunate than could have been foreseen. The 1936-1937 figures stated in the Finance Ministry's 1943 publication, because of not being comparable either with preceding prewar data or wartime data, have misled scholars who have used those figures as a base in studies of wartime finance and inflation. And the divergencies of data have led to charges of financial chicanery.

In their analysis of China's wartime experience with inflation Chang Kia-ngau[12] and Shun-hsin Chou[13] both used as a base the figures for 1936-1937 from the Ministry's 1943 publication, which showed expenditures of C$1894 million. Y. C. Wang, relying on the 1943 figures for expenditures only, gives an incorrect picture of the size of the deficit.[14] The Ministry figure comparable with prewar and wartime figures is C$1167 million for 1936-1937, excluding cash balances at the end of the period. Consequently the quantitative results Chang and Chou show in analyzing the inflation are distorted. Fortunately, their general reasoning and conclusions are not vitiated.

Paauw writing in 1950 to 1952 dwelt upon the discrepancies between the 1934-1935 figures of the Ministry and the Directorate. The Ministry's annual reports, he alleged, were "intended for Western consumption," although he admitted that the Chinese and English versions agree. He considered the Directorate figures "the more primary and hence the more accurate." The Ministry, he charged, "was able to defy the auditing and accounting checks of the Bureau of Budgets, Accounts, and Statistics."[15] Not having the Ministry figures for fiscal 1936 and 1937, he had no way of knowing that while some yearly figures differed considerably the totals of the two sets of figures for the four prewar years are quite similar, as explained above. And he did not know, as did Shun-hsin Chou, that the Directorate compiled its figures from Ministry data. Chou states that he disagrees with Paauw's apparent premise, and that it "does not seem justifiable" to consider the Directorate figures as "an independent version of government accounts, preferable to those released by the Ministry."[16]

Paauw further charged that "the West had no idea of the decline of responsible accounting in Nationalist public finance until the post World War II period," and that there was "fiscal demoralization" and "financial disintegration" after 1933-1934. He accused the government of "obscuring the correct cost of servicing government debt," by failing "to accurately report its expenditure for service of debt after 1933-1934." The inaccurate reporting of bank borrowing, he said, "reflects on the honesty of the financial leaders." He puts forward "the thesis that the financial responsibility and morality of the Nanking regime was deteriorating before the Japanese attack in July, 1937."[17]

These are very serious charges. The divergences in published data, I believe, have been sufficiently dealt with above. These comments refute Paauw's charges of manipulating the data. Certainly, as one intimately concerned with financial operations and currently receiving a flow of the chief data of receipts, payments, and Central Bank accounts, I can recall nothing to support his accusations. The Ministry and Directorate have themselves to thank for the consequences of issuing differing sets of data with unexplained differences. It is not surprising that Paauw should have cherished suspicion in the absence of fuller information. But he should not have equated suspicion with proof. Unhappily his strictures have presented a highly adverse and incorrect picture that, as one China expert stated to me, has influenced the attitude of a whole generation of American scholars toward the National Government.

Besides Paauw's charge that there was large bank borrowing not included in the Finance Ministry's published accounts, Tuan-sheng Ch'ien has stated that the budget for 1937-1938, though presented as balanced at about C $1 billion, did not list about C $400 million of expenditure. This he said was partly for constructive purposes but largely for the military. "How this sum was covered by income," he stated, "was a secret." He assumed that it came "either from the government banks or from resorting to the printing press."[18] Although the charge relates especially to the first year of hostilities, it will be helpful to deal with it.

Chi'en presumably had in mind a statement by Kung in the *Kuo Min News Agency* report of July 1, 1937, that over and above the recently approved general budget of about C $1 billion for 1937-1938 a capital budget of C $400 million was contemplated. The balancing of the ordinary budget was in prospect, said Kung, and the capital budget would include loans whose service would be covered within the general budget.

Kung presumably had in mind the three-year program of development launched in mid-1936, particulars of which were not made public (Chapter 14 and Table 22). The total estimated cost was C $1034 million or an average of C $345 million yearly. Of the C $1034 million C $555 million was for railways, whose finances were mostly outside the general budget.[19] The Railway Ministry was expected to finance its chief programs and Minister Chang was doing so with much success in 1936-1937 (Chapters 14 and 16). External costs were being met with the help of foreign credits. For internal costs railway revenues were supplemented by the Railway Reconstruction Loan of C $120 million, issued in instalments in 1934 through 1938. This loan was secured by pledge of railway revenue, and for the third series of 1936 the Finance Ministry provided a subsidy for four years to help with loan service.

In addition to railways, the remaining items of the three-year program had an estimated cost of C $479 million. These included C $37 million for highways and C $69 million for water conservancy which were in the general budget, under the heading of "Reconstruction" and in part under subsidies to provinces.[20] Deducting these, there remained C $373 million, comprising C $175 million for heavy industry and C $198 million for armaments. Chi'en correctly stresses the military aspect of the expenditures, although intimating that there was something wrong about it despite the threat from Japan. The railway and highway programs were planned in considerable part for strategic purposes as was the program of heavy industry, but these programs were also economically important.

The items for heavy industry and armament, totaling C $373 million for a three-year program, were not detailed in the general budget. A small portion of these items may have been included in the lump sum allocation of C $70 million for "reconstruction" in the 1937-1938 budget. Many or even all of these items may have been included in the ordinary and extraordinary items of "Military Expenses," details of which were never published and which were not available to me. Article 45 of the budget law provided for withholding from publication parts of the budget that should remain confidential.[21] The foreign currency costs for armaments and heavy industry (Table 22) were estimated at C $99 million for armaments, to be paid in cash; and C $104 million for heavy industry, of which C $6 million was to be paid in cash and C $98 million covered by credit. Part of the credit was financed under the German barter agreement, of which the outstanding balance as of mid-1937 was equivalent to a sum of the order of US $40 million; and further foreign credits were under negotiation when the war began (Chapter 15). Besides these foreign currency costs for armaments and heavy industry, there remained Chinese currency costs of C $71 and C $99 million, respectively, a three-year total of C $170 million.

Thus the financing of the costs for armaments and heavy industry in 1936-1938 was as follows:

Foreign currency costs:	
German barter agreement and other foreign credits for heavy industry	C$ 98 million
To be paid in cash (C$99 million plus C$6 million)	105 million
Chinese currency costs to be paid in cash (C$99 million plus C$71 million)	170 million
	C$373 million

These cash payments totaling C $275 million averaged C $92 million yearly.

To summarize on the basis of the foregoing data, the larger part of the extraordinary expenditures of the three-year program of 1936 through 1938 averaging C $345 million yearly was (1) excluded from the general budget but included in the transactions of the Railway Ministry and covered from railway revenue, the Railway Reconstruction Loan, and foreign and local credits to that Ministry; or (2) included in the regular accounts of expenditures for reconstruction, largely for highways, water conservancy, and government enterprises. Cash payments not so covered apparently did not exceed an unpublished cash expenditure averaging C $92 million yearly. Part or all of that may have been included in the global military budget. I cannot be precise as to items involved in the German barter agreement, with which I had little contact.

Furthermore, as explained on pages 95 to 96, the analysis of bank advances to government indicates that there was little room for secret costs. Some data of receipts and expenditures suffered from imperfect and late reporting. But I saw no indications that the Finance Ministry or Central Bank doctored their figures.

Thus there is no substance to the aforementioned charges of chicanery in reports of the financing, nor of concealment except as to a relatively small amount connected with national defense. However, pressure for development, especially for strategic objectives, was growing. As hereafter pointed out, this pressure was a potential source of inflationary troubles, as the experience of many less developed countries has since shown.

Methods and extent of borrowing

After assuming power, the government had needs that were much too urgent to wait for the growth of tax revenues, a matter of months and years. Without borrowed funds the government could not have survived.

Borrowing abroad was out of the question for the time being, although the government hoped to create conditions favorable for foreign loans. Foreign markets were closed to China because of Peking's defaults. Even if China had had good credit, foreign lending hardly existed in the early thirties after the worldwide defaults at the time of the depression. And then there were no programs of aid to less developed countries. China, however, did get timely aid from the two American credits of 1931 and 1933 mentioned above, totaling US $26 million utilized (Chapter 16).

Fortunately, the government was able to borrow domestically beginning in 1927. Shanghai was a rich and growing metropolis where the country's financial resources were centered. Peking's internal bonds had long been traded on the Shanghai Stock Exchange.[22] These bonds were mostly secured on customs and salt revenues after payment of prior obligations. But in 1927 this old debt was partly or wholly in default because of inadequate revenues. Low prices of the issues reflected the difficulties.

There were several procedures for borrowing. The banks bought bonds from time to time for their own account at prices negotiated with the Finance Ministry. In addition, they often advanced cash against bonds, which were sold as the market could absorb them for credit against the advances. The banks also bought bonds to hold as part of the required reserve against notes. Besides there was public demand for bonds for investment and speculation, the latter representing a large part of the market. It was hoped to develop a broad investment market at Shanghai, but continuing internal and external emergencies militated against this.

There were two forms of issues, called "Treasury Notes" and "Bonds" or "Loans." Issues of Treasury Notes predominated up to the debt consolidation of 1936. Issues by years of the Finance Ministry are shown in Table 7 and further details in Appendix 8. Interest and part of the principal of Treasury Notes were paid monthly; hence the par value of each Note gradually decreased. The first issue, the Shanghai 2-1/2 per cent Surtax Treasury Notes, was for C $30 million at interest of 0.7 per cent monthly or 8.4 per cent per annum. Repayment was by 30 equal monthly instalments of C $1 million each. For Bonds, payments were mostly semiannual, with principal retired by drawings. The first major issue of Bonds was the 17th Year Rehabilitation Loan of 1928 for C $40 million, retired by drawings over five years. Because these issues sold at a large discount there was an important lottery feature, since a bond might be drawn promptly for payment at par.

Because of political uncertainties, the bankers insisted upon short-term issues. Thus loans marketed at large discounts had to be redeemed soon at par. This was costly, as discussed on page 98. Repayment became a heavy and growing drain on the

Table 7

Domestic bond issues of the Finance Ministry during 1927 to 1937[a]

	Amount of domestic bond issue (millions)		
	Fiscal year ending June 30	Calendar year	
	For general purposes		For special purposes[b]
1927	C$30	C$70	
1928	106	105	Long-term Currency Loan, to redeem Hankow bank-notes, C$45
1929	163	194	Haiho Conservancy Loan, C$4
1930	114	174	
1931	350	410	Silk Industry Loan, C$6
1932	190	--	
1933	20	124	
1934	254	150	Yu-Ping Railway Loan, C$12
1935	220	240	Szechuan Rehabilitation Loan, C$70; Szechuan Currency Loan, C$30
1936	360	340	Consolidation Loan, C$1460; Szechuan Rehabilitation Loan, C$15; Kwangtung Currency Loan, C$120
1937		--[c]	Port and River Development Loan, Kwangtung, US$2
Totals	C$1807	C$1807	

[a] Source: Finance Ministry.

[b] The Railway Reconstruction Loan of 1936-1938 for C$120 million is treated as a railway loan, although the Finance Ministry provided a subsidy for the first four years for loan service.

[c] First half.

budget. Despite the large growth of revenues the funds available to the government for general purposes steadily shrank. But the government could not drastically cut expenditures because it was deemed vital to put down warlord revolts and Communist subversion. It became only a matter of time until the government would be unable to meet current debt payments, and borrowing would become impossible. Thus, continuing emergencies led to the debt reorganizations of 1932 and 1936 hereafter described.

In addition to the loans issued by the Finance Ministry, loans were issued by the Ministries of Railways and Communications and the National Reconstruction Commission. In 1934, the Railway Ministry issued jointly with the Finance Ministry the 23rd Year Yu-ping Railway Loan of C $12 million secured on salt revenue, which was the First Series of the Railway Reconstruction Loan. The Railway Ministry issued as of February 2, 1936, the Second Series of C $27 million secured on the surplus revenue of the state railways. The Third Series comprised three *tranches* of C $40 million each for issuance as of March 1, 1936, 1937, and 1938. This Third Series is treated as a railway loan, being primarily secured on surplus railway revenues; but the Finance Ministry joined in its issuance and provided a subsidy for four years to cover loan payments until the projected new railways could be completed and produce revenue. Many of the bonds were used as collateral security for advances by foreign and Chinese interests to finance construction.

The Communications Ministry issued in 1935 the 24th Year Electric Power Loan of C $10 million secured on the revenue from international and national communications. That Ministry also contracted from suppliers in 1928 to 1934 a number of short-term loans for telephone and telegraph expansion, equivalent to about C $12 million. The National Reconstruction Commission issued, in 1929 and 1933, three loans totaling about C $10 million for construction of electrical enterprises, secured on the properties and profits of specified enterprises.

Borrowing by the Finance Ministry from the Central Bank and other banks showed considerable turnover of advances and repayments, as shown in Table 8. The net total, 1928 to mid-1937 was C $525 million. Most of this amount was from the Central Bank, whose statement as of June 30, 1937, showed "Loans, discounts, and overdrafts" C $428 million and "Securities owned" C $38 million, total C $466 million. Probably about

C $445 million was credit to the central government, judging from the most recent available breakdown of the item.* Deducting C $445 million of assumed Central Bank advances from the total of C$525 million of net bank advances in 1928 to 1937 leaves C $80 million as an indication of the order of size of advances by other banks as of mid-1937.† But these figures can only be tentative in the absence of fuller information.

Bank purchase of government securities as backing for note issue created an important demand for them. After the currency reform of 1935, when silver was nationalized and withdrawn

Table 8

Bank loans and overdrafts to the government from 1929 to 1937[a]

Year ending June 30	Amount borrowed, millions	Amount liquidated, millions	Net proceeds, millions
1929	--	--	C$32
1930	C$121	C$110	10
1931	185	162	24
1932	109	105	5
1933	226	139	86
1934	395	304	91
1935	436	400	36
1936	607	479	128
1937	336	224	113
Total			C$525

[a] Source: Finance Ministry reports.

*The latest available breakdown of Central Bank advances other than to the central government, as of March 31, 1936, shows a total of C$20 million including C$17 million to banks and most of the rest to provinces.

†The latest available statement of the Finance Ministry's loans from banks other than the Central Bank, as of May 31, 1935, shows a total of C$61 million.

from circulation, note issue of the government banks grew rapidly from C $458 million to C $1407 million in mid-1937. The government banks held large note reserves of cash: foreign currencies, gold, and unsold silver then amounting to about two-thirds of the issue. Their note reserves of government securities were then C $491 million. Part of these securities was delivered to the government banks by other banks, which were allowed to obtain notes by presenting 40 per cent silver and 60 per cent securities (Chapter 10).

The accounts of the general budget included little from the proceeds of foreign borrowing, apparently only the proceeds of the Cotton and Wheat Loan, about C $38 million in 1933 to 1935. The debt transactions of the Railway Ministry were apart from the general budget.

Domestic bond prices, yields, and costs of borrowing

Prices and yields of domestic obligations fluctuated widely in the twenties and thirties. A long period of fluctuations in rates of silver exchange made speculation a way of life, and the bond market was sensitive and speculative. Capital was relatively scarce, although the growth of modern-type banking provided the banks with increasing funds. Data of bond prices and yields are shown in Table 9.

The Shanghai bond market reflected events: revolts and civil wars, Sino-Japanese friction and fighting, and the government's financial situation and prospects. The warlord revolts of 1930 shook the market, but it recovered. Much more serious was the Japanese seizure of Manchuria in 1931, followed by the large-scale fighting at Shanghai early in 1932. That fighting led to closing of the Shanghai market for several months. There followed also the debt reorganization of February 1932, described below, involving extension of maturities and lowering of interest rates on most of the debt. When the market reopened in the spring, prices had fallen drastically.

Apart from the exceptional events of 1931 and 1932, yields in the earlier years through 1933 ranged roughly from 15 to 18 per cent. Thereafter, and especially after the currency reform of November 1935 and the further debt reorganization in January 1936, prices began to climb. In June 1937, on the eve of the quite unexpected outbreak of serious Sino-Japanese fighting, the bond market was strong. Prices rose to an unprecedented level. Yields on the new Consolidated Bonds dropped to about

7-3/4 per cent, at the month's high prices.* Although high by standards in developed countries, such rates were unprecedented in China and well below money rates in less-developed countries generally. The rise in bond prices was partly caused by the demand for bonds deriving from the arrangement whereby for two years banks not having the privilege of note issue could obtain notes by lodging with the government banks 60 per cent in silver and 40 per cent in government bonds (pages 240, 270). It is doubtful that yields as low as about 8 per cent could have developed in the absence of the 60/40 arrangement.

The cost of borrowing was high. Various writers have stated that in 1927 to 1934 the government received in cash no more than 50 to 60 per cent of the face value of obligations issued. The data supporting these charges are not correct. During that disturbed period, the proportion was probably in the range of 60 to 75 per cent, and there was improvement in 1935 to 1937.[23] Precise figures cannot be stated because of lack of comprehensive details of the government's transactions with the banks.

The best available indication of cost is in the indexes of yield of domestic issues (Table 9). These show that average yields in 1928 to 1932 ranged from about 15 to 24 per cent. Thereafter, average yields improved to 11.6 per cent in 1936, to 8.7 per cent in June 1937, and to about 8 per cent at the end of June 1937.

Foreign bond prices and yields

Prices and yields of foreign as well as domestic bonds fluctuated widely in the twenties and thirties, as shown in Tables 10 and 11. The prices were at a low ebb and erratic in the years preceding the Nationalist takeover. Customs-secured foreign debt under the Finance Ministry was duly paid, but the margin of security was small. With the Salt organization disintegrating, salt-secured loans fell into arrears. Railway bonds were mostly in default, because of seizures of revenues and equipment by warlords whom the central government could not control.

In 1927, the approximate range of yields of leading foreign loans was: 1898 4-1/2 per cent Loan (customs-secured), 7 to 11 per cent; Reorganization Loan of 1913 (customs-secured), 9 to

*The yield is calculated on the basis of a bond held to maturity. The bonds were retired by semiannual drawings, in increasing amounts. If yields are figured on a period when half the loan was due to be retired, the yields are about one-half per cent greater. The factor of retirement of drawn bonds by lot also meant that actual yields were somewhat higher on the average.

Table 9

Indexes of domestic bond prices from 1928 to 1937[a]

Year	Yield index based upon 12% per annum = 100		Price index based upon end of July, 1931 = 100	
	Index	Yield, %	High	Low
1928	69.6	17.3	--	--
1929	81.0	14.8	--	--
1930	68,0	17.7	--	--
1931	62.2	19.3	107[b]	55[b]
1932	49.1[c]	24.4[c]	77.7[c]	49.5[c]
1933	71.4	16.8	92.9	58.7
1934	96.8	12.4	109.8	80.1
1935	92.4	13.0	110.4	86.1
1936	103.9	11.6	106.6	97.1
1937 (June)	137.4	8.7	116[d]	104[d]

[a] Source: Index of Sinhua Bank, *The Chinese Economic and Statistical Review*, October 1937, p. 20; average prices from Swan, Culbertson, and Fritz, *Finance and Commerce*- July 21, 1937, p. 66, and August 4, 1937, p. 111. I have not tried to present quotations of individual domestic bonds for the period covered. No single representative issue was outstanding through those years, some being paid off and the terms of others changed by reorganization of the debt structure. Detailed quotations may be found in the Shanghai weekly, *Finance and Commerce* and the *Financial and Commercial Monthly Bulletin* of the Bank of China. *The Central Bank of China Bulletin*, March 1936, pp. 90-92, contains quotations of leading issues from 1927-1935. Quotations of Treasury Notes must be read with the understanding that the principal of each note was reduced monthly by specified amounts.

[b] High in July, low in December, approximate.

[c] Average of January and May-December for yield, and January and April-December for prices—the market being closed for an extended period because of the fighting at Shanghai.

[d] These figures were read from a chart, exact data not being available.

12 per cent; and Shanghai-Nanking Railway Loan of 1903, 11 to 15 per cent.

The vigorous financial measures of the new government brought gradual but irregular improvement. By 1937 the change was striking. At the highs of June 1937, the 1898 Loan with a 1943 final maturity sold in London on a 3-3/4 per cent basis; the 1913 Reorganization Loan with 1960 final maturity yielded

Table 10

London quotations of bonds of Finance Ministry from 1924 to 1937[a]

Year	4½ per cent 1898 Anglo-German Loan		4½ per cent 1908 Anglo-French Loan		5 per cent 1912 Crisp Loan		5 per cent 1913 Reorganization Loan		5 per cent 1925 French Boxer Indemnity Loan	
	High	Low	High	Low	High	Low	High	Low	High	Low
1924	81½	75	--	--	71¼	63¼	--	--	--	--
1925	84¾	70	79½	65½	73½	66	--	--	--	--
1926	77	53	69¼	55½	69½	59	72½	51	--	--
1927	75	51½	48	35½	48¾	31	58¼	43¼	--	--
1928	80¾	66	62¼	36	55	39½	69¼	52¼	--	--
1929	80½	74½	61¾	45	45	42½	69½	59½	--	--
1930	89	77½	65½	42½	54½	28	69½	55	81	67½
1931	90½	72	70	46	52	33½	70½	59	92¼	75
1932	98½	77	76	50½	47½	33	78½	53½	110½	77½
1933	102½	94	91	60	66	37	90¾	60	108¾	77
1934	103¼	100¾	99	89	86½	61	99¾	88¼	98¼	80
1935	105	100	100	96	90¼	71½	99¾	86	101¼	90
1936	104	95¼	101	93½	84	67	95½	81½	101	88½
1937, 1st half	104	102	100¾	99½	94½	82	101¼	94	104½	99
1937, 2nd half	103½	75	100½	88	95½	57	100	61	104¾	70

[a] Source: *The Central Bank of China Bulletin*, March 1938, pp. 81-82.

Table 11

London quotations of railway bonds from 1924 to 1937[a]

Year	5 per cent 1903 Shanghai-Nanking Railway		5 per cent 1908 Tientsin-Pukow Railway[b]		5 per cent 1911 Hukuang Railway[b]		5 per cent 1913 Lunghai Railway	
	High	Low	High	Low	High	Low	High	Low
1924	75	61½	69	55	58¾	45	--	--
1925	68½	54½	57	52	55¼	41¾	34½	17¾
1926	60½	53¼	52	39½	52½	42¾	40	26
1927	48¼	34	33	18	31½	22	21	13¾
1928	67½	38¼	40	22½	42	25¼	34	18¾
1929	67¼	58	43¾	18½	47½	23¼	41	16
1930	63	42	30¼	10¼	35½	20	29	10
1931	60	33¼	30¼	5¼	31½	10¼	20¾	5
1932	43½	27½	27¼	5¼	26¼	11¼	19	5
1933	55	30¼	27¼	12¼	35	18¼	15¼	8¼
1934	80½	55	38½	20¼	47	28½	19	11
1935	86¾	65	36	22	49½	35	19¼	11½
1936	79	65½	55	32	56	44	36	16
1937, 1st half	90½	75	74½	56	75½	55	46	31¾
1937, 2nd half	90½	37	78½	27	78½	33	47½	20

[a] Source: *The Central Bank of China Bulletin*, March 1938, pp. 82-84.

[b] London issue.

4.9 per cent; the Crisp Loan of 1912 with 1952 final maturity yielded 5.5 per cent; and the Shanghai-Nanking Railway Loan of 1903 with 1953 maturity yielded 6 per cent. On the eve of Japan's attack in mid-1937, the London market rated China's credit higher than that of Japan. On July 5, 1937, Japan's 5 per cent Sterling Loan of 1907 with 1947 final maturity yielded 7.5 per cent, and the 6 per cent Sterling Loan of 1924 with 1959 final maturity yielded 6.5 per cent.

Debt readjustment of 1932

Early in 1929, after arriving in China as a member of the Kemmerer Commission, I studied the debt situation. It quickly appeared that the process of issuing at a heavy discount loans repayable at par within a few years, some by equal monthly instalments in 30 months, would soon have to end either in default or a negotiated reorganization of the debt structure. With revenues growing well, China could carry the amounts of debt that seemed in prospect if repayment could be spread over a reasonably long period, e.g., 10 to 20 years. The major obstacle to issuing longer term debt was political. With the government facing warlord and Communist opposition, its future was far from secure. Bankers and the public therefore felt obliged to insist upon short-term debt with high yield.

Finance Minister Soong at once grasped the situation when it was set forth in concrete figures. I presented a succession of refunding plans adapted to the changing financial situation, one of which was embodied in a report of the Kemmerer Commission. The hope was that a plan could be worked out in negotiations with the bankers and bondholders under improved political and financial conditions, preferably to include also a general settlement of foreign and domestic loans in arrears. It was clearly in the long-run interest of creditors, with such a great financial stake, to cooperate in principle in a plan that would ensure the future solvency of the government. But 1930 and 1931 were years of great difficulty. Revolts of warlords, Communists, and dissident political elements continued with little intermission. The climax of difficulties came with the great flood in Central China during the summer of 1931 and with the Japanese invasion of Manchuria in September 1931, followed by the fighting at Shanghai that began late in January 1932.

Japan's action in Manchuria made the financial situation desperate. Revenues fell off, affected both by the Manchurian affair and the deepening worldwide depression. Domestic loan prices slumped seriously, damaging confidence, cutting into bank assets at a time of strain, and making it impossible for the market to absorb the loans on which the government was so largely dependent. Politically China was in a ferment. There was strong agitation by students and considerable popular demand to resist Japan with force in an unequal struggle.[24] But the government feared that moving troops north would bring chaos and grave danger of Communism in the south.[25]

The Sino-Japanese crisis brought peace between the government and the Canton faction which, as described in Chapter 3, had set up a rival "government" and seized the Canton customs. But that faction continued its yen for power. Early in December 1931, I was told in confidence that the government led by Generalissimo Chiang, and whose chief financial and economic officer was T. V. Soong, would shortly resign, to let the dissidents see what they could do. Chiang and Soong were sure that the dissidents would fail, and that the old leadership would soon be back with more authority and greater national unity. Soong hoped that then the debt reorganization, for which I had made a detailed plan, could be used as a chief means to save the situation. I agreed with the prognostication, and, as I had worked under much pressure for several years without rest, took a brief leave in the Philippines until the political situation could clarify. It was agreed that I would return at once when the old group resumed power.

The Canton faction on assuming leadership about the middle of December promptly found themselves unable to manage the finances. Toward the end of December 1931, reports from Nanking indicated that a moratorium on domestic debt payments had been proposed. That action raised a great outcry from bankers and business interests who had subscribed to hundreds of millions of loans. The Shanghai stock exchange closed. The resistance was such that the moratorium proposal was dropped. But the difficulties remained, and on January 21, 1932, Chiang returned to Nanking to take back the leadership. Soong promptly resumed his post as Finance Minister. Their return was in the nick of time. I wrote to a friend that when Soong was out of power "considerable disintegration began," which it would have been much harder to repair "if the opposing faction had been in 'power' for a longer period."

A week later, serious fighting broke out at Shanghai, with

heavy Japanese bombing of the densely populated Chinese-ruled areas. I returned to Shanghai on an American ship that passed up the Whangpoo River while a brief truce was arranged between the opposing forces firing at each other from opposite banks.

The dangerous financial crisis to which events had been leading was at hand. The fighting brought urgent need for funds. But trade was paralyzed in Shanghai where close to half the revenue was collected. Bond prices in January fell about one-fifth to the lowest on record. Further borrowing was impossible. As of January 1932, scheduled debt payments for the year were about C $300 million. That was more than half of the net revenues estimated for the year before the fighting began.* Payments on domestic debts were about C $200 million, of which about C $150 million was for debt retirement. Most of the internal debt totaling about C $800 million was due to be retired within five years.

At last conditions existed making possible a debt reorganization. Urgent negotiations began with bankers and representatives of financial and commercial organizations, including the Bondholders' Association. The eventual plan effective as of February 1 was based on cutting in half the monthly cost of internal debt service and setting monthly payments at C $8.6 million, or C $103.2 million yearly. Interest was at a fixed uniform 6 per cent per annum. Amortization periods were extended to roughly double the former length. All the loans were given customs security, releasing charges on the salt revenue and other internal revenues. The government's mandate of February 24 said:

> This decision ... shall not in any way be altered. Whatever the financial condition of the government in the near or distant future, the fund so earmarked shall never be used for any other purpose than that for which the fund is established.

The public received the plan well. Minister Soong's statement of February 26 called it "evidence to the world of the solidarity of the Chinese people in a period of national crisis." The veteran financial writer E. Kann called it "a scheme which, while not enhancing the investment of bondholders, undoubtedly place [sic] these investments on much firmer ground."[26]

*Revenues in the fiscal year ended June 30, 1932, were C$633 million, or C$553 million after deducting collection costs and refunds.

The plan was rather complicated. I was disappointed because it failed to simplify the debt structure by a consolidation reducing the number of issues from 28, and called for a complicated restatement of the monthly payments on Treasury Notes which carried monthly coupons covering both interest and instalments of principal. But cutting payments to a sustainable basis was of prime importance.

The readjustment provided for later resumption of principal payments on three issues of the former Peking regimes totaling C $48 million: the 6 and 7 per cent Consolidated Loans of 1921, and the Spring Festival Treasury Notes of 1926. Interest was being paid on these loans, but not principal. The plan called for repayment beginning in the fifth year, over 12 years. I had recommended against resuming these principal payments until progress could be made with settling foreign debts in arrears. But the government yielded to pressure from holders of these issues. Fortunately this matter was little noticed, and by the time principal payments began, action to settle the foreign debts was under way.

Soong, in his report of December 15, 1932, said that in contrast with the "incessant issue of domestic loans" before February, the government had since been able to "carry on without resorting to further bond issues." The debt operation had "saved almost [C] $100,000,000 annually in debt charges." In addition, strict economy was necessary:

> In face of the national danger, the government stripped itself of everything for the moment not essential to its existence. Excepting the diplomatic and revenue-collecting services, all civilian departments were drastically curtailed, only the barest skeletons were maintained, and the army alone was provided for.

"It should be a matter of satisfaction," Soong's report said, ". . . . that since February, 1932, for the first time in the 21 years of the Republic, the Government has been able to balance its budget at a time of world economic depression when practically every government has large deficits and when, in addition to the depression, the Government has had to confront the colossal burden of the 1931 floods, the slump in silver, the Japanese seizure of revenue in Manchuria and the attack on Shanghai." Also after the fighting, military expenditures were better controlled. And revenues promptly increased as the government reaped the benefit of continuing efforts to develop the revenue system. Bond prices improved at home and abroad.

Soong was able to conclude that "The striking progress thus achieved offsets all hostile propaganda that China is in a chaotic state with a tottering Government." He stated that "This transformation of the fiscal position puts an end, it is hoped, to a period of borrowing for current expenses which has lasted since the beginning of the Republic." But he recognized that "Financially, the Government is far from being out of the woods."[27]

Surely the balance achieved in 1932 was no mean feat, even though it was to prove temporary.

After the readjustment

In October 1933, Soong resigned as Finance Minister. He had returned only a few weeks before from the United States with the US $50 million Cotton and Wheat Loan. The resignation involved a clash of strong personalities between him and Generalissimo Chiang and disagreement on financial policy. Soong's insistence on the primary need for solid finances could not be reconciled with the insistent demand of the military at most levels for large and loosely controlled funds. Soong's successor was his brother-in-law H. H. Kung who held the post for more than 10 years.

This break between Chiang and Soong, showing their inability to work together, was a grave blow to China. Soong was China's ablest administrator, and he was gaining experience and confidence. But his toughness made enemies. Had the Generalissimo and he been able to continue collaboration, much of the looseness and inefficiency that marked the war and post-war period might have been avoided.

Kung retained a great part of the experienced personnel of the Ministry and continued substantially Soong's policies. But he faced great difficulties. China largely escaped the worldwide depression until 1933. General prices under the silver standard were steady or at times rising, while gold-standard prices elsewhere were falling drastically. But when silver prices rose from 1933, influenced by the beginning of recovery and by the American silver policy, deflation and depression hit China hard. The rising foreign exchange value of the currency was accompanied by a severe drop in internal prices, business failures, and unemployment. Meanwhile, Japanese encroachment and civil strife continued. The Communists were driven from south-central China only late in 1934, and fighting continued in 1935. In addition to large military costs funds were needed to rescue banks and industrial firms hit hard by the depression. Meanwhile the growth of revenues slackened.

The pressure of deficits began again in 1933 and steadily grew. The proportion of deficit to expenditures rose each year, from 12 per cent in fiscal 1933 to 24 per cent four years later. In 1933, loan issues to cover deficit were C $124 million in face value; in 1934, C $150 million; and in 1935, C $240 million. The periods of debt retirement averaged somewhat longer than for issues before 1932, but the payments for amortization were still heavy. Because of the uncertainties, internal and international, market prices heavily discounted the future payments. Yields ranged roughly from 12 to 16 per cent. Revenues could by no means keep up with needs.

Debt consolidation of 1936

By the latter part of 1935 it was clear that a second debt reorganization had to take place. The depression continued. In the second half of 1935, customs revenue slumped seriously and fell short of covering debt charges, largely because of the growing cost of amortizing internal loans. Expenditures continued to be large. The internal situation was relatively stable and improving after expulsion of the Communists to the far northwest. But it was deemed necessary to build more military strength because of Japan's unrelieved encroachment in North China. The gap between revenues and expenditures continued to grow, and the deficit became ever more threatening.

Furthermore, the adoption of a managed currency in November 1935, when the American silver policy forced China to give up the silver standard, made it imperative to control the deficit. The statement announcing the currency reform said that the government planned to balance the budget within 18 months, and was "determined to avoid inflation."

An obvious way to cut expenditure was to lessen the burden of retiring internal debt. Principal payments for 1936 were scheduled at C $126 million, increasing in following years—57 per cent was due within five years. In December 1935, I recommended consolidating the 38 issues, except for a few with special characteristics, into five groups according to nearness of maturity. Maturities of the five groups should be of increasing length. The interest rate, which was 6 per cent on the issues to be consolidated, should remain unchanged.

While Nanking was discussing the problem in January,

rumors circulated in Shanghai to the effect that there might be a reduction of interest or a moratorium. Shanghai was noted as a center for rumors, often devised by speculators. The bond market was nervous and weak despite a calming statement by Minister Kung.

On February 1, Kung made public a proposal by the Bondholders' Association, which embodied an agreement negotiated with the government. As of that date, a Consolidated Loan of C $1460 million in five series was to be issued with customs security. Interest would be 6 per cent, and maturities would be of 12, 15, 18, 21, and 24 years, with drawings each six months. The old issues were classified according to nearness of maturity for conversion into the five new series. All bonds would be converted except the 17th Year Rehabilitation Loan, whose repayment was about to be completed, the 17th Year Long Term Currency Loan, which bore only 2-1/2 per cent interest, and the Haiho Conservancy Loan, which was secured on a local customs surtax at Tientsin. Details of the conversion are shown in Appendix 9.

In addition a new loan, the 25th Year Recovery Loan, of C $340 million was authorized. It carried 6 per cent interest, and was repayable over 24 years by drawing.

The consolidation reduced debt payments by about C $85 million yearly, and it also greatly simplified the debt structure. Five issues replaced 33 older loans that had different schedules and constituted one of the most complicated debt structures in the world. The exchange of securities was duly completed by June.

After the consolidation

The market generally recognized the need for the government's action, but naturally regretted a readjustment under pressure. During 1936, the market was irregular with little net change. But confidence slowly grew, and in the first half of 1937 bond prices rose, especially toward the middle of the year. This rise partly reflected the absence of the pressure from putting new issues on the market. A further factor was the arrangement after the currency reform whereby private banks could obtain bank notes from the government banks by handing over 60 per cent in silver and 40 per cent in government bonds (Chapter 10). The yields of around 8 per cent in mid-1937 were unprecedented in China, where much higher yields had prevailed. Unhappily the improvement was rudely ended by the outbreak of fighting on July 7.

In 1936-1937, the government had no need to issue further loans. The Consolidation Loan included C $191 million of marketable bonds over and and above what were needed to exchange for the older issues. That went almost unnoticed. There was also the Recovery Loan of C $340 million.

The 1936 consolidation gave the government a welcome breathing spell. The success of the currency reform of 1935 greatly strengthened confidence. General internal prices began to recover at once, and by mid-1937 had returned to the 1931 average. Price recovery was necessary to restore the economy to a healthier condition. As the economy improved, revenues grew. In reviewing the events from 1934 to mid-1936, Minister Kung could justly say in his August 1, 1936 report that "... due to timely measures taken by this Ministry and strengthened by the support of the people, the economic structure of the country has not only avoided a crisis of near-panic proportions but actually emerged sounder and stronger than ever."[28]

In mid-1937, on the eve of the war, the 18-month period for balancing the budget had passed, and early balance remained uncertain. Japan's continuing encroachment in North China was cutting into revenue, especially from customs. And military costs were growing because of Japan's action. Also the government was getting into a position where it could pay greater attention to economic development, and that would cost money.

5: Debts and the Rehabilitation of Credit

The debt situation in 1928 reflected the troubles of the preceding generation. Loans equivalent to US $233 million were contracted to indemnify Japan after China's defeat in the war of 1894-1895. Then came the Boxer Indemnity of 1901, equivalent to US $334 million. After the republican revolution of 1911, large sums were borrowed to cover deficits. Successive governments borrowed wherever they could find lenders, foreign or domestic, often at high rates of interest. Beginning in 1899, loans were also issued in Europe to finance railways. By 1928, the internal situation had worsened so far that well over half the old debt was in default, classified as "unsecured or inadequately secured." Only the customs-secured debt administered by the Sino-foreign customs service and the International Commission of Bankers and a small part of the railway debt were being duly paid.

As a result of hundreds of borrowing transactions, the debt structure when the Nationalists took over was probably the most complicated in the world. When I came to China early in 1929, I found it hard to get full and accurate data about the debts. Their administration was divided among the Ministries of Finance, Railways, and Communications. For security the government had pledged customs, salt, and other revenues, along with railway and telecommunications revenues and properties. Nearly three-fourths of the debt was in foreign currencies, mainly sterling.

A summary of the debt position in 1928 and 1937 is given in Table 12, with further details in Appendixes 2 through 9. I consider these data substantially correct, although I cannot be certain of the completeness or accuracy of some of them. Changes between 1928 and 1937 reflect (1) changes in foreign exchange rates, especially from a silver unit equivalent to US $0.47 July 1, 1928, to a managed currency with a rate of US $0.30 as of July 1, 1937; (2) retirement of old debt; and (3) contracting of new debt.

Table 12

Summary of the debt position in 1928 and 1937 (excluding railways in Manchuria)[a]

	Principal outstanding, millions equivalent on: July 1, 1928	July 1, 1937
I. Debt receiving full service		
Foreign currency debt		
Finance Ministry:		
Customs-secured loans, including those secured on French and Belgian portions of the Boxer Indemnity	US$236	US$150
Other Boxer Indemnity, capital amount	81	33
Salt-secured loans	--	75
Debt contracted after July 1, 1928	--	22
Miscellaneous, floating debt	--	9
Railway loans	6	138
Communication loans, other than railways	--	17
Chinese currency debt		
Finance Ministry:		
Peking loans	35	7
Nationalist loans	58	596
Miscellaneous floating debt	--	2
Railway debt, approximate	2	68[b]
Communications debt, approximate	--	5
Other	--	4
Subtotal	US$418	US$1126

Continued

[a]Source: Finance, Railway, and Communications Ministries; Commission of Financial Experts (Kemmerer Commission) reports; Commission for the Readjustment of Finance.
[b]An unspecified part of the equivalent of US$30 million included in this item represents foreign currency debt.

Table 12 (Continued)

Summary of the debt position in 1928 and 1937 (excluding railways in Manchuria)[a]

	Principal outstanding, millions equivalent on: July 1, 1928	July 1, 1937
II. Debt in arrears		
Foreign currency debt		
Finance Ministry:		
Salt-secured loans[c]	84	13
Other Peking debts[d]	64	36
Railway Ministry:		
Loan issues	116	20
Other	33	--[e]
Communications Ministry:	24	--
Chinese currency debt		
Finance Ministry:		
Customs-secured Peking loan issues[f]	22	--
Other Peking loan issues	37	21
Peking Treasury notes	23	16
Other Peking debt, estimated	37	24
Railway Ministry, Peking debts	28	--
Communications Ministry, Peking debts	7	4
Subtotal	US$475	US$ 134
Grand total	US$893	US$1260

[c]Including for 1928 the Hukuang Railway Loan, £5,656,000, which also had railway security, and certain debt to Japanese creditors, namely, the "96 Million Loan," Yen portion, Y32,479,200, and the Tsingtao Treasury Notes, Y13,275,000. The arrears in 1937 consisted of the latter two items, which were left in arrears in view of Japanese encroachment in China.

[d]Excluding the so-called "Nishihara Loans," of which about Y152 million principal sum was outstanding, which the government did not recognize.

[e]Less than US$1 million.

[f]Comprising the 6 and 7 per cent Consolidated Loans of 1921, on which interest only was being paid in 1928.

In summary, the debt being duly paid in 1928 was equivalent to US $418 million (including US $58 million of Nationalist loans of 1927-1928), while that in arrears was equivalent to US$475 million in principal amount, plus large sums of interest.* A total debt burden of about US $2 or less per capita was very low compared with more advanced countries. But for the government of China, as things were in 1928, it was heavy. It continued to be heavy throughout the prewar decade, and debt payments averaged about C $250 million yearly or about 31 per cent of total payments in the general budget. Other debt mainly of railways added about one-fifth to debt payments currently due.

The Nationalists began borrowing at Shanghai in 1927, before their takeover at Peking (Chapter 2). They were repeatedly criticized for contracting fresh loans with the pledge of newly developed revenues, while so much of the old debt was in arrears. But the offsetting argument was that under the former regime there was little prospect of payment of that debt, while the new government recognized it in principle and showed an intention to rehabilitate it once it could consolidate its position. The new loans were essential for success of the new government, as already explained.

Settlement of debts in arrears was a problem of utmost complexity and difficulty. Besides perplexing technical questions, settlement depended on the state of the national finances, which was precarious because of internal disturbances and Japanese encroachments. Throughout I advised all concerned against settlements that China could not carry out. A general settlement with creditors of the chief Western powers and Japan was the preferred solution. But when that became impracticable, how could China avoid inappropriate discrimination? And what should be the policy concerning Japanese claims after Japan's aggressive behavior beginning in 1931?

The remainder of this chapter tells how the situation developed, and describes by a case study the solutions that resulted.

The Boxer Indemnity

By 1928, the Indemnity of 1901 had become not so much a penalty as a means to provide funds for China's benefit.[1] The United States began remitting part of the indemnity in 1908,

*The figures stated here exclude the debt of railways in Manchuria. Until 1931, when Japan seized these railways, their operation and debt were practically the responsibility of the regional regime.

and completed the process in 1924. The first remitted payments were used to educate Chinese students in the United States and to support Tsing-hua University near Peking. In 1925, the China Foundation for the Promotion of Education and Culture was organized to administer the funds, with ten Chinese and five American trustees. The program was broadened to include the support of a variety of educational and cultural programs. The Foundation carefully built up an endowment, and its work continued after cancellation of the Indemnity by treaty in 1943.

After World War I, payments to the foreign governments were cut in half by cancellation of the German and Austro-Hungarian portions and by the renunciation of payments by Russia in 1924. The governments entitled to most of the remaining half followed the American example with action of various degrees of benefit to China. The agreements provided generally for Sino-foreign bodies of administration. The British action under a law of 1925 allocated funds mainly for rehabilitation and development, particularly of railways, with some funds for educational and cultural purposes. The Netherlands remitted the Indemnity in 1925, with 65 per cent for water conservancy and 35 per cent for cultural objects. Belgium, pursuant to an agreement of 1927, arranged issuance of the "1928 Gold Loan" of US $5 million secured on the Indemnity, with three-fourths used for railway purposes and one-fourth as endowment for educational and philanthropic purposes. Japan allocated its portion for scientific and cultural purposes, administered by a Sino-Japanese board that first met in 1926. But friction with China interfered with full use of that portion for the purposes stated.

Use of the French portion brought little benefit to China. An agreement of 1925 provided for issuance of a loan of about US $42 million secured on remitted Indemnity payments. The loan was used mostly to repay creditors of the defunct Banque Industrielle de Chine, with a small part of the payments reserved for educational and cultural uses. Agreements of 1925 and 1933 with Italy allocated funds partly to pay Italian creditors, partly for Sino-Italian enterprises and partly for disposal by China. The minor portions of Spain, Portugal, and Sweden and Norway were not remitted to China, and their payment continued until suspension of transfer of foreign currency debt during the war in 1939.

China used the canceled German and Austro-Hungarian

portions, the renounced Russian portion, and the remitted Italian portion as security for several internal loans in the twenties and thirties. The market regarded such loans as enjoying better security than internal loans secured on the general customs revenues. The balance of the Russian portion after loan payments was remitted to the Treasury for general educational purposes, since the Sino-Russian commission set up pursuant to the 1924 agreement ceased to function after the Nationalist takeover. Most of these four portions became in effect part of the budget of customs revenue and internal debt service.

Apart from the canceled portions and the renounced Russian portion, the capital amount of the Indemnity remaining in 1928 had been greatly reduced by payments from the original US $334 million (equivalent) of 1901. The total in 1928 was US $128 million, comprising US $47 million for the French and Belgian loans, and US$81 million for the rest. By 1937, the capital amount had been further reduced to US$33 million. The reduction resulted partly from payments by China and partly from the settlement with Italy in 1933 that placed remaining payments at China's disposal.

Scheduled yearly payments on the Indemnity, apart from the canceled portions and the Russian and Italian portions, were equivalent to about US $8 million for 1928 to 1931, and about US $11 million for 1932 to 1940.* About 40 per cent of these sums went to pay the aforementioned French and Belgian loans of 1925 and 1928; about 26 per cent for the British portion; and about 17 per cent each for the American and Japanese portions, the other portions being minor.

Salt-secured foreign loans

Resumption of payments on the salt-secured loans as begun in the fall of 1928 involved providing money for a year's service (Chapter 2). There was no plan to make up the arrears that had accumulated since 1926. The districts were mostly sending in their loan quotas, and in the summer of 1929 the Salt administration discussed with me the issue of how the money should be applied. The first question was whether all the funds should go to holders of the senior loan, the Anglo-French Loan of 1908, until regular service was restored. But earlier in 1929 the

*Early in 1932, the government arranged a one-year deferment of payments on the American and British portions, equivalent to nearly US$5 million, in view of the financial difficulties following Japan's attack at Shanghai.

government had paid single semiannual interest coupons of that loan and the Crisp loan of 1912. It had also provided funds for paying a coupon of the Hukuang Railway loan of 1911, which had a limited charge on salt revenue. An element of the problem was that the agreement for the senior 1908 loan created a charge only on the salt revenues of certain provinces—not on the entire salt revenue.

As to interest arrears, my recommendation was to make up with priority the payments on the 1908 senior loan, and to make them up gradually on the other loans. Along with this should go making up the principal arrears, with preference for the 1908 loan. Especially because in 1928 interest payments had been resumed on the 1912 loan, it seemed unwise to stop them until all the large arrears of drawn bonds of the 1908 loan could be paid. I proposed a schedule that Minister Soong approved.

The plan as announced in September 1929 provided for updating at once interest payments on the 1908 loan, along with the principal payment due a year earlier. A single interest payment was also to be made in that month on the 1912 loan. For that loan, four instead of two coupons would be paid in 1930 to bring interest payments to date by the end of the year. Arrears of principal of the 1908 loan were to be paid by the end of 1931 and of the 1912 loan by the end of 1934. Additional funds were to be provided from salt revenues to permit the annual payment of one coupon of the Hukuang Railway Loan of 1911.

It seemed best to announce the plan rather than try to negotiate it with representatives of the holders of the three loans. When the issue was raised, the time before paying dates was short, and secrecy was essential. The plan seemed likely to be well received by bondholders. That proved to be the case. The *North-China Daily News* of Shanghai on September 19, 1929, called it "a common-sense arrangement" showing extension of the government's control throughout China. The plan "represents a definite and conscientious effort on the part of the Ministry of Finance to restore China's credit and do the best that may be done with available resources." Reports from London praised the plan, and prices of the bonds rose. The representative of the bondholders, with whom I had been confidentially in touch well before announcement of the plan, told me that if the plan were carried out "they will build you a monument."

It was not long before events put the plan to the test. For

China, 1930 was a most difficult year. The slump in silver added about 50 per cent to the cost of making loan payments. Thus loan quotas fell short of paying for the needed foreign currencies. And on top of that problem came a serious revolt in North China. Then came the seizure of Tientsin customs revenues described in Chapter 3, and the withholding of salt loan funds in North China by General Yen Hsi-shan, the "model governor" of Shansi Province. Since he charged that the government would use the money for military purposes, the Ministry urged him to remit the quota for loan service to London through a foreign bank, but in vain. To bring pressure, Minister Soong decided to delay the mid-year interest payment due on the 1912 loan, despite the urging of his advisers not to delay. The military situation turned against Yen in September, and the funds were released. The delayed payment was then made, and by the end of 1930 the plan was back on the track.

With all arrears of interest on the 1908 and 1912 loans paid by the end of 1930, regular interest payments continued. But in 1931 even graver difficulties faced China, forcing delay in starting payment of the arrears of principal. Because of these difficulties, the payment of arrears of the 1908 loan was delayed, with only one principal payment instead of two in 1931. Even making one payment was influenced by the fact that Soong was briefly leaving office, to give the Cantonese dissidents the chance they coveted (page 103), and he felt that if the money were left to them they would squander it without benefit to China.

As China's internal and external difficulties continued, it was not until October 1934 that arrears of principal of the 1908 loan were finally paid. Meanwhile, paying arrears of principal of the junior 1912 loan had to wait. In December, Minister Kung announced that from 1935 two principal payments would be made annually on the 1912 loan, instead of one, so that arrears would be eliminated by 1940. He further stated that the charge on salt revenue in favor of the Hukuang Railway loan of 1911 had been increased so that one coupon could be paid regularly each year. Reuter's despatch of January 4, 1935, from London quoted the *Post* as saying that China's action, despite difficulties, showed "a praiseworthy desire to maintain full faith with her creditors."

By mid-1937, before Japan's attack, faithful execution of this plan brought the price of the 1908 loan to par and the 1912 loan close to par. The restoration of these loans, although somewhat delayed by major difficulties, was a notable achievement. It stood out in particular during the depression of the 1930's, when all over the world many loans were falling into default.

Failure of efforts for a general settlement of debts in arrears

The disintegration of China's finances in the 1920's made the defaulted debts of special concern to foreign creditors and their governments. The Peking tariff conference, when it finally met in October 1925, listed payments on these debts as one of the uses of the increased customs revenues, along with making up for abolition of *likin,* payment of current costs of government, and economic development.[2]

During the conference, and for a while after it petered out because of the government's fall in the spring of 1926, the foreign and Chinese experts gave detailed consideration to debt settlement. There was general agreement on issuing a large consolidation loan for which old debts in arrears would be exchanged. Difficult questions related to what debts should be included and on what terms; the interest rate for figuring arrears; the scale of future payments of interest and principal; and procedures to give effect to a plan. Much progress was made toward informal agreement. But the great stumbling block was lack of a Chinese government with solid financial resources that could speak for China and assume realistic obligations for the future. So action stayed in abeyance.*

The Nationalist take over in 1928 raised the hope that at last China could do something to restore her credit. Apart from the justice of paying debts, restoration of credit was important because foreign capital was badly needed for development—before the days of foreign aid such capital had to come from private sources. China's leaders realized that needed foreign capital could not be obtained unless the government's finances were in much better order.

The Kemmerer Commission's 1929 report on public credit, which I prepared, contemplated a settlement negotiated between China and the creditors as a group. The plan contained some features worked out in the 1926 negotiations at Peking.

*Besides the published proceedings of the Conference (Reference 2), there are voluminous Conference documents in the archives of the participating governments. The Chinese government furnished copies of the chief documents to me when I came to China early in 1929, one of my primary tasks being to try to devise and propose a workable means of debt settlement. These documents are the source of the statements in this paragraph.

But I quickly concluded that the order of burden proposed for China in 1926 was unrealistic then and would also have been in 1929. Although the new government had made notable progress in developing revenues it still had a large deficit. The loans contracted beginning in 1927 to finance consolidation of the government's position called for heavy payments to retire them within a brief period—the government being unable to borrow except on such terms. It would have been foolish to invite a breakdown of a settlement by expecting China to assume a burden of payments beyond her reasonable capacity. Hence, in 1929 I proposed payments that in the earlier years were much less than those contemplated in 1926, and increasing *pari passu* with reduction in scheduled loan payments. An alternative schedule of larger payments would apply if refunding the internal loans for payment over a longer period proved feasible.

From abroad criticism continued over the government's borrowing and pledging customs and other revenues for fresh loans while older debts were unpaid. On March 21, 1930, Soong issued a statement declaring a debt settlement "very important." He stated that the government was studying the problem intensively, and that he expected a plan to be formulated during 1930. A settlement should be "in accordance with a general plan," and there was "no intention of dealing with individual creditors or governments except on the basis of such a plan."[3]

Between 1928 and 1930, Japan was the government most concerned about the debt issue. Japan had agreed in January 1929 to accept China's new tariff but not to tariff autonomy. As a condition of agreeing to the latter, Japan pressed in 1930 for assurance that part of the increased customs revenue would be used for payments on debts in arrears. It was hard for China to give any concrete assurance, because of still-aroused feelings resulting from clumsy Japanese military interference with the Northern Expedition at Tsinan in 1928.[4] Soong consequently promised in May that China would convene a conference on or before October 1 at which plans for debt consolidation would be presented and discussed. Meanwhile China had organized the Commission for Readjustment of Domestic and Foreign Debts, composed of leading members of the government, to examine the debt problems and devise plans for settlement. That body succeeded the Peking Commission for the Readjustment of Finance, created after the Washington Conference of 1921-1922.

Pending the debt conference there were discussions with the

creditor countries, mainly Japan. In September, the Japanese minister put forward a plan for a debt payment fund comprising the C $5 million already allocated yearly plus (1) customs revenue freed as existing foreign and domestic loans were paid off, and (2) a sum representing part of the estimated "natural increase" of customs revenue. The plan also suggested that an issue of bonds to consolidate the debts should be considered.*

The two points proposed by the Japanese minister were important, and indicated the most promising basis for international agreement. They were in line with what I had been recommending. Payments on the Boxer Indemnity and foreign loans dropped sharply after 1940, permitting allocation of payments to debts in arrears. In addition, revenues could be expected to grow, thus adding to capacity to pay—although pressure for expenditures would also grow.

The Japanese proposal for a global fund, to be distributed by agreement among the creditors, was in line with the plans discussed at the Peking Conference of 1925-1926. It envisaged cooperation for a general settlement. But agreement on how to divide such a fund involved difficulties. First, there was the matter of what claims would be included by the several countries. The Japanese plan was that the fund would be divided among the creditor nations according to the percentages of the respective national claims, as listed by the Chinese delegation at the Peking Conference. Those claims totaled C $1043 million at the end of 1925. That would have given Japan about 35 per cent, and China about 29 per cent. A serious difficulty concerned inclusion of the Nishihara loans, which are discussed on pages 122 to 126. The C$1043 million figure also included compound interest at high rates. On the other hand, lump sum payments, if they could be agreed, could be used to avoid specifically dealing with the Nishihara loans. China took no action on the Japanese proposal pending the conference, which was delayed because of the serious civil war in North China.

When the conference met on November 15, 1930, the Chinese representatives presented a "Tentative plan without commitment," saying that China "desires to make a comprehensive settlement of its duly contracted obligations that are now in arrears." The memorandum followed the text I proposed except for addition of the phrase, "duly contracted." The clear intent

*These statements are based on documents handed to me by the Japanese minister.

was to hedge concerning the "Nishihara loans." The memorandum proposed payments from customs and railway revenues, except that the salt-secured loans would be cared for according to the plan already described. The customs contribution would be gradually increased. The railways and other communications would carry what burden they reasonably could, supplemented from customs revenue. A prior charge on the customs would be for purposes of rehabilitation. The debts would be retired over not more than 30 years. A procedure for distribution of payments would be proposed after agreement was reached in principle on the other proposals.

The conference lasted only one day. The conferees adjourned to consult their governments, agreeing to meet again when necessary. It was recognized that the governments might negotiate separately with China. Discussion of particulars of a general settlement went forward with a number of governments, especially Japan. And within the Chinese government, discussions proceeded in contemplation of a general settlement. The Finance Ministry made an unsuccessful effort to reach agreement with the Railway Ministry, which sought exaggerated help from customs revenue in settlement of railway debts.

When the conference met in 1930, the internal condition of China was hopeful. But in the spring of 1931 came the Canton revolt and seizure of the Canton customs. In the summer came the very serious floods in central China. In September, Japan marched into Manchuria. So the conference never met again after November 1930.

The failure of international cooperation on debts was a phase of the gradual breakdown of the cooperation envisaged at the Washington Conference of 1921-1922. The failure reflected a trend already well advanced. The events from 1922 to the Japanese occupation of Manchuria beginning in September 1931 have been admirably analyzed by Iriye.[5] The breakdown of cooperation was not the result of intended policy of the governments of Japan, the United States, or Britain. Rather, while envisaging cooperation, they drifted into separate action. Each country had different interests and attitudes vis-a-vis China. Japan refused to see that having a policy for Manchuria different from that for the rest of China would bring a grave clash with China and involve the United States and Britain. Elements in Japan wanted good relations with China and the other two nations, and were ready to work to that end. But Japanese military officers in China took independent action. They brought about an avoidable clash with Chiang's Northern Expedition at Tsinan in May 1928 and in June the assassination of Marshal Chang Tso-lin in Manchuria. Meanwhile, Britain had acted quite independently in dealing with the Kuomintang in south and central China and the threat of radical elements of that party. In 1927, the United States had shied away from joining a plan for eventual cooperative defense of the International Settlement at Shanghai, if needed. Then in July 1928 came the Sino-American treaty that took the lead in granting tariff autonomy to China, followed by separate action by the other powers.

In dealing with China's debts in arrears, the differing interests and attitudes of the powers were such that after 1930 there was no effective consideration of cooperative action. My files on the general settlement of debts in arrears end abruptly in the summer of 1931, just before Japan's Manchurian adventure put an end to the possibility of a cooperative settlement.

Debts to Japan

When Japan agreed at the Washington Conference to restore to China the rights seized from Germany in Shantung Province during World War I, China undertook to pay Y40 million for the railway running from Tsingtao to Tsinan. Payment was by a 6 per cent loan, due December 31, 1937, and with no current amortization; China agreed not to repay "with funds raised from any source other than Chinese."[6] That clause was designed to preserve for Japan the privilege of having Japanese nationals appointed as traffic manager and chief accountant of the line. During the civil wars of 1926 to 1928 and the Sino-Japanese clash at Tsinan in 1928, interest payments fell into arrears. China made up the payments and restored regular debt service in 1929.

Although not mentioned at the debt conference of 1930, a key problem in the search for a general debt settlement concerned the "Nishihara loans."[7] This term was applied to a group of loans to Peking by Japanese bankers in the latter part of World War I and the years immediately following. These loans were soon defaulted and became a political issue in both China and Japan. Pending determination whether the Nationalists would recognize them, and if so in what amount, a general agreement on division of China's payments among creditors was difficult.

The Nishihara loans were an element of Japanese policy to

expand control in China and in particular a hold on Manchuria. The Peking authorities, lacking revenue, were susceptible to Japanese offers. Japan was flush with money from wartime prosperity. Although some of the loans were designated for railways and communications, most of the proceeds went for administrative costs, military outlay, and debt payments. In China there was an outcry against the loans. The Nationalists in particular were outspoken because the loans supported pro-Japanese rulers who wanted to suppress Sun Yat-sen's movement.

The original principal amount was about Y 152 million.* Interest was 7 to 8 per cent per annum. The loans had no effective security, and upon default some original rates were raised to 8 or 9 per cent. Obligations for unpaid interest totaling about Y66 million were also issued, with rates from 8 per cent to as high as 14.4 per cent yearly. After the defaults, the negotiators were denounced in Japan for making bad loans. In 1926, the Japanese government took steps to offer its own bonds in exchange for Nishihara bonds, but it is not clear whether this was done.

After the 1930 conference, I urged informal and confidential discussions with Japan looking toward a compromise settlement of these loans. Otherwise, I pointed out, there probably could be no general debt settlement, and China needed a settlement as a step toward putting her finances in order. T. K. Tseng, the competent general secretary of the debt commission, made similar recommendations. In a memorandum he gave me on November 27, 1930, he said that both in China and Japan "all time honoured procedures were followed," i.e., the loans were duly contracted. China received the money without discount, and the interest rates were normal. But with the loans political issues in both countries, Tseng thus put the dilemma: "The recognition of these loans will mean a political storm in China which may endanger the very foundation of the government, while non-recognition will mean an immediate rupture of our negotiation with Japan." He suggested as a compromise leaving aside part of the loans which the Chinese public considered the more obnoxious, and settling the others. My proposal was for a lump sum debt settlement with Japan not mentioning any specific debts.

*That figure does not include an advance of Y20 million to the Bank of Communications.

Opinion at Nanking was sharply divided on the issue. Even China's promise to hold a debt conference stirred rumblings of opposition, notably by Hu Han-min, the dogmatic and not very practical troublemaker who headed the Legislative Yuan. Hu favored repudiation of the Nishihara loans. He was misled by the idea that a large silver loan by the United States to China, as suggested by Senator Key Pittman, could avoid the need to settle loans in arrears (Chapter 8). Chiang and Soong were ready to consider some compromise in 1930 and 1931. But their freedom to act was hampered by a revolt, as so often was the case in these years in China. In the spring of 1931 came the abortive effect of malcontents to set up a rival "government" at Canton. With the fate of the National Government at stake, and its ability to assume new commitments uncertain, debt negotiations had to wait.

Japan for her part was ready to make concessions to settle these loans. In the fall of 1929, Sadao Saburi was appointed minister to China. He and I were good friends when he was in Washington as counselor of the embassy, and we talked frankly of the problem. One of the duties with which he was charged was to seek a reasonable compromise, as to which he hoped for my sympathetic interest. Unhappily he died mysteriously in Japan a few weeks later. The death was called a suicide but many including Prime Minister Shidehara suspected murder.[8] His death was a great loss because of his character and the regard in which leading Chinese officials held him.

The Shidehara government hoped that Britain and the United States would help to impress upon China the importance of a debt settlement. But Britain was wary of appearing to support Japan on the Nishihara issue, and American action seems to have been held back by the silver controversy. Meanwhile, the moderate Shidehara government was losing ground. Failure to settle the debt question with China was part of the picture, as was the inability to work out a general basis of cooperation with Britain and the United States in debt matters. Discontent in Japan because of the serious effects of the worldwide economic depression weakened the government at a time when the ambitions of the military with regard to Manchuria were growing. In September 1931, Japan's fateful Manchurian adventure began.[9]

The outbreak of serious fighting, as Japan extended her drive for control of China, brought an abrupt halt to discussion of Japanese debts. In 1933, the *Manchurian Daily News* reported that Japan agreed with "Manchukuo" on settlement of part of the Nishihara loans.[10] Clearly the seizure of all of Manchuria and the retention of all its revenues, despite their being charged with contributing to payment of China's customs-secured and salt-secured debts, made it impossible for China to be expected to do anything about the Nishihara loans.

The Railway Ministry, as the finances of some railways improved, began in 1933 to settle several materials and supply debts to Western creditors, summarized in Appendix 5. It was deemed necessary then to take up several railway debts to Japanese creditors to avoid discrimination. Settlements of these Japanese claims totaled about Y60 million, then equivalent to about US $17 million (Appendix 5).

Toward the end of 1934, Japanese creditors pressed the Communications Ministry for debt settlements. The chief debts related to the Peiping and Tientsin telephone systems and to the Shanghai-Nagasaki cable. The original principal of the two debts totaled about Y25 million. The settlement included arrears of interest about equal to original advances, so that the new total of debt was about Y50 million, say US $14 million. The interest rate was reduced from the original 8 and 9 per cent to 6 per cent, but the debt for arrears bore no interest. Payments were to apply first to principal, then to arrears, and then to interest. The payments totalled Y1.8 million yearly, say US $500,000. The settlement seemed within the Ministry's capacity to pay from the proceeds of operations.

In 1935-1936, the Finance Ministry also settled two old and relatively small debts to Japanese creditors dating from 1916 to 1918—the Hua Ning Company Treasury notes and a loan to the Bureau of Printing at Peiping. The original principal sum of each was Y1 million, and interest rates were 8 and 12 per cent, respectively. The settlements, apparently made in the second half of 1936, were based on taking new principal amounts of Y1.88 million and Y1.45 million, respectively, to be paid in equal instalments without interest over periods of ten and eight years, respectively. The total amount outstanding in mid-1937 was Y3.2 million. The American embassy at Peiping reported on November 13, 1935, the settlement of the Printing loan, stating that the loan was made by a Japanese bank represented by Kamego Nishihara. This was not one of the group of large loans of 1918 commonly known as the Nishihara loans (see above). The report of agreement was premature. But the State Department was disturbed, suspecting discrimination. The report was a factor in rejection of China's request to readjust payments on the Flood Relief Loan of 1931. The settlement of these small loans came during Japanese pressure in North China, and the negotiations for the Printing loan were conducted in Peiping by the director of the Bureau and later approved in Nanking.[11]

The terms granted to the various Japanese creditors were more onerous than could have been accepted for settlement of major debts in arrears controlled by the Ministries of Railways and Finance, as to both treatment of arrears of interest and rates of interest for future payments.

As of mid-1937, apart from the Nishihara loans, three larger debts to Japanese creditors were unsettled: (1) the Tsingtao Treasury Notes of Y13.3 million, issued to pay for public properties and other interests transferred by Japan to China in Shantung Province in 1922; (2) the Japanese portion of the "96 million" loan, Y39.5 million, issued in 1922 to refund various debts; and (3) a loan of Y20 million provided to the Finance Ministry through the Bank of Communications in 1918. In 1937 there also remained miscellaneous unsettled debts equivalent to about US $4 million. The total principal amount then unsettled with Japanese creditors was equivalent to about US $24 million, apart from the Nishihara loans. The unsettled debts of course remained in abeyance when the fighting began in 1937, and in 1945 it was assumed that a peace settlement would involve Japan's undertaking responsibility for any settlements with Japanese creditors of China.

Piecemeal negotiations with Western creditors from 1931 to 1935

After Japan's invasion of Manchuria destroyed the possibility of a general debt settlement, negotiations with Western creditors had to be undertaken on an individual basis. Restoration of credit was important and China had to begin somewhere, inevitably making it hard to avoid the charge of discrimination and presenting the risk that early settlements would set a pattern that other creditors would not like but could not easily be changed.

The settlements by the Railway Ministry (Appendix 5) of several materials and supply debts to American, British, and continental European creditors in 1933 and therafter were relatively small and attracted little attention. Little attention was paid also to action of the Communications Ministry early in 1935 in settling several claims on terms much more favorable to China than the aforementioned settlements with Japanese creditors. That Ministry agreed with the Marconi Wireless Telegraph Company on a settlement taking as the basis £170,376, payable in equal monthly instalments during 20 years. Arrears of interest of £305,894 were to be canceled if the payments were all duly made. The Ministry also settled a debt to the China Electric Company, taking as the basis US $900,000, to be repaid in monthly instalments of at least $3000, to retire the debt in not over 25 years. Arrears of interest of US $673,378 were to be canceled if the US $900,000 was duly paid. The Ministry also settled some lesser claims equivalent to about US $200,000. The total of the principal amount taken in these settlements of Communications debts with non-Japanese creditors was equivalent to about US $2 million, and yearly payments about US $150,000.

These settlements did not directly involve the Finance Ministry because the railway and communications finances were separate from the general budget. And the settlements involved no publicly issued bonds. The main blot on China's credit resulted from continuing defaults and low prices of public issues involving the Finance and Railway Ministries.

In 1933-1934, I prepared detailed studies of the chief loans under control of these ministries, and the terms under which I felt that China could reasonably and realistically make settlements. The eventual settlements closely approximated these terms. I also prepared offers with some room for negotiation, but not too far from the terms desired. In the difficult internal and international conditions of the period, I felt that China could make a solid case for lenient treatments in the years prior to 1941, the year when payments on the Boxer Indemnity and other debts decreased. I discussed the problems frequently with leading officials, who wanted to make settlements. But they did not feel ready to act because of the succession of external and internal political crises, continuing large deficits, and the economic difficulties related to the depression and problems of gyrating silver and rates of foreign exchange.

A few weeks after the debt conference of November 1930, Washington instructed Minister Johnson to inform China that the United States could not assent to the approach made by China at the conference until it could know whether American debts would have "just and non-discriminatory" treatment. Beginning in 1932, the American government pressed for a Sino-American claims commission, which would first seek to agree on the amount of American claims even though a plan of payment were not involved. In 1934, the United States gave China lists of claims. China never agreed to set up such a commission, influenced largely by the fear of creating a precedent that might be embarrassing in negotiations with Japan. The State Department records show that for some time it held off pressing American claims in view of China's difficulties and the feeling in China that the American silver policy contributed to them.[12]

From time to time from 1931 to 1935, foreign governments and the representatives of creditors protested China's lack of action on debts in arrears. As fresh internal loans were issued, they protested the pledging for them of China's best security, namely, revenues from customs, salt, and consolidated taxes, while the older debts were ignored.

The breakthrough in attacking piecemeal the problem of settling external debt issues in arrears followed promptly when the success of the currency reform of November 3, 1935, seemed assured. That reform brought a great lift to confidence, after the turmoil of the years when China's economy and finances were at the mercy of the politically governed American silver policy. The effect of that policy in disturbing confidence and thus making more difficult the settlement of debts in arrears has not been generally recognized. Also the internal situation was quiet during the fall of 1935, with no active internal threat to consolidation of the government's authority and the Communists driven to the far northwest.

In September 1935, Sir Frederick Leith-Ross came to China representing the British government (Chapter 9). Shortly after the currency reform of November 3, 1935, he urged the settlement of the Tientsin-Pukow (Tsin-Pu) and Hukuang Railway loans. China hoped for a loan from London, and Leith-Ross made it clear that the possibility of a loan would depend on concrete proposals regarding these loans and a program to deal with other unsettled sterling debts. It was this attitude that led to commencement of negotiations.

Tientsin-Pukow Railway loans of 1908-1910

The largest stake in the loan issues in arrears was British. The British credits to China were mainly public bond issues for railway construction and equipment, secured by pledge of railway properties and earnings. Of Chinese railway debt, mostly issued in London with predominantly British holders, the equivalent of only about US $6 million was being duly serviced in 1928. But the principal amount of British railway loans in arrears equaled a sum of the order of US $75 million, plus large amounts of interest. Other unpaid British advances to the government were equivalent in 1928 to perhaps US $15 million, principal amount, plus unpaid interest.

The largest railway loans in default were the Tientsin-Pukow and Hukuang Railway loans, issued respectively in 1908 to 1910 and 1911. The respective principal amounts outstanding in 1928 were £6,150,000 and £5,656,000, equivalent in total of US $57 million. The Tientsin-Pukow loans were issued mostly in London but partly in Berlin. The Hukuang loan was issued in London, Paris, Berlin, and New York. The "Tsin-Pu" Railway was the important and productive line running from opposite Nanking to Tientsin. The Hukuang Railway was projected to run from opposite Hankow to Canton. But only part of the line was built, from both ends, leaving a gap of about 250 miles in the middle. Part of the loan proceeds was used for purposes other than railway construction. Both the Tientsin-Pukow and Hukuang loans enjoyed the security of the railway revenues along with certain *likin* and other local revenues.

An important clause in similar form in the contracts for both loans provided for contingent security of customs revenue. The substance of the clause was that if *likin* should be abolished in connection with tariff revision an equivalent charge on the increased customs revenue should be substituted.[13] When *likin* was abolished as of January 1931, the bondholders promptly asked that customs revenue be applied to debt service. Repeatedly they pressed their claim, supported by the British, American, and French governments. There was frequent criticism in the press of failure to give effect to the contingent clauses. This was hurtful to China's credit.

The government did not dispute the contingent clauses. But from 1930 to 1935, it felt it was in no position to apply them. First, the state of the finances was too precarious to permit sparing customs revenue, with the yield decreasing after 1931, Japan seizing the revenue in Manchuria, and large deficits persisting. The railways suffered from civil wars, and for several years up to 1932 had little or no net revenue. Furthermore, with so much debt in arrears, the government hesitated to single out debts for special treatment when a general debt settlement was being considered both by China and the foreign governments. Clearly what China might do for individual loans would affect its capacity to deal with the rest of the debt. The British Foreign Secretary, replying in the House of Commons early in 1931 to an inquiry about the contingent clause, said that, "These two loans ... could not be treated independently of the other obligations of the Chinese Government."[14]

As an earnest of intention to do something for the Tientsin-Pukow loans, the Railway Ministry in 1932 undertook to accumulate in the Bank of China from C $90,000 to C $140,000 monthly from the receipts of the line in a fund for payments. But to the end of 1934, average monthly deposits were only C $53,000, which fell far short of ensuring loan service. That was a poor showing because from 1932 the railway, despite being badly over-staffed, made a considerable profit that was diverted to other uses. In the year ended June 30, 1935, net earnings were about C $8 million, but only C $910,000 went to loan service. Full interest payments on the 1908-1910 loans would have required about half of net earnings. The failure to do better resulted from the fact that about one-fourth of the net earnings represented book revenue from military transport and uncollected balances due from other railways, and the rest went for payments to the military, payments on Chinese bank loans and other debts, and capital outlay.

Fortunately, in the latter part of 1935, Chang Kia-ngau was appointed Railway Minister. With his background as a former general manager of the Bank of China, he understood the value of good credit. He was on good terms with Finance Minister Kung and ready to cooperate with him. Chang promptly named as his vice-minister, T. K. Tseng, a capable man who was the best informed Chinese official concerning debts in arrears. Tseng continued concurrently as the general secretary of the Commission for Readjustment of Domestic and Foreign Debts. When in the fall of 1935 the government decided to move actively to settle the debts, Minister Chang, Tseng, and I worked together closely in the negotiations concerning railway debts.

The government made a proposal for both loans on November 11, but nothing was done about the Hukuang loan until early in 1936. The Tientsin-Pukow offer provided for interest beginning at 2-1/2 per cent and rising to 5 per cent in 1940; payments to be made from railway revenue, but interest to enjoy customs guarantee from 1941; and cancellation of interest arrears. The Hukuang offer was similar, but it also involved salt security because the railway had not been completed. It was important that China be conservative in assuming obligations for future payments. While the new currency reform at once gave promise of success, reserves in the early months were too small for comfort. The creditors as well as China had an interest in the success of the reform. Debt settlements that would break down were in no one's interest.

A committee of bondholders was organized in London, and China asked that the German parties interested in the Tientsin-Pukow loans be duly approached through London. The German interest was much smaller than the British. Active negotiations followed through Leith-Ross and a local representative of the committee.

A settlement was announced on February 25, 1936, in the form of an offer to bondholders, acceptance of which their committee recommended. The chief points of the offer were as follows:

> Interest to be paid at 2-1/2 per cent per annum for the first three years, and at the regular rate of 5 per cent thereafter. Principal payments to begin in 1940, starting with 1 per cent of the railways' gross cash earnings and gradually increasing to retire the loan in about 30 years. Four-fifths of the unpaid interest to be cancelled and for the rest non-interest-bearing scrip issued, payable over about 20 years from 1941. All payments to be made from railway revenue, but interest payments to be guaranteed by the customs.[15]

It was also agreed, but not announced, that China would appoint an associate chief engineer and associate chief accountant in whose selection the bondholders' representatives would assist. During the negotiations, these representatives asked for creation of a Sino-foreign Loan Service Committee, which they thought would give them additional protection. The government agreed, realizing that its functions would be only nominal as regarded the mechanics of payment, which are described on page 41. The Committee, however, offered the possibility of being of value in relation to improvement of the overall working of the railway and keeping in touch with its financial operations.

A related debt was an advance of £900,000 to the Tientsin-Pukow Railway by the Deutsch-Asiatische Bank of Berlin for railway construction up to 1916. That advance was partly secured by the pledge of unissued bonds of the loan. Arrangements concerning that advance were discussed during the main negotiations. An agreement was made in November 1936 after difficult negotiations. Arrears of interest were canceled, and £100,000 was to be repaid in three equal yearly instalments; interest on the remaining £800,000 would be at 3 per cent from October 1, 1939, and from that date the railway would pay £50,000 yearly to retire the debt. Of the unissued bonds, £678,000 would be validated, and payments on them would apply on liquidation of the aforementioned payments. The newly validated bonds would be paid under the terms of the settlement of February 1936, but ranking immediately after the bonds included in that settlement.

The successful settlement of the Tientsin-Pukow loans early in 1936 gave impetus to further negotiations. Encouragement came also from the economic improvement following the currency reform of November 1935. In 1936 and 1937, there was a series of settlements covering the chief bond issues in arrears under control of the Finance and Railway Ministries and also various debts not represented by public issues.

Hukuang Railway loan of 1911

A proposal for settlement of the Hukuang Railway loan was given to the representative of the British bondholders in November 1935, as stated above. That proposal was similar to the one for the Tientsin-Pukow debt of 1908 to 1910 because both debts were deemed of similar merit and had contingent claims on customs revenue. But the Hukuang proposal was then ignored and held in abeyance pending progress of negotiations on the senior debt.

On January 13, six weeks before conclusion of the Tientsin-Pukow settlement, the Hukuang offer with the same terms as proposed in November was handed to the American, British, French, and German representatives in China of the bondholders. Interest was to be 2-1/2 per cent per annum, rising to 5 per cent after 1940; interest would be paid from salt revenues until earnings of the railway could cover it, and would be guaranteed by salt revenue and from 1941 also by customs; principal payments after 1941 would be paid from railway revenue within about 30 years; and arrears of interest would be canceled. The British were asked to communicate with the Germans, with whom they were already in touch on the Tientsin-Pukow loans. In March, China modified the Hukuang proposal to be consonant with the Tientsin-Pukow settlement announced February 25.

The difficulties of piecemeal settlement soon appeared. The British and French representatives telegraphed the Hukuang proposal to their principals. Unfortunately the American representative used the trans-Pacific mails. Thus his principals in New York lost the opportunity to consider the proposal well before conclusion of the Tientsin-Pukow negotiation. When the Americans learned of the proposal indirectly through London they were understandably displeased because they appeared to have been left out.

Thus the negotiations with the American side began badly. The Foreign Bondholders' Protective Council assisted somewhat by the American Consortium Group handled these negotiations, and both groups felt that China should make a better offer. The State Department was suspicious and, not knowing how we had worked out on the Chinese side the plan for a series of settlements, wrongly felt that Leith-Ross was responsible for the terms of the proposal and that China planned a separate settlement with Britain.[16]

In March, Sir Charles Addis of the British group told the Americans that in his view the Hukuang loan was no better than the Tientsin-Pukow; that better terms for the Hukuang than the Tientsin-Pukow could not be had; and that China had just cut the interest and lengthened the period of payment of the domestic loans (Chapter 4). China in the British view was trying to "set their railway house in order," and undue foreign pressure might jeopardize precarious stability. The British and German groups were disposed to accept the proposal and hoped for American acceptance. China wanted the representatives of the creditors in the several countries to negotiate jointly; and the State Department wanted the American and other groups to have a common front.[17] But the divergent and tougher view of the American Council led the others to permit the Council to act as the chief negotiator.

The Americans pressed strongly for better terms for the Hukuang loan. In a difficult negotiation, I found myself trading arguments with my good friend and former colleague in the State Department, Francis White, the Council's executive vice-president. White took the position that the Hukuang loan was better than the Tientsin-Pukow loan, rejecting a settlement on similar terms. He contended that the former had been receiving since 1928 partial payments from salt revenue, one coupon yearly, while the latter was almost completely in default. He asked full interest payments at once, with a second coupon paid by the Customs. I argued that the superior salt security of the Hukuang was offset by the superior railway security of the Tientsin-Pukow, and the seniority of the latter's claim on customs revenue. Furthermore, I pointed out that the Hukuang's specific salt security in 1936 covered only 60 per cent of the cost of paying a single coupon. The Tientsin-Pukow was a complete line whose earning power had revived, but the Hukuang was unfinished and with negligible earning power until completed. China simply could not afford to pay another coupon from customs revenue, which was lower because of the depression and also because of Japan's seizure of the Manchurian customs and organized Japanese smuggling in the north. On May 12, 1936, I wrote to White that the government, "having already done something for the Hukuang loan, should not in the circumstances be expected to do more for it immediately upon doing something for another loan." In careful study of the two loans in which I was wholly disinterested, I had concluded before advising the government as to the terms to offer that on balance the loans were quite similar; and the two offers were similar. I was unwilling to see China treat any national or financial group substantially more favorably than another, other things being equal.

The British and German groups would have been unhappy if the Hukuang were preferred. From time to time the British group considered whether to recommend acceptance of the offer regardless of the American attitude. The British Foreign Office agreed with the British bondholders' representatives that the Hukuang security and backing were no better than that of the Tientsin-Pukow, and there were large British holdings of both.[18] The French took no active part, but White said that they agreed with his stand.

Negotiations dragged on for over a year, largely because of the attitude of the American Council. In June 1936, Thomas W. Lamont, head of the American Group, was ready to accept terms no less favorable than those of the Tientsin-Pukow settlement. White disregarded efforts of China and the State Department to have the national representatives of the four countries agree among themselves before communicating with China. White had served in the American Legation in China in the warlord days and did not realize how things had changed. Thus at one stage he queried whether to press China to agree that the Associate Chief Inspector of Salt Revenue should be an American—inasmuch as the Inspector General of Customs was British. Hornbeck quickly pointed out that this was far from appropriate. At times the Council and the American Consortium Group disagreed.[19] While in the United States on leave from September to December 1936, I spent much time in negotiations. I felt that the Council's attitude was obstinate and lacking in appreciation of China's situation. Many in the State Department also felt that the Council should have accepted China's offer without so much delay. Kung threatened to announce the offer without waiting for the Americans.[20]

The Council finally agreed and the settlement was announced April 4, 1937. Lamont was "very much relieved."[21] The result of the long argument was that the terms were quite like those of the Tientsin-Pukow settlement:

> Interest at 2-1/2 per cent per annum in 1937 and 1938, and at the regular rate of 5 per cent thereafter. Principal payments to begin in 1941, and to be completed in 39 years from 1937. Four-fifths of the interest in arrears to be cancelled and for the rest non-interest-bearing scrip issued, payable over about 20 years from 1942. Interest payments to be made from the railway's net earnings and guaranteed out of salt revenue, and from 1941 also out of customs revenue.

It was also agreed, but not announced, that China would appoint a British engineer and a French accountant to work with the railway management. There would be a loan service committee, as in the Tientsin-Pukow settlement.[22]

The Chicago Bank loan of 1919

A default specially hurtful to China's credit concerned the US $5.5 million 6 per cent two-year treasury notes of 1919, issued by the Continental and Commercial Bank of Chicago, and known as the Chicago Bank loan. These notes were issued to refund a loan of 1916, regarding which the State Department issued a statement indicating its interest—hence, the default was specially embarrassing to the American government. The notes of 1919 were widely distributed to American holders. China paid interest for one year only, then the issuing bank advanced funds for one coupon, and the notes went into default in 1921.[23]

Shortly after the currency reform of November 3, 1935, when dollar funds were badly needed to support the reform, China asked the United States to agree to a more favorable schedule of repayment of the Flood Relief Loan of 1931 and the Cotton and Wheat Loan of 1933 (Chapter 15). China felt fully justified in making this request in view of the great importance of ensuring success of the currency reform of November 1935, and the serious damage done to China in 1934 and 1935 by the American silver-buying policy.

China foresaw that Washington was likely to condition extension on some move by China to settle old debts to American creditors. To forestall this action, Ambassador Sze was instructed on November 22 to say that China would make a specific proposal to settle the Chicago Bank and Pacific Development loans, if the United States was favorable in principle to extension. Unfortunately Sze did not state this proposal, and did not so report until December 19.[24]

While telegrams were being exchanged with Sze, the two American agencies concerned indicated to the State Department that they were disposed to extend payments on the 1931 and 1933 loans. The Department on December 19 gave Sze a statement indicating conditional willingness to extend, but recalling that China had not given due consideration to American creditors. The Department hoped for "positive assurances" that China would provide adequate security and begin payments on these debts. The archives now available show that the Department was influenced by the report that China had settled a small Japanese debt mistakenly thought to be one of the notorious Nishihara loans (see page 125). Meanwhile, Sze telegraphed on December 28 proposing that China begin at once full payment of interest on the Chicago loan plus some principal, and advised that John Jay Abbott of the Chicago bank would be in Washington on December 30. Kung rejected Sze's plan as out of line with what China could do for debts generally, and telegraphed a specific proposal that later became the basis of negotiations. But this proposal did not arrive in time to be presented to Abbott, and Sze discussed with him his own plan. The next day, Sze told the Department of Kung's proposal, indicating that he did not like it, and the Department agreed with him.[25]

Until the last moment, it appeared that Washington might accept US $250,000 on December 31 on account of principal of the flood relief loan. On the basis of what I understood to be Minister Kung's views I sent instructions to do all practicable for making the smaller payment, but rather than default to pay in full. Washington finally called for full payment, after gathering somehow that China's paying agents in New York would pay if Washington pressed.[26] Kung was furious and almost fired me. But Hornbeck, who was then head of the State Department's Far Eastern office, later told me that the making of this payment had a most beneficial effect in making possible later substantial aid to China through silver purchases, and in clearing the way for the agreement a few months later to lighten the burden of future payments by China on both the flood relief and cotton and wheat credits.

Sze persisted with his own ideas of settlement of the Chicago loan, and urged that China begin paying some coupons. After talking with the Chicago bank's representative, he proposed remitting a series of lump sums of US $500,000 to pay one coupon yearly (US $165,000) and to buy up bonds by tender. The latter we refused, not wishing to open China to the charge of using funds due the bondholders to buy back bonds at prices that were low because of default. We felt it unwise to do anything short of a definitive settlement.[27]

A slightly improved offer was made to the Bank in March on the general lines of the Tientsin-Pukow settlement of February 25, 1936, and the revised Hukuang offer. That offer was similar to the one for the Hukuang loan. In consideration of asking that the basic interest be reduced from 6 to 5 per cent, China offered to improve the security by pledging either the salt revenue or the consolidated taxes.

The Foreign Bondholders Protective Council, which took over negotiations in May, asked immediate payment of the full amount of the debt. Clearly China could not do that in fairness to other creditors who had to be provided for, and so she rejected the proposal immediately. But there was merit in the contention that a settlement of short-term notes should provide for payment over a shorter period than long-term bonds. The Council also took a stiff position on other points. Negotiations lasted for over 15 months from China's first offer of December 31, 1935. The situation required much of my time during leave in the United States in the second half of 1936. The Council I felt and still feel was obdurate, and failed to appreciate China's financial difficulties and the problems of avoiding unfair discrimination against other creditors. I also felt that the State Department did not appreciate the extent to which China's difficulties were caused by the American silver policy or the importance of success of the monetary reform forced by that policy.

The end result was that in the settlement announced on April 12, 1937, China advanced from five to three years the date for beginning full 5 per cent interest, after payments of 2-1/2 per cent in each of the three years from November 1, 1936; and agreed to retire the notes from 1942 to 1954 by yearly payments of from 5 to 10 per cent, i.e., during 18 years. The debt was to be given salt security, and non-interest-bearing scrip issued for one-fifth of arrears of interest. China also paid in cash US $165,000 to the Chicago Bank, which that bank advanced in 1921 to pay one coupon.

Further settlements of 1936-1937

Two old British loans were brought up for settlement in May 1936: the Marconi Wireless Telegraph Company, Limited, 8 per cent 10 year loan of 1918 for £600,000, and the Vickers, Limited, 8 per cent 10 year loan of 1919 for £1,803,000. An agreement was initialed on July 20, but not announced until October 6, 1936. The delay was considered expedient because, after announcement of the Tientsin-Pukow settlement, Japan pressed for settlement of the Tsingtao Treasury Notes of about Y13 million and the Japanese portion of the "96 Million Loan" of about Y40 million (page 126). Nothing was done about the latter two loans. Because the British loans had no specific security, the terms of settlement were much more favorable to China than the Tientsin-Pukow settlement. All arrears of interest were canceled; interest began at 1 per cent per annum, with gradual increase to 3 per cent in 1942-1943 and thereafter; principal was to be retired over 39 years by payments on an increasing scale from 1941; and the loans were granted security of salt revenue subject to existing charges.

The Pacific Development Corporation loan of 1919 was represented by a note of US $5.5 million, against which actual advances were US $4.9 million.[28] The loan was not sold publicly but was made by a number of American banks and banking houses. It was in default since 1921. Negotiations for settlement were begun about April 1, 1937, as soon as the Chicago Bank loan settlement was agreed. In the absence of Minister Kung, who was attending the coronation in London, I negotiated at Shanghai with the representative of the group banks. They were ready to accept terms similar to those for the Chicago loan, but during the negotiations for the latter, China made it clear that the terms were not a precedent for the other loan. A precedent helpful to China was the settlement on terms favorable to China of the Tientsin-Pukow Railway advance of £900,000 by private German banking interests (pages 131 to 132). I insisted on the point, and reported to Kung. He was able to settle the issue in May in London with Thomas W. Lamont of J. P. Morgan and Company. The terms, as finalized when Kung visited New York and announced July 14, provided for new bonds of US$4.9 million, secured on salt revenue, in exchange for the old 6 per cent obligations. Interest would be 2 per cent in the first year, rising by 1/2 per cent yearly to a maximum of 4 per cent. The bonds would be retired from 1942 to 1954 by yearly payments rising from 5 to 10 per cent. Interest arrears were to be canceled.

The Railway Ministry, as mentioned above, settled a number of debts beginning in 1933 as the finances of a number of railways began to improve. It was hoped to clear the way for further credits which the railways badly needed for rehabilitation and extension. When Chang Kia-ngau became Railway Minister in the latter part of 1935, besides taking part in the aforementioned settlements of railway loans that also involved the Finance Ministry, he also moved actively to settle the major publicly issued loans. The finances of the Railway Ministry were quite separate from the general budget, and the Finance Ministry had not been involved in the settlements made in 1933-1935. But Minister Chang cooperated closely with the Finance Ministry and brought me in to help with negotiations. In his book, *China's Struggle for Railroad Development* (New York, 1943), he has described the negotiations whose results are summarized in Appendix 5. Full data are not available concerning some lesser settlements, especially of miscellaneous debts for railway materials and supplies owed to American, British, other European, and Japanese creditors. Many of these settlements, probably about half in total amount, bore no interest but provided for a series of principal payments. By the summer of 1937, railway debt settlements were equivalent to about US$182 million, including the Tientsin-Pukow and Hukuang loans and scrip for arrears.

Debt situation on the eve of war

Total debt in mid-1937 was equivalent to US $1260 million principal amount, as shown in Table 12. That compared with US $893 million in 1928. The change reflected several things. Most important was heavy internal borrowing, which increased the internal debt receiving service from the equivalent of US $95 million in mid-1928 to US $682 million nine years later. Most of the borrowing was to cover deficits caused by internal disturbances, and thus aid in consolidating the central authority. But a substantial amount, of the order of one-fifth of the increase, was borrowed for such constructive purposes as capitalization of the Central Bank, reform of the currencies of Szechwan and South China, and railway improvement and extension. The borrowing in foreign currency was relatively small, the outstanding amount in mid-1937 being equivalent to US $22 million. That comprised mainly the American Flood Relief and Cotton and Wheat credits of 1931 and 1933, and the British loan to complete the Canton-Hankow Railway, secured on remitted Boxer Indemnity payments.

The changes in debt total in the period would have been greater had not large amounts of old foreign and internal debt been retired. Also, since the comparison is in dollars, the fall in the value of China's currency from about US $0.47 on the silver basis in mid-1928 to US $0.30 in 1937 gives rise to a lesser equivalent for the large internal debt. But that did not mean that the burden of the internal debt was correspondingly reduced, because the net price rise from 1927 to 1937 was of the order of 15 to 20 per cent. As to the foreign currency debt, changes in exchange did not greatly change the dollar equivalent. The larger part of that debt was in sterling, and in mid-1937 exchange was about US $4.95, compared with the par of US $4.8665 in 1928.

Debts in arrears in mid-1937, excluding the unrecognized Nishihara loans equivalent to about US $44 million, were equivalent in principal amount to about US $134 million, of which about half was for foreign and half for internal debts. That was a little over 10 per cent of total debt. That total compared with US $475 million in 1928, a reduction of US $341 million. Part of the reduction represented paying off principal of debts that were settled. Relatively little reflected changes in exchange rates. Most of the reduction reflected settlement of debts in arrears: Finance Ministry, US $76 million; Finance and Railway Ministries (Tientsin-Pukow and Hukuang Railway loans), US$70 million*: Railway Ministry, US$112 million; and Communications Ministry, US $17 million. The total of these debts was US$275 million.

When the fighting began in mid-1937, negotiations to eliminate several defaults that then remained were under way, and had to be suspended. The most important of these concerned the Pukow Port Works 5 per cent loan of 1914 for 150 million French francs. The debts in arrears remaining in mid-1937 are shown in Appendix 7. Had not hostilities supervened most of these debts would soon have been settled, except for Japanese claims held in abeyance in view of Japan's encroachment in Manchuria and North China.

*Including scrip for arrears and the £900,000 bank loan.

6: Fiscal Affairs: Summary and Appraisal

The management of fiscal affairs in the prewar decade shows pluses and minuses that call for appraisal.

Revenues

There is striking contrast between Wellington Koo's pathetic report of 1926, showing less than C $2 million of nonborrowed money available during his tenure of three and a half months as Finance Minister, and conditions a decade later when annual revenue after debt payments was nearly C $700 million. Particular credit goes to Finance Minister Soong for building a productive system of national revenues from 1927 to 1933.

Let us summarize the chief accomplishments. Full tariff autonomy was achieved by international agreements. Rates were raised for greater yield and to some extent for protection. Miscellaneous obstructive levies collected by the Customs service on internal trade were ended. The regional Customs bureaus collecting surtaxes in 1928 were abolished and the revenues were centralized in the national treasury. Regional attempts to seize customs revenue were thwarted, although the seizure by the "Manchukuo" puppets could not be prevented. The Customs service and procedures were integrated into the Finance Ministry with changes that did not infringe agreements. Finally, the way was cleared for Chinese nationals to rise to the upper ranks of the Customs on a merit basis, thus recognizing legitimate claims of nationalism.

The shifting of import duties in 1930 from a silver to a gold basis was of utmost importance. It preserved the real value of the revenue, and increased yield by tens of millions in terms of slumping silver. It was an indispensable means to maintain payment of the foreign and domestic debt, thus maintaining solvency and confidence. Its effects went far beyond improvement of the fiscal situation. By giving the Central Bank experience in international financial operations, it helped to prepare the way for eventual monetary reform—which became a key factor in strengthening the government.

The Salt revenue service was rehabilitated and integrated into the Finance Ministry. In mid-1928, nearly all the salt revenue was appropriated locally. The rehabilitation made it a truly national revenue source, although at the cost of giving some revenue or subsidies to local authorities. In mid-1928, debt payments due from salt revenue were in arrears. Under the new arrangements, as the government began to receive better revenue from salt, it restored regular debt payments along with payment of arrears. Integration of the Salt administration into the Ministry departed from the 1913 Reorganization Loan agreement. But foreign governments and the bondholders did not protest insistently, because the salt revenue situation was so greatly improved, bond prices rose, and payments on the one loan calling for the old procedure (the Reorganization Loan) had been transferred to customs revenue in 1917.

The salt reforms begun in 1928 included tightening the organization in the Inspectorate and the districts, consolidating duties, progressing toward the establishment of uniform rates in the districts, standardizing weights based on the metric system, doing away with tax farming and monopolies and other former malpractices, improving salt works, strengthening prevention of smuggling and bandit seizures, and improving the quality of salt.

The excise tax system was simplified by concentrating taxes on a few widely used items taxed at the source; consolidating the rates; and guaranteeing that the articles would not be taxed further in specified areas. The system was extended as the government broadened its control throughout the country. The substantial abolition of *likin,* the burdensome tax on movement of goods, was an outstanding accomplishment whose success exceeded the expectations of both Chinese and foreign observers. Several drives to do away with illicit or exorbitant taxes led to considerable progress. These measures were of great importance in promoting trade. The principles of partition of revenues between the central and provincial governments as defined in 1928 (Chapter 2) provided guidelines. The financial concessions that had to be made to various provincial authorities were a small price for the progress toward establishment of a nationwide tax system. Administration was improved by bringing in a better grade of men and moving toward a civil service basis. The operation became centralized in the Internal Revenue Administration. Special credit goes to its capable director, Tse Tsok-kai, who worked closely with Adviser Lockhart, to develop that office into a creditable all-Chinese service, alongside the older Sino-foreign Customs and Salt administrations.

Appraising the tax situation as of early 1934, Ambassador Johnson stressed the contrast with 1928. The government, he said, fell heir to a motley collection of taxes, surtaxes, and miscellaneous imposts—there were more than 130 tax bureaus in Shanghai alone. But by 1934, he said, the Customs had "taken notable steps to abolish charges on domestic trade." He thus commented on the overall tax situation:

> A review of the tax situation in China indicates that there has been a very considerable improvement in recent years. Aside from provincial and local taxation, that part of China under the control of the National Government now has a simple, unified and relatively logical system of national taxation. Continual pressure by the National Government upon the provinces has been a potent factor in causing a gradual diminution of irregular and illegal provincial levies and the disappearance of many forms of taxation which formerly burdened and obstructed trade.[1]

Despite the progress, the revenue system as it was developed had important weaknesses. One was inelasticity. Whenever revenue needs increased, the first thought was to raise rates or add a surtax that was supposedly temporary but in practice was not easily ended. Thus various tariff rates were raised and general surtaxes added, bringing about rates that often reduced revenue and caused smuggling that was hard to control. The high tariff rates also increased friction with Japan. They gave an excuse to elements, especially among the military, that sought to make China a preserve where Japanese would enjoy favorable and even preferential treatment. It became easier for such aggressive elements to gain support in business quarters in Japan. Thus China's use of tariff autonomy was one of the factors leading to Japanese encroachment in China after seizure of Manchuria, and to the all-out hostilities that began in 1937.

The salt taxes and the excises, levied on items of wide general consumption, bore heaviest on the mass of the people and were a relatively light burden on the well-to-do. Much the same was true of the customs. When during the war we looked into the possibility of restricting import of luxuries and less essential goods, it was found that nearly all the trade comprised necessities. Revenue needs unavoidably dominated revenue policy in the years under review. And the leaders were so busy with survival of the government in the face of both internal revolt and external aggression that they had little chance to make more basic reforms in the revenue system.

The income tax begun in 1936 was well-intentioned, but must be judged premature in view of difficulties of enforcement. Moreover, it was defective in such matters as trying to reach incomes at too low a level and omitting to tax income from real estate.

The consequences of failure to begin seriously to reform and develop the tax on rural and urban land were serious. A workable land tax should have been a prime aim, both for fiscal reasons and to promote greater social justice. Agriculture in the prewar years has been estimated to engage perhaps 80 per cent of the workers and to give rise to about 60 per cent of the gross national product.[2] Those figures point up the inadequate prewar reliance upon drawing revenue from the agricultural sector. Necessary expenditures could not be fully supported, as D. S. Paauw has pointed out, by "indirect taxation applied to the modern exchange sectors of the economy."[3] The government was able to worry through the prewar decade while the central and provincial governments drew less than one-tenth of their revenue from agriculture, by far the major sector of the economy. But when the war came, the lack of adequate land taxation, while revenues from the coastal and more modernized areas were decimated, made it much harder to deal with inflation.

Furthermore, a reformed tax on both rural and urban land was clearly the most practicable way to apply direct taxation to make the tax system more equitable. Unhappily, that aim was not sufficiently potent in the ruling circles, nationally or locally. The important political power was held by landholding and business elements averse to accepting greater tax burdens and unaware of disastrous possibilities of not moving for greater social justice.

China's failure to reform and develop the land tax is in striking contrast to Japan's action in the early Meiji period, when land tax reform "occupied the best minds in the government over a long period of time." The size and stability of land tax revenue was for many years a chief factor enabling Japan to finance the costs of progress.[4] But in China, the weakness of the Imperial and early Republican regimes, along with the strength of the traditional peasant-landlord-official system, precluded such a reform. And the Nationalists temporarily foreclosed the opportunity to develop the land tax by giving it over to the provinces. Then they were too preoccupied with putting down dissension and dealing with Japan to give adequate attention to land affairs. In addition, the leaders in the field of finance had an urban rather than rural background, and throughout the government there was a predilection for the traditional system. It remained for the Communists with their rural origin to raise large revenue from a heavy draft on land income, supplemented by forced savings in agriculture and commandeering of surplus rural labor for construction.

The progress in the national revenue system in 1928 through 1937 was not matched by progress at the provincial and local level. Although there were improvements there, serious weakness remained at the grass roots, where too often the people were ruled by the military and/or landowning and moneylending elements, and government meant exploitation. Failure to remedy these basic conditions and provide reasonably good government to a greater extent at the local level made it easier for the Communists to gain headway, taking advantage of the disorganization during the war.

The public sector was relatively small in the prewar decade. The proportion of revenue at all levels of government to gross national product can only be estimated roughly. The available data indicate that in 1936 the proportion was about 5.4 per cent, about twice the figure for 1931.[5] That proportion was low for the period compared with other countries, and compares with a fourth and more in many countries today. Even at this low proportionate level, revenues were well short of covering expenditures. Clearly expansion of the public sector was essential to provide the economic infrastructure and social services needed for progress, under the mixed private-public economic system then developing. Yet despite the difficulties of financing costs of development, the momentum of expansion was accelerating, especially toward the end of the prewar decade, as described in Chapter 17.

Expenditures

The new government set itself to build a unified strong China. For that, plus the usual human wish of leaders to keep on leading, the government's survival was a prime goal. Hence there was priority for military outlay, to put down revolting warlords and the Communists and for national defense.

Moreover, the government felt obliged to give subsidies to various provincial and local authorities and/or let them retain some revenues assigned to the central government. That policy was adopted partly because adequate provincial and local revenues had not been developed to meet basic needs. It was also partly the price of maintaining the loyalty of provincial and local authorities. Consolidation of control had to be gradual. Force could not always be used or threatened because warlords or local leaders were usually shrewd enough to call a bluff if they felt that they could. Furthermore, public opinion, which was quite vocal, was becoming hostile to frequent internal use of force, especially as Japan's threat grew. So the government often had to temporize and bide its time. But by 1937 the government had mostly overcome forcible internal resistance to its claim to rule. Bringing Szechwan and South China into the fold was of major importance.

In 1937, two main factors remained to interfere with nationwide centralization. First was the persisting Japanese encroachment in the north. That, besides the control of Manchuria, prevented full control in North China—although in turn it promoted support of the government throughout China. And the Communists, although controlling only a small area in the distant northwest, had adherents in many parts of the country and continued to plot for the day when they might reverse their defeats of the prewar decade.

Action to put down subversive attempts and preparations to resist Japan gave rise to heavy costs involving disproportionate military outlay. That outlay in turn was the main cause of the deficit and heavy borrowing, so that debt payments ranged between 25 and 40 per cent of total expenditure. Since the government could not prevent sporadic revolts or from 1931 onward the Japanese encroachment, efforts to put a ceiling on military costs failed. The financial needs of the military, who dominated the government, primarily determined the amount to be raised by taxes and borrowing. Often they spent money wastefully or diverted it from the intended purpose. Nevertheless, the Finance Ministers strove for restraint and helped to keep some sort of rein on the military. They could do this as members of the Central Political Council and as leaders of the Executive Yuan, which directed the day-to-day operations of government. It was to their credit that Ministers Soong and Kung accomplished as much as they did in this difficult decade, and were able to bring the finances within reach of equilibrium in 1937 on the eve of Japan's attack.

During the decade there was sharp criticism within China of heavy spending for military objects and of the resulting damage to the finances that interfered with use of government funds for such purposes as economic development, education, and social welfare. And a postwar critic of Nanking's financial policies, D. S. Paauw, stated displeasure with what he termed making fiscal decisions "almost exclusively on the basis of non-economic factors," and use of the army "to protect the political and military position of the Kuomintang from the challenge of internal military revolt." Such criticism fails to give weight to the importance of restoring order in China, establishing a government with nationwide authority, and gaining strength to resist both Communism and Japan's attempt at domination. A critic of Paauw's paper, N. S. Buchanan, pointed out that Paauw offered no feasible alternative to the government's course of action; and queried whether Paauw thought it would have been better to have made no attempt to suppress revolts, saying that "it appears hard to believe that to establish order as such was an unproductive expenditure from either the long or short run point of view." Buchanan queried whether Paauw thought that the effort was "undertaken by the 'wrong' group in some sense not clear . . . from his paper."[6]

All too little money remained available for constructive purposes. Yet despite the difficulties, the government was able to allocate in the fiscal years 1934 through 1937 about an eighth of total expenditures for such purposes as construction of roads, civil airports, and port works; water conservancy and river improvement; education; agricultural improvement; and capital for the Central Bank. In addition the Railway Ministry spent about C $100 million to rehabilitate and extend the railways, and the Communications Ministry spent substantial sums to improve telecommunications. Also outside the general budget was the notable program of relief and rehabilitation after the great flood of 1931, costing about C $60 million (Chapter 16). The provinces also allocated considerable sums for railways, roads, and utilities. The government was committed to development, a major tenet of Sun Yat-sen. The progress of rehabilitation and development in the decade was substantial (Chapters 13 and 14).

In 1937 there was extensive planning for future development, which would have gone forward actively if China had been left in peace. In mid-1937, Minister Kung spoke of a new departure, the creation of a special budget for capital expenditure. He said that the ordinary budget was aboutC $1 billion, but that a capital budget of about C $400 million to be raised mostly by borrowing was contemplated (Chapter 4). The balancing of the ordinary budget was in prospect. But the financing of the capital budget would have posed problems, even though the larger part of the borrowing was to be financed from revenues of the Railway Ministry, and service of that part under the Finance Ministry was to be included within the general budget. Elsewhere, adoption of a system of "ordinary" and "extraordinary" budgets has often been a step toward fiscal instability.

It was unfortunate that the government's incessant demand for money absorbed bank resources and savings that otherwise might have promoted private investment in development. Also revenues raised from regressive taxes were used for payments on bonds held by banks and by well-to-do persons. But criticisms must be weighed in the light of both the short-run and the long-run importance of national consolidation.

Deficit management

Receipts and payments for 1928 to 1937 (Table 1) show total deficits of C $1530 million or 21 per cent of total expenditures. Balance was attained only for the calendar year 1932. The situation was better than appears from looking only at the amount and proportion of deficits, in that about two-thirds of the deficits in the prewar decade represented payments to retire earlier debt (Table 13).

The way in which deficits were covered is analyzed in Table 13. More than two-thirds was realized from direct sales of bonds and treasury notes. Most of the rest came from bank loans and overdrafts, these being usually secured by pledge of marketable issues. The total of securities issued for sale and/or pledging to cover deficits was C $1998 million. That amount comprised C $1807 million issued for general purposes (Table 7), and C $191 million of Consolidation Bonds of 1936 issued in excess of the amount needed to exchange for old issues.

Table 13

Analysis of deficit for fiscal years ended June 30, 1929 to 1937[a]

	1929	1930	1931	1932	1933	1934	1935	1936	1937
Borrowing									
Domestic bonds and treasury notes, millions	C$ 69	C$ 91	C$193	C$125	C$ 26	C$ 80	C$164	C$148	C$223
Bank loans and overdrafts, millions	32	10	24	5	86	91	36	128	113
Cotton-wheat loan of 1933, millions	--	--	--	--	--	8	25	--	--
Add: cash balance at beginning of period, millions	--	--	--	--	--	27	60	90	45
Subtotal, millions						207	286	365	381

Continued

Table 13 (Continued)

Analysis of deficit for fiscal years ended June 30, 1929 to 1937[a]

	1929	1930	1931	1932	1933	1934	1935	1936	1937
Subtract: cash balance at end of period, millions	--	--	--	--	27	60	90	110	83
Deficit, millions	100	101	217	130	86	147	196	256	297
Payments to retire debt,[b] millions	67	113	150	160	100	115	125	103	79

[a] Source: Same as Appendix 1. Figures of payments to retire debt for 1931 to 1935 are from the Finance Ministry report for the 23rd fiscal year, p. 16, and for the other years are from my records.

[b] Approximate figures, not including amortization of the Boxer Indemnity other than of loans secured on the French and Belgian portions.

The excess of issues of C $1998 million over deficits of C $1530 million reflects the fact that the government realized on the securities at a large discount. The proportion realized cannot be deduced from simple comparison of these figures, partly because of lack of comprehensive data of the government's transactions with the banks, and partly because an unknown amount of the bonds was unissued as of mid-1937. The proportion realized to 1934 was probably in the range of 60 to 75 per cent, when yields were mostly 15 to 20 per cent. There was considerable improvement between 1935 and 1937, average yields being 13.0 per cent in 1935, 11.6 per cent in 1936, and 8.7 per cent in June 1937 (Table 9). The market demanded short-term high-yield issues in view of internal and external uncertainties. The government had to recognize and adapt to that situation, while trying to remove the uncertainties by consolidating its position. But that took time and was far from easy in view of persisting internal and external difficulties, along with the effects of the great depression and natural calamities. As new short-term loans were issued, the growing charges for amortization gradually absorbed the revenues available for pledging.

The inexorable growth of deficits forced a choice among default, inflationary finance, and readjustment of debt payments. Default, apart from discrediting the government, would have had extremely severe effects on the banks and the public because of large bank holdings of government issues.

Inflation would have been the usual solution under later-type monetary systems, leading to the well-known difficulties of price rise, speculation, exchange depreciation, adverse balance of payments, and exchange control with its accompaniments of distortion and corruption and interference with development. But in China in 1931-1932, no one even thought of inflation as a feasible alternative. Bank notes were redeemable in silver on demand, and an issue of fiat money would have prompty forced inconvertibility. A rising premium on silver would have appeared, in a highly speculative market, and the value of a fiat issue would have quickly fallen. That had been the experience with introducing fiat money under a metallic standard, both in China and elsewhere. In 1935, although an inflationary solution was technically possible after the currency reform, it was never considered. The government was committed by the terms of the reform to balance the finances and avoid inflation.

Consequently the debt reorganizations of 1932 and 1936 were

the best way then available to deal with the fiscal difficulties. The admitted evils of these readjustments were a small price to pay to avoid the alternative evils of general default or inflation. The first reorganization was well accepted as a measure made necessary by the Japanese attack at Shanghai. The second was a means to strengthen the situation after the currency reform of 1935. After both reorganizations, the improvement in the finances justified the action taken, by safeguarding the creditors' interest better than would have any practicable alternative. In 1932, bond prices were higher when the market reopened than before the readjustment. In 1936, the improvement of prices took more time, being retarded by Japan's aggressive action in North China. But in 1937 the improved state of the finances paid off with much higher bond prices than before the readjustment. Both readjustments, saving yearly about C $100 million and C $85 million, respectively, were based on my proposals. I felt then, and still feel, that one of my chief contributions in China was devising means whereby the readjustments could take place with minimum harm and be followed after short interludes by enhancement of credit.

Granted that heavy expenditures were unavoidable, and the difficulty of more rapidly building revenues, I consider in retrospect that Ministers Soong and Kung handled the problem of deficits in a very troubled time with considerable skill. The result after the vicissitudes of 10 years was a spectacular transformation of the fiscal and monetary situation, with the finances within reach of equilibrium in 1937 on the eve of Japan's attack. This was without serious inflation, the general price rise from the beginning to the end of the prewar decade being of the order of a fifth. The contrast between the state of the national finances in 1937 and the chaotic conditions of 1928 is striking.

Rehabilitation of credit

The contrast is also striking between 1927-1928, when well over half of the debt was in default, and 1937 when settlements had been made covering most of that debt. A measure of the change was in bond prices and yields. In 1927-1928, customs-secured foreign loans, which were regularly paid, yielded 7 to 11 per cent; while other loans in arrears sold in the 20's or 30's and even lower. Domestic credit in the early Nationalist years was on about a 15 to 18 per cent basis, with even higher rates in periods of special strain. But by mid-1937, leading loans sold at

London on about a 5 per cent basis, which was considerably better than comparable Japanese loans. In Shanghai, leading internal loans sold on better than an 8 per cent basis in mid-1937, a low rate for less developed countries affected by shortage of capital and a variety of uncertainties.

With only about 10 per cent of the total principal amount of recognized debt remaining in arrears in mid-1937, and negotiations under way concerning some of that, the prospect was that before long the old items would be cleared up. An exception concerned the debts to Japanese creditors, which it would have been hard for China to settle unless Japan moderated her policy toward China. The start of fighting on July 7 was a turning point for debt settlements, along with a great deal more.

In 1928, the government recognized its obligation as a successor to assume Peking's debts. That was done despite the demand of leftists that these be repudiated. And in 1928-1929 it rehabilitated the salt-secured foreign loans. Soong in his annual report for 1928-1929, issued March 1, 1930, said "... it is expected that during the present year it will be possible to formulate some scheme of debt consolidation" (page 7). But then the government waited until the latter part of 1935 to begin a serious effort to settle the major issues. Thus the question arises whether more could and should have been done earlier.

The delay of action is explained by the financial difficulties caused by successive threats of subversion, involving several seizures of customs revenue and detention of salt loan quotas; Japan's seizure of Manchuria and all its revenues in 1931-1932 and encroachments in North China; and the critical monetary and economic situation accompanying the gyrations of silver.

In 1930 to 1935, the foreign governments frequently pressed for action. They were bound to do this because of pressure from their nationals who held unsatisfied valid claims. A chief point made by these governments, while recognizing China's difficulties, was objection to pledge of the best security for internal loans while prior foreign obligations were left in arrears.

From China's viewpoint, this legally valid criticism overlooked the practical situation. Unless the government survived, no one could be paid. The internal loans were essential for survival, and could not have been floated unless well-secured. Had China yielded in 1930 to 1935 to the calls of the foreign governments for settlements, any plan involving considerable payments would have broken down as had the various partial consolidations and refundings attempted by Peking in the 1920's. Without the internal loans of 1927 and following years internal conditions would have reverted to chaos. Some of the government's financial and other policies can of course be justly criticized, as can the policies of almost any conceivable government anywhere. The leaders to my personal knowledge, despite imperfections of some of their policies, desired to settle the debts on terms that China could fulfil.

When during these years there was protest about pledging revenues for internal loans, I called the attention of creditors' representatives to an analogy with the American law concerning preferences of creditors and composition of debts in default. The Supreme Court case of *Fosdick* v. *Schall* (99 US 235) in 1878 and later court rulings held that current outlay needed to preserve an enterprise and maintain its operations could be paid with priority over mortgage debt under certain conditions and for a limited time.

China in 1930-1931 gave much attention to a general debt settlement. But that became impossible after Japan began her Manchurian adventure, and piecemeal settlements became the only feasible action. On that basis, no matter what China might do, it was impossible to avoid the charge of favoritism. China could only strive to be fair in the proposals and agreements, and ask the creditors to understand the difficulties and be tolerant. I felt then and still feel that the chief settlements were on the whole fair in the circumstances. Before 1935, the government should probably have had fuller discussions with the creditors, to explain its problems. But had it made offers of settlement of the major defaulted debts in those years, they would necessarily have been such that the creditors would have rejected them out of hand.

Reviewing the period in 1952, D. S. Paauw is strongly critical of China's action on debts. He said that "... settlement was frequently delayed by Nanking as long as possible, and was made only when considerable pressure was brought to bear."[7] I know of no pressure that could be called "considerable," unless it related to settlement of the relatively small Japanese telephone and cable loans about the beginning of 1935. The United States did bring pressure in December 1935 for settlement of the Chicago Bank loan, but China already had decided to start negotiations on this loan. Paauw did not dig deeply enough into the facts to discover the striking rehabilitation of credit between

1928 and 1937, when so many countries all over the world were going into default. Nor did he appreciate the seriousness of the difficulties confronting the government in those years.

Why did China begin serious action about the debts in the fall of 1935? The initial success of the currency reform of November 3, 1935, gave the leaders confidence that they could carry out a debt settlement. And they felt that foreign credits were desirable if not essential to ensure the continuing success of the reform—although credits proved unnecessary. When Leith-Ross was asked in the fall of 1935 about the possibility of a currency credit from London, he made the obvious reply that a credit would be out of the question if major debts remained unsettled. Those considerations led to the start of negotiations on the Tientsin-Pukow and Hukuang loans, because these had the best right to prior settlement in view of their claim on customs revenue.

We may conclude that China's record in 1928 to 1937, not only in maintaining payment of debts receiving service in 1928 but also in restoring service of debt in arrears equivalent to about US$275 million, was outstanding—especially when compared with the record of many less developed countries whose debts went into default during the depression years. The constructive handling of debt matters in 1935 to 1937 brought commendation at home and abroad. The *Investors Chronicle* of London, quoted in the *North China Daily News* of February 14, 1937, said that, "From the chaos of . . . early days the National Government has achieved a quite remarkable progress."

The foreign debt structure in 1937 was complicated, but the internal debt structure had been greatly simplified and improved by the reorganization of 1936. Minister Kung, in London in 1937 to attend the coronation, discussed there a possible large loan to refund debt and provide fresh capital for development. Some of the debt under the control of the Finance Ministry might well have been refunded, but for example there would have been little point in refunding the 5 per cent Reorganization Loan then outstanding in the equivalent of US $100 million and having 23 years to run. There was a strong case, however, for reforming the railway debt situation. The maze of separate railway loan agreements not only was highly complicated but was an obstacle to the much-needed unification of the railway system. I proposed a plan for exchange of railway obligations into new bonds of several series secured on the revenues of the entire system. The terms of exchange would have depended on classification of old debts according to the following criteria: interest rates, maturities, specific security, record of payments, and market quotations if any.

The fighting that began July 7, 1937, made it impossible to consider Kung's proposals, or other schemes to improve the debt structure.

Fiscal administration

A basic need intimately connected with progress toward a better fiscal system was improvement of government at all levels. While competent and experienced administrators were in short supply in 1928 to 1937, the civil administration was making notable progress. In tax matters during these years, Chinese were advancing to posts of higher responsibility in the Sino-foreign Customs service; the Salt organization was rehabilitated with growing Chinese participation; the Internal Revenue Administration was becoming an effective all-Chinese affair; and burdensome internal taxes on movement of goods were largely abolished. The Finance Ministry was becoming an integrated organization composed of personnel gaining experience.

The Central Bank was a new and vitally important cog in the governmental machinery, as the effective fiscal agent to handle receipts and payments and manage loans, and as an agency able to deal with monetary problems. Under the procedures which the government inherited in 1928, funds for ordinary operations when not held in cash were deposited in various private banks. Collections of customs and salt revenue, on which foreign loans were charged, were deposited in foreign banks in accounts mostly in *taels*. Conversion into foreign currencies was made by the banks without effective competitive bidding to get the best going rates. The government rightly felt that the banks often took advantage of their position to make unearned gains.

After 1928, the Banking Department of the Central Bank became a smoothly running and efficient organization headed by Te-mou Hsi and advised by F. B. Lynch and me. The Bank since its creation in the fall of 1928 was doing well in its handling of funds for service of internal loans. We set out to put the bank in a position to handle also foreign loan service. That involved getting into the hands of the Finance Ministry and Central Bank operations customarily handled by such organs elsewhere. The Ministry's office of loan administration was well directed by Loy Chang. The new procedures had to take account of the terms of existing agreements, and it was essential to move in a way that would strengthen rather than hurt China's credit.

A key reform was adoption of the customs gold unit (CGU) early in 1931. That reform gave the government a regular flow of foreign currency receipts. The selling rates for CGU were adjusted to make it attractive for importers to buy them with foreign currencies as well as with silver, in order to establish balances in the Central Bank in terms of CGU. Duties were then paid by drawing checks on these accounts in favor of the Customs. Before adoption of the CGU system, the Central Bank had arranged to establish accounts with leading banks in New York and London. The foreign currencies received through the CGU system were now accrued in those accounts and also substantial holdings of gold were acquired. The financial officer of the Customs drew checks on the CGU accounts to buy from the Central Bank the foreign currencies needed for loan service.

Some loan agreements had no provisions affecting the right to use this procedure. Under others the government could make direct loan payments in foreign currencies if it "should happen to have gold funds *bona fide* at its disposal."[8] The banks were unhappy because direct payments deprived them of exchange profits. A disagreement on interpretation of the clause was compromised by allowing an extra 1/8 per cent commission on the payments.

Prior to the agreement settling the Tientsin-Pukow Railway loans, the Railway Ministry went into the exchange market to buy foreign currencies for loan service, at times to the detriment of Central Bank operations. Afterward the procedure for handling that settlement provided that the Railway Ministry would deposit funds in local currency each ten days in amounts sufficient to make loan payments, and the Central Bank would then provide the foreign currency required.

Although the procedures developed for handling public funds, including loan payments, concerned what could be termed routine matters, they involved a real growth of administrative experience. And, beyond that, the procedures for foreign loan payments meant that China had progressed to the point where she could recover by evolution the right to operate in such matters as a modern government should. Men were being trained to conduct administration so that they could take over effectively without relying upon foreign participation and advice.

Moreover, these developments in 1929 to 1935 enabled the Central Bank to gain experience in foreign exchange and monetary management that put it in position to give effect to the monetary reform and exchange stabilization of November 1935.

In civil administration there were improvements of importance to the economy and the finances. Establishment of the National Economic Council in 1931 consolidated and centralized functions concerning development that formerly were under charge of various offices. Various functions pertaining to agriculture were also consolidated under the Ministry of Industry. In 1933, a Commission on Administrative Efficiency was created. This Commission led to modest accomplishments in improving procedures, records, and archives; eliminating duplication and consolidation of functions of some offices; and retrenchment.[9] The government planned a civil service system, for which important rudiments already existed in the revenue services. But little was accomplished and plans were mostly on paper in 1937. Abolition of the age-old system of official squeeze was part of the government's policy. Some headway was made in curtailing that system, and I feel that progress to that end was greater than in many other less developed countries where I have had experience. Yet much of the system remained. Its ending was difficult because of the old practice of having far too many poorly paid staff members from whom adequate individual work was not exacted, rather than a lesser number of staff properly paid and held to proper standards. Overstaffing was common in business under the family system, with preference for relatives, as well as in government.

Despite progress in the civil sector there was far too little progress of reform in military finances. There exploitation and inefficiency were far too common, and there was far too little effort to better conditions. The people were tired of the intermittent internal wars. That made it harder for the government to press abusive militarists for reforms by using force when, as often, other means of persuasion were of small avail.

From time immemorial, China's people distrusted government and wanted as little as possible to do with it. They tended to regard officials as mandarins who were in authority to serve their selfish interest rather than the public's. That traditional atmosphere was not conducive to psychological support of government and especially of fiscal policies. Only when people have reasonable confidence in the standards and policies of government are conditions ripe for bettering adequately a system of receipts and payments. Taxes are never popular, and people are the more reluctant to pay them when they see that the burdens are inequitably distributed and the proceeds spent wastefully or corruptly. There were many sincere and loyal men in the government, working to improve conditions. Yet far too many used official position for personal advantage, sometimes subtly but sometimes crudely, especially the military.

Overall, China's fiscal system in 1937 had been remarkably transformed from the chaotic condition of ten years earlier. There were serious defects and weaknesses, but in fiscal matters the government was beginning to be able to act effectively. It was the strongest government in generations. But it had not developed the fiscal structure to a strength that could withstand the enormous strain that began when Japan's attack of 1937 forced the country into more than eight years of bitter war.

Part Three

Monetary Affairs

7: Silver Standard Reform or the Gold Standard?

Monetary reform was clearly needed in 1928, and the new government was committed to action. There were two basic problems: (1) reform of the chaotic monetary circulation; and (2) the choice between staying with silver or moving toward the gold standard.

State of the currency in 1928

China, said the Kemmerer Commission's report, had "unquestionably the worst currency to be found in any important country." It was a heterogeneous mixture of coins, weights, and paper money that varied from place to place. The money was issued by numerous independent authorities, national, provincial, and private. There were a number of different standards of silver, copper, and several kinds of depreciated paper money in various regions. The day-to-day transactions of the mass of the people were largely in terms of copper coins. But China was generally regarded as a silver standard country because most wholesale transactions, a substantial part of the retail transactions, most debts, and the foreign exchange market were on a silver basis.*

The most important silver coins were dollars. Of these there was a great variety, coined at various foreign and Chinese mints. First to come to China were the Spanish Carolus dollars, as early it is said as the 17th century, and some could still be found in circulation in 1928. Others included the American and British trade dollars, Japanese and Saigon dollars, the old Austro-Hungarian Maria Theresa dollars, and Peruvian dollars. But by far the most important were the Mexican dollars, which gave China's currency the popular name "Mex." Chinese mints began coining dollars in 1889, and the supply gradually grew until by 1928 these were a leading part of the circulation. The

*The history of China's currency and the situation in and prior to the 'twenties have been treated at length by various writers, and will only be summarized here. See the Bibliography.

various dollars weighed about 412 to 420 grains each. Fineness varied from approximately 0.890 to 0.900, and the legal fine silver content varied from about 369 to 378 grains. Despite the differences and the slight underweight of some coins, the dollars were generally interchangeable at par. But acceptability varied from place to place. The heavier coins tended to disappear, being melted or exported.

Much of China's silver was in the form of silver "shoes" or *sycee* whose weight was expressed in *taels*, and in bars.[1] Such silver served as bank reserves but was not very suitable for ordinary payments. The *tael* thus was a unit of account. It never really circulated as a coin, although there were instances of *tael* coinage. The *tael's* weight varied from place to place, in the approximate range of 500 to 600 grains. It was in the order of 50 per cent heavier than the silver dollar. Sometimes the *tael* also varied within an area for different transactions. To cite an extreme case, as of 1920:

> One of the most important products of Szechwan is salt, and dealings in this are settled by a *tael* of 556.4 grains, unless it is salt from the Tzeliu well, in which case the standard is 557.7 grains. A transaction in cotton cloth is settled with a *tael* of 555.0 grains, but for cotton yarn the *tael* is 556.0 grains, and for raw cotton the *tael* is 547.7 grains.
>
> This seems confusion, but we are not yet at the end ... Now comes in the question of the fineness of the silver. ... At Chungking three qualities of silver are in common use ... 1,000 fine, .. 995 fine, and "trade silver" between 960 and 970 fine. ... Taking the score of current *tael*-weights ... we have at least sixty currencies possible in this one town.[2]

By 1928 the *tael* had mostly given place to the silver dollar in many parts of China. It continued, however, as an important unit in major centers such as Shanghai, Tientsin, and Hankow, where bank accounts in *taels* as well as in dollars were maintained, backed by silver partly in bars but mostly in *sycee*.[3] Persons having one unit and wanting the other had to effect exchange at rates varying from day to day. In these centers, most wholesale business and larger transactions, such as in local securities, foreign exchange, rents, utility bills, and municipal taxes, were in *taels*. Retail transactions were commonly in dollars when of the order of one dollar or more, while the small day to day transactions of the masses were in coppers.

Subsidiary silver comprised mostly 20-cent pieces, with some 10- and 5-cent coins. This coinage had a silver content less than the dollar. The temptation of overissue to make seignorage gains was not resisted, and it took about six 20-cent coins to equal one dollar—plus or minus a varying number of coppers. These subsidiary silver coins were called "small money," in contrast to the dollar or "big money." In South China, the unit was the dollar of five 20-cent pieces, whose value was in the range of 70 to 75 per cent of the silver dollar.

Attention to silver obscured the copper money situation as a major currency problem. The smaller transactions of the mass of the people, especially in the thousands of villages and the countryside where most of the people lived, were mostly done with coppers of various weights and fineness, and often with copper money notes. Formerly most of the coins were the traditional *cash* with square holes, commonly strung on a string with the *chop* of a money shop. The quality of strings of *cash* varied, and this gave rise to bargaining. These coins had a copper content that made it profitable during World War I for great quantities to be collected and exported. Yet many remained in use away from the chief centers of trade.

In 1901, as a measure of reform, the imperial regime authorized the minting of 1-cent or 10-*cash* coins, modeled after the Hong Kong cent. These first went to a premium and in 1902 were about 80 per silver dollar. But the profit on coinage prompted provincial mints to debase the new cents, and also to issue 2-cent (20-*cash*) coins of proportionately less weight. A generation later, copper cents were around 300 per dollar in Shanghai; 400 or more in Tientsin and Peiping; 600 in Hankow; and 1100 in Yunyang. Issue of copper money notes added to the inflation.

The impact of the inflation of copper money was serious. Wages and incomes in terms of coppers lagged well behind the cost of living. The resulting exploitation of a large part of the population was an important cause of discontent and unrest.

China's silver-copper system was not bimetallic in the sense of the 19th century gold-silver bimetallism of Europe and the United States, because China's silver and copper coins were not tied together at any fixed rates. Rather, both kinds of coins fluctuated constantly according to market conditions.

The circulation of silver dollar bank notes was also important. In 1928, the chief issues were the notes of the Bank of

China and of the Bank of Communications. Notes of the newly created Central Bank began to circulate late in 1928. Other Chinese banks and some foreign banks similarly issued notes. The notes of banks based at Shanghai and Tientsin circulated at par, freely convertible into silver dollars. This paper currency along with the wide use of silver dollars was gradually promoting some measure of unity of the currency. Fractional paper money notes were also common. Most of these were "big money" notes, convertible at face value into dollars or dollar notes. But in the Canton area, and to a small extent in Central China, there were "small money" notes convertible into the depreciated subsidiary silver coins as well as notes in terms of coppers.

In some regions, the currency consisted of depreciated paper issued by provincal banks or currency bureaus. The worst situation was in Manchuria and in Kwangsi and Yunnan Provinces, where depreciation was large and good money had mostly disappeared pursuant to Gresham's Law.

These conditions gave rise to innumerable money shops, taking their toll on a myriad of transactions. Everyone was a buyer and seller of currency. The inconvenience and economic cost of monetary confusion cannot be estimated, but it was high. The money shops sometimes operated as a side line, along with sale of staple goods. Others had large capital and were the local bankers and moneylenders.

Prices and their measurement

As explained above, even as late as the early 1930's, prices were in terms of a great variety of currencies of silver, copper, and paper. Larger transactions prior to the currency reform of November 1935 were in silver; in *taels* and silver dollars up to abolition of the *tael* in 1933, and then in dollars. In October 1934, the silver dollar was divorced from world silver prices, and from November 1935, prices were in *fapi* or legal tender notes, with a managed and stable foreign exchange standard (Chapters 8 and 9). Prior to 1937, the copper standard continued as the chief basis for smaller transactions throughout the country, but in 1936-1937 subsidiary coins pegged firmly to the new currency were being rapidly introduced.

Only partial data are available to show the course of general prices in China as a whole prior to World War I. There is a series of wholesale prices of exports and imports in terms of silver from 1867 compiled from trade returns. Data of that series and of the value of silver from 1870 to 1931 are shown in Table 14.[4] The rise of these prices in terms of silver in that period was more than threefold. That paralleled to a large extent the fall in the world price of silver. The level of American wholesale prices was about the same in 1928 as in 1870, after wide fluctuations.

Table 14

Prices of import and export commodities and the price of silver from 1870 to 1931[a]

Year	Average value of silver content of C$1	Index of wholesale prices of import and export commodities, 1867-1871 = 100
1870	US$ 1.02	98
1880	0.88	84
1890	0.81	97
1900	0.48	155
1910	0.42	205
1920	0.79	252
1927	0.44	277
1928	0.45	286
1929	0.42	297
1930	0.30	330
1931	0.22	340

[a]Source: Silver prices from *Annual Reports* of the U. S. Director of the Mint; price index from L. S. Hsu *et al.*, *Silver and Prices in China* (Ministry of Industries, Shanghai, 1935), pp. 2-4.

The chief indexes are in terms of silver, and from November 1935 in *fapi.* Some indexes in coppers have also been compiled. Official series of indexes in terms of silver compiled by the central government have been published since World War I. In addition, series dating back to 1913 have been prepared by Nankai University for North China; by the University of Nanking for

Shanghai and Tientsin (using for the latter Nankai data); and by the Provincial Bureau of Agriculture and Industry for Canton.[5]

Beginning in 1919, the Bureau of Markets of the Finance Ministry compiled indexes of prices at Shanghai, which were published in monthly bulletins. In 1929, the National Tariff Commission assumed this task. The most important single index was of wholesale prices at Shanghai, reported in terms of *taels* until 1933 and then in dollars. The index covered 153 items, grouped by commodities and by stages of production, and was a simple geometric average. There were indexes of export and import prices, based on 66 and 82 items, respectively, being weighted arithmetic averages. The Commission also compiled and published a cost of living index for Shanghai.

Besides its own indexes, the Bureau of Markets and later the Commission published indexes of wholesale prices for Canton and North China (Tientsin), based on 1926 as 100; and for Changsha, Hankow, Nanking, and Tsingtao based on 1930 as 100. The Canton index was compiled by the Kwangtung Provincial Statistical Bureau; the Tientsin index by Nankai University's Institute of Economics; the Changsha index by the provincial authorities; and the other indexes by the Ministry of Industries. Table 15 shows the chief annual indexes of prices and cost of living from 1921 to 1937. Table 16 shows annual indexes of import and export prices from 1926 to 1936. Monthly indexes for 1929 to 1937 are shown in Appendix 12.[6]

As to prices in the interior in terms of coppers, there are no comprehensive studies. J. Lossing Buck collected data of prices of leading commodities in two inland places that he considered typical, in Chihli and Shansi Provinces, for 1864 to 1923. The indexes showed about a threefold rise of prices in each place in the decade to 1923. Overissue and debasement of copper coins was a chief factor. Opening of communications also led to higher prices for products such as grains.[7]

Agricultural prices took a sharp drop as the effects of the worldwide depression reached China. Ta-chung Liu has prepared an index of agricultural prices for 1931 to 1936 based on a weighted average of prices of leading commodities (Appendix 13). This shows a drop of about 40 per cent from 1931 to the period 1933 to 1936. A study by Buck and his colleagues of the ratio of prices received to prices paid by farmers shows that the ratio improved from 54.9 per cent in 1906, based on 1926 as

100, to 107.6 in 1929. But then it fell sharply, to 68.3 in 1933.[8] Details of a further study for 1929-1937 are summarized in Appendix 13. They are only samples from four widely separated areas. They show wide variations in both prices received and prices paid, especially the former. The terms of exchange of produce for purchases moved against the farmer when he was getting low prices—even though he had more to sell when low prices were caused by glut. For example, at Nanking in 1933, prices received were 60 per cent of those in the base year 1931; whereas, the figure was 85 per cent for prices paid. Because subsistence farming was the rule, crops sold and purchases made are but part of the picture. The rural people were also at the mercy of weather, which could bring famine or flood. The figures in these samples suggest how precarious was the farmer's lot.

Because of lack of modern means of transport most prices in this land of thousands of villages were greatly dependent on local conditions. Prices of ordinary goods of local production and consumption commonly were unbelievably low in terms of foreign currency, as were of course the incomes of those who bought and sold them. A missionary told me that when he went to China in 1900 he could buy a thousand eggs in West China for C $1, which then was worth about half an American dollar. A generation later there were reports that 300 or more eggs could be bought there with a silver dollar.

The generally used price indexes can be criticized as representing the situation at Shanghai and other semimodernized centers, rather than in the countryside and China as a whole. Export and import prices largely reflected world markets and changes in exchange rates. Import items included some items not of great importance to the mass of consumers. The general indexes of wholesale prices are thus affected by including export and import items with others not important in foreign trade.

Ta-chung Liu in his study of national income in 1931 to 1936 prepared a deflator designed to take account of differing price movements in the more modernized and rural parts of the economy. For the former he used an average of wholesale prices in Shanghai and North China. For agriculture he prepared an index weighting leading commodities. The resulting deflator is as follows: 1931, 100; 1932, 77.5; 1933, 67.9; 1934, 63.0; 1935, 63.8; and 1936, 69.0.[9]

The indexes for major cities (Table 15 and Appendix 12),

Table 15

Yearly wholesale prices and cost of living from 1921 to 1937 (1926 = 100)[a]

	Wholesale Prices				Cost of living	
Period	Shanghai	Tientsin	Canton	Shanghai	Shanghai	Tientsin
1921	104.6	88.9	81.0	--	--	--
1922	98.6	86.4	85.1	--	--	--
1923	102.0	90.4	88.6	--	--	--
1924	97.9	93.6	94.0	--	--	--
1925	99.3	97.3	99.9	--	--	--
1926	100.0	100.0	100.0	100.0	100.0	100.0
1927	104.4	103.0	100.8	106.7	101.1	105.6
1928	101.7	108.0	96.8	102.5	93.2	109.5
1929	104.5	111.1	96.7	107.9	102.0	115.7
1930	114.8	115.9	101.4	121.8	116.8	118.8
1931	126.7	122.6	112.6	125.9	113.8	113.8

Continued

Table 15 (Continued)

Yearly wholesale prices and cost of living from 1921 to 1937 (1926 = 100)[a]

Period	Wholesale Prices			Cost of living		
	Shanghai	Tientsin	Canton	Shanghai	Shanghai	Tientsin
1932	112.4	112.9	113.8	119.1	108.1	105.2
1933	103.8	101.0	104.5	107.2	97.2	92.5
1934	97.1	92.3	94.3	106.2	97.4	89.7
1935	96.4	95.5	84.6	106.6	98.7	99.0
1936	108.5	110.6	105.4	113.3	105.0	113.3
1937 (1st half)	123.8	130.0	118.6	118.7	108.8	123.5

[a] Source: Publications of the National Tariff Commission. The wholesale price indexes were compiled as follows: for Shanghai by that body from 1929, and previously by the Bureau of Markets of the Finance Ministry; for Tientsin by Nankai University; and for Canton by the Kwangtung Provincial Government. The indexes of cost of living were compiled as follows: for Shanghai, the left-hand column by the National Tariff Commission, and the other column by the Shanghai Municipal Council; and for Tientsin by Nankai University.

Table 16

Terms of trade from 1926 to 1936[a,b]

	Nankai and adjusted index (1913 = 100)	National Tariff Commission price index: Exports	Imports	Import over export prices
1926	98.6	100.0	100.0	100.0
1927	108.6	106.1	107.3	101.1
1928	100.4	104.5	102.6	98.3
1929	93.1	105.2	107.7	102.3
1930	102.5	108.3	126.7	116.9
1931	116.0	107.5	150.2	135.0
1932	128.6	90.4	140.2	155.2
1933	142.7	82.0	132.3	161.4
1934	136.1	71.7	132.1	184.9
1935	122.9	77.6	128.4	165.6
1936	109.4	96.1	141.7	147.3

[a] Source: Nankai and adjusted index, Chi-Ming Hou, *Foreign Investment and Economic Development in China, 1840-1937* (Cambridge, 1965), pp. 197-198; National Tariff Commission, *An Annual Report of Shanghai Commodity Prices, 1936* (Shanghai, 1937), p. 22.

[b] Manchurian trade excluded after 1931.

despite defects, are the only comprehensive series covering 1921 to 1937. The several indexes of wholesale prices and cost of living differ in detail, but their movements are similar.[10] These indexes, qualified by the less complete data showing the price situation in agriculture, are a serviceable guide to the nature of currency developments and their bearing on the economy.

The silver standard: pro's and con's

The foreign exchange value of China's silver currency fluctuated widely over many years in terms of gold standard currencies, with a falling trend from 1873 until 1932. In 1932, a sharp rise began, augmented by the American silver-buying policy. This policy forced China to abandon the free silver standard in October 1934, and to adot a managed currency system a year later.

In the steadier years, the range of exchange fluctuation was around 10 per cent, but in some years it was 25 per cent or more. From 1873 to 1928, silver exchange rates fell irregularly to less than half their former level in terms of gold. Exchange fluctuations roughly coincided with fluctuations in the world silver price, but not precisely. The exchange and silver markets were free, and silver could be shipped between China and London and New York at a cost of 2 to 3 per cent including interest. That limited the extent to which exchange rates could depart from parity in any extended period. But the divergence was affected by market conditions of the day, and at times was close to 5 per cent. Movements in exchange could be large, and the market was highly speculative.

Both short-term fluctuations in rates and long-term changes in the level of rates had important effects. Fluctuations were of immediate importance to those concerned with foreign trade. They added an element of uncertainty to ordinary business risks. To protect against these fluctuations, traders commonly settled exchange forward, buying or selling foreign currencies for delivery as of a future date. Thus they could cover themselves during the period between payments in one currency and receipts in another.

The process was this. Importers not wishing to speculate on the future exchange rate would fix with a bank, on the basis of the current exchange market, the rate they would later have to pay after their goods arrived. Similarly exporters would fix the rate they would receive from sale of foreign currency at the time when they would be paid for the goods shipped abroad. Thus the banks could count on a demand for and supply of foreign currencies in the future, and set them off. In addition, there were many speculators, both foreign traders and others, who would make future contracts with the banks. And the banks at times would take positions, being overbought or oversold in foreign currencies. Thus an active foreign exchange market developed, centered at Shanghai.

Yet exchange fluctuations were disturbing despite facilities for hedging the risk. For example, an importer who had settled exchange at a rate that proved unfavorable would find it hard to compete with importers who had been more fortunate. And a Chinese buyer of the goods might renege on his contract and perhaps, in the pidgin-English term of the times, disappear to

"Ningpo more far." In any event, the covering of exchange risk was a cost. Existence of the risk led those connected with foreign trade to allow a larger profit margin accordingly.

Longer term changes in the level of exchange, when considerable, spread broadly in the economy and caused dislocations. Although prices in China of goods entering into the import and export trade were sensitive to changes in rates of exchange, the great mass of general prices of goods and services throughout the country was not at once affected. The economy was largely decentralized, and lack of modern transport limited the movement of goods. Thus prices at a given time and place were determined primarily by local factors. But in the more modernized areas a drop in exchange tended to lead to silver imports, adding to bank reserves and the supply of money, and hence tending to raise general prices. Silver would flow out to other parts of the country, adding to the supply of money and credit there. Conversely, rising exchange tended to cause silver exports and to draw silver from the interior to Shanghai, thus causing a deflationary tendency.

Whether exchange depreciation under the silver standard made more adverse the terms of trade has long been the subject of analysis. Falling exchange tends to promote exports, and to discourage imports. It has been argued that, in a country with depreciating exchange, wages and other costs of producing export goods tend to rise only slowly, while exporters receive increasing sums in local currency when converting foreign currencies received. Meanwhile, the argument goes, import costs in local currency tend to be marked up promptly. As a result, it is argued, the country tends to give up a growing proportion of its labor and resources to obtain imports.[11]

This argument that the terms of trade were adverse because of falling exchange has been applied to China. The situation since 1867 has been studied by several scholars, the basic study having been published in 1930 by Franklin L. Ho of Nankai University. He prepared and later revised a series of import and export prices derived from quantities and values reported in the trade returns. Chi-ming Hou has prepared an adjusted index of these data, based on 1913 as 100.[12] This index (import prices over export prices relative to 1931) shows wide fluctuations but little net change in the latter part of the 19th century, the index rising only from 79.0 in 1867 to 82.3 in 1900. But thereafter the trend was unfavorable, rising to 100.4 in 1928 and 109.4 in

1936. Thus the overall deterioration shown for 1867 to 1936 was about 40 per cent. Table 16 shows the Ho-Hou index for 1926 to 1936 together with an index using the export and import price indexes of the National Tariff Commission based on 1926 prices instead of 1913.

But even though th Ho-Hou index shows little net change from 1913 to 1928 and 1936, wide fluctuations continued, nearly all above 100. The index rose to 155.6 in 1920; fell to around 100 in the twenties; and rose again to 142.7 in 1933 before dropping to 109.4 in 1936. The index of Tariff Commission data based on 1926 shows much greater fluctuations, with a rise to a high of 184.9 in 1934 and to 147.3 in 1936.

Hou finds no "causal or even correlational relationship" between the drop in the world silver price and China's terms of trade. Periods of falling silver prices, he believed, were sometimes associated with deterioration in the terms of trade and sometimes with improvement. Hou concluded that factors more weighty than the fall of exchange determined the terms of trade: as to exports, China's competitive position in world markets; and, as to imports, the fact that China provided an insignificant part of the demand for goods whose prices were determined by other factors. Thus he felt that "the terms of trade after the turn of the century were independent of the exchange depreciation."[13] I am inclined to accept this general conclusion. During the deterioration of the terms of trade after 1928, which is much greater when 1926 is the base (Table 16), powerful factors other than exchange depreciation to 1932 and the subsequent rise were at work. Depression abroad impaired capacity to buy China's exports, while rising rates of duty affected import prices.

In appraising the silver standard we must also note that falling exchange from 1873 to 1932 was accompanied by inflation and its usual consequences. thus creditors such as holders of long-term obligations payable in silver lost when silver slumped, to such extent as their purchasing power fell in terms of goods and services bought, but not as measured by the gold value of silver. Conversely obligors, such as borrowers or long-term debtors, gained. after 1932, when the exchange value of china's currency rose and severe deflation set in, the position was reversed.

The silver standard also created uncertainty and risk for the government in budgeting payments on the national debt, nearly three-fourths of which was in foreign currencies. As of 1928, these payments were equivalent to about US $35 million yearly, and restoration of payments on debts in arrears would call for considerably more. Revenues were in silver, including customs duties that were mainly specific. Moreover, in 1928 the falling exchange value of the silver currency seemed likely to continue. In the year from mid-1928 the cost of foreign debt service grew by about C $15 million, or nearly 15 per cent, because of exchange depreciation. It was to remedy this that China placed collection of import duties on a gold basis early in 1930 (Chapter 3).

Looking at the other side, China's use of silver as a standard differing from that of other countries insulated the country to some extent from economic fluctuations elsewhere. This was notably the case in 1929 to 1931, when China largely escaped the worldwide deflation because of being on the silver standard. The silver price fell along with commodity prices generally. Average prices in China actually rose by around one-fourth in that period, while prices fell drastically in gold standard countries. The course of prices in China under the silver standard is treated on pages 166 to 172 and in Chapters 8 to 10. Without question, China had a net benefit from the slump of silver in 1929 to 1931. Internal business was not depressed by deflation, as in gold standard countries. While lower buying power elsewhere reduced demand for China's exports, they were cheapened in terms of foreign currencies and were better maintained than exports of most other countries.

But China in turn suffered acute deflation after 1931. In September 1931 the pound went off gold, followed soon by the currencies of Japan and other countries and later by the dollar. Then came the American silver-buying policy. The resulting rise in the exchange value of China's silver currency drained away large amounts of silver, bringing in deflation and depression. Conditions were aggravated by Japan's seizure of Manchuria, the leading source of exports and whose trade balance with the rest of the world was favorable. Internal disturbances also aggravated the depression, as did the great flood of 1931.

A further argument for staying with silver was that China was accustomed to silver, and that it was harder to tamper with a commodity standard than with a gold-exchange standard. Better to suffer known and measurable evils, it was said, than to risk those that could be much greater.

Intelligent opinion in China favored in principle moving to the gold standard, to join the company of leading nations. It was realized that after the value of silver slipped such countries as India and Japan had abandoned silver for gold. But in China the silver standard was backed by long usage; and the business community was conservative and resistant to change, at least unless it could be done with super-safety. Everyone was quite aware that a change would involve serious problems. The Financial Conference of July 1928 resolved "to work toward ultimate adoption of the gold standard." The issue was highly sensitive, and any suggestion of definite action to that end in 1928-1929 touched off feelings of lack of confidence and led to exchange speculation.

Pre-1929 projects for currency reform

Around the turn of the century there was much interest in currency reform for China. As the price of defeat in the war with Japan in 1894-1895, China had to pay an indemnity, provided by contracting in Europe loans equivalent to US $233 million. In 1901 came the Boxer Indemnity, equivalent to about US $334 million. Payments on this debt of over half a billion dollars had to be made by buying foreign gold currencies with silver of uncertain value. Along with the selfish interest of China's creditors in being paid, China had an interest in being better able to carry the burden and gaining fiscal resources to cover the cost of debt payments. There was also the broader motive of promoting the nation's progress by improving the monetary and fiscal structure.

Sir Robert Hart as Inspector General of Customs urged collection of duties in terms of gold (Chapter 3). He also suggested in 1903 a gold standard for China, but his plan was not worked out on a practicable basis—the subject being outside the fields of administration and fiscal affairs in which his ability was so outstanding.[14]

International attention to the possibility of a gold standard for China was enhanced by Japan's shift from silver to the gold standard shortly before 1900, aided by receipt of the indemnity from China. The United States and the European powers took an interest in the problem. In 1903, China asked the United States to consider the possibility of international cooperation in stabilizing China's exchange with gold standard countries. The American government appointed a commission that studied the problems in China and discussed them in Europe. The members were C. A. Conant, H. H. Hanna, and J. W. Jenks, a leading economist who was a professor at Cornell University. Their proposal was for gradual introduction of a gold-exchange standard, based on a unit equal to US $0.50. The European governments agreed in principle, but there were some reservations as to procedure. In China there was both support and hesitancy. The upshot was that nothing happened.[15]

In 1911-1912, Dr. G. Vissering, President of the Java Bank of Batavia (now Jakarta), served as Monetary Adviser to China. He concluded that immediate and universal introduction of a gold standard or gold-exchange standard in China was not practicable. He recommended that the existing silver currency continue to circulate, but that a gold-exchange standard be started parallel with it. China was used to a variety of money so that a dual currency would be readily accepted. A central bank would be established, which would create a gold unit equal to about US $0.25—a size that he believed most appropriate for China. The public could acquire this stable currency as deposits by paying in silver at the exchange rate of the day. With this silver the bank would acquire reserves in foreign currency. At first the new currency would be a unit of account transferable by check. Later gold bank notes would be issued, then subsidiary coins, seignorage on which would contribute to reserves; and finally the old silver and copper coins would be withdrawn and replaced by new coins. The new unit would be backed by reserves abroad according to principles of the gold-exchange standard. Vissering envisaged that full realization of the projected reform might take 20 to 30 years.[16]

Internal difficulties in China after the revolution of 1911, and the outbreak of World War I, prevented action on this well-devised plan. Other proposals less carefully worked out were put forward by Chinese and foreigners both before and after the Vissering plan, during the last years of the Empire and the period of the Peking regimes. But none of these received serious consideration.[17] In 1929, the subject of currency reform again came to the fore, when at China's invitation Professor E. W. Kemmerer of Princeton University came to China heading the Commission of Financial Experts.

Kemmerer project of 1929

Kemmerer's background of experience as a leading economist and currency expert was impressive. As a young man he presided over the successful introduction of the gold-exchange standard in the Philippines; he had aided several Latin-American countries with monetary reforms; and was the monetary expert of the Dawes Commission on German reparations in 1924. After nine months of work in China, he submitted his project to Finance Minister Soong in November 1929. It was made public the next spring.

The plan proposed a gold standard unit to be called the *sun* (after Sun Yat-sen), without actual gold circulation. The *sun* would be equal to US $0.40, which was the approximate value of the silver dollar in the fall of 1929. The choice of that parity was to permit easy adjustment of prices from a silver to a gold basis. After Kemmerer's departure, silver slumped drastically, and in the spring of 1930 he advised that he felt that the rate of exchange should consequently be lower than US $0.40.

Fiduciary silver *sun* coins would be issued, weighing 20 grams 0.800 fine. The fine silver content of 16 grams, or 246.912 grains, was about two-thirds of that of the current silver dollars. Subsidiary silver coins would be 50- and 20-cent pieces of 10 and 4 grams 0.720 fine. Their fine silver content, per *sun,* would be 222.22 grains or about 60 per cent of that of the current silver dollars. There would also be nickel 10- and 5-cent pieces, and coppers of 1- and 1/2-cent. Subsidiary coins would be firmly held at par by convertibility into the *sun*. The circulation of the old copper 10-*cash* coins would be contracted, to raise this value from around 300 to 200 per *sun*. Probably that would yield a profit because the value of the copper content of the coins mostly exceeded its monetary value.

The currency would be maintained at parity of exchange on the principles of the gold-exchange standard, with the help of a reserve mainly held abroad of at least 35 per cent of the value of gold standard coins in circulation. The reserve would be derived mainly from seignorage profits, which would provide silver to be sold. The eventual gross seignorage profits might reach US $330 million. Although the reform would be mostly self-supporting, it would be desirable to have a loan of US $10 to US $15 millions initially available to add to confidence, and if possible a further equivalent amount that could be drawn upon if necessary. The Central Bank would become a Central Reserve Bank with a monopoly of note issue, which would be backed by a reserve of at least 50 per cent consisting primarily of gold and deposits and short-term gold obligations.

The plan called for gradual introduction of the new currency, starting with the more modernized areas and extended throughout China as conditions might permit. Dates would be set for circulation of the new money, for its exclusive use in new contracts, and for conversion of old contracts at rates to be set.

The Kemmerer report recognized that reform would not be easy. It discussed and rejected other possible procedures. The method used in India in the nineties, of stopping coinage of silver and letting the growth of demand for money raise the exchange value of the currency, was dismissed as unwise. Besides the severe pains of deflation, the plan would interfere with obtaining the seignorage gains on coinage which had to be counted upon largely to create the needed reserve. The report also rejected the idea of unifying the currency on the basis of the silver dollar. The reasons were that this would be costly because of first coining and then recoining; that there would be two currency reforms in succession; and that it would take a long time.

Moreover, provision of a convenient subsidiary coinage involved problems that would be met under any plan of currency reform. It would not be easy to induce the public to accept silver coins whose metal content was below the monetary value. Subsidiary silver had long circulated on the basis of bullion value, and was below parity because it was overissued to gain seignorage profits. New lighter weight silver money would presumably be an important part of the reformed subsidiary circulation. Kemmerer believed it better to deal with this matter under a gold standard plan than first to try to reform the circulation on the silver standard.

In planning a system of subsidiary silver coins, the first problem was to find the right balance between conflicting forces. The silver coins, he believed, would need to be acceptable to the public by not having a silver content whose value was too far below monetary value. But the margin should not be so large as to give great inducement to counterfeiting. On the other hand, the margin should be great enough to prevent melting or export, if the price of silver rose. The solution proposed was a difference of about a third, which was influenced by the belief that the silver price in 1929 showed a downward trend.* A further problem was to devise means to maintain the subsidiary coins at par. That was to be done by ready convertibility into standard

*When the report was presented silver was worth about US$0.50 per ounce, and the melting point of the *sun* would have been US$0.77 3 /4 and of the subsidiary silver coins US$0.86 3 /8.

money, which in turn would be convertible into foreign gold currencies.

Publication of the report on March 30, 1930 was followed by more criticism than approval. The safety of a silver standard based on bullion value appealed to many. China's rulers had a long record of tampering with money. And there was inertia. China could "make do" with silver despite the difficulties which a large part of the people did not appreciate. Critics wondered where China, with her credit at a low ebb, could find the needed reserves abroad. "Faith and Hope," said one critic, ". . . will hardly produce Parity." Silver sales on any scale would further depress the slumping silver price, and the US $330 million which Kemmerer thought eventually might be realized was called "mythical."* With the time-honored practice of hoarding silver, lightweight coins would not be taken at face value. In addition, some provinces had their own mints and the government was not strong enough to prevent their counterfeiting national coins. And the national mint might "squeeze" or overissue the coins.

The exchange market was so sensitive, with silver slumping, that Minister Soong felt it necessary to let it be known that the government had no thought of immediate gold standard reform. In bidding farewell to Kemmerer, Soong expressed the hope that one of his successors as minister could give effect to the plan. Any prospect of early adoption of the gold standard would have been taken to mean large silver sales by China. Indeed the Kemmerer Commission's appointment and its work in 1929 had already added to weakness in the silver market. In 1930, China was one of the chief buyers of silver, and silver imports were large. Early in 1930, many, including Minister of Industries H. H. Kung, who was later to succeed Soong as Finance Minister, urged a duty to check the flow. Such action was clearly unwise because China was one of the largest buyers of silver and a duty would have been a blow to the world silver price. Exchange rates in China would have tended even more sharply downward, following silver.

For China, 1930 was a most difficult year, with internal revolts threatening the government. The worldwide depression

*Official sales of silver, 1935 to 1941, eventually realized US$253 million. Estimated total sales of Chinese silver in 1933 to 1941 were 1155 million ounces, probably equivalent to over half a billion American dollars. (See Table 17 in Chapter 8.)

was deepening. Conditions for basic monetary reform were far from favorable. So the government took no action on the Kemmerer report. But in January the collection of import duties in Customs Gold Units was adopted, to offset the rising cost of foreign debt payments (Chapter 3). That action was a move toward currency reform. But it was indicative of the delicate situation early in 1930 that Soong was unwilling to call the Customs Gold Unit the *sun,* to avoid any implication of a move to implement the Kemmerer report.

Early in 1931, Sir Arthur Salter, Director of the Economic and Financial Section of the League of Nations, visited China to advise on problems growing out of the worldwide depression and on problems of economic development. Conditions had greatly changed since the fall of 1929 when the Kemmerer report was presented. Salter's report[18] pointed out that China may not have lost by being on silver from 1929 to 1931. He analyzed the Kemmerer report in the light of the new situation. He agreed with part of the report, but made some penetrating suggestions for a different approach. Since the report was presented in 1929, silver had fallen by nearly half, and was still weak. He feared that any announcement that China was adopting the gold standard would cause a further precipitous drop, especially since governments such as India, Hong Kong, and Spain that held large amounts of silver might sell. He believed that for convenience China should have a monetary unit smaller than the US $0.40 which Kemmerer proposed, that being the approximate equivalent of the silver dollar in 1929. (Kemmerer advised, after silver slumped, that the new unit should be well below US $0.40.) Probably, said Salter, such a unit both for ease of transition and convenience would best have about the value of the silver dollar in 1931, which was about US $0.20 at its low.

In 1931, Salter also pointed out, financial conditions abroad were unfavorable to arranging the credit needed to support currency reform for China, and he favored a larger credit than Kemmerer proposed. In addition, Salter felt that the reduced demand for China's exports was an unfavorable factor in 1931, and that the reform should await a favorable trade situation. China's internal situation seemed likely to improve, but was still difficult with continuing political troubles, loans in arrears still unsettled, and a serious budgetary problem. The slump in silver made it necessary to rethink the plan for subsidiary silver coins.

He also feared that raising the value of coppers from 300 to 200 per dollar would bring hardship to the poorer classes paid in dollars, since prices in coppers were unlikely to drop *pari passu* with rise of their value in silver. He felt that a first step should be to do away with the *tael* as a monetary unit as a measure of simplification.

As a method of moving to gold, Salter favored a combination of the Kemmerer and Vissering plans. He proposed that the Central Bank open gold accounts with a US $0.20 cent unit, and also issue notes based upon that unit. At first the reserve should be 100 per cent, but as confidence was gained the percentage could be cautiously reduced. Next token coins would be issued. The reforms's progress would be flexible, making use of procedures on the lines of the Kemmerer plan. There need be no pressure to force silver on the market.

In the fall of 1931, two major events took place: Japan's invasion of Manchuria on September 18, and Britain's departure from gold three days later. Apart from anything else, these profoundly important events ruled out for some time the feasibility of gold standard reform. There were several periods of fighting with Japan, the most serious being at Shanghai early in 1932. Internal dissension continued, although lessened by the confrontation with Japan. Further, the uncertainty about the gold value of the pound, dollar, and other currencies led to wide fluctuations of exchange. Until there was a measure of stability in international financial and economic affairs, the major argument that a gold standard would afford exchange stability for China was without weight.

Standardization of the silver dollar and abolition of the tael

In retrospect, the repeated expressions of opinion in favor of abolishing the *tael* as the first step in monetary reform appear as a trend adapted to the conditions of the time. The record shows a persistent view in influential quarters that the silver standard should be improved before moving to gold, the latter being the eventual aim of most of those seriously concerned. Thus the report of the American commissioners in 1903 stated that Britain and Russia favored provision of a uniform currency in China before moving to a fixed gold value. The Shanghai General Chamber of Commerce then took a similar view.[19] In 1928, the National Economic and Financial Conferences favored abolishing the *tael* as a monetary unit, to be replaced by the dollar, before working toward an ultimate gold standard.[20] In 1929, several of Kemmerer's associates on the Commission favored action to abolish the *tael* unit and improve the silver standard as a first step in currency reform. They wanted to take advantage of an opportunity to introduce the big dollar in South China in place of the dollar representing five depreciated 20-cent coins. But Kemmerer preferred leaving the silver standard alone and moving directly to introduce the gold-exchange standard. In 1931 Salter, as mentioned, favored ending the *tael* as a monetary unit.

Despite the shelving of gold standard reform after 1929, the acute drop in exchange promoted active interest in currency matters. In addition, in 1932, the new modern mint at Shanghai was ready to operate, and Clifford Hewitt, a competent American minting technician, was present as an adviser. Three well-qualified Chinese experts spent some time in the Philadelphia Mint in 1931, preparing to act as department heads on return to Shanghai. Designs of new coins were made, and the dies were ready. For years the use of silver dollars had been growing. They were coined by various mints and, along with Mexican and other dollars, were more or less interchangeable despite variations in fine silver content.

In 1932, the range of *tael*-C $ rates widened. For the 11 years between 1921 and 1931 there was little month-to-month variation in average monthly rates between 72.01 and 72.69 *taels* per C $100, with an overall average of 72.31. But in 1932 there was an extreme range of around 8 per cent, between about 68 and 74 *taels* per C $100 (Appendix 11). The high rates resulted from the exceptional demand for dollars because of the Japanese invasion of the Shanghai area early in 1932. After that incident was settled in the spring of 1932, the trend sharply reversed, and rates dropped to previously unknown levels below 70. There was a great flow of silver dollars to Shanghai from the rest of the country. Central China suffered a serious loss of crops from severe floods, and South China had to import rice formerly obtained from Central China. The cheapness of dollars made it profitable to convert large quantities into *sycee*. That tended to correct rates by making dollars scarcer and *taels* more plentiful.

The instability of *tael*-dollar rates caused capricious gains and losses, and in particular the cheapness of dollars caused hardship to debtors in *taels* with assets in dollars. The movement grew to do away with an avoidable element of monetary risk. In

July 1932, Minister Soong appointed a committee of bankers to recommend the weight and fineness of a new silver dollar, the rate for conversion of *tael* obligations to dollars, and measures to promote public understanding of and confidence in the reform. They proposed a dollar weighing 26.6971 grams (412 grains) 0.880 fine, containing 23.493448 grams (362.56 grains) of fine silver. The latter figure was practically equal to the content of the old dollar less estimated minting charges of 1-3/4 per cent.* *Tael* contracts would be converted to dollars at 71.15 Shanhai *taels* per C $100. To promote confidence, the government should assure the free import and export of silver; free coinage of silver, with a minting charge of 1-3/4 per cent; minting of silver bars 999 fine in ingots of C $1000; dismantling all mints but that at Shanghai; and creation of a public board to verify the mint's output.

The recommendation involved a debasement of 1.739 per cent below the legal weight of the old national dollar. The Committee relied on a sample of dollars showing a deficiency of 1.15 per cent in silver content. Advisers Lockhart and Young felt that the sample was too small and urged further tests. These showed that individual coins varied considerably from the standard, but that the newer coins averaged 0.31 per cent light, and the older coins 0.67 per cent. Based on the latter figure the *de facto* debasement would be about 1 per cent.

At the end of 1932 Minister Soong announced that the Central Mint would be opened in March to coin into dollars silver tendered by the public, at a rate of conversion of C $100 for 71.5 Shanghai *taels*. On March 8, 1933, the coinage law was promulgated. It embodied the provisions recommended by the experts as to weight and fineness of the new dollar. Coinage was free but not gratuitous, as a coinage charge of 2-1/4 per cent was fixed. The mint also would make C $1000 "A" bars 0.999 fine, and C $1000 "B" bars 0.880 fine, at a charge of 2-1/4 per cent. A refining charge might be added for certain kinds of silver tendered. Provision was made also for an advisory committee representing the public.

The new dollar coins had an attractive design with the head of Sun Yat-sen on one side and on the other a junk. To make the design harder to counterfeit, the junk was shown against rays of

*China's silver dollar pursuant to the law of 1914 was 0.890 fine and had a fine silver content of 23.909049 grams, equal to 368.97 grains or about 77 per cent of a Troy ounce.

the sun and with three gulls flying overhead. The latter features were promptly criticized, on the ground that the rising sun suggested Japan and the gulls were like the planes that had attacked Shanghai in 1932. So these features were at once removed. Counterfeiting of the dollars did not become serious. With the modern machinery of the new mint, the coins were the finest made in China and making facsimiles was not easy.

On March 10, 1933, Soong announced an official rate of 0.715 Shanghai *taels* per dollar. On April 6 a government measure was announced whereby *tael* transactions were banned and existing contracts were to be settled at .715 per dollar. An export duty of 2-1/4 per cent on silver was also imposed, except that Central Bank bars could be freely exported without duty.[21]

The transition to the new situation was smooth, although some critics had said that a considerable time should be allowed for the new dollar first to become well established. After a few days, exchange was quoted in dollars instead of *taels*. The rate of 0.715 was generally accepted as fair. The matter of debasement caused no difficulty in practice. At first there were objections, especially from some foreign banks and merchants, on the ground that in the past the government had tampered with coinage and that the *tael* as a definite weight was safer than any coin. A "silver clause" stating the weight and fineness of dollars was put in some contracts. But that proved quite unnecessary. The mint did excellent work under the supervision of Lott Wei and Robert J. Grant, formerly Director of the United States Mint, who was engaged to succeed Hewitt as Adviser on Minting. They were aided by the three competent Chinese technicians trained at the Philadelphia Mint. Repeated tests turned up no coins below standard. Some flight of capital was reported, but it was not of much consequence.

The new silver dollars were in great demand, as were also the mint "B" bars of C $1000 each. From March 1933 through October 1935, the mint coined C $133 million in dollars and C $56 million in bars, mostly "B" bars.[22] Despite nationalization of silver by the currency reform of November 3, 1935, coinage of silver dollars continued until the end of the year, about C $5 million more being made. This was partly to keep the mint occupied pending the planned early issuance of minor coins, but also was a sop to public attachment to silver and to show that there was no devaluation of the silver dollar. Furthermore, about C $5 million of "B" mint bars were produced after the reform through June 1936.

The abolition of the *tael* accomplished a real and useful simplification of the currency. And the existence of a modern mint with a qualified personnel cleared the way for basic coinage reform. After the 1935 currency reform, the mint was in position to concentrate on making token coins for use under the managed currency standard, which were issued as from February 1936 as described in Chapter 10.

8: Silver, Down and Up

The drastic slump in silver in 1928-1932 and its sharp rise thereafter gave rise to events that were to prove of tremendous importance to China and the whole world, as discussed in Chapter 12.

Since China produces almost no silver, its stock was practically all imported. Cumulative recorded net imports from 1888 to 1931 were 1037 million fine ounces, mostly in 1920 to 1931. Then the tide turned and from 1932 each of the next ten years showed net exports. The total of recorded exports together with wartime shipments not included in the trade returns was 848 million fine ounces. Estimated sales of demonetized silver from China in 1932 to 1941, including smuggled exports, totaled 1155 million ounces, or more than recorded cumulative imports since 1888. The figures of silver movements are shown in Table 17. Official sales in 1935 to 1941 totaled 550 million ounces (Appendix 15). Private sales including smuggled silver were thus of the order of 600 million ounces.

Slump in silver

From parity with gold at about 16 to 1 before 1873, the gold value of China's silver dollar fell by about half in 20 years. The drop was largely the result of abandonment of bimetallism in favor of gold by several European countries, which led to sales of demonetized silver. And in 1893, India closed her mints to silver. Meanwhile silver production grew. From 1893 to 1928, China's silver exchange fluctuated widely but with little net change. At about the end of World War I, the silver dollar rose sharply and even exceeded the value of the gold dollar, because of abnormal demand for silver and for Chinese goods. During 1920, silver returned to a more normal value, similar to its range from the mid-1890's to 1917. In 1921 to 1928 silver was fairly steady, yet the range of exchange for US $100 was between C $170 and C $250.

The four-year slump that began in 1928 was both sharper and

deeper than the long-time slump from 1870 to 1890, and was comparable to the drop in the early nineties. From about US $0.45 in 1928 the value of the silver dollar fell to below US $0.20 in 1932, the lowest ever recorded. Silver fell to under US $0.25 per fine ounce in New York and 12d. in London. The course of exchange rates from 1920 to 1937 for the American dollar and sterling is shown in Appendix 10. These rates moved in rough proportion to the price of silver until China restricted silver exports in October 1934. Chart 1 shows the wide fluctuations of these rates from 1927 to 1937, and the diverging value of the silver content of the Chinese dollar (0.7555 oz) from October 1934.

The slump after 1928 had several causes. Demand for silver in industry and the arts declined because of the depression. In India, which from time immemorial had been a large buyer of silver for hoarding, demand fell off as the depression cut the demand for Indian exports. Moreover, India became a seller of demonetized silver, along with some other countries, thus adding to the supply. China was a large buyer of silver in 1928-1929, but then her demand slackened along with the reduction of demand for China's exports. Appointment of the Kemmerer Commission, which recommended China's changing from silver to gold, was also a factor that weakened silver in 1928-1929.

Silver loan projects

The slump in silver occasioned a variety of schemes to bolster the price. The earliest to affect China was for a large American loan of silver to China. The general aim of this 1930 project was to take silver off the market at good prices, preferably by organizing an international silver pool. The acquisition and/or repayment of the silver, it was intended, would sharply raise the price. It was also argued that such a loan would bring about a large market for American exports.

A chief proponent of a silver loan was Senator Key Pittman of Nevada, whom Herbert Feis characterized as "that unprincipled man without any genuine concern for the general welfare." Pittman asserted that, with the aid of such a loan, "our commerce with restored China would be increased tenfold, and [the Chinese] would almost immediately consume all our surplus wheat, greatly reduce our surplus production of automobiles, lumber, and manufactured articles, and furnish a demand for more silver, taken with the present demand, than the mines of

Table 17

Net silver imports and exports from 1888 to 1941[a, b] *(In millions of fine ounces)*

	Imports	Exports	Cumulative	Estimates of smuggled exports		Estimated total sales of demonetized silver from China[c]
				Bank of China	E. Kann	
1888-1920	225	--	225	--	--	--
1921	39	--	264	--	--	--
1922	48	--	312	--	--	--
1923	81	--	393	--	--	--
1924	32	--	425	--	--	--
1925	76	--	501	--	--	--
1926	64	--	565	--	--	--
1927	79	--	644	--	--	--
1928	129	--	773	--	--	--
1929	128	--	901	--	--	--

Continued

Table 17 (Continued)

Net silver imports and exports from 1888 to 1941[a, b] *(In millions of fine ounces)*

				Estimates of smuggled exports		
	Imports	Exports	Cumulative	Bank of China	E. Kann	Estimated total sales of demonetized silver from China[c]
1930	81	--	982	--	--	--
1931	55	--	1037	--	--	--
1932	--	9	1028	--	--	--
1933	--	11	1017	--	--	11
1934	--	194	823	15	15	200
1935	--	45	778	174	113	190
1936	--	188	590	30	23	302
1937	--	301[d]	289	--	--	178
1938	--	60	229	--	--	234

(Continued)

Table 17 (Continued)

Silver imports and exports from 1888 to 1941[a, b] *(In millions of fine ounces)*

	Imports	Exports	Cumulative	Estimates of smuggled exports: Bank of China	Estimates of smuggled exports: E. Kann	Estimated total sales of demonetized silver from China[c]
1939	--	20	208	--	--	21
1940	--	17	191	--	--	17
1941	--	2	189	--	--	2
Totals	1037	848		219	151	1155

[a] Source: Customs figures for 1888 to 1933 as converted to ounces (Haikwan *taels* 1 = C$1.558 and C$1 = 0.755 oz.) are from ***Chinese Economic and Statistical Review***, May 1934, p. 8. Figures for 1934 to 1938 are converted to ounces from C$ figures in ***Central Bank of China Bulletin***, Summer 1941, p. 289; and for 1939 to 1941 I have added from my records the amounts of Central Bank exports not shown in published figures because they were confidential during the war period for security reasons. Figures of smuggled exports are converted to ounces from estimates of the balance of payments in the Bank of China's annual reports, and from E. Kann's estimates quoted in Leavens, ***Silver Money***, p. 303. Estimated sales of demonetized silver from China for 1933-1938 are from Handy and Harman's ***Annual Review of the Silver Market***, as quoted by Leavens, ***Silver Money***, p. 354; and for 1939-1941 from my records of Central Bank exports.

[b] The Customs figures of import and export must be taken with some reserve, especially after 1930 in the years when smuggling was rife and during the war period when the Central Bank made shipments confidentially not appearing in the trade returns. Also Customs figures include certain shipments to and from Hong Kong that really represented internal movement between South China and Shanghai. Such shipments affect the figures for 1931 to 1933 in particular. Further, shipments to and from Dairen in Kwantung Territory leased to Japan were treated as internal trade to mid-1932, but after Japan's seizure of Manchuria as external trade. During the second half of 1932 about C$35 million of silver was exported to the leased territory. Were the 1932 figures compiled as before, 1932 would have shown net import.

[c] Data from 1933 to 1938 from Handy and Harman; for 1939 to 1944 from the Central Bank.

[d] All of these exports were in the second half year.

the world could supply." In October 1930, a plan to lend China several hundred million ounces was being considered by a subcommittee of the Committee on Foreign Relations, headed by Pittman. Also in the news was a self-appointed organization with the imposing title of "International Silver Commission," promoted by ex-Senator F. J. Cannon of Utah. They talked of a grandiose but vague plan to lend to China 500 million ounces at low interest, to be provided in instalments for productive purposes.[1]

The idea of a silver loan was promoted in China by Hu Hanmin, President of the Legislative Yuan. Hu and some associates viewed a silver loan as an easy way to solve China's financial problems, and to avoid the need for the stern policies of control, taxation, and debt settlement advocated by Finance Minister Soong. They were equally ignorant of finance and of the procedures at Washington that were requisite for realizing any such scheme.[2]

In October 1930, Hu sent Judge Paul M. Linebarger, an elderly former associate of Sun Yat-sen, to the United States, with some form of mandate from the State Council. Upon reaching San Francisco, Linebarger let it be known that he was seeking a 50-year loan of a billion ounces of silver at 2 per cent interest. When this report was telegraphed to China, Soong at once stated that "there had been no change in the declared policy of the Ministry of Finance not to seek loans abroad until the Government had made a settlement covering foreign and domestic loans in arrears." The silver loan project, he considered, would be "obviously detrimental" to China.[3]

Yet the talk of loan schemes continued in both the United States and China. On January 15, 1931, Pittman stated that his subcommittee would recommend a silver loan, which it shortly did but without eliciting action. It was even reported to China that the loan had been granted. The Chinese minister at Washington, C. C. Wu, explored the subject with Pittman, and indicated partiality to the idea, apparently based on some word from Nanking.[4] The repeated reports from Washington, often far from clear, were upsetting to the Shanghai market.

The attitude in China toward a silver loan was somewhat clarified when Hu resigned early in March. He was placed under house arrest, and later was allowed to go to Hong Kong. On March 15, President Chiang stated that "We must settle our own financial problem and do not wish to contract foreign loans."[5] Yet Pittman persisted, and in the spring went to China to look into the silver situation and with a view to promoting a silver loan.[6] And Linebarger stayed in the United States until mid-1932. His report told of making propaganda for a silver loan, including radio broadcasts. He said that the silver senators "are all high-minded, noble-spirited gentlemen, who regard China with great sympathy.... Hence my mission had an immediate and warm support from these patriotic legislators."[7]

The loan project remained dormant until the latter part of 1933. Then Sir Arthur Salter and Jean Monnet were in China in connection with the work of China's National Economic Council, which had been set up with the aid of the League of Nations to promote development. They and I discussed the possibility of using the unexpended part of the 1933 American Cotton and Wheat Loan (Chapter 16) to buy silver for use in China for productive purposes. I doubted the feasibility of making such an arrangement, and saw difficulties and risks in making foreign exchange arrangements for repayment that would protect China. Pittman would have wanted the loan repaid by buying silver in the market, or otherwise in kind. We prepared, however, a message of inquiry to Washington, which was sent on January 27, 1934, by Finance Minister Kung and T. V. Soong, head of the Council. But nothing came of this move.

China and the depression, 1929 to 1932

For China the depression did not date from 1929 but from the winter of 1931-1932. Until then China was not very seriously affected—less than any other important country. China was almost alone in having rising prices instead of a catastrophic fall. Silver standard prices rose by more than one-fourth, to a peak in the second half of 1931, while in gold standard countries they fell by about one-third (Charts 2 and 3). The drop in the value of silver was mainly in terms of gold rather than goods. The slump in silver accompanied a drop of commodity prices generally in terms of gold, in many cases greater than the drop in silver.[8]

A view commonly taken, chiefly outside China and notably among Americans with a stake in the silver industry, was that the drop in silver was a great disaster for China. Monetary holdings in China were large. The Customs estimated that as of 1931 about 1700 million silver dollars were in circulation (equivalent to about 1280 million ounces, taking C $1 as 0.7555 ounce), of

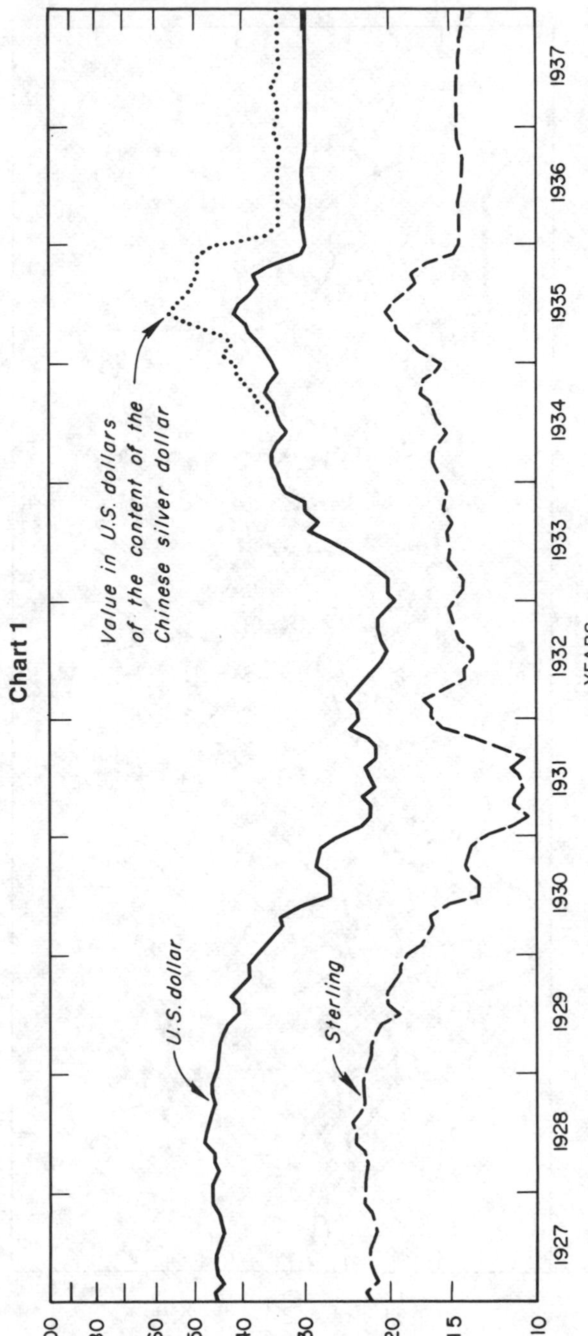

Foreign exchange value of Chinese currency, 1927-1937, and from July 1934 the diverging value in American dollars of the content of the Chinese silver dollar.

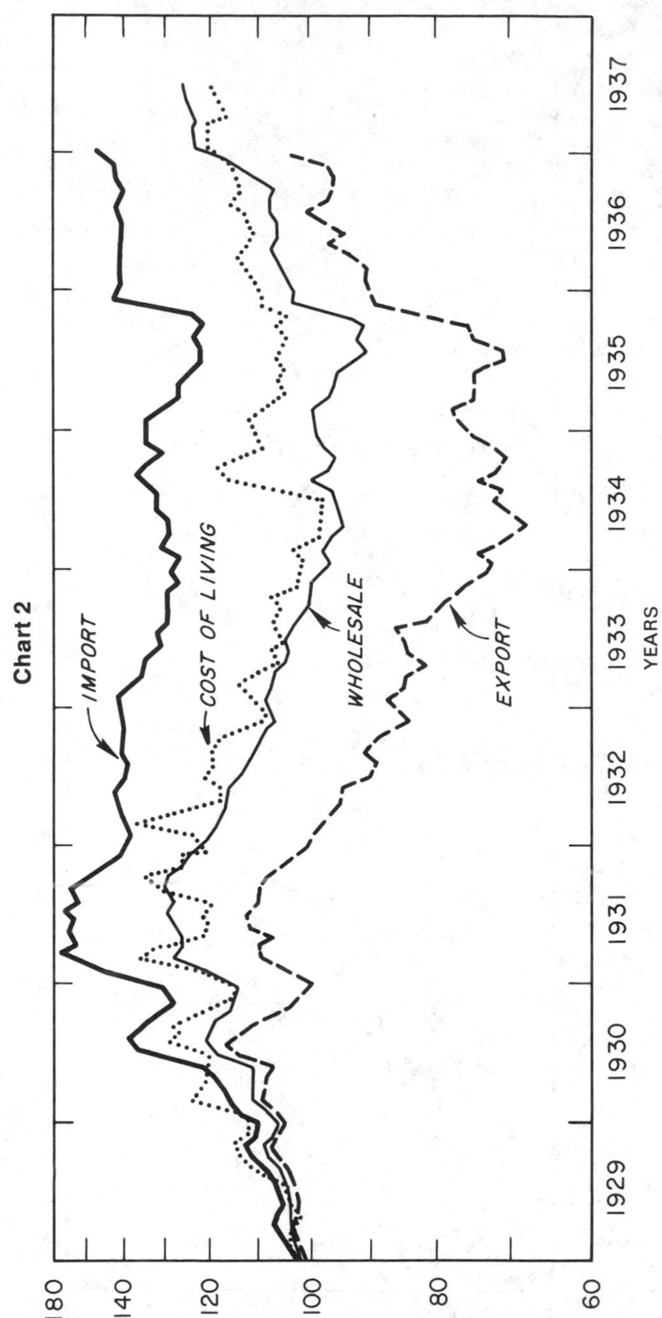

Wholesale, import, and export prices and cost of living at Shanghai, 1929-1937.

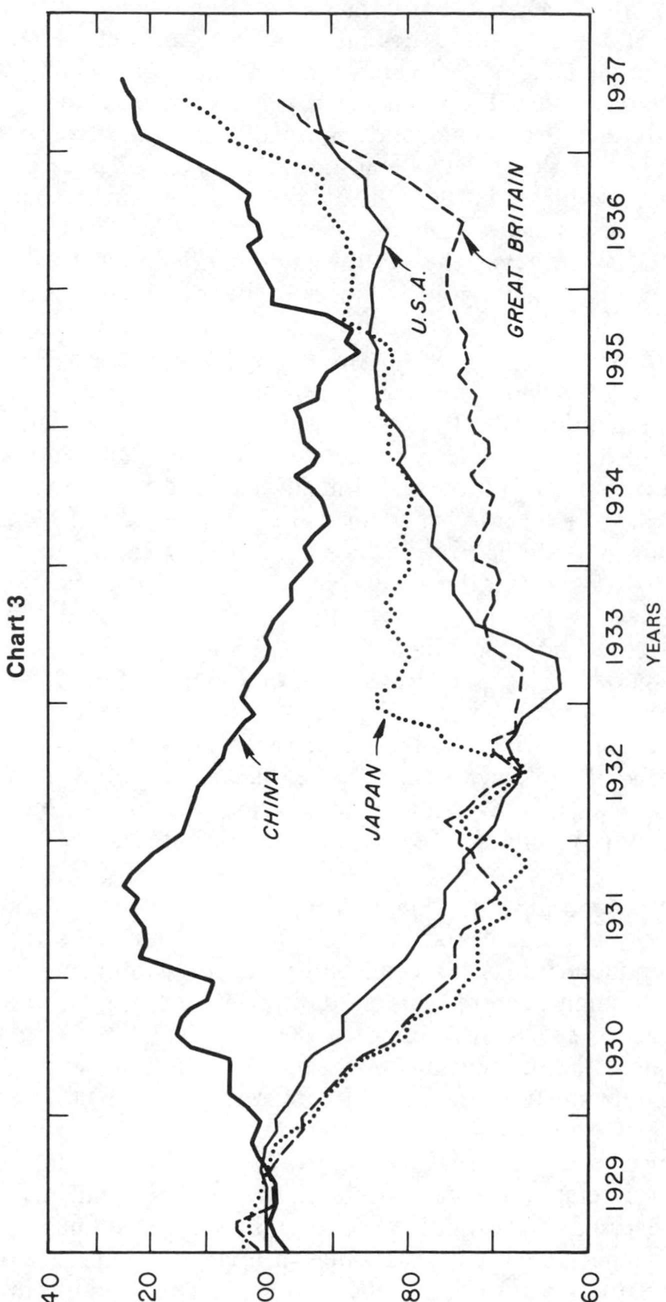

Wholesale prices in China, the United States, Great Britain, and Japan, 1929-1937.

which about 85 per cent consisted of Republican dollars. That figure did not include *sycee* and bars. E. Kann estimated monetary holdings as of 1930 at C $2200 million, or about 1700 million fine ounces. He made a "vague estimate" that, including hoards and ornaments and utensils, the total silver in China might be of the order of 2500 million ounces. Those estimates appear too large, in the light of experience in marshalling silver for conversion into foreign currencies after the currency reform of 1935.[9] Whatever the actual amount, the stock was so large that changes in its gold value as the world price of silver fluctuated were of formidable amounts.

But a slump in the world price could not properly be considered a corresponding loss for China. First the loss was only potential unless the silver were sold. And the calculations of loss were in terms of gold, and not in terms of goods and services (unless imported) for which the silver might be exchanged. The drop in the gold price of silver was accompanied in 1928 to 1932 by a drop in the prices of major goods imported to China. Probably well over half the silver was imported into China when the price was within the "normal" range, say, around US $0.60. Altogether the later official sales in 1935 to 1941 were about 550 million ounces at an average price of about US $0.45 (Appendix 15). The total of private sales was of comparable size, and much of these were when the price was rising in 1933 to 1936. Probably official and private sales in the thirties were at average prices below what the silver had cost in terms of gold. But on balance we certainly cannot assess a catastrophic capital loss in the process.

The economic and other consequences of the slump in silver prices, and the rise that followed, were far more important than any monetary loss that can be figured by comparing prices at which China acquired and sold silver. Time after time the protagonists of silver put forward the argument that falling silver impaired the purchasing power of China and her ability to import. Obviously China paid for imports primarily with the proceeds of exports and other current credits, notably remittances by overseas Chinese.[10] As we shall see, China's imports remained relatively stable while silver was slumping, as exports and overseas remittances were for a time well sustained.

Changes in the external value of a currency operate by their effect, first, on foreign trade and other transactions involving foreign exchange; and, second, on the internal money supply and credit. These changes affect the internal value of the currency only slowly and in less proportion. While China's exchange was falling by more than half in 1929 to 1931, prices rose by about one-fourth. And when deflation set in from the latter part of 1931, the internal price level dropped by about 30 per cent for four years, while the level of exchange doubled.

The Chinese economy was about four-fifths agricultural, and part of that largely a subsistence economy where families consumed much of their own production. Because of lack of modern transportation, large parts of the economy were chiefly affected by local conditions, especially weather and the state of public order. Yet foreign trade was of the order of 6 to 7 per cent of gross national product, and changes in foreign trade had substantial effect. The diverging courses of export and import prices during these periods of great changes in the level of exchange are shown in Chart 2 and Appendix 24. Import prices showed a maximum rise of about half during falling exchange, but were sticky on the decline when exchange rose. Export prices showed only moderate rise while exchange was falling, but fell drastically when exchange rose.

With moderate inflation instead of deflation, economic activity in China was well sustained in 1929 to 1931 despite internal political troubles. Exports had a good competitive position because of the drop in exchange, and until 1932 held up quite well despite the great decrease in purchasing power abroad (Appendix 20). The higher cost of imports because of the drop in exchange acted like a protective tariff. In those years it was responsible for encouraging considerable local production of a variety of goods such as textiles, rubber goods, chemicals, and cosmetics.

Movements of silver both in foreign trade and within China were of great significance in this period. Silver stocks in China were augmented by import of about C $520 million (393 million ounces) in 1928 to 1931, mostly in the first two of these years (Table 17). During these four years reported stocks of silver at Shanghai grew by C $94 million, or more than half (Table 18). About four-fifths of the C $520 million of net imports was distributed in other ports and the interior. This increase in the money supply had a stimulating effect. And the increasing cost of foreign currencies tended to deter those accustomed to invest abroad, so that they sought investments in China. Credit became easy and a boom began in Shanghai real estate and construction. The tide turned in the fall of 1931. September witnessed Britain's departure from gold followed by devaluations

Table 18

Silver stocks at Shanghai from 1927 to 1935[a]

Year-end, millions

End of	
1927	C$142
1928	172
1929	240
1930	262
1931	266
1932	438
1933	547
1934	335
1935	276

End of quarter, millions

	1932	1933	1934	1935
March	C$286	C$472	C$589[b]	C$324
June	369	447	583	341
September	424	460	451	336
December	438	547	335	276[c]

[a]Source: National Tariff Commission, *Annual Report of Shanghai Commodity Prices, 1935*, p. 131, and, for 1932, *Shanghai Market Prices Report*, July-September, 1933, p. 46.

[b]The maximum was C$594 million in April and May 1934.

[c]In November 1935, silver was nationalized. Stocks were handed over to the Central Bank, which gradually sold them.

by Japan and other countries. As a result, exchange rates affecting over half of China's trade rose sharply. Rates for the dollar stayed low until early 1933, when they climbed as the dollar went off gold.

Japan's seizure of Manchuria cut off China from provinces with great agricultural and mineral resources, undeveloped land that was absorbing immigrants from the overpopulated regions, a large export surplus, and the source of 15 per cent of total customs revenue. Japan's attack at Shanghai followed early in 1932. Meanwhile, the government was engaged in the campaign to drive the Communists from Kiangsi Province. A general feeling of insecurity developed, hampering internal and foreign trade. As if these adverse events were not enough, China was visited in the summer and fall of 1931 by the worst floods in generations. Inundation of the most productive agricultural land of Central China caused huge loss.

Added to the external and internal troubles and the vagaries of nature, a new force appeared for stimulating the rise of exchange, with all its consequences for deflation and depression, as the movement grew in the United States to "do something for silver."

"Doing something for silver"

The United States has a long record of "doing something for silver," several times with unforeseen and most unhappy consequences. The senators from seven states that produce silver, acting as a bloc, have repeatedly been able to gain support for silver measures in exchange for support of projects dear to the hearts of others in Congress or the administration. And the silver interests have taken advantage of "populist" sentiment for cheap money and inflation. Issues about the status of silver have tremendously outweighed silver's economic importance. The value of American silver output in 1929 was US $33 million—an amount less than that of the peanut crop, US $52 million!

From 1930, the great depression spawned numerous projects about silver, besides the silver loan schemes already described. I shall only summarize the course of the American silver movement in this period, which has been well analyzed and described elsewhere,[11] and shall pay special attention to its consequences for China. For some time after 1932, Congress was "predominantly silver and inflation-minded."[12] The arguments were to broaden the monetary base by including silver with gold; to promote "controlled inflation"; and, by raising the value of silver, to increase the purchasing power of China and other "silver-using countries," and thus encourage American exports. The aim was a drastic rise in the silver price from US $0.25 per ounce at the end of 1932. Many urged parity with gold at US $1.29 per ounce or even higher.

The profound concern for raising the value of silver to help China is of special interest. It stemmed almost wholly from outside, and continued despite vigorous Chinese protests. There was much feeling in China that an exchange rate around US $0.20 was too low. But I can recall no serious voice raised in China for a sharp and continuing rise. The predominant view favored stability at a moderate level.

As silver slumped during the depression, the idea gained currency in the United States that the slump was highly detrimental to trade with China and the Orient. "The picture of a vast but incapacitated market for American goods became a rosy glow on the horizon of depression"; and even President Hoover stated in October 1930 that, "The buying power of India and China, dependent upon the price of silver, has been affected."[13]

Actually, when American exports to all countries dropped in 1931 by 38 per cent, compared to 1930, exports to China grew by 1 per cent despite a 25 per cent slump in silver.[14]

Many public figures repeated the argument that raising the silver price would help China, ignoring China's relatively good economic performance with cheap silver. A Senate committee almost went into tears, saying that the effect of low silver on China and India "will never be known in its fullest horror. The immediate depreciation of their only stock of money, silver, stopped trade and starved whole provinces. It caused millions of deaths."[15] Of course, the silverites wanted higher silver for their own reasons. One protagonist was the influential demagogue Father C. E. Coughlin, who wanted the United States to "restore the purchasing power of the Orient," and "play the good Samaritan to the lowly Oriental." It appeared in April 1934 that his "Radio League" built up in the name of his secretary a holding of one-half million ounces![16]

On the other hand, economists and others recognized that if the United States would gain by higher general prices, China would not gain by deflation. The boost to American exports for which many silverites hoped was illusory. Higher silver would make it harder for China to compete in export markets, tend to discourage overseas Chinese remittances, and thus tend to reduce ability to import.

The silver agitation and the various projects emerging in Washington were faithfully reported in China. They led to spectacular increases in the silver price, and *pari passu* in rates of foreign exchange for the silver dollar (Chart 1).

The first significant concrete result of the agitation was the silver agreement signed July 22, 1933, during the Monetary and Economic Conference at London. In the spring of 1933, preparatory to the Conference, American representatives conferred at Washington with representatives of a number of foreign governments including China. On May 9 and 10, Finance Minister Soong met with Secretary Hull, Senator Pittman, and other American representatives to discuss silver. According to my memorandums of the meetings, Soong stated that "fundamentally the Chinese Government is most interested in stability of the value of silver," as the wide fluctuations "have caused serious losses." He believed that, "In principle . . . silver should be linked with general prices." He would not be opposed to somewhat higher levels for silver—exchange was then about US $0.24. He favored a conference of silver using and producing countries, for which the silver interests were pushing.

The London silver agreement indicated in its preamble its purpose as "mitigating fluctuations in the price of silver," and its "effective stabilization." It provided for limitations on sales of silver by governments. China undertook not to "sell silver resulting from demonetized coins" during the four years 1934 to 1937. The United States and four other countries agreed to buy from their respective production 35 million ounces yearly. The American share was later set at about 24.4 million ounces. Roosevelt issued a proclamation on December 21, 1933, ensuring a price of US $0.64-1/2 plus per ounce of silver thereafter mined by producers in the United States.[17]

The spirit of the London agreement, to steady the silver price, did not deter the silver protagonists from agitation to do still more for silver. This was fully reported in China, and gave rise to fear in financial circles that the American government would manipulate the world price upward without regard for the principles underlying the London agreement. At first I was hesitant to believe this reasoning. But as the evidence mounted, I proposed on February 23, 1934, that China ratify the agreement only with a reservation. On March 21, China ratified it with the following reservation, which I drafted:

> In ratifying this Agreement, the National Government of China declares that as silver is the basic monetary standard of China, the National Government will consider itself at liberty to take whatever action it may deem appropriate, if, in its opinion, changes in the relative values of gold and silver adversely affect the economic condition of the Chinese people, contrary to the spirit of stabilizing the price of silver as embodied in this Agreement.

The Rogers mission

When Congress assembled in January 1934, a number of proposals on silver were put forward, mostly calling for large American purchases and with strong inflationary implications. Many of the public and many within the Administration were concerned. In February, Morgenthau obtained Roosevelt's consent to send to China Professor James Harvey Rogers of Yale University, who was an official but unpaid adviser to the government on monetary policy.[18] Some in the administration hoped that, because of American sympathy for China, an unfavorable report might check excesses of silver legislation. The attitude of the administration is shown in a telegram of April 21, 1934, from Morgenthau to Rogers then at Shanghai:

> For your personal information, administration is opposing Congressional proposals for remonetization of silver at higher than present

> market prices [about US $0.45 per ounce] on ground that world stocks of disposable silver whose purchase such proposals would involve are incalculable in amount and that adoption of such proposals would interfere with President's monetary program.[19]

Announcing the Rogers mission on March 19, Morgenthau said that there were differing schools of thought as to whether higher silver would increase or decrease American exports to China. Rogers was "to find out which school is right."[20] Silverites called the mission delaying tactics. Senator Burton Wheeler called the mission "the height of asininity," saying that Rogers started "with a prejudice against doing anything for silver, ostensibly to consult Chinese coolies, Chinese merchants, and Chinese manufacturers, but in reality . . . to consult Japanese and British manufacturers as to what our monetary policy should be."[21]

Rogers reached Shanghai on April 10. His mission when announced had been welcomed in China, as a sign that the American government would have some regard for China's vital interest in silver. He interviewed officials and business men and was given full information about the situation and China's views. He telegraphed to Morgenthau on April 21 and 23 that no responsible Chinese opinion favored high silver, but only a minority of importers; that officials and bankers feared a large outflow of silver if the price rose; that higher silver would aggravate China's agricultural depression; and that he found no statistical support for the notion that there was any long-run relation between the silver price and imports, and only a slight short-run relation. The Chinese government would welcome some plan assuring future stability of the silver price.[22]

Rogers traveled extensively in China. He was particularly struck by the agricultural depression. He telegraphed to Morgenthau on May 8 that higher exchange rates curtailed exports, causing agricultural prices to decline. Silver was being drained from the interior to the treaty ports, because "the farmers are in such poor condition that many of them are drawing upon their silver hoards to meet living expenses.' Local moneylenders and native banks were liquidating loans and sending silver to the treaty ports. Also higher silver prices were reducing remittances by Chinese emigrants, who already suffered from depression abroad. He believed that "Any further rise in the price of silver . . . at this time would aggravate this situation." Unless the adverse balance of payments could be checked, he said, considerable silver outflow was likely. A further telegram of May 17 reiterated these views and concluded:

> My firm conviction is that higher silver at this time will add greatly to the difficulties of Nanking government and may even destroy the slight but increasing unification of China which it has been able to accomplish.

Assuming that "a unified China is of high importance to the United States," he suggested that "if the silver price is to be raised further simultaneous consideration be given to a government loan to China." But Washington instructed him not to discuss a loan.[23]

Rogers continued to object to the American silver program. His telegrams reported alarm in Chinese official and financial circles. He hoped that the United States could limit the rise of silver to the average rise in commodity prices, and saw "no excuse for proceeding at a pace that will inevitably create profound disturbance in other countries." On October 17, 1934, he wrote that "to proceed with this new policy [bidding up the silver price] under the present circumstances—before giving the Chinese government an opportunity to adjust itself to the resulting monetary disturbances—seems to me to border very closely on international irresponsibility." And in drafting a letter to Morgenthau, he said that in his opinion "the silver bloc in the United States will soon be rated among the most picturesque clowns in American history."[24]

Rogers planned to make a full report analyzing the problem thoroughly. But events caught up with him. His preliminary warnings were of no avail, and a disagreement with Morgenthau prevented his making the intended report. He had merely "served as an unsuccessful excuse to delay action." While he was investigating and reporting, Roosevelt was capitulating to the silver senators. The key agreement was reached on May 16, 1934.[25]

Silver and politics in 1933 and 1934

Although the silver movement of the thirties was a curious aberration, unquestionably the silverites were strong. The Senate in January defeated by only two votes Senator Wheeler's proposal requiring purchase of 50 million ounces monthly until reserves reached a billion ounces. In April, Senator Elmer Thomas was pushing a similar mandatory plan, to buy 50 million monthly until the price reached US $1.29 an ounce.

Roosevelt and Morgenthau wished no drastic rise in silver, as indicated in the instructions of April 21, 1934, to Rogers quoted above. But Roosevelt did not speak out. His main attention in monetary matters was to gold, which the gold-buying policy had manipulated upward to US $35 per ounce as proclaimed January 31, 1934. Herbert Feis, writing of him in this period, refers to his "apparent indifference to the impact of his action on the commercial and financial situation of other countries." Everest believed that "Probably the president himself never understood that raising the price of silver meant to China the exact opposite of raising the price of gold to the United States."[26]

Furthermore, Roosevelt was disposed to discount protests coming from China, a country on which he considered himself an expert. Records now available shed light on his attitude. On December 6, 1934, he commented to Morgenthau on a report from the Treasury Attache in China, which cannot be found in the records but is described as relating to banking. The president's memorandum said:

> Please remember that I have a background of a little over a century in Chinese affairs. China during the past hundred years has not changed very much if you think of China as an aggregation of four hundred million people . . .
>
> The government of China, because it must use or deal with foreign capital, is obliged to conform with international standards. These standards expressed by the foreign advisers of the Chinese Government . . . represent without question what the banking interests of the world call "orthodox."
>
> You and I know that during the past twenty months our gain has been due to our decision not to accept orthodox advice . . .
>
> China has been the Mecca of the people whom I have called the "money changers in the Temple." They are still in absolute control. It will take many years and possibly several revolutions to eliminate them because the new China cannot be built up in a day.
>
> I am inclined to believe that the "money changers" are wrong and that it is better to hasten the crisis in China—to compel the Chinese people more and more to stand on their own feet without complete dependence on Japan and Europe—than it is to compromise with a situation which is economically unsound and which compromise will mean the continuation of an unsound position for a generation to come.[27]

Domestic politics was also entered in, especially with 1934 an election year. At the cabinet meeting of April 13, 1934, Roosevelt handed Secretary Morgenthau a note saying, "We have worked out a suggestion on silver which I admit is good." Two days later Morgenthau saw him and reported in his Diary that he felt "somewhat discourged because the president was rather conciliatory with the delegation from the Senate and I was worried on account of his attitude." Roosevelt asked the cabinet on April 27 whether he should compromise on silver or try to prevent legislation. The reaction was that it would be better for the congressmen in November elections not to have to live with a veto on silver.[28]

Roosevelt firmly rejected mandatory legislation. But he compromised by agreeing to push silver purchase actively. Arthur Krock of the *New York Times* believed this concession unnecessary, and that the president could have prevented legislation to which he was opposed. But the political motives were decisive. The upshot was the adoption on June 19 of "The Silver Purchase Act of 1934."[29]

The leaders of China were remarkably tolerant of the vagaries of American silver politics. They told Bullitt who visited China in 1934 that they knew the United States "has absolutely no intention ... of trying to mess us up but, nevertheless, it is messing us up terribly."[30] They recognized the United States as a long-time friend, although temporarily misguided on silver, and felt that the United States was on China's side in the confrontation with Japan.

Implementing the silver purchase law of 1934

The silver purchase law prescribed the policy of holding silver in American monetary reserves up to one-fourth of the total of gold and silver reserves. To that end, the Secretary of the Treasury was "authorized and directed to purchase silver, at home or abroad ... upon such terms and conditions as he may deem reasonable and most advantageous to the public interest" (Section 3). To satisfy those who wanted to specify amounts, prices, or time limits, Roosevelt verbally promised to execute the law "enthusiastically and in the spirit in which it was enacted." Morgenthau announced on June 21 that he would carry out the law's purpose "enthusiastically," and buy silver at home and abroad. He said that "What we want is a rise in the price of silver," but not a "sensational" rise followed by collapse. "As it goes up it will stay there." He would, however, guard against speculative activities. Much later, his enthusiasm dampened by sad experience, he called the law "the infamous Silver Purchase Act."[31]

The American silver-buying policy became the primary cause of a steep rise in the price of silver, from its low in 1932-1933 to a peak in mid-1935 that was well over two and one-half times as high. Also, especially in the earlier period, the worldwide trend to recovery from the depression had some influence.

American purchases began in July 1934. In the first four weeks, only 5 million ounces were bought because Morgenthau was away and his subordinate in charge was not in sympathy with the law. But Morgenthau at once stepped up buying, and 48 million ounces were bought in August. Purchases averaged 24 million ounces per month for the next six months, and the silver bought under the act totaled 294 million ounces in the fiscal year ended June 30, 1935. That was in addition to acquisition of 31 million ounces of newly mined American silver and 112 million ounces of silver nationalized as of August 9, 1934.[32]

The Treasury was under great pressure from the silverites to raise the price. That was especially true after April 1935, when under the influence of American buying, the world price approached US $0.64-1/2 plus, which the Treasury was paying for American silver from December 1933—that price having been set pursuant to the London agreement. Roosevelt promptly raised the price for domestic silver by 10 per cent to US $0.7111, and soon thereafter another 10 per cent to US $0.7757. Thinking that the United States would match upward movements of the price, speculators then bid it up in the free market to a peak of US $0.81. But the price fell sharply when the Treasury then refused to buy, and even sold small amounts. After regaining control of the price, the Treasury held it steady for some time at about US $0.65.[33]

By December 1935, Morgenthau had become disillusioned about silver buying. China had completely abandoned the silver standard, followed by Hong Kong; other countries were also unloading silver on the United States. Attainment of the 25 per cent proportion of silver in the American reserves became harder as gold flowed from Europe into currency reserves in the United States for greater safety because of Hitler's disturbing adventures. With Roosevelt's consent on December 9, the Treasury stopped bidding for silver, letting it be known that it would await offers which it might accept or decline. The price for other than American production dropped in six weeks from 65 to 45 cents.[34]

China and the depression in 1932 to 1934

As already noted, China's partial insulation from the worldwide depression ended in the winter of 1931-1932. While most of the world was haltingly recovering, China passed from moderate prosperity to deep depression. Estimates of gross national product were as follows (billions of current C $): 1931, 35.3; 1932, 28.8; 1933, 24.2; 1934, 21.3; 1935, 23.7; and 1936, 25.9. The gross value of the agricultural product was estimated to have fallen from C $24.4 billion in 1931 to C $13.1 billion in 1934. Although the deflation was acute, the physical volume of output changed relatively little, and thus the figures in terms of constant 1931 prices show much less change.[35]

General prices began dropping for three to four years from their peak in the second half of 1931 (Chart 2 and Appendix 12), and exchange rates rose sharply (Chart 1 and Appendix 10). Rising exchange tended to help import trade, making imported goods cheaper. China's masses used relatively few imported items, except kerosene, and many imported consumption goods were used mainly in the treaty ports. But the benefits of cheaper raw materials and other items used in production were more widely diffused. Rising exchange also helped businesses whose costs were mainly for imported items for operations and plant. It helped those receiving local currency and needing to make payments in foreign currencies. Remittances of profits abroad were not relatively great in the disturbed conditions of the time. The government was the chief debtor in foreign currencies, with yearly debt payments equivalent to about US $40 million at exchange rates prior to sterling's devaluation, and other considerable payments for purchases abroad. While the government from 1930 hedged the cost of such payments by collecting import duties on a gold basis, any saving when exchange was rising was minor compared to the injury to the national finances from the deteriorating economy.

Gains by some from rising exchange were much more than offset by other factors in the economy. Ability to import was impaired by diminishing ability to obtain foreign currencies with which to pay. Exporters had to convert foreign currency receipts into decreasing amounts of local currency. While silver exchange was falling, China's exports were relatively well sustained up to 1932, dropping only from C $1070 million in 1929 to C $915 million in 1931 (excluding Manchuria). But when exchange rose strongly, after the devaluation of sterling and the yen, exports fell to C $569 million in 1932 and stayed around that level until after the currency reform of November 1935.

Reduced exports had a damaging effect upon producers, especially of agricultural goods. The injury to China's economy was compounded by floods and especially by Japan's seizure in 1931-1932 of Manchuria with its large export surplus.

Rising exchange had an adverse effect on intangible elements in the balance of payments. The biggest item was overseas Chinese remittances which were ordinarily of the order of C $300 million yearly. There were no accurate figures of these, but Rogers' investigation led him to believe that the total of these increased from C $250 million in 1928 to C $357 million in 1931, and decreased to C $200 million in 1933.[36]

The effects of rising exchange on the economy because of the shrinkage of monetary reserves were of major importance in this period. Of particular importance was the drain of silver to Shanghai from the rest of China, and the drain abroad.

As indicated above, about C $400 million of the C $520 million of silver imported in 1928 to 1931 was added to stocks outside of Shanghai. Beginning in the latter part of 1931, the trend was reversed and silver flowed strongly to Shanghai. Silver stocks there rose from C $266 million at the end of 1931 to C $438 million a year later, C $547 million at the end of 1933, and a peak of C $594 million in April 1934 (Table 18). This increase of C $328 million of Shanghai stocks included net imports to Shanghai of C $18 million from January 1932 through April 1934, although in that period China as a whole had a small net export of silver on balance. Hence the net inflow from the rest of China adding to Shanghai stocks was C $310 million.[37]

The strong flow of silver to Shanghai from the rest of the country after 1931 was both a reflection of troubles in the interior and a cause of further troubles there. There was some flight of capital to Shanghai, whose International Settlement offered greater security at a time of internal and external disturbances. But also there had been serious disturbances in 1929 to 1931, while silver was moving out of Shanghai. The flow to Shanghai chiefly reflected deterioration of the economy in the countryside. World prices of foods and fibers were weak, and China's exports fell because of rising exchange, as explained above, along with continuing reduced demand during the depression abroad. The balance of trade between Shanghai and other areas became adverse. While the prices received by farmers fell, the prices they paid remained relatively high after 1931 (Appendix 13). The rising value of the currency in foreign exchange stimulated competing imports, including agricultural products. Because of the destruction by flood in 1931, the countryside had less to ship to city markets, and silver was shipped to pay for purchases. Money was attracted to Shanghai also by the high returns obtainable on government bonds. And the rising price of silver made it profitable for merchants in the interior to accumulate silver for sale overseas.[38]

The drain of silver contracted credit in the country outside of Shanghai, with resulting price declines, unemployment, underemployment, and business failures. The relatively meager savings were diverted from local expenditure. The income in kind of the rural population alleviated the hardship to some extent. But the rural depression was very acute.

In Shanghai suffering was less at first, and the relatively modern sector continued to grow during the depression. The plethora of money flowing from the rest of the country made credit relatively easy and encouraged speculation in land and building. Shanghai's economy became vulnerable to the contraction following the rise in exchange rates and heavy exports of silver after mid-1934. The result was the grave economic crisis described in the next chapter.

Controversy with Washington

The spate of projects and statements in the United States early in 1934 favoring a rise in the value of silver were fully and promptly reported in China. They caused increasing fears in financial and governmental circles. I urged Minister Kung to make a formal statement to Washington of China's views. But he held back because of wanting to avoid any intrusion in American politics and to avoid risk of offending the American government, which had recently granted the Cotton and Wheat Loan to China (Chapter 16). He asked me to make on his behalf oral representations to be telegraphed through the American consul-general at Shanghai. I did so on February 16, but complied only technically with my instructions on the form of representations by delivering also a "note verbale" confirming what I said. I was sure that China later would be glad to have a written record. This proved to be true since the paraphrased text was made public in October to show a timely objection by China to what Washington later did. The communication of February 16, 1934, stated:

> Since China's currency is silver, China is of course vitally interested in measures affecting its value and international exchange but of course has no desire to intrude upon questions of purely American internal concern. In view of reports here, it may be observed that any action resulting in a rise of China's currency out of relation to other currencies and especially out of relation to world commodities would have deflationary effects in China, further decrease her already reduced exports and so impair her ability to purchase goods from abroad. It would also probably increase the present serious tendency towards heavy silver exports as necessary means of settling large adverse balance. In view therefore of China's vital interest, it is hoped that the Government of China will be consulted in advance if measures concerning silver that might materially affect China's currency and exchange are in fact being contemplated.[39]

Three days later, the Chinese Bankers Associations sent a telegram to Roosevelt in the same sense. It further pointed out that the United States had lowered the value of its money to avert a crisis, and that "Converse applies ... here that any drastic enhancement of silver value ... will result in flight of silver from these shores and bring about credit stringency and collapse of internal commodity level." China was already suffering from a "series of calamities" and "in danger of sinking further into economic depression." They appealed for stability of silver and not drastic enhancement, which would be "likely to bring calamity upon the millions of our people."[40]

Thus began a controversy which, prior to belated efforts to redeem the American position, ranks among the least creditable incidents in American foreign policy. I found myself in the strange position of preparing protests by a foreign government to my own government, whose conduct in the matter at issue I deplored. Washington made no reply of substance to China's representations of February. On August 20, after purchases were pushing silver to higher levels, China pointed out that the United States was departing from the spirit of the London agreement, which contemplated stabilizing silver, and that the outflow of silver was "potentially alarming." China, to safeguard her currency, "would appreciate an indication of the probable policy of the United States in the future purchase of silver."

To this also there was no immediate reply. On September 15, I proposed to Minister Kung that China offer to exchange silver

"MR. MORGENTHAU RECONSIDERS"

North-China Daily News, April 30, 1935.

"ANOTHER IMPENDING COLLISION"

North-China Daily News, October 1, 1934

for gold. Current hardships indicated that China should not maintain the silver standard alone, and China was considering adoption of a gold-based currency. Also the United States desired an increasing proportion of silver in its monetary reserves. His message in that sense, sent on September 23, crossed an American reply that explained the American legislation but contained no assurance helpful to China. On October 5, Kung sent Ambassador Johnson a memorandum, which I prepared, containing a full statement of the situation and the serious problems faced by China. Johnson promptly telegraphed it to Washington.[41]

While these exchanges were taking place, the drain of silver became more and more serious. In the first seven months, C $50 million of silver was exported from Shanghai; in August, C $83 million; and in September, C $36 million—plus about 20 per cent more from other ports. The price of silver abroad rose faster than exchange rates followed. Thus the bullion value of the silver dollar abroad exceeded its exchange value by more than the costs of shipping. In the three months from the end of June to the end of September, silver stocks in the banks at Shanghai fell from C $583 million to C $451 million (Table 18).

An embargo on silver exports was urged in several influential quarters. The government denied intending an embargo. It hoped against hope for American cooperation in avoiding a dire injury to China's economy. (See cartoons.) And China's leaders recoiled from abandoning the free silver standard. Resources to sustain a managed currency were meager and there was no visible chance of foreign aid to support a reform. There was also some advocacy of devaluing the silver dollar, as other countries had devalued gold, but that proposal found no serious support. Yet talk of an embargo or devaluation or nationalization of silver hurt confidence. The market was full of rumors. Close observers of events felt that much of the export of silver, perhaps half, was prompted by fear of such measures and especially by a desire to export silver while this was possible. The prevailing feeling of uncertainty and alarm led many holders of silver in China to convert it to foreign currency while they could.

While weeks passed with no effective word from Washington the government temporized. Early in September it tried to curb speculation and capital flight by issuing an order restricting dealings in foreign exchange to legitimate and normal business and personal requirements. Lacking jurisdiction in the foreign settlements, it could only request the exchange bankers to comply. The order was not effective and made matters worse by hurting confidence.

On October 1, the government pressed Washington for a reply to the inquiry about exchanging silver for gold. When the reply finally came on October 13 it was most disappointing. Although friendly in tone, it gave China no firm assurance. It implied rejection of exchange of silver for gold by stating that free markets were available for those metals.

During the week ended October 13, tension in China grew. Exchange rose sharply to over US $0.37 and 18 pence. But the premium on London silver over the exchange rate rose even more, to 9 to 10 per cent on October 12 and 13. With conditions approaching panic, and in view of the tenor of the American reply, it was clear that China had to rely on herself for protection against the grave injury already suffered from the American silver policy and against the further injury in prospect. October 13 was a Saturday, and Kung decided at once to take action during the weekend. He called an afternoon meeting of financial leaders, governmental and private, that lasted through most of the night. The decision was to cut the tie to silver.

Abandonment of the free silver standard

On October 14, the government announced a duty, effective immediately, of 10 per cent on export of silver dollars and mint bars, less 2-1/4 cent minting charges paid, i.e., 7-3/4 per cent net; and 10 per cent on other forms of silver. In addition, an equalization charge was imposed "equal to the deficiency, if any, existing between the theoretical parity of London silver and a rate of exchange officially fixed by the Central Bank of China, after making allowance for the export duty."

To explain and justify the action, Kung made public on October 14, in agreement with Washington, his communications of September 23 and October 1 and the American reply of October 12. On October 18, he made public the earlier warning and request for consultation of February 16.[42]

The intention in imposing the export duty was to protect the basic silver reserves and to check the rise of exchange that was causing such grave difficulty. By divorcing exchange rates from direct relation to the price of silver abroad China cleared the way for a policy of managing exchange. But a year of extreme difficulty and groping for a policy was necessary before China was ready for a definitive currency reform.

9: Currency Reform of 1935

The export duty on silver effective October 15, 1934, cut the previous link between the value of silver in China and abroad. But internally China remained on the silver standard, with bank notes still redeemable in silver on demand. It was not until November 3, 1935, that China nationalized silver and stabilized exchange, embarking upon a program of disposing of silver to build up reserves abroad.

Working of the flexible duty

The flexible export duty was intended to make export of silver unprofitable. Only about C $10 million was recorded as exported from Shanghai in the first few weeks after October 14, and hardly any thereafter. Recorded exports after 1934 were almost wholly those of the Central Bank for sale to the United States, and these did not take place until after the currency reform of November 1935. Early in 1935 there was a gentleman's agreement that the banks would not export silver.

Although lawful export of silver was checked, smuggling began on a grand scale as the price of silver abroad far exceeded its value in China. Fear of smuggling was a chief deterrent of imposing the duty, and now the fear proved justified. The best estimates were that C $20 million was smuggled out in the last weeks of 1934; C $150 to C $230 million in 1935; and C $30 to C $40 million in 1936 (Table 18). The biggest leak was in North China, where for a time silver was said to be going out at the rate of about C $15 million monthly. The Japanese authorities in the north were hostile to the Central Government. They not merely placed no obstacles to the smugglers, but were reported to have put a branch office of the Manchukuo Central Bank at the Manchurian border to pay a good price for smuggled silver. In May 1935, the Japanese government became more cooperative about checking silver smuggling. Nevertheless in the first nine months of 1935 about 60 million ounces were exported from Japan, most of which clearly had been smuggled out of

China.[1] There was also serious leakage via Hong Kong. The Chinese authorities tried to prevent smuggling by the general public but with little success. The temptation of profit was too great.

Meanwhile, silver abroad showed a rising tendency, from around US $0.50 per ounce before the export duty to a range of about US $0.53 to 0.55 from January to March. China's restriction of export was regarded as bullish for silver. In the spring of 1935, silver moved up sharply, under the strong influence of American buying, to a high of US $0.81 on April 27 and ruling above US $0.70 to mid-year. In August, it fell to around US $0.65 where it was pegged until early December. Then the Treasury dropped it to around US $0.45 where it was pegged until early 1938. By the latter part of 1935, Morgenthau and Roosevelt were becoming disillusioned on silver, and the silver senators were divided and had less political strength.[2]

The duty was intended as a means to check the rise of exchange rates as well as the drain of silver. From around US $0.37-1/2 and 18 pence on October 12 and 13, rates fell by about 15 per cent to about US $0.32 and 15-1/2 pence in the next few days. The sharp drop upset confidence, and the Central Bank operated in the market to restore steadiness. Rates became fairly steady for several weeks around the new level, with a rising tendency. But in March, influenced by rising silver, a sharp climb began to over US $0.40 and 20 pence in July. From that high point rates fell by about a fourth until stabilized by the currency reform of November 1935.

The discrepancy between the internal and external values of silver is shown in Chart 1. With silver at US $0.53 to 0.55 after announcement of the export duty and exchange around US $0.32 and 15-1/2 pence, the silver content of the Chinese dollar was worth abroad about one-fourth more than in China. During the first few days, the Central Bank figured the equalization charge according to the letter of the law. As exchange rates fell, the equalization charge was as high as 14 per cent, on top of the 10 per cent duty.

When the raising of the equalization charge was accompanied by the sharp drop in exchange, the nervousness in the market almost approached panic. Confidence was greater with exchange rising than falling, partly because of the memory of the prosperity in 1919-1920 when silver rose to record heights. But conditions then were entirely different from those of 1934.

The rise of 1919-1920 was caused by abnormal postwar demand for Chinese and Indian exports and a scramble for silver to pay for these. In 1934-1935, the fear was that cutting the historic link to silver would bring inconvertibility and inflation.

The government consequently weakened on the original intent to let the total duty measure the actual discrepancy. To fix the charge, a Foreign Exchange Equalization Committee of three was created, in place of the Central Bank but with Central Bank representation. Beginning October 19, the Committee reduced the charge arbitrarily, dropping it gradually to the approximate range of 6 to 7 per cent and keeping it there until the currency reform a year later. The action was accompanied by a steadying of exchange rates, which probably was more caused by tightness of money than by lowering the equalization charge. The guiding principle at that stage was that maintenance of confidence depended on preventing a further drop in exchange rates and letting them follow the price of silver abroad at a discreet distance. The aim for a time was to prevent the discrepancy between the internal and external value of silver from exceeding about 20 to 25 per cent. It was recognized that there would be some smuggling with such a discrepancy. But it was feared in financial circles that with a larger discrepancy the temptation to smuggle would result in wholesale calls for redemption of bank notes and conversion of deposits to silver, with a serious financial collapse.

Until the early spring of 1935, while the rise in the external silver price was moderate, it was accompanied by a gradual rise in exchange. But in April and May, when the price of silver soared as American buying policy became more aggressive and speculation mounted, the discrepancy for a time exceeded 50 per cent, despite the rise of exchange to over US $0.40 and 20 pence. With silver moving so widely, manipulation of the equalization charge could no longer have much effect. It remained substantially unchanged until the currency reform.[3]

Failure to let the equalization charge reflect the actual discrepancy between the foreign value of silver and the rates of exchange reflected the deep attachment to silver. The fear of excesses of indefinite proportions evoked a series of denials that inflation was being considered. Generalissimo Chiang stated in December that "A paper standard is absolutely unsuitable for China and . . . the government does not intend to adopt such a measure." To enhance confidence the government even imported some small lots of silver early in 1935.

In a memorandum of October 22, 1934, after appointment of the Equalization Committee, I unsuccessfully urged that the total duty be kept in line with the actual discrepancy, both to prevent the lawful outflow of silver and to check deflation, and that exchange be left to find its natural level under the new policy. Money already had been tightened by silver exports, and the tightening seemed likely to continue because of smuggling. There seemed little risk that a decline in exchange would get out of hand. The Central Bank, I believed, should do whatever it found practicable to avoid undue fluctuations in exchange. But no real stabilization would be feasible until there could be a definitive reform, the possibility of which I urged exploring.

Lockhart, Lynch, and I repeatedly urged that the dangers of rising exchange and deflation were much more serious than those from smuggling. We argued against seeking higher rates of exchange by manipulating the equalization charge or by Central Bank support. But we always encountered the strong views that motivated the Equalization Committee. With benefit of hindsight, it appears that as foreigners we did not fully appreciate the force of the market psychology that caused the creation of the Committee and limited its freedom of action.

Whatever the causal effect of changes in the equalization charge, it is clear that greater confidence temporarily followed its reduction and the support of a rising exchange market. Nevertheless, the economic cost of allowing higher rates of exchange was high, and it taught a lesson. The psychology changed by the spring of 1935, when rates fell. An editorial in *Finance and Commerce,* May 29, 1935, said:

> A few months ago there was not a responsible financier in China who would not have held up his hands in horror and distress at the mere idea of a managed paper currency . . . but experience has shown that the money is not particularly sound when the base starts upon a lonely journey skyward and the money cannot follow.

The writer of this comment believed that most financiers had come to feel that a managed currency would be sounder than the existing situation and would give business a chance to recover. He pointed out that the absence of unusual public requests for silver against bank notes "reflects in a wonderful way the confidence which the public have in the paper currency."

China had in reality a form of managed currency after cutting the link to silver abroad. But that was not generally realized, either by the public or even in most financial circles. The manipulation of the equalization charge, and operations of the government banks to support and temporarily even to raise exchange rates, were a form of management although an unsatisfactory one.

Despite the manipulation to keep exchange rates somewhat in line with silver abroad, the operation of the duty helped to check the rise of rates and to moderate the deflation. But further suffering during the year after the duty's imposition was necessary, along with continued negotiations with the United States and exploration of possibilities of foreign aid, before China was ready to accept a fundamental reform.

Deflation and depression, 1934 and 1935

China's depression deepened as silver and exchange rose. Previously, at the peak in 1931, wholesale prices and cost of living in Shanghai were about 30 per cent above the 1926 level. Then deflation carried them down by 30 per cent during three to four years. The low point of indexes of wholesale prices at Shanghai and Canton was in the summer of 1935. The cost of living index at Shanghai bottomed in 1934, and the Tientsin index of wholesale prices showed a double bottom in 1934 and 1935. Samples of prices in rural areas, confirmed by observation and reports, indicate an even worse situation. Prices paid by farmers fell, but generally less than prices received. The latter fell by well over one-third in some areas. (See Chart 2 and Appendixes 12 and 13.)

The agricultural depression was especially important because agriculture occupied roughly 80 per cent or more of the people and produced perhaps two-thirds of the gross national product. Based on the data for estimating gross national product, which permit only rough approximations, Ta-chung Liu has estimated the gross value of the agricultural product as follows (billions of C \$): 1931, 24.4; 1932, 19.2; 1933, 15.4; 1934, 13.1; 1935, 14.7; and 1936, 15.6. For the rest of the product he estimated (billions of C \$): 1931, 10.8; 1932, 9.6; 1933, 8.8; 1934, 8.2; 1935, 8.9; and 1936, 10.2.[4] Liu's data and other information indicate that the production of the relatively modern part of the economy held up better than agriculture in these years.

The most acute crisis was the financial situation centering at Shanghai. The difficulties became more and more serious from the summer of 1934. The serious drain of silver began in

August, and stocks of silver in the banks at Shanghai fell from C $563 million at the end of July to C $335 million at the end of the year (Table 18). Because the silver standard continued internally this drastic contraction of the currency base forced a sharp curtailment of bank credit. The tightening of money was extreme. During 1934, the interest charged by native banks rose from about 6 to 16 per cent per annum, with even higher rates reported. In January 1935, the premium on selling foreign exchange for cash against a month's delivery rose as high as 27 per cent per annum. It became almost impossible to borrow at any rate.

The situation in Shanghai was highly vulnerable from causes not related to American silver buying. There had been no effective regulation of private banking. Loans secured directly or indirectly on real estate and other loans had greatly expanded during the years of easy credit when money flowed to Shanghai. The commercial and native banks were large holders of real estate loans, and defaults piled up. Business failures mounted as debtors were unable to meet their obligations. Throughout the country many factories closed and others worked only on a limited scale. A report of February 4, 1935, from the Central Bank stated that failures included seven small banks, three other financial companies, 58 factories, and 99 stores. The community was shocked in May by the failure of the American-Oriental Bank and its affiliated companies. Later some officers of these organizations were jailed for their actions, but the depression was the occasion for the collapse. Three of the better known medium-sized Chinese banks were in deep trouble, and had to be taken over by the government. The index of prices on the Shanghai Stock Exchange fell by about half in four years from its high in mid-1931. Prices of stocks were cut as holders sold to meet loans. In the early months of 1935, trading on the Exchange almost came to a halt because of the extreme tightness of money, with under 100,000 shares traded in some months.

The commercial banks were in a bind because they held practically no silver in excess of the 60 per cent required as note reserve. Thus they were in no position to increase note issue or add to loans even against good security. The Central Bank could not rediscount because its resources were needed to support its note issue and to finance ordinary government operations. Fortunately there was enough confidence to prevent embarrassing demands for cashing notes for silver or withdrawal of deposits, despite some hoarding of silver and flight of capital. But a run on the banks could have been touched off by any serious untoward political or economic event. Luckily the market for government bonds was reasonably satisfactory, affording some liquidity although limited by the smallness of funds available to buy bonds.

The situation was skilfully sustained by government action in cooperation with the leading banks. The traditional New Year's settlement about February 1, 1935, was said to have been only about 50 per cent of normal, to avoid the forcing of bankruptcies. The government banks provided funds to ease the adjustments among the native banks, which were handicapped by frozen assets even more than the modern-style commercial banks.

In meeting the difficulties the government faced the problem of trying to sustain confidence while maintaining the internal convertibility of bank notes into silver despite the drain abroad. Lockhart, Lynch, and I continued urging that it would be better to prevent a rise in exchange and relieve the extreme tightness of money, and to check falling prices. On March 15 we recommended that Central Bank notes become authorized reserves for banks against note issue, and usable to redeem their own notes and in inter-bank clearings; that the banks be allowed to acquire Central Bank notes by depositing silver, gold, and foreign currencies and also by rediscount of eligible security; and that the Central Bank have the option of redeeming its notes in silver, gold, or foreign exchange at the current rate. To strengthen confidence and support the plan, we urged seeking an exchange credit against pledge of silver, and asking the American government to give an option to buy the silver at the market price but at not less than an agreed minimum. The plan involved a move toward an elastic currency and banking system and a step toward monetary reform. But the government shied away from such action, being impressed with the widespread fear of inflation and an inconvertible paper currency.

Without question, the adoption of the flexible export duty on silver, and the moderating of the rise of exchange rates, prevented a worse deflation. This appears clearly from comparing conditions in China with those in Hong Kong, which stubbornly stuck to silver until after the Chinese currency reform of November 1935. In May and June 1935, the Hong Kong exchange on New York, which before imposition of the export duty had usually ruled about 9 per cent above China rates, rose to more than 40 per cent above them. During the year following September 1934, the maximum fall in the Shanghai wholesale price index was 7 per cent and in the cost of living index 11 per cent. But at Hong Kong the maximum fall in the wholesale price index in that period was no less than 24 per cent (Appendixes 12 and 14). The two chief British banks operating in China and Hong Kong were convinced that China made "a serious mistake" in departing from silver.[5] In November 1934, they proposed a plan to end the export duty and return to the free silver standard. They offered a "credit," which really amounted to little more than authorization to sell £10 million of exchange and cover in London by exporting silver without duty if necessary, with China assuming any loss. The proposal did not merit serious consideration, and the British Treasury disapproved it, realizing that no real solution was possible on the silver standard.

In the latter part of March 1935, the government assumed control of the Bank of China and Bank of Communications and added to their capital. The move centralized control of most of the silver and foreign currencies held by the Chinese banks. It also strengthened the government's hand in supporting the economy when the credit structure was under extreme pressure, and preparing for eventual currency reform. T. V. Soong was put in charge of the Bank of China, and worked closely with Minister Kung. Relations within the Chiang-Soong families were restored in 1935, and for some time thereafter, following the break between the Generalissimo and Soong in the latter part of 1933.

Search for foreign cooperation

During the difficult year after imposition of the silver export duty, China negotiated actively with the United States and Britain in the hope of working out a solution with foreign cooperation. China also considered measures she might take on her own.

Despite Washington's unsatisfactory attitude in October 1934, China persisted in seeking an understanding that would safeguard her currency. On December Kung sent a message to Washington pointing out that the rising silver price was draining away silver, and that China could not allow exchange rates to rise to parity because that would involve extreme deflation.

Adoption of a gold basis would be difficult without a sizable foreign credit. Hence Kung asked that the United States agree not to pay over US $0.45 per ounce for other than American-produced silver. The Chinese currency equivalent would be US $0.34, a rate with which China could live. "If the American government wishes to be in a position to do whatever is desired about silver without hurting China," Kung said, "an alternative would be some form of cooperation to facilitate currency reorganization."[6]

This proposal touched off a flurry of activity in Washington. Undersecretary of State William Phillips sent Kung's message to Roosevelt on December 10, saying that reports showed mounting anti-American feeling in China because of the silver policy. He asked whether Roosevelt wanted to consider any change in policy. A memorandum of December 15 prepared by Ambassador Johnson, who was home on leave, and Herbert Feis, my successor as the State Department's Economic Adviser, concluded that to grant a credit to China would be likely to involve the United States deeply in China's affairs and lead to difficulties with Japan, which claimed primacy in economic relations with China. Hence, the best solution seemed to be to agree to the proposed figure of US $0.45 for foreign silver, and thus relieve China's difficulties. Hornbeck supported that solution pointing out to Secretary Hull that "we cannot at the same time go on with what we are doing and be a 'good neighbor'" to China because "our silver purchasing tends to 'bleed her white.'"[7] In these discussions, it was recognized that the Treasury would continue to buy American-produced silver at bonus prices. It is ironic that a year later the Treasury, tired of the silver-buying fiasco, dropped the price for foreign silver to 45 cents (Chapter 10).

Meanwhile, the Treasury concluded that it was necessary to proceed with silver buying, even though it might finally put China off silver. A solution would be to hold back temporarily with the price at 55 cents, pending agreement with China and congressional leaders. There might be a credit to China for monetary reform.[8]

The upshot when the interdepartmental disagreement could not be resolved was a meeting with Roosevelt. He supported the Treasury and the decision, telegraphed to China on December 18, was to agree to a price of US $0.55, but subject to change on one week's notice. China at once replied that the economic structure could not stand a rise of exchange to the corresponding parity of US $0.41-1/2, an appreciation of nearly one-fourth from the then level; and that "Week notification very short and do not understand why United States might be required make sudden change when regard given to vital importance to China of currency stability."[9]

But even the 55-cent figure proved politically vulnerable. It leaked to the silver senators, who at once made such a fuss that Morgenthau had to cancel it almost immediately. For a brief time the Treasury moderated its purchases, but a renewed rise soon carried silver to a peak of US $0.81 in April, and to a sustained level of over US $0.65 until after China's currency reform in November.

The message of December 18 invited China to send a representative to discuss silver "and related matters." To try to keep the discussions at the technical and nondiplomatic level, the message was sent by the Treasury from the Federal Reserve Bank of New York to the Central Bank of China. China promptly replied that T. V. Soong would come if agreeable to Washington, sailing January 18. Roosevelt approved Soong's coming. But the State Department felt that the visit was likely to end in failure because of obstacles to meeting China's needs. The conclusion was that the United States would be forced to choose between the serious consequences of refusing to help China or of becoming involved in Chinese currency matters in a way that would lead to grave trouble with Japan. Moreover, Senator Pittman, on learning of the proposed visit, insisted that silver policy should not be discussed. So Roosevelt called off the visit on the ground that the exchanges could take place by cable.[10]

The developments of December and January forecast clearly the difficulties of gaining American cooperation. The basic difficulty was the silver law, together with the promises given as to its operation and the greed and stubbornness of the silverites. There was also serious friction between the State and Treasury Departments. And underlying all was Japan's aggressive attitude in East Asia, particularly concerning China.

The record of interdepartmental friction has now been made clear from the Morgenthau *Diaries*, the Hull *Memoirs*, the Roosevelt papers, and publication of the volumes of *Foreign Relations of the United States*. But in 1935 those of us handling matters on the Chinese side could not fully appreciate the extent to which the friction made action by the United States difficult. Morgenthau claimed that the issues were monetary matters to be handled by the Treasury. And he felt that the State Department was unduly timid concerning Japan. The State Department in turn felt that vitally important American relations with China and Japan were involved in a way that gave primary jurisdiction to it and not to the Treasury. The result was compromise action, largely negative but on the whole favoring the Treasury's views. Morgenthau was more assertive than Hull. And as Roosevelt's old friend and former neighbor on their farms in New York State, he had easier access to the president which he did not fail to use.[11]

Some American official representatives in China during this period tended to minimize the effects of silver and to blame the bad situation on speculation and "general economic factors." In March 1934, even Johnson thought that higher silver helped trade and that exchange could rise considerably above its then level of about 35 cents without harm—but he later changed his view as stated above.[12] These persons did not understand the economic consequences of rising exchange, especially when artificially caused and out of line with the movement of world prices. A more perceptive report correctly said that American policy was "rapidly undermining such stability as exists," that anti-American feeling was growing and a boycott of American goods was even urged, and that the silver policy played into the hands of the Japanese militarists.[13] By early 1935 Morgenthau was beginning to become disenchanted about silver. He felt "terribly embarrassed about the thing—I've just been directed as an agent." He said, "If I was on [*sic*] the pay of the Japanese I've been earning my pay."[14]

Grave issues were presented by Japan's claim of primacy in international matters affecting China. That claim was a direct challenge to the open door policy. Japan's position was freshly and aggressively asserted in the famous Amau doctrine enunciated in April 1934. It held that China should progress by her own independent efforts, and opposed joint or individual action by other powers to provide financial and technical aid to China. Such aid if any should come from Japan. The American climate of the middle thirties was strongly isolationist. The State Department believed that the administration could have found little public support if aid to China should bring a serious confrontation with Japan.[15]

Early in February Kung forwarded a far-reaching proposal to

Washington. The rising silver price, he pointed out, was not only disastrous to China's economy, but impaired the government's revenue when it was "making strenuous efforts to stamp out the communist threat in a western province and consolidate its position throughout the nation." China saw no solution except to adopt a new currency system using both gold and silver, to which end "American cooperation is essential." He offered to sell 200 million ounces, saying that in time China might be able to provide the full American requirements of silver. Also he proposed a loan or long-term credit of US$100 million together with a stand-by credit against future delivery of silver, to be used if necessary. He proposed linking the currency to the dollar.[16]

Soong supported the proposal with a strong message saying that if the United States did not help China, the financial system would be in danger of collapse; and that China might be forced to choose between an onerous political and economic settlement with Japan and internal disintegration. "Far more is involved," he said, "than the fate of the present Chinese government or even her economic well-being." Reports from the American legation in China underlined the risks that China might be forced to make a deal with Japan. A telegram of February 17 from Kung to Minister Sze stated that the Japanese were intimating "large loan to meet crisis as part extensive program socalled economic cooperation which amounts to economic domination particularly North China"; and also intimating the making of "joint representations against American silver policy." The Japanese felt that "Western countries will not effectively help China which will be obliged to turn to them." China, said the telegram, was parrying the intimations. Further it said confidentially that China at the appropriate time would not object to discussing a loan with the Consortium. That change in China's long-time strong opposition to the Consortium could only be explained by the desperate state of affairs.[17]

These messages gave rise to continuing disagreements at Washington. Morgenthau persisted in wanting to handle the matters as a monetary problem and negotiate with China, and not be blocked by Japan. He suggested renewing the invitation to Soong to visit Washington. The State Department felt that the United States should not confront Japan flatly on the Amau doctrine. Roosevelt took no clear-cut position—he wanted to offend neither the silverites nor Japan. The result was a reply of

February 26 stating that the United States did not deem it practicable to agree to China's proposal; and inquiring whether China had considered taking up the matter simultaneously with the foreign governments, including the United States, that in the past had shown interest in Chinese financial matters.[18]

Before China could determine a further move, Britain took the initiative, suggesting to the American, French, and Japanese governments an effort to devise a plan for collective aid to China. A March 8 communication to the Chinese government stated that Britain believed that no plan for dealing with China's difficulties "could be really satisfactory unless it contributed to or formed part of" a Sino-Japanese *detente*. But before embarking upon discussions with the other governments Britain wished to know China's views. China replied on March 18, welcoming the British action and stating readiness to participate in discussions with the other governments.[19]

Meanwhile the papers were filled with unverified reports of the possibility of international aid to China and of Japan's attitude. Early in March it was reported on unspecified authority that Japan was ready to grant a loan on condition that China employ Japanese instead of German military advisers, utilize Japanese advisers to the National Economic Council (Chapter 14), and settle debts to Japan including the Nishihara loans. Japanese spokesmen indicated hostility to an international plan to aid China, although moderates within the Japanese government had shown in unpublished discussions a willingness to discuss the subject. Japan's policy continued to be aggressive and dominated by the extremists, and in June China was forced to make the Ho-Umetsu agreement strengthening Japan's position in North China.[20]

London decided that the best hope for finding a solution to China's financial problems lay in having the four powers chiefly concerned designate financial representatives to go to China for discussions in Shanghai. Such discussions, it was hoped, might reduce Japanese apprehensions and lead to improveent of Sino-Japanese relations. France was ready to cooperate, but decided not to send a representative when Japan and the United States held off. On June 10, London announced the sending of Sir Frederick W. Leith-Ross, the Economic Adviser to the British Government.[21] Japan promptly indicated she was not disposed to send a representative. A Japanese spokesman at Peiping said that "American economic aggression in China is more serious than the Japanese military policy."[22]

In Washington, the division between the State and Treasuy Departments continued. The State Department was anxious to send an expert, as repeatedly urged by China. But Morgenthau felt it would be embarrassing. He informed Ambassador Sze that the United States would not send a man: "your people would just crucify him and jump all over him for our silver policy."[23]

Leith-Ross was traveling to China via Canada, and the British intimated that Morgenthau might invite him to go via Washington. But Morgenthau refused. The State Department, however, was anxious to learn what the British were planning, and in particular whether some understanding with Japan was being sought. Undersecretary Phillips wanted to go to Canada to confer with Leith-Ross. But even that was unacceptable to Morgenthau. The State Department was deeply disturbed. Hornbeck wrote on August 8 that while the United States talked about being helpful to China and cooperating, American action indicated "no desire and no intention of *being* helpful or cooperating." The American government would have no cause to complain if the British felt unable to set their Far Eastern policy "on the basis of an unassured, an uncertain, and a not-to-be-relied-upon willingness to cooperate on the part of the United States." British-Japanese arrangements might even be made without American consultation.[24]

Leith-Ross stopped in Japan where he was able to dispel some of the suspicion there as to Britain's policy. But he had no success in sounding the possibility of a Sino-Japanese *detente* or of Japanese financial cooperation in a monetary reform.[25] So moves for international cooperation in help to China came to naught.

Planning currency reform

China's currency situation in 1935 urgently called for reform. There was no chance of satisfactory reform on the silver bullion standard, either at current prices of silver or at a devalued level. And after cutting the external link to silver, exchange fluctuations were wide and highly disturbing. But difficulties of reform were great. These were partly technical, partly in the realm of gaining public acceptance, and partly international.

The technical difficulties could be surmounted, subject to finding means to deal with the issues of public confidence and international affairs. For a long time, plans for comprehensive reform had been ready, on which my colleagues Lockhart and

Lynch and I had been working in close cooperation with Kung and Soong. These plans involved adopting a foreign exchange standard at a level that would not overvalue the currency. The notes of the three government banks would become full legal tender. Bank note issue would gradually be centralized in the Central Bank, which would become a central reserve bank with joint governmental and public ownership. The banking laws would be revised to provide stricter regulation, and a new institution created to lift mortgage loans from the commercial banks. Silver stocks of the banks plus such silver as could be gathered from the public would be nationalized and taken over by the Central Bank to be sold to provide foreign currency reserves. Reserves adequate for the silver standard would be adequate on the new basis, if they could be sold, at a level of exchange that did not overvalue the currency. Some form of credit against silver to be delivered, and if possible a further stand-by credit, would be desirable to assure confidence in a period of transition. Nickel and copper subsidiary coins would be issued to replace the conglomerate and fluctuating silver and copper minor currency. The reform would be buttressed by stabilizing the public finances and settling the debts in arrears. I set forth a detailed plan in a comprehensive report on the eve of Leith-Ross' visit.

His coming, along with the worsening financial situation, galvanized China to action. His appointment was particularly pleasing to me, as we were old friends and I had a high regard for him. We had worked together at Paris in the twenties on problems of German reparations, and had been opposite numbers during American-British financial negotiations. At Nanking the day after his arrival in China, I gave him full information about the situation and what I thought the program should be. I found him in agreement.

During the previous negotiations on currency matters representatives of the United States and Britain asked for particulars of China's plan for monetary reform. No detailed plan was then provided because Britain was discussing the situation with Japan in search of international cooperation, and would have felt bound to inform Japan—which China deemed inadvisable unless Japan's attitude should change. But now Britain alone was working with China on the problems, and Leith-Ross asked what China intended to do.

On October 2, Kung and Soong gave him full particulars of the plan, which was substantially as adopted a month later. It followed the lines set forth above and added important specific details. The government would suspend specie payments; make notes of the government banks full legal tender; limit other issues; adopt a moderately expansionist monetary policy; stabilize exchange at about the average level of 1930 to 1934; seek to sell the silver reserves; enhance public confidence by seeking a foreign loan of £10 million, and creating a special board to supervise currency operations; develop the Central Bank as a Central Reserve Bank; and balance the budget over 12 to 18 months.

It was vitally important to choose a new level of exchange that would not overvalue the currency. Several times I stressed to the government the grave difficulties of Britain from adopting an overvalued level in the twenties, compared to France's advantages from stabilizing at a relatively low level. I was confident that at a proper level, firmly maintained, flighted capital would return in large volume and clinch the reform by adding greatly to the reserves of foreign currency. But as the time for action drew near it was necessary to guard closely the intended rate to avoid speculation. In a confidential memorandum of October 2, I repeated recommendations made for over a year urging a rate in the range of US $0.29 to 0.30 and 14 to 15 pence. That was the approximate average level before distortions from American silver buying.

The choice of a currency standard gave rise to much consideration. Major currencies in relation to each other and to gold had been highly unstable in the thirties. The United States had finally returned to gold but the president still had authority for further devaluation. The pound was still managed but in October 1935 stood at US $4.91 (average), close to the predepression parity of US $4.8665, and was still fluctuating. In 1935, the range was between about US $4.77 and 4.97. China's trade was divided fairly equally between countries based on sterling, which included Japan, and on gold. China had indicated to both the United States and Britain that if a loan for support of a currency reform were provided, the currency could be linked to that of the country providing support.

The issue of linking the currency gave rise to much discussion. Kung told Leith-Ross that the question of a link should be left open, and Leith-Ross did not press for a link to sterling. There was talk in October of a large sterling loan to be issued at Shanghai and quoted on the London Exchange. No such loan was found practicable although, had it materialized, it would have involved a link to sterling. But Morgenthau pressed strongly for a link to the dollar in connection with the silver purchase for which negotiations were active in October and November. He did not wish to be in the politically vulnerable position of providing China with large funds to be used for a link to sterling.[26] The eventual solution was to manage the rate downward to the desired level, and to announce that it "will be kept stable at its present level."

Relations with Japan also entered into choice of a level of exchange. Japan's attitude was bad enough, but it would have been made worse had China adopted a level below that of the yen, whose value averaged US $0.287 in October and November. That was avoided by choosing a level roughly one American cent above the yen.

In 1934 and 1935, China's leaders were receptive to the ideas of currency reform above described. But they had to contend with a market psychology that connected confidence with steady or even rising exchange, despite the deflation involved. In the end extended suffering of more and more acute deflation proved the only way to change the general attitude. When exchange began to fall gradually after its peak in the spring of 1935, the consequences were less serious than had been feared. The drop was about 10 per cent from June to September. The Central Bank was able to withdraw support from the market and accumulate some foreign currencies. In October, heavy speculative buying of foreign currencies and gold, some of it rumored to be by insiders, forced rates down from a high of US$0.38 1/2 to under US $0.31 at the end of the month. The market became so nervous that by Novermber 2 the government felt obliged to act. It seemed clear that the public would accept a stable lower level of exchange, provided that an atmosphere of confidence could be created.

To provide the needed confidence external support in some form was essential. After the somber record of financial distintegration of the twenties, China had had for only a few years a government that showed the capacity to handle financial problems with a measure of assurance and competence. The coming of Leith-Ross provided a needed ingredient. Britain's financial prestige in China remained high despite the pound's troubles. Without British cooperation and public indication of moral support either China would have let matters drift with risk of being forced to an inconvertible paper currency, or would have undertaken the reform with less assurance of success. Leith-Ross' influence was particularly important in stressing the need to develop the Central Bank into a Central Reserve Bank, and to create and maintain budgetary equilibrium to avoid inflation and monetary instability.

American help at last

The high prices of silver gave China a golden opportunity to dispose of silver and convert its reserves into the foreign currencies needed to support a reform based upon stability of exchange. Mexico in 1905 to 1907 and El Salvador in 1919 and 1920 had taken advantage of temporarily high market prices of silver to shift from silver to gold. In 1934 and 1935, China deemed it wise to try to sell large amounts directly to the American government, rather than risk alienating the temperamental Treasury and accept the uncertainties of the market.

Furthermore the situation was so delicate that the government felt that any export of silver would severely shock confidence. Late in 1934, the Central Bank made the first sale of silver to the Treasury through the Chase Bank, 19 million ounces, with the understanding it could temporarily be kept by the latter at Shanghai. Morgenthau was cooperative and delivery was postponed several times by agreement. The Central Bank finally met its commitment by buying silver in London at a higher price, except for 2 million ounces delivered after the currency reform of November 1935.[27] Several times during 1935, China asked the Treasury to buy silver for deferred delivery, to strengthen reserves. But the Treasury always declined.

Only a truly large sale of silver could have made possible a fundamental reform. But in the fall of 1934, as described in Chapter 8, Washington was unwilling to discuss a swap of silver for gold. The silver-buying policy was inexorably forcing China off the silver standard. But the Administration would court the wrath of the silverites had it gotten into the position of helping China to abandon silver. In April 1935, Senator Pittman wrote to Roosevelt that China's threat to do this was "absurd upon its face." In June, the silverites fervently backed a much higher price for foreign silver. A letter of June 20 to the president, signed by 47 senators, urged raising the proportion of silver in the reserves to 25 per cent and raising the price to US $1.29. Roosevelt replied on July 25, citing his intention to follow the silver policy "vigorously and in good faith." The Silver Act was "surcharged with such great possibilities for our national welfare and the advantage of the world, that that duty has been, and will be, discharged in the manner most advantageous to the public interest."[28]

Clearly it was hard for the United States to help China with currency reform while such an attitude continued. The records now available show that during the second half of 1935 the attitude of both Roosevelt and the silver senators changed. The futility and cost of supporting the world price of silver for the benefit of speculators and foreign interests became more and more apparent. Early in November, when purchase of Chinese silver was under negotiation, Roosevelt told Morgenthau that Senator Pittman was "cock-eyed." Morgenthau construed this to be the first indication that the president was less interested in higher silver. And Morgenthau kept Pittman posted about the China negotiations, and obtained his concurrence.[29]

But we in China had no knowledge of the changed and more favorable American attitude when, as a matter of urgent necessity, Kung began on October 8 a new effort to sell silver to the United States.* China, said Kung, was "determined to act now . . . to meet increasingly acute situation which cannot long continue without monetary breakdown." Ambassador Sze was asked to "support proposal with your strongest arguments and convey most earnest plea." The absence of Roosevelt and Morgenthau delayed action until late October. On October 26, Sze was instructed to offer 50 million ounces firm at US $0.65 for delivery within two months, plus 50 million more within the next four months; and to ask for an option for another 100 million during the six months. The proceeds would be used for exchange stabilization. With such foreign currency reserves in hand, Kung at last would be ready to permit the export of the silver without duty, after being previously deterred by fear of the consequences of export.

Morgenthau was receptive but first wanted to know the "new financial and currency program and how funds to be used." He also was suspicious of the Leith-Ross mission. On Friday, November 1, Kung telegraphed the outline of the program, saying that action might be necessary during the weekend. His instructions made it clear that the plan was the "eventuation of a year's consideration," and that there was "no basis for talk of

*The statements and quotations that follow in this section are based on documents in my files unless otherwise indicated.

a Sino-British-Japanese bloc." He referred to the possible loan of £10 million, explaining that if it materialized the currency would be linked to sterling but otherwise there would be no link to another currency. Exchange would be stabilized at a level around US $0.30 and 14-1/2 pence.

Even though negotiations for sale of silver had not been completed, Kung and Soong decided on November 2 that the state of the market made it necessary to effect the reform as of Monday, November 4, Morgenthau's attitude in late October made it seem fairly certain that a sale could be arranged. Ambassador Sze was at once advised of the decision to act. He also was told that Britain would order British banks to conform to China's decree, and asked to express the hope that Morgenthau would influence American banks to do the same.

Meanwhile, on November 2 Sze conferred with Morgenthau after traveling seven hours to the Secretary's home in New York State. With Roosevelt's approval, Morgenthau agreed to buy 100 million ounces—but on several conditions. The proceeds would be used only for currency stabilization. He wanted China to propose a stabilization committee of three, including two American bankers. He also wanted a link to the dollar, with China agreeing to make the currency convertible at a level chosen by China.[30] Kung at once replied that the reform had been announced. China had appointed a Currency Reserve Board of leading Chinese bankers, which was to have an advisory committee including American, British, French, and Japanese bankers. It had also been announced that exchange would be stabilized at the present level, and there was no link to any specified currency.

On November 2 in Shanghai, Ambassador Johnson was advised of China's impending action and the diplomatic representatives of Britain, France, and Japan were similarly advised. Johnson telegraphed on November 4 that Leith-Ross had told him he "had not instigated goverment's decision" and that China had "jumped the gun," but that he considered the plan "essentially a good scheme."[31]

When word of the reform reached Morgenthau, his first reaction was that China went off "half-cocked", lacked "ammunition," and was "playing us for 'suckers' in the belief that they could get our money with which to put their plans through". He persisted in seeking a definite link to the dollar.[32] But China insisted that the silver was offered as a purely financial transaction, without asking a further American commitment. Japan, said Kung, was upset over the currency measure, suspecting a link to sterling, although China worded the decree carefully to avoid a link to any currency. If there were a link to the dollar, he asked, would the United States help to explain to Japan? The message begged Morgenthau to agree promptly. The public had accepted the reform with "surprising readiness," and a break would mean "loss of all confidence in present currency."

Despite this plea, it took ten days after the reform was announced to complete a deal. Morgenthau was worried about criticism from the silverites about helping China to abandon the silver standard. He and Roosevelt backed away from the 100 million figure, and first tried to limit the sale to 20 million ounces. This action was motivated by receipt of word that Hong Kong wanted the Treasury to buy 100 million ounces. Morgenthau experienced revulsion against buying foreign silver, and also suspected a British plot to add both China and Hong Kong to the sterling bloc aided by American purchases of silver.

At that juncture, Sze made an urgent plea to raise the 20 million figure, advising that Japanese banks had raided China's small exchange fund on November 11 and that China immediately needed more foreign currency. Morgenthau's strong dislike of Japan's aggressive action in Asia finally overcame his suspicions of Britain. After consultation with Roosevelt he raised the figure to 50 million. The price was US $0.65 5/8. He asked that China keep his representative fully informed about currency matters during the next twelve months. China accepted these terms.[33] He named as his representative J. Lossing Buck, the well-known agricultural economist of Nanking University.

These protracted negotiations were very frustrating to us in China, especially as we were in the dark concerning the motivation of the New Deal. American action had been a major cause of the difficulties that finally forced China to act. After China acted and success or failure was in the balance, there was an urgent need for usable foreign currencies in place of the ample supplies of silver. And the Treasury was required by law to acquire silver. Morgenthau and Roosevelt were disposed to help China and to counter Japan's aggressive action but steering clear of serious involvement. Although these motives eventually were decisive, Morgenthau's attitude all through his incumbency in this period and after war began in 1937, was colored by a suspicion of China's leaders and their advisers and failure to understand the real nature of China's financial problems. Even after contact with him during the war, and later reading the record in the Morgenthau *Diaries* and other American archives, I find it hard to understand his attitude.

Reform of November 3, 1935

Kung's announcement of November 3 explained that China's currency had been "seriously overvalued." There had been severe deflation, flight of capital, an adverse balance of payments, and impaired government revenue. To prevent the heavy drain of silver, the export duty and equalization charge of October 1934 had been imposed to check the rise of exchange and avert "an immediate calamity." But that measure was clearly temporary. Now the government, "following the precedents of many countries in recent years," was issuing a decree to provide "lasting measures of currency and banking reform," effective November 4.

The decree (Appendix 16) made the notes of the Central Bank, Bank of China, and Bank of Communications full legal tender. "All contractual obligations expressed in terms of silver," it provided, "shall be discharged by the payment of legal tender notes [*fapi*] in the nominal amount due." A Currency Reserve Board was created to control note issue and keep custody of note reserves. "No use of silver dollars or bullion for currency purposes shall be permitted," and all banks, firms, and public and private individuals were required to hand over their silver to the Currency Reserve Board or designated banks. The important provision about foreign exchange was:

> For the purpose of keeping the exchange value of the Chinese dollar stable at its present level, the Central Bank of China, the Bank of China, and the Bank of Communications shall buy and sell foreign exchange in unlimited quantities.

On Monday, November 4, the Central Bank announced opening selling rates of 14-3/8 pence and US $0.29-1/2, slightly below the rates of the preceding Saturday.

The decree declared that the Central Bank would be reorganized as a bankers' bank; the banking system would be strengthened to provide greater liquidity; a special mortgage institution would be created; and measures would be taken to balance the budget, which Kung stated would be done within 18 months. He declared that the government was determined to avoid inflation and would "take energetic measures to deal with speculation and attempts to bring about unwarranted increases in prices." He expressed confidence that "the nation will wholeheartedly support . . . these measures to relieve depression and promote national prosperity."

Because of the system of extrality, the Chinese measure banning silver payments and making banknotes legal tender could not have effect as to most foreigners in China. On November 4, the British ambassador issued a "King's regulation," under authorization of British law, citing the Chinese currency decree and forbidding British nationals to pay in silver any debt or other obligation. The immediate announcement of this regulation gave powerful support to China's move. The requirement that bank notes be accepted as legal tender in place of silver showed strong confidence in the notes. The regulation was taken widely as British endorsement of the currency reform.

Besides the official statement by Minister Kung, Soong as head of the Bank of China issued a strong supporting statement backed by his considerable prestige. He considered the reform a necessary and fundamental remedy for the ills that for some time had been "sapping the vitality and destroying the confidence" of the people. He stressed the importance of exchange stability in place of violent fluctuations, and pointed out that the new level of exchange was the average of the years 1930 to 1934 before "outside influences" forced overvaluation of the currency. He expressed confidence that bank notes would continue to have general acceptance as they had in the past. The new measures, he said, would provide "increased liquidity along sound lines." The government had "a great opportunity to carry through successfully a far-reaching scheme of currency and financial reorganization that will directly increase the well-being of the whole country." He predicted success.[34]

10: Implementing Currency Reform

Adoption of the reform was an audacious move, in view of the bad economic situation, the weak condition of the banks, the government's shrinking revenues and large deficit, continued internal dissension, and Japan's encroachment in the north and unfriendly attitude toward Western aid to China. The reform showed great courage on the part of Kung and Soong. But the situation had become intolerable and the action taken was clearly the best available solution. Careful weighing of the pro's and con's showed a strong probability of success.

The new level of exchange was clearly sound and early reactions to the reform presaged success. But much remained to be done. The nationalized silver had to be brought under central control, and enough converted into foreign currencies and gold to ensure control of exchange rates. A technical problem that could arise at any time was how to maintain rates at the "existing level," not linked to either sterling or the dollar, if the variable pound-dollar rate changed materially. It was necessary to arrange to retire the notes of private banks in exchange for Central Bank notes, and to give effect to monopoly of note issue by substituting Central Bank notes for the large issues of the other government banks. Some of the Chinese banks were so weak that they needed to be rehabilitated by the government or perhaps liquidated. The Central Bank was to be reorganized as a reserve bank. The reform needed to be extended to the distinctive currency area of South China. A convenient nation-wide system of convertible decimal coins was essential to supplant the confusion of fluctuating small money silver, fractional notes, and coppers.

The economic situation called for urgent attention to undo some of the effects of the prolonged extreme tightness of money by moderate expansion of the money supply. And the money supply had to be kept in hand by avoiding unduly large credits to the government, that might dilute the currency to a point endangering stability. The announcement of November 3 said that the budget was to be balanced within 18 months.

Mobilizing nationalized silver

At the time of the reform, the three government banks held about 130 million ounces of silver at Shanghai, and other banks there held about 100 million. A further 100 million was in banks in other parts of China. Thus total bank holdings were about 330 million ounces. Of this amount, foreign banks held 43 million.

The decree required that silver be handed over without any premium. But since it was worth about two-thirds more abroad than in China at the time of the reform, the banks sought a special inducement for exchanging their silver for *fapi*. The solution for the Chinese banks was to give them notes against delivery of 60 per cent silver and 40 per cent of government securities (taken at 80 per cent of market value). Since the banks could continue to receive the interest on the securities deposited, they had the free use of notes equal to two-thirds of the value of silver handed over. The privilege was to extend for two years from the time when the silver was delivered. The arrangement was inflationary because it materially contributed to expansion of the currency.

The foreign banks were offered the same privilege as the Chinese banks for handing over silver. But since they did not generally hold Chinese bonds, they were offered as an alternative an equivalent arrangement for mutual deposits. The Central Bank would pay them 6 per cent while they would pay that bank only 1 per cent per annum, this for a two-year period. All the foreign banks but the Japanese accepted this arrangement and handed over their silver early in 1936. The Japanese were politically motivated, arguing that the reform would fail, and held off. But as the success of the reform became more and more apparent, and because holding the silver was unprofitable, the Japanese banks agreed in the spring of 1937 to hand over their silver on the same terms as the other foreign banks. The arrangement was made by a Japanese economic mission to China, and covered delivery of about C $9 million of silver at Shanghai.

The Japanese military, however, brought pressure to prevent removal of silver from North China amounting eventually to about 40 million ounces. But they did not prevent it from being handed over to the government banks there, on the same terms as had been arranged at Shanghai. That silver remained immobilized throughout the war.[1]

Altogether the government banks took over about 200 million ounces held by other banks at the time of the reform, which was added to the 130 million then held by the government banks. A further 170 million was collected from the public in the 20 months prior to mid-1937. Thus about 500 million ounces was mobilized under the program of nationalization.

Sales of silver

Unsold silver could not support the commitment to stabilize exchange at the level of November 3. The exchange fund was only equal to about US $30 million prior to the sale of 50 million ounces, agreed on November 13 and described in Chapter 9. That sale added US $32.5 million to reserves. Temporarily, the market had technical support from sales of foreign currencies by speculators to take profits on purchases at higher rates. And the level of exchange was favorable because the currency was if anything undervalued. But much larger external reserves were vital to keep rates stable if short-term upsetting factors should develop.

On December 10, Kung asked Morgenthau to buy a further 100 million ounces for delivery before May 1, 1936. But Morgenthau understandably said that he would not consider a further sale until the first 50 million ounces had been delivered. He remembered the sale of 19 million ounces in 1934, of which China felt obliged to cover 17 million in London and had not yet shipped the remaining 2 million. The Chase and National City Banks had each bid for equal parts of the 50 million on November 14 for delivery by February 11, but none of the silver had been shipped. China's leaders still hesitated to ship for fear of upsetting the market, in view of the continued attachment to silver. Reflecting this mood, Kung had even stated three days after the reform that China was not abandoning the silver standard but was only suspending the use of silver money. The mint, he said, was still coining silver dollars for reserve against notes. But Morgenthau's firm stand forced the issue. Shipments of the 50 million were completed between December 21 and January 7, and the 2 million outstanding from the 1934 sale was also shipped. The market took the exports without significant disturbance. Morgenthau was not ready to announce that he had bought the 50 million. So the Central Bank merely stated that the silver had been sold to the two banks to provide additional reserves for exchange stabilization.

Meanwhile, Morgenthau was becoming more and more disillusioned with buying foreign silver. "Siphoning silver out of China" seemed to him "more and more stupid," with someone gaining the difference between the price of 40 cents in China and the 65 cents he paid. With Roosevelt's concurrence, he began to drop the price on December 9. Two days later Pittman told Morgenthau he did not care what was done with the world price if the domestic price were maintained. The world price fell gradually to 45 cents by the second half of January.[2]

In China, the drop was disturbing to confidence because at a price below about 40 cents China could not export silver at a profit. And if the price fell much below 40 cents, it would pay to import silver to acquire *fapi.* A further depreciation of the value of silver reserves would have threatened a serious run on the reserves of foreign currencies and gold. Fortunately for China, the Treasury held the price at 45 cents. *And that was the level China had urged a year earlier for foreign silver.*

China persisted with efforts to sell more silver. Morgenthau's reaction was to complain that he was "kept in complete ignorance" of China's monetary program. That was mystifying to us in China, as the program had repeatedly been explained; and I, under Minister Kung's instructions, was in almost daily touch with Buck. Morgenthau still suspected a deal with Britain, despite explanations that there was no link to sterling and that the program was prepared before Leith-Ross' arrival. We telegraphed another explanation of the program, and Morgenthau was pleased. On February 13, he announced the November sale of 50 million ounces, and commended the success of China's currency reform. He also let it be known that China acquired US $10 million of gold with part of the proceeds of the sale.

Morgenthau proposed that either Kung or Soong come to Washington to discuss silver. The State Department felt it better that a less prominent person come, both because of uncertainty about what the United States could do and because their coming might arouse the suspicions of Britain and Japan.[3] It was agreed that K. P. Chen a prominent banker would come. His instructions, which I drafted, contained a full statement of China's monetary and fiscal situation and program. He was to explain these fully to Morgenthau. At that time the reserves behind China's note issue comprised only 29 per cent in foreign currencies and gold; whereas the American reserves were 82 per cent in gold. China was ready to keep silver as part of the reserves, but wanted to sell up to 200 million ounces. China did not wish to link her currency to any one foreign currency. That was partly because of the monetary uncertainties of the thirties, and partly because a linking would have political implications which China wished to avoid. China was ready to issue fiduciary silver coins, but needed first to have a better idea of the future prospects of silver. A rise in silver might drive the coins from circulation, whereas a fall might threaten counterfeiting.

The American attitude at this time is indicated by a full memorandum given to Morgenthau by Harry D. White.[4] The memorandum favored buying silver from China to support the exchange, as this would help business conditions and benefit American interests. "We do have some responsibility for China's monetary difficulties," it said, "and are in a sense obligated to help her out." While the United States did not want China to link the currency to sterling, White doubted whether a link to the dollar was desirable. China should be asked to mint some coins with silver, to avoid the "onus of having driven silver out of China's monetary system by our silver policy."

Chen arrived in Washington early in April 1936. Morgenthau liked him, and the negotiations went well. He later said that Chen was "everything that a story-book Chinese business man should be and most of them ain't."[5] Morgenthau still had problems with the silver senators, but found them less intractible. The agreement of May provided for purchase of 75 million ounces in eight monthly lots at average prices, which proved to be 45 cents per ounce. The Treasury also agreed to arrange with the Federal Reserve Bank of New York an eight-month credit of US $20 million against 50 million ounces of silver, it being indicated that the credit could be renewed.

Considerable maneuvering was needed to devise a setup that would not arouse the wrath of the silverites. China agreed to hold at least one-fourth of its note reserve in silver; but left open the method of calculation to be able to count silver holdings at their monetary value as fiduciary coin. China also agreed to relax restrictions on the use of silver in the arts.

At this time the price of silver was basically weak, apart from the extraordinary demand from American buying. The Treasury, reflecting the views of the silverites, wanted China to continue the use of silver in her coins. Realizing that coinage matters would be important, K. P. Chen was instructed to say that China was prepared to issue silver coins, provided they could be adequately protected against fluctuations in silver that might lead either to driving the coins from circulation or to counterfeiting. The latter was a serious risk. Besides the cleverness of metal workers, there was the possibility of large-scale coinage either by provincial mints out of control or by the Japanese in North China. Furthermore, extraterritoriality limited China's policing.

China was then thinking of issuing C $1.00 and C $0.50 silver coins 0.500 fine. They could thus be of larger size and more acceptable to the public. Many feared that people would hesitate to accept dollar coins if considerably smaller than the old full weight coins. One plan was to issue "quarternary" coins with silver 0.500 fine plus an alloy of copper, zinc, and nickel, and with a "security rim" to make counterfeiting difficult. The rim had a depression on which beading or lettering could be stamped. Britain had successfully issued such coins. But Chen's mention of this possibility met a highly adverse reaction from Morgenthau. The silverites were bitter about Britain's reducing the silver content of coins from 0.925 to 0.500 shortly after World War I, thus reducing the demand for silver. For China to adopt 0.500 would bring a charge of a secret understanding with Britain.

The Treasury proposed a fineness of 0.720. Kung thought that the matter of fineness had been left open, and his mention of 0.500 fineness at a late stage of the negotiations almost brought cancellation of the tentative agreement, until the suggestion was withdrawn. China had to agree to make fiduciary silver coins 0.720 fine of C $1 and C $0.50, five million of each. The alternative was loss of the vitally needed proceeds from the sale of silver.

The 1936 agreement for the sale of 75 million ounces of silver and a credit against 50 million was a considerable triumph for China. The futility of supporting the price of foreign silver was becoming more and more apparent. Later confidential advices to Ambassador Sze indicated that the Treasury initially thought of buying only 25 million ounces. Morgenthau's announcement of May 18 did not specify quantities, stating that arrangements had been made to buy substantial amounts of silver from China, and to make available dollar exchange for currency stabilization. He stated that China's monetary program was proceeding on sound lines. His favorable attitude toward China during the negotiations was shown by his telling a Japanese financial attaché who called on him that the currency reform in China had "gotten on remarkably well" in a short time. Morgenthau indicated his displeasure at Japan's placing obstacles in the way of the reform, as by the Japanese banks not turning over their silver—which they later did at Shanghai.[6]

A further sale of silver was agreed July 8, 1937. Kung was in Washington after a trip to London for the coronation of George VI. Kung proposed to sell the 50 million ounces pledged for credit, and also 12 million ounces held in San Francisco. Morgenthau promptly agreed to buy the lot at US $0.45 per ounce. When Kung praised him as "a far-sighted statesman," Morgenthau said, "Listen, Dr. Kung, I bought all your silver; you don't have to give me anything more." Kung replied, "Well, I sold the silver to you cheap. I bought your surplus gold."[7] When the agreement was made, neither party knew of Japan's fateful attack of July 7 at the Marco Polo Bridge near Peiping, which ushered in eight years of Sino-Japanese warfare.

Altogether, China's prewar sales of silver to the United States after the currency reform totaled 187 million ounces: 50 million in November 1935; 75 million in May 1936; and 62 million in July 1937. A slightly larger amount was delivered, and the total receipts were US $94 million. To these figures we should add 2 million ounces sold in 1934 but not delivered until December 1935. The latter was the only part of the 19 million ounce sale directly delivered from stocks in China; the remaining 17 million was delivered from purchases in London and did not provide foreign exchange on balance. Further sales of about 3 million ounces were made quietly in London in May 1936 with Morgenthau's approval. Thus total silver sales by the government of China in this period realized nearly US $100 million to provide vitally needed support for the currency reform.

After the hostilities began, Morgenthau bought further large amounts of silver, which in turn were of very great help to China in resisting Japan in the years prior to American involvement in the war. These total wartime purchases were 362 million ounces, which realized US $157 million.[8]

Further details of silver sales are given in Appendix 15.

Working of the currency reform

The reform was generally accepted in China as a courageous act to stabilize exchange and end the disorderly markets that had so long existed. The local press, both Chinese and foreign, commented favorably, and the reform was well received not only in Shanghai but in both North and South China. The British order calling upon British nationals to comply, together with the presence of Leith-Ross, gave a valuable impression of British concurrence if not support. The technical market situation was favorable. Money was tight after the drain of silver and flight of capital. Some speculators who had bought exchange at higher levels sold to take profits and return their funds. Exchange rates showed no tendency to fall. In some places, fear of fiat money caused some rise of prices, a premium on silver, and appreciation of coppers in terms of paper currency. But these happenings did not prove serious. After one month, a commentator in the influential *North-China Daily News* of December 4 said that the government's intentions had met with "almost general approval."

Comments from London praised the reform. American comment was first noncommittal, but became favorable as the reform showed it was off to a good start. Japanese comment however, was critical and even threatening. Official and private financial circles predicted failure, and like Morgenthau suspected a Chinese-British deal involving a loan to China. Japanese commentators repeated the idea that China should rehabilitate her finances by her "own efforts" (which she was doing), although Japan was ready to help. The Japanese War Office saw an "outspoken challenge" to Japan, which might be "compelled to take appropriate steps." There was fear for a time that the Japanese would attempt to set up a special currency in North China. But the success of the reform prevented any such effort. Japanese authorities repeatedly complained about not being consulted, although clearly the matter was within China's sovereign competence and secrecy in such action was obviously essential.* While the foreign governments were not consulted, the chief interested diplomatic representatives were informed before the announcement. The Japanese ambassador was told by Kia-ngau Chang, Deputy Governor of the Central Bank who earlier was a student in Japan and spoke Japanese; the British by T. V. Soong; and the American by me. The French were also advised. The Japanese objections soon quieted down, as the British stated that no loan

*The manager of a Japanese bank, at a luncheon with other bankers at which I was present shortly before the currency reform, berated me for noncommital answers to his probing questions about what the Chinese government intended to do and what I thought it should do. His implication was that I was not a very competent adviser if my solution of the problems was not more definite.

was involved and the reform proceeded smoothly. But a Japanese military spokesman opposed removal of silver from North China. And in May 1936, when it was announced that the United States was buying substantial amounts of China's silver and making arrangements to provide dollar exchange for stabilization, the *Nichi Nichi* of Tokyo said that, "The United States has greatly consolidated the economic situation of China in a manner inimical to Japan."[9]

The immediate test of the reform was in the exchange market. Fortunately no serious threat to maintenance of rates developed in the first 10 days, before Morgenthau's purchase of 50 million ounces of silver doubled China's foreign currency reserves. The US $1.25 million that Japanese banks bought on November 11, word of which induced Morgenthau to raise his purchase of Chinese silver from 20 to 50 million ounces, was not in itself a serious threat to the beginning reserves of about US $30 million. But it highlighted the need for much larger reserves. According to Central Bank data the gold and foreign currencies held by the government banks increased by the end of November to the equivalent of US $45 million, aided by sales by speculators of foreign currencies they had previously bought. At the turn of the year the Central Bank received the proceeds of silver sold to the United States, boosting reserves to US $86 million equivalent at the end of January 1936.

For a time the exchange situation was precarious. The drop of silver from 65 to 45 cents in a few weeks beginning December 9, which Morgenthau engineered, caused nervousness in the Shanghai market as previously described. It cast doubt upon whether the United States would keep on buying foreign silver. Shortly after the decline began, Japanese banks bought exchange heavily, US $2.5 million on December 12. Yet there was no important strain on exchange until May and June. At that time serious Sino-Japanese friction developed in North China, as well as internal difficulties in the south. From May 14 through June the government banks sold exchange equal to about US $40 million. But by then the beginning reserves had been increased by silver sales yielding US $66 million, plus the credit of US $20 million against silver in New York. The Central Bank was a confident seller, even taunting speculators by inviting them to come and buy and promising them that they would lose the costs of their operations—which proved to be the case. The raid gradually petered out and the currency stood stronger than ever.

In mid-1936, the currency outlook was good. The defeated speculators promised to become sellers of the currencies they had bought. Now that the currency had proved its stability flighted capital could be expected to return. Progress was being made in settlement of debts in arrears. Foreign capital showed signs of coming for investment. The successful reorganization of the internal debt was soon followed by a considerable rise of domestic bond prices. The Sino-Japanese situation showed less tension. In July I felt able to return to the United States for the first real leave in seven years.

The precise amount of the foreign currency assets in mid-1936 after the exchange raid is not available. The main item was the US $86 million from deals with the United States, and there were some further foreign currency reserves. The three government banks also held substantial banking funds in foreign currencies. Available information indicates that the total, excluding silver, was then equivalent to between US $100 and US $125 million.

An astonishing increase of external reserves took place from mid-1936 to the outbreak of hostilities a year later. The balance of payments was favorable, and in that year the government banks were able to add to foreign currency reserves funds equal to about US $100 million. In addition there were the large holdings of silver, which potentially could be converted into foreign currencies.

On June 30 1937, on the eve of hostilities, holdings of foreign currencies, gold, and silver totaled the equivalent of US $379 million, as shown in Table 19. These holdings were the total note reserves, plus banking funds abroad of the Central Bank, Bank of China, Bank of Communications, Farmers Bank, and Kwangtung Provincial Bank—the latter two having been added to the list of government banks. The equivalent of banking funds abroad included US $75 million for the Central Bank and US $22 million for the Bank of China and Bank of Communications. The reserves included silver equivalent at US $0.45 per ounce to US $168 million, of which 62 million ounces was sold 10 days later to the American Treasury for US $28 million. Including the latter sum, holdings of foreign currencies and gold as of July 10 were about US $239 million. The remainder of the silver, valued at US $139 million, was eventually sold to the Treasury during the war, plus additional silver collected and sold for US $18 million, except for about 40 million ounces blocked in North China.

Table 19

Holdings of foreign currencies, gold, and silver on June 30, 1937[a]

	Holdings abroad and in transit abroad, millions	Holdings in China, millions	Total holdings, millions
Gold (at US$35)	US$ 32.8	US$ 12.4	US$ 45.2
US dollars	73.9	--	73.9
Sterling (at US$4.95)	92.0	--	92.0
Yen (at US$0.29)	0.1	--	0.1
Silver (at US$0.45 per oz)[b]	49.4	118.3	167.7
Totals	US$248.2	US$130.7	US$378.9

[a] Source: Central Bank of China.

[b] As of June 26, 1937. As of July 10, 1937, China sold 62 million ounces to American Treasury to realize US$28 million. Most of the rest of the silver was sold in 1937 to 1941, during the hostilities.

Some contracts contained a "silver clause," providing for an option of payment in specified silver equivalents. The British "King's regulations" forbade British nationals to pay any debt or other obligation in silver, either themselves or in conjunction with any other person. The Chinese decree ruled out silver payments for Chinese nationals and others not subject to extrality. Other nationals either went along with the Chinese decree or settled by compromise. The failure of the American Supreme Court to uphold gold clauses in contracts probably influenced parties in China to refrain from pressing for application of silver clauses. Also influential was the general welcoming of the reform, the economic revival that followed, and the feeling that the value of the currency would be maintained. I find no record of strict application of the clause, or of cases in China brought to court.[10]

China undertook to maintain the "present level of exchange" and did not adopt a definite parity. The Central Bank's initial rates after the reform at which it would support the currency were 14 3/8d. and US $0.29-1/2 for selling exchange. The buying rates were 14 5/8d. and US $0.30 respectively. These rates reflected a cross rate for fluctuating sterling of about US $4.92, the approximate rate at the time of the reform. But it was not long before the Bank ran into trouble in trying to keep the currency stable in terms of two currencies not stable in terms of each other. Early in February 1936 the dollar-sterling rate rose to about US $5.00. Above US $5.01 the cheapest way to get sterling would be to sell dollars to the Bank and buy sterling at US $5.01. Such arbitrage transactions could quickly exhaust the Bank's sterling reserves and put China on a dollar standard.

The immediate solution was to raise the dollar rate by a half cent. The exchange market was sterling-minded, with more sterling than dollar transactions. The Bank feared that to lower the sterling rate would be deemed a devaluation, and seriously shock confidence. But the action created the false impression that the currency was linked to sterling. So in September, when a rise of the dollar-sterling rate to over US $5.05 called for further action, the solution for the Central Bank was to widen the spread between selling and buying rates for both currencies—to 14-1/4—14-3/4d. and US$0.29-1/2—30-1/2, respectively, to prevent arbitrage dealings through the Bank. That solution avoided the need for further changes in the official rates prior to the war period.

The United States and Japan had indicated to China at various times a wish that China's currency be linked with theirs. Morgenthau was specially insistent that China should not link to sterling, because he would have been attacked politically had he been in the position of buying silver to help China abandon the silver standard and tie up with Britain. China gave no thought to a link to the yen, but considered a possible link to either the dollar or pound in the event of certain kinds of financial help. But no link to either currency was ever close to accomplishment. After the reform, China insisted and maintained publicly that her currency was independent, with no link to any one foreign currency.

The economy responded favorably to the reforms. Particularly striking was the recovery in agriculture. The Bank of China estimated that the value of the main crops in 1936 was C $5.6 billion, an increase of C $1.7 billion or nearly 45 per cent over the average of 1933 to 1935.[11] An early effect of the favorable exchange level was to promote exports, which in the first months after the reform exceeded imports for the first time in many decades. The demand for export goods increased the purchasing power of agricultural producers in particular.

Furthermore, import trade recovered despite the lower level of exchange; in the first half of 1937, imports were 40 per cent greater than a year previously.

Note issue of the government banks grew from C $488 million on November 2, 1935, to C $1,680 million on June 30, 1937, an increase of C $1,192 million (Appendix 17). Those figures include the issue of the Kwangtung Provincial Bank, whose circulation was inflated by a sum of the order of C $100 million equivalent from the time of the reform until the bank was brought under control of the central authorities in mid-1936. Decreases in money supply other than notes of the government banks offset a large part of the overall increase of note issue in the country as a whole. Note issues of the 15 banks under the Currency Reserve Board shrank by C $160 million in the period. Under the program of silver nationalization, the government also mobilized about 500 million ounces of silver, equivalent to about C $665 million, and much of this represented substitution of notes for coin. The silver withdrawn, the increased issue in Kwangtung, and the withdrawal of notes other than those of the government banks, explain about C $925 million of the overall increase of C $1192 million in circulation in the period. Besides, an undeterminable amount of silver coin was withdrawn from circulation for hoarding.

Data of deposits are not available either as of the time of the reform or as of mid-1937. But during 1936, total deposits grew from C $2764 million to C $3523 million, an increase of C $759 million (Appendix 18).

Clearly the total money supply increased after the reform, although precise figures cannot be given because of the lack of data on deposits. The increase was spurred by the arrangement for giving banks notes against 60 per cent silver and deposit of 40 per cent in bonds (page 240). During the exchange raid of May-June 1936, the circulation of the three government banks grew at a rate that offset about half of the contracting effect of sales of foreign currencies to support exchange rates.* The Central Bank and its advisers urged suspending the 60-40 arrangement. But the raid was defeated without serious difficulty and nothing was done.

*The issue of the Central Bank, Bank of China, and Bank of Communications grew by C$77 million from May 16 to July 25, 1936. Exchange sales equivalent to about US$40 million withdrew about C$140 million.

Part of the increased money supply was warranted by the larger demand for money, because of the considerable economic revival that took place after the successful reform. But the money supply grew enough to cause a considerable rise of prices (Appendix 12). Wholesale prices rose by about 30 per cent at Shanghai and cost of living about 15 per cent in the 20 months after the reform. The initial rise was fairly sharp for some items. By mid-1937, prices had recovered to around the average level of 1931, before the deflation began. That relatively moderate reflation cannot be adjudged excessive in view of the need to stimulate and restore the economy. In the first half of 1937, prices seemed to be leveling off. The 60-40 arrangement was due to end in November.

Whether a reasonable degree of price stability could be maintained and exchange kept stable in the long run depended in mid-1937 mostly on two main factors. Could the projected Central Reserve Bank, about to be created by reorganizing the Central Bank, effectively control the money supply? And could the government bring its budget into sufficient balance to avoid excessively borrowing funds created by bank credit? In mid-1937, on the eve of Japan's attack, the outlook for reasonable stability was promising, but uncertainties lurked in the background.

Coinage reform

Following the successful abolition of the *tael* and the introduction of the standard silver dollar in 1933, the government continued with plans begun earlier to reform the subsidiary coinage. It was most important to introduce a uniform and stable decimal coinage in place of the hodgepodge of depreciated and fluctuating silver and copper minor coins and fractional paper money. In 1929, The Kemmerer Commission recommended fiduciary minor 50- and 20-cent coins of silver; 10- and 5-cent coins of pure nickel; and copper coins of 1-, 1/2- and 0.2-cent.

The gyrations of silver soon made it impossible to issue with confidence any fiduciary silver coin. A rise in the price of silver might drive it from circulation, while a decline might create undue risk of counterfeiting. But the plan for pure nickel coins was sound because counterfeiting would be practically impossible, and they would be relatively cheap to make as well as identifiable easily with a magnetic test. So from 1932, plans for nickel coins were actively discussed as were plans for minor copper coins.

After adoption of the variable export duty on silver in October 1934, the active discussion of plans for a new monetary standard involved reform of the coinage system. In June 1935, the government approved plans that my colleagues and I recommended for issuing pure nickel 20-, 10-, and 5-cent coins, together with 1- and 1/2-cent coppers. Dies were ordered from the Philadelphia Mint and nickel blanks from an American company.

Early in 1936, the Shanghai Mint was ready to begin production of the new coins, and they were issued beginning in February. Pursuant to the coinage regulations of January 19, 1936, the pure nickel coins of 20, 10, and 5 cents weighed respectively 6, 4.5, and 3 grams; and the 1- and 1/2-cent coins weighed 6.5 and 3.5 grams, consisting of 95 per cent copper and 5 per cent tin-zinc alloy. The public avidly accepted the new coins. The Shanghai mint produced up to July 31, 1937, about 200 million nickel coins of a total value of about C $21 million, and about 600 million copper coins valued at about C $6 million.

Introduction throughout China of a proper system of subsidiary coins would have been a long and major undertaking. Assuming C $1 per capita, I estimated that more than 10 billion coins would be needed. Their production would occupy the Shanghai Mint for about 17 years on the basis of its maximum capacity in 1937. Unhappily the outbreak of hostilities in August forced the closing of that mint. After the war, plans were made to continue coinage reform. But those plans depended on checking the inflation and attaining a stable currency, which unfortunately was not accomplished.

As described above, China reluctantly agreed at Washington in the spring of 1936 to make silver coins of C $1 and C $0.50, 0.720 fine, and ordered five million of each.* Dies were ordered, and three million ounces of silver was shipped to the United States for coinage. The plan was to issue the 50-cent coins first. There was fear that putting out a new and smaller dollar coin would be regarded as devaluation and damage confidence. There was real risk that a person asked to take a much smaller

*The dollar and half-dollar coins weighed 20 and 10 grams, respectively, with 72 per cent silver and 28 per cent copper. They were, respectively, 35 and 27 mm in diameter and had milled edges like American silver coins. The new dollar was thus considerably smaller than the old one, which weighed 26.6971 grams, 0.880 fine, and was 39-1 /2 mm in diameter. The theoretical melting point of the new coins was US$0.637 per ounce of silver plus costs of melting or shipment. The price of silver did not exceed that figure until about the end of World War II.

coin as equal to the former big dollar would conclude that the government's monetary program was a scheme to cheat him. And such an idea could easily be fomented by troublemakers. The ready acceptance of most paper money was different. The ordinary man, without understanding why, had already found by experience that it passed at full value. The situation suggests a partial analogy to the unsophisticated objections in many quarters in the United States in the middle sixties when half-dollars were issued with reduced silver content and quarters and dimes with none, because of the shortage of silver.

The new silver coins were never issued because they were not ready until after hostilities began in 1937. The coins were later sold to the Treasury as bullion.

Reform of regional currencies

During the thirties, fluctuating local silver and paper currencies persisted in parts of China, particularly in South China where Kwangtung and Kwangsi Provinces had a history of monetary instability, and in Szechwan Province in the west and Shansi Province in the north, both of which suffered from depreciated bank notes. Apart from the government's control, the puppet regime of Manchukuo had its own currency. For a time in the thirties this currency was maintained as a sort of silver exchange currency related to Shanghai. But after China broke with silver in October 1934, Manchukuo currency became related to the yen.

The government reformed the currency of Szechwan in 1934-1935 and the currencies of Kwangtung and Kwangsi in 1936-1937. The Szechwan reform proved especially timely, because that province was to become the headquarters of Free China in 1938, about one year after outbreak of hostilities.

In Szechwan, the government established a branch of the Central Bank, and retired local depreciated notes and miscellaneous silver coins in exchange respectively for Central Bank notes and standard silver dollars. The local note issue was C $32 million, backed by only about C $1 million of cash reserves. These notes were exchanged from September 20, 1935, C $8 of Central Bank notes for C $10 of the depreciated notes. Circulation of local notes was barred from November 20, 1935. Silver currency if of legal weight and fineness was exchanged for Central Bank notes at par, and substandard coins were taken according to an assay. A loan of C $30 million was issued on the security of national revenues collected in Szechwan to buttress the provincial finances. The exchange of currencies went well.[12]

The Canton currency unit had long been the "small money dollar," of five 20-cent pieces debased by overissue. The current value was primarily based on fine silver content, about 70 per cent of that of the "big dollar." But exchange rates fluctuated considerably. Canton also experienced various episodes of paper money excesses during the twenties and thirties. Canton was politically volatile, and disturbances from time to time caused various degrees of depreciation of bank note. Some members of the Kemmerer Commission in 1929 favored putting Canton on the basis of the standard silver dollar, as a first step in reform. But Kemmerer preferred waiting until China could move directly to a gold standard reform. Canton then stayed on the small money basis.

When silver was nationalized in November 1935, Kwangtung Province acted independently, making local notes legal tender and requiring silver to be turned over for notes. On the basis of 1.20 Canton small money dollars for C $1, the Kwangtung government added a premium of 20 per cent on silver, i.e., calling for exchange of big money silver dollars at the rate of 1.44 in small money notes. Announcement of the premium showed a lack of confidence in the local currency, and led to considerable distrust and inflation. It was even reported that local officials borrowed part of the silver reserve of the Kwangtung Provincial Bank, and turned it in to get the 20 per cent premium. Confidence was also affected by the post-reform drop in the silver market in December-January. In November the value of the silver content of C $1 was about C $1.67 in the world market, and it fell to about C $1.15 in the latter part of January 1936. But Canton continued the 1.44 rate and its money depreciated.[13]

After an unsuccessful revolt by the rulers of Kwangtung and Kwangsi Provinces in June-July 1936, the National government took over. At that time, Canton's holdings were 82 million small money dollars and C $19 million in big dollars, a total equivalent to about C $85 million. Circulation then totaled about 232 million of small money notes, more than a threefold increase since November 3, 1935. Kwangsi had about C $10 million of silver of which about 70 per cent was in small coin, and a note circulation of about 18 million in local currency. Exchange on Shanghi was 2.24–1. South China also had a large circulation of Hong Kong notes, estimated at HK $130 million. The Hong Kong dollar was then at a premium of about 8 per cent over *fapi.*[14]

Because of the confused financial situation in South China, there was a delay in merging its currency into the national system. Measures to rehabilitate the local finances and steady the currency were first in order. The Kwangtung finances were in disorder. A considerable part of the revenue came from taxes deemed illegal by the National Government, on opium and gambling. Various local practices also infringed on the national prerogatives concerning customs and salt revenues. Besides withholding national revenues, the local authorities had set up organizations that in effect smuggled imports of sugar and other goods. The National government made sweeping changes to eliminate corrupt activities and personnel. Outlay for the local military was sharply reduced. In the fall of 1936, a rehabilitation loan of C $120 million was issued, secured on the consolidated taxes of Kwangtung Province, and also a loan of US $2 million for port and river improvements in Canton and vicinity.

By the spring of 1937, definitive currency reform could be undertaken in South China. Inflation there had been controlled, and for some months the exchange rate between Canton and Shanghai had been fairly steady around 1.50. T. V. Soong visited Canton, and on June 21 he announced stabilization at the rate of 1.44 small money for C $1. The national currency was to be substituted for the local currency by the end of 1937, and thereafter all transactions were to be based on the former. The Kwangtung Provincial Bank was to become the Canton branch of the Central Bank.[15] In June 1937, plans were made also to extend currency reform to Kwangsi Province by exchanging local notes for *fapi.*

These measures of currency unification were an important part of the government's program of unifying China politically and economically. But unhappily the outbreak of hostilities in July interfered with the execution of the measures in Kwangtung and Kwangsi.

China and gold

Gold coins never really circulated in China although they were made at various times.[16] In the thirties, China was producing a small amount of gold, commonly estimated at about 100,000 ounces yearly. There have been estimates that China then held large accumulations of gold, speculatively and hoarded and in ornaments, but there is no basis for a worthwhile figure. Data for export and import of gold are not dependable. For a time, much gold moved by unrecorded parcel post. Customs figures for the years prior to the adoption of the customs gold unit are in silver terms rather than quantities of gold. Recorded net exports of gold from 1928 to mid-1937 were equivalent to about US $105 million (Table 20).

An embargo on gold exports was imposed in May 1930. Much gold was smuggled-out after the embargo, the amount according to some estimates being comparable with what was recorded. The reasons for the embargo were not clear. I had recommended against it and it was adopted at Nanking in the absence of Minister Soong, who was also opposed to it. The embargo was somehow supposed to alleviate difficulties in the exchange market, because silver was then slumping drastically. An immediate result was that gold was traded in China at various discounts. The Central Bank was able to acquire gold cheaply, and exported some at a profit of 5 per cent or more.

After the first sale of silver to the United States in 1935, China used US $10 million of the proceeds to acquire earmarked gold in New York. By mid-1937, the Central Bank had accumulated US $45 million of gold, of which US $12 million was in China. In July 1937, Minister Kung arranged with Morgenthau a credit up to US $50 million against deposit of gold in New York. Kung wanted to show a holding of gold, even though it might be offset by dollars drawn against it. That credit was renewed periodically for several years during the war until it was liquidated.

Balance of payments

China had a sizable excess of merchandise imports over exports during the prewar decade (Table 20), and this excess had characterized the trade for many years. The figures show the order of the excess, but they must be taken with reservations. Imports were increasingly smuggled when duties were raised several times after 1928. It has been estimated that smuggled imports rose from about 3 per cent in 1929 to 25 per cent in 1935.[17] In addition, some government imports did not appear in the published trade figures. The Japanese seizure of Manchuria in 1931-

Table 20

Balances of trade in merchandise, silver, and gold from 1928 to 1937[a]

Year	Excess of merchandise imports over exports, millions		Excess of:				
	Including Manchuria	Excluding Manchuria	Silver exports, millions	Gold exports, millions	Total of excess, silver and gold exports, millions	Estimated smuggled exports of of silver, millions	Estimated smuggled exports of gold, millions
1928	C$ 319	C$ 483	C$ -166	C$ - 9	C$ -175	--	--
1929	390	550	-165	3	-162	--	--
1930	646	779	-104	26	- 78	--	C$ 23
1931	816	1087	- 71	50	- 21	--	70
1932	867	955	10	109	119	--	90
1933	--	733	14	69	83	--	120
1934	--	495	257	52	309	C$ 20	60
1935	--	343	59	39	98	230	30
1936	--	235	250	41	291	40	--
1937 (first half)	--	123	--	--	--	--	--

[a] Source: Trade data are from Customs reports. Data for smuggled silver are the estimates in Bank of China annual reports. For 1934 to 1936, E. Kann estimated C$20, C$150, and C$30 million, respectively. Data for smuggled gold are the estimates derived from the tabulation in Choh-ming Li's article, "China's International Trade Statistics: An Evaluation," ***Nankai Social and Economic Quarterly***, April 1937, p. 30.

1932 changed the situation greatly by depriving China of a major source of exports. The consequences for the balance of payments of China proper, however, were less serious than the figures would indicate, because part of the exports in effect covered costs of Japanese and Russian investments in Manchuria—especially Japanese after 1931. Appendixes 20 and 21 show the trade figures for China proper and Manchuria.

For a time, an important cause of the excess of merchandise imports was inflow of foreign capital. Carl Remer estimated total foreign investment in China at US $1610 million in 1914 and US $3243 million in 1931.[18] The flow of foreign investment to China was much reduced during the prewar decade, but was growing substantially in the later years of the decade. Japanese investment in Manchuria grew rapidly after 1931. Including Manchuria, the total of private foreign investment was probably little changed in 1937 compared with 1927 (Chapter 16). But Chi-ming Hou has estimated that there were net outpayments on direct investments every year between 1928 and 1936 except for 1930. These payments ranged from C $15 million to C $87 million, and on the average were about 4 per cent of total current outpayments.[19]

In 1928 to 1937, a large flow of remittances from Chinese living overseas accounted for a considerable part of the excess of imports. Estimates of these remittances by years are as follows (millions of C $): 1928, 251; 1929, 281; 1930, 316; 1931, 400; 1932, 300; 1933, 200; 1934, 250; 1935, 260; 1936, 320.[20]

A further large item of the inpayments was foreign expenditure in China. Payments by foreign governments for upkeep of their military, naval, diplomatic, and consular services ranked as largest, being of the order of C $100 million yearly. Support of missions and other philanthropic activities amounted to C $40 to C $50 million. Adding shipping and tourist expenditures, the total of foreign invisible inpayments under these various heads in 1928 to 1937 was in the approximate range of C $150 to C $215 million.*

The cost of foreign debt service during the prewar decade was roughly equivalent to US $40 million yearly, on the average, mostly in sterling. Adoption of the customs gold unit in 1930 hedged the payments as far as concerned the budget. But with

*The Bank of China's estimates in their annual reports range from C$150 to C$215 million in 1933 to 1936.

widely fluctuating exchange rates, from about 11 to 20 to the pound sterling, the cost to the economy in Chinese currency varied widely, roughly between C $80 million and C $160 million yearly. Foreign debt payments ranged between about 3 and 10 per cent of total current outpayments.[21] A substantial part of China's foreign debt, however, was held by Chinese and some estimates put the figure as high as one-third. There is no way to estimate what part of receipts by Chinese of current payments remained abroad.

Trade in silver and gold showed wide variations from 1928 to 1937, first imports and then exports (Table 20). In 1930 and 1931, silver imports increased as the price fell, and the accompanying drop in exchange stimulated exports of merchandise. When silver and exchange rose, a severe drain of silver began, with heavy smuggling following the silver export duty of October 1934. The figures of trade in silver and gold are subject to qualifications explained in Chapter 8. In summary, the customs figures do not reflect the smuggling of silver, or smuggling and unrecorded exports of gold after the export embargo of 1930. Smuggled exports of gold may have been of the same order of size as those recorded.

Capital movements varied widely during the prewar decade. Probably there was little net change in total foreign investment in China between 1927 and 1937, as stated above. A large outflow of capital was reflected in the drain of silver when its value abroad rose. In turn, this capital was largely repatriated after the currency reform, adding notably to external reserves.

After the currency reform, when its success was still uncertain, there were proposals to restrict trade and capital movements. I strongly opposed such action, believing that it would be both hurtful and ineffective. With maintenance of a sound monetary situation, I stated, there seemed to be no reason for China to worry about the balance of payments.

An estimate of the balance of payments in 1936 is shown in Table 21. There are no published official statements of the balance of payments.

Table 21

Balance of international payments in 1936[a]

Receipts from abroad (Inpayments):		
Merchandise exports, recorded	C$706 millions	
Plus: Adjustment for undervaluation and export duty	135	
Subtotal		C$ 841 millions
Gold and silver exports, recorded	290	
Plus: Smuggled exports, estimated	60	
Subtotal		350
Overseas Chinese remittances		330
Foreign expenditure in China:		
Diplomatic, consular, military, naval	100	
Philanthropic	40	
Shipping and tourist	30	
Subtotal		170
Foreign investment in China, repatriation of capital, and income from Chinese investment abroad		150
Total		C$1841 millions
Payments abroad (Outpayments):		
Merchandise imports, recorded	C$941 millions	
Plus: Smuggled imports, estimated	250	
Government imports, unrecorded	120	
Subtotal		C$1311 millions
Foreign debt service		125
Chinese official expenditure abroad		15
Chinese investment abroad and income from investment and business in China remitted abroad		40
Increase of official holdings abroad		350
Total		C$1841 millions

[a] Source: My estimates made shortly after the end of the war. They are based on customs reports and consideration of contemporary estimates by the Bank of China in its annual reports, and E. Kann (see *Finance and Commerce*, March 31, 1937, p. 338, and April 7, 1939, p. 369), and by A. B. Calder, Assistant American Commercial Attache in China.

11: Banking

The use of modern banking practices in China had been growing for some time prior to 1928. The trend continued strongly in the prewar decade. Organization of the Central Bank in 1928 introduced a major new element. It could not only serve as the government's fiscal agent but become an institution to regulate currency and credit.

A full description of the development of banking in China, the various institutions and their functions, and the structure of the money market has been provided by F. M. Tamagna.[1] I shall not duplicate it, and only describe in summary the main elements of the system for convenient reference. I shall deal with developments in private and central banking as they relate to currency matters, the national finances, and economic deelopment.

General banking situation

The banking system in the prewar decade comprised the government banks, provincial and local banks, modern-style private Chinese banks, native banks, and foreign banks. Modern-style banking was fairly well developed in Shanghai and the other treaty ports. It had been concentrated there because these were the chief economic centers, and also because of disturbed conditions in other areas. But, as conditions became more stable during the prewar decade, the Chinese banks were extending a system of branches to the chief cities throughout the country with striking success. In the rural areas, however, where about four-fifths of the people lived, there was no adequate credit system. Agricultural credit was mainly provided by moneylenders, who often were landlords, and by pawnshops and merchants. High interest rates were common, (page 300). The farmer commonly became an urgent borrower about the end of winter when his grain supply ran out. Lenders could take advantage of his urgent need.[2]

The Central Bank of China, which the Nationalists established in 1928, was then the only government bank. It did hardly any commercial business. The Bank of China, established in 1912, had long been the leading Chinese bank. Plans for it to become a central bank never materialized. The Bank of Communications, established in 1907, had also been prominent as a private bank. The Peking regimes were to have subscribed part of the capital of both banks. But they never found the money, and instead became borrowers from them. In 1928, the new government subscribed 20 per cent of the capital of each.[3] In 1935, it took over control of both to strengthen its financial control under the difficult conditions of exchange gyrations and deflation (Chapter 9). The government added C $15 million to its C $5 million holding in the Bank of China, raising the capital to C $40 million and giving the government a 50 per cent interest. It added C $10 million to the holding of C $2 million in the Bank of Communications, raising the capital to C $20 million and giving the government a 60 per cent interest.

The fourth government bank was the Farmers Bank, established in 1933 with head office at Hankow. It made certain advances to agricultural cooperatives and helped in rehabilitation of areas taken over from the Communists in Central China. It also handled certain army funds and was generally regarded as specially close to Generalissimo Chiang. It had the privilege of note issue. Until brought under effective central control early in 1937, the Farmers Bank was a source of worry to the Finance Ministry and Central Bank. Reports of its condition and operations were not made available, and there was fear that it might expand note issue to finance military costs and thus interfere with overall currency policy. A government order of February 1936 limited to C $100 million its issue, of which a considerable part was fractional notes. It was not until a year later that it made regular reports and was brought effectively under the Currency Reserve Board. The head office was transferred to Shanghai from Hankow and the limit on its note issue was removed.

The Central Bank and its advisers urged the great need to develop a system of agricultural credit as a matter of basic importance. But more urgent matters had priority and at the end of 1937 the agricultural loans of the four government banks were only C $35 million, which was roughly half the total rural credit outstanding.[4] The Farmers Bank could have been made an agency to help to develop a nationwide system of agricultural credit. But it would have been necessary to change its character from being an organ created primarily to serve governmental needs. The improvement of agricultural credit was being considered in 1937, but unhappily the outbreak of hostilities prevented much action.

Besides the aforementioned four "government banks," there were two other public financial institutions, the Postal Remittances and Savings Bank and the Central Trust of China. The former began as an organ of the Post Office, but was reorganized and took on the added function of handling part of the remittances by overseas Chinese, which were so important in the balance of payments. The Central Trust was created in 1935 with a capital of C $10 million as a subsidiary of the Central Bank, but it developed considerable autonomy. Its functions were to take charge of certain trust funds such as public employees' savings; to handle governmental purchases, especially military purchases abroad; and later during the war to handle certain controlled exports. As of 1937, the government also had an interest in several modern-style commercial banks, notably in three small banks for which it supplied capital for rehabilitation during the deflation.

The government was thus greatly involved in banking, especially after taking control in 1935 of the Bank of China and the Bank of Communications. Personnel of the Finance Ministry and the National Economic Council were closely identified with these banks, besides the governmental control of the Central Bank and the Farmers Bank. Viewing this situation, George E. Taylor observed in 1936 that "it would be difficult to say where the Government ends and the banks begin."[5] Moreover the banks, as large holders of government bonds, were deeply involved with government.

Most of the provinces had provincial banks and there were several municipal banks. All were relatively small except the Kwangtung Provincial Bank. A number of them issued notes, which commonly depreciated, but the volume of such notes was small relative to silver and to notes of the government banks.

Modern-style private Chinese banks developed rapidly from 1928 to 1937—a total of 124 new banks was established and 23 liquidated. In 1937, there were 164 modern-style banks with 1597 branches. The spreading of branches in the interior, led by the Bank of China, was becoming of great significance as a means to provide modern-type facilities for production and trade. In this period, the capital of the members of the Shanghai Bankers' Association more than doubled—from C $117 million to C $280 million. The headquarters of the largest banks were at Shanghai, but those of a few other banks were in North China and Chungking. Banking resources were highly concentrated, and the leading five banks had about 60 per cent of the total resources of this group of banks.[6]

The growth of this group in the prewar decade was large, and only a little less than that of the Bank of China and Bank of Communications. Up to the currency reform of November 1935 the note issue of this group increased much faster than that of those two banks, but after the reform the issues of this group were being retired. The deposits of the private banks more than doubled from 1928 to the reform, while those of the two banks aforementioned grew 2.8 times (Appendixes 17 and 18).

The modern-style banks provided increasingly important facilities to the economy. Their loans to finance trade and shorter term loans to industry were commonly secured by goods in warehouses, usually in warehouses maintained by the banks rather than by commercial paper. Longer term financing of industry, including private and publicly owned utilities, was usually done by mortgages on the real estate and machinery. The banks also made loans to smaller merchants on personal credit. There was little financing to promote new enterprises. In the thirties, the banks led by K. P. Chen of the Shanghai Commercial and Savings Bank were beginning to finance agricultural credit through cooperatives, mostly credit cooperatives. The security investments were mostly in government bonds. In the latter part of the decade, the private banks helped in financing railway extensions on the security of government bond issues and railway earnings.

The native banks performed the main banking functions throughout China for many years prior to the development of modern-style Chinese banks. They were partnerships of family members or close associates and were strictly local. They took deposits and granted credit. As modern-style banking developed, they commonly held deposits in Chinese and foreign banks and obtained credit from them. They were an important part of the decentralized banking system, with a definite place because of their distribution and their knowledge of conditions and credit where they operated.

The number of native banks declined greatly after 1928, and

they lost much business to modern-style banks. The depression hit them hard and many failed. From 1927 to 1937, the number at Shanghai fell from 80 to 46; and from 1932 to 1937 from 56 to 6 at Nanking and from 540 to 77 at Canton. The total number in 1937 was estimated at about 800, a drop of perhaps half from 1927. Their total capital in 1934 was less than C $100 million, plus substantial reserves. Total assets were of the order of several hundred million.[7]

The foreign banks numbered about 25 in the thirties, and were American, Belgian, British, Dutch, French, German, Italian, and Japanese.[8] Their chief offices and branches were located in the foreign settlements and concessions. Being subject to the laws of their own governments under the system of extraterritoriality, they were not subject to Chinese regulation (except that the Germans gave up this privilege after World War I). They handled primarily foreign trade, and from time to time matters relating to foreign loans and investments in China. They were leading factors in the foreign exchange market, and could always obtain the local currency needed by selling exchange. The functions of the foreign banks in handling deposits and exchange transactions relating to service of foreign loans were mostly transferred to the Central Bank during the period by agreed changes, without prejudice to the holders of the bonds (Chapter 3). Data for the operations and assets of the foreign banks in China were never sufficiently available to permit any estimates of amounts. The indications are that during the prewar decade they were being considerably outstripped by the progress of the modern-style Chinese banks. The Chinese banks were gaining deposits more rapidly than the foreign banks and playing an increasingly larger part in the foreign exchange market.

As of 1936, the available data indicate that the Bank of China, Bank of Communications, and Farmers Bank had a little over half of the total assets and liabilities of the Chinese banks, and the other modern-style Chinese banks about two-thirds of the remaining half. A little over 10 per cent was held by the native banks, and the rest by the provincial and municipal banks.[9]

The government adopted a general banking law in 1931.[10] The Kemmerer project of 1929, which provided for extensive regulation, was shelved because of banking opposition. The law specified requirements as to capital and the permitted kinds of business. Banks were required to make semiannual reports to the

Finance Ministry, which was granted wide discretionary powers of supervision. But there was little effective regulation of banking, and a number of modern-style banks and many native banks got into serious difficulties during the depression. By the time of the currency reform of 1935, the banks generally were in a weak position. Many had their assets immobilized or had deteriorated beyond hope of full recovery and some banks were insolvent. Three of those that were in the deepest trouble were taken over by the government for rehabilitation; those of us concerned with them called them the "three little pigs."

By 1937, the banking situation had somewhat improved. Yet serious weaknesses remained. Most commercial banks were undercapitalized and some were of doubtful solvency. They were largely illiquid, with too much loaned to illiquid debtors. The system of mutual deposits between banks gave a false appearance of liquid cash resources. There was no comprehensive clearing system, no bill market, and still no effective bank regulation.

Minister Kung's announcement of the currency reform of November 1935 stated that measures had been prepared "for strengthening the commercial banking system and giving increased liquidity under sound conditions to the commercial banks so that they may have resources available to finance the legitimate requirements of trade and industry." A special mortgage institution was planned. In 1936-1937, drafts of a revised banking law were prepared and discussed. But the hostilities broke out before action could be taken.

Note issue and deposits

Use of both notes of Chinese banks and deposits in them expanded rapidly in the twenties and thirties despite troubled internal and international conditions (Appendixes 17 and 18). From 1921 to 1928, notes increased from C $96 million to C $309 million, and deposits from C $452 million to C $993 million. During the Nationalist period notes grew more than sixfold and deposits more than threefold. A small part of the increase is explained by the greater inclusiveness of the later data. The larger figures do not reflect a rise in the price level to any great extent.

Note increase from 1928 to the currency reform of 1935 included a considerable expansion of the issue of the newly founded Central Bank. Its notes were generally well received, especially after a run early in 1929 was met by paying out silver without any hesitation. Furthermore, issues of modern-style Chinese private banks at Shanghai grew rapidly. Issues of foreign banks were only a few million dollars, and practically disappeared after the currency reform.

In the 20 months after the currency reform, total circulation more than doubled, from C $765 million to C $1912 million in mid-1937 (page 251). A major factor was substitution of notes after silver was nationalized. The increase was mostly in the issue of the government banks and the Kwangtung Provincial Bank which the government took over in 1936. The total of other issues decreased, despite a large and rapid growth of circulation of the Hopei Provincial Bank under Japanese military pressure. At the time of the short-lived revolt in South China in mid-1936, the generals greatly expanded the Kwangtung Provincial Bank's issue of small money dollars, with resulting depreciation.

The growth of note issue during the twenties and thirties until the time of the currency reform was promoted by two main factors. The demand for notes grew as important parts of the economy were being progressively modernized. And notes were being widely substituted for coin. Note issues of the modern-style government banks and private banks were conservatively managed. More and more people began to find the notes more convenient than the bulky silver dollars. A study based on sampling by the University of Nanking dated August 27, 1935, showed that in 1930 circulation of silver was 68 per cent and paper 32 per cent; whereas in 1935 the figures were 45 and 55, respectively.

After the currency reform, notes were rapidly substituted for nationalized silver. Events showed little basis for the fear that the people would not accept money not linked to silver. They had become used to paper convertible to silver and acceptable interchangeably with it, and did not hesitate to accept paper convertible into foreign exchange at stable rates. This confidence extended into the war period, and paper continued to be acceptable even when exchange depreciated. Acceptance was then aided by the notes being freely convertible into foreign exchange at market rates.

Growth of deposits centered at Shanghai but also occurred in the lesser centers, notably Tientsin, Hankow, and Canton. Fixed deposits grew much faster than current accounts, expanding from 1928 to 1936 in the Bank of China tenfold and in the Bank of Communications fourfold. Deposits also grew along with modernization trends, along with confidence in modern-style banks, and understanding of the convenience of use of deposits as compared with notes and coins. The use of *taels* as uncoined silver money of account until 1933 also promoted bank accounts in *taels*, which were converted to dollars in that year. A further factor was the spread of the network of branches of Chinese banks throughout China.

For the Central Bank, the growth of deposits mainly resulted from its progress as the government's fiscal agent. Until the thirties, collections of customs and salt revenues were deposited mostly in foreign banks. The Central Bank increasingly held provincial funds. It was coming to hold sizable deposits of other banks, although not functioning as a reserve bank. Plans for that were adopted on the eve of hostilities in mid-1937 (pages 271-276).

Foreign banks held large deposits in Chinese and foreign currencies. The Hongkong and Shanghai Banking Corporation held HK $838 million at the end of 1936, but much of this amount was in Hong Kong. In the thirties, the foreign banks held one-third to one-half of the silver in banks in China prior to the large export of silver that began in 1934. That fact suggests backing for large deposits payable in silver. Certainly the foreign banks held hundreds of millions of deposits payable in Chinese currency, plus large deposits in foreign currencies. The depositors, besides foreign enterprises and individuals, included various Chinese businessmen and well-to-do persons. Indications were that, with the progress of modern-style Chinese banks, the deposits in foreign banks during the thirties were not growing and may have tended to decline.

What was the relation between the rapid growth of notes and deposits and general prices? In 1921 to 1928, prices showed little change when note issue more than tripled and deposits more than doubled. That price stability indicated that the expansion reflected a strong trend of financial modernizing, rather than an increase in the supply of money relative to the demands of the economy. From 1928 to the currency reform of November 1935, notes and deposits continued to grow at rapid rates. The price level showed wide variations influenced by the gyrations of silver: a rise of about 30 per cent to 1931, an even larger deflation, and then some recovery. But the net result was that the level of prices on the eve of the currency reform did not differ much from that of 1921 and 1928.

After the currency reform of 1935, credit was deliberately

expanded. Wholesale prices at Shanghai and Tientsin rose by about one-fourth in the 20 months from November 1935, and the cost of living at Shanghai increased about 10 per cent (Appendix 12). The expansion was inflationary, or perhaps better termed reflationary as it restored prices roughly to the level of 1931. An important element in the expansion was the arrangement whereby banks could obtain notes by handing over 60 per cent in silver and 40 per cent in collateral. The circulation was also increased by repatriation of funds, i.e., by selling foreign currencies acquired for speculation or as flight of capital and receiving the equivalent in local currency.

Although the exchange market was strong in mid-1937, despite the rise of prices, and the balance of payments favorable, the expansion of credit was not under effective central control. Such control was clearly needed.

Rise of the Central Bank

The Central Bank's outstanding progress following its creation in October 1928 was an important factor in the growing strength and progress of the central government. In China, as in so many less developed countries, the central banking institution was a positive force for sound financial and economic policies and administration. The chief items in the bank's balance sheet for 1928 to 1937 are shown in Appendix 19.

Part of the Central Bank's activities is described in Chapters 6 and 10 in relation to public administration and monetary reform respectively. Its capital was increased in 1934 from the original C $20 million to C $100 million, partly by using accumulated reserves and profits and partly from an additional subscription by the government. It developed a system of branches and agencies throughout China. As fiscal agent, it was effectively handling the government's receipts and payments and the issuance and servicing of domestic and foreign debts. In 1930, it opened accounts in New York, London, and other foreign centers. It gradually acquired substantial assets in foreign currencies, in part through the development of the system of customs gold units. It managed the silver deals with the United States. It aided in abolishing the *tael* currency of account, in reforming and coinage, and in extending the national monetary system to Szechwan and South China. On several occasions, it intervened in the money market to ease extreme tightness, support banks that were under pressure, and facilitate settlements at the Chinese New Year. It handled a large volume of purchases abroad for the government, issuing the necessary letters of credit and guarantees. In 1933, it established a research department. The expansion of its activities is shown by the growth of its balance sheet from C $47 million at the end of 1928 to C $1477 million as of June 30, 1937.

Adoption of the currency reform of November 1935 opened a new era. For some time previously, the Central Bank had operated in exchange to steady the market and reduce fluctuations. By 1935 it had become probably the largest operator in foreign exchange at Shanghai. With experience thus gained, it quickly showed itself able to take charge of stabilizing exchange rates in the face of considerable difficulties. It opened an account at the Federal Reserve Bank of New York early in 1936.

Yet at the time of the currency reform there were serious weaknesses in the system. Basic improvements were needed to put the Central Bank in a position to perform effectively the closely related tasks of managing money and credit internally and maintaining the currency in the markets for foreign exchange. Recognizing this need, Minister Kung's statement at the time of the currency reform of 1935 contained important declarations. The Central Bank was to take over gradually the note issue of all other banks, and "after a period of two years will enjoy the sole right of note issue." It was to be reorganized as the Central Reserve Bank, and instead of full government ownership was to be "owned principally by banks and the general public, thus becoming an independent institution, devoting itself chiefly to maintaining the stability of the nation's currency." It was to "hold the reserves of the banking system and . . . provide centralized rediscount facilities for the other banks." And Kung declared the government's intention to avoid inflation and bring the budget into balance within 18 months.

Control of the supply of money was of primary importance. Although in 1935 notes and coins were still used almost exclusively by the great mass of the people, the more advanced parts of China had reached a stage of economic development in which bank credit had become widely used. Thus a need existed to centralize control of bank credit, as well as of note issue.

When the Central Bank commenced note issue in 1928, the notes of the Bank of China and the Bank of Communications were well established in public favor. Because of the difficulty and risk of transporting silver and maintaining reserves at all branches, the place of redemption of each note of these two banks was specified as Shanghai, or Tientsin, or Tsingtao. The

Central Bank, however, undertook to redeem notes only at Shanghai. Its issue was conservatively managed and grew steadily. By November 1935, its issue exceeded that of the Bank of Communications, and was gaining on that of the Bank of China. The development of the issues of the various banks is shown in Appendix 17.

In the 20 months following the currency reform, little progress was made toward the objective of exclusive Central Bank issue. The circulation of private banks was being rapidly retired. But in total issue the shares of the Bank of China and Bank of Communications decreased only slightly. The amount issued by the Farmers Bank grew about sevenfold, as that bank was not brought under central control until early in 1937. The issue of provincial banks grew, because the Kwangtung Provincial Bank was out of control for some time, as was the Hopei Provincial Bank, which was under Japanese pressure. The upshot was that between November 3, 1935, and mid-1937 the Central Bank issue increased only from 18 to 20 per cent of the total (Appendix 17).

Clearly it was highly important to perfect centralized control of issue as a basic measure to safeguard stability of prices and exchange rates. I urged centralization by making use of the Currency Reserve Board's power to "control the issue and retirement of ... notes," pending creation of the Central Reserve Bank. But to no avail. Under the 60-40 plan of note issue (Chapter 10), the government banks other than the Central Bank could profit much from issue, and these banks had strong influence. And it was taking time to control the Farmers Bank as well as the Kwangtung Provincial Bank, which later involved reform of the South China currency. When efforts for central control of note issue lagged, hopes had to be pinned to early creation of the Central Reserve Bank.

The banking system as it had developed in China was inflexible. Banks had to keep a reserve of 60 per cent in cash and 40 per cent in securities against notes. Although there was no specified reserve against deposits, the rigid limit on notes interfered with needed elasticity of credit. There was no development of rediscounting by the Central Bank; nor was there a bill market of worthwhile proportions. Development of a bill market was important to provide for controlled liquidity of credit. Greater overall flexibility of credit was needed to meet seasonal and emergency needs.

The system whereby the government banks bought and sold exchange to maintain stability was likewise in need of centralization. The action of the banks was coordinated by the Central Bank and proved effective, but it was clumsy to have more than one bank responsible. Moreover, a difficulty prior to the reform was that the Central Bank did not handle all the government's foreign business. In particular, the Railway Ministry for some time before 1935 failed to abide by a governmental order to work only through the Central Bank, and at times bought exchange without regard to what the Central Bank was doing in the market.

As its resources grew, the Central Bank became more and more a lender to the government. A further growing practice, which the Central Bank's operating management and advisers deplored, was arranging for the bank to guarantee performance of certain of the government's purchase contracts abroad. Besides reflecting on the government's credit, the practice involved the bank in politically determined liabilities that could be indefinitely extended. Regulation of all forms of governmental use of Central Bank credit was necessary to avoid endangering the currency. It was clearly urgent to concentrate on the project of transforming the Central Bank into the proposed Central Reserve Bank.

Planning a Central Reserve Bank

To plan the announced reorganization of the Central Bank as China's Central Reserve Bank, Minister Kung named an expert committee early in 1936. Its members were Deputy Governor Jian H. Chen, General Manager Te-mou Hsi, T. L. Soong of the Manufacturers Bank, Cyril Rogers who was loaned by the Bank of England, and advisers Lynch and Young. The plan proposed in June was designed to take account of modern experience as adapted to China's special needs and problems.[11]

The plan provided for balanced ownership: 40 per cent by government, with no voting or dividend rights; 30 per cent by Chinese banks; and 30 per cent by the Chinese public. The aim was to avoid complete domination by any one interest, governmental, banking, or private, while protecting the government's legitimate interest in being satisfied as to control of policy. To that end the government would appoint one of the eleven directors; approve appointment of the governor and deputy governor, who would be directors; and approve appointment of the four directors elected by the public shareholders, three of whom would be actively engaged in agriculture, commerce, and industry respectively. Thus the government would have a voice in selection of seven of eleven directors. The remaining four would be elected by the banks, and one of them would not be a banker.

Capital would be C $50 million instead of the C $100 million of the Central Bank. In the past, that bank was readily able to earn a good return on its capital with the aid of profits gained from operations in widely moving foreign exchange rates, and from export of gold bought in China below the price abroad. But such profits were not to be expected in future, especially with exchange held stable and with the prospect of lower interest rates as the financial market became better developed. The experts felt that the new institution should be able to determine its policies on the basis of the needs of the market and the general interest, without feeling pressed to make a profit to cover dividends on an amount of capital that did not seem to be needed under the new plan. Moreover, with the private banks undercapitalized, to require them to subscribe 30 per cent of a capital of C $100 million would needlessly strain their resources. Finally, the repayment of C $50 million of capital to the government would help the Finance Ministry.

The planning of relations to exist between the new bank and the government gave rise to a major problem. It was most important to avoid endangering the currency by direct borrowing from the new bank. From 1928 to 1936, the government came to lean heavily on the Central Bank. By the end of 1935, most of the C $407 million of its loans, discounts, overdrafts, and securities owned (Appendix 19) represented advances to the Finance Ministry and various governmental organs. The prospect was that the government would need to have recourse to borrowing for some time to come. In 1936, China had not fully recovered from the depression. There were occasional flare-ups of internal revolt, and Japan continued to apply pressure in North China. Doubt grew whether the budget could be balanced in 18 months as contemplated by Kung's statement of November 3, 1935.

The guiding principle as to borrowing was that credit should come essentially from savings of the public rather than creation of it by the banks. To that end, the committee emphasized that all governmental borrowing should pass through the hands of the new bank, but that it should neither subscribe to the issues nor lend to banks to help them to subscribe. Rather, the new bank should see to it that the new issues were placed with the private banks and the public.

The plan, however, recognized the government's need for temporary accommodation. The proposal was that the government be entitled to borrow up to one-sixth of the revenue of the previous fiscal year, but subject to repayment during the current fiscal period either from revenue or from borrowing from the public.

The plan called for revision of the system of note issue and reserves. The existing 60 per cent requirement of reserve against notes was deemed too high, and there was no provision for reserve against deposits. It also appeared that the total cash reserve could be less than 60 per cent with unification of the note issue. The committee proposed a reserve of 40 per cent against notes plus deposits, with provision for temporary reduction accompanied by the raising of interest rates to meet special demands that might arise, e.g., those at the time of the New Year's settlements.

Commercial banks would be required to maintain with the new institution a reserve of 10 per cent against demand deposits and 5 per cent against time deposits. That reserve would provide the basis for a convenient clearing system. Because the banks were weakened by the years of depression, the banks would be allowed time to bring their reserve deposits up to the required figures. Also some of the security reserves against notes which certain banks had transferred to the Currency Reserve Board were either of types unsuited for the purpose, such as mortgages and real estate, or comprised such items as bonds and shares that had depreciated. Since those assets should become the property of the new bank, the plan was that the government take them over for liquidation, issuing an equivalent amount of non-interest-bearing bonds, with possible recourse against the respective banks.

The foreign banks could not specifically be brought under the plan. But the plan was flexible enough to permit them to come into the system by making deposits with the Central Reserve Bank. The committee believed that they would do this to facilitate clearing, and also that many of them would wish to take advantage of credit facilities in local currency.

Taking account of the weakness of the private banks, the committee recommended adoption of a revised comprehensive banking law. The committee had met difficulties in getting adequate information about the banking situation, and recommended a system of regulation and periodic reports. The committee gave considerable attention to preparation of a project for such a law.

The plan for the reserve bank was debated at Nanking for a year. It was finally adopted by the Legislative Yuan on June 25, 1937, with a few modifications. Details of transitional measures were also included in it. Voting rights were given to the government's shares to provide for greater control; the period for withdrawal of notes other than of the Central Bank was fixed at four instead of two years; reserves against notes and sight deposits were reduced from 40 to 35 per cent; and the provision for temporary government borrowing was set at one-fourth instead of one-sixth of the previous fiscal year's revenue. But the essential elements of the committee's plan were approved.

Unfortunately, the Sino-Japanese hostilities broke out within two weeks of the plan's adoption. It had to be held in abeyance, and the planned Central Reserve Bank, which could have had great possibilities for improving China's financial system and economy, never came into being. During the hostilities, the Japanese puppet regime in Central China created its "Central Reserve Bank," making use of the name and some of the plan devised in 1936-1937. That bank's career was brief and inglorious.[12]

12: Monetary Affairs: Summary and Appraisal

Comparison of the conditions of 1928 and 1937 in the field of currency and banking showed a change that was indeed striking. In that brief period, the situation was being transformed and modernized to the great benefit of the people of China and of other countries having interests in China. In 1937, nevertheless, much remained to be done to improve the situation.

Currency

The new government when it took over in 1928 clearly saw the need for reforming the currency. Currency reform involved unifying and standardizing the chaotic circulating medium and bringing the standard of value into a stable relation to the monies of leading countries. Attaining these ends was far from easy. Strong dissident and separatist elements were disturbing the internal situation, and externally there were the grave difficulties with Japan beginning in 1931. The worldwide depression of the thirties was accompanied by first the acute drop and then the sharp rise of silver. Devaluation of the pound and then the dollar created further abnormal fluctuations and uncertainties in rates of foreign exchange.

The first major decision was to adopt the customs gold unit (CGU) early in 1930, following the advice of the Kemmerer Commission. The fiscal effects of this decision were of major importance. Customs revenue was substantially increased at a time when silver was slumping, thus providing sorely needed income when severe internal and external troubles plagued the government. It made possible the preservation and improvement of the government's credit, helping to maintain payments on the foreign debt. It paved the way for eventual settlement of most of the debts in arrears. But the effects of the CGU on the currency were specially important. The manner of operation of the CGU system provided a flow of foreign currencies to the Central Bank. That afforded valuable experience in foreign exchange operations as well as in administration of debt service.

The advisers hoped that the CGU would be a step toward adopting the gold standard. To that end CGU notes were issued. But they did not enter into general circulation, and their use was mostly for payment of customs duties.

The next major decision, in 1933, was to abolish *taels* as units of account and unify the currency on the basis of the standard silver dollar. The transition took place smoothly. It wiped out at a stroke the confusion of obsolete units having values that varied from place to place and even within some financial centers. Abolition of the *tael* units was facilitated by completion of the Shanghai Mint equipped for efficient coinage. After issuance of standard silver dollars, preparations followed to issue fiduciary nickel and copper coins on a decimal basis and firmly held at parity with the standard dollar.

Paradoxically, the depression and the gyrations of silver led to basic currency reform. Early in 1935 I wrote to a friend that "the American silver action may even prove a blessing in disguise if it leads without undue delay, and without financial collapse, to a really constructive monetary reform." While silver was slumping it seemed impossible to sell enough on the world market to permit China to obtain foreign currency resources adequate to back a nationwide currency reform with exchange stabilization. Only a windfall could suffice, such as the strong rise of silver in 1904 to 1907 that permitted Mexico to adopt the gold standard.[1] But China would have to sell much more silver than did Mexico. For a time, the only practicable approach to currency reform in China seemed to be to issue a new and solidly backed currency unit on a moderate scale and let it make its way. But even that plan was a dubious expedient when the values of the dollar and pound were so uncertain during the depression.

It was the American silver buying policy that made possible, and necessary, the currency transformation in China. The transformation was possible because it gave China the prospect of selling large amounts of silver at good prices and without breaking the market. And necessary because the suffering in China caused by the artificial rise of silver out of line with the rise of world prices in general became intolerable. A particularly objectionable phase of the American silver movement was the callous disregard for the vital interests of a friendly state. That attitude was compounded by the repeated claim that raising the value of silver would help China, even though the Chinese government and overwhelming opinion in China called the claim fatuous.

The decisive break with silver was the adoption in October 1934 of the flexible export duty. Such a duty brought about abandonment of the free silver standard and led to variable exchange rates that were managed after a fashion. It made almost inevitable a definitive reform as soon as the public was psychologically ready and external conditions suitable. The attachment to silver died hard. To condition the public for fundamental action took a year of economic distress and uncertainty, while exchange rates were for a time manipulated to follow more or less the gyrations of silver. Even after announcement of the reform of November 1935, Minister Kung stated, hoping to allay nervousness, that China was still on silver and that the mint was making silver dollars (which it soon discontinued). And it was some weeks before he felt ready to allow export of silver to deliver the sales made to the United States shortly after the reform. The silver was exported only after Secretary Morgenthau properly said that he would not discuss further sales until the silver already sold was delivered.

The external conditions for basic reform seemed auspicious when in the latter part of October Morgenthau indicated that he was favorable to a large purchase of China's silver. China was consequently encouraged to act even though negotiations were still pending. The exchange market was so disturbed that action to end the uncertainty seemed necessary. The technical state of the market was also favorable to stabilizing action. The plans were ready, having been under preparation for months. So China acted resolutely and the response was favorable.

The reform of November 3, 1935, nationalized silver and made notes of the Central Bank, Bank of China, and Bank of Communications full legal tender for all obligations in terms of silver. Use of silver as currency was forbidden, and all banks, firms, and the public were required to hand over their silver to the Currency Reserve Board or designated banks. The three banks were to buy and sell foreign exchange in unlimited quantities to keep the Chinese dollar "stable at its present level." The rates announced by the Central Bank were 14-3/8 pence and US $0.29-1/2, slightly below the level of the preceding business day. The Central Bank was to be reorganized as a true central bank, the banking system was to be strengthened, and measures were to be taken to balance the budget within 18 months.

The British government gave indirect but powerful support to the reform by issuing a "King's regulation" citing China's action, and forbidding British nationals to pay in silver any debt or obligation.

At the time of the reform, banks in China held 330 million ounces of silver, including 43 million in foreign banks, which in due course they turned over. About 170 million were collected from the public, making a total of about 500 million. Of the latter sum, 191 million was sold to the American Treasury before July 10, 1937, for US $94 million. The first sale of 50 million ounces a few days after the reform to produce US $32.5 million was of crucial importance, because on November 3 China had only the equivalent of about US $30 million to support exchange. Further sales followed in 1936 and 1937. During the war, the balance of the silver was sold to the Treasury, together with additional silver collected, to realize a further sum of US $157 million. Altogether the Central Bank sold to the Treasury 553 million ounces to realize US $252 million.[2]

Once exchange was stabilized, the way was cleared for coinage reform to provide stable fiduciary coins in place of the fluctuating depreciated subsidiary silver and copper coins. New nickel and copper coins were issued, with the mint working a 24-hour day, and the public avidly accepted them. This reform gave effect to long-prepared plans. In connection with American silver purchases, the Treasury insisted that China issue silver coins of C $1 and C $0.50. Coinage of these was begun, but had to be canceled when hostilities broke out.

The first sale of silver to the American Treasury followed by further sales ensured success of the monetary reform—provided China buttressed it by the needed internal measures. The Treasury's action was partly an act of conscience, to try to remedy some of the damage done to an innocent friendly country; partly to help a country with which the United States had long had an almost sentimental relation; and partly influenced by displeasure with Japan's aggressive moves against China.

Success of the reform exceeded expectations and the following 20 months up to outbreak of hostilities showed a remarkable transformation. For the first time in history, China had stable rates of foreign exchange, firmly maintained by the Central Bank around the level of November 4, 1935. China carefully avoided a link to either the dollar or the pound. After dollar-sterling rates fluctuated, the Central Bank widened the spread of rates to avoid having to tie to one or the other.

For a time the outlook for exchange was precarious, especially when Washington allowed the world silver price to drop from 65 to 45 cents in December-January. But confidence strengthened after the price was held well above the parity of the silver dollar. Speculative attacks were met without worry. And the United States continued support by buying more of China's silver at 45 cents. The balance of payments became favorable so that China gained large sums of foreign currency. These amounts along with the proceeds of silver sales brought currency reserves to the equivalent of US $379 million in mid-1937. In urging adoption of the reform, I was encouraged by the experience of France in the twenties, some of which I had personally observed. Then the choice of a favorable level of exchange brought speculative covering and repatriation of capital that greatly strengthened external reserves.

American silver policy in this period is a monument to the silver interests, who were politically powerful even though their American product was of less value than the peanut crop. They cleverly allied themselves with the influential advocates of some degree of inflation as a measure of recovery from depression. The hopeless notion of giving silver a status along with gold as a basic monetary metal led to purchase of more than 1.7 billion ounces of silver for about one billion dollars.[3] In 1934, before the Silver Purchase Act, my friend Neil Carothers, with tongue in cheek, recommended "that the government call a conference of the silver interests and offer complete surrender. Ask them what sum in cash they will take to withdraw from politics—and give it to them. Whatever they ask, the bargain will be cheap at the price."[4]

While the United States was able to absorb so large a needless cost without great fundamental damage, the consequences for China went far beyond what could have been foreseen when the Silver Purchase Act was adopted in 1934. A near result was the departure from silver and the adoption of a successful reform with a stable exchange level for the first time in history. Without the American silver measure, there is doubt whether China could have put through a comprehensive reform. The immediate effects of the reform were highly favorable—in clearing the way for economic recovery and accelerated progress, increased foreign trade, and coinage reform. In internal affairs, the government's ability to use generally accepted bank notes for expenditures all over the country gave it a great advantage over regional dissenters who had no such opportunity. Broadly, the success of the reform gave the government greater strength and prestige both at home and abroad.

The long-term effects of the currency reform were to prove far greater than the immediate effects. Japanese expansionists were not slow to declare that the American support of China's reform had strengthened China "in a manner inimical to Japan."[5] A few weeks after the outbreak of hostilities, F. P. Lockhart, Counsellor of the American Embassy stationed at Peiping, analyzed the reasons for Japan's aggressive policies. He said:

> The Japanese military have long harbored the belief that the Chinese program of unity, economic development and military advancement, which has been moving forward for several years with marked success, constituted a threat to the future security of Japan and that a postponement of the present process of destroying that program would only mean that its destruction would be all the more hard to achieve later on.[6]

Also of utmost importance were the effects of eight years of war on China's newly adopted managed currency. In *China and the Helping Hand* I wrote (page 34):

> . . . the managed currency system, which had started out with so much promise, made it easy to issue paper currency for war needs. Under stress of war, an inflation followed which the government found itself unable to control. Although Japan was ultimately defeated, galloping inflation became a major cause of the government's downfall. If by staying on a silver basis China had found herself unable to make prolonged resistance to Japan, the later events of World War II and its aftermath would certainly have been different. Whether for better or for worse is an interesting intellectual speculation.
>
> Thus it is ironic and indeed frightening that an American policy promoted by special interests, and apparently when adopted of rather minor importance to the United States, changed world history in a way that could not have been foreseen.

Banking

The National Economic and Financial Conferences, convened at Nanking shortly after the new government's takeover in 1928, called for creation of a strong Central Bank and strengthening of the banking system. The Central Bank was promptly established and made notable progress in the years prior to mid-1937. The banking system showed weaknesses in those years under the strains of depression and disturbances. Yet growth of modern-style banking resources outpaced the country's economic growth by a wide margin. The prospects for a much improved banking system were good in 1937.

The Central Bank proved itself as a major factor in the government's progress in the prewar decade. It handled well the management of the government's money. For a time, the funds of some public organs, notably the railways, were handled independently. But by 1937 the integration of the finances was being accomplished. Adoption of the CGU enabled the Central Bank to improve procedures of foreign debt payments and other payments in foreign currencies, while gaining experience in foreign exchange operations. Thus, when China was forced to abandon the silver standard in 1935, the Central Bank was able successfully to take general charge of operations to manage exchange rates.

Although the Central Bank functioned well as the government's fiscal agent and manager of exchange rates, there were still two major weaknesses in 1937. It had not yet become a true central bank in relation to control of the supply of money and credit. And it was too much involved in financing a government that was continuously in deficit.

The project to convert the bank into the Central Reserve Bank, as approved on the eve of outbreak of hostilities, dealt with both these problems. One can only speculate about what might have happened if the reserve bank project had taken effect. There would have been problems in controlling private bank credit. The plan whereby banks could obtain banknotes against delivering 60 per cent silver and 40 per cent securities was inflationary but profitable to the banks. To end it, as the advisers urged, would have met opposition. Centralization of note issue in the Central Bank also made little headway in 1935 to 1937 because the other government banks expanded issue. The original plan set a limit of two years for giving the Central Bank the monopoly of issue, but the plan of June 1937 extended this limit to four years. The other government banks were reluctant to give up the issue privilege. During the war, the Central Bank's monopoly of issue was not effected until June 30, 1942.

Control of government borrowing from the Central Bank also presented difficulties. The plan of 1937 provided that deficits would be financed basically by selling securities paid for from the savings of the public rather than by Central Reserve Bank credit. That bank, however, would be permitted temporarily to finance current needs up to one-fourth of the previous fiscal year's revenue. In 1937, there were ambitious plans for economic development with government support. Fortunately there was no active internal revolt then. But the government was determined to strengthen and modernize the armed forces in view of Japan's continuing aggressive designs. Such a program was costly.

Whether the Central Reserve Bank, had it been created, could have adequately held in check governmental recourse to it for financing must remain speculative. Certainly the pressures would have been strong for excessive use of central bank credit, endangering in time the stability of the currency, as postwar experience has shown in so many countries. But in the first half of 1937, revenues were improving with economic recovery and stabilization of the public finances was within reach.

In the field of private banking there were positive and negative elements. The sixfold growth of note circulation and threefold growth of bank deposits during the prewar decade mostly reflected greater use of modern financial instruments and growth of the economy. Only in the latter part of the period did it reflect a relatively small degree of inflation, or reflation. The spread throughout China of a network of branches of modern-style banks made possible collection of savings. The Chinese and foreign banks were able to finance reasonably well the needs of the more important enterprises engaged in production and in domestic and foreign trade.

The government established collaboration with the private banks in 1927. That step provided a most important means to finance the government's urgent needs while it was striving to unify the country and develop the revenue system. Unfortunately, the government's borrowing diverted capital from private production and trade to expenditure in putting down subversive movements and preparing to confront Japanese aggression. Given the importance of creating order and political unity and security, the costs cannot be termed unproductive. On the contrary, they were in principle designed to lead to a situation in which production and trade would have better opportunity to progress. There was loss because part of the outlay was used wastefully or corruptly. But the end result in greater public order and unity, and in clearing the way for financial and economic reforms, justifies on the whole the general policies followed.

In the prewar decade, the Chinese modern-style banks grew partly in substitution for native banks, whose number and importance shrank. The decline of the latter reduced the credit facilities of numerous small traders and producers who were not in position to obtain credit at a modern-style bank.

Another serious weakness was the undue concentration of banking facilities in the treaty ports and lack of adequate rural credit facilities. Rural loans were commonly less for financing production and improvements than for personal needs, such as to tide over the period from late winter when food stock ran out until the new crops were ready. The personal needs were also for funerals, weddings, and in such emergencies as looting by troops or bandits. Recourse to local moneylenders often meant usurious charges.

In 1937, the commercial banks were undercapitalized and often illiquid, largely as a result of the years of depression. Plans for regulation and improvement of the situation were under consideration in 1937. There was a plan for a mortgage institution to assume real estate obligations, with which various commercial banks were heavily burdened. There were also plans to improve the facilities for agricultural credit. That was of prime importance because the abuses of usury and exploitation gave rise to acute discontent that made the people receptive to communism.

Unhappily the outbreak of hostilities prevented fruition of the plans to improve the credit system, by creation of the Central Reserve Bank and of agencies for mortgage and rural credit.

Part Four

Modernization and Development

13: Planning, Policy, and Organization

Deep public and scientific interest in economic growth is largely a phenomenon since World War II. Yet in prewar China there was a strong urge for modernization and development, although with groping for means to attain these ends. China's lag behind the more-developed nations distressed the many who remembered their country's past preeminence in many fields.

In introducing the treatment in Chapters 13 and 14 of modernization and development, I would explain that my participation in Chinese affairs concerned primarily fiscal and monetary matters and less extensively matters of development. And I was concerned with operations rather than research. Although I had a close relation to some matters of the economy, I was not in a position to gather primary data on the economy in general. Hence, as to matters with which I was not immediately concerned, I rely on published data and the work of others. More remains to be done to describe the state of China's economy and the extent of its progress in the prewar decade. Yet it seems worthwhile to make a first approach to show the overall situation, as indicated by data now readily available. Many primary source materials were lost during and after the war; others, if they still exist, are in Mainland China. Exploitation of materials that do exist elsewhere would involve extensive study of data, notably those in Chinese, for which others than this author are more competent. Nevertheless, I believe that this presentation shows substantially what happened, and that further studies are not likely to change basically the general view offered.

This Chapter, after briefly discussing the antecedent conditions affecting the course of economic development, deals with planning, policy, and organization. Chapter 14 deals with the economy in relation to the major branches of production, transport, and trade, together with capital formation. Chapters 15 and 16 deal primarily with foreign technical and financial aid and investment, but these topics are also necessarily involved in the discussion of the economy.

Background

The course of economic development in China during the prewar decade has to be viewed in the light of antecedent conditions. During the last decades of the empire, governmental and social attitudes toward development were not conducive to progress. Early modern-style enterprises in shipping, telegraphs, textiles, and banking were not viewed by government as means to development. Rather they were regarded primarily as sources of revenue. The private investors and managers, moreover, were not oriented to initiative and risk taking. Instead of providing reserves for depreciation and reinvesting profits at least in part to build up the enterprises, they withdrew money for more immediately lucrative investments such as in pawnshops and moneylending. They sought to benefit their families through nepotism. Feuerwerker has pointed out that an "institutional breakthrough" was needed, to replace "the traditional Chinese preoccupation with dividing a static economic pie" with attention to increasing its size; and to substitute criteria of managerial ability and success for "over-riding obligation to family and clan."[1]

Analyzing the obstacles to development in the later imperial period, Feuerwerker enumerates foreign competition, governmental weakness, lack of capital, technical backwardness, and deficient motivation. Importers had the advantage of almost nominal tariffs, and many goods could be produced abroad more cheaply than was possible in China. China had to rely heavily on foreign technicians since Chinese technicians were few and their increase slow. The government was too weak to be capable of promoting a serious effort to modernize, even if it had the motivation. And motivation in the community was far from strong enough to transform the traditional system of family ties, the low status of merchants, and official perquisites and squeeze. Capital was meager, and a great part of such savings as there were was put into buying land and moneylending. After China's defeat by Japan in 1894-1895, the heavy war indemnity paid by borrowing in Europe, plus the heavy Boxer Indemnity of 1901, drained away much capital.

China's slowness to modernize contrasted strikingly with how Japan met the challenge of the modern world. Japan had a strong government in a much smaller country. The Meiji rulers promptly resolved to modernize and persisted in their effort. To meet costs of the program, they promptly reformed the land tax to draw large revenue from what was for long the major sector of the economy. Consequently, Japan developed solid finances, and the government was strengthened accordingly. By the turn of the century, Japan was able to gain tariff autonomy, develop industries, eliminate extrality, adopt the gold standard with the aid of the indemnity paid by China after the war of 1894-1895, and develop enough military strength to defeat Russia.[2]

China's revolution of 1911 and the downfall of the imperial regime created a much improved environment for modernization. Notable growth of industry began. World War I isolated China from many sources of imports, and local production was therefore encouraged. John K. Chang's study shows a compounded rate of industrial growth of 13.4 per cent from 1912 to 1920. After slackening in the early twenties, active growth resumed and accelerated in the latter part of the prewar decade.[3]

In the prewar decade, conditions and institutions unfavorable to economic progress continued from the older days to a substantial extent. These detriments included the general absence of modern agricultural techniques, unjust incidence of the local land taxes, frequent exploitation by local moneylenders and landlords, the tendency to invest savings in land and moneylending rather than in business enterprises, too great a reliance upon family enterprise with its practice of nepotism rather than corporate business organization, lack of proper accounting methods, the tendency in both family and corporate business to distribute earnings rather than reinvest a suitable proportion, shortage of qualified technicians in nearly all lines of economic activity, frequent internal disturbances, and absence of the rule of law.

A fundamental economic factor was the general poverty and low average income, which afforded little if any margin for the accumulation of capital. Pressure of population constantly pushed the people against the minimum of subsistence. And these conditions were made worse because of the heritage of the warlord era of the twenties, with its widespread disturbance of local conditions and looting by bandits and undisciplined troops along with conscription of laborers.

Besides the social, institutional, and economic problems, there were strong unfavorable factors in the overall environment for development in the prewar decade. Following 1929, the world was in the grip of a deep depression and in 1931 very serious trouble with Japan began. The costs of coping with internal and external difficulties drew heavily upon savings and left little money for development.

Despite the difficulties, there was a new factor of utmost importance: the positive approach to development taken by the Nationalist government. Achievements in development in the prewar decade were considerable, and momentum was gaining on the eve of the outbreak of hostilities in mid-1937 as the following account will show.

Planning and policy

Planning as it developed in the Nationalist period did not mean a program of detailed control and regulation of economic activities. Rather it was a setting of goals and delineation of the governmental policies, functions, and programs designed to achieve them.

Sun Yat-sen was the father of planning China's development. His plan to carry out this put forward at about the end of World War I was designed "both to develop China's own productive forces and to absorb the industrial capacity of the foreign Powers." He envisioned building 100,000 miles of railways; a million miles of roads; three large-scale ports, "capable of equalling New York in the future," for the north, center, and south of China; improvement of other ports, rivers, and canals and building new canals; improvement of telegraph and telephone systems; industrial development including plants for iron and steel and cement; development of mineral wealth; improvement of agriculture; irrigation and reforestation; and colonization of outlying underdeveloped regions.[4] Sun contemplated large-scale foreign participation in China's economic development, but had no concrete plans as to how to accomplish it. Although his ideas seemed grandiose and visionary, subsequent events despite setbacks are vindicating the broad elements of his conception except as to foreign participation.

Finance Minister Soong's *Annual Report,* dated March 1, 1931, covering the fiscal year 1930, after stressing the urgent need for solid finances, turned to the great importance of what was termed "reconstruction" (pages 10-11). In the public mind, reconstruction meant not only rebuilding and remodeling but also the whole process of modernization and strengthening the nation, including promotion of economic development, mass education, and public health. Soong wanted "a positive programme of systematic and coordinated expansion extending through a series of years." He said:

> Surely a case has been made for discarding the haphazard, unrelated, and clashing programmes of the various branches of the Government, and the creation of a really effective planning organization which would guide the productive forces of the country, co-ordinate the activities of the ministries, and rigidly map out the essential ends which for a given course of years each of the different components is obliged to pursue.

Beginning in 1931, the government gave much attention to planning, involving creation in June of the National Economic Council and collaboration with the League of Nations (Chapter 15). In May, the National People's Convention announced a ten-point program based on Sun's principles, which named specific time goals for various programs and gave details as to objectives in industry and agriculture. In August, a grandiose ten-year plan was announced listing categories of projects, with goals whose attainment would require decades—such as a merchant marine of 8 million tons, industrial power plants to produce 20 million horsepower, and during ten years 120 million tons of iron and steel. But Chiang, when inaugurating the National Economic Council, proposed a more realistic three-year plan. Work would begin on some of the more urgent projects such as water conservancy in the Hwai River region and certain roads. Plans would also be made concerning the course to be followed in industrial development, for land reform and agricultural development, and for reforms in education. As to public health Chiang included the concrete three-year plan already approved by the government.[5]

Chiang's planning, in line with Sun's ideas but in contrast to the later plans of the Communists, viewed China as "an integral part of the world economic system, profoundly affecting world conditions and affected by them."[6] The trend in China to planning was influenced by the example of Russia and later Germany, internal subversive actions, and the threat of Japan.

The question arises whether China's leaders had a general philosophy of development. Chiang in his address of November 15, 1931, when the National Economic Council was being set up, said (page 1):

> The National Government presumes that the National Economic

> Council will wish to be guided by the consideration that China, while obviously remaining predominantly an agricultural country, needs to secure rapidly an industrial development on a considerable scale, and to do this largely under plans promoted and aided by Government action.

In proposing the three-year plan, the items were listed as follows: public works, education, land reform and agricultural improvement, industrial development, financial policy, and public health and medicine. In practice, the approach was essentially pragmatic because of preoccupation with affairs other than development, along with limitation of funds. There was emphasis on public works, notably transport and water conservancy, and strategic industry.

The planning contemplated a mixed economy, with the government encouraging and aiding private enterprises and also engaging in a variety of undertakings. The line between public and private enterprise was not clearly drawn. Sun gave two differing indications for guidance. In 1921, he wrote that "all matters that can be and are better carried out by private enterprise should be left to private hands which should be encouraged and fully protected by liberal laws. . . . All matters that cannot be taken up by private concerns and those that possess monopolistic character should be taken up as national undertakings."[7] But in *San Min Chu I* in 1923 he took a more socialistic view of how to promote industry. The shift in his view was apparently influenced by his contacts with Communism and his reading of Marxist-Leninist literature.[8] In his Canton lectures in the second half of 1923, transcribed for the *San Min Chu I*, he said:

> If we do not use state power to build up these enterprises but leave them in the hands of private Chinese or of foreign business men, the result will be simply the expansion of private capital and the emergence of a great wealthy class with the consequent inequalities in society . . . The state should lead in business enterprises and set up all kinds of productive machinery which will be the property of the state . . . If the industries are carried on by the state, the rights and privileges which they bring will be enjoyed by all the people.[9]

The policies in the prewar decade reflected both aspects of Sun's views. The general policy was stated as reserving to government the public utilities and heavy industries, which were those closely related to defense, and leaving light industries to private initiative. Thus there were prolonged negotiations for an iron and steel plant in which the government would work with a private German group, but the fighting in 1937 prevented fruition of the project. Yet in the prewar decade, the Ministry of Industries repeatedly advocated projects for various state-operated factories. These projects included some light industries, and that Ministry participated in operating an alcohol distillery. In the later years of the decade, the government exercised various degrees of supervision or control over production of wood-oil, antimony, tungsten, and matches. The China Merchants Steam Navigation Company, with its long checkered history, was taken over as a state enterprise in 1932. In addition, through what later has been called "bureaucratic capitalism," high officials acted as chief officers in the Bank of China, Bank of Communications, and Farmers Bank. Besides some provinces engaged in a variety of enterprises, notably Shansi, Kwangtung, and Kwangsi. In 1936, Kwangtung was operating more than 25 enterprises whose products included sugar, cement, textiles, chemicals, fertilizer, paper, and soft drinks.[10] All in all, the trend of events indicated that there would be exceptions to the policy of leaving light industries to private capital, and in some cases joint governmental and private participation.

Both before and during the prewar Nationalist decade, China had the services of hundreds of foreign technicians, engineers, and other specialists. And an increasing number of Chinese gained competence by training and experience in the various fields of communications, industry, agriculture, and trade. Through the work of these Chinese and foreigners, a great volume of plans was produced relating to river conservancy, irrigation and drainage, port improvements, railways, roads, airways, telecommunications, industry, agriculture, and defense.

The estimated requirements of the chief fields of development for 1936 to 1939 were C $1034 million (Table 22). The distribution was 54 per cent for railways, 19 per cent for armaments, 17 per cent for heavy industry, and the balance for water conservancy and highways. Over half the costs represented payments in China. The larger part of the costs both in China and abroad was to be covered by loans and credits.

During the war, and especially after victory was assured, the government developed much larger comprehensive plans for

Table 22

Estimated costs of a development program for 1936 to 1939[a]

	Total, millions	Payments in China, millions	Payments abroad, millions	
			Credits	Cash
Railways	C$ 555	C$335	C$154	C$ 66
Highways	37	25	4	8
Water conservancy	69	55	10	4
Heavy industry	175	71	98	6
Armament	198	99		99
Totals	C$1034	C$585	C$266	C$183

[a] Source: Received from Central Bank of China, apparently data of the National Economic Council.

reconstruction after war losses and for new development. Rehabilitation plans submitted in 1944 to the United Nations Relief and Rehabilitation Administration called for imported requirements of US $945 million and the aid of over 2000 foreign experts. Internal costs were estimated at C $2.7 billion in terms of prewar currency. Plans for development were brought together in the summer of 1945 in a detailed scheme calling for total external costs of about US $2 billion. About 40 per cent was for transportation and communications, and over half for industry and mining. Agriculture was to be helped by the production of fertilizers, insecticides, tools and equipment and by processing industries. Inasmuch as agriculture engaged about four-fifths of the population, the Nationalist planning gave it inadequate attention, as did the Communists later. Moreover, the planning for the postwar period was far from realistic, in that it failed to take account of the need for ending the galloping inflation before solid development could begin. There was no adequate plan for raising the huge amount of internal funds, roughly equal to external funds needed, on a noninflationary basis. What foreign funds and foreign aid could do, as compared with internal effort, was greatly exaggerated.[11]

The prewar and wartime planning became available to the Communists, and many of the planners and technicians also joined them, either from a belief in development primarily by state activity or from necessity. Thus the planning in these years should receive credit as the foundation for part of what the Communists have since accomplished constructively.

Organization for development

Three organizations were set up to be specially concerned with economic development: the National Reconstruction Commission; the National Resources Commission; and the National Economic Council, already mentioned.

The Reconstruction Commission was created in 1928 under the leadership of Chang Ching-kiang, who for some time was governor of Chekiang Province. That Commission gave special attention to the development of electric utilities in Nanking, Hangchow, the region between Nanking and Shanghai, and Hankow. It promoted railway construction in Chekiang and Anhwei Provinces, development of local transportation in Nanking, and improvement of the coal industry in central China. It set up the Model Irrigation Administrative Bureau. The promotion of electric utilities was aided by loans of several millions. Current funds for the Commission's activities were provided from the national budget and from local sources. The Commission also received advances of several millions from the Board administering remitted British Boxer Indemnity funds.

The National Resources Commission began work as the Defense Planning Committee under the headquarters of the Army Chief of Staff. In 1935, the Commission was transferred to the National Military Council and became the National Resources Commission, but with little change in internal organization. The scope of its activities changed gradually from defense planning to development of basic industry, but it still emphasized strengthening the economy for defense. In 1936, the Commission prepared a three-year plan to develop a number of industries including iron and steel, copper and other metals, chemicals, and electrical equipment. Of the estimated cost of C $230 million, about one-third was to be derived from the general budget and the rest from foreign loans. But actual appropriations in the first two years were only about C $30 million, only a part of which pertained to the prewar period. Before the war, the Commission was primarily interested in planning; after hostilities began, it took an active part in transfer of industries away from areas threatened by the enemy, and construction and operation of strategic industries behind the enemy lines.[12]

The National Economic Council (NEC) was created pursuant to a decision taken early in 1931, following the recommendation of Sir Arthur Salter of the League of Nations. Prior to formal inauguration two years later, a Preparatory Office performed some of the work intended for the NEC. The NEC became the most important organ for promoting development. Its organization came to include the Bureau of Roads, Bureau of Hydraulic Engineering, Bureau of Agriculture, Cotton Industry Commission, Sericulture Improvement Commission, Cooperatives Commission, and Central Field Health Station.

Experts from the League of Nations played an important role in the work of the NEC (Chapter 15). The NEC cooperated actively with a number of provinces, notably in highway construction, agricultural activities, and rural rehabilitation. The NEC supervised expenditure of most of the proceeds of the American Cotton and Wheat Loan of 1933, amounting to C $38 million, along with other funds from the national budget and provincial sources.

14: The Economy

This Chapter discusses developments in the major fields of production, transport, and trade, together with national income and capital formation. Although Chapters 15 and 16 deal primarily with foreign technical and financial aid and investment, these subjects necessarily are involved to some extent in this Chapter. I recognize of course that although the relation of foreign personnel and finance to events was influential, it was likewise peripheral because the course of events depended primarily on Chinese attitudes, policies, and activities. The economy was dualistic—predominantly traditional but with a small and growing modern sector.

Agriculture[1]

The 75 to 80 per cent of China's families depending on agriculture for livelihood in the prewar period faced enormous problems, most of which are still critical. About one-fourth of the world's population must eke out support on only about 7 per cent of the world's cultivated land. China's area includes a large proportion of rough terrain, and rainfall is capricious in many regions. The great rivers are hard to control, frequently causing serious floods. Only a little more than 10 per cent of the area is under cultivation, although much of it is extremely rich. Another 5 per cent is marginal land whose utilization is difficult because of scanty or irregular rainfall or other conditions. Nearly half the cultivated area was irrigated, and much of that terraced.

The relentless growth of population has long pressed against the limited resources. Some authorities believe that standards of living have become progressively lower during the last two hundred years. Numbers increased substantially in the generation preceding the Nationalist takeover. As numbers grew, land was divided into uneconomic miniplots, with the average farm perhaps 3-1/2 acres and a third or more less than 1-1/2 acres. These conditions led to high density of labor on the land. Yields per acre were high but productivity of labor was low. The man-hours needed per acre were many times greater than in the United States. Only by dint of unremitting labor have China's people been able to feed themselves, at a rather low level of nutrition. Many serious famines could not be relieved because of poor transport. The rural sector had to feed the cities, except that coastal cities found it cheaper to import some food than to get full supplies locally. Marketing was wasteful, with losses of 5 to 20 per cent from improper storage and handling, pests, moisture, and adulteration. Besides these handicaps agriculture prior to the Nationalist takeover received nothing from the government sector, while being a major source of revenue and having to support the armies.

The economic and social aspects of Chinese agricultural conditions were not seriously and broadly studied prior to the work begun during the twenties by J. Lossing Buck and his associates at Nanking University.[2] Their investigations indicate that about half the farms were owner-operated, the proportion being considerably more in the north, and less in central and south China. Rural credit, which was commonly seasonal, was meager. According to a survey of 1933, modern and native banks provided only about 10 per cent of total rural credit. The rest was provided by merchants, landlords, local moneylenders, and pawn shops.[3] Lenders charged rates in the general range of 20 to 40 per cent yearly and in some cases more. Sometimes relatives or friends loaned money at the more moderate rates. Rural debt was a serious problem, especially during the acute deflation of 1931-1935. Land taxes were inequitable, bearing more heavily upon the poorer households while many well-to-do evaded a proper share of the burden. Some landlords collected extortionate rents from tenants. Local government all too often was bad, with farmers suffering at the hands of predatory officials.

The National Government inherited an agricultural situation that had become acute in the extensive areas affected for many years by marching and countermarching of warlord armies. Manpower was drained away by conscription, crops and other property were looted, and livestock was slaughtered which also reduced the supply of fertilizer. During the confusion, long established systems of flood control and granaries were neglected. These conditions continued, especially in the north and northwest, during the warlord revolts of 1929 to 1931 and sporadically thereafter on a lesser scale during the period of relative internal peace from 1932 to mid-1937. The losses resulting from the protracted internal disturbances were a major cause of the rural distress so widely noted in the thirties. A further cause was the serious long-time inflation of the copper currencies generally used in the countryside. Then came the acute deflation of 1931 to 1935, which greatly hurt many rural areas.

These causes of rural discontent often have had inadequate attention, compared to the commonly expressed emphasis on exploitation.

Various observers felt that China was in the throes of an acute rural crisis. They drew pessimistic conclusions about trends and the possibility of serious social disorders if not revolution. Thus Professor C. Dragoni of the League of Nations mission to China, writing in 1934, feared that the peasantry might yield easily to Communism, and considered it "essential to devise and resolutely to apply agricultural policies which will prevent the growth of discontent." His report set forth an excellent program of action.[4]

The importance of land reform and the improvement of agriculture were emphasized by Sun Yat-sen. His goal as set out in 1924 was that "each tiller of the soil will possess his own fields." He urged greater use of machinery, pest control, better techniques, improved transport, and prevention of natural disasters.[5] Various Kuomintang pronouncements supported action to these ends.[6] The government's policy contemplated no radical change in organization of peasant agriculture; its aim was rather to improve the existing system on the lines urged by Sun Yat-sen.

During the prewar decade there was only a beginning in the overall improvement of rural and socio-economic conditions. Good laws were enacted. The comprehensive land law of 1930 embodied a broad program for agricultural reforms and improvement, and another excellent land law was adopted in 1937. The law of 1930 had various provisions to encourage owner operation instead of tenancy. It included a limitation of rent to "37.5 per cent of the main produce from the land," and of taxes of 1 per cent on value of improved land.[7] Tawney pointed out that "as far ... as programmes are concerned, all the agrarian reforms carried out in other parts of the world in the course of the last century are now part of the official policy"; but that, "Whether political conditions, administrative machinery and financial resources are such as to enable them to be applied in practice, is a different question."[8]

Unhappily, the law of 1930 remained largely a dead letter. The government was too preoccupied with internal and external emergencies to promote large-scale progress in basic reform and improvement of rural conditions. Furthermore, most of the leaders had an urban background and were not oriented toward rural affairs, and they had an empathy with landowning and financial interests. Thus, for example, when Chekiang Province under the governorship of Chang Ching-kiang tried to apply the rent reduction to 37.5 per cent, the effort failed because of the opposition of the rural gentry.

Despite the failure to deal fundamentally with socio-economic rural problems, both the national and some provincial governments took steps to promote improvement of the agricultural economy. The national government convened a congress on agricultural economics in December 1929, following which it created the Ministry of Agriculture and Mining, later merged into the Ministry of Industry. It created in 1933 the Rural Rehabilitation Commission, which made basic studies of marketing, land tenure, and rural credit. The Commission's work helped to make generally known the importance of the rural economy and the need for reforms. Several provincial governments had programs to improve agriculture, including establishment of experimental *hsiens* for crop improvement, cooperative credit, and tax reforms. These programs contributed to gains in production of rice, wheat, and cotton so that imports of these items decreased considerably in the latter prewar years.

Special credit for stimulating national and provincial action on agriculture and promoting improvements belongs to Nanking University. Agricultural research, instruction, and training of experts were developed there beginning in 1920, with the aid of Cornell University and the Rockefeller Foundation. A number of Cornell professors spent time in China. Pioneer work was done in plant breeding and improving varieties of seeds and in developing pesticides.[9] On the economic side, J. Lossing Buck and the Chinese and American experts associated with him at Nanking University did valuable work as mentioned above in surveying land utilization and agricultural conditions generally. The College of Agriculture of Southeastern University (later National Central University), under the direction of P. W. Tsou, also had a part in stimulating governmental interest and action.

Of special importance was the development of a system of crop reports and statistics. This work was begun in 1929 at Nanking University, and taken over by the National Agricultural Research Bureau upon its creation in 1932. That bureau drew its staff members mostly from Nanking University and Southeastern University. Beginning in 1931, China had for the first time comprehensive reports on acreage and production of crops, based on data from observers in each *hsien* of the provinces of China proper.[10]

The Agricultural Bureau's data show for 1931 to 1937 in China proper an average production of 131 million metric tons of the chief food crops, including 51 million of unhulled rice, 23 million of wheat, 50 million of miscellaneous grains, and 7 million of sweet potatoes. But the figures were underestimates because owners of farm land under-reported area under cultivation to evade land tax. Buck's data indicate a much higher production of rice—88 million tons—and somewhat higher figures for the other items. For all of mainland China, but without adjustments for under-reported cultivated areas in Manchuria, Sikong, and Sinkiang, he estimates a total of 182 million metric tons (taking sweet potatoes at their grain equivalent). He concludes, on the basis of his estimates of population before the war and in the fifties, that the food grains available per capita in the prewar period were somewhat greater than in the Communists' "Great Ten Years, 1949-1958."[11] Estimates by Ta-chung Liu and K. C. Yeh, using different methods, show a broadly similar conclusion.[12] Such comparisons should be qualified by noting that distribution among the population in the Communist period was more even than in the prewar period. The "Great Leap Forward" caused a very serious drop in output after 1958. After recovery from the Leap the Communists moved to strengthen agriculture by increased use of modern implements and machinery, rural electrification, and especially a several-fold increase in use of chemical fertilizer. There is disagreement among the experts as to production in the last half of the sixties, but it appears that the acute shortages of the post-Leap period no longer existed.

The Agricultural Research Bureau developed in the thirties improved varieties of rice, wheat, corn, potatoes, and cotton, and a significant area was planted with improved seed. The Bureau also developed production of insecticides and sprayers. It established experiment stations, demonstration farms, and extension systems in a number of provinces. Many of the provincial governments showed interest in agricultural improvement, setting up institutes and extension procedures, although their resources were meager. Organization of farmers' agricultural improvement associations began in 1930, and these spread rapidly. The government set up inspection stations to standardize exports of tea, silk, and wood oil. A uniform system of weights and measures based on the metric system was adopted. Thus the *picul* whose weight had varied much from place to place was fixed at 50 kilograms, and the *catty* at 1/100 kilogram or 1.1023 pounds.

In organizing cooperatives and improving facilities for rural credit, there was a modest beginning, followed by considerable progress. Both public and private agencies promoted cooperatives, including the Ministry of Industry, which took over the former Ministry of Agriculture and Mining; the National Flood Relief Commission; the National Economic Council; the China International Famine Relief Commission; and various banks. The first bank to loan to cooperatives was the private Shanghai Commercial and Savings Bank, through the interest and efforts of its head, K. P. Chen. About 40 per cent of the cooperatives were set up under government auspices, 20 per cent by semigovernmental agencies, and the rest by banks and private agencies. Most were credit cooperatives, along with some of producers and consumers and for marketing. The number of societies grew from 2796 with 56,000 members in 1931 to 46,983 with 2,140,000 members in 1937.[13] Through cooperatives and the activities of several banks, rural credit facilities at moderate rates were increased.

Many of the senior experts who later worked in Taiwan with the Joint Commission on Rural Reconstruction gained their training during the prewar decade in the work described here. Their experience and tradition played a large part in the remarkable growth of agricultural production and improvement of rural conditions in Taiwan after 1950.

In 1934, the government embarked on a comprehensive program of rural rehabilitation in Kiangsi Province after the Communists were driven out. The aim was to clean up local government, lend money at reasonable rates, and provide free services of education, health, and agricultural improvement. A beginning was also made with a land survey, looking toward reform of the land tax. The program was good, but the funds and personnel were too limited and time too short to give it effect on a large enough scale. Haldore Hanson writing in the *North-China Daily News* of July 4, 1937, said that the program in Kiangsi "answers every problem of the farmer except over-population," but he commented as follows:

> General Chiang [Chiang Kai-shek] and a few hundred sincere followers are trying to push through a reform program against the historical inertia of 10,000,000 other officials, national, provincial and local. At present it seems that it cannot be done till the masses are educated to push from the bottom, demanding a higher standard of government.

Governmental action in other fields was important to agriculture. During the prewar decade, rail transport and road transport, in particular, were improved and expanded. Tax reforms included abolition of *likin* (transport tax) as from January 1, 1931, the decree having substantial observance despite the fears of skeptics. Many miscellaneous burdensome taxes were ended or reduced, notably abolition in 1931 of coast trade duties, transit dues, and native customs charges on junk-borne trade. Specially important was the work of the National Flood Relief Commission in relief and rehabilitation after the great flood of 1931 (Chapter 16). By providing work relief to millions with payments in kind from the American wheat loan of 15 million bushels, dykes were rebuilt and improved, and local rehabilitation was accomplished with great success.

In summary, the rural population were exceptionally hard working and knowledgeable according to their lights, but were handicapped by the very adverse relation of numbers to resources. Besides the urgency of population control there was a basic need for technological improvements, because overall the technology had changed little for centuries. The farmers needed better seeds, pest control, much larger use of fertilizer, irrigation and flood control, credit for seeds and fertilizer and tools, better marketing and transport, along with peace and order in the countryside and reforms in tenancy and taxation. The farmers alone could not generate very rapidly the resources and technology needed for progress. The government was committed to progress on these lines. The beginnings in the thirties were promising, and some of the programs were of the kind that could take hold rather quickly. An indication of progress is that imports of agricultural machinery and parts grew from a total of about C$400,000 in the three years from 1932 to 1934 to

C $660,000 in 1935 and over a million in 1936; and imports of pumping machinery and parts grew from C $750,000 in 1932 to C $2.5 million in 1936. Another indication is the reduction of imports of wheat, rice, and cotton during the last years before the outbreak of hostilities. But the time span which events allowed for operation and expansion of the reforms was too short for their impact to be weighed. How rapidly some rural reforms can progress is shown by the postwar experience in Taiwan.

The efforts during the prewar decade in improving agriculture were thus most worthwhile and promised much for the future. Franklin Ho considers that "China was on the road toward a 'take-off' in the development of her agricultural economy during the decade from 1927 to 1937"; and that "had there been no communist rebellion within and no foreign aggression without, she could have been able to overcome all the traditional resistances to a steady and accelerated development of her agricultural economy."[14] Buck considers that improvement of agriculture in China in the thirties ranked high compared with progress in other less-developed countries. But only a beginning had been made when war supervened, and by 1937 there had been little change in the overall rural situation. Agriculture ranked low in the scale of priorities for development as compared with transport and industry, and its budget was well under 1 per cent of the total. The Nationalists, like their successors on the mainland for so long, greatly downgraded agriculture.

Industry

Handicraft production was much more important than modern-type industry in the prewar decade, and the economy as a whole, weighted heavily by agriculture, was overwhelmingly traditional. Estimates indicate that handicraft and modern-type industry together were contributing only about one-tenth of the gross domestic product. In that tenth, handicraft production predominated. Modern-type industries were mainly light industries, those for textiles being much the largest. Factory-type industries together with utilities and mining employed in 1933 only about two million workers, and contributed only between three and four per cent of the gross national product.[15]

In China, both the Nationalists and the Communists have charged that foreign trade and investment, which were associated with development of modern-type industries, caused a decline in the handicraft sector. Data of the year-to-year trend of handicraft production are not sufficient to permit quantitative estimates. But careful studies of scholars indicate that while the share of handicrafts in *total* industrial production was declining, there was probably no absolute decline. Economic modernization hit hard some handicraft industries, but others were able to co-exist quite well.[16]

Foreign investment played a large part in the introduction and development of industry. Foreigners introduced modern technology and trained many Chinese, who proved good imitators. Foreign financing and enterprise provided much of the structure of transport and communications, utilities, and financial services, which were essential to modernization. In modern-type mining and utilities, foreign capital was dominant from the beginning of development, although participation of Chinese capital was growing. In the important cotton textile industry, foreign capital had about one-third of the product in 1933. In that year, foreign-owned firms produced 35 per cent of the total value of factory products. Details are shown in Table 23.

Modern-type industries, Chinese as well as foreign, were concentrated in the treaty ports. These afforded greater law and order than the interior, and also had advantages of communication by waterways. But this location was strategically vulnerable, and in some cases distance from raw materials such as cotton led to waste in utilization of resources. Industry was primarily for production of consumer goods, and there was relatively little heavy industry in China proper. A factor stimulating industry after 1928 was the sharp rise of tariff rates under tariff autonomy. Rates were raised more for revenue than protection, but the protective effect was necessarily present.[17]

The most comprehensive quantitative study of the data of industrial development in Mainland China between the fall of the empire and the Communist take-over is that of John K. Chang. His analysis indicates the following compounded growth rates in Mainland China in various periods: 1912-1949, 5.6 per cent; 1926-1936, 8.3 per cent; and 1928-1936, 8.4 per cent. These data include Manchuria where Japan, largely for strategic reasons, poured in capital and personnel for rapid industrialization. The growth rate in Manchuria therefore became faster than in China proper: 8.3 per cent per year in 1926 to 1936 and 9.3 per cent per year in 1931 to 1936. In the latter

Table 23

Gross product in 1933 of factory industries having more than 30 employees and using power, including Manchuria[a]

Industry	Chinese		Foreign		Total	
	Number of factories	Value of product, (millions)[b]	Number of factories	Value of product, (millions)[b]	Number of factories	Value of product, (millions)
Woodworking	18	C$ 3.8(20)	48	C$ 14.7(80)	66	C$ 18.5
Machine works	222	20.1(61)	40	12.7(39)	262	32.7
Metal	82	61.0(92)	17	5.4(8)	99	66.4
Electrical instruments	5	11.3(57)	19	8.4(43)	74	19.7
Transportation	29	5.2(43)	16	7.1(57)	45	12.3
Bricks, earthenware, etc.	105	15.4(51)	64	14.7(49)	169	30.1
Water, gas, electricity	603	117.5(47)	65	133.3(53)	668	250.8
Chemicals	159	77.5(68)	78	36.2(32)	237	113.7
Textile[c]	808	592.5(67)	72	294.1(33)	880	886.5
Clothing	165	37.5(88)	15	5.2(12)	180	42.7
Leather, rubber	85	38.2(76)	28	11.9(24)	113	50.2

Continued

Table 23 (Continued)

Gross product in 1933 of factory industries having more than 30 employees and using power, including Manchuria[a]

Industry	Chinese		Foreign		Total	
	Number of factories	Value of product, (millions)[b]	Number of factories	Value of product, (millions)[b]	Number of factories	Value of product, (millions)
Food, drink, tobacco	493	377.5(65)	136	208.2(35)	629	585.7
Paper, printing	37	47.6(74)	50	17.0(26)	287	64.6
Scientific and musical instruments	74	5.6(90)	6	0.6(10)	80	6.2
Miscellaneous	32	4.8(82)	20	1.0(18)	52	5.8
Total	3167	C$1415.5(65)	674	C$770.7(35)	3841	C$2186.2

[a] Source: Adapted from Chi-ming Hou: *Foreign Investment and Economic Development in China, 1840-1937* (Cambridge, 1965), p. 129. The data are derived from Ou Pao-san, *Corrections to China's National Income* (1947), pp. 130-133.

[b] Percentage of the total value of the product in parenthesis.

[c] The most important item of textile production was cotton spinning, whose value for Chinese mills was C$384.2 million and for foreign-owned mills C$280.7 million.

period in Manchuria, the net value added in mining, industry, and electric power more than doubled.[18]

If Manchuria is eliminated, Chang's figures for China proper show a compounded growth rate of 6.4 per cent for industrial development in 1926 to 1936, and 6.7 per cent for 1931 to 1936. Thus, there was a definite acceleration of growth in the latter period, when the National Government became more firmly established after putting down the major warlord revolts. Chang presents year-by-year figures for China proper only for 1926, 1931, and 1936.[19]

For China, including Manchuria, Chang has constructed one index based on gross value of output and one on net value added. He uses 1933 as the base because value-added data are most readily available for that year. The two indexes show a similar movement in the prewar years, although there are considerable differences after 1936. Chang uses the data for net value added in his computations. His indexes for 1927 to 1936, converted to 1927 as a base, are shown in Table 24.

Chang's data for China, including Manchuria, show overall growth in every year from 1927 to 1936. The value-added index more than doubled. For China proper, the index grew by 86 per cent in 1926 to 1936. Growth in that period is most creditable, considering that it included not only disturbed internal and external conditions, but also the years of depression. We may compare this with the situation elsewhere at the time. The world index of mining and manufacturing, excluding Russia, fell from 100 in 1929 to 63 in 1932, and recovered only to 96 in 1936. General indexes of production in the United States, France, and Germany fell from 100 in 1929 to 54, 69, and 53, respectively, in 1932, and recovered to 88, 79, and 106 by 1936. The United Kingdom, which devalued in 1931, showed a much smaller drop to 84 in 1931 and 1932, and recovery to 116 in 1936. Japan, which followed the United Kingdom in devaluation, showed a drop of only 9 per cent from 1929 to 1931. From 1931, the index for Japan nearly doubled by 1937, showing a compounded growth rate of nearly 10 per cent.[20] That was a foretaste of Japan's rapid growth in the postwar recovery.

Chang's items are (a) mining and metallurgy (coal, iron ore, pig iron, steel, antimony, copper, gold, mercury, tin, and tungsten); (b) manufacturing (cotton yarn, cotton cloth, and cement); and (c) fuel and power (crude oil and electric power). He has compiled the data from the sources which he deemed most

Table 24

Industrial production from 1926 to 1936[a]

I. China including Manchuria

Year	Gross value of output		Net value added	
	Millions of 1933 C$	Index 1927 = 100	Millions of 1933 C$	Index 1927 = 100
1927	670.1	100.0	245.1	100.0
1928	725.6	108.4	260.8	106.5
1929	773.8	115.4	278.2	113.7
1930	821.1	122.5	296.4	121.1
1931	886.9	132.1	320.0	130.6
1932	921.5	137.5	334.1	136.3
1933	1006.3	150.1	369.7	151.1
1934	1042.6	155.6	395.0	161.5
1935	1104.1	164.6	441.8	180.2
1936	1227.4	183.2	499.1	203.6

II. China proper and Manchuria

	China proper	Manchuria
1926	100.0	100.0
1931	134.4	174.4
1936	186.1	378.0

[a] Source: John K. Chang, ***Industrial Development of Pre-Communist China*** (Chicago, 1969), pp. 60-61, 103. Indexes in part I are here converted from 1933 to 1927 as the base. Yearly figures other than those shown in part II are not stated.

reliable. There are some gaps filled by estimates, and the data are of uneven quality. He recognizes the difficulties and fully explains the limitations. In the main computation, he weights the several series based on 1933 gross prices and net value added. He presents alternative series based on 1925 and 1952 prices, but these show little difference for the prewar period.

He estimates at 40 per cent the coverage of industrial production, because of lack of data for other items. Important industries omitted are cigarettes, matches, flour, food and beverages, wool, silk, paper, leather, and chemicals. But available data indicate that they grew on the average at a rate similar to that of the composite index. He points out that major studies of earlier industrial growth in the United States and elsewhere have had to use a coverage of the order of 40 per cent.

Clearly modern-type industries grew notably during the prewar decade. I see no reason to doubt that Chang's analysis of growth substantially indicates the situation in that period, despite some data being admittedly imperfect. His index data are broadly in line with indexes of other indicators of economic development in China proper, including items other than for industry, which I compiled (pages 426 to 429) in Table 27. These data other than of physical production of goods support the view that an important part off the economy was being steadily modernized and mechanized. Electric power output in China proper more than doubled in the decade. Bank deposits in 1928 to 1937 at constant prices more than tripled. Railway ton-kilometers of manufactures grew 36 per cent and of mineral products 49 per cent in 1932 to 1936, earlier comparable data not being available. Imports of capital goods increased by 34 per cent in 1932 to 1936, despite the deflation during most of the period.[21]

In considering factory development, the definition of "factory" as used in the various compilations has to be considered. In Table 23, a factory is defined as having more than 30 workers and using power. Liu and Yeh define a factory as a manufacturing establishment using power, regardless of the number of employees. On that basis they estimate the number of factory workers in 1933 as 1.13 million.[22] A report of the government's Statistical Bureau, apparently using the less restrictive definition of factory, gave the following data[23] as to the most important industries established in China from 1928 to 1936:

	Number of factories	Capital, millions	Number of workers
Machinery	377	C$ 8.7	17,065
Chemicals	434	43.9	54,512
Textiles	1160	202.2	293,706
Agricultural products	855	58.1	40,226
Totals	2826	C$312.9	405,509

Progress of industrialization was affected by both negative

and positive factors. Despite a commendable rate of industrial growth, much faster than that of the economy as a whole, the economy remained mostly traditional and undeveloped in 1937. Industry's contribution to overall growth remained small. While agriculture, as indicated on pages 305 to 306, was developing potential for much progress, the actual progress realized was small relative to the total rural economy. Industrial growth was held back by illiteracy and the low level of education. A relatively small proportion of advanced students specialized in technical and scientific subjects. Other factors retarding industrial growth were the low buying power of consumers who were predominantly rural; poor transport; and continuing sporadic internal disorders, even though these notably lessened during the prewar decade.

On the positive side, the government for the first time was taking an interest in promoting industrialization and modernization generally, as explained in Chapters 13, 15, and 16. In this it was backed by a strong urge for modernization on the part of the business and intellectual community, along with the industry and adaptability of workers. During part of the period, falling exchange gave protection additional to that afforded by higher tariffs. Banks, which were becoming more and more closely involved with government during the prewar decade, provided financial and at times supervisory support of industry. Foreign credits were becoming available.

In addition, the government was creating an environment increasingly favorable to industry. Abolition of *likin* and other taxes obstructive to movement of goods internally was helpful. Communications were being improved by expansion of postal and telegraph services, rehabilitation and extension of railways, and creation of a network of airlines. Weights and measures were being standardized on the basis of the metric system. Organizations under the Ministry of Industry were promoting use of national products. These developments were creating a nation-wide market. The successful currency reform of 1935 was unifying the currency nationally, providing stable rates of foreign exchange without overvaluation, and a convenient and dependable money for the people. Import duties, although primarily set for revenue, afforded substantial protection. The country was becoming more and more unified, except for Japan's interference in the north. A strong factor for greater progress in all sectors was the abating of civil wars and improved internal order. Meanwhile, Japan's attitude, although a threat to progress, was a stimulus to accelerated development of a stronger industrial base. All these things brought an economic upsurge that was clearly evident from the latter part of 1935 until interrupted by the hostilities.

Railways

China's railways existing in 1927 had been built in large part by funds from several foreign countries during the international scramble for concessions and spheres of influence from the late nineties to World War I. But dislike of the foreign penetration led the central government and the provinces to build about 40 per cent of the lines. On the eve of the Nationalist takeover, China had 7683 miles of line, including Manchuria.[24] The length was meager for one of the largest nations in area and the largest in population. Because the lines came into being under a variety of agreements with foreign interests, each was built and operated as a separate unit. Nevertheless, some progress in centralization was made in accounts and procedures, in statistical reports, and in interchange of equipment and arranging through traffic.

The railways were profitable from the start since there was a dire need for better transport. River and canal traffic was highly developed and relatively cheap even using manpower. But away from waterways, goods had to move mostly by human effort: on men's backs, commonly on a pole with one man carrying two bundles or two men one bundle, or by wheelbarrow or cart. Animals were also used extensively. These modes of transport were dear. J. E. Baker estimated that in the twenties average rail costs were under C $0.01-1/2 per ton-kilometer, and that for man-powered barrows or carts the cost was at least ten times as great, and for man-carriage 20 to 30 times.[25]

Thus the railroads could tap heavily populated and productive areas ready for large movement of goods and people. In the more stable years up to the mid-1920's, the railways had very favorable operating ratios of costs to revenues, sometimes even below 50 per cent, and met their obligations. But for several years prior to 1928, the railways were in confusion. Warlords used the lines for military purposes, thus interrupting service. From 1925 to 1929, the number of locomotives in China south of the Wall decreased by 26 per cent, passenger cars by 31 per cent, and freight cars by 53 per cent, partly because of equipment removed to Manchuria.[26] Warlords also seized revenues, and most of the loans contracted abroad to build the lines were in default from the early twenties. The original financing arrangements commonly provided for extensive foreign technical aid and supervision in operations and finance. But such supervision could not be very effective in disturbed conditions.

The new government was anxious for improvement of railway operations and great expansion of the railway network, influenced by the plans of Sun Yat-sen. A separate Railway Ministry was set up headed by his son, Sun Fo. But conditions were far from favorable for rehabilitation and extension. Repeated revolts by warlords and regional authorities continued to interrupt railway service for military use, with hoarding, diversion, and damage of rolling stock. Government military forces used about 15 per cent of the passenger miles in 1932 to 1936 for troops, and a further large amount for supplies, while coping with disturbed conditions.[27] The military did not pay cash, and the cost became a book entry treated as an advance to the government. China had capable men experienced in railway operation and construction, but the railways were a political ploy. Personnel was greatly expanded to care for political favorites, many of whom were wished on the railways by officials of other branches of government. Added to the difficulties was the Japanese seizure of the railways in Manchuria. Finally, the railways were financially autonomous and not subject to whatever discipline the Finance Ministry could exert.

Nevertheless, there was progress with railway rehabilitation and services were restored and improved. Total operating revenues grew from C$117 million in 1928 to C$171 million in fiscal 1935-1936 (the price level being about the same in the two periods). Freight ton-kilometers grew from 1931, when the data were first reported, to 1935-1936 by about two-thirds for mineral products and about one-third for other items. Operating ratios were 67.3 per cent in 1927 and 64.5 per cent in 1935-1936. But here the results fell far short of the remarkable earlier ratios —51.2 per cent average in 1916 to 1925.[28] These ratios showed the great potential of railway development with proper management.

Costs of rehabilitation had to be met in the first instance from the internal flow of funds. With debts in default and disturbed conditions, lenders were not ready to come forward even had not the depression intervened. As revenues improved, they were used for the growing expenses of the various lines and the Railway Ministry and for capital improvements and extensions. Meanwhile, creditors were vexed for several years by the continual disregard of their claims (pages 128 to 130).

There was progress with extension of lines. For this there was great pressure both for strategic and economic reasons, in view of the meagerness of the railway network. Thus the government proceeded with new construction as a political necessity. There was also considerable provincial initiative. Governor Yen Hsi-shan of Shansi Province built about 400 miles of meter-gauge line between the north bank of the Yellow River and the Peiping-Suiyuan Railway in the north. This line was constructed and financed by the province at a cost of C $16 million. Southwest of Shanghai, Governor Chang Ching-kiang of Chekiang Province actively promoted lines in that province and Kiangsi. This project involved the eventual building of about 500 miles of lines. Much of this line was first built with light 35-pound rails, which were later replaced with those of the 63-pound type generally used on other lines. Provincial resources for this project were supplemented by support of the central government, using part of the proceeds of the Railway Reconstruction Loan issued in China in three series beginning in 1934. The Bank of China and other Chinese banks also made advances, and credits were obtained from the remitted British Boxer Indemnity funds and from German interests (Chapter 16).[29] Altogether in the prewar decade, about C $100 million was expended for extension of railways.

Of special importance was completion of the Canton-Hankow line. The internationally issued Hukuang Railway Loan of 1911 was made just before the revolution, and only about two-thirds of it appears to have gone into actual construction. A gap of 252 miles was left. The closing of this gap was financed with the help of remitted British Boxer Indemnity funds (Chapter 16).[30] The construction in difficult mountainous country was done entirely by Chinese engineers, and the through railway opened in the fall of 1936. This line proved of great importance after hostilities began in 1937, both to move troops and, until the capture of Canton in the fall of 1938, to bring in war supplies via Hong Kong.

Also important was the westward extension of the Lunghai Railway. This trunk line running west from the China Sea at

Haichow north of Shanghai was intended to open up the distant west and northwest eventually. In 1930 to 1934, the Railway Ministry extended the line for 125 miles to Sian, besides developing a new port at Lienyuan to replace the harbor near Haichow which had silted up. The Ministry continued with the westward extension, aiming eventually to traverse Sinkiang Province in Central Asia.[31]

Other extensions included lines from Nanking westward to Wuhu on the Yangtze River; from opposite Wuhu northward to Tienkian on the Wei River; and a link from Soochow to Kashing, south of Shanghai on the line to Hangchow. Furthermore, between 1927 and 1931 in Manchuria, 858 miles was built with wholly Chinese investment; 397 miles with Sino-British investment; and 689 miles with Sino-Japanese investment. These lines, totaling 1944 miles, were lost when Japan seized Manchuria in 1931, along with the Japanese-owned South Manchuria Railway of 709 miles and the Russian-owned Chinese Eastern Railway of 1073 miles, which Japan soon acquired from Russia.[32]

Altogether in the decade to mid-1937 a total of 2328 miles of railways was added in China proper, an increase of 47 per cent.[33] In 1937, plans for much more construction were interrupted by the hostilities.

Besides extensions of lines, the Railway Ministry procured a train ferry to operate at Nanking across the Yangtze River. The ferry made possible through train service between Shanghai and Peiping. Remitted British Boxer Indemnity funds equivalent to about US $7 million financed the ferry and purchase of equipment and materials for various lines. That was in addition to providing from these funds a sum equivalent to more than US $20 million to finance completion and improvement of the Canton-Hankow railway. A major bridge nearly one mile long was built across the Chientang River near Hangchow, with two decks, one for the railway and the other for road and pedestrian traffic. Unhappily, this bridge had to be destroyed a few weeks after completion early in the Sino-Japanese hostilities in the fall of 1937. Plans were drawn for another major bridge, to cross the Yangtze at Hankow, but war came before construction could begin. The Communists have since built this bridge with Russian help.

Despite rehabilitation and extensions, the railways continued to suffer from serious defects in organization, operation, and financial structure. There were about 15 more or less independent lines whose length varied from about 100 to less than 1000 miles. The system was top-heavy with executives and excessively staffed. The structure hampered normal interchange of rolling stock and created friction. Thus operations were costly and wasteful. Each railway had its special agreements relating to debts incurred for construction, equipment, and supplies. Some lines were charged with debts contracted for other lines. Thus the debt structure was highly complex.

For a considerable time after 1928, nearly all the debt remained in default. The creditors became impatient as they saw their claims ignored while improving revenues were used not only for basic rehabilitation but for capital improvements and extensions. Beginning in 1933, the Railway Ministry settled a number of material and supply debts; however, nothing was done for several years about the publicly issued bonds that were quoted at low figures in the markets. Finally, from 1935 to 1937, settlements were made covering most of the debt (Chapter 5 and Appendix 5). The rest would doubtless have been settled before long had not hostilities interfered, except that nothing could have been done about certain Japanese claims so long as serious friction continued.

Kia-ngau Chang began a program of reform after becoming Railway Minister in the latter part of 1935. He took a leading part in negotiating settlements of the publicly issued debt and other claims. He introduced improved accounting and statistical control, with a revised budgetary system. Daily and monthly reports were required on prescribed forms covering revenues, traffic, and cargo awaiting transport. The accounts of all lines were audited and adjusted. Standard budgets were prescribed for cash and materials. A General Railway Fund Ledger was set up as from January 1, 1937. A centralized system of purchasing and stores accounting was also introduced. Plans were adopted to reduce staff. Many improvements were made in signaling systems, maintenance of lines and equipment, bridge strengthening, addition of loops and sidings, and addition of rolling stock. In the year from May 1936 to May 1937, the number of locomotives, freight cars, and passenger cars increased by about 15 per cent in each category. From the first half year of 1935 to that of 1937, operating revenue grew from C$85.8 million to

C $91.9 million, while expenditure fell from C $54.2 million to C $46.9 million.[34]

Despite these important reforms, the serious structural defects continued. In 1929, W. B. Poland of the Kemmerer Commission urged combining the railways into six operating systems. One of them was for Manchuria. He also advocated centralizing and improving financial control, and settling and refunding debts in arrears. In 1935, General F. D. Hammond made a full report in which he analyzed the defects of the railway setup and made concrete proposals to improve operations. These included grouping the lines into five or preferably four systems, each divided into districts. He said that any plan to "bring real benefit both to the railways and to the bondholders" should "... amalgamate the railways administratively and financially; ... simplify the existing tangle of foreign loans; and ... provide new capital for development."[35]

In 1937, the Ministers of Railways and Finance asked me to study and make recommendations concerning the railway debt structure. Unhappily the hostilities erupted before completion of my report of October 1937, and prevented action on it. I proposed exchange of most of the outstanding railway obligations for four or five new series of bonds, secured by the revenues and assets of the system as a whole. The terms of exchange would reflect the position of old obligations as to interest rate, adequacy of security, nature of amortization provisions, the record as to payment of interest and principal, and market quotations if available. In the past, the pledge of security of specific railways had not given the results expected of it. The security of the railway system as a whole, backed by the government's desire to improve and maintain its credit as shown by growing evidence, I believed, would be more valuable to creditors than retention of the pledge of security of specific lines.

The prospects for the railways were bright in 1937. Besides Minister Chang's active program of reforms, the restoration of railway credit cleared the way for renewal of foreign investment in Chinese railways. As described in Chapter 16, Ministers Chang and Kung were able to interest European capital in large-scale railway financing, aided by the China Development Finance Corporation. The American Export-Import Bank was prepared to aid in financing the purchase of locomotives. There had already been substantial foreign investment in the railways between 1935 and 1937. Had not war come, the railways would have been greatly expanded and improved pursuant to agreements whose fruition was then prevented.

Roads

In 1920, nonurban China had only about 100 miles of roads suitable for motor traffic. In 1920 to 1921, Baker and his associates supervised the building of 850 miles of road in North China, using workers paid by famine relief funds sent by the American Red Cross. Then and later this method of work relief proved of great value in China. Political and military leaders became interested in road building, and a Good Roads Association was formed. By 1927 there were about 18,000 miles of road.[36]

Road building became an important concern of the new government. A National Highway Planning Commission was organized in 1929. By 1932, mileage had risen to 44,000. In that year the National Economic Council took over the responsibility and organized its Bureau of Roads. Construction was pushed forward, and by the end of 1936, the total length had risen to 69,000 miles including about 15 per cent in Manchuria and Mongolia. Roads under construction totaled about 10,000 miles and roads projected totaled about 30,000 miles.[37]

Prior to 1932, each province devised its own road program without much reference to what was done elsewhere. The Bureau of Roads set out to plan a road system, open remote areas, coordinate provincial road building with the plans of the central government, provide technical aid to the provinces, prepare uniform engineering standards and traffic regulations, and assist in financing. The bureau had helpful advice from M. S. Okecki, representing the Communications and Transit Organization of the League of Nations, and his assistant F. I. M. Bourdrez. Up to the end of 1936 about 15,000 miles was built under the auspices of the Bureau of Roads, and over half of this mileage was surfaced. Often it was found that building relatively short stretches could connect local road systems. The Bureau of Roads worked closely with the provincial governments. It provided standard specifications and technical aid, together with loans not exceeding half the cost. From 1932 to 1936, the National Economic Council loaned C$12 million to 15 provinces for road building.[38] The Bureau also paid attention to coordinating the road system with railways and waterways.

Most of the road building was in central and northwest China. The first emphasis was in the provinces adjacent to the Shanghai area, and then it was extended to other provinces in central China. These regions were both the most productive part of the country and the places where the government had the most authority. Specially important was the road from Sian to Lanchow in the northwest, the Si-Lan Road, about 500 miles through difficult terrain. A primitive dirt road with occasional gradients as high as one-third was converted into a motor highway. During the war, it proved a key link in the route traversed by military supplies from Russia. The China International Famine Relief Commission, supported by American gifts, provided part of the costs for the Si-Lan Road, as well as some supervisory services. The government provided part as did local civil and military authorities.[39]

Some road building was done by soldiers throughout this period, but they should have been used on a much larger scale in such work. Great masses of troops ill-fitted for real warfare were maintained and (for the most part) paid. The chief *raison d'etre* of a great part of such forces was to maintain the power, and often in devious ways the income, of local and regional leaders. Repeatedly I and others urged making greater use of troops in productive projects, but with relatively little result. Road building was also done by farmers in the off season. Later, during the war, labor was conscripted on an enormous scale for such projects as the Burma Road and the northwestern road to Russia.

By far the larger part of the roads was unsurfaced. Surfacing was mainly by the use of gravel and broken stone because asphalt and concrete were too expensive. The constant maintenance needed to keep graveled or unsurfaced roads in usable condition was usually lacking. Surfaced roads were often in bad repair and dirt roads were frequently unusable for motor traffic.

The central authorities also promoted ancillary traffic facilities and services, e.g., gasoline stations, first aid stations, car repair facilities, training of drivers and mechanics, road signs, road telephones, and uniform licensing of vehicles for participating provinces. To that end, a National Highway Traffic Commission was created under the National Economic Council with representatives of the provinces of Central China.

Gasoline imports grew from 13 million gallons in 1927 to 46 million in 1936. From 1927 to 1936, the registration of passenger cars grew from 16,012 to 27,465, trucks from 1901 to

11,917, and buses from 1015 to 8060. In 1937, there were several hundred private bus companies and many provincial and municipal lines.[40]

Although road building and motor traffic increased rapidly, less than 100,000 miles of road including projects under way and 47,000 motor vehicles of all kinds were meager for a huge country. Nevertheless, roads were a factor for unification. They gave greater mobility to government personnel and especially military forces, which had many more vehicles than the dissident elements. Roads were also located with a view to the possibility of having to fight Japan.

The building of roads under pressure for military and strategic, rather than economic, reasons had its evil side. A report of the British Commercial Counselor said:

> Undertaken often with the assistance of forced labour (the corvee system has been instituted in sixteen provinces), built on land which has been in many cases confiscated from the peasant owners without compensation, and along routes already served by railways or waterways, their use forbidden, in some cases, to barrows and carts carrying produce, and allowed only to motor-bus companies which have purchased a monopoly, there is no doubt that the immediate result of their construction has been to place further burdens on local industry and agriculture.[41]

Most of the rural people who were taxed to pay for roads or impressed for labor gained little immediate benefit. Sometimes, when roads created better routes and facilities for goods and passengers, unemployment resulted among porters, carters, and workers in water transport. Commercial uses were slow to develop and many roads were underused.

Despite the drawbacks, use of roads by the public was growing in 1937. Maintenance was improving, and imports of automotive equipment were increasing. The development of road transport for persons and goods promised to become of significant benefit to the overall economy.

Airways

During the twenties, there were sporadic efforts to establish air services for passengers and mail. These efforts were frustrated largely because militarists seized the planes. But civil aviation made tremendous progress in the prewar decade.

The serious development of civil aviation began in the spring of 1929 when Railway Minister Sun Fo signed with a subsidiary of the Curtiss group of companies a contract for establishing air services.[42] But friction developed at once with the Communications Ministry, which was finally awarded jurisdiction. In July 1930, that ministry signed a 10-year contract leading to creation of the China National Aviation Corporation (CNAC), which was to play an outstanding part in aviation progress both before and during the war years.

CNAC was capitalized at C $10 million, and was owned about 55 per cent by the Chinese government and 45 per cent by the American interests. The government appointed four of the seven directors, the president and one vice-president, the managers of the business and financial departments, and the assistant manager of the operations department. The American partners named another vice-president, the manager of the operations department, and the assistant managers of the other two departments.

CNAC had difficulty in getting started successfully, and for a time lost money. In 1933, Pan American Airways took over the enterprise and actively pushed its development. By 1935, CNAC was operating profitably.

CNAC began development of a network of routes serving the leading cities. First in 1929 was the Shanghai-Nanking-Hankow route, later extended up the Yangtze River to Chungking, and to Chengtu and Kunming. The route to the north was developed from Shanghai to Peiping, also serving Tsingtao and Tientsin. Then came the service to Canton with some flights including coastal ports en route. A link to world air routes was established by flights to Hong Kong and Hanoi. At the beginning, the service to river ports used only single-motored Loening amphibian planes, which flew about 100 miles per hour. Stinson single-motored land planes, somewhat faster, were used on routes in central and north China, and Sikorsky and Dolphin amphibians on the Canton run. In 1935, several Douglas DC-2's were added, and these more efficient planes made possible large reductions in fares. Planes were equipped with efficient homing devices tuned to radio beacons, to cope with the difficult weather conditions. CNAC's progress from 1929 to 1936 is shown by the increase in the number of kilometers flown (from 93,000 to 2,466,000); passengers carried (from 354 to 18,567); number of passenger kilometers (from 107,000 to 12 million); and amount of mail carried (from 3932 to 70,806 kilograms).[43]

The company undertook to train Chinese personnel in all branches of aviation and to use them as soon as qualified men were available. Employment of Chinese pilots began with American-born Chinese. But the company's slow progress in training Chinese-born pilots led to justifiable complaints on the Chinese side. There was, however, good progress in training Chinese radio operators, mechanics, and airport operators. The number of Chinese personnel trained by CNAC in the various branches of civil aviation grew, and formed a valuable nucleus for the continuing development of aviation in China.

In 1931, the Eurasia Aviation Corporation was created under an agreement with the German Lufthansa. The Ministry of Communications named six directors and the Germans three. The first service was in May 1931, from Shanghai to Manchouli on the Russian border of Manchuria. This was to be the first leg of a service to Berlin. This route had to be dropped, however, after Japan's invasion of Manchuria a few months later. Eurasia then hoped to develop a service to Europe via Central Asia. But the line could get no farther than Lanchow in the northwest, because of disturbed conditions in Sinkiang Province and lack of agreement with Russia. Eurasia developed services between Lanchow and other points in the west and northwest and Shanghai, Peiping, and Kunming. Its operations were on a smaller scale than those of CNAC but showed rapid growth: an increase of kilometers flown from 1932 to 1936 (11 months only) from 254,000 to 911,000; passenger kilometers flown from 326,000 to 3,123,000; passengers carried from 589 to 5115; and mail from 1750 to 26,961 kilograms.[44] Eurasia first used single-motored and later three-motored Junkers planes.

Another airline, Southwest Aviation Company, operated in South China from 1933, with headquarters at Canton. It was organized by the provincial governments of Kwangtung and Kwangsi. Besides connecting several leading cities in South China, it flew to Hanoi to connect with the service of Air France to Europe. That company operated four small British planes.

In October 1936, Japanese pressure in North China forced the authorities at Peiping to agree to the creation of the Huitung Air Navigation Company. This Japanese airline, which had nominal Chinese participation, operated between Tientsin and Peiping, Manchukuo, and Japan. The planes, pilots, and technical personnel were Japanese. The Chinese public boycotted the line, and it mainly served Japanese military and civilians.[45]

The arrangement for shared Chinese and American participation in the working of CNAC worked well, on the whole, as I was able to observe first hand while serving during the war as a director of the company. The plan was well designed, and its success was due to the cooperative attitude on both sides, and particularly to the ability and tact of William L. Bond, the American vice-president. CNAC came to enjoy a high reputation for the quality of its operations under difficult pioneering conditions. In the Eurasia enterprise, Sino-German cooperation worked well, and Eurasia's operations were also good under difficult conditions.

Although at the working level cooperation was generally good, at times it left much to be desired in relations with the higher level of government. Shortly before the war the National Aviation Commission, a military body, sought to control civil aviation and used some heavy-handed tactics. CNAC managed to resist successfully. But pressures for nationalization threatened to become greater, until outbreak of hostilities showed clearly that China was best served by keeping CNAC as a civil operation and maintaining the existing arrangements.

The progress of civil aviation in China during the prewar decade was of major importance. Even with the relatively slow planes then used, journeys formerly taking days or weeks could be accomplished in hours or in a day or two. And dependable, cheap airmail service enormously improved the pattern of communications. To an important extent, air services made up for the meagerness of the railway and road net. The economic advantages of these services were great. Even more important was the political significance. By bringing distant regions into closer contact, political unity and national solidarity were promoted.

Foreign trade

Foreign trade per capita was very low. Lack of knowledge of the size of the population prevents precise figures, and in any event they would be somewhat arbitrary because of wide variations in exchange rates. But assuming for purposes of this calculation a population of 500 million, the per capita value of total foreign trade in the twenties in China proper was roughly US $2.00 to 2.50, and in the depression period, 1932-1936, about US $1.00 (Appendix 20). In the latter years, total foreign trade of China proper was between about 6 and 8 per cent of estimated gross national product.[46] In the prewar decade, as earlier in China's history, foreign trade was an important factor promoting the country's modernization. It linked the economy with the outside world.

The trade statistics in my judgment are quite reliable as to recorded trade. But smuggling became more and more important after 1928 when duties were raised several times. The ratio of customs revenue to imports rose from almost 4 per cent before 1929 to about 25 per cent in 1934 to 1937. Choh-ming Li estimated that import totals should be raised by the following amounts because of smuggling: 1929, 3%; 1930, 5%; 1931, 8%; 1932 and 1933, 10%; 1934, 15%; and 1935, 25%.[47] For 1936, smuggling was even greater than before because of organized Japanese smuggling in North China (Chapter 3). Smuggling became so great that it must be taken into account in interpreting the published figures.

Interpretations must also note whether the published figures before 1932 include the trade of Manchuria, since from 1932 it was not included. The trade of China proper in 1921 to 1937 and the trade of Manchuria in 1926 to 1937 are shown in Appendixes 20 and 21. In 1926 to 1931 Manchuria's total trade was about 30 per cent of that of China proper. Manchurian trade increased greatly after 1931. Partly this resulted from Japan's activities in pushing development in Manchuria and promoting its exports. Also an important factor was that deflation there was countered by the devaluation—in line with sterling—of the Japanese yen and of the Manchurian currency which became tied to the yen. From 1932 through mid-1937, that region's trade expanded to nearly 60 per cent of that of China proper.

The total value of the foreign trade of China was greater in the twenties than in the thirties, whether measured in Chinese or American currency. The slump was not peculiar to China because the index of world trade fell from 100 in 1929 to about a third of that figure by 1934. From 1928 to 1931, the dollar value of the total trade, including Manchuria, fell by nearly half reflecting chiefly the world-wide depression. But in terms of Chinese currency the total value actually grew, reflecting the drastic depreciation of silver exchange and an internal price rise of about a fourth. After 1931, when the exchange value of China's currency rose sharply accompanied by severe deflation, the value of the trade of China proper shrank greatly in terms of both Chinese and American currency. From 1928 the successive increases in import duties tended to reduce foreign trade.

The greater part of both handling and financing foreign trade was in foreign hands, largely British, during the prewar decade. But Chinese were taking a growing part, often brought in as partners of foreign firms. In financing the Bank of China in particular was becoming more and more important. It established branches at London, New York, Hong Kong, and Singapore. Also the government more and more bought directly from firms in Europe and America. And there was some tendency to government trading, as through the China Vegetable Oil Corporation, the China Silk Corporation, and the barter trade with Germany developed from 1935 to 1937.[48]

China's foreign trade comprised a great variety of goods. (The chief items in 1935 and 1936 are shown in Appendix 22.) Imports included many kinds of manufactures, raw materials, and foodstuffs. Imports of foodstuffs varied with the crops, but part of the imports came to ports where Chinese products could not compete with foreign products having cheap water transport. Thus Chinese wheat available at Shanghai could supply the four mills for only part of the year. Average rice imports were around 2 per cent of production.

Net imports of capital goods in China proper grew from C $108 million in 1932 to C $144 million in 1936 in terms of constant 1932 prices. Imports of railway and communications equipment at current prices grew from C $21 to C $56 million; vehicles and parts from C $11 to C $24 million; communications equipment from C $15 to C $24 million; electrical machinery and parts from C $6 to C $11 million; and miscellaneous machinery and parts from C $28 to C $49 million.[49]

Exports comprised a wide variety of goods, of which about five-sixths were agricultural products. Mineral exports included tin, tungsten, and antimony. Fabricated goods were only a minor part of exports. China was an exporter as well as an importer of foodstuffs. About one-sixth of total exports consisted of foodstuffs, important items being eggs and egg products, groundnuts, fruits, and vegetables. Other major agricultural exports included fibers (silk, cotton, and wool), various oil seeds, tea, hides, skins, and leather. The government was moving to help the trade to improve the quality of silk and tea, exports of which had greatly shrunk from their former preeminence. Loss of Manchuria after 1931 was a heavy blow to export trade, especially because of the importance of export of soy beans and their products. Expansion of exports in which China had a comparative advantage, to an extent that would significantly promote economic development by covering the costs of needed imports, was clearly a difficult prospect especially after 1931. The stabilization of exchange rates in 1935 at a favorable level, however, helped greatly in recovery of the export trade.

Indexes of quantity of foreign trade were prepared by Franklin Ho of Nankai University.[50] These indexes, based on 1913 as 100, rose by 1928 to 131.5 for imports and 156.1 for exports. From 1928 to 1931, quantities were fairly well sustained, at 129.9 and 136.5, respectively. But for the period after 1931, interpretations of these indexes must recognize the exclusion of Manchuria. The drop in 1932 of the index for China proper to 106.0 for imports and 100.8 for exports largely reflects omission of Manchurian trade, which included large exports of soy beans, bean cake, and coal and imports of textiles, flour, gunny bags, raw cotton, and iron and steel products. By 1936, the index for imports fell to 77.9. That drop apparently reflected to a large extent the effect of rising rates of duty. The index for exports, however, showed recovery to 125.6 in 1936.

China's terms of trade showed secular deterioration over the years 1867 to 1936 (Chapter 7). The Ho-Hou index based on 1913 prices shows a deterioration of about 40 per cent during the period. For 1927 to 1937, that index shows little net change, but an index based on 1926 prices shows a large deterioration (Table 16).

Changes of distribution of trade by countries in 1927 to 1937 (Appendix 23) are subject to important qualification to indicate what really happened. The British Empire's share, which was the largest, fell from about 32 to 27 per cent. That included the trade of Hong Kong, part of which represented transit trade of China between the Canton area and other points. From 1932, goods shipped through Hong Kong were shown in the figures according to actual origin instead of as Hong Kong trade. Thus Hong Kong's share in the distribution of trade with China fell from about 17 per cent before 1932 to about 10 per cent thereafter. Direct trade with Britain grew from about 8 to 10 per cent of the total. Trade with the United States and continental Europe grew, respectively, from about 15 to 23 per cent and about 13 to 20 per cent. Except for Japan, the trade with other countries showed little change between 1927 and 1937.

Japan's share of the total trade was about one-fourth before 1932, but it fell to 12 to 15 per cent between 1933 and 1937. There were several causes. In 1931, Japan provided 57 per cent of Manchurian imports and took 45 per cent of the exports.[51] Elimination of this trade after 1931 from the published Chinese customs statistics meant that Japan's share became a smaller proportion. Japanese trade also shrank because of boycotts. Rising tariffs were adverse to Japanese trade, and were a factor in promoting smuggling of both Japanese and other goods. Finally, the organized and open Japanese smuggling in the later part of the prewar decade largely involved goods from Japan and Formosa. Thus, much Japanese trade went unrecorded.

Japan's China trade in the prewar decade, according to Japanese figures, was nearly a fifth of Japan's total and was second to trade with the United States. After 1931 Japan's exports to Manchukuo boomed. But this gives a misleading impression of benefit to Japan, as it largely represented exports of capital that were eventually lost.

National income and capital formation

Internal and international conditions from 1927 to 1937 were far from favorable for growth of national income and capital formation. While the data for measuring these parameters are far from satisfactory, studies of the available data by competent scholars indicate the general situation.[52]

Kung-chia Yeh's study shows for China, including Manchuria in 1931 to 1936, a gross domestic product averaging about C $30 billion at 1933 prices, with only a moderate increase as shown in Table 25. The figures are supported by detailed examination of value added in the several branches of economic activity. Nearly two-thirds derived from agriculture. About 10 per cent derived from manufacturing, mining, and utilities, and of this about two-thirds represented handicraft production. The rest represented transport and communications, trade, construction, rents, and financial, personal, and governmental services.[53]

Capital formation in 1931 to 1936 according to Yeh's computation of 1964 averaged C $1.49 billion gross in constant 1933 prices, and about C $0.46 billion net, as shown in Table 26. Liu

Table 25

Domestic product (including Manchuria) from 1931 to 1936 in constant 1933 prices[a]

	Domestic product, billions, in indicated year					
	1931	1932	1933	1934	1935	1936
Agriculture	C$18.59	C$19.66	C$19.34	C$17.11	C$18.79	C$19.89
Manufacturing						
Factories	0.57	0.62	0.63	0.66	0.72	0.82
Handicraft	2.10	2.05	2.04	1.89	1.93	2.03
Mining	0.19	0.19	0.21	0.22	0.26	0.28
Utilities	0.11	0.13	0.13	0.15	0.16	0.18
Construction	0.40	0.41	0.44	0.44	0.46	0.49
Transportation and Communications						
Modern	0.41	0.40	0.43	0.47	0.53	0.58
Old-fashioned	1.17	1.26	1.21	0.99	1.08	1.12
Trade						
Stores	1.89	1.75	1.75	1.66	1.72	1.82
Peddlers	0.92	0.97	0.96	0.87	0.94	1.00

Continued

Table 25 (Continued)

Domestic product (including Manchuria) from 1931 to 1936 in constant 1933 prices[a]

	Domestic product, billions, in indicated year					
	1931	1932	1933	1934	1935	1936
Government	0.84	0.79	0.84	0.93	1.00	1.07
Finance[b]	0.06	0.06	0.06	0.07	0.08	0.09
Personal services	0.34	0.34	0.34	0.35	0.35	0.36
Residential rent	1.01	1.02	1.03	1.04	1.06	1.07
Net domestic product	28.60	29.65	29.43	26.85	29.08	30.80
Depreciation	0.98	1.02	1.02	0.97	1.05	1.10
Gross domestic product	29.58	30.67	30.45	27.82	30.13	31.90

[a] Source: Kung-chia Yeh: *Capital Formation in Mainland China, 1931-36 and 1952-57* (unpublished dissertation, Columbia University, 1964), p. 183.
[b] Only that portion of net value added not included elsewhere is given here.

Table 26

Domestic capital formation from 1931 to 1936 in constant 1933 prices[a]

	Domestic capital formation, billions, in indicated years						
	1931	1932	1933	1934	1935	1936	1931-1936 average
Gross fixed capital formation:							
Buildings and structures	C$0.91	C$0.92	C$1.01	C$1.01	C$1.05	C$1.14	C$1.01
Producers' equipment	0.36	0.36	0.40	0.45	0.48	0.54	0.43
Total	1.27	1.29	1.42	1.46	1.52	1.69	1.44
Net change in inventories	--	.20	0.08	- 0.34	0.07	0.26	0.04
Gross domestic capital formation	1.27	1.49	1.50	1.12	1.60	1.95	1.49
Less: Capital consumption	0.98	1.02	1.02	0.97	1.05	1.10	1.02
Net domestic capital formation	0.29	0.47	0.48	0.15	0.55	0.85	0.46

[a] Source: Kung-chia Yeh: "Capital Formation in Mainland China, 1931-36 and 1952-57" (unpublished dissertation, Columbia University, 1964), p. 76a.

and Yeh presented in 1965 a revised and slightly higher figure for 1933, namely, C $1.596 billion gross and C $0.51 billion net.[54] Gross capital formation according to these data averaged about 5 per cent of the gross domestic product, and net capital formation about 2 per cent.

Earlier estimates of capital formation in the prewar period vary considerably. Simon Kuznets in 1946 estimated gross domestic capital formation in 1936 at C $1.735 billion, with net of C $0.700 billion. Several other estimates, showing average yearly gross national capital formation in 1931 to 1936, are Kuznets, C $1.280 billion; Wu Ching-chao, C $1.188 billion; Hsing Mo-huan, C $1.6 billion; Wu Cheng-ming, C $0.966 billion; and Ou Pao-san, C $1.061 billion.[55] But Ou made a radically lower estimate of net capital formation, showing negative figures for each of the six years. His estimates of national income average about C $21 billion, or about two-thirds of Yeh's figure. He considers that capital consumption was large, 1933 being a year of depression. He makes large deductions for depreciation, especially in agriculture and housing. Furthermore, he deducts C $0.192 billion for reduction in stocks of silver and gold. His revised figures for 1933 show a negative figure of C $0.621 billion for capital formation. He points out that American estimates of capital formation in the United States in 1933 were negative. Yeh disagrees with Ou and thinks that each of the six years showed positive capital formation.[56]

I have not tried to make an independent estimate of national income and capital formation, but consider Yeh's figures as the most comprehensive and dependable. Certain comments are in order.

China in the prewar decade was clearly at an early stage of economic development, with the modernized industrial part of the economy producing only about 3 per cent of the national product. While that part was progressing at a rate that was good considering the obstacles, achievement of a good overall rate of progress depended on upgrading the agricultural sector that produced about two-thirds of the total national product. Here there were factors inhibiting much saving. The ratio of good land per person was under one-half acre. By dint of great effort, most of the rural population could barely maintain minimum subsistence. They had barely enough food grains and little other food, barely enough clothing and low-grade housing, and could do little more than maintain their simple tools and other productive equipment. Little was available for emergency needs or improvement. They generally lacked improved seeds, pesticides, fertilizer, and credit facilities, although measures to remedy these lacks were gaining momentum in the thirties.

Buck investigated savings in the rural areas and his finding may be taken as illustrative. His samples indicated that 21 per cent of the farms had savings, which averaged C $192 per family with savings. The savings comprised hoarded money, stored products, and loans of money or in kind. The mean size of families was 5.21 persons.[57] Assuming for purposes of calculation a total population of 500 million and a rural population of 400 million, there were 77 million rural families of which 21 per cent or 16.2 million had savings of C $192 per family. On the basis of that rough calculation, the total savings of farmers were about C $3.1 billion.

The prewar rate of gross capital formation, estimated by Yeh at about 5 per cent of the gross domestic product, may be compared with postwar rates in Mainland China and Taiwan. For 1952 to 1957, Yeh estimates a rate of about 18 per cent for Mainland China. This higher rate is striking because the average level of consumption was probably no greater than or even below that of the prewar decade. The higher rate was largely due to imposition of forced saving at the cost of holding down consumption. Yeh points out that the Communists also tapped latent sources of savings that were not formerly used because of institutional constraints. In 1952 to 1957, these sources included reduction of wedding and funeral expenses; holding down consumption in good years; reduction of the larger consumption of the well-to-do; better health services; and more even food distribution which increased the productive capacity of the very poor. The government also organized labor brigades for large-scale improvements of irrigation and conservancy. Furthermore, depreciation was less in 1952 to 1957 because the newer capital was younger.[58] Above all, there was internal peace, maintained by stern measures.

Overall growth in mainland China in 1952 to 1957 has been estimated by competent experts at about 6 per cent yearly, an excellent rate considering the great difficulties of rehabilitation. But then came the Great Leap Forward and a calamitous retrogression. It appears that there was no overall growth from 1958 to 1965. After some recovery the Great Cultural Revolution caused another setback. The economy has since improved, aided by good crops. The regime has discontinued providing statistical information since the Great Leap, and estimates of growth and capital formation since 1957 are hard to make with confidence.[59]

Taiwan under its free enterprise system and with the benefit of large American aid has shown outstanding growth of the gross national product in each year since 1951. The official figures, which Neil H. Jacoby considered substantially correct, showed for 1951 to 1965 an average compounded yearly rate of 7.6 per cent and per capita growth of 4.2 per cent. Gross domestic savings at constant prices grew nearly fivefold from 1951 to 1964, and were 12 per cent of GNP in 1951, rising to a somewhat larger percentage in the sixties.[60]

15: Foreign Advisory and Technical Aid

Prior to 1927, China had long received considerable foreign aid in technical affairs and administration. China was following the earlier example of Japan, which in about 1875 after the Meiji restoration employed more than 500 foreigners as advisers and regular officials.[1] China's Sino-foreign Customs service dated from 1854 and her Salt revenue administration from 1913. Sir Robert Hart helped in setting up the postal service, which later became independent of the Customs. In 1928, the Peking regime had about 20 foreign advisers in different departments; the Customs had a foreign personnel of about 240; and the Salt and Posts had about 50 and 100, respectively.[2] The total was more than 400.

The Nationalists continued to make extensive use of foreign advice and technical aid. But the pattern changed. The new government moved much more aggressively to have Chinese take over administrative posts as rapidly as it deemed them qualified to do so. T. V. Soong's policies concerning the Customs and Salt service are discussed in Chapters 2 and 3. The result of the changes was that during the prewar decade the number of foreigners in these services and in the Posts was roughly halved. The prewar objective of the government was to nationalize these services by orderly evolution over a period of years. The process was eventually completed as a result of the shattering events of the war period.

The Nationalists made much greater and more effective use of foreign advisers and specialists than had their predecessors, in both civil and military affairs. Some were engaged directly; others were recommended by foreign governments; and still others were provided by the League of Nations through its programs of technical cooperation. In civil affairs, the number totaled about 65, including about 35 League experts from several European countries and 17 American members of the Kemmerer Commission. In military affairs, the total was more than 175, mainly Germans but including Americans, Frenchmen, and

Italians. The number of advisers and specialists in China at any one time was much less than the total, because many served for relatively short periods. The best results, however, were realized with the help of those who stayed for extended periods.

Foreign advisory and technical aid in military affairs is discussed in this chapter, partly to make more complete the coverage of the work of foreign personnel in the period, but also because the military situation both internal and vis-a-vis Japan was so important a factor affecting the finances and economy.

Financial affairs

The discussion of fiscal and monetary matters in preceding chapters has dealt specifically with the participation of foreign advisers and experts. In this chapter, I shall summarize and consider it in the overall setting.

In the field of finance, aid was provided by the Kemmerer Commission in 1929, and thereafter by several of its members who were engaged to advise China. Other foreigners who aided in relation to financial policy were Sir Arthur Salter and Maurice Frere of the League of Nations; Sir Frederick W. Leith-Ross who came in 1935 representing the British government; Edmund (later Sir Edmund) Hall-Patch of the Leith-Ross mission; and Cyril Rogers of that mission, who remained to advise on central banking matters.[3] In more specialized matters, Clifford Hewitt served as a minting expert, succeeded by Robert J. Grant; J. F. Freeman was an accountant in the Central Bank; and Carl F. Bartz served as a cotton expert in the Central Bank in connection with handling the cotton bought by China under the American Cotton and Wheat loan of 1933 (Chapter 16).

The Commission of Financial Experts, commonly called the Kemmerer Commission, was arranged by Sun Fo when visiting the United States in the fall of 1928. It was significant that China turned to the United States for financial advice. The chief European powers had had much friction with China over many years, and were regarded as colonialists. Japan's civilian leaders were following a moderate policy toward China, but the pointless intervention of the military in Shantung Province during the Northern Expedition in mid-1928 still rankled. A further factor was that China's leaders in Nanking hoped to clear the way for an American loan for rehabilitation and development.

The Kemmerer Commission arrived in China early in 1929 for

one year. The new government, besides facing political uncertainties, lacked experience in financial policy and administration and was short of qualified personnel. Fortunately for the Commission, its contact with the government was through Finance Minister Soong, whose ability and resourcefulness at once impressed the Commission's members. His attitude was that China was entering a new era, and that the new government should measure up to its opportunities and responsibilities both at home and abroad. Information on many financial matters was not easy to obtain, but the government departments with few exceptions responded as best they could to calls for data. The Commission rendered full reports on the main branches of fiscal and monetary affairs.* Most reports included drafts of specific legislation or regulations to give effect to the recommendations.

Kemmerer's plan of currency reform remained in abeyance, as described in Chapter 7. Several of the Commission, while deferring to Kemmerer as a currency authority of world renown, would have preferred moving to the gold standard by stages, starting with reform of the existing silver currency. The onset of the depression, the slump in silver, continuing internal disturbances, and from the fall of 1931 the friction with Japan, made obsolete important parts of the plan. These events also interfered with giving effect to several of the Commission's plans such as projects for settling debts in arrears; rehabilitation of railway finances; reform and development of land taxation; and conversion of the Central Bank into a central reserve bank. The plan of banking regulation was strongly opposed by Chinese bankers and little was done in that field during the prewar decade.

The chief results of the Commission's work were realized with the help of members who were engaged for work that continued for some time: F. A. Cleveland, first as budget expert but soon named as Associate Chief Inspector of Salt Revenue; Oliver C. Lockhart as Financial Adviser with special reference to taxation, and in 1935 to succeed Cleveland in the Salt administration; F. B. Lynch as Adviser to the Central Bank; and me as Financial Adviser with special reference to public credit and currency. Benjamin B. Wallace and William Watson stayed for shorter periods as advisers on tariffs and accounting, respectively.

A most important fiscal reform emanating from the Commission's work was the collection of import duties on a gold basis

*These reports are listed in the Bibliography.

which I first proposed in May 1929 (Chapter 3). This reform greatly benefited the revenue, and made it possible to preserve and strengthen the government's credit at home and abroad. The reform also led to important progress in administrative procedures in the Finance Ministry and Central Bank, shifting responsibility for management of debt service from the Customs and foreign banks to the Finance Ministry and Central Bank. This change was accomplished without impairment of the rights of creditors. Moreover, it fitted in with legitimate national aspirations and removed a possible grievance that might have stimulated drastic and unwise nationalistic action. A rise in bond prices followed, which was stimulated by measures begun in 1929 to pay the arrears of service of salt-secured loans.

The Commission's proposals for taxation, which were developed by Lockhart, fitted well into the program of reform already begun by Soong. Lockhart continued as Financial Adviser, and by close relations with the revenue authorities, who were competently led, he was able to exert considerable influence on policies and administration. One result was the development of a respected service to operate the consolidated taxes on factory products. The position of the older commodity taxes collected throughout the country remained less satisfactory because they were less adaptable to central control and administration remained largely the prerogative of local authorities. The Commission recommended against an income tax on the ground that China was not yet ready to operate it efficiently. The wisdom of this conclusion was proved when an income tax introduced in 1936 disclosed serious defects and fell far short of success, despite hard work by many of those charged with its collection.

Unhappily the Commission's recommendation of reforming the land tax, beginning with surveys and a proper system of registration, failed to receive attention. Failure to progress in this area was costly. A solid fiscal system could be built only by drawing large revenue from agriculture, which was by far the largest part of the economy. Moreover, abuses in land taxation contributed to the rural discontent that gave the Communists an opening for winning the rural masses.

Cleveland and later Lockhart took over administrative work in the Salt revenue service. Both helped to improve the organization and procedures, although the subsequent great growth of revenue was largely the result of the widening authority of the government. They also helped in effecting better control of salt production and trade and in eliminating long-standing abuses.

Cleveland prepared the Commission's proposals for improved budgetary and accounting procedures of the government. These proposals were adopted to a considerable extent by administrative decisions. But operation of the procedures was far from adequate because of lack of qualified personnel in the civil branches and especially because of failure to bring about fiscal control of the military. By 1937, there had been considerable improvement, and real budgeting and accounting were becoming feasible if accepted by the military.

The Commission's proposals for reorganization of the internal debt which I prepared and later revised as conditions changed, were the basis of major refunding operations in 1932 and 1936. These operations reduced yearly charges for debt retirement by around C $100 million and C $85 million, respectively. These savings were of great importance to the hard-pressed government. The first readjustment avoided suspension of debt service in the difficult conditions accompanying the Japanese attack at Shanghai in January 1932. The second buttressed the currency reform of 1935. Both readjustments involved pressure on the representatives of bondholders, but proved to be in their longer run interest as bond prices improved to levels that, by mid-1937, put interest yields on internal bonds on what for China was an unprecedented low yield of 8 per cent and less. These readjustments were an alternative to meeting revenue needs by inflation.

As to foreign debt in arrears, the government adopted my plan, which was recommended by the Commission in 1929, for making payments current on the chief salt-secured loans. The full operation of the plan was delayed by the temporary regional seizures of loan quotas. But the interest arrears were soon eliminated, and the payment of arrears of drawings was nearly completed when hostilities began in 1937.

The Commission's proposals for settlement of debts in arrears, other than salt-secured, were not workable after both China and the foreign powers abandoned the idea of a general negotiated settlement (Chapter 5). I then prepared plans for piecemeal settlement of the chief individual debts, and these plans became substantially the basis for the eventual settlements. These plans were shelved until the currency reform improved the economic outlook and brought home to the government the importance of action to improve credit abroad. The progress of that reform and the beginning of recovery from the depression, along with improved internal political conditions, made action feasible. The settlements had to involve reduction of current interest, largely on a temporary basis, as well as reduction and in some cases cancellation of arrears of interest. Nevertheless, the regularization of payments on debts in arrears equivalent to about US $275 million, and improvement of prices of leading foreign loans to about a 5 per cent basis in 1937, represented a considerable accomplishment. China's improved credit made possible moves to attract foreign investment in economic development.

In development of the Central Bank, Lynch played an important part, working closely with T. M. Hsi, the general manager of the Banking Department. Lynch and I devised the procedures to take maximum advantage of adoption of the customs gold unit—to develop assets in foreign currencies and use such funds directly for service of foreign debts and other payments in foreign currencies. The latter procedure was substituted for purchase of exchange in the open market, which often had been done in ways that added to the government's cost. The Central Bank became an important operator in foreign exchange, and thus was in position to handle the operations connected with introducing and strengthening the currency reform of 1935.

In no field were foreign advice and technical aid more important than in dealing with monetary problems. Key instances related to adoption of the customs gold unit in 1930; coping with the gyrations of silver and abandonment of the free silver standard in 1934; planning the currency reform of 1935; and implementation of that reform including sales of silver to the American Treasury, exchange operations to maintain stability at the new level, and the project for conversion of the Central Bank into a central reserve bank. Lynch, Lockhart, and I were active in these matters, notably in preparation of the plan for the currency reform of 1935. Sir Frederick Leith-Ross brought British prestige and his own competence to aiding in that reform, including issuance of the King's regulation calling on British nationals to use bank notes as legal tender instead of silver. He performed an important service in stressing to the government and public the basic importance of fiscal stability to maintain the soundness of the new managed currency from 1935. Similarly he stressed the importance of converting the Central Bank into a Central Reserve Bank. His associate Rogers, on leave from the

Bank of England, took the leading part in preparing and promoting the project for the reserve bank.

In all these matters of finance, foreign advice and technical aid would have been of little avail had not the Chinese leaders, notably Soong and Kung and their associates, been ready to seek and accept advice besides initiating action and contributing to plans themselves. Sometimes in weighing policy they did not accept certain proposals for reasons of their own or because foreigners could not always be aware of the ramifications of situations in a country not their own. At other times, they improved the proposals that the foreigners made.

Aid by the League of Nations

The League's aid antedated the Nationalist period, but was greatly increased in 1931 to 1935. In 1922 to 1930, several visits to China were made by League representatives, especially members of the Health Section in relation to problems of epidemics and quarantine. Among these representatives was Dr. Ludwig Rajchman of Poland, Director of the Health Section. For about 15 years he had much contact with China, and in the thirties was prominent in the controversy over China's relations with the League and its members, especially in Japan. His appointments were technical. But he was in China when Japan began to take over Manchuria in 1931. His active help to T. V. Soong in presentation of China's cause to the League gave rise to the charge that thereafter his work in China was political as well as technical.

In January 1931 Rajchman, who had recently arrived in China, proposed inviting two League experts to China. They were Sir Arthur Salter, the British Director of the League's Economic and Financial Organization, who was then in India, to discuss the effect on China of the world depression; and Robert Haas, a Frenchman, Director of the Transit and Communications Organization, to discuss problems of inland waterways and land reclamation. Minister Soong consulted me about the proposal, wondering whether their coming might involve the League too deeply in China's affairs. I reassured him, saying that I felt that he and his associates could control such matters and that the experts could be helpful. He and the Generalissimo invited them, and their visit was arranged. I wrote to a friend on April 4, 1931: "I think the League would like to take over China's rehabilitation. But I think T. V. will want to do the job himself." There were indications that the League would have liked to take over financial advisory work from the Americans. But we had and retained the government's confidence, and never felt that we were likely to be displaced.

Salter arrived in March 1931, accompanied by Maurice Frere, a Belgian financial expert. I had known both in Europe when they and I were concerned with problems of German reparations in the mid-1920's, and thought well of their competence. Salter submitted an excellent report, *China and the Depression* (Nanking, 1934), which I have discussed in Chapter 7. Haas made proposals on water conservancy, especially for control of the Hwai River, whose flooding frequently caused great damage. Rajchman's proposals related to improvement of procedures of quarantine and epidemic control, and medical education.[4] The visit of these experts led to continuing helpful collaboration between China and organs of the League.

An early result of the League's activity was the decision in April 1931 to create the National Economic Council (NEC), headed by Chiang and under Soong's active direction. Its function was to promote development by selecting the most urgent projects, establishing an order of priority, and elaborating and implementing a plan of development. Chiang and Soong invited the League's collaboration in the NEC's work, especially by providing expert advice, in training Chinese and in improving the educational system.[5]

The League's Council at Geneva warmly welcomed the invitation. Japan's representative, Kenkichi Yoshizawa, moved its approval thus showing the good will of Japan's civil authorities four months before the military seized the initiative by their attack in Manchuria. Yoshizawa said that Japan was "entirely in sympathy with the Nanking Government's efforts to reorganize the country." He noted that the plan was technical and not political, namely to aid China in "the development of the natural resources of the country and the well-being of the Chinese people." He said that he was convinced that the League would invite Japan's participation, especially "as regards the advisers to be appointed."[6]

The NEC was slow in starting its work because of internal disturbances, flood disaster, and the Manchurian affair, all of which marked 1931 as a most difficult year. The NEC set up a preparatory office, but was not formally inaugurated until the fall of 1933.

Meanwhile, in the summer of 1933 Soong was in Europe to attend the World Economic Conference in London. On June 28, he addressed a communication to the League's Council concerning aid in China's reconstruction. After expressing appreciation of the help already granted, he said that China wished to push the program "in a few provinces which will serve as models for the rest of the country." He requested the Council to nominate a technical representative "to be accredited to the National Government and its National Economic Council." On July 18 the Council agreed to appoint an agent, whose work would be "of a purely technical and entirely non-political character," to serve for one year.[7]

The Council appointed Rajchman as its representative. Minister Johnson promptly predicted that this appointment would "doom effort of League to the suspicious attention and opposition of the Japanese." Japan, recalling Rajchman's activities in China during the League's controversy over Manchuria, at once charged that the League's program was political, meaning anti-Japanese. The Rajchman appointment became a factor in growing Japanese opposition to League aid in China's rehabilitation. The opposition extended to all forms of non-Japanese aid, notably American.[8]

The Rajchman issue came to a head in the spring and summer of 1934, when his report was about to be issued. On April 23, the Japanese representative at Geneva stated that Japan had "the impression that Dr. Rajchman's report involved a program which particularly in its financial elements was either implicitly or explicitly politically antagonistic to Japan." American Minister Hugh Wilson reported on May 15 that in the League's China Technical Committee there seemed to be "a certain amount of dissatisfaction with Rajchman's alleged political activities in China." The end result was that Rajchman's appointment to China was not renewed when it expired July 31.[9] The League did not again have a technical representative in China with a continuing mission, and the scale of its work decreased although Haas did make an additional visit in the first part of 1935 to maintain contact.

In July 1933, Soong, besides asking the League to send a technical representative, discussed with the League further measures of aid to China. He hoped to have the League help to form a Consultative Committee of Chinese and foreign members to deal with economic reconstruction. He asked Jean

Monnet, who later was to gain distinction as a chief architect of European integration, to head this Committee and to come to China. Soong conceived of the plan as helping to give effect to a recommendation of the Lytton Commission, named by the League to try to devise a settlement of the Manchurian affair, that peace in the Far East needed "a strong central government in China," a requisite for which would be "temporary international cooperation in the internal reconstruction of China."[10] But Soong's plan aroused strong Japanese hostility. It was dropped when Thomas W. Lamont and Sir Charles Addis, the American and British financiers whom Soong wanted to join the Committee, declined to serve. The failure to organize the Committee derived from doubt whether it could succeed without Japanese participation, from Lamont's banking connection with Japan, and from the Consortium agreement relating to international participation of Western powers and Japan in Chinese financing.[11] But Monnet came to China despite the failure of Soong's original project, and helped in the formation of the China Development Finance Corporation.

The League's collaboration, prior to formal activation of the NEC, extended beyond the already described work of Rajchman, Salter, and Haas. In 1931-1932, the League sent a mission to advise on improvement of education and intellectual intercourse between China and foreign countries. The mission's report, prepared after a stay of three months, contained numerous proposals for betterment of the educational system. It stressed what it considered "the remarkable, not to say alarming, consequences of the excessive influence of the American model on Chinese education." While concluding that "the cultural conditions of Europe are more suitable than American conditions for adaptation to Chinese requirements," because of the greater strength of tradition in Europe, it urged that China's educational system should essentially reflect Chinese culture and traditions rather than foreign. The aim should be "to prepare students for a life of useful work in China."[12] Some who read the report wondered whether the League was seeking to supersede American influence in China.

Even though the United States was not a member of the League, it was noteworthy that the League sent no American experts to China. Soong named me as adviser to the NEC, but as matters developed I did little in that capacity. It was a bit ironical, in view of the attitude of some League personnel to

Americans, that funds to effect much of the work with which League experts were connected in 1931 to 1935 came from the American Flood Relief Loan and the Cotton and Wheat Loan.

Besides the educational mission to China, the League arranged for the summer 1932 European visit of a Chinese educational mission. To follow up this exchange of missions, the League sent M. Fernand Maurette of the International Labor Office to China for a brief stay in the spring of 1934. In addition, three European professors were provided for an extended stay at Central University in Nanking, in geology, geography, and English literature.[13]

Besides its activities in education, the League, prior to formal activation of the NEC, sent three European engineers to China to study public works projects. A Polish road expert, M. S. Okecki, was appointed for a stay of considerable time. Recognizing the pressing need of agricultural reform, the League sent Professor Carlo Dragoni of the University of Rome and an assistant in 1932-1933. Of special importance was the work of Sir John Hope Simpson, who came on the League's recommendation in November 1931 to act for several months as the director of flood relief.[14] The League also sent two advisers on civil service reform, one British and one German. But they were not able to accomplish much at the Examination Yuan.[15]

After its activation, the NEC had some important accomplishments with the collaboration of League experts.[16] Funds were provided from the proceeds of the American Cotton and Wheat Loan, and the budget of C $15 million for 1934 included C $6.8 million for roads, C $2.5 million for developments in the northwest, C $1.9 million for rural rehabilitation in Kiangsi Province, C $1.75 million for improving cotton and silk production, and C $0.5 million for public health.

Road building was largely done by the provinces, in cooperation with the Bureau of Roads created in October 1933. The NEC's standard contribution was 40 per cent of cost. Subsidies by the NEC to seven provinces in central China were about C $4 million from 1931 to April 1934, and with this help a total of about 2000 miles of roads was built. First of these subsidies was for a three-province project in the lower Yangtze region, followed by a seven-province project in adjoining areas. The program was extended to the west and northwest, where several main highways were built.[17] The NEC conducted experiments with different kinds of construction and trained highway engineers.

The work of the NEC in the undeveloped northwest, besides road building, related to irrigation, animal husbandry, health and veterinary services, and agricultural cooperatives.

The NEC's first work in water conservancy was largely the extension of the 1931-1932 flood control projects in the Yangtze Valley. This additional work was so effective that renewed high water in 1935 did little damage. Water conservancy was traditionally handled by regional and *ad hoc* bodies, and at times there was confusion and shifting of responsibility. In 1934-1935, centralized control was vested in the NEC, which provided subsidies. The greater part of the work was in the hands of five chief bodies: the North China River Commission, the Yellow River Commission, the Hwai River Commission, the Yangtze River Commission, and the Kwangtung Conservancy Board. The NEC arranged for regional representation in its work, which covered flood control, irrigation and reclamation, and improvement of inland waterways. It set up procedures of research and inspection.[18]

The Cotton Industry Commission was established in 1933 under the NEC. Its purpose was to improve and develop cotton production, which provided the largest part of China's needs, as well as the important textile industry. The Commission included members from cotton-growing, textile, and banking circles. It gave special attention to the improvement of cotton cultivation, research in seed varieties, control of pests, and use of fertilizer. Plantings of improved seed increased from about 100,000 acres in 1934 to about 500,000 in 1936. Inspection bureaus were set up to promote standardization of cotton; cooperative ginning and baling were developed through cooperatives; and a central office was created to facilitate better transportation, marketing, and spread of information.[19]

The Sericulture and Filature Improvement Committee was set up under the NEC early in 1934, and had the benefit of help from Benito Mari, an Italian expert provided by the League of Nations. China's silk industry, long of great importance, was declining largely because of deterioration of silkworms. To bring about improvement the Commission conducted research on bettering their quality through model egg-producing stations, established a training school for demonstrators to help farmers, and promoted use of better silk-reeling machines.[20]

In health, the League's collaboration extended over the longest period and helped with much constructive work. The National Quarantine Service was created in 1930 under direction of Dr. Wu Lien-teh. Emphasis was placed on control of epidemics and communicable diseases. A key factor in the medical program was the Central Field Health Station created in 1931. Personnel were trained as public health officers and nurses, sanitary inspectors, midwives, and hospital staff. Materials were prepared and circulated for health propaganda in schools and by posters and radio. Facilities were provided for experimentation and testing, especially to study parasitology, and to prepare vaccines and sera for human and animal diseases. The organization collaborated with a number of provinces and with local authorities on problems of sanitation, preventive medicine, and medical relief. It provided expert help in sanitary engineering including water supply and sewage disposal. It created clinics. The Central Hospital was established at Nanking in 1930, and set up in larger quarters in 1933. Attached to the hospital were schools of nursing and midwifery and a system of medical internship. League doctors specially helpful in the health program were Dr. B. Borcic and Dr. A. Stampar.[21]

Besides the help of League programs in connection with the central government, the extensive work with provincial and local authorities was important. Dr. Stampar said after a visit to the northwest that "The example of the National Economic Council has fired the local authorities," and that "most important progress was made in the awakening of a real interest on the part of the local governments and local population in the reconstruction activities."[22]

When the NEC was first established, Generalissimo Chiang's opening address stressed land reform and agricultural improvement as of great importance "from the economic, social and political points of view." Experts working with the NEC prepared good reports in this field. Dragoni reported that "The concentration of property that has gone on in many regions in the last 50 or 60 years is dangerous for the well-being of the rural classes." Agricultural policies must be found, he said, to prevent growth of discontent that would "gravely endanger social and political stability." Dragoni made a wide range of solid recommendations.[23]

Two important group studies were made of conditions in the provinces. In 1933-1934, Max Brauer, E. Briand-Clausen, and A. Stampar studied the problems of rehabilitating Kiangsi Province after expulsion of the Communists. Their excellent recommendations covered much of the same area as those of Dragoni, namely, reform of land tenure and taxation. They also dealt with problems of local government, education, and economic development.[24]

Early in 1934, a group of foreign and Chinese experts headed by Salter studied the situation in Chekiang Province, south of Shanghai. This group dealt extensively with land problems, about five-sixths of the province's activity being agricultural. They found a distressing state of affairs resulting from the depression and overpopulation. They made a wide range of proposals for improvement.[25]

The recommendations of the experts in these groups were excellent. Some progress was made in rehabilitating the depressed silk, tea, and cotton production; in expanding agricultural cooperatives and improving their quality; and in rehabilitating Kiangsi Province. And the recovery from depression in 1935 to 1937 alleviated part of the rural distress.

But progress was far from adequate with the fundamental and comprehensive agricultural reforms needed. These changes involved the collection of additional basic information, adequate land registration, reform of land tenure and land taxation, improvement of production, and rural credit. Above all, a suitable administrative organization was needed to make the reforms effective. Unfortunately, problems relating to deflation and financial reforms, internal political affairs, and Japan's aggression in the north occupied the government's chief attention in 1933 to 1937. The leaders were not sufficiently aware of the vital need for fundamental agricultural reform. And their predominantly urban background and landholding bias were not conducive to emphasis on rural economic and social problems. Hence, progress toward agricultural improvement and social progress affecting four-fifths of the people fell far short of what was desirable, up to the time when Japan's attack in 1937 forced concentration on survival. Whatever the explanation of the government's prewar failure in this basic area, the consequence was that wartime disruption added to the preexisting distressed conditions and left people open to accepting the blandishments of the Communists.

Military affairs

Military operations both internal and vis-a-vis Japan, together with strategic preparations, vitally affected the finances and the economy during the prewar decade. In the field of military affairs, an important role was played by foreign experts, chiefly Germans but also Americans, Frenchmen, and Italians.

After Generalissimo Chiang broke with Russia in 1927, the Russian military advisers left. Even before completion of the Northern Expedition, Chiang replaced them with Germans. F. F. Liu, a former Chinese officer, has given a good account of the work of the German advisers and their influence and I shall only summarize here.[26]

China copied the imperial German system of having the military free of civilian control, as did Japan. By 1937 there were about 300,000 troops in German-trained units, including 80,000 in first-class units with German-made weapons. There were plans to strengthen air power and build a navy with German aid. When Japan attacked in mid-1937, China was becoming a much stronger power.

The first German military adviser to come to China was Colonel Bauer in 1927. After an initial visit to China he recruited an unofficial group of 46 officers, thus beginning a program of strengthening the Nationalist armies with German aid. Bauer was credited with helping to devise the strategy that allowed Chiang to win a quick victory over the Kwangsi warlords in Central China in the spring of 1929. Later in 1929 Bauer died in China from smallpox. He was followed by Lieutenant-Colonel Hermann Kriebel and then by General Georg Wetzell. In 1934-1935, General Hans von Seeckt visited China. He had won fame in preparing Germany to become a strong military power despite the restrictions imposed after World War I. When von Seeckt left China because of ill health, he was succeeded by General Alexander von Falkenhausen. Altogether 137 German military advisers served in China, with a maximum of 64 at one time. About 30 were there when hostilities began in 1937. The number of Germans in this work was exceeded only by the number of foreigners in the Customs service.[27]

The German advisers helped in training officers and men and in improving equipment. Especially influential was von Seeckt. He stressed the need for quality and development of a good corps of officers, and until 1937, about 2000 officers were graduated from the army staff college.[28] He also recommended reform of army finance with uniform and strict procedures for budgets and audit, but unfortunately little was done. He urged the need for industrialization including an armaments industry.

In Germany, industrialists pushed the program of military aid to China. With the help of the advisers, they got orders for weapons and for machinery and equipment for arsenals and munitions plants. A revolving credit under a barter agreement was set up as described in Chapter 16. At first, the German government took no part in the program, stating that it was not sending officers to China and indicating that their going to China was against its wishes. But it soon concluded that the experience of the officers in China helped toward German rearmament, besides providing markets. Among the leaders who took an interest in the program were Ludendorff, Goering, von Blomberg, and Beck.

But German views on China policy were divided. Elements favoring Japan finally won out. In April 1936 and June 1937, Germany signed trade agreements with Manchukuo, and in the latter part of 1936 signed the anti-Comintern pact with Japan. Yet, the German military advisers remained and served China loyally until pulled out by Hitler a year after the outbreak of the hostilities.[29]

The French had in China for a time an instructional team headed by General Balny. Their emphasis was on defense and the lessons of World War I, in contrast to the German emphasis on a war of movement.[30]

China's need for a military air force became clear early in 1932 when Japanese planes, with unimpeded control of the air, wrought havoc on almost defenseless Shanghai. Robert M. Short, an American volunteer pilot killed in that fighting, became a hero. A campaign to raise funds to buy military planes was promoted by the China Aviation League, and a number of planes were bought from funds subscribed all over the country. Soon after the fighting ended, T. V. Soong with Generalissimo Chiang's approval sought expert American help. I was asked to handle negotiations with the American government, having participated for some time in matters concerning civil and military aviation.

The State and War Departments would not permit a mission of American air officers, having regard to neutralist feeling and the wish to avoid involvement with Japan. So American help was volunteered by the Department of Commerce, a member of whose staff at Shanghai was Edward P. Howard, a former air force major. He proposed engaging on American recommendation a group of civilian experts with experience in the air force.

They would establish a school to train new Chinese personnel, give a refresher course to pilots already in the air force, and help to reorganize existing facilities. They would order immediately the training planes and other equipment needed for China. None of the group would be asked or allowed to take part in any belligerent action.

The record now available shows that the State Department was opposed to even a mission of American civilians to give training in military aviation. But the negotiations between China and the Commerce Department had gone so far that the State Department felt unable to take any action.[31] While negotiating with Howard on behalf of China, I did not know that the State Department opposed even a civilian mission.

Soong agreed to the Commerce Department's proposal. In mid-1932, Colonel John H. Jouett and a staff of nine pilots, four mechanics, and one secretary arrived in Shanghai on a three-year engagement. They proceeded at once to Hangchow, 135 miles south of Shanghai, to the school's location. Some preparations had already been made, but the field had no potable water supply, no electricity, and no facilities for plane maintenance and repair. Nevertheless, the Jouett group was able to commence a refresher course for air force pilots and begin training the first new class by about mid-September. By the end of the year, a large hangar was near completion, a machine and engine overhaul shop was completed, the school buildings had been remodeled, officers quarters were nearly ready, a deep well was dug, electricity was supplied, and an operations center with a radio station was functioning. The Americans were pleased with the caliber of the cadets. They felt that within a few years China would have the nucleus of an effective air force.[32]

The Jouett group was responsible for notable accomplishments. The school they established trained several hundred new pilots, and gave refresher instruction to old pilots, after setting physical and mental standards and rejecting men not competent to fly. A group of Chinese flying instructors was trained, as were maintenance mechanics and a number of doctors for aviation medicine. Jouett, in a report of September 15, 1934, said:

> The Central Aviation School . . . now contains complete modern hangar facilities; complete repair depot sufficient in size and facilities for the maintenance and upkeep of all School airplanes; adequate and sanitary living quarters for cadets, guards, and the instructional staff; . . . a thoroughly up-to-date School building,

> with modern class-rooms and modern instructional equipment. All other necessary adjuncts, such as photographic building, mechanics' school building, meteorological station, etc., have been provided. The entire school is thoroughly modern, up-to-date and functioning well.

Jouett also helped to formulate a five-year program of aviation development, with estimated costs, and provided recommendations and studies on policies of procurement and defense.[33]

But all this was accomplished in the face of great difficulties: friction within the mission; erratic support on the Chinese side; and competition from the Italian air mission that arrived in the latter part of 1933 upon the invitation of Kung. The mission's troubles are worthy of discussion because they shed light on the problems of an alien group then working in China and on the weaknesses in China's government.

Jouett's contract of July 25, 1932, signed by the Generalissimo, provided that "The functions and scope of work of the director and the group shall be specified in a separate agreement." Jouett and I promptly proposed the draft of such an agreement. Yet despite repeated efforts on our part nothing was done. Failure to define the mission's status and functions by the contemplated agreement became later a source of difficulty.

There was friction within the mission, and at times insubordination to Jouett. Such developments could be expected in a group living under confined conditions in the interior of China, away from the bright lights of Shanghai and not under formal military discipline. There was also friction between Americans and Chinese at the school, resulting partly from language difficulties and partly from differences in culture and the need for the Americans to exercise authority in a foreign country.[34]

Under Soong's dynamic leadership, the mission's work went fairly smoothly for about six months. But his assumption of responsibility in military aviation clashed with the prerogatives of the director of the Bureau of Aeronautics, who incidentally was pro-American. After a few months, Soong dropped out of the picture, apparently because of friction with Generalissimo Chiang. The Bureau's director was replaced, according to Jouett, by a general who was "completely ignorant and uninformed as regards aviation matters and not at all prone to ask for advice or to listen when given." That general's successor some months later, Jouett stated, was no better.[35]

But more trouble for the Jouett group was still to come, as a rival aviation mission was invited from Italy. When H. H. Kung was in Italy in 1933, he called on Mussolini, who greatly impressed him and is said to have remarked that "Since the time of Marco Polo, China and Italy have had cultural affinity." Italy provided remitted Boxer Indemnity funds to buy Italian planes. The Italian mission was headed by General Roberto Lordi, who brought a staff of 20. He was recalled in the summer of 1935 for reasons that were not clear. He was succeeded by General Scaroni, who flew to China in a Savoia-Marchetti plane that Mussolini presented to Chiang. Italian manufacturers formed an Aeronautic Consortium to supply an aviation factory at Nanchang, and financed delivery of materials and machinery valued at about US $1.5 million. The coordinated Italian effort contrasted with what an American official report called "the reported cut-throat competition and sharp practices among American aviation interests in China," complicated by "the alleged demanding and accepting of 'squeeze' by Chinese officials."[36]

With the arrival of the Italians, the position of the American group deteriorated. The Italians had avowed military status with a general as leader and the backing of their government. They made their headquarters at Nanchang and cooperated in Chiang's anti-Communist drive. Their salaries, much lower than those of the Americans, were paid from Boxer Indemnity funds. Japan apparently did not object to the presence of the Italians, but she objected strongly to the work of the Americans. In 1935 the Italian group began to lose favor. They lost face when word spread about an incident in which the Generalissimo chose to use his Boeing plane with an American pilot in place of the plane presented by Mussolini.[37]

The American group had no official backing, and the State Department viewed their presence unfavorably. Their position suffered from the failure of the Chinese government to make the contemplated agreement with Jouett to define the mission's responsibilities. The draft agreement provided that any foreign advisers or experts concerned with military aviation should be "subordinate and responsible" to him. Even though that draft had not been formally approved, he felt that it was mutually understood that he was the principal foreign adviser on aviation. He felt that he and his group had laid a good foundation after over a year of hard work, and that China's efforts in aviation would be dissipated by having two different systems of training and development. He wrote me that his concern was "not so much on the personal side as . . . on the question of seeing what we have built up possibly torn down." He talked with the Generalissimo, who he stated gave him to understand that he was the senior adviser and would be consulted about assignment of duties to the Italians.[38] Nevertheless, in April 1934, the Bureau of Aeronautics was removed from Hangchow to Nanchang where Chiang made his headquarters for the drive on the Communists. Lordi was appointed chief adviser to the Bureau.[39]

Six months later, the American military attaché, Colonel W. S. Drysdale, reported that Generalissimo Chiang indicated that he was not entirely satisfied with the work of the Jouett mission. Drysdale gathered that he felt the Americans were more interested in sale of American planes than in building up the air force. Drysdale suspected a fine Italian hand, stating that "It is significant that this same idea . . . was given to an American correspondent by one of the Italian aviation mission." Drysdale referred to an accumulation of small frictions at the school, and said that the American group were "being severely criticized by the controlling Chinese officials," despite the "excellence of their work."[40] It was no surprise that the Jouett mission's work ended in June 1935 when the contract expired, although two or three members remained in other capacities.

F. F. Liu, the Chinese military historian, praised the work of the Americans, saying that Jouett's "small instructional team . . . laid a sound foundation for the Chinese through his introduction of the highly efficient American air-training system." Captain (later General) Evans F. Carlson also praised their training work, but said that the "experiment with Italian aviation was not successful." He said that "A reliable Chinese informant has stated that after the departure of the Italian mission from Nanking none of the elaborate aerial survey mosaics, which the Italians had made of the Nanking-Hangchow-Shanghai triangle, was to be found."[41] Colonel (later General) Claire L. Chennault charged that these surveys were sold to the Japanese for a handsome price. He found the Chinese air force in a sad state when he reached China a month before the fighting began in 1937. He caustically criticized Mussolini's mission but found the graduates of Jouett's school to be quite competent.[42]

The Italian mission left China after the outbreak of Sino-Japanese hostilities. Mussolini was moving toward closer relations with Japan. The Italian group at Nanchang was reported to have openly discussed the possible seizure of part of central

China in case of revolution or war leading to the country's partition.[43]

Chennault's arrival shortly before the outbreak of hostilities ushered in a new phase in Chinese military aviation. But this phase mostly coincided with the war period. Chennault retired from the American army in the spring of 1937, and accepted China's invitation to survey China's aviation needs. A believer in pursuit aviation, he had not been able to sell his ideas on air tactics to his American superiors. His views on the vulnerability of unescorted bombers to attack by properly trained and equipped pursuit pilots were vindicated later in a costly way by losses of Japanese bombers in China and Burma, German bombers in the Battle of Britain, and British and American bombers over Europe.

It was a pity that China's military aviation did not benefit as it could have from foreign expert advice in the prewar period. The government failed to support the capable Jouett group by assigning good officers for overall supervision of the program. Indeed, not only in the prewar period but even during much of the war, I saw from considerable contact with the problems that many higher officers in charge of military aviation were poorly qualified and not ready to take advice from those who could help them. The episode of Mussolini's air mission showed a damaging eclecticism on China's part. It led to costly experimentation that set back progress. China would have been much better off to have declined Mussolini's offer, relied on the Jouett group for aid and advice, and extended their contract.

Miscellaneous foreign aid

The Sino-foreign Customs service, besides its fiscal operations, continued during the prewar decade to perform other long established functions of basic economic importance. With the help of foreign experts, it maintained aids to navigation such as lighthouses, and helped to keep ports and rivers in safe and usable condition. The Posts, which the Customs established in 1878 and for a time supervised, became an excellent service as an independent organization with the help of foreign experts of various nationalities.

Foreign experts also rendered important services in other branches of the civil government. The Railway Ministry had the help of several experts, some appointed under loan agreements and others directly engaged. John Earl Baker helped that Ministry set up and operate a system of accounts and records. William B. Poland, the railway finance expert on the Kemmerer Commission, put forward helpful proposals for the better working of the railways. Brigadier F. D. Hammond, recommended by the British government, made an excellent survey of the railways in 1935, with recommendations for reorganization and improvements. H. H. Love served as agricultural adviser under the Minister of Industries. R. E. Lewis was an adviser to the Foreign Ministry. Paul M. Linebarger, a former associate of Sun Yat-sen, acted as legal adviser to the government. Attilio Lavigna, on recommendation of the Italian government, visited China in 1933 to advise on reform of the penal code. For two or three years, the city of Nanking had a group of American advisers on planning and administration. William H. Donald, an Australian, was for a time adviser to the "Young Marshal" Chang Hsueh-liang and later to Chiang Kai-shek. Donald was influential during the later years of the prewar decade through his close relations with Generalissimo and Madame Chiang. He participated in the negotiations for release of Chiang after the Young Marshal's forces seized him at Sian in December 1936.

Although Soong's plan to promote development with the help of a Consultative Committee under the League of Nations failed in 1933, he continued with his plan to have Jean Monnet come to China. Monnet arrived in 1934, and worked with the NEC. His chief contribution was in helping to form the China Development Finance Corporation (Chapter 16). The objective was to provide a framework for obtaining Chinese and foreign capital, either singly or jointly, for development.

In the study of agricultural problems, J. Lossing Buck had an outstanding part. At the University of Nanking, a mission-sponsored institution, he pioneered field examination of agricultural conditions. He and his associates worked closely with governmental authorities. Of special importance was their promotion of the system of nationwide crop reporting, which the government successfully introduced. Largely through Buck's efforts, the University of Nanking became a center for training agricultural experts and promoting agricultural progress. His publications are standard referenceson conditions in the prewar decade.[44]

Many foreigners rendered important help in connection with famines and floods. The most important episode concerned the great flood of 1931 (Chapter 16). Besides Sir John Hope Simpson's splendid work as director of the program, special mention should be made of the planning and administrative work of John Earl Baker as well as the work of Colonel George G. Stroebe, who served as chief hydraulic engineer of the Yangtze River Board. Colonel and Mrs. Charles A. Lindbergh happened to be in China at that time, and volunteered to make an aerial survey and photographic flight. American pilots of CNAC and the air force of the British Navy also helped with aerial surveys.

In dealing with rural rehabilitation and reconstruction, China had long benefited from the experience and idealism of Westerners, notably American missionaries and other philanthropically minded foreigners in cooperation with like-minded Chinese. These activities, largely on a volunteer basis, had on the whole the encouragement and support of government at both the national and local levels. Pioneer work was done by the China International Famine Relief Commission (CIFRC), organized as a Sino-foreign group at the time of the great famine in the northwest in 1921-1922. By 1930, the CIFRC had administered C $33 million, provided in roughly equal parts by the general public of China, American gifts, and the Chinese government. In these operations, important work was done by continuing personnel: O. J. Todd in engineering and Dwight W. Edwards in administration and field work.[45]

The major principle of help was work-relief, whereby goods were paid in kind in proportion to work done that was beneficial to the community. The community was to repay if possible the funds provided. The CIFRC expanded its program to promote and finance with loans rural credit cooperatives, whose spread was rapid especially in North China where there were 200,000 members by 1936.

After the twenties the Commission's work declined, as the validity of its program was recognized by the government. More and more, the government took over the preventive projects such as water conservancy, and also began to supervise the cooperative movement. The CIFRC participated actively in the road program of the NEC. The CIFRC operated in wide areas of China, and built or improved 3825 miles of road and 290 miles of irrigation ditches, dug 5036 wells, built 904 miles of dykes, and accomplished other miscellaneous work. It spent altogether about C $50 million.[46]

Missionaries not only took an active part in the CIFRC, but became deeply involved in other phases of the rural reconstruction movement in the thirties. During the Kiangsi campaigns against the Communists, Generalissimo and Madame Chiang came into close touch with missionaries. They enlisted missionary aid in 1933 in rehabilitation of recovered areas, under the Generalissimo's program coupling 70 per cent economic and 30 per cent military action. The aim was to give special attention to improvement of agriculture, rural credit, sanitation, and literacy. The program of missionary cooperation began in Kiangsi Province as a pilot project in the spring of 1934, but met with difficulties limiting its success until interrupted by the war.[47]

In plans of rural rehabilitation the government was also influenced by James Yen (Yen Yang-ch'i), who with foreign help pioneered in the twenties an attack on illiteracy with his Mass Education Movement and 1000 character program. In his model village experiment at Tinghsien in Hopei Province, he came to appreciate the need for careful study of rural needs to deal with problems of economics, health, culture, and government. Chiang was impressed by Yen and hoped to apply his ideas on a much larger scale. But this, like so much more, could not be brought to fruition because of the war.[48]

The Rockefeller Foundation had long operated in China, and by 1934 had invested US$37 million in health work, mostly in developing the Peking Union Medical College as a first-class institution. In 1934, after prolonged investigation, the Foundation granted US$1 million for a program to promote rural rehabilitation. Emphasis was on grants to strengthen selected institutions to train men for work in raising the economic, social, health, and cultural standards in rural areas. The aim was to combine studies with practical contact with and study of conditions in the field. The Foundation also hoped to improve coordination of existing programs. But the work was only getting started when the war came.[49]

Mention should also be made of important foreign participation in the development of civil aviation. Great progress was made (Chapter 14) with the help of Americans working through the China National Aviation Corporation and of Germans working through Eurasia Corporation.

16: Foreign Private Investment and Financial Aid

Prior to the 1930's, the concern of foreign governments with investments in China related to protection and promotion of the interests of their nationals, as holders of Chinese obligations and of direct investments in China. Especially around the turn of the century, the promotion phase also concerned spheres of influence. But beginning in the 1930's new trends began that have since developed greatly. Governments began participating with their nationals in credits for sale of capital goods. And the United States provided two direct governmental credits to China in 1931 and 1933. Involvement of foreign governments, in a positive way, raised serious international issues especially in relation to Japan.

Attitude toward private foreign investment

Chinese opinion has long been critical of the effects of foreign trade and investment on China. Many have regarded foreign investment as a symbol of foreign invasion, closely related to the system of unequal treaties, which provided for foreign settlements, open ports, extrality, and extremely low tariffs. Under the Manchus, the Nationalists, and now the Communists, criticism has continued of what has been characterized as imperialism and the effort to make China a colony or quasi-colony. The main charges have been that foreign trade and investment involved interference in Chinese affairs, brought ruin to handicraft production and disrupted agriculture, drained away wealth through the adverse trade balance and remittance abroad of income from investments, and through competition held back growth of Chinese industry.

Chi-ming Hou, in a broad examination of these matters, concluded that foreign investment was beneficial to China on the whole. It brought modern technology and provided capital, which were scarce in China. Foreign investment stimulated Chinese private enterprise to develop modern-type production and trade, often using technicians and managers trained in foreign enterprises in China. The system of treaty ports provided areas of law and order where Chinese enterprises could flourish. The fear of foreign domination led the government to develop industries of military importance, such as arsenals.[1]

Hou does not accept the view that the traditional sector of handicrafts, small mines, and transport declined sharply as a result of foreign investment. Although this sector may have declined relatively, he sees little reason to believe that there was an absolute decline. On the contrary, modern-type production often created a demand for products of handicrafts and helped to promote technical improvement of their methods of work. Railways helped traditional production by giving better access to internal and external markets and reducing costs of transport.[2] China's terms of trade worsened from 1867 to the thirties, yet he considers that this deterioration resulted from forces in world markets rather than from growth of foreign trade and investment. There was considerable outward remittance of profits. On balance however, the effect of foreign investment was constructive, and "foreign capital played a significant role in bringing about whatever economic modernization existed in China before 1937."[3]

Sun Yat-sen and after him Chiang Kai-shek were strongly critical of what they regarded as foreign economic oppression; nonetheless, they and their associates favored utilizing foreign capital as an aid to development but without involving foreign control. And the Communists later turned to Russia for credits and technical aid.

Avoidance of foreign control in connection with investments was a guiding principle of Nationalist policy. In earlier decades, railway loan agreements had provided for extensive foreign control of operations and finances. But such provisions became largely unworkable in the disorderly years before the Nationalist takeover. In relation to direct foreign investments, the general aim of the Nationalists was that Chinese citizens or the government have at least half the ownership and a majority in the directorates in enterprises in which foreign capital participated. These principles could not be applied in the treaty or open ports, but were operative elsewhere.

Kung, speaking in New York in July 1937, offered foreign investors "a hearty welcome and the full protection of my government." Skeptics in China wondered whether his colleagues in the government would support these words, and whether any change in the theretofore restrictive policy as to direct investments outside the treaty ports would result.[4]

The China Consortium

In 1920, the China Consortium was organized on American initiative, in the hope that it would not only contribute to checking and controlling national rivalries, but also afford a workable procedure to provide foreign capital for proper purposes in China. American, British, French, and Japanese banking groups participated with the approval of their governments. The objects were to forestall efforts by any group to obtain preferential advantages, to pool options for loans such as those for railway building, and in general to promote cooperation among the powers and avoid friction. The agreement related to the issuance of public loans other than in China. The groups were to take equal shares if they wished to participate, but they could decline to do so.[5]

When the Consortium was being formed, Japan tried to exclude Manchuria and Mongolia from the arrangement. After long negotiations, a formula was found which excluded from Consortium obligations the South Manchurian Railway and its then existing branches and subsidiary mines, and certain other specified railways in the area. Other projected railways in the area were to be within the Consortium's scope. The United States and Britain also assured Japan that they would not countenance "any operation inimical to the vital interests of Japan."[6]

The organizers of the Consortium hoped for formation of a Chinese banking group to cooperate with them. But the Chinese government and opinion in China objected. They regarded the Consortium as creating a financial monopoly, and feared that it might lead to further foreign encroachment or possibly involve favoring a particular faction in China as against others.* The Consortium was unable to make any loans, partly because of China's opposition, but in any event the disturbed internal conditions of the twenties and the parlous state of China's finances practically precluded borrowing. The Consortium, however, was able to block some proposed transactions.[7] After the American government granted to China the Cotton and Wheat Credit of 1933, financial circles in Britain and Japan charged that it was contrary to at least the spirit of the Consortium.[8]

Issues concerning the Consortium remained mostly quiescent

*In 1935, China's desperate economic situation during the silver crisis led Kung to indicate that China was ready to discuss a loan with the Consortium if foreign financial aid could be had (page 227).

until the possibility of public issuance of Chinese loans appeared in 1936-1937. When the financing of railways in southeast China by British capital came up for active consideration about the beginning of 1937, the Japanese members of the Consortium wanted to participate. Japanese officials in China approached the Minister of Railways and the authorities in Canton. But in view of Japan's seizure of Manchuria and her encroachments in North China, Japanese participation was out of the question. The Japanese group finally joined the American and French groups in May in agreeing not to share in the loan for the Canton-Meihsien Railway and leaving the project to the British group. The agreement for the Pukow-Sinyang Railway was signed on August 4 with a clause (Article 29) conditioning issuance of the loan upon agreement with the other groups.[9] Temporarily there appeared to be some mellowing of the Japanese attitude of looking askance at any form of non-Japanese foreign participation in projects of development in China.

The changed situation early in 1937 as compared with 1920, and the difficulties with Japan, led the British government and the British group of the Consortium to conclude that the Consortium should be dissolved. In February 1937 the British Foreign Office told the American Embassy that "instead of promoting the economic progress of China as its authors intended," the Consortium "was now an obstacle which stood in the way of such action." Besides the problems involving Japan there seemed no chance of a change in the basic Chinese attitude toward the Consortium.[10]

The State Department was reluctant to see the scrapping of the agreement, and desired that neither it nor the American group take any responsibility for dissolution. The Department with Roosevelt's approval decided "with sincere regret" to offer no objection. Washington hoped for substitution of some form of loose association of the financial groups to maintain the principle of cooperation. The French and Japanese groups were consulted in May and June about possible dissolution. But no word as to their attitude was received before the outbreak of hostilities, and the issues of dissolution and organizing a less formal procedure for future cooperation stayed in suspense.[11]

The China Development Finance Corporation

A procedure that could be substituted for the Consortium, with active Chinese participation, was through the China Development Finance Corporation (CDFC). Soong's hope in 1933 to enlist larger League of Nations aid in economic reconstruction in China failed, largely because of Japanese hostility (pages 344 to 345). Jean Monnet, who came to China despite the failure of the project for League aid, worked with Soong and others to prepare the plan for the CDFC. Yakichiro Suma of the Japanese legation in Nanking told him that Japan would not permit the plan for the Corporation to be realized. Other threats were made to leading officials and bankers. The project for creating the Corporation apparently was a factor in the issuance of the Amau Declaration in the spring of 1934, opposing non-Japanese technical and financial aid to China, a declaration that Suma claimed to have recommended. Chiang felt he would have to drop the plan to create the Corporation if it would lead to Japanese seizure of Peiping and Tientsin. But the Chinese decided to stand firm, and the Corporation was created and announced about June 1, 1934.[12]

The Corporation's purpose was as follows:

> . . . in conjunction with Chinese banks and financial interests abroad, to assist and collaborate in enterprises private and public for the development of commerce and industry for which long term credits are required, . . . and facilitating an ordered flow of capital into the work of China's reconstruction.[13]

It intended to provide machinery to finance projects deemed worthwhile with both Chinese and foreign capital. The capital of C$10 million was subscribed by 14 Chinese banks, together with a number of individuals including Soong and Kung. The powerful Hongkong and Shanghai Bank agreed to cooperate.[14]

The CDFC at once began to prove its usefulness as a means of Sino-foreign financial cooperation (pages 369 to 371). Certain loans in which it participated were issued in China rather than abroad, hence no question arose about the Consortium. In 1937 loans were proposed to be issued in London in which the CDFC was to participate, along with members of the Consortium groups. Had not the war supervened, the CDFC would have been in a position to help to arrange the participation of Chinese and foreign capital, in cooperation, for projects of development on a considerable scale.

Extent of foreign private investment, 1927 and 1937

There was no great change in the total of foreign private investment in China proper in 1937 as compared with 1927. In the later years of the decade foreign investment was increasing, with the prospect of further large increase if conditions remained stable. Also there was growing Japanese investment in Manchukuo after 1931.

No detailed study of the position as of 1927 is available. Carl Remer's thorough study as of 1931 showed a total for China, including Hong Kong and Manchuria, equivalent to US $3243 million.[15] That was roughly double the figure in 1914 before World War I. Remer defined foreign investment as "a source of income owned by a 'foreigner' who may live in China or outside of China." Business investment was 79 per cent of the total and holding of government obligations the rest. The largest category of investments was in transportation, and other important categories were foreign trade, manufacturing, real estate, and banking.

Direct foreign investment was mostly confined to the treaty ports, especially Shanghai, and the open ports. Foreign capital had the leading position in a number of modern-type enterprises, including mining of coal and iron ore, electric power, and cigarettes. Yet Chinese enterprises were well able to coexist, and were spreading steadily into the interior. They produced 65 per cent of the gross value in manufacturing as a whole in 1933 (Table 23), and the proportion was fairly stable in the prewar decade. In banking foreign capital had the leading position in the twenties. But during the prewar decade Chinese banks progressed rapidly and were forging to the front. Geographically, 34 per cent of the foreign capital was allocated to Shanghai and 27 per cent to Manchuria.

British investments were 37 per cent, Japanese 35 per cent, and American 6 per cent. Russian investments in 1931 were 8 per cent, mostly in the Chinese Eastern Railway which was sold to Japan in 1935. Investments in China were but a small part of the foreign investments of the Western capital-exporting countries, but in the case of Japan were about four-fifths.

As of 1936, Chi-ming Hou presents an estimate of US $3483 million for China including Hong Kong and Manchuria, based on Japanese studies. It is hard to draw definite quantitative conclusions from the fact that this figure is US $240 million larger than Remer's figure for 1931. A main part of the increase probably represents growth of Japanese investments in Manchuria by Y1163 million, equivalent to US$328 million at average exchange rates of 1932 to 1936. The 1936 estimates show 40 per cent Japanese, 35 per cent British, and 9 per cent American, while Russian investments were practically eliminated by the sale to Japan of the Chinese Eastern Railway.[16]

There was some disinvestment in China during the silver crisis of 1933 to 1935, when considerable foreign capital left China. Also various foreign enterprises failed. No useful estimate of amounts is possible. The estimates of balance of payments in the annual reports of the Bank of China enumerate as unaccounted for outpayments totaling C $891 million for 1934 to 1936, of which some part was disinvestment of foreign capital.[17]

On the other hand, there was fresh foreign capital investment in a number of lines, encouraged in part by the higher tariffs from 1929. In cotton textiles there was steady growth, and Japanese investment in particular grew greatly: from 1.29 million spindles and 9625 looms in 1927 to 2.14 million spindles and 28,915 looms in 1936. The 1936 figures do not include 211,600 spindles in Manchuria. In British mills, the number of spindles did not change greatly, being about one-tenth of the Japanese, but the number of looms increased from 2348 to 4021.[18] Many foreign-owned machine works were established to produce such items as electrical equipment, motors, light machines, and bicycles. Beginning in 1931, there was sizable American and German investment in civil aviation. Furthermore, especially during the depreciation of silver exchange in 1930 to 1933, there was considerable foreign investment and speculation in Shanghai real estate, induced by the cheapness of the currency.

The years from 1934 to 1937 saw the beginning of a considerable inflow of capital (pages 367-376). This inflow was partly the result of the participation of agencies of foreign governments. The chief object of investment was the railways. Actual foreign credits for railways in these years were of the order of US $40 million equivalent, and still larger credits were in prospect when the war came. There were also German barter credits for a variety of goods, the amount of these in mid-1937 being equivalent to the order of US $40 million.

Foreign credits for railways and industrial development, 1934 to 1937

Beginning in 1934, private foreign investors took a growing part in providing funds, first for railway extension and rehabilitation of existing lines and then for development of a variety of industries. Foreign government agencies participated by underwriting part of the risk of some credits. Previously in 1931, the trustees of the remitted British Boxer Indemnity funds began to finance railway needs, and they continued an active program. The first private investors in this period were the Germans, but soon British, French, Belgian, and Czechoslovak interests were participating. American interests were slow to participate, but began to do so in a relatively small way in 1937. By mid-1937 foreign interests had undertaken or agreed to undertake a large amount of financing, especially of railways, and more was in prospect when the hostilities supervened.

German industrialists looked to China for markets in 1934, when their trade with Russia fell off because of Russo-German friction. The firm of Otto Wolff set up a Shanghai office, acting for a consortium whose credits to China would be guaranteed up to 70 per cent by the German government. The first contract in June, in which Wolff joined with the Bank of China, was for materials and equipment for the Chekiang-Kiangsi Railway. The German part of that credit was C $8 million. Further similar German credits of C $10 million followed for extension of that railway. The security for these advances was pledge of assets and revenues of the railway, together with bonds of the Railway Reconstruction Loan issued in series between 1934 and 1937.[19]

Other credits by a group of German industrialists, to provide materials for a 623-mile extension of the Chekiang-Kiangsi Railway through Hunan to Kweichow in Kweiyang Province, were agreed in the latter part of 1936 after long negotiations. Credits of about C $40 million were contemplated. Surveys were made and preliminary work begun, but relatively little of the line had been built when hostilities began. Construction continued during the early part of the war, advances by the German group totalling C $3.6 million. A further German credit, whose operation was prevented by the war, was agreed to late in 1936 with the Siemens-China Company to provide materials to the value of C $10 million to strengthen the bridges of the Peiping-

Hankow Railway. The materials were to be delivered over six years, with payment over 13 years with 6 per cent interest. The agreement had to be canceled before any deliveries were made.[20]

German firms also provided a variety of industrial and military equipment. In 1936, von Reichenau, an intimate of Hitler, came to China representing Hapro, a concern controlled by the German War Ministry. The result was an agreement to provide China with industrial materials of military importance, including a steel mill, which did not materialize because of outbreak of hostilities. Arsenals were expanded and modernized with machinery to produce German-type weapons. China was also to receive naval equipment including submarines for which Hapro contracted.[21]

The German credits were provided under barter arrangements begun in 1935, whereby China paid interest and principal instalments by delivery of goods. Germany was specially interested in getting tungsten and other minerals for rearmament. In 1937, German exports to and imports from China about doubled from the 1932 to 1934 level. German credits to China under the barter agreement were sizable, the maximum reached in mid-1937 being equivalent to US $40 million plus or minus 20 per cent according to Bloch's estimate.[22]

At this time, China's relations with Germany were paradoxical. In June 1937, Minister Kung visited Berlin and was quoted as saying that "China considers Germany to be her closest friend." Leading Germans reciprocated these sentiments. But many in both countries did not take account of a contrary trend in German policy. In April 1936, Germany made a trade agreement with Manchukuo, and later in that year Ribbentrop signed an anti-Comintern agreement with Japan. This trend proved to be decisive, and German material help to China as well as military advisory help soon petered out.[23]

The readiness of German interests to grant credit in 1934 encouraged credits by other foreign interests. In mid-1934, the Hongkong and Shanghai Banking Corporation joined with the Central Bank, Bank of China, and Bank of Communications in a loan of £1.5 million for completion of the Canton-Hankow Railway. That loan was secured on the remitted British Boxer Indemnity funds, regarded as prime security. The trustees for these funds had previously agreed to advance a total of £4.7 million for that railway, of which that loan was a part. The balance of the £4.7 million was provided in part from accumulated funds held by the trustees and in part from loans by the trustees to be repaid out of future railway revenues or from future remitted indemnity instalments. The trustees also provided the equivalent of about US $7 million to finance the Nanking-Pukow train ferry and materials and equipment for various railways.[24]

In November 1934, the British and Chinese Corporation, which long had had an interest in Chinese railways, arranged for the issuance of a loan of C $16 million for completion of the Shanghai-Hangchow-Ningpo Railway, including the long bridge over the Chientang River near Hangchow. The China Development Finance Corporation joined in the project as organizer of the syndicate. The financing was then planned in Chinese currency because of the stringency of the London market, but had to be postponed because there was also stringency at Shanghai. Both the British and Chinese financiers made some advances for the project pending issuance of the loan. It was finally issued in the spring of 1936 for £1.1 million, the approximate sterling equivalent. It was a 25-year loan at 6 per cent, issued at 88, and secured on the railway revenues and 70 per cent of the bridge tolls. A by-product of the loan was adoption of administrative improvements in railway operations. The British side complained of unduly high overhead costs on the existing railway and also on the Shanghai-Nanking line. Minister Chang saw to it that these costs were reduced by a substantial amount. He was already determined to improve railway operations, and completed an extensive program of reforms on the various railways.[25]

In the latter part of 1935, French interests began negotiations for funds to aid in the extension of railways in southwest China. France had considered that this area was a French sphere of influence, and the railway from Indochina to Kunming had been French financed. But the Chinese negotiators were careful to avoid giving any recognition to the idea of such a sphere. After more than a year of negotiations, agreements were concluded between the French interests and the Chinese side represented by the China Development Finance Corporation, the Railway Ministry, and Szechwan Province. The major project was the Chungking-Chengtu line in that productive and densely populated province. The French group was to provide C $34.5 million for imported materials, together with costs of transporting and setting them up in China. The credits were backed by the French Government Credit Insurance Department. Chinese banks participated through the China Development Finance Corporation, and were to have a part in the building and operation of the railway under the general supervision of the Railway Ministry. The project represented joint Chinese and French governmental and private action. Unhappily, the outbreak of hostilities interfered with the project, although considerable work on the right-of-way was done during the war. I have no information indicating that any French funds were provided.[26]

A further project in which French interests were planning to join with the China Development Finance·Corporation concerned a railway between Kunming, the terminus of the line from Indochina, and Kweiyang. It would have provided an important link between Yunnan Province in the far southwest and the rest of China, once the westward extension to Kweiyang had been completed. The country was rugged and the estimated cost was about C $120 million, of which about half would have been provided by a loan of £4 million. Negotiations were well under way when war came.[27]

The Railway Ministry agreed with a Belgian group in August 1936 to finance materials for a line of 447 miles from Paoki, to connect with Chengtu the Lunghai Railway whose construction Belgian interests had largely financed. Advances were to be 450 million Belgian francs, equivalent to about US $15 million. But only preliminary work was done, and as of June 30, 1937, no advances had been made under the credit.[28]

Arrangements were also made in 1936-1937 with a Czechoslovak group to provide 63-pound rails to replace the light 35-pound rails used for the initial construction of the Chekiang-Kiangsi Railway. The credit was for CGU2.3 million equivalent to about US $1.5 million. The new rails were laid in the spring of 1937, and the improved line became of great value as soon as hostilities began. The Bank of China, Farmers Bank, and Chekiang banks provided a credit of C $2.8 million for local currency costs.[29]

Much the largest program for extension of the railways was being worked out with British interests in 1936-1937 until suspended by the war. To facilitate sale of capital goods, an office of the British Export Credits Guarantee Department was established at Shanghai. Credits that might total £15 million were under active consideration with the approval of the British government. Two important agreements with the British and

Chinese Corporation were signed, taking advantage of the presence in London of Finance Minister Kung and Railway Vice-minister T. K. Tseng. Besides the two ministries, the China Development Finance Corporation participated on the Chinese side. The first agreement of July 30, 1937, concerned a loan of £3 million at 5 per cent for 30 years to build a line in a northerly direction from Canton to Meihsien. A few days later, an agreement was signed for another loan of £4 million on similar terms. This loan was to be used to build a line to connect Pukow on the Yangtze River opposite Nanking, where there was a train ferry, with the Hankow-Peiping line north of Hankow. Both loans were to be secured on the assets and revenues of the railways and also on salt revenue. The negotiations contemplated further large credits for other projects. The eventual aim was to link the Canton-Meihsien line with the Chekiang-Kiangsi Railway, thus connecting with Shanghai and other parts of south-central China. It was also planned to build a westward line from the Canton area into Kwangsi Province. These projects became possible because of the collapse of the dissident elements in south China in mid-1936. The government wished to solidify its position there by promoting economic development, as well as by improving communications with its position of greatest strength in central China. Furthermore, the lines would have had considerable strategic importance vis-a-vis Japan.[30]

A further well-advanced project to be financed by British financial and commercial interests in China along with Chinese commercial banks, with some aid from British Boxer Indemnity funds, was to connect Nanking with the Chekiang-Kiangsi Railway. British interests were also to provide £800,000 for improving the Shanghai-Nanking Railway, per an agreement of June 1, 1937. Both projects were blocked by the war.

Despite the activities of Europeans, American interests were slow to join in credit granting. In 1935, a privately organized American Economic Mission to the Far East, headed by W. Cameron Forbes, went to China to investigate possible means for American participation in China's development. The mission was much impressed by the evidence of progress. Upon returning home, Forbes tried hard to gain the support of large companies and the government in some schemes to finance large-scale credits to China. But private interests were not ready for serious action. And Washington was worried about a possible confrontation with Japan. When Forbes approached the State Department in April 1936 he found a negative attitude.

Washington was unfavorably impressed by China's handling of the settlement of debts in arrears, despite China's beginning a serious effort at settlement in the latter part of 1935.[31] In my view, as explained in Chapter 5, Washington and the negotiators for the creditors failed then to appreciate China's constructive action on debt matters and the significance of the monetary and fiscal reforms of 1935-1936.

By 1937, as evidence of China's progress became more and more clear, Washington changed its view. In the spring, President Warren L. Pierson of the Export-Import Bank visited China and was favorably impressed. That Bank agreed to finance half the cost of locomotives sold by American companies. The total cost was about US $1.5 million, and the credit was for five years at 6 per cent. The Bank of China guaranteed payment. In July 1937, Kung was in Washington and found the Bank favorable in principle to granting much larger credits for industrial goods. But then came the war and nothing further was done.[32]

To summarize, railway credits granted and used in 1934 to 1937 were equivalent in total to about US $40 million. Under German barter agreements, the outstanding credit to China as of mid-1937 for industrial and military purposes equaled a sum of the order of US $40 million. Thus the total foreign credit utilized in this period equaled about US $80 million. In addition, credits for railways agreed but not used, granted by Belgian, British, French, and German interests, were equivalent to about another US $80 million. Further railway credits by British and French interests equivalent to about US $35 million were under negotiation or contemplated. There was also a good prospect of large American credits for railways and other capital purposes. Had it not been for the war, China's economic development would have benefited from very considerable foreign support.

Other foreign loan projects in 1937

Minister Kung's visit to Europe and the United States in 1937 attracted much favorable attention to China. There was widespread recognition that China had reached a turning point and that conditions were developing in which both foreign private and governmental financial support would become mutually advantageous. The chief factors causing the changed atmosphere were the success of China's currency reform of 1935; the settlements covering most of the defaulted foreign debt;

recovery from the depression; and the fact that the country was becoming more and more unified under a government of growing strength and stability. While issues with Japan were grave and unsettled, political developments in Japan in the spring of 1937 gave ground for hope of a better attitude on Japan's part, before the hope was so rudely shattered by the events of July-August 1937.

Kung's mission was to attend the coronation of George VI, but he had in mind grand plans for foreign loans. He talked of borrowing as much as £120 million in London to refund the more than C $2 billion of internal loans. Most of these bore 6 per cent interest, and in mid-1937 were selling on about an 8 per cent basis. His scheme was to borrow if he could at lower rates —he talked of 4 per cent—and save a large amount on current interest—he talked of C $80 million yearly.[33] Anticipating that questions of customs security might arise, he took with him to London Sir Frederick Maze, Inspector-General of Customs.

In London, negotiations progressed rather far. On June 21, the Foreign Office gave the American ambassador a memorandum stating that Britain was favorably disposed toward a loan of £10 to £20 million, with a first *tranche* of £10 million, provided the loan was part of a well considered program of stabilizing the currency and maintaining sound finances. The loan would not be used for current budgetary purposes but could be used over a period of time for gradual redemption of internal bonds. Creation of the proposed Central Reserve Bank as a nonpolitical institution, which Kung stated was intended, should precede issuance of a loan. China would be expected to agree to maintain the Customs administration as then constituted and resume recruitment of foreign Customs personnel. Issuance of the loan would be subject to clearance with the Consortium, unless the Consortium were meanwhile dissolved as Britain proposed.[34]

The Hongkong and Shanghai Bank wrote to Kung on July 30 reciting those terms in substance. The letter also stated that the loan would be secured on customs revenue and that the loan proceeds would be disposed of in consultation with an adviser to the Central Reserve Bank (who presumably would have been Cyril Rogers). Issuance of the loan and the terms would depend on London market conditions and on the Consortium placing no obstacles. Kung's reply of August 3 said that the matter would receive his careful attention. London press despatches of

August 4 and 5 said that there was agreement in principle for a loan of £20 million, to be drawn upon as needed and probably to be used to convert internal loans. On August 12, the British Foreign Office told the American embassy that China would accept the conditions, but that the tension in North China forced postponement of consideration.[35] The next day major warfare broke out at Shanghai.

Kung's attitude then to the British loan proposal involving customs security, maintenance of and strengthening the Sino-foreign Inspectorate General of Customs, and consultation with an adviser to the Central Reserve Bank about use of the loan proceeds was significant. It contrasted with his strongly nationalistic attitude in 1942 when the wartime American and British loans of US $500 million and £50 million, respectively, were being negotiated. He then refused to agree with Washington on any form of consultation. And he characterized the British suggestion that their credit be secured on postwar customs revenue as a "colonial attitude."[36]

Kung's ideas in 1937 also foreshadowed another phase of what took place more than four years later. Ambassador Bullitt in Paris thus reported Kung's talk with him in June: "He was prepared to promise that the money would not be taken out of England. So long as he should have such a credit in England he could issue notes which would serve the same purpose as cash."[37] In 1941-1942, when seeking large American and British loans for war purposes, Kung argued that having large reserves abroad even though not drawn upon would greatly support the currency and hold back inflation.[38] Had the British credit of 1937 and the other credits then under consideration materialized, policy issues would probably have developed between Kung and his advisers as they did in the 1941 to 1944 period on how far the mere holding of large resources abroad could permit a sound expansion of credit and deficit financing in China.

From England, Kung went to the United States where he arranged with Morgenthau for further large purchases of silver (Chapter 10). He also arranged a procedure to draw up to US $50 million against gold held in the United States. And he completed settlement of the old Pacific Development Loan (Chapter 5). Meanwhile, reports from London kept Washington posted on the favorable progress of preliminary loan negotiations. Expecting that the American government would be approached about further credits, and to take action parallel to that contemplated in Britain, the State Department began formulating its position. Hornbeck reacted favorably, although pointing out that there would be both advantages and disadvantages, economic and political. The administration could make up its mind what to do, he felt, if the question arose after being brought up by American financial interests.[39]

In the United States, Kung's search for credit centered on his request for US $50 million for capital goods for transport and for industry to be bought over two years on five years' credit. His proposal was for the Export-Import Bank to take half the notes, the American supplier one-fourth, and Chinese banks one-fourth. The Bank was favorable in principle to credits to China but wanted to consider each case specifically. An initial credit of US $10 million was brought up for first consideration. On August 9, the State Department offered no objection, subject to the Bank's decision that the credit was sound from the business angle. Two days later, the Bank postponed action in view of the worsening situation in the Far East, and no further action was taken.[40]

Kung meanwhile returned to Europe and continued there his solicitation of credits. Previously he had obtained from European banks three credits equivalent in total to US $12 million against pledge of 35 million ounces of silver.[41] That action was taken because of uncertainty about American purchases, prior to his sale concluded with Morgenthau in July. On August 12, the press reported that French banks agreed to credits of 200 million francs equivalent to about US $8 million for currency support. In Czechoslovakia, it was officially announced in August that the Skoda Works had granted a credit of 1.5 billion crowns, equivalent to about US $50 million. This credit was reportedly in part for war materials and in part for rolling stock, with deliveries to be made over a period up to six years. The credit was to be secured on customs revenue ranking after the proposed large British loan. The French and Czech credits were dropped in view of war developments.[42]

It was also reported that in the spring of 1937 China ordered two lots of 30 planes each from France on six years' credit. Apparently some were received in China, and others were detained in Indochina because of Japanese pressure after the outbreak of hostilities.[43]

It is clear that, had it not been for the war, China was embarking upon a new phase of borrowing that involved both private interests and governmental agencies in Europe and the United States. The credits could have promoted development if carefully used. But if they were not to be accompanied by prudent fiscal and monetary policies, serious difficulties might arise. There was need to raise revenue sufficient to cover the internal costs of using the foreign funds, as well as to buy the foreign currencies needed for interest and amortization of the foreign loans; to maintain a balance of payments that would permit acquiring the needed foreign currencies for loan payments; to control overall expenditure; and to control credit to the private sector. Whether these things could have been done, in view of the strong drive for development and greater military strength, was in the lap of the gods.

Flood relief and rehabilitation in 1931-1932

The measures to cope with the great flood of 1931 were noteworthy for two reasons. First, the Chinese government took large-scale effective action to deal with a major natural disaster. And second, for the first time China received sizable external governmental aid in the form of the American wheat credit.

In the twenties, private financial and technical aid was predominant in flood relief and rehabilitation. In particular, the China International Famine Relief Commission did effective work with Sino-foreign cooperation (pages 321, 358). After the National Government replaced the preceding ineffective regimes, it took over more and more responsibility in this area, while continuing to rely to a large extent on the voluntary effort of private organizations and individuals.

The Yangtze Valley flood of 1931, according to the report of the National Flood Relief Commission, not only surpassed any in China's unhappy history of floods, but was "the greatest flood on historical record" (page 3). An area of 65,000 square miles was seriously flooded and 5000 less seriously. That area is greater than all of England and about equal to the combined area of New York, Connecticut, and New Jersey. The people in distress numbered about 25 million. Thousands were drowned when dykes broke, and many millions had to migrate for much of the winter. In the flooded areas, the average maximum inundation of fields was nine feet, and 45 per cent of the farm buildings in these areas were destroyed. The total loss was estimated at C $2 billion, including C $900 million loss in crops.[44]

Immediate steps on a huge scale were needed to provide food, shelter, and protection from epidemics. Furthermore, the area had to be rehabilitated and its productivity promptly restored. John Earl Baker, a senior expert with long experience in helping to cope with disasters, gave an interview on August 1 to American correspondents at Shanghai. He urged that China seek to buy from the United States on credit a large amount of wheat for flood relief. A week later, Baker outlined to me his detailed ideas of what should be done. Based on our discussion, I gave Minister Soong a memorandum of August 10 proposing an active governmental program. The immediate need was to find out the main facts, first by aerial survey and from reports based on surface investigation. Next were measures of relief and rehabilitation. I endorsed Baker's proposal to try to buy 15 million bushels (450,000 tons) of wheat from the United States on liberal terms, a quantitative estimate that proved to be remarkably correct. The wheat was to be used "primarily as wages for work done to repair the damage and prevent recurrence of floods." The government was also to appoint a high-grade man to take charge of the work.

Soong with characteristic energy at once approved these proposals and began to put them into effect. By mandate of August 14, the National Flood Relief Commission was created, with Chinese and foreign members and with Soong as chairman.

As of first urgency, I at once arranged with the China National Aviation Corporation for an aerial survey. The British Navy also made survey flights, using the seaplanes of a vessel at Hankow. In September, Colonel and Mrs. Lindbergh arrived in China with their seaplane after a flight from the United States on the Arctic Circle route, then a considerable adventure. They offered to survey and report on the flooding, and made several flights. Their report with maps and photographs, along with the data from other surveys, were of great value in determining the dimensions of the problem.[45] The publicity resulting from these flights helped to elicit contributions from the United States. Reports of conditions in the various areas were sent in by local *hsien* magistrates under instructions. Customs officers and personnel from branches of the Bank of China, Socony-Vacuum Oil Company, and foreign mission stations also sent in reports as did observers on American naval vessels.

Negotiations with the United States began on August 15. Minister Johnson recommended that Congress be presented with a proposal to provide the wheat as a gift, but this plan was not accepted in Washington.[46] An agreement of September 25 with the Federal Farm Board covered the sale and purchase of 450,000 short tons of wheat, to be loaded at Pacific Coast ports from that date through March. At the Board's option, half might be in the form of flour and eventually nearly half was so delivered, this reflecting pressure of American millers. The prices were to be current market prices f.o.b. port of loading. Payment would be made in three equal instalments at the end of 1934, 1935, and 1936, with interest at 4 per cent. American vessels would be used, other conditions being equal.

How to meet costs in China was a serious problem. The Legislative Yuan adopted a plan on September 11 for issuing a flood relief loan of C $80 million. They proposed buying grain from Manchuria—days before the Japanese attack! Soong wanted an issue of only C $10 million, knowing that it would not be practicable to market the larger amount. This and other clashes between the Executive and Legislative Yuans brought out the fact that the latter, as I pointed out in a letter of August 31 to Soong, "is an appointive rather than a representative body, and in reality is a committee whose power in drafting legislative projects may result in measures embarrassing to, or in conflict with, the action of those responsible for conduct of the affairs of government." The final decision of the government was to issue as a first instalment a relief loan of C $30 million. But flotation of any loan became impossible when the Japanese attack in Manchuria on September 18 created turmoil.

To provide for emergency needs of relief, the government adopted a 10 per cent surtax on customs revenue effective December 1, 1931. From August 1, 1932, the rate was to be 5 per cent, earmarked for payment of the American loan. But the government's general fiscal needs continued urgent, and from that date surtaxes continued to total 10 per cent including a 5 per cent revenue surtax. For immediate relief needs the Hongkong and Shanghai Bank provided at 7 per cent interest a sterling credit up to £140,000, equivalent to about C $2 million, repayable from the surtax. The surtax produced C $15 million up to July 31, 1932. A surtax on railway passenger fares produced several hundred thousand dollars.

Private gifts in China and abroad produced C $7.5 million. Also received were important gifts of medical supplies, rice and prepared foods, clothing, and other useful items. The Italian government granted from Boxer Indemnity funds US $200,000 for purchase of tools, under an agreement I negotiated with Count Ciano, then consul general at Shanghai. The first lot of 15,000 shovels left Venice on November 14, and further lots of tools and equipment promptly followed. But they did not begin to arrive in Shanghai until January, and before that tools had to be purchased to supplement those locally available.

The relief administration was hard-pressed for cash. In the emergency, the American government agreed to the sale of wheat and flour to realize funds for relief. This was a tremendous help, and 132,000 tons or 34 per cent of the 446,000 received were sold to realize C $10 million.[47] Washington also agreed to the use of 5000 tons of the wheat to aid refugees from the Japanese attack at Shanghai early in 1962.

To take administrative charge of relief the League of Nations at China's request made available Sir John Hope Simpson, who had long experience in relief work in India and Greece. He was an admirable choice. He arrived in China on October 20, and was named director-general of the program. Prior to his arrival, I had been giving full time to administrative and policy work in the relief program, and after helping to brief him I returned to financial duties.

The operation was a splendid example of Sino-foreign cooperation. The China International Famine Relief Commission provided personnel and overhead expenses to repair or rebuild 134 kilometers of dykes in the central Yangtze region. The Chinese-Foreign Famine Relief Committee of Shanghai received a subsidy of wheat which it supplemented with funds to repair a number of breaches in the Grand Canal.[48]

In field work, many of the foremen and gang leaders were recruited among the refugees. Most of the engineering work for dyke building was done by Chinese engineers, many of whom received crash training for their specific work on dykes. In administrative work, numerous individuals both Chinese and foreign participated on a volunteer basis, receiving only traveling expenses. These included university students, missionaries, business men, and also numerous local volunteers. Local guilds and the Red Swastika Society helped. The Commission worked through local charitable organizations when possible. Nanking University, under the direction of J. Lossing Buck, surveyed economic and social conditions in the flooded areas. Provincial governments conducted relief operations on a considerable scale. Many local magistrates and gentry took part in the program.[49]

There were, however, many cases of "obstructive tactics of the local civil authorities and notorious members of the gentry." Often the Commission's representatives had to fight hard to put into effect the program of relief and dyke building. Many local officeholders had the old ideas of exploitation of their positions for personal benefit. There was also considerable interference by bandits and Communists, who were in some force in many parts of the disaster area. A number of staff were killed or kidnaped. Armed guards had to be provided in some places at considerable cost, and in a few cases disturbed conditions precluded conduct of the program.[50]

Despite difficulties, a vast task of relief and restoration was accomplished. Total expenditures were about C $70 million, spent mostly by the Flood Relief Commission. The operation involved large-scale organization of transport, distribution, and engineering. Food, clothing, shelter, and medical attention were provided for millions. Free relief benefited about five million of the destitute. But the outstanding feature was work relief. An average of 900,000 men and women worked on rehabilitation projects each day, and the maximum at one time was 1.4 million. The earthwork done in six months totaled 153 million cubic meters, or two-thirds that of the Panama Canal. It was equivalent to a wall two meters wide and two meters high around the earth at the equator. Construction included 7430 kilometers of dykes, 288 kilometers of channels, and extensive masonry and culverts.[51]

Labor relief in kind had both advantages and disadvantages. Requiring labor in exchange for food served the double purpose of getting work done and avoiding the evils of free hand-outs. Import of large amounts of wheat and flour into the distressed areas checked profiteering and price rises, thus substantially relieving those who could afford to buy. But physical distribution of wheat and flour and making payments in kind required a huge organization. There were unavoidable losses in transit. Rice eaters often had trouble in learning to use wheat and flour, and commonly sold those foods even at a sacrifice to buy rice, although they would eat them rather than starve. Wheat and flour distribution had to be supplemented by cash payments to buy other necessities such as salt, vegetables, and fuel. On balance, however, labor relief in kind was of enormous advantage.

Mistakes were unavoidable in such a huge project conducted in an emergency and under disturbed conditions. But as one close to the operation, I can testify that the overall operation was highly creditable to its leaders, administrators, and staff. Funds and wheat were carefully handled and abuses were relatively minor. Despite the government's enormous financial difficulties in 1931-1932, no funds allocated for relief were diverted to other governmental uses. Politics was mostly prevented from intruding. Occasional losses to thieves, bandits, and peculators were far more than offset by the faithfulness of nearly all the staff and their bravery in the disturbed areas.[52]

The total debt for wheat and flour was US $9,212,828.46. The one-third instalments due at the end of 1934 and 1935 were duly paid, despite the great financial stringency of the period. The 1936 instalment was refunded in that year and a revised schedule included with payments on the 1933 Cotton and Wheat Loan. Payment in full of both of these was completed during the war.

The effective relief program was of broad economic and political significance. It saved countless lives and restored the damaged economy. Reconstruction of dykes and other measures of rehabilitation were so successful that there was record production of rice in 1932. The Flood Relief Commission's report stated that farm rehabilitation "inspired the peasant population with renewed hope and courage, and has, to a great extent, counteracted the tendency to Communism which was powerful all through the Yangtze Valley." The report concluded that the operation "brought forcibly to the notice of the affected population the fact that this National Government has been inspired by an interest in the well being of the common people," leading them to regard the government "with more interest and more respect." Thus "a political result of the first magnitude" was achieved.[53]

The observations of a writer in the *North-China Daily News* of December 29, 1932, confirm the Commission's appraisal. The program "represents the symbol of central authority in an area where Nanking's relations with the peasant farmers . . . were of a shadowy nature at the most." It was "no mere coincidence that the great dyke system should have been completed almost at the same time that a large area in Hupei, Anhwei, and

Honan has been cleared of Communists." The work "brought home to the people . . . the expression of a government's desire to help them in their direst need."

American cotton and wheat loan of 1933

In 1932-1933, after the success of the flood relief operation, there were active negotiations for credits to buy both wheat and cotton from the United States. A representative of the Grain Stabilization Corporation came to China in the summer of 1932, and I negotiated with him at great length. When an agreement seemed near, Washington suddenly called off the project for reasons that were not clear.

The Roosevelt administration after taking over early in 1933 invited a number of foreign delegations to come to the United States for conferences on economic matters. Minister Soong was invited, and Washington suggested that I come with him. We arrived early in May. I prepared a tentative plan for two credits of US $5 million each for wheat and cotton. But it immediately appeared that Washington had much larger ideas, aiming to absorb surplus stocks and raise the prices of these commodities, which were then about 75 cents per bushel and 8-1/2 cents per pound respectively. The idea of a sizable commodity credit had been promoted in Washington in April by Jean Monnet, whom Soong had invited to come to China to advise on matters concerning economic development.[54] Washington suggested a credit of US $50 million. I was asked to handle negotiations with the Reconstruction Finance Corporation (RFC) because Soong's contact with them would have stirred publicity. After two weeks of intense negotiations agreement was reached on May 29.

The agreement provided for a credit of US $50 million. Of this amount, four-fifths was for cotton and the balance for wheat, of which at least 40 per cent was to be taken as flour. The credit was for three years, with an indication that payments might be extended for two additional years, and interest was 5 per cent. The credit was secured on the consolidated taxes, plus a charge on the 5 per cent flood relief surtax junior to the charge for the flood relief loan of 1931. At least half the shipping was to be in American vessels and at least half the insurance with American insurance companies. The RFC reserved the right to approve China's purchasing agents. The latter clause caused some difficulty. I successively proposed the names of competent agents, but each was vetoed until persons were found whose appointment would be of political advantage to the Washington administration. China set up purchasing and handling organizations in New York, Houston, and Portland as well as at the Central Bank in Shanghai. In the United States, the accounting and procedures were supervised by Price, Waterhouse and Company, which also made a final audit.

Insurance gave rise to problems. The Central Bank of China first arranged with an American company in China for coverage at competitive rates. That brought a quick objection from the RFC, on the ground that the intention was to give the business to companies in the United States. I pointed out to Stanley Reed, then Chief Counsel of the RFC (later Justice of the Supreme Court) and with whom I had negotiated, that China was within her rights. He agreed but urged dealing with companies locally. There were signs that failure to go along would lead to obstructive tactics on the American side. So it was deemed necessary to concur. I was advised to confer with a certain insurance broker in New York. On going to his office, I found that James Roosevelt was at the conference.

After announcement of the loan on June 4, both political and financial issues were raised. There was an outcry in Japan on the ground that the United States was bolstering an unfriendly government in China. But Washington maintained that the credit was commercial, and that the action was "to aid the price situation at home." At first Japanese mills in China bought loan cotton, but then were told to desist. These mills were major users of American cotton, and their action was largely responsible for the reduction of the cotton credit to US $10 million early in 1934. In China, the dissident Canton faction protested the arrangement, claiming that it would be used to buy arms to fight them. Japan seized on this claim to allege that the credit would foment trouble in China. The credit was one of several things involved in Japan's growing opposition to Western efforts to strengthen China.[55]

The financial issues concerned the Consortium agreement and China's debts in arrears. There was no conflict with the text of that agreement because no public loan was involved. But not only in Japan but also in Britain there were complaints, and the London *Times* of June 7 charged that the RFC credit "seemed to impinge on the policy of international cooperation envisaged by the Consortium." The State Department and also the American officers of the Consortium felt that the RFC's action was "not inconsistent with obligations of the United States Government relative to the Consortium agreement." That agreement did not contemplate possible governmental credits to China. But they were not happy about whether the credit was in accord with the spirit of the agreement.[56] Arguments concerning the Consortium did not disturb China, which refused to recognize or deal with it.

Another financial issue concerned China's debts in arrears. In July 1933, the British, French, and Japanese financial groups objected to pledging of the 5 per cent customs surtax on the ground that it contravened the claim of the Hukuang Railway loan on customs revenue. The American group did not join the protest, holding that the surtax was an entirely new tax.[57] But they as well as the State Department were unhappy about China's delay in settling debts in arrears.

On December 31, 1935, an instalment of about US $3 million of the Flood Relief Loan of 1931 was payable. That was just after the currency reform and China was short of reserves to combat Japanese and other speculative raids on the currency (Chapter 10). At my suggestion, Ambassador Sze under Kung's instructions asked on November 19 for extension of the period of payment of principal of both the 1931 and 1933 loans, proposing to continue interest payments at the prescribed rates. Washington refused China's request in order to bring pressure for debt settlements, even though China indicated her intention to proceed with negotiations (Chapter 5).

By an agreement of May 28, 1936, the outstanding balances of the 1931 and 1933 loans were consolidated into a single obligation of US $16.6 million, with payments extended through 1942. For China that was an important relief, especially in view of the need to support the currency reform. Under the original agreements, principal payments scheduled in 1936 and 1937 totaled US $17 million. The 1936 agreement reduced those payments to US $3.4 million.[58] China repaid both loans in full during the war despite her grave financial difficulties.

To handle sales in China, the Central Bank organized two syndicates comprising the chief importers of the commodities. Administrative difficulties were considerable but were solved fairly well. There was criticism of the credit by the importers, who felt that it interfered with normal channels of trade and may have even lessened sales of the commodities. The allocation of US $40 million for cotton had not seemed too far out of line because in the two seasons of 1930-1932, when prices were low, imports of American cotton had been 885,000 and 750,000 bales, respectively. During the loan negotiations in May 1933, we were advised from China that 600,000 bales could be used, the price of which seemed likely to reach US $40 million. The chief reason for reducing the cotton credit to US $10 million was that the Japanese mills, which were users of 60 to 70 per cent of American imports, were not allowed to buy. Furthermore, the depression in China was deepening in 1933-1934, and China had a bumper crop. In the season of 1933-1934, imports of American cotton were 425,000 bales. Loan cotton bought with the US $10 million from July 1933 through October 1934 was 159,536 bales.[59]

All the US $6 million credit for wheat was used. But of the US $4 million credit for flour, only US $1.1 million was used. The flour could not be sold competitively except at sizable loss. China fell behind in buying and sought to modify the agreement. In the spring of 1935, the balance of the credit for flour was canceled.

The total expended under the credit was US $17.1 million, to buy and ship 159,536 bales of cotton, 10,769,340 bushels of wheat, and 338,000 barrels of flour. China realized net proceeds of about C $38 million. There was a net operating loss of 0.5 per cent on cotton, 0.1 per cent on wheat, and 3.5 per cent on flour, or 0.6 per cent overall. The average interest cost to China was 8.6 per cent per annum.[60]

The problems raised by the credit led the State Department to feel that it had caused the American and Chinese governments "no end of trouble"; had been of doubtful benefit to China; and had led to "widespread criticism abroad" especially on the part of Japan.[61] But from China's standpoint, the positive factors much outweighed the detriments. Money gotten at an average cost of 8.6 per cent per annum was helpful at a time when internal loans could be floated only with great difficulty and at a cost of the order of 15 per cent. The net proceeds of about C $38 million were used for a variety of constructive purposes, largely through the NEC. These included highway building, water conservancy, rehabilitation of areas recovered from the Communists, public health, and education. And the operation was conducted without scandal or corruption.[62]

China complied with its undertaking to use the loan proceeds only for constructive purposes. Edgar Snow has stated that the proceeds "were of decisive value to Chiang Kai-shek's civil war against the Reds, according to reports of foreign military observers."[63] That could not have been through direct use for military purposes, although some of the funds were used for rehabilitation of areas recovered from the Communists. The available details, which cover the two fiscal years ended June 30, 1935, show the following uses: highways, C $8.9 million; water conservancy, C $6.9 million; agricultural rehabilitation, C $3.6 million; rehabilitation in Kiangsi Province, C $2.8 million; education, C $1.5 million; public health, C $1.4 million; construction and miscellaneous, C $7.0 million; total, C $32.1 million.[64] Without the proceeds of the credit, little money could have been found for these purposes. Hence the money could scarcely be deemed substitutable to free other funds for military purposes. Snow's statement may be interpreted to mean that the government's use of the loan proceeds reduced the Communist threat by demonstrating ability to promote rehabilitation and other activities helpful to the people's welfare and the country's development.

Of much importance was the help to morale in China. Upon my return to China after conclusion of the loan agreement, several high officials told me that American aid to China was most heartening at a time of strong Japanese pressure, attempted internal subversion, and acute economic depression.

17: Modernization and Development: Summary and Appraisal

Sun Yat-sen's vision of a united China, freed of servitudes and advancing on all fronts, sparked the movement for rehabilitation and progress that led to the Nationalist takeover. A striking characteristic of the prewar decade was the government's desire to promote modernization and development, coupled with growing ability to do so as it gained authority and experience. No previous regime had the desire and ability to attempt this on a nationwide scale.

Conditions and institutions unfavorable to progress continued from older days to a large extent. Capital was in short supply and the tendency was to invest in land and moneylending rather than in enterprises involving risk. Qualified managers and technicians were scarce. China met the modern world with a weak and decadent monarchy, succeeded by warlords, and those rulers had little desire or capacity to reform faulty social, economic, and governmental institutions. Japan, in contrast, had a strong regime that promptly adopted basic reforms.

In the prewar decade, overall conditions were far from favorable for development. Repeated subversive movements against the government although unsuccessful were disturbing. Serious clashes with Japan were costly and unsettling. After 1929, the world was in deep depression. The effects of depression on China were delayed because the slump in silver prevented deflation until the latter part of 1931. But then the rise of silver, pushed out of line with general prices by American silver buying, brought a severe financial and economic crisis. Fortunately, the currency reform of November 3, 1935, reversed the situation. From then until outbreak of fighting in mid-1937, China enjoyed unprecedented progress.

The tone for development was set in 1931 by T. V. Soong's call for systematic and coordinated planning and by the creation of the National Economic Council. The ambitious program included land reform and agricultural improvement, industrial development, improvement of communications, water conservancy, education, and public health. Plans contemplated a mixed economic system of public and private enterprise, reserving to government the public utilities and the heavy industry closely related to defense but leaving light industry to private enterprise. In practice, the action was not consistent, with some joint public and private enterprises and some governmental participation in light industries.

Through the work of hundreds of Chinese and foreign technicians, a great volume of plans was produced for river conservancy, irrigation and drainage, port improvements, railways, roads, airways, telecommunications, agriculture, industry, and defense. Requirements for costs of a three-year program were estimated in 1937 at about C$1 billion. The plans, which were expanded comprehensively during the war, were often quite detailed. These plans became available to the Communists, and many planners and technicians joined them either from a belief in development mainly by state action or from necessity. These plans and technicians deserve credit for providing the nucleus for much that the Communists later accomplished.

The economy

Agriculture, conducted mostly by traditional methods with unremitting labor, engaged 75 to 80 per cent of China's families and produced nearly two-thirds of the national product in the prewar decade. According to Ping-ti Ho, population pressure has caused "an almost progressive deterioration in the national standards of living since the late eighteenth century."[1]

At the time of the Nationalist takeover, the rural situation had become acute especially in the wide areas involved in the civil wars of the warlord era. The people suffered from conscription of manpower, heavy surtaxes on land, looting of crops and other property, and slaughter of livestock, which also meant reduced fertilizer supply. These conditions, followed by continuing internal strife and the acute deflation of 1931 to 1935, were major causes of the distress in the countryside. Also abuses were common in landlord-tenant relations, although at least half the farms were owner-operated, more in the north and less in the central and southern areas. Rural credit was meager and costly, and many moneylenders exploited the borrowers. Land taxation bore heaviest on the poorer households. Local government all too often was bad.

The great need of land reform and improvement of agriculture was urged by Sun Yat-sen and also in various pronouncements of Nationalist officials. The proclaimed aim was for reforms rather than radical change in the system. The government created the Ministry of Agriculture and Mining, later merged into the Ministry of Industry. J. Lossing Buck and the Chinese and American experts associated with him did pioneer work in agricultural research, promoting the training of experts, improving varieties of seeds and plants, developing use of pesticides, and thus encouraging modern practices. They devised a system of comprehensive crop reports and statistics, which the government soon took over. An Agricultural Research Bureau was created, and experiment stations, demonstration farms, and extension systems were set up in a number of provinces. Inspection stations were established to standardize exports of tea, silk, and wood oil. Cooperative credit societies were organized, and grew to have over two million members by 1937. Banks began lending to cooperatives. A comprehensive program of rural rehabilitation was begun in Kiangsi Province after expulsion of the Communists in 1934. But funds and personnel for agricultural improvement were generally too limited to permit a wide effect. An indication of progress in agriculture was the rapid growth of imports of agricultural and pumping machinery.

The government adopted excellent land laws. But the leaders were too preoccupied with internal and external emergencies to devote enough attention to basic improvement of rural conditions. Besides, most of the leaders had urban and not rural backgrounds, along with an empathy with landowning and financial interests. Yet, despite failing to deal in a large way with agricultural improvement, which was a huge problem calling for intensive effort over decades, the progress in several fields was significant. Had not the war supervened, the results would have been more and more apparent.

In other fields, governmental action benefited agriculture. Rail, water, and road transport was greatly improved. Many burdensome taxes were removed or reduced, notably abolition of *likin* (transport tax) from January 1, 1931, a reform whose success much exceeded expectations. Furthermore, coast trade duties, transit dues, and native customs charges on junk-borne trade were abolished. In 1931-1932, the program of flood relief aided by the American wheat loan of 15 million bushels made possible rehabilitation of a large area of the central Yangtze basin and construction of more than 7000 kilometers of dykes together with other works. A daily average of 900,000 workers was engaged in this program and largely paid in kind. Of great underlying importance was the improvement of public order, especially in the latter part of the decade. China's farmers could always recover rapidly from their troubles, given good weather and conditions of peace and order.

Buck and other experts estimate that agricultural production in the thirties before the outbreak of hostilities in 1937 was as great or greater than Communist production during part of their rule on the mainland, although distribution has been more even than prewar and in the most recent years production has increased.

The rural population was hard-working and knowledgeable according to their lights. Their greatest needs, besides the primary importance of peace and order and justice in land taxation, were for better seeds, pest control, fertilizer, improved arrangements for credit and marketing, irrigation and flood control, and better transport. The farmers alone lacked the ability to generate the resources and technology needed for improvement. The government was committed to promote progress on these lines. But, like the subsequent experience of the Communists, agriculture had too low a priority. Many of the agricultural reforms planned by the government could have taken hold rapidly. A beginning had been made, and in Buck's opinion improvement of Chinese agriculture in the thirties ranked high as compared with progress then in other less developed countries. But time was needed, and time ran out when the hostilities began.

Handicrafts and modern-type industry together produced about one-tenth of the national product in the prewar decade. Handicrafts were the greater, and factory-type industries, utilities, and mining contributed only three to four per cent of the total product. Studies indicate that, contrary to common charges, handicraft production did not absolutely shrink although its share in the total was declining. Foreign capital and enterprise played a large part in industrial development, by providing for several decades much of the structure of modern-type transport, communications, utilities, mining, and financial services. Modern-type industries, both Chinese and foreign, were concentrated largely in the treaty ports, because they afforded greater law and order than in the interior. Rising tariff rates under tariff autonomy after 1928 gave protection although rates were raised more for fiscal reasons.

A study of industrial development by John K. Chang indicates that substantial progress took place between the fall of the empire and the Communist takeover. He estimates compounded growth rates for industry, mining, and electric power as follows: 1912 to 1949, 5.6 per cent; 1926 to 1936, 8.3 per cent; and 1928 to 1936, 8.4 per cent. These figures include Manchuria, where Japan strongly promoted development after 1931 for strategic reasons. Eliminating Manchuria, the data for China proper show a growth rate of 6.4 per cent for 1926 to 1936 and 6.7 per cent for 1931 to 1936. There was overall growth in every year from 1927 to 1936 in the indexes, including Manchuria. For China proper the index grew by 86.1 per cent from 1926 to 1936 (Table 24). Although some of Chang's data are admittedly imperfect and incomplete, I consider that his figures substantially indicate what was happening, in the light of indicators of growth other than of physical production, e.g., establishment of factories, bank deposits, trade, and railway traffic.

For this period, China's record was strikingly better than that of most other countries. Indexes in leading industrial countries showed either a loss or at most a small gain between 1929 and 1936. An exception was Japan, where there was a small decline from 1929 to 1931, but a compounded growth of nearly 10 per cent from then to 1937—a foretaste of the rapid postwar growth.

Although modern-type industry grew at a good rate, its contribution to overall growth was small because of its small share in the total economy. The economy as a whole in 1937 remained mostly traditional and undeveloped because of the preponderance of agriculture and old-style handicrafts and transport. The predominantly rural consumers had small buying power. Growth was retarded by illiteracy, low average level of education, shortage of qualified managers and technicians, poor transport, and continuing though decreasing internal disorders. But, on the positive side, the government was taking an interest in promoting modernization, backed by important elements of the business and intellectual communities. Workers were industrious and adaptable. Banking was developing rapidly to provide financial support, and foreign credits were becoming available. The government was creating an improving environment by tax reforms and improvement of transport and communications. The currency reform of 1935 ended the severe deflation and provided stable rates of exchange. There was no overvaluation and exports were expanding. Coinage reform and the spread of the national currency to displace regional systems were also constructive. Gradual strengthening of central control and improvement of internal order created an improving environment for modern-type industry.

The railways were in confusion in 1927-1928, following years in which warlords used the lines for military purposes, removed and sequestered rolling stock and supplies, and seized revenues. Most of the loans secured on the railways were in default. The new government gradually rehabilitated the lines, restoring and improving services. Ton-kilometers of freight grew from 1931, the first data available, to 1935-1936 by about two-thirds for mineral products and one-third for other items. The operating ratios of costs to revenues were 67.3 per cent in 1927 and 64.5 per cent in 1935-1936. But these ratios failed to match the remarkable earlier average of 51.2 per cent in 1916 to 1925, partly because hungry politicians expanded railway personnel to care for favorites.

During the thirties, the railway finances gradually improved. Increasing net revenues made possible settlement of most of the defaulted debt, and the rest would probably have been settled had not hostilities supervened. Also the railways were able to provide security for new credits from both foreign and domestic sources to improve and expand the railway system. The credit guarantee systems of several European governments and the United States were being made available to help to finance substantial purchases of materials and equipment. Minister Chang, in particular, was able to introduce important economies and reforms between 1935 and 1937. These changes included reduction of staff, stricter control of expenditures, centralized purchasing and stores, better maintenance of ways and equipment, and addition of rolling stock.

There was considerable extension of lines, notably completion of the Canton-Hankow railway, building of new lines southwest of Shanghai in Chekiang and Kiangsi provinces, and the westward extension of the Lunghai trunk line north of the Yangtze River. In the prewar decade, a total of 2328 miles of line was built in China proper, an increase of 47 per cent. Plans for further construction were well under way when interrupted by the hostilities in 1937. Plans were also being formulated to amalgamate the railways administratively and financially and to simplify the complicated debt structure.

The road system made notable progress in the prewar decade, growing from about 18,000 to 69,000 miles including Manchuria. Much more was under construction and projected. Most of the road building was in central China and the northwest. Most roads were surfaced only with gravel and broken stone and maintenance was a problem. Facilities for traffic were being extended by providing service stations, road signs, and repair shops. Gasoline imports grew from 13 million gallons in 1927 to 46 million in 1936, registration of passenger cars grew by 70 per cent, and the number of trucks and buses grew sixfold and eightfold, respectively.

Roads were built largely for strategic purposes, and commercial uses other than transport of passengers were slow to develop. Road building placed further burdens on many local communities and caused some unemployment of porters, carters, and persons engaged in water transport. But general use of roads was growing, maintenance was improving, and their development promised in time to be of material gain to the overall economy.

Air services, starting from practically nothing, made great progress in the prewar decade. Beginning in 1929, the China National Aviation Corporation (CNAC), in which Pan-American Airways acquired about 45 per cent interest and the government had the rest, developed a network of routes connecting the leading cities. Lesser but important operations were the Sino-German Eurasia company; the Southwest Aviation Company based in Canton; and the Japanese-operated line connecting North China cities, Manchukuo, and Japan. CNAC and Eurasia provided good service as Sino-foreign enterprises under cooperative arrangements that mostly worked well under difficult pioneering conditions. The air services were of major importance, helping to make up for the scantiness of railway and road communications. Fast air mail service was of great economic benefit. Specially important was the political significance, by bringing closer contact throughout the country and promoting unity and solidarity.

Further evidence of progress was improvement of telegraph, telephone, and postal communications. In 1936, there were 89,415 kilometers of telegraph lines. From 1932 to 1936, the length of telephone toll lines increased from 9303 to 47,084 kilometers, and the number of telephone poles from 179,423 to 543,728. The number of postal offices increased from 42,484 at the end of 1932 to 73,690 in mid-1937.[2]

Foreign trade never exceeded about US $3 per capita at the peak, and at the low of the depression was much less. Between 1931 and 1936, the foreign trade of China proper was about 6 to 8 per cent of the national product. Trade in the thirties was less than in the twenties. That decrease reflected the worldwide depression as well as the rising tariff rates that brought the ratio of revenue to imports from 4 per cent before 1929 to about 25 per cent in 1934 to 1937. Foreign trade contributed importantly to modernization, providing a link to the outside world. Net imports of capital goods grew materially during the thirties. Exports improved materially after the currency reform. But their expansion in the lines in which China had a comparative advantage, sufficient in amount to increase importantly the resources to finance needed imports, presented problems and would have called for careful and extended effort.

China's gross domestic product is difficult to estimate because the data are unsatisfactory. Kung-chia Yeh estimated it for 1931 to 1936 at an average of about C $30 billion at 1933 prices. Nearly two-thirds derived from agriculture; about 10 per cent from manufacturing, utilities, and mining; and about two-thirds of the 10 per cent represented handicraft production. The rest represented transport, communications, trade, construction, rents, and financial, personal, and governmental services. Capital formation in those years according to the computation by Yeh and Ta-chung Liu averaged about C $1.596 billion gross and about C $0.51 billion net. These figures were about 5 and 2 per cent, respectively, of gross domestic product.

While the modernized part of China's economy was progressing at a good rate in the prewar decade, modernized industry, transport, and communications contributed not over about 5 per cent of the total product. Upgrading the overall rate of progress depended on progress in the overwhelmingly important agricultural and traditional sectors. The process was bound to be slow, considering the adverse ratio between land and population, backward technology in agriculture and other traditional production and services, illiteracy, and general inertia. Mainland China after 1949 under the Communists attained for a time a much higher rate of gross capital formation, which Yeh has estimated at about 18 per cent of gross national product in 1952 to 1957 compared with about 5 per cent in China proper in the thirties. The rate of yearly growth in Mainland China appears to have been about 6 per cent in 1952 to 1957. The Great Leap Forward led to severe retrogression after 1958. By 1965 the economy had largely recovered. But then came the Great Cultural Revolution and a further setback. There has since been a recovery but suppression of information prevents concrete estimates of growth since the Leap began.

In Taiwan, with a system of free enterprise and with large American aid, the average yearly growth rate from 1951 to 1965 was over 7 per cent and the rate since then has been greater. Gross domestic savings were 12 per cent of gross national product in 1951 and have since risen somewhat.

Stagnation or growth?

The case for economic stagnation during the prewar decade has been vigorously argued by Douglas S. Paauw. His argument, in summary, is that the agricultural sector remained backward; that the government showed little inclination or capacity to effect social reforms, especially in agriculture; that while there was progress in transport, communications, and electric power, industry made little progress, and was largely in the hands of "bureaucratic capitalism"; that inflow of foreign capital decreased; that the climate for growth was less favorable than in the earlier period of imperialism; and that heavy expenditures for political unification and defense, assumed apparently to be unwarranted, absorbed savings, stifled growth, and relegated economic development to a secondary role. He concluded that "the government had less capacity to promote economic development in 1937 than a decade earlier"; and that it is doubtful that it could have "solved China's traditional problem of economic stagnation with more political control and less Japanese aggression."[3]

"The record," charged Paauw, "shows little more than the continuance of economic stagnation during the Nanking period."[4] His charges have had a measure of influence, and it is regrettable that he made them without being familiar with major parts of the record. The data herein presented refute his argument. His treatment of the economy and misleading strictures on financial policy and action show strong anti-Nationalist bias (*infra*, pages 83 to 92, 148, 155 to 156).

Table 27

Indicators of economic development (excluding Manchuria)

	1927	1928	1929	1930
1 Electric power, million Kwh	772	882	1017	1112
2 Coal, million metric tons	14.2	15.4	15.2	15.8
3 Tin, thousand metric tons	10	8	8	7
4 Cement, thousand metric tons	498	608	753	691
5 Cotton yarn, thousand bales	2127	2175	2298	2401
6 Cotton cloth, thousand bolts of 40 sq. yds.	8999	13768	14780	16180
7 Railway ton-Kilometers excluding minerals,[b] million metric tons				
8 Railway ton-Kilometers, minerals,[b] million metric tons				
9 Motor roads,[c] length, thousand miles	18	19	22	29
10 Gasoline imports, million gallons	11.0	15.2	21.7	24.0
11 Fuel oil imports, thousand long tons	151	214	163	142
12 Chinese steamships, thousand gross tons		291	334	415
13 Chinese shipping entered and cleared in foreign and domestic trade,[d] million gross tons,	25.0	37	30	29
and proportion of total, per cent	(19.8)	(23.9)	(19.3)	(18.8)
14 Ditto, foreign trade [d]	3.1	4.4	4.4	4.2
	(7.4)	(9.4)	(8.5)	(8.5)
15 Ditto, domestic trade [d]	22	32	26	25
	(20.2)	(30.4)	(24.6)	(23.7)

Continued

from 1927 to 1936[a]

1931	1932	1933	1934	1935	1936	*%
1287	1195	1422	1541	1569	1724	9.4
18.0	18.9	18.8	20.9	23.6	26.2	7.0
9	7	8	8	10	13	3.0
687	621	727	838	1027	1243	9.6
2360	2424	2447	2382	2137	2148	--
23013	23255	28344	28831	30298	35448	16.5
	1600	1664	1787	2304	2260	9.0
	2029	2063	2448	2932	3030	10.5
41	44	45	53	60	69	16.1
27.0	22.0	31.3	39.7	41.0	45.5	17.1
222	235	336	402	392	313	8.4
	577	625		675		12.8
33	34	37	41	42	44	6.5
(20.4)	(25.0)	(27.1)	(29.3)	(29.2)	(30.5)	
5.0	4.3	4.6	6.8	7.6	7.4	10.2
(9.7)	(9.7)	(11.2)	(15.2)	(15.8)	(16.4)	
28	30	32	34	34	37	5.9
(25.5)	(32.6)	(33.9)	(36.0)	(35.8)	(36.9)	

*Annual growth rate compounded.

Continued

Table 27 (Continued)

Indicators of economic development (excluding Manchuria)

	1927	1928	1929	1930
16 Air-Kilometers flown, thousands			93	531
17 Membership of cooperatives,[f] thousands				
18 Index of bank deposits current and fixed, excluding Central Bank, at 1928 prices		100	111	123
19 Index of note circulation, at 1928 prices [g]		100	110	119
20 Index of industrial production, including Manchuria	100	108.4	115.4	122.5
21 Ditto, excluding Manchuria, 1926 = 100				
22 Net domestic product including Manchuria, 1931-1936, in constant 1933 prices, billions of C$				
23 Agriculture, do.				
24 Nonagriculture, do.				
25 Gross domestic capital formation, do.				

[a] Sources for indicated items:

1. For 1927-1931, *The China Annual* (The Asia Statistic Company, Shanghai, 1944), p. 945; for 1932-1935, Yen Chung-p'ing, ed.: *Selected Statistics on the Economic History of Modern China* (Chung-kuo chin-tai ching-chi shih t'ung-chi tzu-liao hsuan-chi), Peking, 1955, p. 130.

2. Geological Survey of China: *General Statement on the Mining Industry*, No. 5 (Nanking, 1935), pp. 34-35, and No. 7 (Chungking, 1945), p. 4.

3. Yen, *Selected Statistics*, pp. 139-140.

4 to 6. John K. Chang, *Industrial Development in Pre-Communist China*, pp. 119, 122-123.

7 and 8. *Statistics of Chinese National Railways, 1935-1936* (Nanking, 1937), pp. 78-79. The figures for 1934-1936 are for fiscal years ended June 30.

9. National Economic Council, *Annual Report, 1935* (Nanking, 1936), p. 12; and *Annual Report, 1936*, extract in *The China Year Book, 1939*, p. 514. Figures are converted from kilometers.

10 and 11. Maritime Customs reports, *passim*.

12. Yen, *Selected Statistics*, p. 229, quoting Ministry of Communications, *Statistical Yearbook*.

13 to 15. Maritime Customs reports, *passim*.

16. Maritime Customs: *The Trade of China*, 1936, v. 1, part 1, pp. 91-92.

from 1927 to 1936

1931	1932	1933	1934	1935	1936	*%
716	948	1438	2038	2701	3460	--[e]
56	151	185	558	1004	1644	--[e]
130	159	202	248	290	326	15.9
102	137	173	222	325	492	22.0
132.1	137.5	150.1	155.6	164.6	183.2	7.0
134.4					186.1	6.4
28.60	29.65	29.43	26.85	29.08	30.80	1.4
18.59	19.66	19.34	17.11	18.79	19.89	1.5
10.01	9.99	10.09	9.74	10.29	10.91	1.8
1.27	1.49	1.50	1.12	1.60	1.95	8.9

*Annual growth rate compounded.

17. Tsung-kao Yieh, *Industrialization of Wartime China*, unpublished memorandum received in 1942.
18. Appendix 18.
19. Appendix 17.
20 and 21. Chang, *Industrial Development in Pre-Communist China*, pp. 60-61, 103.
22 to 24. Table 25.
25. Table 26.

[b] Data for years before 1932 are not available.

[c] Including roads in Manchuria which in 1935-1936 were about a tenth of the total. No breakdown for earlier years is available, but indications are that the proportion was smaller in those years.

[d] The figures in the first column are the averages of 1926-1927. For Chinese shipping, 1926 was an abnormally low year in foreign trade and 1927 in domestic trade.

[e] No percentage rates are stated because growth started from scratch.

[f] Mostly rural credit societies.

[g] The increase of note issue up to the currency reform of November 1935 was somewhat similar to increase of deposits. After the reform, much of the increase reflected substitution of notes for silver money.

Some of Paauw's points are justified. Agriculture was the major part of the economy, and certainly most of it was relatively stagnant during the decade despite important trends that were beginning to bring about a forward movement. There was some shrinkage of foreign investment during the silver crisis of 1933 to 1935, and the slackening of inflow during the depression is understandable. But he failed to recognize that foreign investment was resuming on a considerable scale in the latter years of the prewar decade. The indications were that there was not much change in the total amount of foreign investment as of 1937 compared with 1927, as explained in Chapter 16. Paauw ignores the activities and promise for the future of the National Reconstruction Commission, the National Resources Commission, the National Economic Council, and various provincial governments. It was especially important that the government was taking a positive attitude toward development, and improving the economic climate by progress in political unity and by fiscal and monetary reforms. Clearly there is no support for the surprising charge that the government "had less capacity to promote economic development in 1937 than a decade earlier."

The most important available indicators of economic development are shown in Table 27. They confirm that there was relatively little growth in the overall economy because of the weight of agriculture, handicrafts, and traditional transportation. But they show good rates of growth in many indexes of modernization. The indications are that improved statistical coverage did not greatly affect the data. The compounded yearly rates of growth are high for modern communications, 9.0 to 16.1 per cent, while air communications grew spectacularly from practically nothing before 1929. Electric power grew yearly by 9.4 per cent, cotton cloth 16.5 per cent; coal 7.0 per cent; cement 9.6 per cent; and industry, mining, and utilities as a whole 6.4 per cent. Bank deposits grew 15.9 per cent,* and gross domestic capital formation 8.9 per cent from 1931 to 1936. The number of memberships in cooperatives, mostly for agricultural credit, was relatively small but grew rapidly in the later years of the prewar decade.

Chi-ming Hou has pointed out that the modern sector of the economy showed a linear trend of long-term growth over many

*Here there is a small increase of coverage because data for provincial and municipal banks, 6 per cent of the total for 1932, were first included in that year (Appendix 18).

years. He cites a number of indexes, which include Manchuria, showing compounded yearly rates of growth as follows: physical quantity of imports and exports from 1867 to 1932, 2.5 and 2.4 per cent, respectively; railroad mileage from 1894 to 1937, 10.3 per cent; pig iron and coal production of modern mines from 1900 to 1937, 9.8 and 8.2 per cent respectively; and cotton yarn spindles from 1890 to 1936, 11.6 per cent. I concur with him in the view that fundamental forces of development were at work, which operated under widely different political conditions.[5]

Clearly both internal and external forces of modernization were gaining strong momentum after the currency reform of 1935. The prevalent feeling of accelerating progress was restrained, however, by uncertainty about what Japan might do.

Part Five

Conclusion

18: Overall View of the Nation-Building Effort

Transition from a traditional to a modern-type economy, accompanied by an effort to create a strong central authority in place of regional and local centers of power, can never be smooth. In China during the prewar decade, consolidation and progress had to face the stubborn problems, which have since continued, of huge numbers, adverse relation of numbers to resources, high illiteracy, language differences, strong regionalism, poor transport and communications, and difficulties of foreign relations. The nation-building effort had to be undertaken in the setting of disruption, losses, and costs resulting from many years of civil and foreign wars. Furthermore these conditions were compounded by traditional weaknesses arising from extensive economic exploitation and bad government. Besides these factors, China's effort in the prewar decade was made harder because of the worldwide depression and gyrations of exchange rates caused mostly by external forces. And aid from external private and governmental sources was relatively small.

On the economic side, industrialization and modernization of production and transport are bound to disturb various established activities. In the early stages, they usually involve poor labor conditions and exploitation of workers. On the political side, while the basic pride of race and sense of unity of the Chinese people are remarkable, the country is not easy to govern by a unified national authority. The Nationalists found this out in the prewar period, and their successors on the mainland have since been discovering it.

The experience of the prewar decade necessarily shows a mixed picture. Appraisals of the nation-building effort in fiscal affairs, monetary affairs, and modernization and development are given in Chapters 6, 12, and 17, respectively. In the pages that follow I comment further on the national effort and the foreign role, and present an overall appraisal and a balance sheet of negative and positive aspects as of 1937. I shall not ordinarily support with references the statements in this chapter because they are generally based on the preceding more detailed discussion.

National effort and the foreign role

In a country's modernization and development, by far the chief factor must be the effort of the leaders and its people. But progress can be much greater with the wise use of foreign personnel, the technology they can bring, and external resources.

In China during the prewar decade, most of the foreign personnel for advisory and administrative aid were directly engaged and paid by China. The League of Nations provided some personnel, and foreign governments recommended only a few experts. There were no loans by foreign governments except the two American commodity credits of 1931 and 1933 of which US $26 million was utilized, and there were no governmental grants, except remitted Boxer Indemnity annuities, which China had paid and was paying. But backing of private foreign investment by governments was beginning in the latter part of the decade. With that support private foreign investment was gaining considerable momentum, although it probably provided no net increment during the period.

During much of the decade, progress in modernization and development was handicapped while the government struggled for survival against great odds. Countering the leaders' drive for nationwide authority were the warlords, who stood to lose perquisites if not position. Their huge and mostly inefficient armies were a costly drain on resources, often a source of disorder, and practically useless except to support their leaders in power. The government from the time of its takeover tried as a major policy to get rid of the warlords. Some were defeated and eliminated or reduced in power after civil wars that sometimes were hard fought. But the public wearied of civil strife, especially after Japan's seizure of Manchuria. Thus, the government found it advisable to rely increasingly on procedures to extend the central authority by inducing regional leaders to conform by pressure, naming to prestigious posts, subsidies, or revenue adjustments. Yet execution of the policy was a huge task and took time. Many local or almost private armies were left that could not easily be eliminated. T.V. Soong thus excoriated the system after the debacle in resisting the Japanese drive into Jehol Province in 1933:

> The blame lies not so much with individuals but in the system which permits the existence of vast armies of ill-fed, ill-armed and ill-trained soldiery which in time of crisis degenerate into helpless mobs. . . . of the small band of competents [educated youth] very few have been drawn into the army. Until our military leaders could be made to discard 18th or 19th century conceptions of warfare and begin training a modern army in earnest, so long will the national defence be lacking.[1]

Rivals within the party, especially the Canton faction, staged several serious revolts. And throughout the Communists and the Japanese militarists had their own programs for China in conflict with those of the Nationalists.

The government's effort to consolidate power in the face of the repeated internal and external threats was costly and kept the finances in an almost constant state of crisis. Attention was diverted from the need for internal reforms and development. The protracted struggle with warlords and Communists and from 1931 with Japan made it harder for the government to create conditions that would have made the country less receptive to Communism. Chiang realized the importance of reconstruction and said that the anti-Communist effort should be 70 per cent political and 30 per cent military.

Concentration on consolidation and survival contributed to the neglect of agriculture where the problems were so huge. The leaders with their largely urban background were not oriented toward dealing fundamentally with rural problems, and their attitudes were slanted toward the landowning and financial interests. There was no serious effort to reform and develop the taxation of land, although about two-thirds of the national product came from agriculture.

The performance in modernization and development was necessarily spotty. Yet despite difficulties, the government was able to progress with important reforms, to plan actively for the future, and in the latter part of the prewar decade to obtain moderate resources at home and abroad for rehabilitation and development.

Of crucial importance was the effort of the Nationalists, begun soon after their takeover, to strengthen the finances far beyond what had ever before been seen in China. They built productive revenues, made arrangements to borrow domestically on a large scale, and created and developed the Central Bank. It is hard to find a more spectacular financial transformation than that from Peking's situation in 1927 and the Nationalists' first fiscal year, 1928-1929. The revenue available for disposal, after customs debt payments, grew from a few millions yearly to hundreds of millions. Later a decisive turning point was the currency reform of 1935, whose success in stabilizing exchange and checking deflation invigorated the economy and created stronger confidence in the future. Administratively during the decade, the government's offices were steadily improving in efficiency, and the Central Bank was playing a key part. The government, as personnel gained experience and confidence, was beginning to be able to act as a modern government should. The progress in banking, industry, and communications was noteworthy. While agriculture lagged, there were beginnings of improvement of the kind that could take hold and spread quickly.

Foreign administrative and technical aid and advice were greatly relied upon in the prewar decade. The Peking regimes had long had the help of foreign administrators and technicians in the Customs and Salt revenue services. During the prewar decade, these continued to give loyal and efficient service. Besides collecting and disposing of revenue, the Customs had for many years provided aids to navigation and helped with port and river improvements, and the Customs had started the postal service. Under the regime of higher tariffs, the Customs developed a service to protect against smuggling, which was effective as far as conditions permitted. The Nationalists continued the use of foreign personnel in these fields. However, they moved to integrate the services more closely into the government, and to substitute Chinese for foreigners in administrative and technical duties, including the most senior posts, as rapidly as they deemed nationals to be qualified. Also the Finance Ministry and Central Bank took over the handling of foreign debt service under procedures that Lynch and I helped to devise. In this matter and in the case of the Customs, the changes were made without infringing loan agreements.

The integration of the Sino-foreign Salt service into the Finance Ministry in 1928 involved changes inconsistent with the Reorganization Loan agreement of 1913. But the infringement was of small practical importance, because loan payments were being regularly made from customs revenue, to which these had previously been transferred under provisions of that agreement. The resumption of payments on other salt-secured foreign loans in 1928 and the notable improvement in administration of salt revenue benefited these loans. The prices of both customs secured and salt-secured foreign loans rose greatly between 1928 and 1937. Although the changes affecting the Customs service did not infringe agreements, there were nationalistic moves to alter the setup of the Salt service without regard to clearly implied commitments at the time of the settlement in 1936-1937 of several debts in arrears for which salt security was pledged. Minister Kung resisted these moves, but the pressure and intrigue continued within the Salt organization.

The Nationalists made much better use of foreign advice, in both civil and military affairs, than had their predecessors. The best results from foreign advisory and technical personnel were generally obtained through the work of those who stayed for periods of several years. They were thus able to get a real grasp of the problems, to gain the confidence of the officials with whom they worked, and also directly or indirectly to guide and train them. Much less was accomplished from the good, or sometimes bad, reports written by those staying for shorter periods—the reports were often merely filed.

The new government at once turned to Americans for financial advice. The United States had stood aside from the imperialistic acts of the European powers, Russia, and Japan in the taking of territory, and had little part in the establishment of settlements and concessions, although Americans accepted their privileges.[2]

The Soong-MacMurray treaty of 1928 was the first agreement for tariff autonomy and set a precedent for other countries. Also China's leaders hoped that financial rehabilitation would clear the way for an American loan. Sun Fo in his visit to the United States in the fall of 1928 took steps to engage the Kemmerer Commission of financial experts. The Commission made comprehensive proposals in 1929 for reform. Although some of these proposals became obsolete because of the onset of the depression, the slump in silver, the continuing civil war, and the Japanese aggression, others remained pertinent. The results of the Commission's work were mainly realized with the help of members engaged for further periods by the government.

The Finance Ministry under T. V. Soong started an excellent program of revenue building even before the capture of Peking. Soong induced the foreign tobacco and oil companies to pay taxes by offering a guarantee against further taxation in areas that were expanded as the government extended control. The policy of excise taxes on a few items of wide consumption was in the course of acceptance before the Kemmerer Commission came. In the field of taxation, Oliver C. Lockhart was able to provide valuable guidance in development of this policy and in improving administration, which was brought under a newly created Internal Revenue Administration. In tariff matters, his influence was for moderation and maximization of revenue. But here he was listened to less because of the inclination of the Ministry to raise various rates beyond the levels of greatest yield.

The operation of the Salt revenue administration presented great difficulties during the prewar decade because various local rulers wanted to keep all or most of the revenue. Soong devised the system of getting loan quotas from the districts, which worked well most of the time. He and Kung worked hard to make deals with the local rulers to extend central control, at times arranging subsidies in place of receipts from collections. Thus the better yield from improving administration benefited the national treasury. There was also considerable effort to get rid of long-established abuses in the salt trade. To this end, the government had great help from the foreign personnel, who felt less the pressures that bore so often on the Chinese administrators. Cleveland and later Lockhart, as foreign co-chiefs of the Salt service, and the foreign personnel cooperated with their Chinese associates to effect great improvement in operations.

In fiscal affairs foreign advice was specially important in bringing about collection of import duties from 1930 in terms of gold, at a time when silver was slumping sharply (Chapter 3). This action preserved the security of the foreign and internal loans and added many tens of millions to the government's free revenue. Previously the Central Bank had been little more than the government's fiscal agent. But after creation of the customs gold unit the Bank received a flow of foreign currencies. This had two major consequences. It enabled the Finance Ministry and the Bank to take over administration of foreign debt service from the Customs and foreign banks, thus avoiding the former aspects of a receivership. Also the Bank was able to gain experience in foreign exchange operations and to build up assets in foreign currencies. That proved of vital importance for management of the currency when monetary reform became possible in 1935.

Also foreign advice was of great importance in preparing the plans for the two reorganizations of the internal debt in 1932 and 1936 (Chapter 4). The first, forced by the Japanese invasion of Manchuria and the fighting at Shanghai, brought about savings of about C $100 million in 1932. The second was needed to buttress the currency reform of 1935, after acute depression and shrinkage of revenues, and saved about C $85 million in 1936.

These measures may be regarded as a substitute for inflationary finance. In particular, the government undertook, in connection with the currency reform of 1935, to avoid inflation and stabilize the finances. While the debt reorganizations were regrettable, such action was the choice of the lesser evil. The measures were vindicated by the rise of domestic bond prices, after an interlude, to higher levels and by an improved budgetary situation. It can be argued that the government should have stabilized the finances by spending less and taxing more. Both Ministers Soong and Kung strove for such a solution, but they could not avoid being confronted with the situations described here. In retrospect, I do not regret having proposed the solutions adopted in 1932 and 1936.

A further field where foreign advice was specially important concerned rehabilitation of debts in arrears (Chapter 5). In 1928, Soong announced resumption of service on the salt secured foreign issues, after devising the system of loan quotas from the districts. The Salt administration then in the first instance merely paid the oldest global payments in arrears without regard to priorities or distinctions between interest and principal. When the matter was brought to me in 1929 I proposed giving priority to arrears of interest, and clearing them as soon as practicable. That seemed calculated to benefit a larger number of bondholders and help China's credit more than to apply so large a part of the payments to pay a relatively few who held drawn bonds. The announced scheme adopting that basis was welcomed by the representatives of the bondholders, and resulted in early payment of interest arrears and of most arrears of principal before the hostilities supervened.

When plans for a general settlement of debts in arrears foundered, my plans for separate negotiation and settlement of the chief debts were based on doing what was feasible for the creditors while having regard for what it seemed that China could pay. The eventual settlements of these debts under charge of the

Finance Ministry and of that Ministry jointly with the Railway Ministry were quite similar to these plans.

Altogether, debts equivalent to about US $275 million were settled. The prices of all bonds consequently rose greatly, and in mid-1937, the best foreign loans were on about a 5 per cent yield basis, which was better than that of similar Japanese foreign obligations. By that time, most of the debts in arrears had been rehabilitated, and the rest would doubtless have been settled but for the war, except that settlements with Japanese creditors would have awaited changes in Japanese policy and actions vis-à-vis China.

In currency matters, foreign advice and support were essential, but could only be helpful when coupled with the Chinese contribution of ideas, understanding, and readiness to act decisively, especially on the part of Finance Minister Kung and Soong, then head of the Bank of China. The Kemmerer plan of reform was soon outdated by events, and his idea of selling silver to provide needed reserves became practicable only after the United States became a large buyer of silver. The upgrading of the standard silver dollar and abolition of the *tael* unit of value was mostly on Chinese initiative, although backed by the foreign advisers subsequent to Kemmerer's departure. The details of the change were worked out by a Sino-foreign group that Soong named. Sir Arthur Salter with his wealth of experience gave helpful advice during this period on the relation between silver and the depression.

The currency reform of 1935 depended for success on a carefully prepared plan and on Chinese readiness to act vigorously to cure an intolerable deflation, coupled with firm British support and buttressed by American purchase of silver. The presence of Sir Frederick W. Leith-Ross, Economic Adviser to the British Government, was crucial, bringing the aura of British financial prestige as well as his own competence. The immediate British issuance of a King's Regulation requiring British nationals to accept the legal tender notes instead of silver was a key factor in promoting confidence. The plan as to level of exchange, sale of silver to obtain reserves abroad, and action by the Central Bank to operate the reform was substantially what I had been advocating for months. In the final form, it embodied ideas contributed by Kung and Soong, staff members of the Central Bank and Bank of China, and Advisers Lynch and Lockhart. I described the plan to Leith-Ross immediately after his arrival, and he was in general accord with it. He and his associates Cyril Rogers and E. Hall-Patch helped by contributing ideas, stressing especially the reorganization of the Central Bank as a reserve bank and controlling governmental expenditure. Following the monetary reform, Leith-Ross explained that it was not his plan, but that he thought it good and promising of success. In 1936, Kung named a Sino-foreign committee, of which Rogers, Lynch, and I were members, to prepare a plan to convert the Central Bank into a Central Reserve Bank. The government adopted the committee's plan with few alterations in June 1937, but outbreak of fighting prevented action.

The currency reform of 1935 was followed by a remarkable economic recovery, helped by bountiful crops. Agricultural prices also improved, with benefit in the countryside. The success of the reform was a major factor in the betterment of the overall situation, politically as well as economically, in 1936-1937.

By 1937, the government was becoming more and more able to handle financial problems effectively. I viewed my function as trying to work myself out of a job. In the spring of 1937, I arranged to shorten my contract so that either party could terminate it on 90 days' notice. I felt that I would be able to leave in view of the progress of currency reform, internal debt reorganization, and settlement of debts in arrears. Also nationalism was becoming more assertive, and I felt that the time to withdraw was approaching. But when the hostilities began I felt obligated to stay for the duration.

In disaster relief and rehabilitation foreign personnel, partly on a volunteer basis and backed by foreign contributions, had a chief part in the earlier period. But during the prewar decade, Chinese governmental personnel and financial support and management became increasingly important, along with private Chinese participation. At the time of the great flood of 1931, Minister Soong through the National Flood Relief Commission energetically gave effect to the proposals which Baker and I developed. The conduct of the program was a splendid example of cooperation by governmental and private agencies and individuals, both Chinese and foreign. Administration after the early weeks was under the excellent direction of Sir John Hope Simpson whom the League of Nations recommended.

In economic development, contributions came from many technicians, Chinese and foreign, in the fields of transportation, communications, river and port improvement, water conservancy, development and reforms in agriculture, and expansion of industry. These persons provided numerous plans to which the government gave effect in part in the prewar decade and to some extent during and after the war. These plans, and some Chinese personnel involved in their preparation and partial execution, became available to the Communists as a highly valuable nucleus for their programs.

J. Lossing Buck and his associates, many of the Chinese whom he had trained, pioneered the collection and analysis of data on agriculture. With governmental support, which was all too scanty, they set up systems of statistics and reporting. They also promoted the introduction of better seeds, and pesticides, agricultural extension, and cooperation especially for increased rural credit facilities. The results would have been increasingly felt had time been granted for changes that were bound to be a matter of decades.

In preparing for systematic planning and promotion of development the creation of the National Economic Council was of great importance. The idea came from Sir Arthur Salter, and Generalissimo Chiang and Soong and their associates accepted it avidly. The European experts of the League of Nations, who came under the auspices of the NEC, were well-qualified. They helped especially in planning and to some extent execution of road building, agriculture and rural reforms, irrigation and water conservancy, public health, and education.

In devising a procedure for financing development, credit goes to Jean Monnet for helping to create the China Development Finance Corporation, with the strong support of Chiang, Soong, and Kung. This agency was beginning to prove its flexibility and usefulness in attracting foreign capital in cooperation with Chinese capital when the war so rudely put an end to the pending projects—the chief of which were for extension and improvement of the railways. The CDFC in a way supplanted the old Consortium that China throughout rejected. The Consortium was about to be dissolved in 1937, and it lapsed after hostilities began.

In civil aviation, the Ministry of Communications with cooperation of foreign capital and technical personnel developed a network of airways that was of great and growing importance for the economy and a factor for national consolidation. The China National Aviation Corporation in which Pan-American

Airways had about 45 per cent interest was a form of Sino-foreign cooperation that worked well but was threatened shortly before the war by pressures from the military for nationalization. Eurasia with Sino-German cooperation was a lesser enterprise that also contributed to betterment of air communications.

The foreign role in military affairs should be noted because German advisers in particular helped greatly to strengthen the armies under reliable central control, which provided an important factor for national unification and peace and order. Their influence was for better training, discipline, and equipment and for elimination of abuses that were wasteful and sapped the military strength. In military aviation, the unofficial Jouett mission trained well a nucleus of men for a modern-type force. The mission's work was undermined and brought to a close, unhappily for China, by introduction of the rival Italian mission accepted at Mussolini's urging and which did more harm than good for China.

Foreign private capital with partial govermental guarantee took a growing part in 1934 to 1937 in providing funds to China in association with Chinese capital. The foreign capital was largely in the form of credits for railway construction and improvement but to some extent for industry. British and German interests were specially active, the latter especially under the Sino-German barter agreement. The Chinese capital came from governmental and private banks and also from issues of the Railway Reconstruction Loan. Foreign credit used in this period was equivalent to about US $80 million, and the carrying out of agreements concluded or in contemplation for railway and industrial purposes would have raised the total to about US $200 million had not war come. In addition, a loan of £20 million by private British interests for currency support was then under negotiation in accord with the British government.

In the promotion of development, American governmental and private participation lagged much behind that from Europe. The Department of State was slow to recognize the greatly improved situation in China and also feared a confrontation with Japan. But American private firms, stimulated by the National Foreign Trade Council, showed interest, which gave rise to the Forbes economic mission of 1935. The resulting project was to create a syndicate of American firms with governmental support. But the Department of State discouraged this move. Only in the spring of 1937 did serious American interest appear. Had not fighting begun in mid-1937, substantial American private investment, notably through export of capital goods, was likely with backing of the Export-Import Bank and acquiescence of the Department of State.

The effects of foreign investment on China have been a field of controversy. It has been charged under the Manchus, and the Nationalists, and now the Communists, that it was imperialistic, damaged handicrafts and agriculture, retarded growth of Chinese industry, and drained away wealth. Chi-ming Hou after broad study of these matters reached the conclusion, with which I agree, that foreign investment on the whole was beneficial. It was a force for innovation by bringing modern technology, providing scarce capital, stimulating private Chinese enterprise to develop modern-type industry and trade, and helping to train Chinese workers, technicians, and managers. Hou sees no reason to think that traditional production declined absolutely, although it may have declined relatively. The idea that foreign capital could be beneficial is implicit in the views of Sun Yat-sen and Chiang Kai-shek. While opposing what they regarded as foreign economic oppression, they favored use of foreign capital —without foreign control—to aid development.

There was considerable drain abroad of funds from China after 1895 because of payments on loans floated in Europe to discharge the indemnity to Japan after the war of 1894-1895 and on the Boxer Indemnity of 1901. But conclusions on this situation must be qualified because in the thirties Chinese were estimated to hold perhaps one-third of the foreign loans, and most of the Boxer Indemnity was remitted for China's benefit. The burden of external debt payments relative to the balance of international payments was much less serious than the budgetary problem of providing the local currency for debt payments, chiefly on the heavy internal debt.

Foreign investment did not go into production of agricultural and mineral goods for export and cause a lopsided development as in some less developed countries. Rather it was related to development of foreign trade, railways, shipping, utilities, light industries, mining for mostly local consumption, and financial services. There was little foreign investment in industry and trade outside of the treaty ports,which Tawney called "islands of privilege."[3] Indications from partial data were that foreign firms on the average were reinvesting in China 30 to 40 per cent of profits.

In summary, China's nation-building effort in the prewar decade shows what can be done primarily by national initiative, aided by foreign personnel and a moderate amount of external resources. The resourcefulness and drive of the leaders in the face of great odds was an outstanding feature. They built up the national finances from a level of a few million dollars available yearly to a budget around C $1 billion that was becoming nationwide. They introduced basic fiscal and monetary reforms. Inflation was shunned and the currency was stabilized without overvaluation, thereby ushering in a period of accelerated progress. The government left the economy fairly free, while taking the initiative in planning and promoting economic development. The government was changing by evolution rather than revolution various inherited servitudes and practices that interfered with China being master in her own house. The government was developing the country's infrastructure notably transport and telecommunications. The body of trained civil servants was growing. There was considerable progress in public health activities and promotion of education. Chinese private enterprise was becoming more and more active, with increasing experience and know-how in industry and finance. In mobilizing private Chinese capital for productive investment, there were modest beginnings.

In contributing to progress in the prewar decade, the advice and administrative aid by foreign personnel clearly played a most important part. Without them and the extent of their effective use the course of events would have been quite different, as the record set out in the preceding pages shows.

Large-scale foreign technical and material aid to less developed countries, such as has taken place in the postwar years, did not then exist. China received no grants apart from remitted Boxer Indemnity, which still consisted of payments by China. The external resources provided were only moderate but were most timely. The American flood relief credit of US $9 million was crucial for rehabilitation of a key area of central China when the government's survival was in the balance. And the US $17 million realized from the Cotton and Wheat Loan of 1933 gave a thrust to development, through the work of the National Economic Council, and provided a strong boost to morale. The American purchases of silver from the Central Bank involved no credit. But they gave support to the currency at a critical time, after the silver-buying policy had wrought great harm to China's economy by draining away reserves and aggravating an already acute deflation. Foreign private investment was not a chief factor in much of the decade, but its growth in 1934 to 1937 stimulated by governmental credit guarantees abroad was becoming a strong factor for development.

China's prewar experience affords a useful lesson with regard to postwar efforts to promote the progress of the less developed countries. China was not seeking instant development without effort. There was indeed some overemphasis of the potential of foreign financial aid. But this was outweighed by the strong national urge for modernization, the growing willingness and capacity of the government to encourage and support a strong internal effort, and the readiness of China's leaders to accept foreign expert advice. Had peace continued, China had the prospect of great benefit from the inflow of foreign funds and technology.

Contemporary appraisals

Observers in 1937 were impressed by China's progress and prospects. But in previous years many comments were pessimistic. Until 1936-1937, American diplomatic officials in China as well as the State Department were not hopeful of the government's viability. They were influenced by continuing internal dissension and lack of unity, financial and economic difficulties, delay in taking action about debts in arrears, laxness of some officials, and Japanese pressure. Although the foreign embassies had offices in Nanking, the ambassadors still kept official residences in the Legation Quarter in Peiping. Meanwhile, the action in modernization and development centered mainly in the Yangtze Valley and South China. The atmosphere of the Legation Quarter tended to make for slowness to appreciate how greatly China was changing from the older days. Even two months after the currency reform of November 1935, Ambassador Johnson considered the situation "even more precarious" than in mid-1935, and the reform's "probable effect . . . not regarded with optimism." In mid-1936 when South China elements revolted he thought that developments were "working for the disintegration of China."[4]

The American appraisal changed radically during the year preceding the outbreak of hostilities in mid-1937. Factors causing the change were the clear success of the currency reform, progress of settlement of debts in arrears, progress in economic rehabilitation and development, the government's ascendency in

South China after collapse of the revolt of mid-1936, the defeat of the Japanese puppets in Suiyuan Province later in that year, and the way in which Chinese opinion rallied to Chiang after his release from the Sian kidnaping in December.

In 1937, American official reports became optimistic. In April, Johnson said that "An observer ... cannot but be impressed by the energy with which the Chinese government is pushing its program of economic reconstruction on all fronts, agricultural, industrial and communications." Johnson believed that "an era of economic development under National Government leadership has begun." The long-term credits from Britain, Germany, and France recognized this, he said, and queried whether the United States "should not participate more actively." The currency reform he now considered a success, and general conditions were improving. He said that "there is no armed opposition to the government anywhere, except as instigated by Japan," and the Japanese elections of April 30 might indicate moderation of what he termed "the policy of armed invasion." He thought it probable that "China's economic, social and political development is being accelerated to a marked degree by the fact and fear of Japanese encroachment."[5]

In June, he again reported optimistically. "The ideal of national unity," he said, "is rapidly becoming a part of China's national consciousness." He saw indications that the people "have come to realize the necessity, for their own salvation, of joining together in forming a real nation under effective government." But he cautioned that the results of the Sian kidnaping of Chiang, settlement of which involved the beginning of collaboration with the Communists, were yet uncertain.[6]

The American Commercial Attache stated the following in his *Annual Economic Report* for 1937:

> At the beginning of 1937, China faced a more favorable outlook in internal political unity, currency stabilization, economic reconstruction, agricultural betterment and improved social and cultural conditions than for many years past ... An even more glowing picture concerning the future of commercial and economic advancement in China was presented on July first.

He cited the improvement of communications; the interest of foreign countries in granting long-term credits; the linking of China with the United States and Europe by regular air services and radio-telephone; and the increase of imports in the first half year by 45 per cent over that period in 1936, including a large rise of automotive imports. Specially important was "the advancement in industrial expansion which ... characterized the country as a whole."[7]

The British Commercial Counsellor in China was also optimistic. In the spring of 1937 he wrote: "That Chinese private interests can adapt themselves to modern economic needs is shown by the growth of a number of enterprises, such as Chinese insurance companies, the flour industry, the Chinese cotton industry, the electrical industry and many others." He noted "the increasing, justified confidence which the Chinese themselves as well as the world at large have in the future of this country, a confidence based on the remarkable growth of stability achieved in recent years and the improved political, financial and economic conduct of affairs—government and private."[8]

The London *Economist* commented in July 1937, just after fighting began in North China:

> All observers seem to be agreed that China has been pulling round with remarkable success during the last year or two. The Central Government's authority has been becoming rapidly more effective over an ever wider area, for example in the Far South. The financial and economic condition of the country has been distinctly improving . . . Have the Japanese army now made up their minds to swallow China whole before she is completely herself again? If so, they will probably find . . . that it is easier to start a war than to wind it up.[9]

Also I venture to quote my own appraisal, written shortly after the outbreak of hostilities in 1937:

> The ten years prior to June 1937, a brief period in the life of a nation, had seen in China a transformation with few parallels in history. In 1927 the internal situation was chaotic. The country was torn by civil war and ravaged by banditry. There was no central authority to speak for the country. Railways were disrupted and largely in the hands of warlords. Roads and airways were almost nonexistent. There was no uniformity of currency, no decimal monetary system. Mediaeval fiscal practices were the general rule, with only the rudiments of a system of modern financial administration. The government could not strengthen itself because of inadequacy of revenue sources, and could not develop adequate revenues because of lack of authority. Internationally, China was viewed as a liability and numerous schemes were proposed for dealing with the "problem of China" and for accomplishing measures of reconstruction.

> The success of the Nationalist movement broke the vicious circle and opened the way for the soundest type of reconstruction—a building-up based primarily on China's own efforts. These ten years have seen the spread of the Central Government's authority to all parts of the country. Warlords have been defeated, have thrown in their hands or have become loyal members of the government. Although communism had not been entirely eliminated, it had ceased to be a factor of first importance by the middle of 1937. Banditry was being gradually exterminated. The railway system was restored and its administration improved, new lines were built, and a comprehensive scheme of development was being carried out. Air lines covered in hours distances previously requiring days or weeks. Currency reform had become a reality instead of an aspiration. Adequate public revenues and a modern system of financial administration were being developed. The reforms of the past ten years bear comparison with the financial measures adopted in the early days of the American Republic.
>
> On the whole, China's progress had acquired a momentum that was remaking the country and carrying it along in spite of difficulties. China was becoming a stronger factor in the world situation, and potentially a notable addition to the stabilizing forces in a period of extreme world-wide difficulty. In this situation came the Japanese seizure of Peiping and Tientsin and the hostilities following the despatch of the Japanese fleet to Shanghai. The full results of these measures of aggression are for time to show. There can be no doubt, however, that the interruption of China's progress in self-development is one of the great tragedies of history. [10]

Besides Western appraisals, we may cite that of Russia, as evidenced by policy in 1936 and the early part of the Sino-Japanese war. Russia, facing a threat from Japan, recognized that Chiang was the symbol of China's nationalism and her growing unification and progress. At the time of Chiang's kidnaping at Sian in December 1936, Russia urged successfully that he be released unharmed. Despite Chiang's stalwart anti-Communism, Russia saw that he was the outstanding leader. Ambassador Bogomolov told an American journalist in Shanghai in April 1937 that the Soviet view was that Russia "would do well to support the Nanking Government as the stabilizing and paramount force" in China. When the hostilities began, Russia was prompt to give large aid to the National Government, and gave no material aid of consequence to the Chinese Communists until the end of the war.[11]

The balance sheet

Appraisal, after a generation, of China's nation-building effort and its status on the eve of hostilities in 1937 shows clearly negative and positive factors.

The government inherited in 1927-1928 a situation of great difficulty. Almost continuous conditions of emergency confronted it during the prewar decade. Some measures of rehabilitation, reform, and development such as fiscal and monetary reforms showed results fairly soon. But others such as improvement of agriculture and of the level of public administration required many years. The stormy ten-year period saw progress in some areas and promising beginnings—but also failures and frustrations. Ambassador Nelson Johnson once remarked to me that the National Government never had a real chance to show what it could do.

Surprisingly, much postwar comment of scholars as well as publicists either dismisses the decade as mere continuance of an era of confusion or ignores the notable accomplishments during the period and the promising situation in 1936-1937 as described in the preceding pages. It has been and is the fashion of many both in academic circles and more widely to say that the government's tenure on the mainland was an abject failure and that its fall was inevitable. It has, for example, been called a "miserable remnant of feudalism."[12] Many more similar comments could be cited. The arguments are that the government was corrupt and exploitative, dominated by militarists, gangsters, business men and "bureaucratic capitalism"; that it wasted money for civil wars to protect its position; that it worked through a group at the top and failed to develop an image and ideology that gained broad support of intellectuals and the masses; that rural areas were ruled in the interest of landlords and moneylenders; that social conditions in both rural and urban areas were dreadful, with the ruling classes unmindful of the welfare of the masses for whom Sun Yat-sen had concern; and that the humiliations of which the unequal treaties were a symbol could not yield to evolution, as in Japan, but only to revolution.

Many of the criticisms contain a measure of validity. The government's overall position left much to be desired. By past standards, the government was a great improvement. Nevertheless, China suffered from bad government. The military unduly dominated policy at the national level. There was too much of "the old school tie"—dependence on political and military veterans of the revolution. Their formal loyalty was reliable, but all too often they were incompetent, reactionary, and/or corrupt. Too little effort was made to enlist men of good will from all elements and regions. Serious thought of how to broaden the government's base was little in evidence. Progress in administration was taking place and many members of the government strove for high standards. But even the best branches of government were burdened with superfluous personnel—analogous to the many family shops that were run to see how many they could support. Pay of officials and employees generally was so low as to offer temptation to "squeeze." Most efforts to set up tight staffing with adequate pay foundered because of opposition and inertia. On the whole, the government was proving a poor organizer. A basic weakness was the lack of involvement of the mass of the people in the processes of government, a program greatly developed by the Communists. The government failed to identify with the people, but rather stood above them. Clearly the tutelage which Sun Yat-sen envisaged would have to continue for some time.

In the hinterland progress in reform of government lagged. The provincial and local governments, with some notable exceptions, made less advance than the National Government. An observer who traveled widely in outlying parts of Central and South China in the winter of 1936-1937 reported a lack of public spirit and even obstructionism on the part of the "small-official class," who tended to consider themselves mere jobholders and not public servants. But he noted that "The firmer the control of the Central Government over a province, the greater the progress it has made." He was impressed by regional language differences, which tended to cause the people to regard other Chinese with a different dialect as strangers and foreigners. He saw overpopulation as the greatest obstacle to improving the lot of the masses, who had a "desperate struggle for existence." Banditry he found rife, with most local military leaders doing little about it.[13]

The government's base was diverse. The military in general and some others were authoritarian. They tended to stress the Confucian virtues. Some were influenced by the fascist experiments in Germany and Italy. Military elements tended to be allied with the rural gentry and landlords. The civilian leaders of the government were more progressive and more in line with modern trends. Many of them had received education in the West, especially in the United States. Their influence was for reforms and modernization, economic development, and sound finance. They were allied with the urban interests of bankers, traders, and industrialists. Some intellectuals were in the government or supporting it; some were critical but broadly in favor of a free system; and some were Communists or well to the left. The government was having difficulty with the younger generation. The students were strongly nationalistic, but the activists' aims were largely impracticable, especially in wanting the government to resist Japan at all costs even though unready. A minority of students joined the Communists.

Moreover, the five-yuan organization of government proved a poor structure. The effective decision-making and operating organs were the Executive Yuan and its Ministries, and the National Military Council. The other Yuans lagged far behind the Executive Yuan in importance. The Judicial Yuan had a logical place, but the Control Yuan and Examination Yuan had little influence. The Legislative Yuan was not really a representative body; rather it was a sort of politically constituted committee that, in a period of tutelage of uncertain duration, could and at times did work at cross purposes with those responsible for operations. It did, however, do useful work from time to time in drafting laws.

The rule of China in the prewar decade has commonly been called that of the Kuomintang, to which under the Organic Law the National Government was subservient. According to my observation the Kuomintang Party as such was far less important than the government as a factor in national affairs in those years, and was tending to decrease in importance and become almost nominal. Most leading officials but not all were members of the party. But they operated as a group better described as the National Government than as the Kuomintang.[14] (The reader will note few references to the party in this account of the financial and economic record.) In local affairs, however, the Kuomintang played a larger part than in national affairs.

Chiang Kai-shek, while the outstanding personality and leader, was not a dictator in the ordinary sense. His word had great and often decisive weight as to governmental policies and action. But, in a government reaching for nation-wide control, his task of leadership was delicate and difficult. It called for great political skill, and the government was by no means only his shadow, as some writers have suggested. His prewar accomplishments in leading the drive for unification and progress were so impressive that, had he died before the breakdown of the wartime and postwar years, there would have been little controversy in according him recognition as one of the great constructive leaders of his time.

After the Nationalists' takeover in 1928 Chiang and his associates had to give priority to consolidating the new regime and unifying with a stable government, rather than to economic and social reforms. Building a national state had to come first. The alternative was reversion to the chaos of the warlord era.

Unification during the decade involved military action that was costly and diverted resources from economic and social development. Here there is a dilemma. Without military action against the revolts would the country have fallen apart again as in the twenties? Or would alternative use of resources have been feasible in a way that would have checked political and social unrest? It is hard to be sure. I can only record that at the time I was convinced that the militarists and politicians who were rival claimants to power were much inferior to the government's leaders and lacking in ability to build a strong nation. The Communists were disciplined and determined but would have brooked no real compromise, and in mid-1937 did not appear to be a significant military threat. I felt that more attention should have been given to making a model area of the region immediately tributary to Shanghai, with the expectation that the influence of accomplishments there would radiate into the rest of the country, with expanded central authority. Under actual circumstances, occasional use of force to prevent disruption and promote unification seemed the best available procedure. Whatever the faults of the action taken, it was a notable achievement to reverse the previous trend to separatism, and attain the degree of unification reached by 1937.

The government's social policy was certainly inadequate, and the rural situation was particularly acute. But the civil wars of the twenties and 1930-1931, together with the deflation that followed—aggravated by the American silver-buying policy—were important causes of the distress so widely noted. These causes have been underplayed at the expense of the commonly heard charge of exploitation. Certainly drastic changes were essential to improve the lot of the rural masses, notably control of the increase of population, a measure not generally agitated anywhere in the prewar period. The government's program did not involve fundamental change in the system, but rather reforms through rent limitation, encouragement of owner-operated farms, fairer taxation, technical improvements, and rural credit. The measures adopted and contemplated were good, and could have produced considerable improvement, given time. But action was slow, there was opposition by vested interests, and there was not enough time to show major results before the war.

In China, a special situation resulted from the humiliations of many decades—the seizures of territory by European powers, Russia, and Japan, and the unequal treaties granting special rights and privileges to foreigners. The government made a good beginning in recovery of China's national rights by negotiation and evolutionary changes. It recovered tariff autonomy, arranged for payment of certain taxes by foreign enterprises, and integrated into the Finance Ministry the Customs and Salt revenue services, with their partly foreign personnel, and the administration of debt service. Little could be done, however, about the foreign settlements and concessions, leased territories, and the extra-territorial rights of foreigners. Continuation of these understandably irked nationalistic sentiments, although the arrangements originated in part because China wanted to segregate and not be bothered with the "barbarians". On balance these arrangements were temporarily advantageous to the economy, and to change them was difficult in the prewar years. Japan was in no mood to give up any privileges but rather wanted to increase them for her special benefit. And the friendly foreign governments were not prepared to give up the rights pending improvement in China's administration of justice and maintenance of public order. But Germany and Austro-Hungary had given up their rights by treaty after World War I, and Russia had voluntarily relinquished them in 1924. The government in 1937 hoped to recover these rights not by drastic action but by evolution, as happened in Japan around the turn of the century.

A far more stubborn problem concerned the right of foreign powers to station troops on Chinese soil. This became mainly an issue with Japan, and it was the clash of Japanese and Chinese troops at the Marco Polo Bridge on July 7, 1937, that ushered in eight years of bitter warfare. As to this problem, during the prewar decade China could only play for time to gain greater economic and military strength, and hope for a basic shift in the international situation.

The Pacific War enabled China to end the unequal treaties. At the war's close the relics of imperialism had disappeared except for the position of Hong Kong, which the Communists have not seriously tried to change, and the minor area of Macao.

The extreme xenophobia of China since the war is rooted to a considerable extent in the nationalism that the war stimulated so greatly. Also the Communists have strengthened it by intense propaganda; it has been excited by the wars in Korea and Vietnam and friction with Russia. Before the Sino-Japanese hostilities active nationalistic feelings were certainly growing. But then the leaders of the government and public felt a need for the friendship and aid of foreign nations, partly because of Japan's attitude and partly to promote national development. There was in 1937 a real prospect that China would become a stablilizing factor in Asia.

A potential cause of weakness, which has not received much attention from critics, was the possibility of over-straining the finances. The movement for development was gaining so much momentum in 1937 that it could have overstrained the budget and led to financial excesses of the kind that have vexed so many less developed nations in the postwar years. The currency reform with a managed currency opened the possibility of immoderate creation of credit with resulting inflation. It was conceivable that this would have happened, with unhappy consequences such as have afflicted in the later period advanced as well as less developed countries.

While in mid-1937 there was a good chance of reasonable stability for some time, inadequate attention was being given to providing the internal resources needed for development. As to the public sector, large foreign credits for railways and industries were pending. These could not have been used without expending sums of the same order of size in local currency. The existing tax system could not easily have been expanded to cover these costs. How to mobilize resources from the agricultural sector that provided close to two-thirds of the national product was a thorny problem that was hardly faced.

The problem of obtaining a surplus from China's largely subsistence economy, with pressure of excessive population, was bound to remain stubborn. The rate of savings in the prewar decade was relatively low. A high rate of savings was difficult to attain in a brief time without the sort of ruthless authoritarianism practiced later on the mainland. Conclusions as to the Communist performance since 1949 must be imperfect and partly conjectural because of suppression of quantitative data. The industrial growth in 1952-1959 was clearly remarkable. Yet the overall record of the economy for two decades was tarnished by blunders and giving primacy to politics and dogma over economics. A recent study indicates that as of 1969 India's performance, without harsh compulsion, compared well with that of Communist China.[15] Had the Nationalists been granted the opportunity, their past record and resourcefulness suggest that they could have found means to promote sustained growth within the framework of a fairly free economic system.

In several important respects the Nationalists were developing the modern-type structure necessary for building a strong nation with a good rate of growth in a fairly open society. The country was being tied together more closely by improvement of telecommunications, radio, and transport. Favorable factors in the private sector were the progress of banking (including spread of branches in the interior), the beginnings of a capital market at Shanghai, growing attention to the needs of the rural economy, and the trend toward a nation-wide market. Primary and advanced education and literacy were improving, although at a rate that would have taken much time to overcome the overwhelming illiteracy and general backwardness.[16] Ways to improve agriculture were becoming well understood, and there was a good potential for gradual growth of output. Industry also had the potential for continuing the growth already under way. The government was gaining strength and experience and improving the level of administration. Growth of a modern-type nucleus of armed forces under central control with increased mobility worked to maintain internal peace and strengthen the government.

China's transformation in the prewar decade shows conclusively that the Nationalist nation-building effort cannot be called a failure. Whatever the government's weaknesses, by 1937 it survived a series of acute crises, consolidated its position in most of the country after putting down regional separatists, developed the nucleus of a strong army under central control, was able to speak internationally for China, built up the revenues almost from scratch to about C $1 billion (about US $300 million), organized a budgetary and administrative system, developed a market for internal borrowing, settled most debts in arrears, reformed the currency system and coinage on a nationwide basis, organized and developed a central bank, rehabilitated and improved transport and communications, began agricultural reforms, and had under way a growing and promising program of development in which both domestic and foreign capital and technical aid participated. Although the economy as a whole showed little growth in the decade because of the great weight of traditional agriculture, handicrafts, and transport, the aggregate should not obscure the great progress in many fields. Compounded yearly growth rates in 1927 to 1936 (Table 27) were 9.4 per cent for electric power, 8.4 to 17.1 per cent for modern-type communications with air communications growing spectacularly from nothing, and for a limited but representative group of industries including utilities and mining (in 1931 to 1936) 6.7 per cent. For bank deposits the rate was 15.9 per cent, with slightly more coverage but with relatively little net price change in the period. These growth rates were accomplished despite worldwide depression, when most economies were deteriorating or only slowly recovering.

Was the fall of the Nationalist Government inevitable, as various persons have asserted with a sort of Marxist determinism? Certainly in mid-1937 there was no appearance of internal breakdown but rather growing strength. The government had strong backing of nationalistic sentiment, especially after the surprising degree of success in resisting the Japanese attack at Shanghai in 1932. This was qualified by the views of many who wanted stronger resistance to Japan's encroachment even though China was far from ready for so grave a step. Ambassador Johnson reported in May 1937 that it was the prevailing idea in China that "Chiang's leadership is necessary to the nation's survival".[17]

While China's internal situation appeared stabilized as of mid-1937, there were two major uncertainties. The consequences of the United Front with the Communists, following Chiang's release from the kidnaping at Sian at the end of 1936, were yet to be revealed. And there was the threat from Japan—although that seemed to be easing after the success of moderate elements in Japan's election in the spring of 1937.

No one can say with assurance what might have been in

China. Had no major war come, there was in 1937, I believe, no more reason to expect the government's overthrow than there is today to expect radical revolution in the many advanced countries experiencing acute social unrest and student agitation. The government indeed lacked representative institutions, was authoritarian, often suppressed dissent, and was understandably rough in dealing with attempted subversion. Today, apart from Western Europe, most of North America, Australasia, India, and Japan, a similar situation characterizes the governments of most countries, and democracy as we know it is absent. Most of the less developed countries are plagued by various forms of age-old abuses and exploitation, inadequate social concern, and lack of effective programs of social welfare. Many of these countries have political revolutions of one kind or another from time to time, often with little more than a shift from one governing group to another, and sometimes a social revolution but only rarely Communism. Whether deep-rooted ills can be remedied without drastic change is often controversial. But when orderly evolution can take place, even though its processes may be slow and the extent of progress often discouraging, it can avoid the overwhelming excesses and injustices that inevitably accompany revolution.

The prospect in China as it appeared on the eve of the hostilities in mid-1937 was for evolutionary change and growth. Certainly China was then progressing on a broad front, with no apparent likelihood of collapse. But then came the holocaust of eight years of warfare. As to the consequences, I cannot do better than quote what I wrote in 1963:

> Clearly the causes of Nationalist collapse on the mainland were rooted in events of the war. The causes comprise Japanese aggression, Russia's operations, the acts and omissions of China and China's friends, and the aggression of the Chinese Communists.[18]

Appendixes

Appendix 1

Receipts and expenditures from July 1, 1928 to June 30, 1937[a]

	1929	1930	1931	1932	1933	1934	1935	1936	1937
	Receipts for years ending June 30, millions								
Revenue									
Customs	C$179	C$276	C$313	C$370	C$326	C$352	C$353	C$272	C$379
Salt	30	122	150	144	158	177	167	184	197
Consolidated taxes									
Rolled tobacco	28[b]	37	46	62	54	71	68	89	110
Cotton yarn			2	17	15	18	16	23	23
Flour	2	4	4	6	6	6	5	6	5
Matches			1	3	4	5	9	10	10
Cement				1	1	2	3	3	5
Cured tobacco						4	4	4	5
Tobacco and wine tax	4	7	9	8	10	13	11	15	15
Stamp tax	3	5	6	5	5	8	7	10	9
Income tax									7
Mining tax						2	4	4	4

Continued

Appendix 1 (Continued)

Receipts and expenditures from July 1, 1928 to June 30, 1937[a]

	1929	1930	1931	1932	1933	1934	1935	1936	1937
	Receipts for years ending June 30, millions								
Bank note tax					3	2	2	2	
Collections by provincial governments	77[c]	11	4		5			2	
Government property receipts						3	2	9	3
Government enterprise receipts[d]				1	20	18	61	67	13
Government administrative receipts						3	11	12	8
Profit on government business enterprises[d]		1	1	2	2	2	1	10	9
Miscellaneous	12	21	25	15	5	4	21	78[e]	68
	334	484	561	633	614	689	745	801	870
Refunded revenues (–), and recovery from suspense (+)		- 1	- 3	-14		- 1		+16	
	334	484	558	619	614	689	745	817	870

Continued

Appendix 1 (Continued)

Receipts and expenditures from July 1, 1928 to June 30, 1937[a]

	1929	1930	1931	1932	1933	1934	1935	1936	1937
(totals brought over from previous page)				Receipts for years ending June 30, millions					
	334	484	558	619	614	689	745	817	870
Proceeds from borrowing									
Domestic bonds and treasury notes	69	91	193	125	26	80	164	148	223
Bank loans and overdrafts	32	10	24	5	86	91	36[f]	128	113
Cotton-wheat loan of 1933						8	25		
Cash balance at beginning of fiscal year:									
Customs and Salt services						26	40	73	
Depositories						2	19	17	45[g]
Total	C$434	C$585	C$775	C$749	C$726	C$896	C$1031	C$1182	C$1251

Continued

Appendix 1 (Continued)

Receipts and expenditures from July 1, 1928 to June 30, 1937[a]

	1929	1930	1931	1932	1933	1934	1935	1936	1937
	Expenditures for years ending June 30, millions								
Party	C$ 4	C$ 5	C$ 5	C$ 4	C$ 5	C$ 6	C$ 6	C$ 8	C$ 7
Civil expenses									
National Government Council	4	2	2	2	2	3			
Executive Yuan and subsidiary organs	22	30	30	23	36	2			
Legislative Yuan and subsidiary organs	0.5	1	1	0.6	1	2			
Supervisory Yuan and subsidiary organs	0.4	0.6	1	0.8	1	2			
Judicial Yuan and subsidiary organs	0.5	0.4	0.1			1			
Examination Yuan and subsidiary organs	0.2	0.6	1	0.6	1	1			
Other civil establishments			5	2	3	5			
National Government Council and subsidiary organs							16	15	18

Continued

Appendix 1 (Continued)

Receipts and expenditures from July 1, 1928 to June 30, 1937[a]

	1929	1930	1931	1932	1933	1934	1935	1936	1937
	Expenditures for years ending June 30, millions								
Interior	C$	C$	C$	C$	C$	C$ 4	C$ 5	C$ 13	C$ 13
Foreign affairs						10	9	11	10
Financial		45	60	66	55	72	69	67	64
Education and cultural						13	32	37	42
Judicial							4	4	3
Industrial						2	7	7	3
Communications						5	7	6	5
Mongolian and Tibetan affairs						2	2	3	2
Reconstruction						7	26	88	54
Capital for government banks	20						74		
Capital for other government enterprises							1	33	29
Subsidies, provincial and local	4	6	19	23	29	26	55	99	86
Subsidies, other	1	1	0.3	0.4	2	6			

Continued

Appendix 1 (Continued)

Receipts and expenditures from July 1, 1928 to June 30, 1937[a]

	1929	1930	1931	1932	1933	1934	1935	1936	1937
				Expenditures for years ending June 30, millions					
Transfers to local authorities from the Salt Revenue Inspectorate		C$ 36	C$ 48	C$ 48	C$ 37	C$ 23			
Transfers to Special Funds from the Salt Revenue Inspectorate				1	1	1			
Compensation and awards						1	C$ 2	C$ 2	C$ 3
Famine relief		10		2	2	4	1		
Miscellaneous	C$ 1								
Military expenses, current fiscal year	147	245	312	255	262	327	330	390	521
Military expenses, previous fiscal years				49	59	46	58		
Military expenses, disbursed directly by provinces	62								
Miscellaneous	1			1					

Continued

Appendix 1 (Continued)

Receipts and expenditures from July 1, 1928 to June 30, 1937[a]

	1929	1930	1931	1932	1933	1934	1935	1936	1937
					Expenditures for years ending June 30, millions				
Debt service									
Loans	C$ 121	C$ 159	C$ 241	C$ 239	C$ 170	C$ 203	C$	C$	C$
Domestic bonds							141	186	192
Foreign loans							62	62	63
Bank loans and overdraft							30	5	7
Indemnity	39	41	49	31	40	42	32	36	38
Debt readjustment fund							5	5	5
Refund of principal and interest on bonds and notes held by Treasury							– 32		
Net additions to reserves and suspense items, less refunds	7	2			– 7	22	1	– 4	
Cash balance at end of fiscal year:									
Customs and Salt services					26	40	73	65	
Depositories					2	19	17	45	83[e]
Total	C$ 434	C$ 585	C$ 775	C$ 749	C$ 726	C$ 896	C$1031	C$1182	C$1251

[a] Source: Data through 1935 are from the published reports of the Finance Ministry, and for 1936 and 1937 from Ministry data currently supplied and stated to be final. Blanks in the table indicate either zero or a sum less than C$0.5 million.

Prior to fiscal 1935, costs of revenue collection were stated as deductions from revenue, and thereafter as expenditures, as explained in the ***Report for the 23rd Fiscal Year, July 1934 to June 1935***, Ministry of Finance, Nanking, p. 16n. Here these costs are treated as expenditures.

[b] Includes revenue from kerosene and gasoline, the tax on which was thereafter collected as import duty.

[c] Includes C$62 million of "National revenue collected by provinces and directly disbursed for military expenses."

[d] Most of "Government enterprise receipts" is from railways, including the value of transport services for the military. A corresponding amount is included under military expenditure. These were not cash transactions. Most of "Profit on government business enterprises" is from the Central Bank.

[e] This item according to a letter of July 23, 1937, to me from the Accountant General of the Finance Ministry comprises (millions of C$): refund from loan service fund, 10; refund of principal and interest on bonds and treasury notes held by the Treasury, 14; proceeds of sale of bonds and treasury notes issued in previous years, 12; balances carried forward from various accounts of the Salt Inspectorate, 19; other, 23; total, 78.

[f] The Finance Ministry's published report for fiscal 1935 lists C$83 million from bank loans and C$55 million for overdrafts, and subtracts C$102 million for "Repayment of bank overdrafts from last year," leaving net proceeds of C$36 million under these heads.

[g] The accounts do not show for either the beginning or end of fiscal 1937 any separate item of cash balances of the Customs and Salt administrations, which were shown for previous periods. Much the larger part of such balances was with customs.

Appendix 2

Foreign currency debt under charge of the Finance Ministry receiving service as of July 1, 1937, principal outstanding in 1928 and 1937

Date of loan	Name	Terms as of July 1, 1937		Security from which paid	Principal outstanding, thousands	
		Date of final payment	Interest rate, per cent		July 1, 1928	July 1, 1937
	Receiving service as of July 1, 1928					
1895	Franco-Russian	1931	4	customs	£2,316	--
1896	Anglo-German	1932	5	customs	£3,429	--
1898	Anglo-German	1943	4½	customs	£8,970	£4,308
1913	Reorganization	1960	5	customs	£23,641	£20,179
1925	Gold Loan	1948	5	customs	US$ 42,016	US$ 27,570
1928	Gold Loan	1941	6	customs	US$ 4,987	US$ 1,420
		Total, approximate equivalent			US$236,000	US$150,000
	In arrears as of July 1, 1928, but on which payments were resumed					
1908	Anglo-French	1938	4½	salt	£2,750	£500

Continued

Appendix 2 (Continued)

Foreign currency debt under charge of the Finance Ministry receiving service as of July 1, 1937, principal outstanding in 1928 and 1937

1911	HuKuang Railway[a]	1975	2½ to 5	salt	£5,656	£5,656
1911	ditto, scrip	1961	--	salt	--	£442
1912	Crisp	1952	5	salt	£4,584	£3,931
1918	Marconi Notes	1975	1½ to 3	salt	£600	£600
1919	Vickers Notes	1975	1½ to 3	salt	£1,803	£1,803
1919	Chicago Bank	1954	2½ to 5	salt	US$ 5,500	US$ 5,500
1919	ditto, scrip	1954	--	salt	--	US$ 1,006
1919	Pacific Development	1954	2 to 4	salt	US$ 5,500	US$ 4,900
		Total, approximate equivalent			US$ 86,000	US$ 75,000
	Contracted after July 1, 1928					
1930	Sino-French Educational advance	1948	6	customs	--	US$ 265
1931-1933	U. S. Government Relief and Cotton and Wheat Loans	1942	5	customs surtax	--	US$ 14,700
1934	Canton-Hankow Railway	1947	6	customs	--	£1,164
	Miscellaneous				--	Y3,022
		Total, approximate equivalent			--	US$ 22,000
		Grand total, approximate equivalent			US$322,000	US$247,000

[a] This loan was also secured by railway revenue, but pursuant to the settlement of April 5, 1937, interest was being paid from salt revenue.

Appendix 3

Railway debt (excluding railways in Manchuria) as of 1928 and 1937[a]

I. As of July 1, 1928

Date of loan	Foreign currency debt	Interest rate, per cent	Principal outstanding, thousands	Approximate equivalent in US$, thousands
	Bond issues receiving full service			
1899	Peking-Mukden Railway	5	£978	
	″, Double Track Loan	8	£218	
1902	Cheng-Tai Railway (Shansi)	5	Fr.fr. 11,383	
				US$ 6,000
	Bond issues receiving irregular interest payments			
1904	Shanghai-Nanking Railway	5	£2,900	
1908	Shanghai-Hangchow-Ningpo Railway	5	£750	
1923	Tsingtao-Tsinan Railway	6	Y40,000	
				US$ 36,000

Continued

Appendix 3 (Continued)

Railway debt (excluding railways in Manchuria) as of 1928 and 1937[a]

Date of loan	I. As of July 1, 1928 Foreign currency debt	Interest rate, per cent	Principal outstanding, thousands	Approximate equivalent in US$, thousands
	Debt receiving no payments			
	Bond issues[b]			
1912	Lunghai Railway	5	£4,000	
1920	"	8	B.fr. 137,743	
1920	"	8	Fl. 30,750	
1925	"	8	B.fr. 21,250	
1903	Pien Lo Railway	5	B.fr. 23,500	
1907	Canton Kowloon Railway	5	£1,112	
1911	Peking-Hankow Railway	5	Y9,340	
1908-1910	Tientsin-Pukow Railway	5	£6,150	
1905	Honan Railway	5	£496	
				US$ 80,000
	Loans and advances for railways not built			12,000
	Miscellaneous loans and advances			7,000
	Material and supply debts			14,000
	Continued			US$155,000

Appendix 3 (Continued)

Railway debt (excluding railways in Manchuria) as of 1928 and 1937[a]

I. As of July 1, 1928

Foreign currency debt	Principal outstanding, thousands	Approximate equivalent in US$, thousands
(Total brought over from previous page)		US$155,000
Chinese currency debt		
Debt receiving service	C$ 2,000	
Debt in arrears:		
Bond issues	5,000	
Loans and advances, foreign creditors	10,845	
" , domestic creditors	30,596[c]	
Material and supply debts	11,408	
	C$59,849	US$ 28,000
Total		US$183,000

Continued

Appendix 3 (Continued)

Railway debt (excluding railways in Manchuria) as of 1928 and 1937[a]

II. As of January 1, 1937[d]

Foreign currency debt	Approximate equivalent in US$, thousands
Foreign currency debt receiving service:	
Loans and advances[b]	US$115
Debts for materials etc.	23
Foreign currency debt in arrears[e]	20
Chinese currency debt receiving service:	
Railway Reconstruction Loan, 1934-1936	22
Loans and advances, debts for materials etc.	46
	US$226

[a] Source: Railway Ministry.

[b] Excluding the Hukuang Railway Loan of 1911, payments on which were made from salt revenue by the Finance Ministry; and, as of 1937, the Canton-Hankow Railway Loan of 1934, secured on remitted British Boxer Indemnity funds and paid from customs revenue.

[c] Including C$4 million of advances not allocated between foreign and domestic creditors.

[d] Details of the railway debt as of January 1, 1937, are shown in Arthur N. Young, *China's Wartime Finance and Inflation, 1937-1945*, pp. 338-340, 342.

[e] The principal amounts of the chief items in arrears were Shanghai-Nanking Railway loan of 1903 on which interest payments were being made but with some delay, £2,784,000; Kaireng-Honan (Pienlo) Railway loan of 1903, on which interest was currently paid but principal was in arrears, French francs 23,500,000; and railway equipment loans equivalent to about US$5 million.

Appendix 4

Debt of the Communications Ministry and of miscellaneous government organs as of 1928 and 1937[a]

	Principal outstanding, thousands	Approximate equivalent, thousands
I. As of July 1, 1928, all in arrears		
Cable loans	£282	
Telegraph, wireless, and telephone loans	Y40,222	
	£702	
Miscellaneous	C$14,200	
		US$30,000
II. As of January 1, 1937, receiving service[b]		
Communications Ministry:		
Telegraph, wireless, and telephone loans	Y49,019	
	£153	
China Electric Company Loan	US$ 814	
Other (nearly all in US$)	US$ 1,533	
	Continued	US$17,000[c]

Appendix 4 (Continued)

Debt of the Communications Ministry and of miscellaneous government organs as of 1928 and 1937[a]

	II. As of January 1, 1937, receiving service[b]	
Chinese currency debt	C$16,990	5,000
	Total	US$22,000
Other government organs, mainly the National Construction Commission	C$13,144	US$ 4,000
	III. As of January 1, 1937, in arrears	
Miscellaneous certificates of indebtedness and bank advances, Peking governments	C$12,220	US$ 4,000

[a] Source: Communications Ministry, Finance Ministry.

[b] Excluding debts of C$34 million of the China Merchants Steam Navigation Co., in which the government owned stock.

[c] The reduction compared with 1928 results largely from depreciation of the yen from US$0.46 to US$0.28-1/2.

Appendix 5

Railway debt settlements from 1929 to 1937[a, b]

Date of		Name or description	Interest rate, %		Terms of settlement		
Original loan	Settlement		Original	As per settlement	Year of final payment	Principal amount	Treatment of interest arrears
1922	1929	Tsingtao-Tsinan Railway loan	6	6	1937	Y40,000,000	Paid in 1929
Various	10/1933	Peiping-Hankow Railway debts to American Car Company; Baldwin Locomotive Works; Andersen, Meyer & Company	10-15	5	[c]	US$ 4,305,302 C$437,571	Figured at 6% simple interest
Various	Various	Do., miscellaneous foreign creditors				US$ 700,000[d]	
1918-21	4/1934	Peiping-Suiyuan Railway loan	7-7½	6	[c]	Y5,000,000	About 3/5 canceled
Various	7/1934	Do., debt to Mitsui Bussan Kaisha		[e]	[c]	Y7,612,000	Principal plus interest reduced by nearly half
Various	Various	Do., miscellaneous foreign creditors, mostly American				US$ 7,500,000[d]	

Continued

Appendix 5 (Continued)

Railway debt settlements from 1929 to 1937[a, b]

Date of		Name or description	Interest rate, %		Terms of settlement		
1912-22	4/1935	Kiukiang-Nanchang Railway loans	5	5	1946	Y18,045,915	Apparently some reduction. Interest arrears to be paid off without interest after principal retired
1911	4/1935	Peiping-Hankow Railway Loan	5	5	1952	Y9,340,000	Apparently some reduction. Interest arrears to be paid in three years, whereupon payments would go to regular debt service
1918	4/1935	Kaomei-Hsuchow Railway loan[f]	8			Y20,000,000	
1913	5/1935	Tatung-Chengtu loan	5	2	1955	£637,128 Fr.fr. 4,699,956	Debt reduced to 48½% of original principal plus interest arrears

Continued

Appendix 5 (Continued)

Railway debt settlements from 1929 to 1937[a, b]

Date of		Name or description	Interest rate, %		Terms of settlement		
1914	8/1935	Shanghai-Fengching loan	6	6	1942	£375,000	About 1/3 of interest arrears canceled
1905	5/1936	Honan (Taokow-Chinghua) loan	5	2½-5	1963	£495,700 £44,613[g]	4/5 of interest arrears canceled, noninterest scrip issued for 1/5
1919-20		Do., Ching-Meng and "100 Wagons" loan			1948	£178,960	Principal plus arrears figured at 3% to be repaid without interest
1907	8/1936	Canton-Kowloon Railway loan	5	2½-5	1986	£1,111,500 £122,265[g]	4/5 of interest arrears canceled, noninterest scrip issued for 1/5
	8/1936	Lunghai Railway[h]:		1½-4	1982		Interest arrears canceled
1913		Sterling loan	5			£4,288,200	
1920-23		Guilder loan	8			Fl. 31,483,000	
1920-23		Belgian franc loan	8			B.fr. 137,743,000	
1925		French franc loan	8			F.fr. 21,250,000	

Continued

Appendix 5 (Continued)

Railway debt settlements from 1929 to 1937[a, b]

Date of		Name or description	Interest rate, %	Terms of settlement		
1924		C$ loan	8		C$5,000,000	
1914	1/1937	Nanking-Hunan Railway loan[i]	5	1951	C$6,100,000	Some arrears of interest included; see note i
Various	Various	Tientsin-Pukow Railway, miscellaneous materials debts			US$ 5,500,000[d]	
Various	Various	Miscellaneous materials debts			US$ 3,500,000[d]	
		Total, approximate equivalent at exchange of 1937			US$112,000,000	

[a] This table does not include the settlements of the Tientsin-Pukow and Hukuang Railway loan issues, which also involved the responsibility of the Finance Ministry.

[b] Source: Railway Ministry; Commission for Readjustment of Domestic and Foreign Debts; Chang, *Railroad Development*, pp. 161-172.

[c] Depending on railway earnings.

[d] Approximate equivalent. The terms of the settlements are not available.

[e] The new debt total to be retired by payment of promissory notes due monthly.

[f] Particulars of the settlement are not available.

[g] Scrip issued in respect of interest arrears.

[h] The several loans listed were settled on the terms stated on this line. In exchange for various unfunded debts, £288,200 of additional bonds of the Sterling loan was issued.

[i] There were two advances, taken in the settlement at C$2.5 million and C$3.6 million, respectively, including a substantial amount of interest arrears. The former sum would bear no interest, and be repaid by 1951 by yearly payments. Of the latter sum, C$2.2 million would bear 1 per cent interest, it being contemplated that the C$3.6 million would be paid from proceeds of a loan to be negotiated.

Appendix 6

Internal loans as of 1937

Date of loan	Name of loan	Scheduled date of final redemption	Interest rate (%)	Security from which paid	Principal outstanding July 1, 1937 thousands
1928	17th Year Long Term Currency Loan	1953	2½	Customs	C$ 37,125
1929	Hopei Conservancy Loan	1939	9.6	Tientsin customs surtax	800
1934	23d Year Yuping Railway Loan[a]	1943	6	Subsidy from salt revenue to provincial government	9,600
1935	24th Year Szechwan Rehabilitation Loan[a]	1944	6	Subsidy from salt revenue to provincial government	61,600
1936	25th Year Szechwan Rehabilitation Loan[a]	1951	6	Subsidy from salt revenue to provincial government. Also tobacco, wine and business taxes in Szechwan	14,400
1936	25th Year Kwangtung Currency Readjustment Loan[a]	1966	4	Consolidated taxes collected in Kwangtung	118,800

Continued

Appendix 6 (Continued)

Internal loans as of 1937

Date of loan	Name of loan	Scheduled date of final redemption	Interest rate (%)	Security from which paid	Principal outstanding July 1, 1937 thousands
1936	25th Year Consolidation Loan		6	Customs	
	Class A	1948			148,350
	Class B	1951			148,500
	Class C	1954			346,500
	Class D	1957			544,500
	Class E	1960			257,400
1936	25th Year Recovery Loan	1960	6	Customs	336,600
	Miscellaneous				4,138
	Total				C$2,028,313
1937	Kwangtung Harbor Loan	1953	6	Canton customs surtax	US$ 2,000

Grand total, approximate equivalent at exchange of July 1, 1937: US$606,000,000

[a] These loans were authorized by the National Government, for purposes primarily affecting the regions mentioned, and secured either on subsidy from the government to provincial or local authorities or on specified revenues collected in the respective regions.

Appendix 7

Debt in arrears: Original principal amounts as of July 1, 1937[a]

Date	Name	Foreign country chiefly interested	Original principal amount outstanding as of July 1, 1937 thousands
	FOREIGN DEBT		
	Finance Ministry: Funded external loans		
1912-1914	"Skoda" or "Ex-Austrian" loans	Italy and other European countries	£3,500[b]
1913	Pechili Provincial loan, guaranteed by the Central Government	Belgium	£500
1914	Pukow Port Works loan	France	French francs 100,000
1922	Tsingtao Treasury Notes	Japan	Y13,300[c]
1922	96 Million, yen portion	Japan	Y32,479
	Unfunded external debt		
1918	Bank of Communications Japanese loan	Japan	Y20,000

Continued

Appendix 7 (Continued)

Debt in arrears: Original principal amounts as of July 1, 1937[a]

Date	Name	Foreign country	thousands
1919	Kiousin debt	France	French francs 4,473
1921	Marconi loan, coupon No. 5 advance	Great Britain	£24
	Miscellaneous, approximate equivalent	Various	US$ 6,000
	Total, approximate equivalent at exchange of July 1, 1937		US$49,000
	Railway Ministry		
1903	Shanghai-Nanking Railway[d]	Great Britain	£2,784
1903	Kaifeng-Honan (Pienlo) Railway[d]	Belgium	French francs 23,500
1916-1920	Chuchow-Chingchow Railway Advances (Siems & Carey loan)	United States	US$ 1,150
1922	Railway Equipment Loan (Paotow-Ninghsia Railway)	Belgium	£800
	Total, approximate equivalent at exchange of July 1, 1937		US$20,000
	Grand total		US$69,000

Continued

Appendix 7 (Continued)

Debt in arrears: Original principal amounts as of July 1, 1937[a]

INTERNAL DEBT

Date	Name	Amount
	Finance Ministry: Funded internal loans	
1920	Famine Relief Loan	C$ 1,610
1921	Consolidation bonds	
	1st Year National Loan	12,150
	8th Year National Loan	1,210
1922	96 Million, dollar portion	56,391
	Total	C$ 71,361
	Unfunded internal loans	
Various	Treasury notes, Peking	C$ 52,140
Various	Miscellaneous items, Peking, approximate	80,000
	Total, approximate	C$132,000

Continued

Appendix 7 (Continued)

Debt in arrears: Original principal amounts as of July 1, 1937[a]

Date	Name	Amount
	Former Peking Communications Ministry	
1921	Certificates of indebtedness	C$ 7,880
Various	Bank advances, etc.	4,339
	Total	C$ 12,220
	Grand total,	C$216,000
	approximately equivalent at exchange of July 1, 1937 to	US$65,000
	Grand total, foreign and internal debt in arrears, approximate equivalent at exchange of July 1, 1937	US$134,000

[a] This tabulation does not include the Japanese "Nishihara Loans," which the National Government did not recognize. See the comment regarding them in chapter V.

[b] Approximate. Since this compilation deals with original principal amounts, the figure here used is based on the amount of loans issued in 1912-1914, and not on the amount of bonds issued under a 1925 arrangement, which at once went into default.

[c] Approximate.

[d] Interest was being paid on these loans; on the Shanghai-Nanking loan with some delay.

Appendix 8

Domestic loan issues of the Finance Ministry from 1927 to 1937[a]

Date of issue	Amount, millions	Title	Interest rate, %	Final maturity	Security	Remarks
1927						
5/1	C$30	Shanghai 2½% Surtax Treasury Notes	8.4	12/1929	Shanghai customs 2½% surtax	Payable in 30 monthly instalments, principal and interest, from 7/31/1927
10/1	40	″, 2d issue	9.6	4/1933	″	″, 40 instalments from 1/31/1930
1928						
4/1	16	17th Year Rolled Tobacco Tax Treasury Notes	9.6	11/1930	Rolled tobacco tax	″, 32 instalments from 4/30/1928
5/1	6	17th Year Military Purposes Loan	8	12/1938	Stamp tax	The first Nationalist issue paid semiannually
6/1	4	″, second instalment	8	12/1938	″	
6/30	40	17th Year Rehabilitation Loan[b]	8	6/1933	Kerosene and gasoline tax	The security was transferred to customs early in 1929

Continued

Appendix 8 (Continued)

Domestic loan issues of the Finance Ministry from 1927 to 1937[a]

Date of issue	Amount, millions	Title	Interest rate, %	Final maturity	Security	Remarks
1928						
7/1	C$ 9	Tientsin 2½% Surtax Treasury Notes	9.6	3/1931	Tientsin customs 2½% surtax	Payable in 30 monthly instalments, principal and interest, from 10/31/1928
10/25	30	17th Year Short Term Treasury Loan	8	9/1935	Customs	Secured on customs revenue formerly assigned for German share of Boxer Indemnity
11/30	45	17th Year Long Term Treasury Loan	2.5	9/1953	Customs	Issued to redeem bank notes issued by the then defunct leftist Hankow regime
1929						
1/8	10	18th Year Famine Relief Loan	8	12/1938	Customs	
2/1	50	18th Year Troop Disbandment Loan	8	1/1939	Customs	
3/1	24	18th Year Rolled Tobacco Tax Treasury Notes	8.4	1/1932	Rolled tobacco tax	Payable in 34 monthly instalments, principal and interest, from 4/30/1929

Continued

Appendix 8 (Continued)

Domestic loan issues of the Finance Ministry from 1927 to 1937[a]

Date of issue	Amount, millions	Title	Interest rate, %	Final maturity	Security	Remarks
1929						
4/21	C$ 4	Haiho Conservancy Loan	8	4/1939	Tientsin customs 5% surtax	For conservancy work in the Tientsin area
6/1	40	18th Year Customs Treasury Notes	8.4	7/1934	Customs	Payable in 62 monthly instalments, principal and interest, from 6/30/1929
9/1	70	18th Year Troop Reorganization Treasury Notes	8.4	12/1937	Customs	" , 100 instalments, from 9/30/1929
1930						
1/1	20	19th Year Customs Revenue Loan	8	12/1939	Customs	
3/1	24	19th Year Rolled Tobacco Tax Treasury Notes	8	3/1933	Rolled tobacco tax	" , 36 instalments, from 4/1/1930
9/15, 10/7	80	19th Year Customs Short-Term Treasury Notes	9.6	5/1935	Customs	Payable in 52 monthly instalments, principal and interest, from 8/31/1930

Continued

Appendix 8 (Continued)

Domestic loan issues of the Finance Ministry from 1927 to 1937[a]

Date of issue	Amount, millions	Title	Interest rate, %	Final maturity	Security	Remarks
1930						
11/1	C$50	19th Year Rehabilitation Short-Term Treasury Notes	9.6	4/1936	Customs	", 66 instalments, from 11/30/1930
1931						
1/1	60	20th Year Rolled Tobacco Tax Treasury Notes	8.4	6/1937	Rolled tobacco tax	", 78 instalments, from 1/31/1931
4/1	80	20th Year Customs Short-Term Treasury Notes	9.6	7/1939	Customs	", 100 instalments, from 4/30/1931
4/15	6	20th Year Kiangsu-Chekiang Silk Industry Loan	8	10/1938	Export duty on raw silk	
6/1	80	20th Year Consolidated Tax Treasury Notes	9.6	11/1937	Consolidated taxes	", 78 instalments, from 6/30/1931

Continued

Appendix 8 (Continued)

Domestic loan issues of the Finance Ministry from 1927 to 1937[a]

Date of issue	Amount, millions	Title	Interest rate, %	Final maturity	Security	Remarks
1931						
8/1	C$80	20th Year Relief Treasury Notes	9.6	1/1938	Salt revenue	″, 79 instalments, from 8/31/1931
9/1	30	20th Year Relief Loan	8	8/1941	Customs surtax	
10/1	80	20th Year Short-Term Currency Loan	8	10/1941	Customs	Secured on customs revenue formerly assigned for German share of Boxer Indemnity
1933						
3/1	20	22d Year Patriotic Treasury Notes	6	11/1936	Rolled tobacco tax	Payable in 45 monthly instalments, principal and interest, from 3/31/1933
10/1	100	22d Year Customs Treasury Notes	6	3/1946	Customs	″, 150 instalments, from 10/31/1933
11/1	4	22d Year North China War Relief Short-Term Loan	6	7/1938	Salt surcharge at Changlu	Principal and interest payable quarterly

Continued

Appendix 8 (Continued)

Domestic loan issues of the Finance Ministry from 1927 to 1937[a]

Date of issue	Amount, millions	Title	Interest rate, %	Final maturity	Security	Remarks
1934						
1/1	C$50[c]	23d Year Customs Treasury Notes	6	12/1940	Customs	Payable in 84 monthly instalments, principal and interest, from 1/31/1934
6/1	12	23d Year Yu-ping Railway Loan	6	5/1943	Salt revenue	Issued jointly by Finance and Railway Ministries, as the First Series, Railway Reconstruction Loan[d]
6/30	100	23d Year Customs	6	6/1945	Customs	
1935						
2/1	120	24th Year Consolidated Tax Treasury Notes	7.2	1/1946	Consolidated taxes	Payable in 132 monthly instalments, principal and interest, from 2/28/1935
4/1	100	24th Year Currency Loan	6	3/1945	Customs	
7/1	70	24th Year Szechuan Rehabilitation Loan	6	6/1944	Salt revenue in Szechuan	

Continued

Appendix 8 (Continued)

Domestic loan issues of the Finance Ministry from 1927 to 1937[a]

Date of issue	Amount, millions	Title	Interest rate, %	Final maturity	Security	Remarks
1935						
8/1	C$30	24th Year Szechuan Currency Readjustment Treasury Notes	6	11/1940	Consolidated tax, stamp, wine and tobacco taxes in Szechuan	Payable in 64 monthly instalments, principal and interest, from 8/30/1935
11/1	20	24th Year Flood-Labor Relief Loan	6	10/1947	Customs	
1936						
2/1	150	25th Year Consolidation Loan, A	6	1/1937	Customs	
2/1	150	″, B	6	1/1940	Customs	The Consolidation Loan was issued in five series in exchange respectively for the issues listed
2/1	350	″, C	6	1/1943	Customs	
2/1	550	″, D	6	1/1946	Customs	
2/1	260	″, E	6	1/1949	Customs	
3/1	340	25th Year Recovery Loan	6	2/1960	Customs	

Continued

Appendix 8 (Continued)

Domestic loan issues of the Finance Ministry from 1927 to 1937[a]

Date of issue	Amount, millions	Title	Interest rate, %	Final maturity	Security	Remarks
1936						
4/1	C$15	25th Year Szechuan Rehabilitation Loan	6	3/1951	Salt, wine and tobacco, and business taxes in Szechuan	
10/1	120	25th Year Kwangtung Currency Readjustment Loan	4	3/1966	Consolidated taxes in Kwangtung	
1937						
4/1	US$2	26th Year US Dollar Port and River Development Loan	6	4/1953	Customs surtax at Canton	

[a] Source: Ministries of Finance and Railways.

[b] Half of this loan was issued in December 1928.

[c] This loan was originally announced as C$100 million but half was canceled to be replaced by the 23d Year Customs Revenue Loan.

[d] This was the First Series, Railway Reconstruction Loan. The Railway Ministry issued the Second Series, but the Finance Ministry joined the Railway Ministry in issuing the Third Series. The latter is treated as a railway issue because the Finance Ministry provided no specific security but only a subsidy for the first four years to tide over the period until the newly built railways would have earnings.

Appendix 9

Classification of internal debt consolidated as of February 1, 1936[a]

Name of loan	Amount consolidated, millions	Maturity before consolidation	
		Mo.	year
Series A, 12 years			
22d Year Patriotic Treasury Notes	C$ 4.7	11	1936
25th Year Short Term Treasury Certificates[b]	100.0	12	1936
18th Year Customs Treasury Notes	7.9	7	1937
22d Year North China War Relief Short Term Loan	2.2	7	1938
15th Year Public Safety Loan[c]	2.0	1	1939
19th Year Customs Short Term	33.0	1	1939
Subtotal	149.8		
Series B, 15 years			
19th Year Rehabilitation Short Term Treasury Notes	25.8	11	1939
15th Year Austrian Indemnity Treasury Notes[c]	1.5	12	1939
24th Year Szechuan Rehabilitation Loan	27.6	11	1940
23d Year Customs Treasury Notes	37.5	12	1940
20th Year Rolled Tobacco Tax Treasury Notes	37.7	1	1941
Subtotal	130.1		
Series C, 18 years			
18th Year Troop Reorganization Treasury Notes	36.3	6	1941
20th Year Consolidated Tax Treasury Notes	56.8	9	1941
20th Year Short Term Currency Loan	71.2	10	1941
20th Year Relief Treasury Notes	58.5	10	1941
20th Year Kiangsu-Chekiang Silk Industry Loan	4.5	4	1942
18th Year Famine Relief Loan	5.3	6	1942
17th Year Military Purposes Loan	5.2	9	1942

Continued

Appendix 9 (Continued)

Classification of internal debt consolidated as of February 1, 1936[a]

Name of loan	Amount Consolidated, millions	Maturity before consolidation	
		Mo.	year
18th Year Troop Disbandment Loan	C$ 27.0	1	1943
20th Year Customs Short Term	56.6	1	1943
Subtotal	321.4		
Series D, 21 years			
19th Year Customs Revenue Loan	12.8	12	1943
7th Year Long Term Loan[c]	19.8	12	1943
20th Year Relief Loan	24.0	2	1944
Italian Indemnity Fund Certificates[b]	34.6	1	1945
24th Year Currency Loan	100.0	3	1945
23d Year Customs Revenue Loan	98.0	6	1945
Russian Indemnity Fund Certificates[b]	111.9	12	1945
24th Year Consolidated Tax Treasury Notes	112.6	1	1946
Subtotal	513.7		
Series E, 24 years			
22d Year Customs Treasury Notes	86.0	3	1946
24th Year Flood-Labor Relief Loan	20.0	10	1947
7% Consolidated Loan[c]	8.1	11	1947
6% Consolidated Loan[c]	32.0	12	1947
15th Year Spring Festival Treasury Notes[c]	8.0	1	1948
Subtotal	154.1		
Grand total	C$1,269.0		

[a] Source: Finance Ministry.

[b] Not publicly issued. Details of the Short Term Treasury Certificates and the Russian Boxer Indemnity Certificates are not available, except that the latter were for an advance by the Central Bank. The Italian Boxer Indemnity Certificates were issued in January 1934 for C$44 million as a loan from banks, with interest of 8 per mille per month (9.6 per cent per annum), with principal and interest payable in monthly instalments to January 1945. Interest was secured on customs revenue, and principal on customs revenue formerly assigned to the Indemnity.

[c] Peking Government issues.

Appendix 10

Foreign exchange rates from 1920 to 1937 (telegraph transfer selling rates)[a]

	Sterling (pence per C$)		U. S. dollars (cents per C$)	
A. By years, 1920-1937				
Period	High	Low	High	Low
1920	80.25	33.98	115.54	48.79
1921	35.79	25.30	58.55	41.02
1922	31.45	26.03	58.40	48.77
1923	29.26	26.03	54.21	49.29
1924	30.19	26.94	57.08	49.19
1925	28.38	26.11	57.48	52.61
1926	26.94	19.52	54.00	39.34
1927	23.14	20.78	47.33	42.35
1928	24.58	22.23	50.09	45.02
1929	22.45	18.10	45.43	36.83
1930	17.79	12.14	36.92	24.54
1931	17.17	9.85	26.30	19.88
1932	17.81	13.33	25.00	19.09
1933	16.19	13.98	34.31	19.47
1934	18.50	14.63	37.88	31.19
1935	20.94	14.38	42.13	29.50
1936	14.56	14.25	30.25	29.44
1937	14.75	14.13	30.25	29.44
B. By months, 1928-1937				
1928	High	Low	High	Low
January	22.59	22.23	45.83	45.11
February	22.41	22.23	45.38	45.02
March	22.23	22.23	45.30	45.30
April	22.59	22.23	46.14	45.42
May	24.58	22.59	50.09	45.93
June	23.86	23.14	48.53	47.08
July	23.22	22.95	47.26	46.44
August	23.14	22.77	46.57	45.86
September	22.77	22.41	45.89	45.08
October	22.95	22.59	46.42	45.70
November	22.77	22.77	46.03	46.03
December	22.77	22.41	45.83	45.11

Continued

Appendix 10 (Continued)

Foreign exchange rates from 1920 to 1937 (telegraph transfer selling rates)[a]

	Sterling (pence per C$)		U. S. dollars (cents per C$)	
	B. By months, 1928-1937			
1929	High	Low	High	Low
January	22.45	22.09	45.43	44.62
February	22.08	21.72	44.60	43.97
March	22.10	21.92	44.65	44.38
April	21.88	21.16	44.29	42.77
May	21.34	20.62	42.86	41.60
June	20.41	19.88	41.18	41.11
July	20.64	20.10	41.73	40.57
August	20.49	20.13	41.07	40.62
September	20.52	19.44	41.04	39.24
October	19.26	19.08	38.97	38.70
November	19.13	19.08	38.81	38.81
December	19.19	18.10	38.91	36.83
1930				
January	17.79	16.89	36.92	34.22
February	17.10	16.56	34.64	33.56
March	16.93	15.85	34.30	31.69
April	16.76	16.40	33.96	33.33
May	16.56	14.13	33.56	28.62
June	14.03	12.41	28.07	25.10
July	13.35	12.91	27.26	26.17
August	14.04	13.31	28.44	26.98
September	14.43	13.80	29.25	27.97
October	14.09	13.72	28.54	27.81
November	13.97	13.61	28.30	27.57
December	13.40	12.14	27.08	24.54
1931				
January	12.09	10.82	24.40	22.10
February	11.03	9.85	24.31	19.88
March	11.94	10.31	24.15	20.90
April	11.37	10.64	23.01	21.56

Continued

Appendix 10 (Continued)

Foreign exchange rates from 1920 to 1937 (telegraph transfer selling rates) [a]

	Sterling (pence per C$)		U. S. dollars (cents per C$)	
B. By months, 1928-1937				
1931	High	Low	High	Low
May	11.03	10.12	22.34	20.52
June	11.64	10.00	23.55	20.28
July	11.70	10.70	23.66	21.67
August	10.79	10.42	21.84	20.94
September	13.05	10.51	22.47	20.39
October	14.36	12.90	23.45	20.99
November	16.69	14.33	26.30	22.49
December	17.17	15.73	24.32	22.15
1932				
January	16.77	15.96	23.77	22.96
February	17.81	16.45	25.00	23.53
March	16.72	14.57	24.28	22.75
April	14.35	13.75	22.72	21.84
May	14.39	13.69	21.93	20.71
June	13.78	13.52	21.06	20.28
July	13.93	13.33	20.51	19.64
August	14.97	13.85	21.68	20.22
September	14.99	14.38	21.66	20.61
October	15.22	14.61	21.30	20.68
November	15.36	15.00	21.13	19.71
December	15.79	13.83	20.08	19.09
1933				
January	14.45	14.13	20.42	19.66
February	14.51	13.98	20.54	19.47
March	14.84	14.21	21.77	20.20
April	16.19	14.16	24.25	20.31
May	15.50	14.50	25.13	24.06
June	15.63	15.00	27.25	25.13
July	15.63	14.88	31.00	27.94
August	15.19	14.69	29.13	26.94

Continued

Appendix 10 (Continued)

Foreign exchange rates from 1920 to 1937 (telegraph transfer selling rates) [a]

	Sterling (pence per C$)		U. S. dollars (cents per C$)	
	B. By months, 1928-1937			
1933	High	Low	High	Low
September	15.50	15.25	30.94	28.44
October	15.50	15.25	30.81	28.75
November	15.56	15.13	34.31	31.25
December	15.88	15.18	34.06	32.75
1934				
January	16.44	16.00	34.69	33.06
February	16.81	16.13	35.63	33.75
March	16.56	16.13	35.38	34.38
April	16.25	15.31	35.00	32.94
May	15.56	14.63	33.19	31.19
June	16.25	15.50	34.25	32.50
July	16.31	16.00	34.44	33.69
August	16.88	16.13	35.44	33.88
September	17.56	16.94	36.63	35.38
October	18.50	15.69	37.88	32.38
November	16.31	15.88	34.31	33.06
December	16.94	16.31	34.88	33.75
1935				
January	18.00	16.94	36.38	34.50
February	19.06	17.32	38.56	35.13
March	20.31	18.69	40.38	37.44
April	20.94	18.38	42.00	36.88
May	20.56	20.13	42.13	40.63
June	20.50	19.13	42.00	39.38
July	19.19	18.00	39.56	37.25
August	18.38	17.38	38.00	36.06
September	18.88	17.81	38.81	36.81
October	18.81	14.88	38.50	30.56
November	15.00	14.38	30.81	29.50
December	14.50	14.38	29.81	29.50

Continued

Appendix 10 (Continued)

Foreign exchange rates from 1920 to 1937 (telegraph transfer selling rates)[a]

	Sterling (pence per C$)		U. S. dollars (cents per C$)	
	B. By months, 1928-1937			
1936	High	Low	High	Low
January	14.53	14.38	29.94	29.63
February	14.53	14.38	30.19	29.94
March	14.50	14.40	30.19	29.94
April	14.50	14.50	30.00	29.88
May	14.50	14.38	30.00	29.75
June	14.38	14.38	30.13	29.88
July	14.40	14.38	30.13	30.06
August	14.40	14.38	30.19	30.13
September	14.41	14.25	30.25	29.50
October	14.50	14.31	29.50	29.44
November	14.56	14.50	29.69	29.50
December	14.56	14.44	29.75	29.50
1937				
January	14.61	14.53	29.81	29.75
February	14.59	14.50	29.81	29.56
March	14.63	14.60	29.81	29.69
April	14.63	14.50	29.88	29.75
May	14.53	14.50	29.88	29.81
June	14.52	14.36	29.78	29.53
July	14.75	14.28	29.75	29.58
August	14.53	14.28	30.25	29.50
September	14.53	14.37	30.13	29.63
October	14.36	14.27	29.88	29.55
November	14.25	14.13	29.75	29.50
December	14.25	14.17	29.69	29.44

[a] Source: Sterling rates for 1920 to 1932 and dollar rates for 1929 to 1932 were compiled by E. Kann, sterling rates for 1920 to 1928 being taken from his compilation in *China Year Book, 1929-30*, p. 296. Sterling rates for 1920 to 1928 were originally in Shanghai *taels* and are converted to C$ at 72.3 *taels* per C$100, the approximate average rate for the period, since *tael*-C$ rates year by year are not available (See Appendix 11). Dollar rates for 1920-1928 are from the report of the Commission of Financial Experts (Kemmerer Commission), *Project of Law for the Gradual Introduction of a Gold-standard Currency System in China* (Shanghai, 1929), Appendix A. Rates for 1933 to 1937 were compiled by the Central Bank of China.

Appendix 11

Average rates of Shanghai taels *per C$100 from 1921 to 1933*[a]

Average monthly rates, 1921-1931

January	72.24	April	72.34	July	72.09	October	72.46
February	72.01	May	72.39	August	72.28	November	72.69
March	72.15	June	72.06	September	72.34	December	72.69

Averages by months, 1929-1933

	1929	1930	1931	1932	1933
January	71.825	71.863	72.163	71.750	71.334
February	71.788	71.988	72.295	73.538	71.447
March	71.875	72.025	72.363	71.925	71.495
April	71.725	72.075	72.767	70.450	71.500
May	71.725	71.988	72.951	70.188	(Tael
June	71.625	71.963	72.748	69.338	abolished)
July	71.800	72.705	72.530	69.225	--
August	71.900	72.919	72.513	68.838	--
September	72.000	73.132	72.488	69.313	--
October	72.000	72.700	72.700	70.400	--
November	72.200	72.559	72.550	71.013	--
December	72.400	72.455	72.313	71.381	--
Average	71.905	72.364	72.532	70.613	71.444

[a] Source: For 1921 to 1931 averages, E. Kann; for 1929 to 1933 data, Central Bank of China.

Appendix 12

Monthly wholesale prices and cost of living from 1929 to 1937 (1926 = 100)[a]

	Shanghai				Tientsin	Canton
	Wholesale prices					
Period	General index	Exports	Imports	Cost of living	Wholesale prices	Wholesale prices
1929						
January	101.7	103.4	102.6	104.2	111.4	--
February	103.2	103.8	105.6	104.8	112.9	--
March	104.1	104.2	107.1	103.7	112.8	--
April	103.1	102.4	106.1	102.7	110.7	--
May	102.6	104.5	104.9	103.6	110.0	--
June	103.0	104.1	105.4	105.4	110.2	--
July	103.4	105.5	106.7	105.9	111.0	--
August	104.8	105.8	108.7	111.7	111.0	--
September	106.6	108.2	111.7	114.1	111.3	--
October	107.4	108.9	112.5	114.6	111.0	--
November	106.1	106.1	110.6	111.9	110.3	--
December	105.5	104.8	110.1	111.5	110.1	--
1930						
January	108.3	106.4	114.6	113.6	110.6	--
February	111.3	109.2	115.8	124.1	113.9	--
March	111.3	108.7	117.0	122.2	114.3	--
April	111.2	108.5	119.2	120.8	113.4	--
May	111.0	106.8	122.3	120.7	114.8	--
June	117.5	114.0	136.0	120.2	118.6	--
July	120.4	116.8	137.7	129.5	120.5	--
August	119.6	113.0	135.6	126.9	120.2	--
September	118.4	110.4	133.3	128.1	118.3	--
October	115.4	104.3	127.8	121.3	116.0	--
November	114.1	102.2	129.2	115.8	115.0	--
December	113.6	99.7	131.3	113.8	114.5	--
1931						
January	119.7	103.2	145.5	120.9	118.2	--
February	127.4	109.1	157.8	136.0	122.2	--
March	126.1	109.9	153.2	132.2	124.0	--

Continued

Appendix 12 (Continued)

Monthly wholesale prices and cost of living from 1929 to 1937 (1926 = 100)[a]

	Shanghai				Tientsin	Canton
	Wholesale prices					
Period	General index	Exports	Imports	Cost of living	Whole-sale prices	Whole-sale prices
1931						
April	126.2	107.4	154.6	121.3	124.5	--
May	127.5	111.3	153.3	120.3	125.0	--
June	129.2	111.7	156.1	121.0	124.8	--
July	127.4	109.8	152.1	119.2	123.3	--
August	130.3	109.5	154.0	130.9	123.8	--
September	129.2	108.4	149.2	135.3	123.5	--
October	126.9	105.6	145.3	127.3	121.3	--
November	124.8	103.5	141.0	125.2	120.5	--
December	121.8	101.2	138.9	121.2	119.4	--
1932						
January	119.3	99.8	137.8	122.8	117.3	117.2
February	118.4	98.1	139.2	136.4	118.7	116.7
March	117.6	96.4	140.6	127.2	117.7	117.0
April	116.7	94.8	142.0	117.2	118.3	116.8
May	115.7	94.7	141.6	117.5	116.6	116.6
June	113.6	90.6	139.2	121.3	113.7	116.1
July	111.8	88.7	138.8	118.7	112.0	115.3
August	111.3	91.1	140.5	119.0	110.9	114.5
September	109.8	88.9	140.4	118.2	109.1	114.4
October	108.7	86.9	140.1	113.5	107.1	108.3
November	106.9	84.0	140.0	108.7	106.5	107.1
December	107.5	86.1	141.1	108.0	106.7	106.3
1933						
January	108.6	87.5	141.5	110.5	108.6	108.8
February	107.6	85.5	138.6	113.4	108.0	108.8
March	106.7	84.7	134.8	111.2	106.2	108.2
April	104.5	81.4	133.8	106.3	102.5	106.0
May	104.2	84.3	131.2	106.8	101.3	104.9
June	104.5	85.1	131.7	105.4	102.6	104.6

Continued

Appendix 12 (Continued)

Monthly wholesale prices and cost of living from 1929 to 1937 (1926 = 100) [a]

Period	Shanghai: Wholesale prices: General index	Shanghai: Wholesale prices: Exports	Shanghai: Wholesale prices: Imports	Shanghai: Cost of living	Tientsin: Wholesale prices	Canton: Wholesale prices
1933						
July	103.4	86.2	129.7	106.6	101.4	103.0
August	101.7	81.3	129.6	107.2	98.1	103.6
September	100.4	79.6	129.0	106.0	96.8	104.7
October	100.3	77.0	129.8	106.9	94.9	102.3
November	99.9	75.8	126.5	103.2	94.0	101.4
December	98.4	73.0	128.4	102.6	92.6	98.8
1934						
January	97.2	71.8	127.1	101.8	91.6	99.8
February	98.0	74.2	130.9	103.5	92.1	100.4
March	96.6	71.3	128.7	98.9	91.1	100.1
April	94.6	68.2	129.3	99.0	89.2	98.6
May	94.9	69.7	131.8	98.5	89.4	98.0
June	95.7	71.8	131.5	98.5	89.5	92.5
July	97.1	70.9	133.9	106.9	90.9	92.5
August	99.8	74.2	136.3	115.7	94.8	94.6
September	97.3	71.5	134.5	118.1	92.5	91.6
October	96.1	70.3	131.1	113.3	92.3	90.4
November	98.3	72.0	134.8	108.8	93.0	87.0
December	99.0	75.3	135.0	110.4	95.0	86.2
1935						
January	99.4	77.2	135.1	110.9	96.1	86.4
February	99.9	78.0	132.0	109.0	96.9	87.2
March	96.4	74.9	127.0	104.8	95.8	85.5
April	95.9	74.7	127.2	106.1	95.3	83.8
May	95.0	75.0	123.9	105.6	95.1	81.1
June	92.1	70.4	122.1	105.9	93.4	80.2
July	90.5	71.0	121.8	105.2	91.8	80.8
August	91.9	74.7	123.5	104.6	91.2	81.7
September	91.1	75.4	120.7	105.4	90.7	82.0

Continued

Appendix 12 (Continued)

Monthly wholesale prices and cost of living from 1929 to 1937 (1926 = 100)[a]

	Shanghai				Tientsin	Canton
	Wholesale prices					
Period	General index	Exports	Imports	Cost of living	Whole-sale prices	Whole-sale prices
1935						
October	94.1	80.6	123.7	103.9	94.2	81.9
November	103.3	89.6	142.7	109.2	100.9	92.3
December	103.3	90.0	141.5	109.3	102.5	94.0
1936						
January	104.3	90.8	141.1	111.0	104.1	95.6
February	105.6	90.2	141.2	112.0	107.1	98.3
March	106.4	92.4	140.8	114.1	110.5	99.4
April	107.3	97.3	140.9	111.7	111.5	100.9
May	105.8	94.5	140.3	111.1	109.1	102.3
June	106.1	97.5	140.7	111.8	108.1	110.5
July	107.2	100.7	141.8	112.2	109.6	112.9
August	107.4	97.6	140.0	115.5	109.3	109.5
September	107.0	95.9	140.1	113.5	108.7	108.9
October	109.7	96.1	142.3	114.0	111.5	108.7
November	113.0	97.1	142.9	114.9	115.1	109.6
December	118.8	102.9	147.6	117.5	122.8	111.3
1937						
January	121.6	--[b]	--[b]	120.1	126.3	115.7
February	122.9	--	--	120.1	128.9	118.0
March	123.0	--	--	116.8	129.7	117.5
April	123.9	--	--	117.4	134.1	119.8
May	125.1	--	--	118.7	130.4	119.8
June	126.1	--	--	119.0	130.4	118.7

[a] Source: See Table 15, pages 170 to 171. The Shanghai cost of living index is that of the National Tariff Commission.

[b] Issuance of indexes of export and import prices was suspended pending revision, and not resumed because of outbreak of hostilities in July 1937.

Appendix 13

Agricultural prices from 1929 to 1937[a]

I. Index, 1931-1936

Year	Index	Year	Index
1931	100	1934	56
1932	72	1935	57
1933	61	1936	60

II. Prices received and paid by farmers, 1929-1937 (1931 = 100)

	Nanking, Cheng Hwa Men		Wuchin, Kiangsu		Suhsien, Anhwei		Szechwan, 11 places	
	Received	Paid	Received	Paid	Received	Paid	Received	Paid
1929	--	--	109	95	--	--	78	76
1930	110	81	122	105	84	91	83	82
1931	100	100	100	100	100	100	100	100
1932	86	95	93	97	89	99	84	92
1933	60	85	71	81	57	77	73	83
1934	65	77	86	79	47	63	83	85
1935	77	77	97	74	57	60	85	--
1936	82	89	101	94	75	69	115	--
1937 (first half)	89	97	109	103	87	76	152	--

[a] Source: I. Ta-chung Liu: *China's National Income, 1931-36* (Brookings Institution, Washington, 1946), pp. 11-12n. This index, Liu stated, "is based on a simple arithmetic average of the prices of rice, wheat, other grains, beans and peas, rapeseed, sesame, sweet potatoes, peanuts, tobacco and cotton, weighted by their respective quantities in the current year."

II. *University of Nanking Indexes*, compiled by W. Y. Yang, Bulletin No. 54 (New Series), Chengtu, January 1941, *passim*. I have converted the index figures for Wuchin and Szechwan to the 1931 base used in the other indexes. The number of items used for prices received and paid respectively was: Nanking, 18 and 28; Wuchin, 7 and 51; Suhsien, 38 and 73; Szechwan, 2-6 and 2-7. The method was weighted aggregative, except for Szechwan where it was simple geometric. Some data go back to 1894.

Appendix 14

Wholesale prices at Hong Kong from 1922 to 1938 (1922 = 100)[a]

By years

1922	100.0
1924	106.8
1931	136.6
1932	122.4
1933	103.5
1934	93.6
1935	77.9
1936	103.1
1937	131.1
1938	130.6

By months

	1932[b]	1934	1935	1936	1937	1938
Jan.		97.8	83.4	97.4	114.5	138.9
Feb.		96.1	84.3	97.7	117.3	137.4
Mar.	132.0	92.9	76.1	101.8	122.0	137.8
Apr.		92.6	77.9	102.2	127.4	136.7
May		95.6	73.1	103.3	128.1	
June	126.7	97.4	71.1	100.9	131.2	
July		93.0	73.4	106.8	130.1	
Aug.		95.3	69.4	104.4	135.3	
Sept.	117.2	91.2	73.3	103.0	143.3	
Oct.		92.0	72.6	106.9	143.1	
Nov.		91.3	85.4	103.7	139.6	
Dec.	113.7	88.2	94.2	109.1	141.2	

[a] Source: Statistical Office of Exports and Imports, Hong Kong Government; *Economic Facts*, University of Nanking, October 1936, pp. 95-97, 105, and June 1938, pp. 432-444, for certain figures for 1935-1938 which are here reconverted to their original base; and the *Hong Kong Blue Book* for the breakdown of quarters for 1932. Investigation at Hong Kong indicated that no further data are available in records there that survived the war.

[b] Data are by quarters.

Appendix 15

Silver sales from 1934 to 1941[a]

Date of agreement	Amount, oz		Price, U. S. cents per oz	Net proceeds
	A. To July 10, 1937, Chinese data			
	Contracted	Delivered from stocks in China		
November 1934	19,000,000	2,506,000[b]	53.3[c]	US$ 1,340,000[c]
November 1935	50,000,000	50,208,396	65.17 and 65.03	32,256,865
May 1936	75,000,000	75,629,077	45	34,033,085
July 1937	62,000,000	62,514,710	45	28,131,620
Totals	206,000,000	190,858,183		US$ 95,761,570
	B. After July 10, 1937, Chinese data			
1937-1941	362,101,578[d]		--[e]	US$157,164,000
	C. Totals, Chinese data			
1934-1941		552,959,761[f]		US$252,925,570[f]

Continued

Appendix 15 (Continued)

Silver sales from 1934 to 1941[a]

D. American Treasury data

Date of agreement	Amount purchased, oz	Cost
1934	19,506,000	US$ 10,427,997
1935	50,115,000	32,166,303
1936	66,975,000	30,157,000
1937	130,026,000	58,512,000
1938	265,892,000	115,530,000
1939	33,341,000	13,787,000
1940	5,142,000	1,800,000
1941	805,000	282,000
Totals	571,802,000	262,662,300
Less: Adjustment for 17,000,000 ounces delivered from purchases in London	17,000,000	9,087,997
	554,802,000	US$253,574,303

[a] Source: Chinese data are from the records of the writer, who participated in the operations, except that American Treasury data are incorporated for 1940-1941 because the Chinese records are incomplete. Treasury data are from A. S. Everest's book, ***Morgenthau, the New Deal, and Silver*** (New York, 1950), page 178, and are derived from the Morgenthau *Diaries*. Actual deliveries varied slightly from contractual amounts because of varying outturn in refining etc. The two sets of data could probably be reconciled if fuller Chinese data were available.

[b] A total of 17 million ounces was delivered from purchases in London, and not from stocks in China.

[c] Approximate average figures derived from data in heading D of the table.

[d] Mostly amounts contracted for but including some items of actual deliveries.

[e] About 150,000,000 ounces at US$0.45; about 200,000,000 at US$0.43; and about 12,000,000 at US$0.35.

[f] Approximate because of combining contractual amounts and deliveries.

Appendix 16

Currency reform: Decree of November 3, 1935

To conserve the currency reserves of the country and effect a stable monetary and banking reform, and to prevent a financial catastrophe, the Government, following the precedents of many countries in recent years, has decreed, as follows:

1. As from November 4, 1935, the banknotes issued by The Central Bank of China, The Bank of China, and The Bank of Communications shall be full legal tender. Payment of taxes and discharge of all public and private obligations shall be effected by legal tender notes. No use of silver dollars or bullion for currency purposes shall be permitted; and, in order to prevent smuggling of silver, any contravention of this provision shall be punishable by confiscation of the whole amount of silver seized. Any individual found in illegal possession of silver with intention to smuggle it shall be punishable in accordance with the law governing acts of treason against the State.

2. Banknotes of issuing banks, other than The Central Bank of China, The Bank of China and The Bank of Communications, whose issue had been previously authorized by the Ministry of Finance, shall remain in circulation, but the total outstanding banknotes of each bank shall not exceed the amount in circulation on November 3, 1935. The outstanding banknotes of these banks shall be gradually retired and exchanged for Central Bank of China banknotes within a period to be determined by the Ministry of Finance. All reserves held against the outstanding banknotes, together with unissued or retired notes of these banks, shall be handed over at once to the Currency Reserve Board. Notes previously authorized and in process of printing shall also be handed over to the said Board upon taking delivery by the banks.

3. A Currency Reserve Board shall be formed to control the issue and retirement of legal tender banknotes, and to keep custody of reserves against outstanding banknotes. Regulations governing the said Board shall be separately enacted and promulgated.

4. As from November 4, 1935, banks, firms, and all private

and public institutions and individuals holding standard dollars, other silver dollars, or silver bullion, shall hand over the same to the Currency Reserve Board or banks designated by the Board in exchange for legal tender notes, at face value in the case of standard silver dollars, and in accordance with the net silver content in the case of other silver dollars or silver bullion.

5. All contractual obligations expressed in terms of silver shall be discharged by the payment of legal tender notes in the nominal amount due.

6. For the purpose of keeping the exchange value of the Chinese dollar stable at its present level The Central Bank of China, The Bank of China and The Bank of Communications shall buy and sell foreign exchange in unlimited quantities.

The measures set forth above are designed for economic rehabilitation. The Central Bank of China will be reorganized to function as a bankers' bank. The general banking system will be strengthened, giving increased liquidity to the commercial banks under sound conditions, so that they may have resources available to finance the legitimate requirements of trade and industry. Measures have been prepared to create a special institution to deal with mortgage business; and steps will be taken to amend the present legal code affecting real estate mortgages so as to make real estate more acceptable as security for loans.

Plans of financial readjustment have been made whereby the National Budget will be balanced. Also with the centralization of note issue, the provision of adequate reserves against the legal tender currency, and a system of rigorous supervision, confidence in the currency will be strengthened. It is hoped that the nation will wholeheartedly support the Government in measures to promote the national prosperity. The Government will take drastic measures to deal with speculation and attempts to bring about unwarranted increase in prices, and with any action intended to hamper the execution of the measures set forth in this decree.

Appendix 17

Note issue of Chinese banks from 1928 to 1937[a]

	Amount issued, millions										
	1928	1929	1930	1931	1932	1933	1934	1935	1935	1936	1937
1. Government banks											
								(November 2)			(June 30)
Central Bank of China	C$ 12	C$ 15	C$ 23	C$ 25	C$ 40	C$ 71	C$ 86	C$136	C$180	C$340	C$383
Bank of China	172	198	204	192	180	180	201	187	286	459	518
Bank of Communications	68	69	83	81	82	83	103	105	176	295	336
Farmers Bank						2	6	30	30	162	208
2. 15 banks brought under the Currency Reserve Board, November 1935[b]											
	57	68	104	95	120	156	174	232	175	100	72
3. Provincial and municipal banks not included in 2[c]											
Kwangtung Provincial Bank[d]					28	33	33	30	63	170	235
Others[e]					17	24	59	40	50	90	140

Continued

Appendix 17 (Continued)

Note issue of Chinese banks from 1928 to 1937[a]

	Amount issued, millions										
	1928	1929	1930	1931	1932	1933	1934	1935	1935	1936	1937
4. Other banks[f]											
					C$ 5	C$ 5	C$ 5	C$ 5	C$ 5	C$ 15	C$ 20
Totals											
Government banks	252	282	310	298	302	336	396	458	672	1,256	1,445
Others	57	68	104	95	170	218	271	307	293	375	467
Grand total	C$309	C$350	C$414	C$393	C$472	C$554	C$667	C$765	C$965	C$1,631	C$1,912

[a] Source: Central Bank of China statements; Bank of China; Finance Ministry; Currency Reserve Board; and Wei-ya Chang, *Money and Finance of China*, pp. 157-158; for certain provincial issues. Data for "other banks" under headings 3 and 4 are lacking before 1932, and for later years may not be complete. Under all headings, some figures received at different times do not agree, and I have mostly used the most recent data. A few figures are estimated.

[b] These banks, and for the more important their percentages of total issue as of November 2, 1935, were China and South Seas Bank (31); National Industrial Bank of China (23); Commercial Bank of China (12); Ningpo Commercial and Savings Bank (8); Agricultural and Industrial Bank of China (6); Hupei Provincial Bank; National Commercial Bank; Land Bank of China; Commercial Guarantee Bank of Chihli; Chekiang Provincial Bank; Shensi Provincial Bank; Bank of Agriculture and Commerce; Dah Chung Bank; Honan Provincial Bank; and Frontier Bank of Tientsin. The China and South Seas Bank's notes were the responsibility of the Four Banks Joint Treasury, comprising that bank and the Kincheng Bank, Yien Yieh Commercial Bank (Salt Bank), and the Continental Bank. The figures for the end of 1935 and 1936 are estimated from data as of dates near the year-end; the figure for 1937 is as of May 29.

[c] The provincial banks of Chekiang, Honan, Hupei, and Shensi were brought under the Currency Reserve Board in November 1935 and are included under 2.

[d] The figures are converted from Kwangtung currency at approximate rates of exchange on Shanghai at the respective periods.

[e] The chief of these were the provincial banks of Hopei, Hunan, Shansi, Kiangsu, and Kwangsi. Much the largest issue was that of Hopei, which under Japanese military pressure expanded its issue after mid-1936 from a few million to a reported C$55 million June 30, 1937. (See *Finance and Commerce*, February 23, 1938, p. 149.) The reduction as of November 2, 1935, resulted from national takeover of Szechwan issue, figures of which are included only for 1934.

[f] The chief of these were the New Futien Bank of Yunnan and the Yu Ming Bank of Kiangsi. The New Futien Bank's notes depreciated and are here converted at their approximate equivalent in national currency, eventually 10 to 1.

Appendix 18

Deposits, current and fixed, in Chinese banks from 1921 to 1937[a]

	Deposits, millions									
	1927	1928	1929	1930	1931	1932	1933	1934	1935	1936
Government banks, except Central Bank of China										
Bank of China										
Current accounts	C$ 91[b]	C$223[b]	C$255[b]	C$310[b]	C$288	C$242	C$338	C$295	C$465	C$559
Fixed deposits	40	52	55	70	174	234	211	252	344	505
Bank of Communications										
Current accounts	72	103	103	121	127	142	166	180	261	348
Fixed deposits	44	47	56	52	60	70	75	107	126	191
Farmers Bank	--	--	--	--	--	--	8	16	53	155
Subtotal	247	425	468	553	649	688	798	850	1,249	1,758

Continued

Appendix 18 (Continued)

Deposits, current and fixed, in Chinese banks from 1921 to 1937[a]

	Deposits, millions									
	1927	1928	1929	1930	1931	1932	1933	1934	1935	1936
Government banks, except Central Bank of China										
Commercial banks[c]	C$205	C$568	C$672	C$834	C$972	C$979	C$1,158	C$1,376	C$1,264	C$1,415[d]
Provincial and municipal banks[e]	--	--	--	--	--	103	118	151	251	350[f]
Total	452	993	1,141	1,387	1,621	1,766	2,074	2,377	2,764	3,523
Central Bank of China[g]	--	15	40	66	90	154	227	249	596	714

[a] Source: For 1921 to 1931, Bank of China, *An Analysis of the Accounts of the Principal Chinese Banks, 1921-1931* (Shanghai, 1933), pp. 55, 64, 315-316. After 1931, ***Chinese Bankers Yearbook, 1936***; which is quoted in F. M. Tamagna ***Banking and Finance in China*** (New York, 1942), pp. 131, 155, 160, 172; ***Finance and Commerce***, July 14, 1937, pp. 42-43; Central Bank of China.

[b] Adjusted; prior to 1931 "Forward contracts sold" are included in this heading, and the 1931 breakdown shows them constituting about one-third. Hence the figures prior to 1931 are reduced by one third as an estimated adjustment.

[c] The data for 1921 to 1931 are less comprehensive than thereafter, but the items thereafter added are relatively small in total. This heading includes what the ***Bankers Yearbook*** calls "Special banks," whose business did not differ materially from that of those classified as "Commercial banks."

[d] Estimated from data for banks that had about three-fourths of the deposits in 1934-1935.

[e] Data not available before 1932.

[f] Estimated.

[g] Most of the Central Bank's deposits were governmental. A breakdown for mid-1935 shows about 75 per cent governmental, 21 per cent banking, and 4 per cent private. The breakdown for other dates is not available. A great part of the private deposits was in CGU, for paying customs duties.

Appendix 19

Condition of the Central Bank of China from 1928 to 1937[a]

		Assets, millions				
			Reserves against notes			
Year ended December 31	Cash on hand and in transit	Amount due from banks	Cash	Securities	Loans, discounts, overdrafts	Securities owned[b]
1928	C$ 8	C$ 10	C$ 8	C$ 3	C$ 4	C$ 10
1929	14	19	10	6	15	9
1930	15	42	19	3	28	1
1931	16	22	19	6	75	--
1932	39	50	33	7	98	--
1933	65	57	58	13	143	--
1934	53	56	68	18	85	155
1935	87	176	119	61	154	253
1936	50	225	222	118	477	38
June 30 1937	C$117	C$416	C$244[c]	C$132[c]	C$428	C$ 38

Continued

Appendix 19 (Continued)

Condition of the Central Bank of China from 1928 to 1937[a]

	Liabilities, millions			
December 31	Capital, reserve, individual profits	Notes in circulation	Deposits	Total assets and liabilities, millions
1928	C$ 20	C$ 12	C$ 15	C$ 47
1929	20	15	40	87
1930	21	23	66	124
1931	23	25	90	145
1932	27	40	154	249
1933	36	71	227	364
1934	104	86	249	478
1935	104	180	596	932
1936	109	340	714	1,231
June 30				
1937	C$118	C$383	C$924	C$1,477

[a] Source: Central Bank statements which through June 30, 1936, are contained in the Finance Ministry's annual reports.
[b] Securities owned comprised almost wholly government items.
[c] From Currency Reserve Board reports as of June 27, 1937.

Appendix 20

Foreign trade excluding Manchuria from 1921 to 1937[a]

	Trade in millions C$			Trade in millions US$			
	Imports	Exports	Total	Imports	Exports	Total	Average value of C$ in US$
1921	1,233	698	1,931	628	355	984	0.510
1922	1,284	764	2,048	714	425	1,138	0.556
1923	1,251	868	2,119	658	456	1,114	0.526
1924	1,389	878	2,267	732	463	1,195	0.527
1925	1,242	876	2,118	707	498	1,205	0.569
1926	1,473	934	2,407	737	467	1,204	0.500
1927	1,298	980	2,278	569	430	1,000	0.439
1928	1,530	1,047	2,577	705	483	1,187	0.461
1929	1,620	1,070	2,690	679	448	1,127	0.419
1930	1,723	944	2,667	515	282	797	0.299
1931	2,002	915	2,917	448	205	653	0.224
1932	1,524	569	2,093	331	123	454	0.217
1933	1,345	612	1,957	385	175	560	0.286
1934	1,030	535	1,565	351	182	534	0.341
1935	919	576	1,495	336	211	547	0.366
1936	941	706	1,647	280	210	491	0.298
1937 (first half)	606	483	1,089	180	143	323	0.297
1937 (total)	953	838	1,791	284	250	534	0.298

[a]Source: ***The Trade of China, 1936: Introductory Survey***, p. 16, and other Customs publications. Exchange rates are from Federal Reserve System, ***Banking and Monetary Statistics*** (Washington, 1943), p. 667.

[b]Approximate.

Appendix 21

Foreign trade of Manchuria from 1926 to 1937[a]

	Imports	Exports	Total	Imports	Exports	Total	Average value of unit in US$
		In millions C$			In millions US$		
1926	279	413	692	140	207	346	0.500
1927	280	451	731	123	198	321	0.439
1928	333	498	831	154	230	383	0.461
1929	352	512	864	147	215	362	0.419
1930	318	450	768	95	135	230	0.299
1931	231	502	733	52	112	164	0.224
		In Manchurian yen					
1932	301	616	917	85	173	258	0.281
1933	515	423	938	132	108	240	0.256

Continued

Appendix 21 (Continued)

Foreign trade of Manchuria from 1926 to 1937[a]

	Imports	Exports	Total	Imports	Exports	Total	Average value of unit in US$
	In Manchurian yen			In millions US$			
1934	594	448	1,042	176	133	309	0.297
1935	604	421	1,025	173	121	294	0.287
1936	692	603	1,295	201	175	376	0.290
(first half)	408	358	766	118	103	221	0.288

[a] Source: For 1926 to 1931, compiled from Customs publications; for 1932 to 1935, from ***Japan Year Book, 1936***, p. 1179; for 1936 and 1937, from ***Japan-Manchukuo Year Book, 1938***, p. 870. The currency values shown for 1932 to 1937 are for the Japanese yen, with which the Manchukuo yen was at parity. Exchange rates are from Federal Reserve System, ***Banking and Monetary Statistics*** (Washington, 1943), pp. 667, 673.

Appendix 22

Principal imports and exports in 1935 and 1936[a]

Imports, millions

		1935		1936
Metals and ores		C$87.4		C$108.1
Candles, soap, oils, fats, waxes, gum and resins:				
Kerosene	C$37.6		C$39.9	
Gasoline, etc.	19.6		22.6	
Liquid fuel	19.5		16.2	
Other	25.0		26.4	
Subtotal		101.7		105.1
Machinery and tools		65.9		60.0
Books, maps, paper and wood pulp		53.1		57.5
Cotton and manufacturers thereof:				
Raw cotton	40.9		36.1	
Cotton piece goods	20.6		12.1	
Other	7.2		6.1	
Subtotal		68.7		54.3
Vehicles and vessels		30.6		52.5
Chemicals and pharmaceuticals		37.4		51.8
Cereals and flour:				
Rice and paddy	89.6		26.7	
Wheat	34.9		11.8	
Wheat flour	6.0		4.7	
Other	5.5		6.0	
Subtotal		135.9		49.2
Miscellaneous metal manufactures		34.8		46.7
Dyes, pigments, paints and varnishes		37.6		41.2
Wool and manufactures thereof		20.4		29.3
Timber		34.8		28.9
Sugar		27.7		20.5
Flax, ramie, hemp, jute and manufactures thereof		13.1		18.0
Fishery and sea products		19.0		17.8
Tobacco		11.3		17.4
Animal products, canned goods and groceries		11.8		9.4
Silk (including artificial and manufactures thereof)		8.0		9.4

Continued

Appendix 22 (Continued)

Principal imports and exports in 1935 and 1936[a]

Imports, millions				
	1935		1936	
Medicinal substances and spices		8.7		8.7
Wood, bamboo, rattans, coir, straw and manufactures thereof		7.5		7.6
Coal, fuel, pitch and tar		9.2		7.4
Fruits, seeds and vegetables		6.9		5.8
Others		87.7		134.9
Total		C$919.2		C$941.5

Exports, millions				
Textile fibres:				
Silk	C$40.5		C$44.5	
Raw cotton	21.7		28.2	
Sheep's wool	14.2		15.4	
Ramie	6.2		8.0	
Others	14.7		16.9	
Subtotal		C$97.4		C$113.0
Animals and animal products:				
Eggs and egg products	32.1		41.8	
Bristles	16.2		25.3	
Intestines	9.0		10.9	
Other	22.9		26.0	
Subtotal		80.3		104.0
Oils, tallow and wax:				
Wood oil	41.6		73.4	
Oils (others), tallow and wax	15.7		18.0	
Subtotal		57.3		91.4
Ores, metals and metallic products:				
Tin	20.4		26.8	
Antimony	8.0		9.9	
Wolfram	6.7		9.3	
Other	8.5		10.7	
Subtotal		43.6		56.7

Continued

Appendix 22 (Continued)

Principal imports and exports in 1935 and 1936[a]

Exports, millions

	1935		1936	
Yarn, thread, plaited and knitted goods		42.5		47.5
Seeds:				
Groundnuts	19.6		10.9	
Sesamum seed	16.6		18.6	
Other	12.8		11.3	
Subtotal		49.0		40.8
Hides, leather, skins (furs)		23.6		40.5
Tea		29.6		30.7
Cereals and cereal products		18.9		24.8
Piece goods		18.9		24.1
Vegetables and vegetable products		14.6		16.6
Fuel		8.6		13.0
Tobacco		9.0		10.1
Fruits		8.5		9.9
Medicinal substances and spices		9.1		9.8
Other		65.0		72.8
Total		C$575.8		C$705.7

[a] Source: Compiled from Customs reports.

Appendix 23

Distribution of total foreign trade from 1921 to 1937[a]

	Great Britain	Hong Kong	British Empire, total	United States	Europe	Japan	Other
1921	11.8%	25.0%	42.5%	17.3%	5.9%	24.9%	9.3%
1922	11.3	25.1	41.9	16.4	7.7	24.0	10.0
1923	9.6	24.9	41.1	16.5	8.4	24.1	9.9
1924	9.7	23.0	38.5	16.1	10.8	24.1	10.5
1925	8.1	16.7	30.9	16.4	11.1	27.9	13.7
1926	8.6	10.9	27.8	16.8	11.6	27.3	16.4
1927	6.8	19.6	32.2	14.8	11.1	25.7	16.2
1928	7.9	18.5	32.0	15.1	12.8	24.9	15.2
1929	8.4	16.9	32.1	16.1	13.0	25.2	13.7
1930	7.7	16.9	33.8	16.4	12.6	24.5	12.7
1931	7.7	15.9	31.9	17.7	13.1	23.8	13.5
1932	9.4	10.6	26.2	18.7	13.4	17.9	23.8
1933	9.7	11.7	31.7	20.2	14.5	12.7	20.9
1934	10.7	10.9	29.2	21.9	15.2	13.7	20.0
1935	9.5	9.3	28.2	21.3	16.9	14.6	19.0
1936	10.4	8.5	26.2	23.0	20.3	15.4	15.1
1937	10.6	10.7	27.8	23.7	21.5	12.9	14.1

[a] Source: Central Bank *Bulletin*, December 1937, p. 337.

Appendix 24

Export and import wholesale prices at Shanghai from 1926 to 1936 (1926 = 100)[a]

	Exports	Imports	Terms of trade (imports exports)
1926	100.0	100.0	100.0
1927	106.1	107.3	101.1
1928	104.5	102.6	98.5
1929	105.2	107.7	102.4
1930	108.8	126.7	116.3
1931	107.5	150.2	139.7
1932	90.4	140.2	155.3
1933	82. --	132.3	161.5
1934	71.6	132.1	184.9
1935	77.6	128.4	165.6
1936	96.1	141.7	147.0

[a] Source: Appendix 12.

Appendix 25

Goods carried on railways from 1932 to 1936[a]

		Tonnage (thousands of metric tons) Products of Indicated Industry				
Yen	Total[b]	Mines	Agriculture	Forests	Animals	Manufactures
1932	26,065	14136	3374	527	379	3113
1933	27,076	13712	3638	469	405	2994
1933-34	29,113	15605	4208	465	437	2990
1934-35	32,959	16869	5820	478	484	3529
1935-36	34,364	18169	4923	432	519	3812
		Ton-Kilometers (millions of metric tons)				
1932	3,629	2029	790	82	82	696
1933	3,727	2063	839	79	88	657
1933-34	4,235	2448	975	77	95	641
1934-35	5,236	2932	1324	92	109	778
1935-36	5,290	3030	1178	82	121	878

[a] Source: *Statistics of Chinese National Railways, 1935-1936* (Nanking, 1937), pp. 78-79.

[b] Including goods carried for government and for railway operations.

Notes

Notes

Chapter 1

[1]R. H. Tawney, *Land and Labour in China* (London, 1932), p. 12.

[2]For the best comprehensive description of these rights and interests, see W. W. Willoughby, *Foreign Rights and Interests in China* (Baltimore, 1927).

[3]*China Year Book, 1928*, p. x.

[4]*Ibid.*, pp. 543-552.

[5]S. F. Wright and J. H. Cubbon, *China's Customs Revenue Since the Revolution of 1911* (Shanghai, 1935), pp. 410-441.

[6]Chow Tse-tsung, *The May Fourth Movement* (Cambridge, 1960).

[7]For a full account of Russian activities in this period, see Robert C. North, *Moscow and Chinese Communists* (Stanford, 1953).

[8]Akira Iriye, *After Imperialism: The Search for a New Order in the Far East, 1921-1931* (Cambridge, 1965), pp. 55, 44.

[9]*Ibid.*, p. 41.

[10]*China Year Book, 1928*, pp. 616-618.

[11]Paul K. T. Sih, ed., *The Strenuous Decade: China's Nation-Building Efforts, 1927-1937* (New York, 1970), p. 10.

C. Martin Wilbur after study of the available data on the Nanking incident concluded: "Responsibility for the incident is still uncertain." Ping-ti Ho and Tang Tsou, eds., *China in Crisis* (Chicago, 1968), vol. 1, book 1, pp. 249-250 n.

[12]*Foreign Relations of the United States*, 1927, vol. 2, p. 5. Hereafter cited as *FRUS*.

[13]*China Year Book*, 1929-30, p. 1181.

[14]F. F. Liu, *A Military History of Modern China* (Princeton, 1956), p. 47.

[15]For the text of important documents see *China Year Book, 1928*, pp. 799-824.

Chapter 2

[1]See *Organic Law of the National Government of the Republic of China* (Nanking, 1928); and *Civil Code of the Republic of China*, Book 1, *General Principles*, translated by Ching-lin Hsia and James L. E. Chow (Shanghai, 1929).

[2]*China Year Book, 1929-30*, p. 629; for the resolutions adopted, see *ibid.*, pp. 629-632.

[3]*Ibid.*, p. 633.

[4]Iriye, *After Imperialism*, p. 41.

[5]The only text of this memorandum available to me is a French translation in J. R. Baylin, *Emprunts Interieurs Chinois* (Peking, 1929), pp. 21-28.

[6]The authoritative work on these matters is Stanley F. Wright, *China's Struggle for Tariff Autonomy, 1843-1938* (Shanghai, 1938). For further particulars regarding the operation of the Customs service and disposal of the revenue, see Wright and Cubbon, *China's Customs Revenue Since the Revolution of 1911.*

For material on international developments during this period, see Iriye, *After Imperialism*, pp. 71-88.

[7]See Wright, *Tariff Autonomy*, pp. 602-623.

[8]*China Year Book, 1928*, pp. 645-646.

[9]*Ibid.*, pp. 759, 766.

[10]Iriye, *After Imperialism*, pp. 246-248.

[11]For the agreement on the Salt Administration, see the Reorganization Loan agreement in J. V. A. MacMurray, *Treaties and Agreements with and concerning China, 1894-1919* (New York, 1921), vol. 2, pp. 1009-1029.

[12]For Wilson's statement, see *ibid.*, p. 1025.

[13]Details of the working of the Administration are given in *China Year Book, 1929-30*, pp. 671-672. For early developments see S. A. M. Adshead, *The Modernization of the Chinese Salt Administration, 1900-1920* (Cambridge, 1970).

[14]See *ibid.*, pp. 672-675, for the statements quoted in this and the preceding paragraphs.

[15]For data in this section, I have drawn upon my files; Finance Minister, *Annual Report for the Fiscal Year July 1928 to June 1929; China Year Book, 1928; China Year Book, 1929-30;* and Yau-pik Chau, *Taxation Reforms of the Chinese National Government in the Decade 1927-37* (unpublished doctoral dissertation, University of Chicago, 1945).

[16]For the text of the charter, see *China Year Book, 1929-30*, pp. 312-315.

[17]See Richard Feetham, *Report to the Shanghai Municipal Council*, (Shanghai, 1931). For a discussion of these matters, including a full statement of Chinese views, see *Problems of the Pacific, 1931*, edited by Bruno Lasker (Chicago, 1932), which contains a report of the Institute of Pacific Relations' Conference at Shanghai and Hangchow in 1931.

[18]*FRUS*, 1928, vol. 2, pp. 453-454.

[19]Iriye, *After Imperialism*, p. 239.

[20]*Ibid.*, pp. 192-214, 239-253.

[21]*Ibid.*, pp. 242-253.

Chapter 3

[1]MacMurray, *Treaties and Agreements*, vol. 1, pp. 105-109.

[2]*North-China Daily News*, November 9, 1933.

[3]For an account of the complicated procedure used, see Wright and Cubbon, *China's Customs Revenue Since the Revolution of 1911*, Chapter I.

[4]*FRUS*, 1923, vol. 1, pp. 551-579; 1924, vol. 1, pp. 409-416.

[5]*China Year Book, 1928*, pp. 645-646.

[6]See for example *Far Eastern Review*, August 1932, p. 348.

[7]Wright and Cubbon, *China's Customs Revenue Since the Revolution of 1911*, p. 173; Wright, *Tariff Autonomy*, pp. 344-346, 354, 363-371.

[8]Wright, *Tariff Autonomy*, p. 685.

[9]*Chinese Year Book, 1936-37*, pp. 891-945, and Chao-ying Shih, "Smuggling in North China," *Information Bulletin of the Council of International Affairs*, vol. 1, May 21, 1936.

[10]For a history of the salt tax and details of some matters discussed here see Yau-pik Chau, *Taxation Reforms of the Chinese National Government*, Chapter III. See also Esson M. Gale, "Public Administration of Salt in China: A Historical Survey," *Annals of the American Academy of Political and Social Science*, vol. 152, November 1930, pp. 241-251; and Albert Feuerwerker, *China's Early Industrialization* (Cambridge, 1958), pp. 50-51.

[11]F. A. Cleveland, *Digest of . . . Statistical Review of the Work of the Inspectorate of Salt Revenue from 1913 to 1933 Inclusive* (Shanghai, 1934), p. 29.

[12]*Ibid.*, p. 9.

[13]Statements of receipts and payments in the Reports of the Minister of Finance, *passim*.

[14]*North-China Daily News*, April 10, 1936; Salt Inspectorate, *Advance Annual Report for 1937*, p. 3.

[15]See *Shanghai Evening Post and Mercury*, February 11 and 12, 1932, June 22, 1937.

[16]See State Department file 893.51 Salt funds /155, despatch of December 21, 1936, from American embassy, Nanking.

[17]For an account of developments during the war affecting the Salt administration see Arthur N. Young, *China and the Helping Hand, 1937-1945* (Cambridge, 1963), pp. 42-48, 96-99, and *China's Wartime Finance and Inflation, 1937-1945* (Cambridge, 1965), pp. 34-39, 48-53.

[18]Finance Minister, *Report for the 18th Fiscal Year, 1929-1930*, p. 5.

[19]T. V. Soong, "Taxation Policy of the Nationalist Government," *St. John's Echo* (Shanghai), January 1929.

[20]State Department file 893.00PR /41, despatch from American legation, Nanking, January 12, 1931.

[21]State Department file 893.512 /1312, despatch from American legation, Nanking, January 24, 1934.

[22]See H.G.W. Woodhead, "Plain Speaking on Opium," *Shanghai Evening Post & Mercury*, June 2, 1934; and articles in that publication, October 21 and 22, 1935, by Garfield Huang; State Department file 893.114 Narcotics /1687, 1829, 1855, 1900, 1990, 2013, despatches from American embassy, Nanking, August 12, 1936, to June 22, 1937.

[23]Marcus Mervine, "Japanese Concession in Tientsin and the Narcotic Trade," *Information Bulletin of the Council of International Affairs* (Nanking), February 11, 1937, p. 83; *North-China Daily News*, June 4, 1937.

[24]*China Year Book, 1924*, p. 805.

[25]For a translation of the law see *Chinese Year Book, 1936-37*, pp. 667-682.

[26]Hart's plan of reform was naive. He proposed a uniform tax regardless of the kind of land, and had no plan for assessment or valuation and no machinery for collection. He had the ingenious idea of a "chain letter" plan to extend the reform throughout China. First a team would be trained to begin in one province, and, after starting the plan, the team would train teams to go to other provinces to train more teams—to spread the plan with geometric progression. Hart's plan is in *Reports of the Chinese Customs Service*, Special Series No. 26 (1904), and also in the *North-China Herald*, April 15, 1904.

[27]For an account of the history and status of the land tax to 1918, see Huang Han-liang, *The Land Tax in China* (New York, 1918).

[28]Lossing Buck, Owen L. Dawson, and Y. L. Wu, *Food and Agriculture in Communist China* (New York, 1966), p. 9.

[29]*Annexes to the Report to the Council of the League of Nations of Its Technical Delegate on His Mission to China . . . until April 1, 1934* (Nanking, 1934), pp. 73-108, especially pp. 107-108.

[30]Y. L. Wu, *China's Economic Policy: Planning or Free Enterprise?* (International Economic Research Center, New York, 1946), pp. 22-23.

[31]*Chinese Year Book, 1936-1937* (2nd issue), p. 1258.

[32]*Ibid.*, pp. 691-693.

[33]Ta-chung Liu, *China's National Income, 1931-1936* (Brookings Institution, Washington, 1946), p. 11; also Ta-chung Liu and Kung-chia Yeh, *Economy of the Chinese Mainland; National Income and Economic Development, 1933-1959* (Princeton, 1965), p. 66.

[34]E. H. Norman, *Japan's Emergence as a Modern State* (New York, 1940), pp. 138-144.

[35]These are the estimates of Ta-chung Liu, in *China's National Income, 1931-1936: An Exploratory Study* (Washington, 1946), pp. 54-55, 70. He states that, "Missing data for certain provinces in some years are made up by using data for the same province or for a province with similar population in the nearest year." He estimated *hsien* figures by making similar adjustments.

For further details see Directorate General of Budgets, Accounts and Statistics, *Statistical Abstract* (Chung-hua Min-kuo t'ung chi t'i yao), 1940, pp. 151-155. Incomplete data of actual receipts and expenditures for 1931-1936 are given in *Chinese Year Book, 1936-37*, pp. 702-710, and in *China Year Book, passim*. A law of 1932 required provincial and local governments to obtain the Finance Ministry's approval for changes in taxes and for public loans (*Kuo Min News Agency*, November 20, 1932).

[36]For data on distribution of receipts, see *Chinese Year Book, 1936-37* (2nd issue), pp. 704-705.

[37]*Ibid.*, pp. 692, 696-699. See also the budget law of August 1932, Articles 78-94.

[38]*China Year Book, 1929-30*, pp. 646-647.

Chapter 4

[1]Finance Minister, Report, 1928-1929, pp. 3, 10.

[2]*North-China Daily News*, June 12, 1932.

[3]The estimates of expenditures are those of Ta-chung Liu, *China's National Income, 1931-36*, pp. 54-55. For partial data on distribution of provincial expenditures see *Chinese Year Book, 1936-37* (2nd issue), pp. 702-709.

[4]*China Year Book, 1928*, pp. 553-560.

[5]*Annexes to the Report to the Council of the League of Nations of Its Technical Eelegate on His Mission to China . . . until April 1, 1934*, pp. 152-153.

[6]*Ibid.*, pp. 74-77.

[7]F. E. Lee, *Currency, Banking, and Finance in China* (Department of Commerce, Washington, D.C., 1926), pp. 133-134.

[8]Data in this and the preceding two paragraphs are from a report of the Department of Accounts received February 13, 1931, and a memorandum of William Watson of November 20, 1931.

[9]Y. C. Wang, *Chinese Intellectuals and the West* (Chapel Hill, North Carolina, 1966), p. 453; D. S. Paauw, "Chinese Public Finance during the Nanking Government Period" (unpublished doctoral dissertation, Harvard University, 1950), p. 123n.

[10]These figures are also presented in Chang Wei-ya's useful book, *The Money and Finance of China* (Taipei, 1951), pp. 138-140, and some writers have cited them from this source.

[11]See Appendix 1 and also the tables and comment in Young, *China's Wartime Finance*, Appendix A, pp. 330-334.

[12]Chang Kia-ngau, *The Inflationary Spiral: The Experience of China, 1939-1950* (New York, 1958).

[13]Shun-hsin Chou, *The Chinese Inflation, 1937-1950* (New York, 1963).

[14]Chang in *The Inflationary Spiral*, p. 16, derived the figures for fiscal 1937 from Chang Wei-ya's *The Money and Finance of China*, which gives the figures in the Finance Ministry's aforementioned 1943 publication. Chou's figures in *Chinese Inflation*, pp. 62, 72, are similar. His tables overlook the fact that fiscal years through 1938 ended June 30; that the second half of 1938 was a separate fiscal period; and that thereafter fiscal and calendar years were the same. For Y. C. Wang's figures see his *Chinese Intellectuals and the West*, p. 456.

I published Ministry figures for the two prewar fiscal years in a table summarizing the fiscal results for 1931 through 1937 in *China's Economic and Financial Reconstruction* (Committee on International and Economic Policy and The Carnegie Endowment for International Peace, New York, 1947), pp. 30-35. The 1937 figure of payments was given as C$1138 million instead of C$1167 million (Appendix 1) because in 1947 all of my records were not available. Because of the lack of officially published Finance Ministry figures for fiscal 1936 and 1937 and for purposes of comparison, I included the basic figures of receipts and expenditures in *China and the Helping Hand*, p. 435, published in

1963 after Chang Kia-ngau's and Chou's books but before Wang's. I also included a summary of the data from 1929 to 1937 and details for fiscal 1936 and 1937 in *China's Wartime Finance and Inflation* (1965), pp. 12, 331-334.

[15]D. S. Paauw, "Chinese National Expenditures during the Nanking Period," *Far Eastern Quarterly*, November 1952, pp. 10, 21, 23. See also his unpublished doctoral dissertation, Harvard, 1950, *passim*.

[16]Chou, *Chinese Inflation*, p. 287.

[17]Paauw, *Far Eastern Quarterly*, November 1952, pp. 10, 24, and Harvard thesis, p. 124.

[18]Tuan-sheng Ch'ien, *Government and Politics of China* (Cambridge, 1950), p. 213. This is an adaptation of a two-volume work (in Chinese) published in China in 1939.

[19]Payments for government transportation were included in the budgets of the military (mostly not paid in cash) and other departments. Receipts from railway profits (largely representing the value of military transport not paid in cash) made up two-thirds of the C$21 million budgeted as receipts from government enterprises for 1936-1937, and presumably a similar proportion of C$23 million budgeted for 1937-1938. The budget for 1936-1937 also included C$78 million as payments for railways. The breakdown of the budget for 1937-1938 is not available, but the C$70 million for "Reconstruction" presumably included some payments for railways. For details of the budget for 1936-1937 see *Chinese Year Book, 1936-37* (2nd issue), pp. 589-597. A summary of that budget and of the one for 1937-1938 is in *China Year Book, 1939*, pp. 342-343.

[20]*Chinese Year Book, 1936-1937* (2nd issue), pp. 596-597.

[21]See *China Handbook, 1943*, p. 199, for a summary of the budget law adopted by the Legislative Yuan in September 1932 and revised in April 1937. See also Chi'en, *op. cit.*, pp. 206-210. The Legislative Yuan at its meeting on June 25, 1937, complained about lack of details of the lump sum appropriation of C$70 million for Reconstruction, and asked that details be provided in future except for secret items that were to be reserved under Article 45. See *Kuo Min News Agency*, June 27, 1937.

[22]For a history of internal borrowing, see E. Kann, "China Internal Loans of Today and Yesterday," *North-China Daily News*, January 1, 1930.

[23]See Leonard G. Ting, "Chinese Modern Banks and the Finance of Government and Industry," *Nankai Social and Economic Quarterly*, October 1935, p. 591; and Frank M. Tamagna, *Banking and Finance in China* (New York, 1942), p. 217, referring to Ting. The figures cited in both these publications are from Chu Hsieh, "Problems of China's Public Finance" (1934). See also Y. C. Wang, *Chinese Intellectuals and the West*, p. 436.

Chu as quoted by Ting charged that from May 1927 to January 1932 the government received only C$539 million against an issue of C$1006 million. Total issues for general purposes in that period were not C$1006 million but C$953 million (Appendix 8). Special issues in that period whose proceeds were not incorporated in treasury receipts were C$45 million of 2-1 /2 per cent bonds exchanged to redeem depreciated notes of the leftist Hankow regime, C$4 million for the Haiho Conservancy Board, and C$6 million for the silk industry. The C$539 million seems derived from adding to the C$478 million received from bonds and treasury notes in the four fiscal years to June 30, 1932 (see published Ministry annual reports), the C$61 million from loans for the year ended May 31, 1928 (see *China Year Book, 1929-30*, pp. 646-647). No loans were issued in the period from January to June 30, 1932, when the situation was disrupted and the Stock Exchange closed for several months because of the Japanese attack at Shanghai. Moreover, the Ministry reports state that it received C$71 million from bank loans and overdrafts, presumably secured by the bond issues, in the aforementioned four years. Adding C$71 million to the C$539 million gives C$610 million, or 64 per cent of C$953 million of obligations issued for general purposes.

Another charge (see Tamagna who referred to Chu) is that in 1927 to 1934 the government received only C$809 million against issues of C$1465 million. From May 1927 through June 1934, loan issues for general purposes actually totaled C$1127 million (Appendix 8), to which should be added a loan of C$44 million borrowed from banks in January 1934 but not publicly issued, making a total of C$1171 million. That excludes

C$100 million issued as of June 30, 1934, which presumably pertained to the immediately following fiscal period, and the Yuping Railway loan of C$12 million. Receipts from loan issues through June 1934, including the aforementioned C$61 million in 1927-1928, were C$645 million. In addition, C$248 million was received from bank advances, presumably secured by the bond issues, through June 1934. Total receipts of C$893 million were 76 per cent of the nominal total of C$1171 million.

The conclusions above must be qualified to the extent if any that there was bank borrowing not covered by collateral securities. Definite data as to this are not available, but indications are that there was little if any such borrowing.

[24]On student agitation see John Israel, *Student Nationalism in China, 1927-1937* (Stanford, 1966).

[25]See Soong's conversation on December 8, 1931, with Willis R. Peck of the American embassy at Nanking. Soong pleaded for the United States to take some action to counter Japan's move. State Department file 893.51 /5574.

[26]*North China Daily News*, March 2, 1932.

[27]*Report for the 19th and 20th Fiscal Years, July 1930 to June 1932*, pp. 1-2, 10, 12.

[28]*Report for the 21st and 22nd Fiscal Years, July 1934 to June 1935*, p. 19.

Chapter 5

[1]For a detailed account of the Boxer Indemnity to 1935 see Wright and Cubbon, *China's Customs Revenue since the Revolution of 1911*, pp. 169-287, 442-591. See also the published annual reports of The China Foundation for the Promotion of Education and Culture, and annual and semiannual reports of the Board of Trustees for the Administration of the Indemnity Funds Remitted by the British Government.

[2]Proceedings, *The Special Conference on the Chinese Customs Tariff* (Peking, 1928), pp. 150-151.

[3]*Kuo Min News Agency*, March 21, 1930.

[4]See Iriye, *After Imperialism*, pp. 193-205, for a discussion of the Tsinan affair.

[5]*Ibid.*

[6]For the agreement see Carnegie Endowment for International Peace, *Treaties and Agreements with and concerning China, 1919-1929* (Washington, 1929), pp. 83-84, 87-88.

[7]For the best account of the making of the Nishihara loans and of the action of Japan and China at the time see F. C. Langdon, *The Japanese Policy of Expansion in China, 1917-1928* (unpublished doctoral dissertation, University of California, Berkeley, 1953), pp. 31-82 and 109-110. See also Arthur G. Coons, *The Foreign Public Debt of China* (Philadelphia, 1930), pp. 73-75, 85-86, 91-93; and Iriye, *After Imperialism*, pp. 32, 68, 281-282, 289. For the texts of the Nishihara agreements, see MacMurray, *Treaties and Agreements*, 1918 /4, 7, 9, 11, 14, 15, 16.

The statements concerning these loans are based on the aforementioned sources; data of the Chinese Commission for Readjustment of Finance, and the Commission for Readjustment of Domestic and Foreign Debts; and documents supplied to me by Japanese representatives and conversations with them.

[8]Iriye, *After Imperialism*, p. 263.

[9]For a valuable analysis of the events discussed in this paragraph, see James B. Crowley, *Japan's Quest for Autonomy* (Princeton, 1966), pp. 1-121, and from the Japanese side, Iriye, *After Imperialism*, pp. 278-293.

[10]*Manchurian Daily News*, August 23, 1933.

[11]State Department files 893.51 /6061, 6069, despatches from the American embassy November 13, 1935 and January 8, 1936; 893.48 /1026, memorandum of December 14, 1935.

[12]*FRUS*, 1931, vol. 3, pp. 1034-1046;1932, vol. 3, pp. 621-627;1933, vol. 3, pp. 628-629; 1934, vol. 3, p. 543; 1935, vol. 3, pp. 754-757; also State Department files 893.51, Contractual obligations /18A, January 3, 1931, and /34, July 29, 1935.

[13]For the contracts see MacMurray, *Treaties and Agreements*, 1908 /1; 1910 /4; 1911 /5. The contingent clause is Article 9 in each agreement.

[14]*Reuters News Agency*, despatch from London, February 5, 1931.

[15]For the full text of the offer and fuller details concerning this debt and the debt of £900,000 mentioned in a following paragraph, see Chang Kia-ngau, *China's Struggle for Railroad Development* (New York, 1943), pp. 155-159.

[16]*FRUS*, 1936, vol. 4, pp. 584-586; State Department files 893.51 /6120A, 6126.

[17]State Department file 893.51 /6126, 6157, and 6204, March 31, April 29, and July 11, 1936; *FRUS*, 1936, vol. 4, p. 583.

[18]*FRUS*, 1936, vol. 4, pp. 587-589; State Department file 893.51 /6210-6211, July 11-15, 1936.

[19]State Department files 893.51 /6201, June 29, 1936, /6258, October 28, 1936, and /6317, March 2, 1937.

[20]State Department files 893.51 /6336-6338, March 22-23, 1937.

[21]State Department file 893.51 /6347, March 25, 1937.

[22]For the text of the offer see *FRUS*, 1937, vol. 4, pp. 671-672, and Chang, *Railroad Development*, p. 161.

[23]For the text of the agreement see Carnegie Endowment, *Treaties and Agreements with and Concerning China*, pp. 1-11.

[24]Letters from Kung to Sze, October 12 and 14, 1935; telegrams from Sze to Kung, November 20, from Kung to Sze, November 22, and from Sze to Kung, December 19, 1935.

[25]Telegrams exchanged between Kung and Sze, December 19-31; State Department files 893.48 /1021-1027, 1033, December 14-31, 1935.

[26]Telegrams exchanged between Kung and Sze December 28-31, 1935; Central Bank of China telegram to Chase Bank, New York, December 30, 1935; State Department file 893.48 /1033, December 31, 1935.

[27]Telegrams from Sze, December 30, 1935, January 13 and 20, 1936; telegrams from Kung to Sze, January 6 and 23, 1936.

[28]For the text of the agreement see Carnegie Endowment, *Treaties and Agreements*, pp. 11-21.

Chapter 6

[1]State Department file 893.512 /1312, despatch 2481 of January 24, 1934.

[2]For data on national product see Ta-chung Liu, *China's National Income, 1931-36*, p. 12.

[3]See D. S. Paauw, "Chinese National Expenditures in the Nanking Period," *Far Eastern Quarterly*, November 1952, p. 7. Paauw's discussion of revenue policy, besides making the point quoted above, charges the government with "inability and unwillingness to develop an economically rational tax structure"; stresses the regressive nature of the revenues; and argues that the fiscal policies "were predominantly repressive of economic development" (pp. 6, 3). His discussion shows inadequate appreciation of the difficulties. It mostly ignores the constructive aspects summarized in this chapter and detailed in preceding chapters, notably the striking contrast between the low state of the national finances just prior to the Nationalist take-over and the improvements in the following decade.

In addition, his charge regarding repression of development gives undue weight to measures affecting such a small proportion of the economy, apart from anything else. N. S. Buchanan made this point in commenting on Paauw's paper (*ibid.*, p. 45). Paauw overlooks the lift to production and trade caused by fixing definite taxes under the consolidated tax program, and suppression of *likin* and other irregular charges throughout much of China. Whatever the repressive effect on development, the modernized industrial sector was able to progress in the prewar decade at an annual compounded rate estimated at 6.4 per cent for 1926 to 1936, and 6.7 per cent for 1931 to 1936 (Chapter 14).

[4]Norman, *Japan's Emergence as a Modern State*, pp. 138-144.

[5]This calculation is necessarily rough. The imperfections of data of revenues of the provinces and special municipalities are stated in Chapter 3. Since *hsien* data are available only for 1936-1937, the figures for previous years are here taken as a constant proportion of provincial and special municipal revenues. For the figures of gross national product here used see *Liu, China's National Income*, p. 10.

[6]*Far Eastern Quarterly*, November 1952, pp. 13, 16, 45-46.

[7]D. S. Paauw, "Chinese National Expenditures in the Nanking Period," *Far Eastern Quarterly*, November 1952, p. 6.

[8]See the Reorganization Loan agreement of 1913, Article 10, Macmurray, *Treaties and Agreements*, vol. 2, p. 1011.

[9]Ray Chang, "Trends in Chinese Public Administration," *Information Bulletin of the Council of International Affairs*, February 21, 1937.

Chapter 7

[1]The word *tael* is not Chinese, and apparently derives from the Malayan *tahil* or the Indian *tola*. The Chinese expression for that unit of weight is *liang* (ounce). The chief form of *tael* silver was *sycee* or ingots of about 50 *taels*. These were called shoes from resemblance to the shoes of women with bound feet. The ingots were made by a few private smelting firms which were trusted, and bore their *chop* certifying the content. *Sycee* is said to be derived from the Cantonese pronunciation of *hsi ssu*, meaning fine silk. See the article by E. Kann in *China Year Book, 1929-30*, p. 287.

[2]H. B. Morse, *Trade and Administration of China* (New York, 1920), pp. 164-165.

[3]For further particulars as to the Shanghai *tael* see John Parke Young, "The Shanghai Tael," *American Economic Review*, December 1931, pp. 682-684.

[4]There are also some discontinued series such as that of W. C. Wetmore for 1873-1892, and the Japanese Commission for the Investigation of Monetary Systems for 1874-1893. See Franklin Ho, "Prices and Price Indexes in China," *Chinese Economic Journal*, May 1927, pp. 429-463.

[5]See Franklin Ho, "Prices and Price Fluctuations in North China, 1913-1929," *Chinese Social and Political Science Review*, October 1929, pp. 349-358. For the University of Nanking data see the 360-page mimeographed publication compiled by W. Y. Yang, *University of Nanking Indexes* (Bulletin 54, New Series, January 1941). This document contains, besides various indexes, a list of wholesale prices of individual commodities in leading cities including considerable data on a monthly basis. Some of the data go back to 1913. I have lodged a copy of this document at the Hoover Library at Stanford University.

[6]The several indexes of prices and cost of living for the various cities are found in the following publications: Bureau of Markets, Finance Ministry, to 1929, and thereafter the National Tariff Commission; The *Shanghai Market Prices Report* (quarterly), 1923-1933; the monthly bulletins of these organizations, *Prices and Price Indexes in Shanghai*; and the Commission's *Annual Reports of Shanghai Prices*, 1934-1936. Most publications were suspended after hostilities began in 1937. For price data after that time, see Young, *China's Wartime Finance and Inflation*, pp. 347-358.

[7]J. Lossing Buck, "Price Changes in China," *Journal of the American Statistical Association*, June 1925.

[8]J. Lossing Buck, *Land Utilization in China* (Chicago, 1937), p. 319. The indexes for 1906-1933 are shown in Chi-ming Hou, *Foreign Investment and Economic Development in China, 1840-1937* (Cambridge, 1965), p. 266.

[9]Liu, *China's National Income, 1931-36, passim*. See also Appendix 13.

[10]This is shown graphically in the chart in the *Annual Report of Shanghai Prices, 1935*, p. IV, and is discussed there on pp. 14-18.

[11]See C. A. Conant, J. W. Jenks, and Edward Brush, "The Influence of Falling Exchange upon the Return Received for National Products," an argument submitted in 1903 to the Mexican Monetary Commission, report of the U. S. Commission on *Stability of International Exchange* (H.R. Document 144, 58th Congress, Second Session, Washington, 1903), pp. 431-439; also printed in *Bankers' Magazine*, May 1903.

[12]For the original study see Franklin L. Ho, "Index Numbers of the Quantities and Prices of Imports and Exports and of the Barter Terms of Trade in China, 1867-1928," *Chinese Economic Journal*, September 1930, pp. 1013-1041. For the revised series through 1936 see *Nankai Social and Economic Quarterly*, July 1937, pp. 346-347. For Hou's revision of Ho's data see Hou, *Foreign Investment and Economic Development in China, 1840-1937*, p. 198.

An element of uncertainty arises with regard to these indexes because the data after 1931 do not include prices of goods entering into Manchurian trade. But it seems doubtful that the overall price situation was significantly affected by this trade.

[13]Hou, *op. cit.*, pp. 199-204.

[14]Hart's suggestions regarding a gold standard are set forth in *North-China Herald*, July 3, 1903, and in *Stability of International Exchange*, pp. 226-229.

[15]See *Stability of International Exchange, op. cit.* This important document contains the first report of the American commissioners dated October 1, 1903. It also contains full documentation of the commission's work in China and Europe. The final report of the commissioners dated October 22, 1904, is entitled, *Report on the Introduction of the Gold-Exchange Standard* (Washington, 1904). It contains further data regarding the problems of China and other silver using countries. See also D. H. Leavens, *Silver Money* (Cowles Commission, Bloomington, Indiana, 1939), pp. 131-132.

[16]G. Vissering, *On Chinese Currency*, vol. I (Batavia, 1912); *On Chinese Currency: The Banking Problem*, vol. II (Amsterdam, 1914). See also Leavens, *Silver Money*, pp. 131-132.

[17]Leavens, *Silver Money*, pp. 132, 195, 199-200. The 1929 report of the Commission of Financial Experts (Kemmerer Commission): *Project of Law for the Gradual Introduction of a Gold-Standard Currency System in China, together with a Report in Support Thereof* (Shanghai, 1930), Appendixes H and I, contain fuller particulars of the various plans for currency reform from 1903 to 1929.

[18]Sir Arthur Salter, *China and the Depression* (National Economic Council of China), May 1934, pp. 90-116.

[19]*Stability of International Exchange, op. cit.*, pp. 15, 34.

[20]*China Year Book, 1929-30*, pp. 632-634.

[21]Regarding these measures see *Kuo Min News Agency*, December 30, 1932, March 5 and 9, and April 6, 1933; *Finance and Commerce*, Shanghai, April 12, 1933, pp. 405-407; and Leavens, *Silver Money*, pp. 202-205.

[22]*Report of the National Government Central Mint from its opening through June 30, 1935*, p. 14, and records of Central Bank.

Chapter 8

[1]Herbert Feis, *1933: Characters in Crisis* (Boston, 1966), p. 237; *New York Times*, October 9, 1930; *North-China Daily News*, November 26, 1930. Pittman's statement is quoted by Iriye, *After Imperialism* (p. 283), from a speech on October 8, 1930, among the Pittman papers in the Library of Congress.

[2]Hu's plan is set forth in detail in *Finance and Commerce*, February 4, 1931.

[3]*North-China Daily News*, October 31, 1930; *Reuter News Service*, January 12, 1931.

[4]*Reuters*, January 15, 1931; *North-China Daily News*, January 11 and 19, 1931; United Press despatch from Washington, January 22, 1931; *New York Times*, February 12, 1931.

[5]*China Press*, March 16, 1931.

[6]A letter of May 11, 1931, from John Parke Young to this author told of a talk with Pittman, who said he was "on his way to China to look into the silver situation, and . . . to see if China wants a silver loan and how they want it."

[7]*Report of the Legal Adviser of the National Government of China* (mimeographed), July 16, 1932.

[8]*Effect of Low Silver*, hearings before the Committee on Coinage, Weights, and Measures, 72d Congress, 1st Session, on H. R. 72 (Washington, 1932), Part 2, p. 274.

[9]For E. Kann's figures see *Chinese Economic Journal*, April 1931, pp. 410-411. The Customs estimate is in *Decennial Reports, 1922-1931* (Shanghai, 1933), vol. II, p. 11. In mid-1938, after efforts to collect silver for export for war purposes, the Bank of China and Bank of Communications estimated that prior to outbreak of fighting in August 1937 total silver stock in all forms was equivalent to about 900 million ounces. See Young, *China's Wartime Finance*, pp. 190, 400. Recorded exports from 1932 to mid-1937 plus Kann's estimate of smuggling totaled about 600 million ounces (Table 17). Adding that to the 900 million equals 1500 million, which compares with Kann's estimate for 1930 of 1700 million ounces of monetary silver and his "vague estimate" of 2500 million ounces of total silver.

[10]For an analysis of the economics of this issue see T. J. Kreps, "The Price of Silver and Chinese Purchasing Power," *Quarterly Journal of Economics*, February 1934, pp. 245-287.

[11]For the best accounts see D. H. Leavens, *Silver Money* (Cowles Commission, Bloomington, Indiana, 1939), and A. S. Everest, *Morgenthau, the New Deal, and Silver* (Columbia University, New York, 1950). Leavens also gives a comprehensive account of the American experience with silver from 1789 to 1938. For an account of Secretary Morgenthau's relation to the silver movement from 1933 to the outbreak of Sino-Japanese hostilities in 1937, see also J. M. Blum, *From the Morgenthau Diaries: Years of Crisis, 1928-1938* (Boston, 1959), pp. 183-228, 479-480.

[12]Everest, *op. cit.*, p. 37.

[13]Everest, *Morgenthau and Silver*, p. 101.

[14]H. M. Bratter, *The Silver Market*, Department of Commerce, Trade Promotion Series No. 139, 1932, p. 56.

[15]Quoted by Kreps, *Quarterly Journal of Economics*, February 1934, p. 247.

[16]Everest, *op. cit.*, pp. 38, 42.

[17]See *Executive Agreement Series*, No. 63, Washington, 1934, and Leavens' *Silver Money*, pp. 374-378.

[18]For an analysis and description of the Rogers mission to China, and for the loan of documents relating thereto, I am indebted to Byrd L. Jones, the author of *James Harvey Rogers: An Intellectual Biography, 1886-1939*, an unpublished doctoral dissertation presented at Yale University, 1966. Most of the citations in this section are from the aforementioned documents.

[19]State Department file 033.1100 Rogers, James H., telegram of April 21, 1934.

[20]*New York Times*, March 20, 1934.

[21]*Congressional Record*, 78, Pt. 5, p. 4814.

[22]State Department file 033.1100, Rogers, James H., telegrams of April 21 and 23. *FRUS*, 1934, vol. 3, pp. 430-440, contains the texts of several of Rogers' telegrams.

[23]*Ibid.*, telegrams of May 17 and 18, 1934. See *FRUS*, 1934, vol. 3, pp. 434-437.

[24]Jones, *op. cit.*, pp. 254-255; also one of Rogers' papers that Jones thought may have been a draft of a final report.

[25]Jones, *op. cit.*, pp. 260-265; Everest, *Morgenthau and Silver*, p. 43.

[26]Feis, *1933*, p. 287; Everest, *Morgenthau and Silver*, p. 103.

[27]Franklin D. Roosevelt Library, Hyde Park, New York, file 150 China, 1933-1942.

[28]Morgenthau *Diaries*, Book I, pp. 43-49.

[29]Blum, *Morgenthau Diaries, 1928-1938*, pp. 185-187; *New York Times*, May 20, 1934. Later, in April 1935, Roosevelt stated, "I have at least 65 votes. I can positively defeat any silver legislation" (quoted by Everest, *Morgenthau and Silver*, p. 52, from *Morgenthau Diaries*, April 26, 1935, Book V, p. 28).

[30]Morgenthau *Diaries*, Book II, pp. 338-343, undated comment in early 1935.

[31]See Everest, *Morgenthau and Silver*, p. 46, and Washington despatch to the *New York Times*, June 21, 1934, quoted in Leavens, *Silver Money*, p. 266. Everest, pp. 36-46, and Leavens, Chapter XXVI, give a full account of these matters. See also Morgenthau, "The Morgenthau Diaries, III," *Collier's*, October 11, 1947, p. 79.

[32]Everest, *op. cit.*, pp. 48-54; and Leavens, *Silver Money*, p. 273.

[33]Everest, *op. cit.*, pp. 51-62.

[34]Everest, *op. cit.*, pp. 60-61.

[35]Ta-chung Liu, *China's National Income*, pp. 10-14. The totals are about 10 per cent greater when adding estimates for Manchuria, Jehol, Sinkiang, Mongolia, and Tibet, and for 1931-1936 are respectively (billions of current C$), 38.9, 31.7, 26.7, 23.5, 26.1, and 28.5. Liu makes it clear that the data permit only approximate estimates.

[36]Jones, *op. cit.*

[37]Of C$520 million of silver imported to China in 1928-1931, C$369 million came to Shanghai and C$151 million to other ports. In those years the net outflow from Shanghai to the rest of China was C$251 million. Hence the increase of stocks in China outside of Shanghai in those years was C$402 million.

Different sources give varying figures of silver stocks at Shanghai and of internal silver movements, but the differences are not major. The figures here given are from Tables 17 and 18; "Movement of Silver in Shanghai," Directorate of Statistics, Nanking, August 25, 1934; *Chinese Economic Journal*, February 1, 1933; and *Finance and Commerce*, February 1 and 8, 1933, and February 7, 1934.

[38]See Hsu *et al.*, *Silver and Prices*, pp. 57-58, and Chang, *The Inflationary Spiral*, p. 183.

[39]For the text of the correspondence between the two governments see *FRUS*, 1934, vol. 3, pp. 423-424, 440-450.

[40]*FRUS*, 1934, vol. 3, pp. 424-425.

[41]For the text see *FRUS*, 1934, vol. 3, pp. 446-449.

[42]See reference 39.

Chapter 9

[1]*Shanghai Evening Post*, April 11, 1935; *North-China Daily News*, May 30, 1935; Everest, *Morgenthau and Silver*, pp. 112-113.

[2]See Everest, *Morgenthau and Silver*, pp. 51-78 for an account of Treasury operations, based on the Morgenthau *Diaries*.

[3]After the currency reform the equalization charge was raised to as much as 58.5 per cent in November and December 1935. When in December and January the American Treasury let the silver price fall sharply, the charge was lowered accordingly, and in 1936-1937 ranged mostly from zero to 6 per cent, although raised considerably at times in response to temporarily higher prices for silver at London. For a detailed record of the charge see Bank of China, *Financial and Commercial Monthly Bulletin, passim.*

[4]Liu, *China's National Income*, p. 10.

[5]See the report of the Chairman of the Hongkong and Shanghai Banking Corporation, *North-China Daily News*, February 27, 1935.

[6]*FRUS*, 1934, vol. 3, p. 455.

[7]State Department file 893.515 /372, December 16, 1934.

[8]Morgenthau *Diaries*, Book I, pp. 295-301, December 16, 1934.

[9]*FRUS*, 1934, vol. 3, pp. 457-458, 461-462. Borg, *op. cit.*, pp. 123-124. The quotation is from my records.

[10] See *FRUS*, 1934, vol. 3, p. 461, and 1935, vol. 3, p. 526; and Everest, *op. cit.*, p. 108.

[11] See Blum, *Morgenthau Diaries:* 1928-1938, *passim;* Cordell Hull, *The Memoirs of Cordell Hull* (New York, 1948), *passim;* Everest, *op. cit.*, pp. 107-110; Borg, *op. cit.*, pp. 123-128, which cites the Roosevelt papers and *FRUS;* and *FRUS*, 1935, III, pp. 535-537, 599-602.

[12] Russell Buhite, *Nelson T. Johnson and American Policy Toward China, 1925-1941* (unpublished doctoral dissertation, University of Michigan, 1965), pp. 204-205.

[13] See *FRUS*, 1935, vol. 3, pp. 578-579, 588, and 593-594 for reports from China.

[14] Morgenthau *Diaries*, Book II, pp. 338-343, undated in early 1935.

[15] For an excellent account of the Amau doctrine and the American attitude see Borg, *op. cit.*, pp. 46-99.

[16] For the text see *FRUS*, 1935, vol. 3, pp. 533-534.

[17] *FRUS*, 1935, vol. 3, pp. 37, 45, 532-533. The telegram of February 17, 1935, is from my records.

[18] *FRUS*, 1935, vol. 3, pp. 542-543. For a detailed account of the in-fighting at Washington at this stage see Borg, *op. cit.*, pp. 124-128.

[19] *FRUS*, 1935, vol. 3, pp. 542-566. The communications of March 8 and 18 are in my records.

[20] *North-China Daily News*, March 1, 3, 7, 1935; Borg, *op. cit.*, pp. 128-129.

[21] For Leith-Ross' account of his mission, see his autobiography, *Money Talks* (London, 1968), Chapter 15.

[22] *North-China Daily News*, June 11, 14, 1935.

[23] Morgenthau *Diaries*, Book IX, p. 15, August 8, 1935; telegram August 9, 1935, Sze to Kung.

[24] *FRUS*, 1935, vol. 3, pp. 328-330, 567-568, 591, 595, 599-607, 609-616; State Department file 893.51 /6035-1 /2, August 8, 1935. For a more detailed account of the State-Treasury controversy see Borg, *op. cit.*, pp. 131-132.

[25] *FRUS*, 1935, vol. 3, p. 619.

[26] *FRUS*, 1935, vol. 3, pp. 632-633, 637-638.

[27] *FRUS*, 1935, vol. 3, pp. 582, 585.

[28] Franklin D. Roosevelt Library, Hyde Park, New York, file 229, June-December 1935, Boxes 8 and 9.

[29] *Ibid.*, Box 9; Morgenthau *Diaries*, Book XI, pp. 17-22, 37-44.

[30] *FRUS*, 1935, vol. 3, pp. 632-633.

[31] *FRUS*, 1935, vol. 3, p. 631.

[32] *FRUS*, 1935, vol. 3, pp. 632-633, 637-638.

[33] Everest, *Morgenthau and Silver*, pp. 111-112; *FRUS*, 1935, vol. 3, pp. 641-642.

[34] *Kuo Min News Agency*, November 4, 1935.

Chapter 10

[1] Young, *China's Wartime Finance*, pp. 136, 166, 171, 174-176, 189-190.

[2] Morgenthau *Diaries*, Book XIII, pp. 89 and 218, December 8 and 11, 1935.

[3] State Department file 893.51 /6070, Hornbeck's memorandum, January 17, 1936.

[4] Harry D. White papers at Princeton University, undated memorandum on "China" (evidently early 1936), pp. 42-43.

[5] Morgenthau, *Diaries*, April 1940, v. 255, p. 183.

[6] *FRUS*, 1936, vol. 4, pp. 477-479.

[7] Everest, *Morgenthau and Silver*, p. 118.

[8] Young, *China's Wartime Finance*, pp. 133, 189-192, 368.

[9]*North-China Daily News*, November 6, 9, 14, 1935; *Reuter News* despatch, May 20, 1936.

[10]For a detailed discussion see D. H. Leavens, "Silver Clause in China," *American Economic Review*, December 1936, pp. 650-659.

[11]*Annual Report* of the Bank of China, *North-China Herald*, April 7, 1937, p. 27.

[12]Records of the Finance Ministry. See also *Chinese Year Book, 1936-37* (2nd issue), pp. 694-696.

[13]For developments in South China in this period see A. B. Lewis and Lien Wang, "Currency Changes in Canton," *Economic Facts*, September 1936, pp. 46-65; E. Kann, "Paper Money in South China," *Finance and Commerce*, October 13, 1937, pp. 285-289; Finance Division, Bureau of Foreign and Domestic Commerce, Washington, "Monetary Developments in China since November 3, 1935," October 1936, pp. 31-34; and *Chinese Year Book, 1936-37* (2nd issue), pp. 698-699.

[14]Reports from the Customs Commissioner at Canton, June 17 and 22, 1936.

[15]For the government's order see *Kuo Min News Agency*, June 22, 1937. I advised caution in procedure to effect the exchange of a larger for a smaller unit, pointing out the risk that unscrupulous dealers would try to transfer prices unchanged to the new larger unit. I recalled the unfortunate American experience in Puerto Rico in 1899-1900 in hastening the introduction of the dollar in substitution for a silver unit worth 40 per cent less, which caused much suffering and discontent. I recommended active publicity and requiring the posting of price quotations in the old and new currencies according to the official rate.

[16]E. Kann, *Illustrated Catalog of Chinese Coins* (Hong Kong, 1954), pp. 422-442.

[17]Choh-ming Li, "China's International Trade Statistics: An Evaluation," *Nankai Social and Economic Quarterly*, April 1937, p. 20. Li disagreed with Remer and others that exports were considerably undervalued after 1904.

[18]C. F. Remer, *Foreign Investments in China* (New York, 1933), p. 73.

[19]Hou, *Foreign Investment and Economic Development in China*, pp. 17, 99.

[20]The estimates for 1928 to 1930 are from Remer, *Foreign Investments in China*, pp. 221-222; for 1931, from E. Kann, *Finance and Commerce*, November 25, 1931, p. 7; for 1932, from the author; and for 1933 to 1936 from the Bank of China's annual reports.

[21]Hou, *op. cit.*, p. 209.

Chapter 11

[1]F. M. Tamagna, *Banking and Finance in China* (Institute of Pacific Relations, New York, 1942). See also Kia-ngau Chang, *Inflationary Spiral*, pp. 172-184, for a briefer analysis.

[2]For an account of conditions of rural credit see Tawney, *Land and Labour in China*, pp. 58-63.

[3]For the history of banking to 1928 see E. Kann's account in *China Year Book, 1929-30*, pp. 307-310; and the chapter by Kia-ngau Chang in Sih, ed., *The Strenuous Decade*, pp. 129-140.

[4]*Central Bank Bulletin*, January 1946, p. 123.

[5]George E. Taylor, *Reconstruction Movement in China* (Royal Institute of International Affairs, London, mimeographed report, 1936), p. 28.

[6]Tamagna, *Banking in China*, pp. 160, 185.

[7]Tamagna, *op. cit.*, pp. 13-23, 57-88; Kia-ngau Chang, *The Inflationary Spiral*, pp. 172-174; G. H. Chang, "A Brief Survey of Chinese Native Banks," *Central Bank of China Bulletin*, March 1938, pp. 25-32.

[8]See Tamagna, *op. cit.*, Chapter VI.

[9]*Ibid.*, pp. 62, 138, 155, 160, 172.

[10] *Chinese Economic Journal*, May 1931, pp. 533-542.

[11] *Report of the Committee . . . on the Reorganization of the Central Bank of China*, June 8, 1936. A copy of this report has been lodged at the Library of the Hoover Institution on War, Revolution, and Peace, at Stanford University.

[12] See Young, *China's Wartime Finance*, pp. 151-153, 165, 177-186, 366.

Chapter 12

[1] E. W. Kemmerer, *Modern Currency Reforms* (New York, 1916), Part V.

[2] Young, *China's Wartime Finance*, p. 368.

[3] Leavens, *Silver Money*, p. 273.

[4] Neil Carothers, "Incredible Silver," *Journal of the American Bankers Association*, quoted in *Finance and Commerce*, June 6, 1934, pp. 662-663.

[5] *Reuter's News* despatch, May 20, 1937.

[6] *FRUS*, 1937, vol. 3, pp. 545-547.

Chapter 13

[1] Albert Feuerwerker, *China's Early Industrialization* (Cambridge, 1958), pp. 242-243. This work gives an excellent account of the reasons for backwardness in development in the later imperial period.

See also Dwight H. Perkins, "Government as an Obstacle to Industrialization: The Case of Nineteenth Century China," *Journal of Economic History*, December 1967, pp. 478-492. He stresses internal instability, meagerness of fiscal resources, and the fact that the government did little to promote progress.

[2] Feuerwerker, *ibid.*, pp. 43-44; E. H. Norman, *Japan's Emergence as a Modern State* (New York, 1940), pp. 138-144; W. W. Lockwood, *The Economic Development of Japan* (Princeton, 1954), pp. 3-19.

[3] John K. Chang, *Industrial Growth in Pre-Communist China: A Quantitative Analysis* (Chicago, 1969), p. 71.

[4] Sun Yat-sen, *Memoirs of a Chinese Revolutionary: A Programme of National Reconstruction for China* (Philadelphia, 1919), pp. 179-181. See also his *International Development of China* (New York, 1922).

[5] *Chinese Economic Bulletin*, May 23, 1931, pp. 261-263, and June 27, 1931, pp. 326-330; Tze-hsiung Kuo, *Technical Cooperation between China and Geneva* (Information Bulletin of the Council of International Affairs, Nanking, July 1, 1936), pp. 5-9; Chiang Kai-shek's opening address, National Economic Council, November 15, 1931 (Nanking, 1931), pp. 4-7, 11-14.

For an analysis with more details of these earlier plans see Y. L. Wu, *China's Economic Policy: Planning or Free Enterprise?* (Sino-International Economic Research Center, New York, 1946), pp. 34-38.

[6] Chiang Kai-shek, Address to the National Economic Council, *op. cit.*, p. 5.

[7] Sun Yat-sen, *International Development of China* (New York, 1922), p. 11.

[8] As to Sun's relations with Communism, see Shao Chuan Leng and Norman D. Palmer, *Sun Yat-sen and Communism* (New York, 1960), e.g., p. 74.

[9] Sun Yat-sen, *San Min Chu I* (The Three Principles of the People), translated by Frank W. Price (Institute of Pacific Relations, China Committee, Shanghai, 1927), pp. 438-443. This book records a series of lectures in 1923.

Y. L. Wu in *China's Economic Policy* analyzes Sun's views and points out the shifts and confusion in his writings. Wu's conclusion is similar to mine above, and he also felt that Sun was not urging socialism but rather a mixed economy with a considerable degree of state participation.

[10] See *Chinese Economic Bulletin*, July 19, 1930, p. 37, and October 11, 1930, p. 192; *Kuo Min News Agency*, April 2, 1931, July 12, 1931, and November 29, 1935; Annual Reports of the American Commercial Attache, 1934, pp. 19-20; 1936, pp. 23-24; 1937, p.

25; *FRUS*, 1937, vol. 4, pp. 583-584; despatch 413, April 6, 1937, from Ambassador Johnson on "Trend to State Capitalism" (State Department file 893.00 /14107).

[11]Young, *China and the Helping Hand*, pp. 368-369, 377, 389-396, 422. I have lodged at the Hoover Institution on War, Revolution and Peace at Stanford University data of the Nationalist planning for the postwar period.

[12]See *Monthly Journal*, National Resources Commission (Tzu-yuan Wei-yuan-hui Yueh-k'an), first issue, April 1, 1939; and Y. L. Wu, *China's Economic Policy*, pp. 37-38.

Chapter 14

[1]For comments and data relating to agriculture the writer, not an expert on the subject, is indebted to J. Lossing Buck, Owen L. Dawson, Franklin Ho, and Ramon H. Myers; but they of course have no responsibility for this presentation.

[2]See Buck's account of this in Sih, ed., *The Strenuous Decade*, pp. 172-173.

[3]*The Chinese Year Book, 1936-37*, Second Issue, p. 1263.

[4]Annexes to the *Report to the Council of the League of Nations of Its Technical Delegate on His Mission to China* (Nanking, 1934), p. 175. For a detailed account of agricultural conditions as of 1931 by an experienced scholar, see Tawney, *Land and Labour in China.*

[5]Sun Yat-sen, *San Min Chu I*, pp. 456-458.

[6]Chiang Kai-shek's views in support of agrarian reform are shown in his message of 1934 to the Executive Yuan, whose text appears in the report of the technical delegate of the League of Nations, pp. 21-23.

[7]*Chinese Year Book, 1936-37* (2nd issue), p. 1258.

[8]Tawney, *Land and Labour in China*, p. 84.

[9]See T. H. Shen, *Agricultural Resources of China* (Ithaca, New York, 1951), p. 355.See also Buck account in Sih, ed., *The Strenuous Decade*, pp. 172-193.

[10]*Ibid., passim.*

[11]J. L. Buck, O. L. Dawson, and Yuan-li Wu, *Food and Agriculture in Communist China* (New York, 1966), pp. 48-51, 58-59.

[12]Ta-chung Liu and K. C. Yeh, *The Economy of the Chinese Mainland: National Income and Economic Development, 1933-1959* (Princeton, 1965), pp. 43-55.

[13]Chen Han-seng, *Gung Ho! The Story of the Chinese Cooperatives* (Pamphlet 24, Institute of Pacific Relations, New York, 1947). The figures of growth of cooperatives are from an unpublished memorandum by Tsung-kao Yieh, *Industrialization of Wartime China*, which I received at Chungking in 1942.

[14]Sih, ed., *The Strenuous Decade*, p. 203. Besides Taiwan, a case of rapid agricultural progress is Iran in the sixties. See Charles Issawi, "Iran's Economic Upsurge," *Middle East Journal*, Autumn 1967, pp. 447-461.

[15]Year-by-year data of industrial production as a whole in China proper are not available. The most comprehensive study of modern-type Chinese-owned industries was made as of 1933 by D. K. Lieu, *Report on a Survey of Chinese Industry* (National Resources Commission, Nanking, 1937). This study covered China proper, but did not include foreign firms.

Concerning industrial development in general and the relative positions of traditional and modern-type production see Chang, *Industrial Development in Pre-Communist China*, Chapter V; Kung-chia Yeh, *Capital Formation in Mainland China: 1931-36 and 1952-57* (unpublished doctoral dissertation, Columbia University, 1964), p. 225; Chi-ming Hou, *Foreign Investment and Economic Development in China, 1840-1937* (Cambridge, 1965), *passim;* Ta-chung Liu and Kung-chia Yeh, *Economy of the Chinese Mainland* (Princeton, 1965), pp. 66-69; and Nai-ruenn Chen and Walter Galenson, *Chinese Economy under Communism* (Chicago, 1969), pp. 10-22.

[16]Hou, *op. cit.*, pp. 1-6, 165-168, 186-188, 218-219.

[17] For further discussion of these matters see G. C. Allen and Audrey Donnithorne, *Western Enterprise in Far Eastern Economic Development: China and Japan*, Chapters IX and X (London and New York, 1954); and Hou, *Foreign Investment and Economic Development*, pp. 130-136 and 216-219.

[18] Chang, *Industrial Development*, pp. 71, 99.

[19] *Ibid.*, chapters IV-VI, and Chang's article with a similar title in *Journal of Economic History*, March 1967, pp. 56-81.

[20] *Statistical Yearbook of the League of Nations* (Geneva, 1938), pp. 175-176.

[21] The figures of imports of capital goods are from Yeh, *Capital Formation*, p. 307. I have converted his figures on the basis of 1932 prices.

[22] Liu and Yeh, *Economy of the Chinese Mainland*, pp. 139, 188.

[23] Statistical Bureau of the National Government, *Statistical Abstract of China*, February 1941, p. 38, quoted by Tsung-kao Yieh in a memorandum on "Industrialization of Wartime China," received in 1941, p. 1.

[24] Kia-ngau Chang, *China's Struggle for Railroad Development* (New York, 1943), pp. 76, 85. For an account of the development of China's railways in the pre-Nationalist period, see pp. 23-76. See also H. J. von Lochow (former adviser to the Ministry of Communications), *China's National Railways* (Peiping, 1948); and Arthur G. Coons, *The Foreign Public Debt of China* (Philadelphia, 1930), pp. 27-44.

[25] J. E. Baker, "Transportation in China," *Annals of the American Academy of Political and Social Science*, vol. 152, November 1930, p. 165.

[26] Data of the Railway Ministry, as furnished to the Kemmerer Commission.

[27] *Statistics of the Chinese National Railways, 1935-1936*, Part VII, p. 66.

[28] *Statistics of Chinese National Railways, 1928*, pp. 2, 20; *1929*, p. 1; *1932*, p. 84; *1935-1936*, pp. 1, 32, 77. Data for 1936-1937 are not available because of the hostilities.

[29] Chang, *Railroad Development*, pp. 76-80, 142-143. For an excellent detailed account see Ling Hung-hsun's paper, "A Decade of Chinese Railway Construction (1926-1936)," in Sih, ed., *The Strenuous Decade*, pp. 255-288.

[30] *Ibid.*, pp. 77-78; Coons, *Foreign Debt*, pp. 34-38.

[31] Chang, *Railroad Development*, pp. 80-81.

[32] *Ibid.*, pp. 81-85.

[33] Chang lists 6047 miles of railways in China proper as of the end of 1935. His account shows the following mileage built in the Nationalist period to that date: Shansi, 420; Chekiang-Kiangsi to Yushan, 221; Lunghai extension to Sian, 125; Weinan Railway, Anhwei, 134; Nanking-Wuhu, 120; Soochow-Kashing, 46;total 1066. Thus deducting these extensions, mileage was 4981. He lists 1262 miles built from the end of 1935 to July 7, 1937. Thus total construction was 2328 miles, an increase of 47 per cent. Chang, *Railroad Development*, pp. 80-82, 86-88.

[34] Chang, *Railroad Development*, p. 181; see pp. 172-182 for details of the various reforms in procedures and control.

[35] F. D. Hammond, *Report on the National Railways of the Republic of China*, September 2, 1935 (Nanking, 1936?), p. 146.

[36] Baker, *op. cit.*, pp. 160-162.

[37] The annual report of the National Economic Council for 1936 provides the following yearly figures of total road mileage, here converted from kilometers to miles: 18,000 in 1927; 19,000 in 1928; 22,000 in 1929; 29,000 in 1930; 41,000 in 1931; 44,000 in 1932; 45,000 in 1933; 53,000 in 1934; 60,000 in 1935; and 69,000 in 1936.

For a detailed account of the road building experience in China see the Reports of the Bureau of Roads to the National Economic Council, and the Council's Reports, 1935 and 1936, the latter quoted in the *China Year Book, 1939*, pp. 513-514; and two *Information Bulletins* of the Council of International Affairs, Nanking: "Highways in China," by Lawrence M. Chen, November 21, 1936, and "Highway Construction and Transport in China," by T. K. Chao, August 4, 1937. The *Annexes* to the Report to the Council of the

League of Nations of its Technial Delegate in China, pp. 108-113, deal with road building and related problems in Chekiang Province in 1932. See also A. Viola Smith, "Motor Roads in China," Trade Promotion Series No. 120, Department of Commerce (Washington D.C., 1931).

[38] T. K. Chao, *op. cit.*, p. 157.

[39] *Shanghai Evening Post and Mercury*, February 5, 1935.

[40] Gasoline figures from Chao, *op. cit.*, pp. 164-165. Vehicle figures from *Economic Handbook of the Pacific Area, 1934*, p. 161; and *Economic Survey of the Pacific Area*, Part 2, p. 44, both edited by F. V. Field (Institute of Pacific Relations, New York, 1934 and 1941, respectively).

[41] Quoted by George E. Taylor, *Reconstruction Movement in China* (Royal Institute of International Affairs, mimeographed, London, 1936), p. 24.

[42] For the agreement, see *China Year Book, 1929-30*, pp. 484-490.

[43] The figures are from Maritime Customs, *Trade of China, 1936*, vol. I (Part I), pp. 91-92. For further details on aviation in China see *China Year Book, passim;* and Lawrence M. Chen, *Aviation in China* (Council of International Affairs, Information Bulletin III, no. 12, Nanking, May 1, 1937).

William M. Leary, Jr., of the University of Victoria, British Columbia, has in preparation a full study of development of aviation in China.

[44] *Maritime Customs, op. cit.*, p. 92; and *North-China Herald*, February 10, 1937, p. 244.

[45] Chen, *Aviation in China*, pp. 272-273.

[46] This computation relates the figures in Appendix 20 to GNP as estimated for China proper in Liu, *National Income*, p. 10. Inclusion of Manchuria raises the overall proportion of foreign trade to national product in 1932 to 1936 to about 10 per cent because of the relatively greater foreign trade there. See Liu, *op. cit.*, p. 10, and Appendix 21.

For a general discussion of China's foreign trade see Yu-kwei Cheng, *Foreign Trade ane Industrial Development of China* (University Press of Washington, D.C., 1956).

[47] Choh-ming Li: "China's International Trade Statistics: an Evaluation," *Nankai Social and Economic Quarterly*, April 1937, p. 20.

[48] As to barter trade see Kurt Bloch, *German Interests and Policies in the Far East* (Institute of Pacific Relations, New York, 1940), pp. 26-29.

[49] Yeh, *Capital Formation*, pp. 305-308.

[50] The indexes, which include Manchurian trade through 1931, are found in *Nankai Social and Economic Quarterly*, July 1937, pp. 346-347, and are reproduced by Hou in *Foreign Investment and Economic Development*, pp. 231-232.

[51] Yu-kwei Cheng, *Foreign Trade and Industrial Development of China* (University Press of Washington, D. C., 1956), pp. 48-49. This book contains a detailed analysis of the nature and development of the trade in 1913-1936, pp. 27-52.

[52] Colin Clark in *The Conditions of Economic Progress* (1st ed., London, 1940) made a rough estimate of China's national product in the period 1925 to 1934. He estimated agricultural income at C$18.7 billion and nonagricultural income at C$5.8 billion, a total of C$24.5 billion (pp. 44-46). A pioneer study is that of Ta-chung Liu, *China's National Income.* A further comprehensive study of China's national income is that of Ou Paosan, *China's National Income, 1933* (Shanghai, 1947). Ou later wrote, "A New Estimate of China's National Income," *Journal of Political Economy*, December 1946, pp. 547-554, and presented a fuller analysis in *Capital Formation and Consumer's Outlay in China* (unpublished doctoral dissertation, Harvard University, 1948). Kung-chia Yeh developed the subject further in *Capital Formation in Mainland China* (unpublished doctoral dissertation, Columbia University, 1964), and in a chapter on "Capital Formation," in Alexander Eckstein, Walter Galenson, and Ta-chung Liu, *Economic Trends in Communist China* (Chicago, 1968), pp. 509-547. See also Liu and Yeh, *Economy of the Chinese Mainland*, pp. 66-68, 226-230.

[53] Yeh, *Capital Formation*, p. 183 and *passim*.

[54] Liu and Yeh, *Economy of Mainland China*, p. 228.

[55] For a list of the estimates see Yeh, *Capital Formation*, pp. 109-110. He gives the following references: Simon Kuznets, *Estimate of Prewar Savings in China, 1946*, and *Crude Estimate of Capital Formation in China, 1936*, 1946; Wu Ching-chao, *Plan for China's Industrialization* (China Institute of Pacific Relations, Chungking, 1945); Hsing Mo-huan, *Some Preliminary Observations on China's National Income and Related Problems* (New York, 1947); and Wu Cheng-ming, "Crude Estimate of Capital Formation in China," *Central Bank Monthly*, November 1946, pp. 1-19.

[56] Ou Pao-san, *Capital Formation and Consumers' Outlay in China* (unpublished dissertation, Harvard University, 1948), pp. 136, 143-144; Yeh, *Capital Formation*, pp. 108-117.

[57] Buck, *Land Utilization in China*, pp. 466-467, 370.

[58] Yeh, *Capital Formation*, pp. 76-96, 149-157, 176-181.

[59] Alexander Eckstein, Walter Galenson, and Ta-chung Liu, *Economic Trends in Communist China* (Chicago, 1968), pp. 8-12.

[60] Neil H. Jacoby, *U. S. Aid to Taiwan* (New York, 1966), pp. 85-86; *Free China Weekly*, December 8, 1968, and September 28, 1969.

Chapter 15

[1] G. C. Allen and A. G. Donnithorne, *Western Enterprise in Far Eastern Development: China and Japan* (London, 1954), p. 270.

[2] *China Year Book, 1928*, pp. 1249-1262.

[3] Alberto de Stefani, former Finance Minister of Italy, visited China briefly in 1937 on Mussolini's recommendation. He was attached to the National Resources Commission and was concerned primarily with economic development. See F. M. Tamagna, *Italy's Interests and Policies in the Far East* (Institute of Pacific Relations, New York, 1941), p. 18.

[4] *Kuo Min News Agency*, April 28, 1931.

[5] *Ibid.*, April 27, 1931.

[6] *Ibid.*, May 22, 1931; Tze-hsiung Kuo, "Technical Cooperation between China and Geneva," *Information Bulletin of the Council of International Affairs* (Nanking) July 1, 1936, pp. 4-5.

[7] *Report to the Council of Its Technical Delegate on His Mission in China* (Nanking, 1934), pp. 5-7.

[8] *FRUS*, 1933, vol. 3, pp. 494, 502. For an excellent detailed account of these developments see Dorothy Borg, *The United States and the Far Eastern Crisis of 1933-1938* (Cambridge, 1964), pp. 60-99.

[9] *FRUS*, 1934, vol. 3, pp. 128, 145-155, 381, 395-402, 418.

[10] *Report of the Commission of Enquiry of the League of Nations*, 1932, Chapter IX, point 10.

[11] For a detailed account of this episode see Borg, *op. cit.*, pp. 63-65.

[12] C. H. Becker, M. Falski, P. Langevin, and R. H. Tawney, *Reorganization of Education in China* (League of Nations' Institute of Intellectual Co-operation, Paris, 1932), pp. 25, 28, 113.

[13] Kuo, *Technical Cooperation between China and Geneva*, pp. 12-15; Chiang Kai-shek, *Opening Address*, National Economic Council, November 15, 1931 (Nanking, 1931), p. 12.

[14] Kuo, *op. cit.*, pp. 13-14.

[15] *FRUS*, 1933, vol. 3, p. 523.

[16] See *Report to the Council of the League of Nations of Its Technical Delegate on His Mission in China from Date of Appointment until April 1, 1934;* and *Annexes* (Nanking, 1934). The volume of Annexes contains the text of many of the principal reports of League experts. See also *Annual Report of the National Economic Council, 1935* (Nanking, 1936), and Kuo, *op. cit.*

[17]Kuo, *op. cit.*, p. 13.

[18]*Kuo Min News Agency*, September 30, 1934, June 23, 1935.

[19]*Chinese Year Book, 1936-37* (2nd issue), pp. 382-384.

[20]*Ibid.*, pp. 384-386.

[21]*Report of the Technical Delegate and Annexes, passim; Report of the NEC 1935*, pp. 17-21; Kuo, *op. cit.*, pp. 9-11.

[22]*Kuo Min News Agency*, June 4, 1935.

[23]*Annexes to the Report to the Council of the League of Nations of Its Technical Delegate*, pp. 220, 175. For Dragoni's reports see pp. 167-226.

[24]*Ibid.*, pp. 41-69.

[25]*Ibid.*, pp. 73-166.

[26]F. F. Liu, *Military History of Modern China*, pp. 60-102. See also Kurt Bloch, *German Interests and Policies in the Far East* (Institute of Pacific Relations, New York, 1940), pp. 12-16.

[27]Liu, *op. cit.*, pp. 61-63, 91-102; Bloch, *op. cit.*, pp. 13-15. Liu gives Bauer's first name as Walter; Bloch as Max.

[28]Liu, *op. cit.*, p. 88.

[29]See Young, *China and the Helping Hand*, pp. 16-18, 59-60.

[30]Liu, *op. cit.*, pp. 106-107.

[31]See State Department files 893.20 /310, 315, 320, March-June 1932. For a full account of this mission see W. M. Leary, Jr., "Wings for China: The Jouett Mission, 1932-1935," in *Pacific Historical Review*, November 1969, pp. 447-462.

[32]See report by Trade Commissioner E. P. Howard, December 16, 1932, State Department file 893.20 /407.

[33]Jouett has given an account of his mission in an article, "War Planes Over China," *Asia*, vol. 37, December 1937, pp. 827-830.

[34]State Department files 893.20 /396, 494, and 497, of November 19, 1932, May 6, 1934, and September 12, 1934, respectively.

[35]State Department file 893.20 /361; Jouett's report of September 15, 1934.

[36]*FRUS*, 1934, vol. 3, p. 316, and State Department file 893.20 /497, 564; F. Tamagna, *Italy's Interests and Policies in the Far East* (Institute of Pacific Relations, New York, 1941), pp. 19-21.

[37]State Department file 893.20 /541, 558.

[38]Letters to me of September 18 and October 24, 1933.

[39]Tamagna, *op. cit.*, p. 19.

[40]Report to Chief of Staff Douglas MacArthur, November 21, 1934, *FRUS*, 1934, pp. 315-317.

[41]Liu, *Military History*, pp. 174-175; Evans F. Carlson, *Chinese Army* (Institute of Pacific Relations, New York, 1940), p. 46.

[42]Chennault said that the Italian school "graduated every Chinese cadet who survived the training course as a full-fledged pilot regardless of his ability"; whereas the Americans rejected incompetents. The Italian assembly plant, he said, turned out fighter planes that were worthless in combat, and bombers usable only for transport. Claire L. Chennault, *Way of a Fighter* (New York, 1949), pp. 37-38. See also Young, *China and the Helping Hand*, pp. 24-26.

[43]Tamagna, *op. cit.*, p. 21.

[44]See especially J. Lossing Buck, *Land Utilization in China* (Shanghai, 1937). See also the studies contained in *Economic Facts*, the monthly publication of the University of Nanking.

[45]See A. J. Nathan, *History of the China International Famine Relief Commission* (Harvard East Asian Monographs, No. 17, Cambridge, 1965); and *The CIFRC 15th Anniversary Book, 1921-1936* (Peiping, 1936). Concerning Todd's work see Jonathan

Spence, *To Change China: Western Advisers in China, 1620-1960* (Boston, 1969).

[46]See Nathan, *op. cit.*, pp. 74-77.

[47]For a full account of this episode, see James C. Thomson, Jr., *While China Faced West: American Reformers in Nationalist China, 1928-1937* (Cambridge, 1969).

[48]*Ibid., passim.*

[49]*Ibid., passim.*

Chapter 16

[1]Hou, *Foreign Investment*, pp. 216-220.

[2]*Ibid.*, pp. 183-188.

[3]*Ibid.*, p. 216, 219-220.

[4]*North-China Daily News*, July 8, 1937.

[5]See Carnegie Endowment for International Peace, *Consortium: The Official Text of the Four-Power Agreement for a Loan to China and Relevant Documents* (Washington, 1921); and F. V. Field: *American Participation in the China Consortiums* (Chicago, 1931).

[6]Field, *op. cit.*, pp. 154-164.

[7]See *Ibid.*, pp. 167-170, for the Consortium's record to 1931 and the attitude in China.

[8]See the London *Times*, June 7, 1933.

[9]*FRUS*, 1937, vol. 4, pp. 587-592.

[10]Chang, *Railroad Development*, pp. 124-126; *FRUS*, 1937, vol. 4, pp. 568-569.

[11]*FRUS*, 1937, vol. 4, pp. 568-592, 606, 614, 624.

[12]See State Department file 893.50A /101, Ambassador William Bullitt's despatch of July 7, 1934, from Moscow reporting a talk with Monnet giving background of his activities in helping with the creation of the Corporation; see also State Department file 893.50A /56.

[13]*North-China Daily News*, June 1, 1934.

[14]See Monnet's talk with Bullitt, State Department file 893.50A /101, July 7, 1934.

[15]C. F. Remer's *Foreign Investments in China* (New York, 1933), pp. 58, 62, 69-79, is the source for statements in this and the next two paragraphs.

[16]Chi-ming Hou, *Foreign Investment*, pp. 10-17, 235.

[17]Bank of China, *Annual Reports, 1934*, pp. 13-14; *1935*, pp. 25-26; *1936*, pp. 19-20.

[18]Hou, *op. cit.*, p. 88.

[19]Kurt Bloch, *German Interests and Policies in the Far East* (Institute of Pacific Relations, New York, 1940), pp. 23-26; Chang, *Railroad Development*, pp. 79-80, 97, 115.

[20]Chang, *op. cit.*, pp. 79-80, 111-116, 140-141.

[21]Bloch, *op. cit.*, pp. 23-29; Liu, *Military History*, pp. 101-102.

[22]Bloch, *op. cit.*, pp. 27-29.

[23]Bloch, *op. cit.*, pp. 31-33, 35-40; Liu, *op. cit.*, pp. 101-102; Young, *China and the Helping Hand*, pp. 17-18, 59-60.

[24]Reports of the Board of Trustees of the British Boxer Indemnity, 1931-1936, *passim.*

[25]*Chang, Railroad Development*, pp. 98-102, 172-179.

[26]*Ibid.*, pp. 102-111; memorandum of April 2, 1937, from the China Development Finance Corporation.

[27]Chang, *op. cit.*, pp. 133-140.

[28]Data of Railway Ministry; Chang, *op. cit.*, pp. 120-122.

[29]Chang, *op. cit.*, pp. 142-143.

[30]Information from Railway Ministry; Chang, *op. cit.*, pp. 116-120, 122-133, 141-142.

[31]For an account of the Forbes mission and the American attitude see Borg, *The United States and the Far Eastern Crisis of 1933-1938*, pp. 256-266.

[32]*FRUS*, 1937, vol. 4, pp. 584-586, 595, 612-613, 618-619.

[33]*Ibid.*, pp. 603-604; *North-China Daily News*, June 14, 1937.

[34]*FRUS*, 1937, vol. 4, pp. 605-606.

[35]*Ibid.*, pp. 619-620; *North-China Daily News*, August 6, 1937.

[36]Young, *China and the Helping Hand*, pp. 226, 231.

[37]*FRUS*, 1937, vol. 4, p. 604.

[38]Young, *China and the Helping Hand*, pp. 218, 231-233.

[39]*FRUS*, 1937, vol. 4, pp. 608-609.

[40]*Ibid.*, pp. 616-619; State Department file 893.51 /6418, July 12, 1937.

[41]Young, *China and the Helping Hand*, pp. 31, 62, 79.

[42]*North-China Daily News*, August 12, 1937; *FRUS*, 1937, vol. 4, p. 622.

[43]See *FRUS*, 1938, vol. 3, p. 352.

[44]For a full and excellent account of the flood relief operation see *Report of the National Flood Relief Commission, 1931-1932* (Shanghai, 1933).

[45]See Anne Morrow Lindbergh: *North to the Orient* (New York, 1935), pp. 199-225. The original motion picture films taken by Colonel Lindbergh with my camera are in the Millar aviation collection at the Occidental College Library.

[46]State Department file 893.48 /308, August 26, 1931.

[47]Flood Relief Commission's *Report*, p. 305.

[48]*Ibid.*, pp. 130-131.

[49]*Ibid.*, pp. 65, 80, 88-90.

[50]*Ibid.*, pp. 87-88, 127, 136-137.

[51]*Ibid.*, pp. 138-139, 190. Address of Chairman Soong, December 28, 1932 (mimeographed).

[52]There was some criticism by importers and traders because the operation was conducted by officials and volunteers. See *The Commercial Review*, Portland, Oregon, October 25, 1932, for unfounded charges by a "Chinese importer visiting in Portland."

[53]Flood Relief Commission's *Report*, pp. 103, 193-194.

[54]See State Department file 893.48 /717 on Monnet's call in April 1933.

[55]State Department files 893.48 /794, conversation of Secretary Hull with the Japanese ambassador, August 10, 1933; and 893.48 /858, telegram January 1, 1934, from American embassy, Peiping; *FRUS*, 1933, vol. 3, p. 512.

For a good account of the development of Japanese policy as to China's reconstruction and Western participation therein see Borg, *The United States and the Far Eastern Crisis*, pp. 55-99.

[56]*FRUS*, 1933, vol. 3, pp. 509-511, and 1934, vol. 3, pp. 135, 384; and State Department files 893.48 /727, 729, 730 containing memoranda of May 1933.

[57]State Department files 893.51 /5823, 5833.

[58]Finance Ministry, *Report, 1934-1935*, p. 10.

[59]The figures are from *Report of Operations* of the Chinese American Cotton Syndicate to the Central Bank of China, September 11, 1935.

[60]Report of Accounting Division, Central Bank, September 11, 1935.

[61]State Department files 893.515 /372, 402; *FRUS*, 1934, vol. 3, p. 384.

[62]For a preliminary report on the credit see Finance Ministry's annual *Report*, 1932-1934, pp. 13-14.

[63]Edgar Snow, *Red Star over China* (Grove Press, New York, 1961), p. 415.

[64]Data of the Finance Ministry received October 19, 1935. The Finance Minister's report for the fiscal years 1932-1934 states (p. 14) that C$15 million of the loan proceeds was transferred to the Central Bank for currency reform. But this was later turned over to the NEC.

Chapter 17

[1]Ho and Tsou, editors; *China's Heritage and the Communist Political System*, vol. 1, book I, p. 9.

[2]Directorate General of Budgets, Accounts, and Statistics; *Statistical Abstract*, 1940, pp. 171-172, 178.

[3]Douglas S. Paauw: "The Kuomintang and Economic Stagnation, 1928-1937," *Journal of Asian Studies*, vol. 16, February 1957, pp. 213-220. See also his article, "Chinese National Expenditures in the Nanking Period," *Far Eastern Quarterly*, November 1952, pp. 3-26.

[4]Paauw, "Economic Stagnation," p. 214.

[5]Hou: *Foreign Investment*, p. 126.

Chapter 18

[1]*Kuo Min News Agency*, in *North-China Daily News*, March 7, 1933.

[2]A Soviet writer has made the charge, absurd on its face, that all American policies toward China aimed to displace Britain and Japan and "clear the way for American capital." See M. I. Sladkovskii; *History of Economic Relations Between Russia and China* (Davey, New York, 1967), reviewed by Walter Galenson in *American Economic Review*, March 1968, p. 227.

[3]Tawney, *Land and Labour in China*, p. 13.

[4]See *FRUS*, 1933, vol. 3, pp. 170-174, 491-493; 1934, vol. 3, pp. 344-348; 1935, vol. 3, pp. 306-309, 503-506; 1936, vol. 4, p. 232.

[5]*FRUS*, 1937, vol. 4, telegram of April 16, despatches of April 21 and May 7, 1937, pp. 581-583, 594.

[6]*FRUS*, 1937, vol. 3, despatch of June 10, 1937, pp. 111-112.

[7]American Commercial Attache, *Annual Economic Report for 1937* (Washington, 1937), pp. 1-4.

[8]Quoted in G. C. Allen and A. G. Donnithorne, *Western Enterprise in Far Eastern Economic Development: China and Japan* (London, 1954), pp. 28-29.

[9]*The Economist*, London, July 24, 1937, p. 167.

[10]Arthur N. Young, "China's Financial Progress," in *Foreign Policy Reports* (Foreign Policy Association, New York), April 15, 1938, p. 35.

[11]See Young, *China and the Helping Hand*, pp. 18-22, 26, 54-57, and on pp. 455-456, notes I, 1, and II, 10-14, for references to support the statements in this paragraph. Stalin was following a consistent policy. He is reported to have expressed the view in 1927 that Chiang and the Right were capable, had the chief military force, had political skill, and could raise money for their operations; they "have to be utilized to the end, squeezed out like a lemon, and then flung away." See Harold Isaacs, *The Tragedy of the Chinese Revolution* (Stanford, 1951), p. 162.

[12]E. F. Goldman, *Crucial Decade* (New York, 1956), p. 117.

[13]W. Lewisohn: "The Modernization of China," *North-China Herald*, February 3, 1937, p. 258. His preceding articles were in the weekly issues from December 16, 1936, to January 27, 1937.

[14]See Melville T. Kennedy, Jr., *The Kuomintang and China's Unification, 1928-1931* (unpublished doctoral dissertation, Harvard University, 1958); also Ch'ien *Government and Politics of China*, pp. 147-149, 161.

[15]Nai-ruenn Chen and Walter Galenson, *The Chinese Economy under Communism* (Chicago, 1969), state: "Considering the tremendous cost of boom and bust to the Chinese people, it is not at all clear that the Chinese performance was superior to the Indian" (p. 60).

[16]For an account of prewar developments see Theodore H. E. Chen, "Education in China, 1927-1937," in Sih, ed., *The Strenuous Decade*, pp. 289-314, 328-329.

[17]*FRUS*, 1937, vol. 3, p. 90, despatch of May 11, 1937.

[18]Young, *China and the Helping Hand*, p. 421. For further analysis of the war-rooted causes of the Nationalists' collapse on the mainland, see *idem*, pp. 421-426.

Bibliographic Note

Bibliographic Note

Here I indicate the chief sources relating to the subject matter of this book, to aid those wishing to look further into the subjects treated. It is not practicable to list here all the sources used or the great volume of materials in several languages relating to financial and economic matters in China in the prewar decade. A detailed listing as of 1954 is in *Economic and Social Development of Modern China: A Bibliographic Guide*, by Tungli Yuan (Human Relations Area Files, Yale University, New Haven, 1954). John K. Fairbank prepared *Modern China: A Bibliographic Guide to Chinese Works, 1898-1937* (Cambridge, 1950). Japanese materials are included in *Checklist of Archives in the Japanese Ministry of Foreign Affairs, Tokyo, Japan, 1868-1945* (Library of Congress, Washington, 1954). Other full bibliographies are in Ta-chung Liu and Kung-chia Yeh, *The Economy of the Chinese Mainland: National Income and Economic Development, 1933-1959* (Princeton, 1965), pp. 713-757; and Chi-ming Hou, *Foreign Investment and Economic Development in China, 1840-1937* (Cambridge, 1965), pp. 275-296.

Chinese official records on financial and economic matters published for the prewar decade are not extensive in most fields, and much of the unpublished materials was lost during and after the war. The texts of many documents, statistics, and historical and current data are found in the *China Year Book*, issued from 1912 to 1939, and *The Chinese Year Book*, issued for 1935-36 and 1936-37. A chief source for this book is the papers I collected and preserved without loss while serving as Financial Adviser from 1929 through the war period. These papers in English and Chinese comprise letters and telegrams, memoranda, reports, statistics, periodicals, pamphlets, and books. The Chinese government has consented to my use of these materials.

General works giving background include the following: H. B. Morse, *The Trade and Administration of China* (New York, 1920); W. W. Willoughby, *Foreign Rights and Interests in*

China (2 volumes, Baltimore, 1927); J. V. A. MacMurray, *Treaties and Agreements with and Concerning China, 1894-1919* (2 volumes, Carnegie Endowment for International Peace, New York, 1921); a supplement to MacMurray's compilation with the same title, *1919-1929* (Carnegie Endowment, Washington, 1929); Tuan-sheng Ch'ien, *Government and Politics of China* (Cambridge, 1950); and F. F. Liu, *Military History of Modern China, 1924-1949* (Princeton, 1956). A good summary entitled "The Economic Heritage" is contained in Nai-ruenn Chen and Walter Galenson's *The Chinese Economy under Communism* (Chicago, 1969), pp. 1-32. C. Martin Wilbur gives a good account of internal political developments in his chapter entitled "Military Separatism and the Process of Unification under the Nationalist Regime," in *China in Crisis*, Ping-ti Ho and Tang Tsou, editors (Chicago, 1968), vol. 1, book 1, pp. 203-263. The movement for modernization and reform in China is discussed in Tse-tung Chow's *The May Fourth Movement: Intellectual Revolution in Modern China* (Cambridge, 1960); and student activism in John Israel's *Student Nationalism in China, 1927-1937* (Stanford, 1966).

A broad account of prewar events is contained in *The Strenuous Decade: China's Nation-Building Efforts, 1927-1937*, edited by Paul K. T. Sih (St. John's University Press, Jamaica, New York, 1970). This comprises papers on international, political, financial, economic, and educational topics.

As to China's financial and economic relations with the United States, the yearly volumes of *Foreign Relations of the United States* (cited as *FRUS*) and the archives of the Department of State contain much information. Relations during the latter half of the prewar decade are thoroughly analyzed in Dorothy Borg's *The United States and the Far Eastern Crisis of 1933-1938* (Cambridge, 1964). The volumes of the officially published British record, *Documents on British Foreign Policy, 1919-1939*, contain little on financial and economic matters. Relations with countries of Europe are covered in the following: Irving S. Friedman, *British Relations with China, 1931-1939*; Kurt Bloch, *German Interests and Policies in the Far East*; and Frank M. Tamagna, *Italy's Interests and Policies in the Far East* (these three published by the Institute of Pacific Relations, New York, 1940, 1940, and 1941 respectively). As to China's relations with Japan, Dorothy Borg's book contains much, and other books are Akira Iriye, *After Imperialism: The Search for a New Order in the Far East* (Cambridge, 1965); and James Crowley, *Japan's Quest for Autonomy* (Princeton, 1966). A large amount of international, political, economic, and financial information is contained in *Memoranda Presented to the Lytton Commission by V. K. Wellington Koo, Assessor* (3 volumes, New York, 1932-33).

In fiscal matters, as well as financial and economic matters generally, the Finance Ministers' *Annual Reports* contain basic data and comment for the period July 1, 1928, to June 30, 1935. For the period from then until outbreak of hostilities in mid-1937 the reports were in preparation, but not completed for reasons explained in Chapter 4. The published reports in my judgment are as accurate and complete on financial matters as the data permitted, as are also the unpublished accounts for the period from July 1, 1935, to June 30, 1937 (Appendix 1).

Unfortunately, two official publications issued in Chinese during the war contain figures of receipts and payments in the fiscal years 1934 through 1937 which differ from the definitive figures of the Finance Ministry. The Directorate General of Budgets, Accounts, and Statistics issued the *Statistical Abstract* (Chung-hua min-kuo t'ung chi t'i yao) at Chungking in 1940, having published in 1936 and 1937 data for fiscal years 1934 and 1935 based on Finance Ministry data but differently presented. And the Finance Ministry issued at Chungking in 1943 the *Public Finance Yearbook* (Ts'ai-cheng nien-chien, hsu-pien). In Chapter 4, I discuss the differences, and how they have misled several writers who did not have access to the Finance Ministry's unpublished data for 1935 to 1937, which were on a basis comparable with similar data for preceding and subsequent years. These two publications of 1940 and 1943 should be read in the light of my comments in Chapter 4.

As to fiscal procedures, the Commission of Financial Experts (Kemmerer Commission) submitted in 1929 reports and projects of law on *Financial Planning, Budget Preparation, Budget Enforcement, Accounting, Fiscal Control, Supervisory Inspection and Audit* (2 volumes); and on *Setting up a Department of National Debt within the Ministry of Finance.* F. A. Cleveland prepared in 1932 an edited English text of the *Chinese Budget Law* of that year.

Current developments in taxation are described in the Finance Ministry's *Annual Reports.* Minister T. V. Soong wrote "The Taxation Policy of the Nationalist Government,"

St. John's Echo (St. John's College, Shanghai), January 1929, pp. 58-61. The Kemmerer Commission submitted in 1929 four reports on taxation as follows: *Report on Revenue Policy; A Special Consumption Tax on Portland Cement; A Special Consumption Tax on Matches;* and *A Documentary Stamp Tax.* Yau-pik Chau wrote *The Taxation Reforms of the Chinese National Government in the Decade 1927-1937* (unpublished doctoral dissertation, University of Chicago, 1945), dealing with customs, salt revenue, and internal taxation generally.

In the field of customs, the official publications of the Inspectorate General of Customs and other publications under its auspices are comprehensive and dependable. The Inspectorate published the tariffs in force, monthly trade data, and yearly reports for calendar years containing both full trade and financial statistics and comment on events. The *Decennial Reports, 1922-1931* (two volumes, Shanghai, 1933) contain not only a detailed account of developments at each port but also a history of trade from 1834 to 1931. Of historical importance also is the *Proceedings of the Special Conference on the Chinese Customs Tariff, 1925-1926* (Ministry of Foreign Affairs, Peking, 1928).

Under the auspices of the Customs, senior officials published important historical works: S. F. Wright, *China's Struggle for Tariff Autonomy, 1843-1938* (Shanghai, 1938); and S. F. Wright and J. H. Cubbon, *China's Customs Revenue since the Revolution of 1911* (Shanghai, 1935). The Kemmerer Commission submitted in 1929 reports and projects of law on the following subjects: *Tariff Law; Increasing the Customs Revenue from Import Duties, . . . Simplifying Import Duties, and . . . the Eventual Abolition of Customs Duties Levied upon the Internal Trade;* and *Placing Customs Duties on Imports from Abroad upon a Gold Basis.* A study from early times through 1948 is: Yu-kwei Cheng: *Foreign Trade and Industrial Development of China* (University Press of Washington, D. C., 1956). Choh-ming Li wrote "China's International Trade Statistics: an Evaluation," *Nankai Social and Economic Quarterly*, April 1937, pp. 1-23. On Japanese-sponsored smuggling in North China, *Chinese Year Book, 1936-37, Second Issue*, contains an account by P. T. Chen, "The North China Smuggling Situation," pp. 891-945. This was reprinted as a booklet, with a supplement.

The Chief Inspectorate of Salt Revenue issued Annual Reports for calendar years. F. A. Cleveland as Associate Chief

Inspector prepared in 1934 a *Statistical Review of the Work of the Inspectorate, 1913-1933, with Special Attention Given to the Evaluation of Results Achieved during the Last Five Years.* In 1935, he wrote *The Problem of Putting the Principle of the New Salt Law into Effect.* An historical account of salt taxation was written by Esson M. Gale, "Public Administration of Salt in China: A Historical Survey," *Annals of the American Academy of Political and Social Science*, vol. 152, November 1930, pp. 241-251. S. A. M. Adshead wrote *The Modernization of the Chinese Salt Administration, 1900-1920* (Cambridge, 1970).

There has been little analysis of the fiscal situation in the prewar period. *Chinese Year Book, 1936-1937, Second Issue*, contains an account by P. T. Chen, "Recent Financial Developments in China (1934-1936)," pp. 548-778, which was reprinted as a booklet. Douglas S. Paauw wrote an unpublished doctoral dissertation at Harvard, 1950, *Chinese Public Finance During the Nanking Government Period*, and an article, "Chinese National Expenditures in the Nanking Period," *Far Eastern Quarterly*, November 1952, pp. 1-23. Y. C. Wang in *Chinese Intellectuals and the West* (Chapel Hill, North Carolina, 1966), pp. 422-464, analyzes financial performance in the administrations of Finance Ministers Soong and Kung. The latter two and other postwar writers were misled on some matters by the aforementioned official publications of 1940 and 1943. (See Chapter 4). Prior to these postwar writings, I published two pamphlets that analyze fiscal matters and present approximations of some figures for 1935 to 1937: *China's Financial Progress* (Foreign Policy Association, Foreign Policy Reports, New York, April 15, 1938), and *China's Economic and Financial Reconstruction* (Committee on International Economic Policy and Carnegie Endowment for International Peace, New York, 1947). These figures did not come to the notice of the latter two writers mentioned above.

As to debts, the texts of foreign loan agreements are found in the aforementioned MacMurray's *Treaties and Agreements with and Concerning China, 1894-1918*, and in the supplement with the same title, 1919-1929. The Railway Ministry issued in 1931 at Nanking *Railway Loan Agreements* (3 volumes), with texts in English or French and Chinese. The Commission for the Readjustment of Finance set up at Peiping in 1923 issued in 1927 a *Resume of Work Done*, listing its published and unpublished studies on debts, revenues, and financial policy. The

Kemmerer Commission submitted in 1929 a *Project of a Public Credit Rehabilitation Law, Together with a Report on the National Debt of China and the Rehabilitation of China's Credit* (2 volumes); and a *Project of Organic Law Setting up a Department of National Debt within the Ministry of Finance.* The Bank of China published *Chinese Government Loan Issues and Obligations* (Shanghai, 1930) dealing with both foreign and domestic issues; and *Chinese Government Foreign Loan Obligations* (Shanghai, 1935) giving the texts of agreements in English or French and Chinese, together with amortization tables and loan quotations. The issues of the *China Year Book* contain tables of loans prepared by Eduard Kann. Kann's tables also were published from time to time in *Finance and Commerce* (Shanghai). He also published *History of China's Internal Loan Issues* (Shanghai, 1934). A general discussion of the foreign debt is in Arthur G. Coons' *Foreign Public Debt of China* (Philadelphia, 1930).

As to currency, data on conditions prior to the Nationalist takeover are found in F. E. Lee, *Currency, Banking, and Finance in China* (Department of Commerce, Washington, 1926); and E. Kann, *Currencies of China* (Shanghai, 1926), and *Illustrated Catalog of Chinese Coins* (Hong Kong, 1954). Projects of reform are discussed in Commission on International Exchange, *Report on the Introduction of the Gold-Exchange Standard into China and Other Silver-Using Countries* (58th Congress, 2d Session, Doc. No. 144, Washington, 1903); and *Report on the Introduction of the Gold-Exchange Standard into China . . . and Other Silver-Using Countries*, Submitted to the Secretary of State (Washington, 1904); G. Vissering: *On Chinese Currency* (Batavia, 1912); and Kemmerer Commission: *Project of Law for the Gradual Introduction of a Gold-Standard Currency System in China* (Shanghai, 1930). That Commission also made two brief reports dealing with copper coins and miscellaneous monetary matters.

On the problems relating to silver and China in the prewar decade, the most comprehensive account is by Dickson H. Leavens: *Silver Money* (Cowles Commission, Bloomington, Indiana, 1939). Other references are Sir Arthur Salter, *China and the Depression* (National Economic Council, Nanking, 1934), and *China and Silver* (New York, 1934); Handy and Harman, *Annual Review of the Silver Market* (New York); United States Director of the Mint, *Annual Report*

(Washington); *Effect of Low Silver*, Hearings before the Committee on Coinage, Weights, and Measures, 72d Congress, 1st Session, on H.R. 72 (Washington, 1932); T. J. Kreps, "Price of Silver and Chinese Purchasing Power," *Quarterly Journal of Economics*, February 1934, pp. 245-287; and L. S. Hsu et al., *Silver and Prices in China* (Ministry of Industry, Shanghai, 1935). The *Annual Reports* of the Finance Ministry contain a record of current developments on monetary matters. The Shanghai Mint issued in 1935 *The National Government Central Mint and a Brief Review of Its Operations*, which were from its opening in March 1933 through June 30, 1935. As to the American action on silver, a full account is given in A. S. Everest, *Morgenthau, the New Deal, and Silver* (Columbia University, New York, 1950); and a further account from Secretary Morgenthau's angle, in John M. Blum, *From the Morgenthau Diaries: Years of Crisis, 1928-1938* (Boston, 1959).

The currency reform of 1935 is discussed, with basic documents, in the Finance Ministry's *Annual Report* for 1934-1935. A further documentation is in the publication of the Currency Reserve Board, *New Monetary Policy of China* (Shanghai, 1936). Other contemporary treatments include Wei-ying Lin, *New Monetary System of China* (Shanghai, 1936); Liang-li Tang, *China's New Currency System* (Shanghai, 1936); Dickson H. Leavens, *Silver Money* (cited above), Chapters 28-30; Finance Division, Bureau of Foreign and Domestic Commerce, *Monetary Developments in China Since November 3, 1935* (Washington, 1936); and Arthur N. Young, *China's Financial Progress* (cited above), pp. 30-33.

Official indexes of prices and cost of living in the chief cities are found in the following publications: Bureau of Markets, Finance Ministry, to 1929, and thereafter the National Tariff Commission, *Prices and Price Indexes in Shanghai* (monthly); also in *Shanghai Market Prices Report* (quarterly, 1923-1933); and *Annual Reports of Shanghai Prices*, 1934-1936. The University of Nanking published a compilation of leading indexes some of which run from 1913 to 1940: W. Y. Yang, *University of Nanking Indexes* (Bulletin No. 54, New Series, Chengtu, January 1941). That university also issued from 1936 a monthly publication, *Economic Facts*, which contains extensive price data, including prices paid and received by farmers. Nankai University issued the *Nankai Weekly Statistical Service* containing prices in North China, their data going back to

1913. Franklin L. Ho of that University published "Prices and Price Indexes in China," in *Chinese Economic Journal*, May 1927, pp. 429-463; studies of terms of trade: "Index Numbers of the Quantities and Prices of Imports and Exports and the Barter Terms of Trade in China, 1867-1928," *Chinese Economic Journal*, September 1930, pp. 1013-1041; and a revised series of terms of trade through 1936 in *Nankai Social and Economic Quarterly*, July 1937, pp. 346-347. Chi-ming Hou made a revision of the latter series in his *Foreign Investment and Economic Development in China* (Cambridge, 1965), p. 198. In *China's Wartime Finance and Inflation, 1937-1945* (Cambridge, 1965), I have presented the chief price data for 1937-1945 inclusive, and also some data for 1948, pp. 347-358.

As to commercial banking, Eduard Kann presented a history to 1928 in the *China Year Book, 1929-30*, pp. 307-310; and F. E. Lee covered most of that period in *Currency, Banking, and Finance in China* (Department of Commerce, Washington, 1926). Frank M. Tamagna's *Banking and Finance in China* (New York, 1942), contains background data and an account of developments in banking and credit in the prewar decade and the first war years. The Bank of China issued in 1933 *An Analysis of the Accounts of the Principal Chinese Banks, 1921-1932*, and issued similar analyses yearly thereafter. The *Chinese Bankers' Yearbook* contains details of the condition of the leading Chinese banks. The Bank of China's *Monthly Bulletin* contains current data on banking and other financial subjects, as do its *Annual Reports* and those of the Bank of Communications and the Hongkong and Shanghai Banking Corporation. The Central Bank of China published semiannual financial statements and from 1935 issued a quarterly *Bulletin* of articles and statistics. That bank's charter is found in *China Year Book, 1929-30*, pp. 312-315. The Kemmerer Commission submitted in 1929 a *Project of a General Banking Law* and a *Project of Law for the Creation of the Central Reserve Bank of China.* In 1936, the *Report of the Committee . . . on the Reorganization of the Central Bank of China* was submitted by a joint Chinese-foreign committee, which report became the basis of the plan adopted in 1937 but which the war prevented from entering into effect.

The state of the economy in the early part of the prewar decade (1931) is described by J. B. Condliffe in *China Today: Economic* (World Peace Foundation, Boston, 1932); and by R. H. Tawney in *A Memorandum on Agriculture and Industry in*

China (Institute of Pacific Relations, Honolulu, 1931), which formed the basis for his *Land and Labour in China* (London, 1932).

The movement for economic development and modernization of China was strongly influenced by Sun Yat-sen who wrote *Memoirs of a Chinese Revolutionary: A Programme of National Reconstruction for China* (Philadelphia, 1919); *International Development of China* (New York, 1922); and *Three Principles of the People* (San Min Chu I), translated by Frank W. Price (Institute of Pacific Relations, China Committee, Shanghai, 1927). The effort of the Nationalists in giving effect to Sun's ideas is described, *passim*, in the Finance Ministry's *Annual Reports*. Much more fully it is described in documents relating to the work of the National Economic Council: *Opening Address* [by Chiang Kai-shek] *Delivered at the First Meeting on November Fifteenth in the Twentieth Year of the Republic of China* (Nanking, 1931); and further in the *Report to the Council of the League of Nations of Its Technical Delegate on His Mission in China from Date of Appointment until April 1, 1934*; and *Annexes* to that Report. The Council also published *Report on the Work of the Preparatory Office of the National Economic Council* (Shanghai, 1933); and *Annual Reports* for 1935 and 1936. Appraisals of the Nationalist effort are given by George E. Taylor, *Reconstruction Movement in China* (Royal Institute of International Affairs, London, 1936); W. Lewisohn, "Modernization of China," *North-China Herald*, weekly from December 16, 1936, to February 3, 1937; Douglas S. Paauw, "Kuomintang and Economic Stagnation, 1928-1937," *Journal of Asian Studies*, February 1957, pp. 213-220; Ta-chung Liu and Kung-chia Yeh, *The Economy of the Chinese Mainland, National Income and Economic Development, 1933-1959* (Princeton, 1965); and Y. L. Wu, *China's Economic Policy: Planning or Free Enterprise?* (Sino-International Economic Research Center, New York, 1946, pamphlet 4).

Factual data on development are found in a wide variety of sources. These include *China Year Book; The Chinese Year Book; Annual Reports* and *Monthly Reports* of the American Commercial Attache in China (Department of Commerce, Washington); *Chinese Economic Yearbook* (Chung-kuo ching-chi nien-chien, Ministry of Industries, Nanking, 1934); *China Industrial Handbooks:* Chekiang, Hunan, Kiangsu, Shansi, Shantung (Ministry of Industries, Shanghai, 1933-1936); D. K.

Lieu, *Report on a Survey of Chinese Industry* (Chung-kuo kung-yeh tiao-tsa pao-kao, National Resources Commission, Nanking, 1937); Directorate General of Budgets, Accounts, and Statistics, *Statistical Abstract of the Republic of China, 1935, 1940* (Chung-hua min-kuo t'ung chi t'i yao, Nanking, 1935, and Chungking, 1940); Liu and Yeh, *Economy of the Chinese Mainland* (cited above); Yu-kwei Cheng, *Foreign Trade and Industrial Development of China* (cited above); and Chung-p'ing Yen, *Selected Statistics on the Economic History of Modern China* (Chung-kuo chin-tai ching-chi shih t'ung-chi tzu-liao hsuan-chi, Peking, 1955). On Japan's development, which contrasts strikingly with that of China, W. W. Lockwood wrote *Economic Development of Japan: Growth and Structural Change, 1868-1938* (Princeton, 1954); and E. H. Norman wrote *Japan's Emergence as a Modern State* (New York, 1940).

On national income and capital formation a pioneer study is by Ta-chung Liu, *China's National Income, 1931-36, An Exploratory Study* (Brookings Institution, Washington, 1946). Pao-san Ou wrote *Capital Formation and Consumers' Outlay in China* (unpublished doctoral dissertation, Harvard University, 1948). Kung-chia Yeh wrote *Capital Formation in Mainland China, 1931-36 and 1952-57* (unpublished doctoral dissertation, Columbia University, 1964), and with Ta-chung Liu wrote *Economy of the Chinese Mainland* (cited above).

As to foreign investment, the standard work covering the period to 1931 is Carl F. Remer, *Foreign Investments in China* (New York, 1933). A later comprehensive work is Chi-ming Hou, *Foreign Investment and Economic Development in China, 1840-1937* (cited above). G. C. Allen and Audrey Donnithorne wrote *Western Enterprise in Far Eastern Development: China and Japan* (London and New York, 1954).

On agriculture, Library List No. 85 of the National Agricultural Library of the Department of Agriculture, *Publications on Chinese Agriculture Prior to 1949* (Washington, 1966), lists 888 items. A full historical account is in Dwight H. Perkins, *Agricultural Development in China, 1368-1968* (Cambridge, 1969), together with a bibliography, pp. 366-380. Earlier standard works are J. Lossing Buck, *Land Utilization in China*, three volumes including statistics and an atlas (University of Chicago and University of Nanking, 1937); R. H. Tawney, *Land and Labour in China* (cited above); and T. H. Shen, *Agricultural Resources of China* (Ithaca, New York, 1951). Under the auspices of the National Economic Council, studies were made of current conditions: *Report on Agricultural Reform and Development in China*, by C. Dragoni; *Report on a Survey of Certain Localities in Kiangsi*; and *Report on the Economic and Financial Situation of Chekiang Province.* Participants in the studies leading to the latter two reports included Franklin L. Ho and Sir Arthur Salter. These three reports and other data were published in 1934 in *Annexes to the Report to the Council of the League of Nations of Its Technical Delegate on His Mission in China.* Franklin L. Ho wrote "Rural Economic Reconstruction in China," *Nankai Social and Economic Quarterly*, July 1936, pp. 469-535. Comparisons of the agricultural situation in the prewar years and under the Communists have been made: Tachung Liu, C. Twanmo, and K. C. Yeh, *Production of Food Crops on the China Mainland: Prewar and Postwar* (Rand Corporation, RM 3569, PR 1964, Santa Monica, California); and J. Lossing Buck, Owen L. Dawson, and Yuan-li Wu, *Food and Agriculture in Communist China* (New York, 1966); and Liu and Yeh, *Economy of the Chinese Mainland* (cited above). Considerable data on prewar agriculture are contained in the *Report of the China-United States Agricultural Mission* (Office of Foreign Agricultural Relations, Department of Agriculture, Washington, 1947). James C. Thomson, Jr., wrote *While China Faced West: American Reformers in Nationalist China, 1928-1937* (Cambridge, 1969), dealing with the work of missionaries and plans for rehabilitation of rural Kiangsi Province after expulsion of the Communists. Ramon H. Myers wrote *The Chinese Peasant Economy: Agricultural Development in Hopei and Shantung, 1890-1949* (Cambridge, 1970). For a comprehensive discussion of agriculture in the prewar decade see the papers by Buck, Ho, and Shen in Sih (ed.), *The Strenuous Decade*, pp. 171-236.

On industrialization, the background is discussed in Albert Feuerwerker's *China's Early Industrialization* (Cambridge, 1958); and in Dwight H. Perkins' article, "Government as an Obstacle to Industrialization: The Case of Nineteenth-Century China," *Journal of Economic History*, December 1967, pp. 478-492. On the more recent phase, John K. Chang's *Industrial Development in Pre-Communist China* (Chicago, 1969) provides a quantitative analysis covering the period 1912 to 1949.

As to railways, the Ministry issued yearly from 1915 through 1935-1936 *Statistics of the Chinese National Railways*, the earlier titles being slightly different. The Kemmerer Commission submitted in 1929 *Report on Railway Finance*, and in 1935 F. D. Hammond submitted *Report on the National Railways of the Republic of China.* On the history of the railways H. Lin Cheng wrote *Chinese Railways: A Historical Survey* (Shanghai, 1935). Minister Kia-ngau Chang gave a full account in *China's Struggle for Railway Development* (New York, 1943). A later work is by H. J. von Lochow, *China's National Railways* (Peiping, 1948).

On general problems of transportation, J. E. Baker wrote "Transportation in China," *Annals of the American Academy of Political and Social Science*, vol. 152, November 1930, pp. 160-172. On roads, A. Viola Smith wrote *Motor Roads in China* (Trade Promotion Series, No. 120, Department of Commerce, Washington, 1931); and Lawrence M. Chen wrote *Highways in China* and T. K. Chao wrote *Highway Construction and Transport in China* (Information Bulletins of the Council of International Affairs, Nanking, November 21, 1936 and August 4, 1937, respectively). On aviation, Lawrence M. Chen wrote *Aviation in China* in the aforementioned series of Bulletins, May 1, 1937. W. M. Leary, Jr., wrote "Wings for China: The Jouett Mission, 1932-1935," *Pacific Historical Review*, November 1969, pp. 447-462; and has in process a study of development of civil aviation in China.

Periodicals containing data on financial and economic matters include *Central Bank of China Bulletin* (quarterly); Bank of China, *Financial and Commercial Monthly Bulletin*; Directorate of Statistics, *Statistical Monthly*; Ministry of Industry, Bureau of Foreign Trade, *Chinese Economic Journal* (monthly from 1927), and *Chinese Economic Bulletin* (weekly through 1935); Nankai University, *Nankai Social and Economic Quarterly, Monthly Bulletin on Economic China*, and *Nankai Weekly Statistical Service*; University of Nanking, *Economic Facts* (monthly); *Finance and Commerce* (Shanghai, weekly); *North-China Daily News*, and *North China Herald* (Shanghai, weekly).

Index